The Book of Psalms

From Suffering to Glory

Volume 2: Psalms 73–150

God's Manual of Spirituality

Philip Eveson

EP BOOKS

(Evangelical Press) Unit C, Tomlinson Road, Leyland, England, PR25 2DY

www.epbooks.org
epbooks@10ofthose.com

EP Books are distributed in the USA by:

JPL Books
www.jplbooks.com
orders@jplbooks.com

and

10ofThose Ltd
www.10ofthose.com
sales.us@10ofthose.com

British Library Cataloguing in Publication Data available

ISBN 978-1-78397-021-6

Unless otherwise indicated, Scripture quotations are from the New King James Version (NKJV)®. Copyright © 1982 by Thomas Nelson, Inc. Used by permission. All rights reserved. Some Scripture quotations are the author's own translation.

To Jen

Preface

The Psalms have been very much a part of my life from early childhood, especially through hearing the Metrical Version of some of them each Lord's Day. Others were memorised from the Authorised Version of the Bible. They have been a wonderful source of comfort and encouragement over the years through the ups and downs of life. The academic study of the Psalms has in no way dampened my enthusiasm for this biblical treasure. It has been a delight to lecture and preach from this book and preparing this commentary has been a labour of love and of great spiritual benefit.

It must be well over ten years ago that David Clark of Evangelical Press set me the task of producing this commentary for the Welwyn series. More recently, Graham Hind, the managing director of Evangelical Press, has given me every encouragement and has even allowed me the unique privilege of extending the commentary over two volumes! It has been the task of Trudy Kinloch to edit the manuscript and I am grateful for all her input and advice. Mr David Bond kindly directed me to literature concerning early Jewish music and I greatly appreciated his help in that area. I pray that the commentary will contribute a little more to an understanding of the text and that the message of the Psalms will challenge and convict as well as bring comfort and hope. Above all, I trust it will lead to a deeper appreciation of our Lord's inner life as the suffering Messiah as well as of the glory that followed.

A special word of thanks must go to my dear wife Jennifer, who has been my best friend and support for forty-five years. She has read through various drafts of this commentary, checked all my references and often suggested better ways of expressing my thoughts.

Philip H. Eveson
Wrexham
August 2014

Contents

Book Three

The Book of Psalms is divided into five parts and they are commonly described as books. In Books One and Two (Psalms 1–41 and 42–72) the emphasis fell on the highs and lows of David's life and encouraged the people to look forward to David's greater son, the LORD's Anointed, and to his universal reign. In book Three the psalms express very poignantly the confusion and concerns of God's people as they try to come to terms with their sad and sorry situation without homeland, temple and king. But they also contain expressions of trust in God's faithfulness and encourage the people to look in anticipation for God to make good his promises despite their own unfaithfulness.

In this central book all but one (Psalm 86) are associated with the Levite musicians—Asaph (Psalms 73–83), the sons of Korah (Psalms 84–85, 87–88) and Ethan (Psalm 89). They were part of the original music leadership group appointed by David (1 Chronicles 15:16–17; 2 Chronicles 5:12), and their descendants continued to function in the music department of temple worship through to the time of the building of the Second Temple after the return from exile (2 Chronicles 20:19; Ezra 2:41; Nehemiah 11:22). The Levites were also involved in building the walls and gates of Jerusalem and in their dedication (Nehemiah 3:17, 22; 7:1; 12:27–43), which may explain why the city and its sanctuary become major concerns in this selection of psalms. Following the return from Babylonian exile, Jerusalem with its completed temple, walls and gates, is depicted as a holy city for a holy people (Nehemiah 11:1, 18). The closing chapter of Nehemiah's book, however, reveals how far short the city and its people fell from the ideal. These psalms first encouraged the Jews not to give up hope but to look expectantly to the realisation of the prophetic messages. They continue to speak to Christians as members of the heavenly city as they work towards its growth and final glory in the new creation.

Psalm 73

Concerns and Convictions

When the introductory and concluding psalms are removed (Psalms 1-2 and 145-150), Psalm 73 occupies the halfway point of the whole collection and begins a series attributed to Asaph.

Asaph was one of David's leading Levite musicians who composed psalms under the influence of the Spirit (see Psalm 50 for details). It may be that Asaph spoke prophetically in some of these psalms of the future destruction of Jerusalem and its Temple, using conventional language of the time,[1] and they would have been especially appreciated during the exile when the Jews were removed to Babylon and their city and temple were destroyed. King Hezekiah commanded the Levites to sing praises to the Lord using 'the words of David and Asaph the seer' (2 Chronicles 29:30). On the other hand, Asaph may stand for a later family member for we know that his descendants were involved in temple worship after the return from Exile (see Ezra 2:41; 3:10; Nehemiah 7:44; 11:22). These Asaph psalms were probably collected together during the Exile.

With city and temple destroyed, Psalm 73 encourages a new spiritual way of thinking with the Lord himself as the people's inheritance and the need to trust him even when life looks bleak for God's people in comparison with the prosperity of the enemy. Here then is a psalm that is of immense value to Christians going through difficult and testing times when the temptation is to give up and wonder whether living the Christian life is worthwhile. Like the opening psalms of Book Two (Psalms 42–43), Psalm 73 indicates that believers do not live on a bed of roses and can be discouraged and troubled in various ways. This in itself is an encouragement: to know that the Bible records the experiences of those in similar situations. However, the Bible does not leave us just with sympathetic examples but rather shows how God's people took themselves in hand and in this way presents us with principles that can be applied to our own difficult circumstances.

Asaph is a very honest person and he shares the thoughts that bothered him and how he dealt with them but everything he says is framed by his opening and concluding words of confidence in God. In a number of respects the psalm echoes the two introductory psalms (Psalms 1–2) and clears up misunderstandings concerning the prosperity of the godly.

There are three main divisions introduced by the same word in the original ('Truly/Surely', verses 1, 13, 18) and in all three the 'heart' as a person's innermost being is prominent (verses 1, 7, 13, 21, 26).

Truth confessed (verse 1)
Asaph begins with his triumphant conclusion and then tells us in the rest of the psalm how he came to such a strong conviction. To say that 'God is good' might appear glib when life is treating us well but when that confession is tested in times of adversity it becomes more real and meaningful. I remember being at the bedside of a lady missionary dying of cancer. As she lay in her weakness her only words whispered into my ear were, 'God is good'.

God acts true to his nature. Only God is good and that good is expressed in temporal and spiritual benefits particularly in the context of God's special covenant relationship with his people (see Jeremiah 33:11; Nahum 1:7; Psalm 86:5; 100:5). The 'Israel' that Asaph has in mind is true Israel, those who are 'pure in heart' (see Psalm 24:4), who are faithful to God and without hypocrisy. Their words and actions arise from a life that is in a right relationship with God.

Temptation to doubt (verses 2–12)
'But as for me' (verse 2) introduces Asaph's testimony in which he reveals how near he came to denying the strong conviction of verse 1.

The familiar picture of the godly person walking with God, as in Psalm 1, lies behind the picture of 'feet' that had 'almost stumbled' (literally 'turned aside') and 'steps' that had 'nearly slipped' (see Psalm 56:13).

As in Job's case, the temptation is to deny the justice and integrity of God when life's experiences seem so unfair. Godly Asaph, who has tried to live as described in Psalm 1, is perplexed and tempted to be 'envious' of the 'wicked' and 'boastful' people (verse 3; see Psalms 1:1; 5:5; 75:4). While life seemed hard for this man of God, he watched the arrogant in their 'prosperity' (verse 3; literally 'peace') where everything seemed to go well for them. Devilish thoughts like this can come into our minds but as we learn from Asaph he rejected them; he did not sin by accepting them and taking them to heart.

A description of the wicked is given in detail from verses 4 to 12 to highlight the severity of the temptation the psalmist felt. The 'well-being' they enjoy covers physical health and strength (verses 4–5) which leads them to become even more arrogant and violent (verse 6). The original of verse 7 suggests not so much enjoying everything they set their hearts on but possessing a cruel spirit overflowing with scheming thoughts. They scoff and threaten oppression (verse 8) and from a position of superiority they make their voice felt far and wide (verse 9). Verse 10 is difficult but perhaps the thought is that God's people are brought back to an Egyptian-like situation, to experience the worst excesses of the wicked and to drink to the dregs the consequences of an oppressive regime (see verse 14 for more detail). The wicked behave in this way because they think God is not interested and so they can get away with their violent activity (verse 11). Like the deists of 18th century Britain they think that God has left his creation to tick away without the need for him to intervene. They are similar to the practical atheists of Psalm 14. The final verse sums up Asaph's problem as he looks out on the wicked: 'There they are, these wicked people, forever at ease and increasing in wealth'. Their position seems to run contrary to the teaching of Psalm 1.

Turning point (verses 13–17)

Asaph tells us of his strong temptation to give up. He says in effect, 'What's the point of being godly when it appears that the wicked are enjoying God's favour while I'm being afflicted and experiencing God's judgment?' (verses 13–14). A person who came before God with 'clean (innocent) hands' and 'a pure heart' (verse 13) could expect blessing from the LORD (see Psalm 24:4–5) but Asaph is knowing only plague and punishment all day of every day (verse 14). The same temptation to curse God and die also came to Job whom God himself describes as an upright, godly person.

But the psalmist does not accept that tempting solution otherwise he would never have come to the conclusion with which he starts the psalm. As in Psalms 42–43 he takes himself in hand and begins to see the consequences if he were to express openly the thoughts that troubled him. He would have been unfaithful to the community of faith (literally 'the generation of your sons', verse 15; see Psalm 24:6). When Nehemiah was tempted by a false associate to escape for his life he resisted when he considered the consequences of such an action on his people. 'Should such a man as I run away?' (Nehemiah 6:11). How important it is that we consider the damage we might do to God's people by expressing our doubts and uncertainties in public. Let us learn to keep our troubling thoughts to ourselves (unless we are seeking help for ourselves) until we have clearer light on the subject.

Though he resists expressing to others his troubling thoughts, Asaph's mind is in great turmoil. He is concerned to have answers to God's mysterious providential workings. It is interesting that we do not question God about the good things that come to us out of the blue, but only when bad things happen to us for no apparent reason. The Preacher declares that it is not possible to fathom God's ways, though a person 'toils' to discover them (Ecclesiastes 8:17) and Asaph was finding this out for himself as he tried to understand. He found it a 'toilsome' or 'painful' task (verse 16).

Relief came when he entered 'the sanctuary' (verse 17; see Psalm 20:2), the earthly counterpart to God's heavenly residence (in the original 'sanctuary' is plural as in Psalm 68:35). It was in the sanctuary that people were made aware of God's power and glory (Psalm 63:2) and it was toward the sanctuary that they lifted up their hands in prayer (Psalm 28:2). It is through this means that the psalmist came to 'understand (or rather 'consider') their end'. True religion does not by-pass the mind; it is no opiate; it is not mysticism or emotionalism. In the sanctuary he reflected on what God had already revealed and gained a fresh appreciation of the destiny of the wicked. The Bible has much to say on this subject. The first psalm closes with the truth that the ungodly will perish (Psalm 1:6). Unless we turn and believe in God's way of salvation, we all deserve to 'perish' (John 3:16) and Jesus warned that there is a broad road that leads to destruction and many are on it (Matthew 7:13).

As Christians assemble together as a church, where God's word is carefully proclaimed, the sacraments rightly administered and love and care for God's people is seen in action, God has promised to be with them. Here too Christians find encouragement and are reminded of eternal truths.

Triumph of Faith (verse 18–26)

Right thinking about God and the wicked (verses 18–20)

From this spiritual perspective the psalmist now sees not the present success of the wicked but their underlying situation and ultimate state. Their position looks pleasant and prosperous but the reality is quite different. In God's overall providential activity they are set on 'slippery' ground or placed in situations that are 'false' and full of 'flattery' (see Psalm 12:2) and are caused to fall into 'deceptions' (which fits the context better rather than emending to give 'destruction' in verse 18).[2] As Alec Motyer puts it, 'they will find themselves to have been victims of a "total deception". Their abrupt and complete end with its accompanying "terrors" is astounding as the exclamation "how ...!" suggests' (verse 19).

Verse 20 makes clear God's active involvement in the judgment on the wicked. How illusory was the prosperity of the wicked—an 'image' or 'shadow' (see Psalm 39:6) despised by God. Using anthropomorphic language, the sovereign God's present inactivity toward the wicked is likened to him being asleep (see Psalm 44:23). Of course, God neither slumbers nor sleeps (Psalm 121:4), but that is how it appears. The sceptics through the ages have attributed God's inactivity to impotence or lack of care. The psalmist says that it is not because he is lacking in power or justice or because he is unloving that he fails to act against the wicked, but because he is sleeping. In other words, God is waiting his moment to act. He works according to his timetable not ours and when that time comes he will certainly 'awake' to action. He has done that throughout history and all those expressions of judgments are but warnings of the final day of judgment (see 2 Thessalonians 1:6-10).

Right thinking about himself (verses 21–22)

Asaph is very honest 'before' or 'with' God. He realises that his own reaction to the prosperity of the wicked has been wrong. His heart was 'grieved' or 'bitter/soured' and his 'mind' (literally 'kidneys', suggesting his inner being) 'vexed' or more literally 'pierced'. He goes further and confesses how stupid and ignorant he has been, becoming as irrational as cattle or a clumsy giant of a creature ('beast'; literally 'behemoth' see Job 40:15).

Right appreciation of God's grace (verses 23–26)

God's people are aware of their imperfections and failures and freely confess them but they are also so grateful that God does not abandon them when they begin to slip and slide backward. With George Matheson they can sing *O Love that wilt not let me go*. Asaph is still 'before' or 'with' God and the reason why he has not fallen (see verse 2) is because he is held by God's own 'right hand' (verse 23; see Psalms 18:35–36; 37:24; 63:8). As the Lord encouraged Israel and Cyrus (Isaiah 41:10, 13; 45:1) with protection and support by his powerful grasp of them, so Asaph is aware of that same hand upholding him. He is assured that the Lord will 'guide' him 'with' (or 'in') his 'counsel' either in the sense of advising and pointing him in the right direction or in the sense of directing him 'in the counsel' or 'purpose' God has planned for him (verse 24). The goal toward which he is moving is to be taken to 'glory', which could mean eventual 'honour' on earth, but the verb 'receive' or 'take me' as well as the sequence of thought from verse 23, suggests being taken to the glory of the heavenly presence of God (see Genesis 5:24; Psalms 16:11; 49:15) in contrast to the destiny of the wicked (verses 17–20).

If, as he is now assured, he has God as his provider and protector what other support does he need! (verse 25; see Psalm 16:2). Like Enoch, life for Asaph, even in this frustrating world, meant being in fellowship with God—this was his delight and satisfaction. Outwardly and inwardly ('My flesh and my heart') he may be a spent force but God is 'forever' his 'strength' (literally 'the rock of my heart') and his 'portion' (verse 26). This 'portion' originally referred to land inheritance in Canaan allotted to each tribe, which meant rest, sustenance for living and a future. The Levites owned no land because the Lord himself was to be their 'portion or inheritance', by receiving part of the offerings made by the people to God (Numbers 18:20–24; Deuteronomy 10:9; Joshua 18:7). Asaph the Levite took to heart this provision and like David looked to the reality to which it pointed, by confessing that he rested in the Lord for his livelihood, security and future (see Psalm 16:5–6).

Truth affirmed (verses 27–28)

Asaph concludes by drawing a contrast between those who are 'far' from God, who commit spiritual 'prostitution' by serving other deities (verse 27; see Hosea 1:2) and those like Asaph who come 'near' to God (verse 28). Paul speaks of Gentile believers who were once 'far off' but who 'have been brought near by the blood of Christ' (Ephesians 2:13). The destiny of the wicked is again emphasised—they 'shall perish', they are 'destroyed' or 'cut off' by God. On the other hand, those like Asaph, who have made the sovereign GOD (Yahweh) their 'refuge' (see Psalm 2:12) find God to be the 'good' they desire, the total sum of happiness, and celebrate the fact by declaring all God's amazing acts particularly his saving works. Asaph is a representative of God's true Israel who can testify that coming to God and seeking his help is a 'good' thing to do because God is good to his people despite difficult and testing experiences, as the first verse has indicated. As the hymn-writer put it:

> Thee to praise, and Thee to know,
> Constitute my bliss below;
> Thee to see, and Thee to love,
> Constitute my bliss above.[3]

Asaph, as a representative of the Israel of God, points us to the Lord Jesus Christ, who is the true Israel (Isaiah 49:3), who, as the Suffering Servant, knew what it was to feel the temptation to give up (see Isaiah 49:4a), yet shook it off by reminding himself of his God and trusting that he would be vindicated by him (Isaiah 49:4b).

Psalm 74

A Cry for God to Remember

Pictures of Warsaw after it was flattened by bombs during World War II give some idea of what Jerusalem was like after the Babylonians had destroyed it. This psalm like the book of Lamentations reflects the time after the Babylonians had destroyed Jerusalem and its Temple in 587 BC, described in 2 Kings 24-25. The devastation had been so complete that questions began to be asked whether there could ever be a restoration. In this teaching psalm ('Contemplation', see Psalm 32) attributed to 'Asaph' or a descendant of his belonging to the same prophetic and musical tradition, the grief of the poet captures the emotional state of people who had a deep concern for the cause of God on earth. If Psalm 73 parallels Psalms 42-43, there are also parallels between Psalm 44 and this psalm, but unlike Psalm 44 where God's rejection of his people had brought them disgrace for no apparent reason, this psalm does not plead innocence but is concerned with the effects of the disaster on God's reputation. It is a psalm that Christians can use in their prayers. God's honour is at stake as the enemies of God and his people mock the sorry state of the professing church in the West.

Besides the name Asaph, the psalm uses several words that link it with the previous psalm including 'sanctuary', 'right hand' and 'violence/cruelty', but whereas in Psalm 73 the first person singular predominates with Asaph speaking his own thoughts on behalf of Israel, here he expresses the community's thoughts (see Psalms 42–43 and 44). The deep distress felt by the people at the loss of sanctuary and city is expressed again in Psalm 79. It also bears similarities to Psalm 89, the final one in Book Three.

The passionate plea (verses 1–3)

The psalm begins with a perplexing cry to God, 'Why have you cast off ...' or 'rejected ...' (see Psalm 60:1) a people described as 'the sheep of your pasture?' (verse 1; see Psalms 79:13; 100:3). The Shepherd of Israel who cares for his flock and protects from attack (see Psalms 23:1–6; 80:1) has abandoned them to the enemy. But it is the permanent, enduring nature of the rejection that so perplexes the people—it looks like it is 'for ever' (see Lamentations 5:20; Psalms 44:23; 77:8) although they have been led to believe that the Lord will 'not cast off for ever' (Lamentations 3:31). The psalmist is not questioning the correctness of their punishment by God but he is concerned as to why there is no let up in his smoking 'anger' (see Psalm 18:15; Deuteronomy 29:20) that keeps them in their sorry condition.

Out of the anguish comes the prayer that God would 'remember' (verse 2; see verses 18, 22) and intervene on behalf of his people. With echoes of the Red Sea victory song (Exodus 15:1–18), a variety of expressions are used to press home the close association that exists between God and Israel:

1. They are a 'congregation' (verse 2; see Psalm 1:5), an 'assembly' or 'community' gathered together by God at the time of the exodus. Asaph refers to that great event 'of old' when God 'purchased' or more literally, 'acquired' (see Exodus 15:16; Psalm 78:4) Israel as a holy nation and special treasure (Exodus 19:5–6; Deuteronomy 7:6).

2. In the parallel line a more unusual phrase is used to describe the special relationship—'the tribe of your inheritance' (verse 2; see Jeremiah 10:16; 51:19). Israel as a whole is seen as God's tribe, his own family grouping. Not only is God Israel's inheritance (Psalm 16:5; or 'portion' Psalm 73:26) but Israel is God's inheritance (Psalm 28:9). It accords with the spiritual heart of the covenant with Israel where God states: 'I ... will be your God, and you shall be my people' (Leviticus 26:12). These are the people God 'redeemed' from Egyptian bondage (Exodus 15:13; Psalm 77:15).

3. The final argument that Asaph uses in his plea is even more

persuasive for he moves from thinking about God's people to the place where God had specially chosen to live among his people—'Mount Zion' (Psalms 48:2, 11; 78:68; 135:21). God had withdrawn his presence and allowed the sanctuary to be destroyed and so, using very vivid imagery, Asaph urges God not merely to look down from a distance but actually to take the trouble to journey to the ruined area, to 'lift up his feet[4] to the perpetual (or 'for ever' as in verse 1) desolations' and to see the irreparable damage (literally 'evil') done to 'the sanctuary' or 'holy place' (verse 3; see Psalm 73:17). Asaph's hope is that God will be moved to show compassion and that his anger will be aroused against the enemy that has done this. The wording suggests that the fall of Jerusalem had happened some time back.

Above all the concerns that grieve us, what should affect us most should be the state of his church and the resulting dishonour that is brought to God's holy name. We are encouraged to take our complaints to God and to use the same type of arguments as we plead with God, which include our relationship to him, the grace and power shown in his redeeming work through Christ and the sorry condition of God's cause in our land.

The situation described (verses 4–11)

It is the evil done to the Temple that is portrayed in some detail in these verses. This is what God would see when he visited the site. Instead of Israel's voices ringing out in praise to God it is God's adversaries that roar like lions (see Lamentations 2:7) from God's 'meeting place' or 'assembly place', referred to in the law as 'the tent of meeting' (Exodus 25:8), the sanctuary where God had appointed to meet with the assembly of his people (verse 2; Lamentations 2:6). In place of the signs that pointed to God's presence in the temple such as the ark of the covenant, the enemy had set up ensigns or 'banners' (see Numbers 2:2) of their own presence.[5] The wanton destruction of all the specially carved wood around the walls of the Temple (see 1 Kings 6: 29–36) is depicted graphically and with eyewitness detail in verses 5 and 6. The whole demolition process including the setting alight of the 'sanctuary' (see 2 Kings 25:9) was sacrilege: it had been 'defiled' (verse 7).

All the terms for the Temple are used and God's ownership of it is emphasised to reinforce Asaph's cry to God: 'the sanctuary' or 'holy place' (verse 3), 'your meeting place' (verse 4), 'your sanctuary' (verse 7), 'the dwelling place of your name' (verse 7; see Deuteronomy 12:11) and 'all the meeting places of God' (verse 8). The destruction of the Temple was the result of the enemy's deliberate plan ('They said in their hearts', verse 8) so that there was no possibility of Israel meeting with God in the land—the whole of God's meeting place (the plural form of verse four's 'meeting place' probably emphasises every part of the Temple complex) was destroyed by fire.

'We do not see our signs' may refer either to religious signs (see verse 4) or to special tokens of God's interest in them including the gift of prophecy. God reveals his secrets to his servants the prophets (Amos 3:7) but there are no longer any prophets among them (Lamentations 2:9) who know 'how long' (or 'until when') the situation will last. Jeremiah, the last of the true prophets of the Lord in Jerusalem, was taken into Egypt by Jews who refused to accept his God-given messages (Jeremiah 43:1–7). It is part of God's judgment when there is a famine 'of hearing the words of the LORD' (Amos 8:11). When king Saul inquired of the LORD, there was no answer 'either by dreams or by Urim or by the prophets' (1 Samuel 28:6).

In view of this sad state of affairs, the cry goes up 'how long'—'until when O God will the adversary scoff?' (verse 10). Again, the chief concern is God's honour. He is being despised; his name is being blasphemed. Is this also going to be 'for ever', as permanent as Israel's rejection in verse 1 and the sanctuary desolations of verse 3? The questioning continues in verse 11 with a 'why' question as in verse 1 but it introduces a call for action. There is no loss of faith in God's ability to change the situation. The powerful divine 'right hand' that was at work at the time of the exodus (Exodus 15:6.12) is not thought to have become weak. Rather, it has been withdrawn and so the prayer is that God will intervene and 'destroy' the enemy.

When all things seem against us and the future of the church looks bleak we are encouraged to direct our concerns to God knowing that he can and will destroy all his enemies and bring honour to his name.

The past recalled (verses 12–17)

The account of God's powerful deeds of the past, echoing again the Red Sea song of Exodus 15, is presented as yet another argument in moving God to action in the present. The passage emphasises God's activity by stressing 'you' seven times in the original (at the beginning of verses 13 and 14, twice in 15, the middle of 16 and twice in 17). Asaph, still speaking on behalf of Israel, moves from the plural 'we' (verse 9) to 'my' (verse 12) as he appeals to God as 'King from of old', similar to the 'Contemplation of the sons of Korah' in Psalm 44:1 and 4 (see also Psalm 68:19, 24). From earthly rulers like Nebuchadnezzar attention is drawn to the sovereign ruler of the universe who works a fulsome 'salvation' (the word is in the plural) for all to see 'in the midst of the earth'. He is the one who reigns everlastingly (Exodus 15:18).

Both the exodus event from the Red Sea to the Jordan (verses 13, 15) and the creation and Flood accounts are alluded to in these verses, where waters are divided and dried up (Genesis 1:6–10; 8:7, 14; Exodus 14:16, 21–22; Psalm 66:6). The language used is also reminiscent of the Ancient Near-Eastern stories of the gods and their victories over the tyrannical waters, the 'sea serpents' (verse 13; see Psalm 148:7) and the seven-headed sea monster, 'Leviathan' (verse 14; Isaiah 27:1). It was no mythical tale what God did in dividing the Red Sea and breaking Egypt's power, which is likened to those hideous creatures, (see Psalm 87:4; Isaiah 51:9; Ezekiel 29:3) resulting in Pharaoh's dead soldiers becoming food for the wild desert animals (verse 14, where 'people' is used of 'creatures' as in Proverbs 30:25). John's vision uses the sea monster image to depict the devil as the representative of all wicked rule that persecutes the church of God and whose end is the lake of fire (Revelation 12:3, 9; 20:2, 10).

The God who has made and reigns over the waters is also the one to whom 'day' and 'night' belong and who established the 'sun', which is also referred to by the unusual word 'light' or 'luminary' as in the creation account (verse 16; see Genesis 1:14–16). The 'borders of the earth' (verse 17), as in Psalm 104:9, suggest the edges of the land that God has set so that the sea is prevented from over-running the earth (Genesis 1:9–10). This along with the forming of the seasons, 'summer and winter' also recalls the covenant made with all creation after the Flood (Genesis 8:21–22; 9:9–17). Creation, the Flood and its aftermath, and deliverance from Egyptian slavery are all brought to God's attention testifying to his power and sovereignty and supplying compelling reasons why he should act in the present crisis.

The passionate plea (verses 18–23)
For the first time God's covenant name 'LORD' (Yahweh/Jehovah) is used, appropriate in view of the reference to the 'covenant' (verse 20). Having confessed faith in God's kingship and power, Asaph, as he

continues to represent his people, makes a final fervent plea in a series
of positive and negative appeals. A number of concerns are presented:

First, the honour of God is at stake—The psalmist mentions again
the scoffing of the enemy and how they have despised God's name
('reproached ... blasphemed your name', verse 18; see verse 10 where
the same two verbs are found). Defiling the sanctuary and profaning
God's person are closely associated (see Leviticus 20:3). God is called
to 'remember' this as well as remembering his people (verse 2). Like
the fool of Psalms 14 and 53 the enemy is dismissing God as irrelevant
to daily life and behaving as if God has no interest in world affairs.
The closing verses likewise remind God how the 'fool' ridicules
('reproaches') him daily and the psalm urges God to 'Arise', as if from
a bed of slumber (see Psalms 44:23-26; 73:20), and 'defend' his cause
('plead your own cause', verse 22). Supporting this call to 'remember'
there again comes a plea not to 'forget' (see verses 18-19) the enemy
voices and 'tumult' or 'noise' that rise up against God 'continually'
(verse 23; see verse 4). Can God continue to allow the enemy to boast
and mock God? It is a strong plea with which to end the psalm.

Second, God's people are vulnerable—They are likened to a helpless
'dove' in the face of a 'wild beast' and so there comes an emotional
appeal for God not to forget 'for ever' (see verses 1, 3, 10) his 'poor'
godly people (see Psalms 9:18; 35:10) who are dear to God's heart (see
Song of Solomon 6:9). A little later after referring to the violence of
the proud foreign oppressors (verse 20) Asaph again draws attention to
God's 'poor and needy' (see Psalms 37:14; 40:17; 70:5). These are ones
the Messiah takes pity on and saves (Psalm 72:13). He prays that God
will not allow his 'oppressed' people to 'retreat in disgrace' ('return
ashamed') but instead, to have much cause to 'praise' God's name (verse
21).

Third, there is a covenant to bear in mind—Asaph appeals to the
special relationship between God and Israel (verse 20). The Sinai
covenant they had broken and the final curse attached to it is what
they were presently experiencing (see Leviticus 26:27-39). But that did
not mean God had finished with them. The 'covenant' promises made
to Abraham, Isaac and Jacob remained and the law and the prophets
had spoken of a future beyond the final curse (Leviticus 26:40-45;
Deuteronomy 30:1-10; Amos 9:11-15; Micah 4:1-5). He therefore
calls on God to 'Have respect to' or 'look to the covenant' with a view
to fulfilling those remaining obligations. In support of this appeal,

reference is made to 'the dark places of the earth' filled not with 'pastures of grass' and sheep (Psalms 23:2; 68:13) but with 'pastures of violence' ('habitations of cruelty', verse 20). The argument is that the whole earth is in deep gloom and full of violence instead of being 'filled with the glory of the LORD' (Numbers 14:21; Habakkuk 2:14) which God is committed on oath to establishing. That same promise still applies and we look to the day when Satan's kingdom of darkness and brutality will give way to God's rule through his Messiah and the earth will be full of the knowledge of the Lord as the waters cover the sea (Isaiah 11:1–9).

Israel's experience of abandonment points forward to that crucial and far worse rejection that Jesus knew when he hung on the cross to atone for his people's sins (see Psalm 22:1; Mark 15:34). We are warned to escape from the final and eternal abandonment when our Lord and Judge will say, 'I never knew you; depart from me, you who practise lawlessness!' (Matthew 7:23).

Psalm 75

Sovereign Supreme

The rise and fall of civilizations is a subject that intrigues historians, and many theories are suggested for the collapse of societies like Rome or the Maya civilization of the Central American region. Here we are taught that behind all the events of history there is a God who 'puts down one and exalts another'. How different the psalm is to the previous one! In place of God's distance and inactivity with regard to his people there is a strong awareness of God's presence and involvement in human affairs. It may come from a later period during Israel's exile for there are echoes of Daniel's book with God's kingship emphasised in the rise and fall of empires and the eventual victory of God's people over their foes.

This is the third in a series of Asaph psalms that began with Psalm 73. It is a 'Song' but whether the phrase 'Do not Destroy' (see Psalms 57–59) refers to the tune for the musical director ('The Chief Musician') it is impossible on our present knowledge to be certain. As in the poems of Hannah and Mary (1 Samuel 2:1-10; Luke 1:46-55) this one speaks of God 'putting down' one and 'exalting' another.

Various 'voices' are detected in the psalm and commentators are not all agreed on their identity. First, Asaph speaks with the rest of the congregation ('we'; verse 1), closely followed by a word from God (verses 2-3). The 'Selah' (end of verse 3) suggests a pause, with perhaps

Asaph himself speaking in verses 4 and 5, although some think God continues to speak to the end of verse 5. All seem agreed that the psalmist's voice is heard in the following lines (verses 6-8) and the psalm ends with Asaph speaking as a representative of his people ('I'; verses 9-10), although some have thought it is God's voice in the final verse.

Praise for God's wonderful acts (verse 1)

The psalm begins and ends with praise. It is an important part of worship to 'give thanks' to God for his extraordinary saving activity (see Psalm 9:1). For the old covenant people the great event of the past was the redemption from Egyptian bondage (Exodus 3:20; 15:11). Believers under the new covenant praise God for the events surrounding the death and resurrection of Jesus, God's Son, to redeem us from the bondage of sin and Satan. In Psalm 73:28 Asaph came near to God to recount all his works, whereas here we find God's 'name' or personal presence is 'near' to his people as the story of his wonderful deeds are recounted (see Psalm 34:18). The angel of God's presence was with Israel at the time of the exodus from Egypt and it is stated, 'my name is in him' (Exodus 14:19; 23:20-21). That same divine presence and self-disclosure was seen most wonderfully and fully in the Word made flesh (John 1:14, 18).[6]

God's time for justice (verses 2-3)

Here is a reassuring word from God encouraging his people despite appearances (see Psalm 74) to trust God and not despair. God has his set times for action as he explained to his people in Egypt (Exodus 9:5) and later through Daniel. The word 'proper (or 'set') time' (verse 2) can mean either an appointed place (see Psalm 74:4, 8) or an appointed time such as special seasons (Genesis 1:14) and holy festivals (Leviticus 23:2). God determines when things happen. There is a set time for favouring Zion (Psalm 102:13) and 'at the appointed time' the end will come (Daniel 8:19; 11:27, 35). Jesus the Messiah came into the world at the date set by the Father, in the 'fulness of time' (Galatians 4:2, 4).

As in Habakkuk's prophecy, the 'proper time' is used in the context of a concern for justice over the wicked—'the vision is yet for an appointed time' (Habakkuk 2:3). We can rest content that the God who is in overall control will intervene at the right time in his purposes and when he judges (the 'I' is emphasised in 'I will judge') it will be fair and just ('uprightly', verse 2; see Psalm 50:6). God, and no other, rules the world so that when the earth and its inhabitants 'melt' ('are dissolved' verse 3; see Psalm 46:6) in fear, it is God himself who is the basis of stability and moral order. There is no need to despair when 'foundations' are being destroyed (see Psalms 11:3: 82:5), for it is God not any human magnate who is upholding all things (see 1 Sam 2:8–9).

A word to the boastful (verses 4–5)

These verses could be continuing God's word but it is more likely in view of the 'Selah' at the end of verse 3, the special introduction, 'I said' (verses 4), and the fact that there is no break after verse 5, that the psalmist now addresses the boasters in the light of God's word in verses 2–3.

The 'wicked' are addressed, especially rulers who boast in their pride and arrogance as if their lofty positions of influence are due to their own abilities. They are the ones mentioned in Psalms 1 and 2 (see also Psalm 73:3). 'Horn' is a symbol of strength and is used in the book of Daniel to symbolise kings (Daniel 7:7, 8, 24; 8:3, 21). The idea behind the image of a 'stiff neck' (verse 5) is of an unrestrained person pushing forward with his neck stretched out like a player in a rugby scrum. It stands for a person who is 'insolent' or 'arrogant' (see Psalms 31:18; 94:4) and the word for 'stiff' is translated 'arrogance' in Hannah's prayer (1 Samuel 2:3).

God rules and dispenses justice (verses 6–8)

'Exaltation' ('uplifting', verse 6) is the term emphasised in these verses and picks up terms from the same word family that we find in the previous two verses ('lift up' and 'on high'). Look where you will, east, west or south[7] there is but one supreme ruler. Are we ultimately in the hands of ruthless rulers like Nebuchadnezzar, subject to the whim of dictators like Stalin and Hitler, or to sinister impersonal fatalistic forces? No! 'God is the Judge' (verse 7; verse 2). In other words, it is God alone who is in charge to establish justice in the earth. He alone makes the decisions about who should gain or lose power. He alone has the ability 'to put down' ('make low') and to 'exalt' ('lift up') as Hannah stated in her prayer (1 Samuel 2:7) and Mary in her hymn of praise (Luke 1:52). After God revealed to Daniel the secret of Nebuchadnezzar's dream concerning the world empires, Daniel acknowledged in prayer that God was the one who 'changes the times and the seasons; he removes kings and raises up kings' (Daniel 2:21).

Unusual for this part of the collection from Psalms 42 to 83 (see Psalm 42), God's personal name 'LORD' (Yahweh/Jehovah; verse 8) is used as the solemn theme of God's just judgment is brought to our attention. This divine judgment is symbolised by a 'cup' (see Psalm 11:6). God is likened to a royal cupbearer whose job was to select and serve wine to the king (see Nehemiah 1:11). The 'wine' is 'red' or better 'fermented' or 'foaming up' (verse 8; see Psalm 46:3 of the 'troubled' waters) and 'fully mixed' with herbs and spices or perhaps other alcoholic liquor to give it real potency. Then it is poured out and 'the wicked of the earth' will drink and 'drain' the cup to its very dregs. Isaiah uses a similar picture and calls it a 'cup of fury' (Isaiah 51:17; see Jeremiah 25:15, 17). John sees God's end-time judgment on the rebellious worldly system as 'the cup of the wine of the fierceness of his wrath' (Revelation 16:19; 18:6). How amazing then to be told that our Lord Jesus endured the cup of God's wrath in the place of sinners so that all who believe in him might be spared that awful future (Mark 14:36; John 18:11)!

Praise to the God who encourages his people (verses 9-10)

In contrast to 'the wicked of the earth', Asaph, speaking as the representative leader of God's people, is emphatic ('But I') in his commitment to go on declaring or retelling (see verse 1) 'for ever' the truth about God's rule and justice and to 'sing praises' ('make music'; see Psalm 66:4) to 'the God of Jacob' (verse 9; see Psalm 20:1). Picking up again words like 'horns' (verses 4-5), 'the wicked' (verses 4-8) and 'exalted' or 'lift up' (verses 4-5, 7), God's covenant community have confidence that through God they can 'cut off' (verse 10) enemy strength and be powerful 'without aggression' and be raised up 'without pride'.[8] This is so different to earlier expressions of despair at the fall of Jerusalem that describe how God had caused the enemy to rejoice over them and had 'exalted the horn' of their adversaries (Lamentations 2:17). God's people are viewed in the singular as the 'righteous' one (verse 10), just as the nation can be described as 'Jacob' (verse 9; Exodus 19:3; Isaiah 2:5-6) and Israel can be viewed as God's son (Exodus 4:22-23). The psalm ends by reminding us of Psalm 1 where the wicked end in ruin while the righteous ones are in a most happy position.

The phraseology used in the closing verse is a further reminder of Hannah's words. Her prayer begins by praising God that her 'horn' is exalted in the Lord and ends with a prophetic plea that God would 'raise the horn of his anointed' king (1 Samuel 2:1, 10). The help that came to Hannah in her need is a small example of what the Lord would do through the Anointed One of David's family line as Mary and Zacharias' prophetic poems relate (Luke 1:46–55, 68–79). In view of these associations, the closing words of our psalm point us to Jesus who through his work on the cross has disarmed principalities and powers and triumphed over them so that all who belong to him are more than conquerors (Colossians 2:15; Romans 8:31, 37–39). As Jesus the righteous one has been raised to glory so those who are united to him are accounted righteous and raised up and made to sit together in the heavenlies and will be raised bodily to the glory of the world to come (Philippians 3:9; Ephesians 2:5–6; 1 Corinthians 15:20–21, 42–43).

Psalm 76

The Awesome God

This psalm follows naturally from the previous one with its theme of God's just control over the affairs of this world bringing encouragement and hope to God's people. Many including the ancient Greek translators of the Psalms have concluded that its original setting was God's miraculous intervention and victory over Sennacherib's Assyrian army (2 Kings 19:35-36). On the other hand, the psalm may well have in mind the 'wondrous works' of Psalm 75:1 when at the time of the exodus God rescued his people from Pharaoh's chariots and horses (verses 6-7; Exodus 15:3-7, 11, 18). Our psalm also bears some resemblances to Psalms 46 and 48. Perhaps the psalm is meant to recall all God's saving activity with an eye to God's end-time judgment.

The psalm impresses upon us that we are dealing with the true and living God who is to be feared, whose righteous anger will destroy his enemies and bring deliverance for his oppressed people. The persecuted Church of Jesus Christ throughout history has held firmly to this belief in the face of great tribulation and still does. John's vision in the last book of the Bible was written for those facing devilish opposition to assure them that God has his day of vengeance and that his people will have great cause to praise him for 'the Lord God omnipotent reigns' (Revelation 19:1-6).

Again, we have another psalm belonging to the 'Asaph' collection and while the term 'Psalm' implies musical accompaniment, the 'Chief Musician' is given clear directions to use 'stringed instruments' for this 'Song' (see Psalms 4 and 67).

God's protection of his people (verses 1–3)

The God who actually does exist and is not a figment of human imagination or evolutionary development can only be known if he decides to reveal himself. At the time of the exodus, God made himself known to Moses and Israel (Exodus 3:1–4:17; 15:11) and then to Pharaoh and the Egyptians (Exodus 5:2; 14:4, 18). But this psalm draws attention to God's special relationship with his people associated with the central sanctuary in Jerusalem. It was to the chosen nation, made up of 'Judah' and 'Israel' (verse 1), that God revealed himself more fully ('known') and his majestic presence ('name'; see Psalm 75:1) was more clearly appreciated ('great'; see Psalm 95:3). The following two verses explain how this was the case.

Verse 2 provides a good example of one of the typical features of Hebrew poetry, synonymous parallelism, where the second line reinforces the first (see Psalm 2). 'Salem' (elsewhere only found in Genesis 14:18 and Hebrews 7:1–2), and 'Zion' (Psalms 2:6; 74:2) both refer to Jerusalem, and the two terms, 'tabernacle' (see Psalm 27:5) and 'dwelling-place', to the sanctuary first set up by David in his capital city (2 Samuel 6:17). These two words, 'tabernacle' and 'dwelling-place', for God's residence in Jerusalem are unusual and both are associated with a lion's lair or den (Job 37:8; Psalms 10:9; 104:22; Jeremiah 25:38; Amos 3:4). They suggest that God's earthly home was to be seen as a makeshift, temporary place like the 'huts' or 'booths' that the people made out of branches during the festival of tabernacles. Perhaps in this context the terms are used to view God's presence in Jerusalem like a lion in its den ready to pounce on its prey (Isaiah 31:4; Jeremiah 25:38; Amos 1:2). The psalms have already drawn attention to God's choice of Zion (Psalms 46:4–5; 68:15–18) and to his residence and activity there (Psalms 9:11; 14:7; 20:2; 48:2–3; etc.).

It was in his victories over well-armed opponents that God was known and the greatness of his character acknowledged by his people. As the enemies came against them God destroyed all their weapons of war (see Psalm 46:9). The description is vivid with the 'arrows' (literally 'flames', verse 3) pictured as flashes or bolts of lightning. God brings peace to Salem whose name resembles the word for peace (Hebrews 7:2). As the introductory Psalm 2 has shown, the enemies of God are constantly making attempts to fight against him and his Anointed. We are also taught that to fight against Messiah's people is to fight against the Messiah himself (Acts 4:23–31; 9:5). Spurgeon aptly comments, 'no weapon that is formed against the church shall prosper' and the 'Selah' gives opportunity to pause and reflect on this truth before going on to expand on the defeat of God's enemies.

God's power over his foes (verses 4–6)

God is now directly addressed ('You', verse 4) and, as in the previous psalm, called 'God of Jacob' (verse 6; see Psalm 75:9). The verses celebrate his power in the destruction of the enemy. Victory over his foes shows him 'glorious' or 'illustrious' (literally 'enveloped in light', verse 4; see Psalm 104:2) and 'excellent' ('majestic'; see Psalm 8:1, 9). The thought of God as a lion in its den (see verse 2) helps us to appreciate the phrase 'mountains of prey' (verse 4). People are sometimes depicted as prey (see Psalm 124:6; Nahum 2:12). The imagery suggests that the hills around Jerusalem are filled with the corpses of the enemy as a result of God's intervention on behalf of his people (see Isaiah 5:29; 31:4; 37:36), revealing how superior he is to the hostile forces. A more literal translation catches the meaning: 'Glorious you are, majestic from the mountains of prey'.

The 'stout-hearted' enemy (see Isaiah 46:12) that expected to take spoil were themselves taken as spoil ('plundered', verse 5; see Exodus 15:9). Valiant fighting men were unable 'to lift a hand' but had 'sunk into their sleep' which, if literal, is contrary to what one would expect from an enemy about to attack (see Isaiah 5:27) but it could be referring to their death (Psalm 13:3; Nahum 3:18). The reason for this turn of events is the power of God's 'rebuke' (see Psalms 9:5; 18:13–15; 20:1) which led to 'chariot and horse' falling silent. It recalls the Red Sea incident (Exodus 14:23–28; 15:1) which Isaiah uses to illustrate the new exodus from Babylon (Isaiah 43:17; 50:2). The 'dead sleep' either refers to falling into a deep sleep (Judges 4:21), the result of supernatural action as in the case of Adam and Saul (Genesis 2:21; 1 Samuel 26:12) or, as our translation rightly suggests, to the sleep of death. We are taught, as Calvin aptly observes, that whatever natural abilities people may possess, God is able to deprive them of their powers and 'by the mere breath of his mouth to subdue and dissipate all assailants'.

God's presence in judgment (verses 7–9)

The psalmist continues addressing God but the focus moves from praising God's power to praising his righteous wrath. It is God and God alone who is to be feared—revered by his people (Isaiah 8:13) but a terrifying prospect to his enemies. When God's anger is aroused who can stand one's ground in opposition to him? (see Psalms 1:5; 2:12; 130:3). It may appear to God's enemies that he is not concerned when the wicked triumph over the godly but there is a day of reckoning. There is a time for God's anger to be revealed—'when once you are angry' (verse 7).

The God who dwells among his people in Zion is the one who is in 'heaven' (verse 8; Matthew 6:9): a close link exists between the two as there also exists between his being in heaven and with each repentant person (see Isaiah 57:15). It was 'from heaven' that God's 'sentence' or 'decision' ('judgment' verse 8) was heard that led to the destruction of the enemy so that on 'earth' it resulted in 'fear' and a stillness and quiet that comes after war (see Joshua 14:15; 2 Kings 11:20). Verse 9 alludes to the same event emphasising its solemn nature—'God arose to judgment'. He stood up to pass sentence and take action. Defeating the foes led to deliverance for God's 'oppressed' or more accurately, his helpless 'humble poor' followers the world over (Psalms 9:12; 22:26; 74:19, 21). God commenced his work of salvation with one nation that blessing might come to the whole world. Through Jesus the Messiah the great enemy has been defeated and 'mournful, broken hearts rejoice, the humble poor believe'.[9] Another pause is appropriate at this point ('Selah', verse 9) before proceeding to the final verses.

That wrath that consumed Pharaoh's army at the Red Sea and which brought dread to the surrounding nations and led to God's delivered people revering him (Exodus 15:7, 11, 16) is a picture and warning of the wrath to come. There is an end-time judgment when the wrath that is revealed already (Psalm 90:7-11; Romans 1:18) will give way to its final awesome expression when God consigns all those opposed to his rule to unending, conscious punishment (Revelation 14:10-11; 20:10-15) and ensures the eternal safety of God's people.

God's proper dues (verses 10–12)

Worship in the form of praise and homage to this awesome God is the appropriate response. Human wrath that rages against God and persecutes his people is employed by God to redound to his honour and praise. Even the remnants of such wrath God can use to his glory, like a king securing his sword around his waist to enhance his majestic splendour—'with the remainder of wrath you shall gird yourself' (verse 10; see Psalm 45:3). The supreme demonstration of this truth was at the cross of Jesus. There we see human fury in all its ugliness directed toward the Son of God. But in God's gracious purposes that atrocious act brought honour to his name in the salvation of sinners (Acts 2:23; Ephesians 1:3-14). For the people of God in all ages it is a comforting thought that no human or demonic activity is outside of God's control. The 'kingdom shall be the Lord's' and not only in Judah will God be known (verse 1) but 'the earth will be filled with the knowledge of the glory of the Lord as the waters cover the sea' (Obadiah v. 21; Habakkuk 2:14).

In view of all God's gracious activity on behalf of his people, what should we 'render to the Lord for all his benefits'? (Psalm 116:12). Promises made to 'the Lord' their God in times of trouble are to be kept when deliverance comes ('Make vows ... and pay', verse 11). It is an indication of a thankful, grateful spirit to dedicate ourselves to his service, but let us be true to our word.

When God delivered Hezekiah and his people from Sennacherib's army in answer to the prayers of the king and Isaiah the prophet, 'many brought gifts to the Lord at Jerusalem and presents to Hezekiah king of Judah, so that he was exalted in the sight of all nations thereafter' (2 Chronicles 32:23). While gifts came from God's people, 'presents' or 'tribute' came from the surrounding nations, thus enhancing Hezekiah's reputation. This seems to be the meaning here where 'all who are around him' (verse 11) are those over whom the 'Awesome One', the one 'who ought to be feared' (literally 'the Fear'; see Isaiah 8:13) is victorious. They are urged to show their allegiance (see Psalm 2:10-11) by offering 'presents' or 'homage gifts' (see Psalm 68:29; Isaiah 18:7). The idea is similar to the picture presented in Psalm 72:10-11 and Revelation 21:24.

The final verse, like Psalm 2, includes a warning that God is 'awesome to the kings of the earth' for he has the power to 'cut off' the lives of rulers as a grape cluster is 'gathered' or 'cut off' from the vine (Leviticus 25:5). Israel's history bore witness to this when the Lord saved his people at the Red Sea and 'Israel saw the Egyptians dead on the sea-shore' (Exodus 14:30) and when the Assyrian army was cut down and Sennacherib himself struck down (2 Chronicles 32:21). Those reading this psalm in the aftermath of the Babylonian invasion and destruction of Jerusalem and its temple, whose feelings are conveyed in such poems as Psalm 74, would have been encouraged to pray on like Daniel and keep trusting the true and living God. Christians, too, experiencing untold suffering at the hands of cruel authorities, can likewise have confidence in the God who has won the decisive battle at Calvary's cross, and can therefore be assured of the day when the enemies of God's rule will have all been defeated and the 'kingdoms of this world have become the kingdoms of our Lord and of his Christ' (Revelation 11:15).

Psalm 77

Consolation through Contemplation

Have you ever had doubts about God? Doubts do not normally appear when all is going well. It is in times of adversity and trouble that we can be plagued with thoughts that make it difficult to worship God. What an encouragement that such a psalm as this exists as part of God's Word to us and for us to use in prayer to God! God is so kind and understanding. He knows our frame and remembers how weak we are.

This is a psalm to help distressed believers find real comfort in stressful times. The psalm is also a pattern prayer that the persecuted church can use in communal worship. As Calvin perceptively comments, 'It is not the private grief of some particular individual which is here expressed, but the lamentations and groanings of the chosen people'. Like so many psalms of this type, it begins with lament and ends on a more positive note. There is no hint of the particular occasion that gave rise to the poem but it bears resemblances to Psalm 74 and the prayer of Habakkuk (Habakkuk 3). Whenever the psalm was actually written, it would certainly have come into its own in that period following the fall of Jerusalem in 587 BC and during the Babylonian captivity of the Jews.

The heading includes a reference to 'Jeduthun' (see Psalm 39) who, with Asaph and Heman, belonged to a family of Levites appointed by

40

David to lead the singing in the sanctuary. As in Psalm 62 the wording is literally 'on' or 'according to' (not 'To') suggesting that the psalm is to be sung to music associated with Jeduthun (2 Chronicles 5:12). Both before and after the Babylonian exile, the families of Asaph and Jeduthun continued to have responsibilities for music in the temple (2 Chronicles 35:15; Nehemiah 11:17). The 'Selah' (verses 3, 9, 15) helps to mark out the divisions within the poem with the words 'remember' and 'meditate' appearing in each of the first three sections (verses 3, 6, 11, 12).

Thoughts that trouble (verses 1–3)

Just as Israel 'cried out' on account of their bondage in Egypt (Exodus 2:23–24) so the psalmist 'cried out' to God 'with full voice' ('my voice ... my voice') that God would hear his urgent cries. The phrase 'and he gave ear' (verse 1) would be better translated 'that he may give ear', for it indicates in this context the reason for his praying rather than the result. Day and night in his distress he 'sought' help from the sovereign God ('Lord') with hands outstretched in supplication (1 Kings 8:22). Holding the hand out for long periods can cause numbness but as the phrase 'without ceasing' (verse 2) in the original suggests, Asaph made sure that 'it was not numb'. Human consolation however well-meaning was unacceptable. The psalmist's state was like that of Jacob mourning over Joseph who 'refused to be comforted' (verse 2; Genesis 37:35).

Why is the psalmist 'troubled' or 'agitated' (see Psalm 46:3, 6) and his spirit 'overwhelmed' or 'fainting' when he thinks about ('remembered') God and meditates ('complained', see verse 6)? Perhaps he is overawed by God's inscrutable ways. Job, in his grave situation, exhibited a similar agitated state of mind when God seemed so inaccessible (Job 23:15–16). The psalmist is in the situation of Israel before God acted to deliver them. It was at least eighty years after their groans and cries were first heard that the people were rescued under the leadership of Moses and Aaron.

Thoughts that depress (verses 4–9)

The psalmist's anguish continues in verse 4. Although he was making urgent appeals to God day and night (verses 1–3), his sleeplessness he believes is due to God holding open his 'eyelids' (literally, 'the guards of my eyes') and his 'troubled' state makes it impossible for him to 'speak' in praise of God and of his power (Psalm 137:1–4). His mind turned to think of better times ('days of old ...', verse 5), reminiscing nostalgically 'on the years of long ago' and he remembered as he lay awake 'in the night', the kind of 'song' or 'music' with which he used to praise God (verse 6).[10] The psalmist depicts a similar desperate state in Psalm 42:4 and as in that psalm, the antidote to despondency is not to listen to self as it recounts the good old days. 'Hankering after the past is', as Motyer puts it, 'no remedy for the present and no recipe for the future'. As he talked to himself ('I meditate within my heart', verse 6; see verse 12) he searched earnestly to understand God's ways. It led him to raise serious questions about God that he lists in the following verses (verses 7–9). They cannot be easily dismissed as mere rhetorical questions that expect the answer 'No'. There are echoes from previous psalms as, with remarkable honesty, Asaph expresses the temptation he had to doubt the very character of God. He thinks the unthinkable. The second question in each of the three verses underlines the point made in the first half of each verse—'cast off' parallels 'favourable no more'; 'mercy' parallels 'promise', etc.

The book of Lamentations, written after the collapse of Jerusalem into the hands of the Babylonians asserted 'For the Lord will not cast off for ever' (Lamentations 3:31) yet the psalmist, using the same words, seems unsure as he asks whether the sovereign Lord will 'cast off ('reject') for ever?' (verse 7). This has been a concern in a number of psalms and is sometimes introduced with the question 'Why?' (Psalms 43:2; 44:9, 23; 60:1, 10; 74:1). Will God no longer be 'favourable' ('be pleased with', verse 7) in the way he showed his goodwill in the past (see Psalm 44:3)?

The next question is even bolder. God's 'mercy' (or 'loving-kindness', verse 8; see Psalms 17:7; 26:3) is his 'unfailing love' and the whole of Psalm 136 celebrates the fact that it lasts 'for ever'. Yet the psalmist questions whether such loving commitment has 'ceased' to be perpetual (see Psalm 74:1, 3, 19). God's special relationship to Israel is in mind here as the supporting line indicates with reference to his 'saying' or 'promise'. The psalmist may be thinking not only of his covenant promise to Abraham (Genesis 17:7) but also of the one made to David (2 Samuel 7:12–16). Has God's word of promise 'failed' or 'come to a close' for all future generations ('for evermore', verse 8)?

In continuing to debate with himself, as Calvin puts it, the psalmist asks whether God has 'forgotten to be gracious' and 'shut up', in the sense of 'withheld' his 'tender mercies', his 'compassion' (verse 9). It is at this point that he introduces God's 'anger' (see Psalm 74:1), which as Kidner points out, is only aroused by sin. All these references to God's character were revealed when Moses asked to see God's glory (Exodus 34:5–7). The psalmist is tempted to question these very basic truths concerning God and his relationship with his people. Christians down the centuries have been tempted to ask similar questions in times of deep distress: does God care and if he does why does he not act to put an end to these things? While it is better to express our doubts particularly to God and not bottle them up it does not bring comfort. The psalmist's crying out to God and audacious questioning has not settled anything. There are occasions when prayer is not the first resort especially when we are full of troubled thoughts. The next section reveals the way forward and the 'Selah' at this point suggests a pause and a change of mood and thought.

Thoughts that encourage (verses 10–15)

It is best to take verse 10 as the pivotal point in the psalm with the first part—'And I said, "This is my anguish"'—looking to the depressing things said in the previous verses and the second part—'the years of the right hand of the Most High'—preparing for the fresh way of looking at the past.[11] There is also a shift at this halfway point from 'I' to 'you', from self to God. It is not by questioning God or by looking to past experiences and wistfully longing for those earlier times but by thinking of God as the one who has acted in history that comfort comes. This is how the prophet Habakkuk found comfort by reminding himself of Israel's redemptive history (Habakkuk 3:3–15). Confidence was renewed, hope revived, the heart gladdened, enabling psalmist and prophet to go on in spite of circumstances. The Christian has a redemptive history of which Israel's history was but a pale reflection.

Asaph refers to God as the 'Most High', a description that draws attention to his sovereignty over the nations (Genesis 14:18–22; Numbers 24:16; Deuteronomy 32:8 and found twelve times in the book of Daniel; see Psalm 7:17). It was the powerful 'right hand' of this universal ruler that was in evidence at the Red Sea (Exodus 15:6, 12; Psalms 17:7; 20:6). Asaph is determined now to 'remember' the 'works' and 'wonders' of 'the LORD' (verse 11) and in doing so he uses the covenantal name, 'LORD' (Yahweh/Jehovah), rare in these particular psalms (see Psalm 42), nevertheless precious to God's people, especially from the time of the exodus (Exodus 3–4). John Newton expressed the truth that for the believer the very name of Jesus is a sound 'sweet' to his ears, one that 'soothes his sorrows, heals his wounds and drives away his fear'. With this special name in mind, the psalmist reflected (for 'meditate' see Psalm 1:2 and for 'talk' or 'muse' see above on verse 6) on God's extraordinary activity in Egypt and at the Red Sea in order to redeem them from bondage and was immediately encouraged. Like those songwriters of old, Christians can look to what God has actually done in history and find hope and consolation. Our faith is based not on cleverly devised myths or the ideas of mystics and philosophers but on an historical event. God's redeeming work is accomplished through the actual life, death and resurrection of Jesus the Messiah, God's Son (2 Peter 1:16; 1 Corinthians 15).

The allusions to the exodus event continue almost to the point of quotation. Verses 13 and 14 echo the song of Moses and the people: 'Who is like you, O LORD, among the gods? Who is like you, glorious in holiness, fearful in praises, doing wonders?' (Exodus 15:11). It is for this reason we should translate more literally, 'Your way, O God, is in holiness' rather than 'in the sanctuary'. God's way of dealing with his people is characterised by holiness. God's holiness is what makes God, God. He is unique. That otherness of God was revealed in the destruction of Pharaoh's army and the deliverance of Israel. The God of Israel cannot be compared with anyone else. He alone is 'great' (Deuteronomy 7:21; Psalms 48:1; 95:3). His greatness was witnessed at the Red Sea when the signs and 'wonders' (see verse 11) reached a climax in the judgment on the Egyptians. The surrounding 'peoples' will hear of the 'strength' of God's 'arm' (see Exodus 15:6; Psalm 37:17) with which he 'redeemed' his people (verses 14–15; see Exodus 6:6; 15:14). Even at the end of the judges' period, the Philistines were well aware of what happened to the Egyptians at the hands of Israel's deity (1 Samuel 4:7–8).

God's people are here referred to by the unique expression 'the sons of Jacob and Joseph' (verse 15). A similar usage is found in Obadiah's prophecy (verse 18) where again 'the house of Jacob' and 'the house of Joseph' refer to the whole nation of Israel, Judah included.

At the time of the exodus, God made clear his sovereign power in human affairs by informing Pharaoh that he had been raised up 'that I may show my power in you, and that my name may be declared in all the earth' (Exodus 9:16). A different word for 'declared' (verse 14) is used here (literally, 'to make known') but the thought is the same. This is an historical fact, witnessed and acknowledged by many peoples and no figment of Israel's imagination. Recalling these points brought great encouragement to faith. In the same way there are eyewitnesses to Christ's death and resurrection so that a Christian's faith rests solidly on what happened in our world at a particular moment in history, significant enough to divide that history into 'before' and 'after' the event. This is a good moment to pause ('Selah', verse 15) and consider the 'arm of the Lord' that appeared in the person of God's Son Jesus Christ to pay the costly price for the redemption of his people from bondage to sin, Satan and the curse of the law (Isaiah 53; Romans 3:24; Galatians 3:13; Hebrews 2:14-15; 1 Peter 1:18-19; Revelation 5:9).

Thoughts that burst into praise (verses 16–20)

As in Psalm 74 the psalmist waxes lyrical as he describes God's amazing victory at the Red Sea. It is as if Asaph were present as an eyewitness. God's power over the turbulent waters and the sea, a frequent theme in the Bible, is celebrated in these verses (see Psalms 18:7-16; 29:3-4; Habakkuk 3:3-15). The fearful sights and sounds of Sinai (verses 17-18; see Exodus 19:16-18) that spoke of God's awesome presence is used to impress upon us God's intervention and powerful activity in the salvation of his people. God's 'way' which is 'in holiness' (verse 13) was also 'in the sea' (verse 19; see Habakkuk 3:15) to effect deliverance for his people, but his 'footsteps were not known'. He passed through 'the great waters' yet no one could later trace his footprints at the scene. The phrase also suggests that God's ways are inscrutable and 'past finding out' (Romans 11:33). Augustus Toplady's great hymn comes to mind:

A Sovereign Protector I have,
Unseen yet for ever at hand,
Unchangeably faithful to save,
Almighty to rule and command.

With the song of Moses again in his thoughts (Exodus 15:13), Asaph brings his poem to a close by relating how God led and guided the people he had redeemed (verse 20). This is no anticlimax but an encouragement to believe that as God acted powerfully against Israel's foes and shepherded his people through human agents like Moses and

Aaron (Exodus 12:50; Numbers 33:1; 1 Samuel 12:6; Micah 6:4), so God can do the same in the particular crisis that the psalmist is facing.

As believers today, when the powers of darkness seem overwhelming, we remember how God acted in Christ at the cross to defeat the devil and his henchmen, rising triumphant over death. As Israel praised God after their deliverance from Pharaoh's army so John views the church praising God in the song of Moses and of the Lamb, for the greater victory accomplished through the Lamb's redeeming work (Revelation 15:3–4). We are encouraged in the present when faced with opposition and persecution to take to heart Jesus' words, 'Do not fear, little flock, for it is your Father's good pleasure to give you the kingdom' (Luke 12:32). Believers are 'more than conquerors' through him who loved us and are enabled to be triumphant in the worst of situations.

Psalm 78

Preaching the Old, Old Story

History is considered by many to be boring and uninviting. Perhaps this is because of the way it has been taught in the past, while for others it may be due to the spirit of the age, which despises the past and lives only for the moment. As Christians, this kind of thinking must be resisted for Christianity is based solidly on what has happened in the past and history is meant to teach us lessons from which we would do well to learn.

Psalm 78 is the second longest psalm and is often associated with Psalms 105, 106 and 136 as historical psalms, but whereas those poems are clearly in the form of hymns of praise to God that draw on Israel's history, this psalm is a sermon directed to God's people. Like Moses preaching to the people of Israel in the plains of Moab shortly before his death, (Deuteronomy 1:1–5) this psalm recounts Israel's history with the purpose of encouraging, warning and exhorting his own generation to faithful obedience rather than defiant rebellion. The heading states that this is a 'Contemplation of Asaph'. There are thirteen 'contemplation' (*maskil*) psalms (see Psalms 32, 42, etc.), the previous one being Psalm 74. Asaph (see Psalm 73), one of the chief sanctuary musicians of the David-Solomon era, was father to a family of Levites who had a prophetic function that not only included expressing praise to God but the ability to bring words of exhortation and direction from God to the people. The Chronicler draws our attention to these men throughout his work (1 Chronicles 16:5; 25:1-5; 2 Chronicles 20:14-17; 34:30; see 2 Kings 23:2). The Levites were also given the task of teaching God's law and this psalm is full of references and allusions to that law.

After an introduction that presents the preacher's purpose in writing, the psalm reviews the history of Israel to the time of David, pulling no punches as attention is drawn alternatively to the people's rebellion and ingratitude, and to God's continued goodness and faithfulness in the face of great provocation.

The history of Israel from the exodus to the time of David is reviewed in two parallel sections, verses 9-39 and 40-72. Both sections begin with failure due to forgetfulness (verses 9-11, 40-42), then highlight God's wonderful acts (verses 12-16, 43-55), Israel's sin and God's judgment (verses 17-33, 56-64), and end by drawing attention to God's compassion and continuing plans for his people (verses 34-39, 65-72). The review begins and ends with a reference to Ephraim and his failure and rejection, with the object of highlighting God's choice of Judah, Zion and David.

Statement of intent (verses 1–8)

Asaph, the Levite preacher-prophet (2 Chronicles 29:30), calls his people's attention ('Give ear ... incline your ears', verse 1) to the sobering yet encouraging message ('law' is used in the general sense of 'instruction') he has been given to deliver. He speaks like the wisdom teacher (Proverbs 7:24) but even more like Moses in his song where he also draws on Israel's early history to teach his people (Deuteronomy 32).

In verse 2 Asaph continues to emphasise that what he has to say is important. Like a prophet or wisdom teacher he will 'open' his mouth (see Proverbs 1:23; 31:26; Ezekiel 3:27; 33:22) and 'utter' ('pour out') his authoritative word. He describes what he has to say as a 'parable' and 'dark sayings' (see Psalm 49:4; Proverbs 1:6). The past can be 'a tangle of events' that needs explaining, a 'riddle' or mystery that needs interpreting. From Israel's history ('of old'), he desires to impart profound truth, showing that their story has a meaning. This verse is used by Matthew to show that Jesus in his teaching fulfils a pattern or type visible in Asaph's psalm of instruction (Matthew 13:34-35). Asaph is not only explaining patterns in redemptive history but is himself,

Matthew is saying, part of Scripture which Jesus fulfils when he uses parables.

The language of verse 3 brings to mind Psalm 44 but the situation is different. In the earlier psalm the account of God's activity in the past led to the question of why God was not acting in their present crisis but here the concern is to show from Israel's history their repeated rebellious responses to God's gracious activity.

Asaph sees himself as part of an important chain in which the story of Israel's redemptive history is passed on from parents to children. Telling 'the generation to come' (verses 4 and 6) was not a mere cultural tradition for present and future generations to encourage, but a divine obligation ('he commanded', verse 5), instilled into the people from the very beginning (Exodus 10:1-2; 12:26-27; Deuteronomy 4:9; 6:20-25). Christian parents likewise have a sacred duty to teach the faith to their children (Ephesians 6:4). Timothy's mother and grandmother took their responsibilities seriously in teaching him the holy Scriptures (2 Timothy 3:15), described here as the 'testimony' and 'law' that God 'established' and 'appointed' in 'Jacob' (verse 5; with 'Israel' in the parallel expression the terms emphasise the one nation made up of the twelve tribes). The content of the sacred tradition, which makes 'the LORD' (Yahweh/Jehovah) worthy of praise, includes his revelatory word ('testimony', 'law', verse 5; see Psalm 19:7-10) and his amazing deeds ('his strength' and 'wonderful works', verse 4).

The purpose of declaring or recounting this history to future generations is stated positively in verse 7 and negatively in verse 8. Instead of the stupidity of looking to useless objects (Psalm 49:13), it will encourage them to have a 'simple confidence' ('set their hope') in God,[12] not forgetting the basic ingredients of their relationship: God's 'works' of grace and power and their obedience to 'his commandments'. Put negatively, the story they pass on will act as a warning not to behave like their ancestors who were 'a stubborn and rebellious generation' (see Deuteronomy 21:18). The reason for the people's rebellion is given: their 'heart' was not 'set ... aright' ('not established' or 'firm') and their 'spirit' was not 'faithful to God'. Despite all their good intentions there was a problem in their innermost being. They needed 'a circumcised heart' (Deuteronomy 10:16; 30:6), what Jesus described as a new birth from above (John 3:3-10). Asaph's recital of Israel's history will reveal both God's grace and Israel's rebellious nature.

First Review of Israel's history (verses 9–39)

A. Israel's forgetfulness (verses 9–11)

These verses correspond with verses 42–44 to form a fitting preface to each historical survey that follows. Both begin by pointing out the main lesson to be learnt from Israel's history—the people's unfaithfulness despite God's gracious activity. There is deliberate ambiguity in the use of the name 'Ephraim'. It is introduced here to represent the whole of Israel as an example of the nation's rebellious spirit that the bulk of the psalm highlights. It is also employed to represent the northern tribes' divisive, anti-Christ spirit that opposed the king 'after God's own heart' and it is with that background in mind that the name appears again in the final section of the psalm (verse 67).

Ephraim's representative status was due to the fact that from the beginning it was the dominant tribe (Genesis 48:17; Deuteronomy 33:17), allotted a central location in Canaan, and described by Ralph Davis as 'a prima donna among the tribes, a corporate Diotrephes (3 John 9),'[13] proud and domineering (Judges 8:1-3; 12:1-6). Joshua and Samuel were among its famous sons (1 Chronicles 7:27; 1 Samuel 1:1, 19-20). The name, Ephraim, was also associated with the northern tribes and when the great split took place after the death of Solomon, Ephraim's importance was recognised for it was used frequently by Hosea as a synonym for the northern kingdom of Israel as distinct from the southern kingdom of Judah (Hosea 5:3, 11-14; 6:4; etc.). But even prior to that final break Ephraim was among the northern tribes slow to accept David as king (2 Samuel 2:8-11) and it was an Ephraimite, Jeroboam, who rebelled against Solomon's rule and who eventually became king of the breakaway state in the north (1 Kings 11:26; 12:1-33). Ephraim's name appears again in the closing section of the psalm (verse 67) so that it frames the two reviews and indicates a second reason for Asaph's recital of Israel's history—to show how Ephraim's prominence was transferred to Judah.

The 'day of battle' (verse 9) could either refer to Israel's defeat by the Philistines when they destroyed the sanctuary at Shiloh, situated within Ephraim's borders, and captured the ark of the covenant (see verses 60-61; 1 Samuel 4-6) or to Israel's defeat by the Philistines when Saul was killed (1 Samuel 31), the event that opened up the way for David to become king. In both cases Israel, though equipped for battle ('armed ... carrying bows', verse 9), 'turned back' or 'fled' from the scene. Both situations were due to Israel's disloyalty to the 'covenant of God' (verse 10) and failure to remember God's acts, those 'wonders' or extraordinary deeds (verse 11), that had originally delivered them from slavery and in the light of which they were to live obedient to God's 'law' (see Exodus 20:1-2). It is in view of God's saving mercies that Christians are called to serve God (Romans 12:1-2).

B. God's amazing activity (verses 12–16)
The references to 'wonders' (verse 11) leads into a recital of what God did at the time of the exodus from the plagues which their ancestors, the original eye-witnesses, saw (verse 12; see Exodus 3:20) to the Red Sea incident (verse 13; see Exodus 15:8), not forgetting 'the cloud' that led them by day and the 'light of fire' by night (verse 14; see Exodus 13:21-22). 'Zoan', called Tanis by the Greeks, was an ancient capital city of Egypt in the Nile Delta. It is used here along with a reference to its countryside ('field'), to represent the seat of Pharaoh's power and influence (see Numbers 13:22; Isaiah 19:11, 13; Ezekiel 30:14).

God's miraculous power was also seen in providing for the people's needs in the wilderness. He not only 'split' ('divided', verse 13; see Exodus 14:16, 21) the sea, he also 'split' (verse 15) the rocks to provide water in abundance (see Exodus 17:6) and on more than one occasion (verse 16; see Numbers 20:8-11).

Paul calls attention to the cloud, the sea and God's provisions as an indication of the privileges Israel received and sees them as types and analogies of the Corinthian believers' favoured position in Christ in order, as in the psalm, to draw out the same spiritual lessons and as a warning to the people not to give way to temptation (1 Corinthians 10:1-4).

C. Israel's sin (verses 17–20)
Instead of encouraging the people to live obediently, God's gracious and powerful deeds had only served to make them more defiant in their rebellion against the 'Most High' (verse 17; see Psalm 7:17; Deuteronomy 32:8). No sooner had they come out of Egypt than they 'tested God in their heart' (verse 18). What they expressed with their lips was an indication of a sinful rebellious nature. While Moses showed how the people grumbled against him and Aaron (Exodus 15:24; 16:2; 17:2-3; Numbers 14:2), the psalm, true to its statement of intent (see verses 1-8), emphasises that the real target was God himself

(see verses 17–19). They had a basic distrust of God, which led them to test his powers rather than simply to rely on him to provide their needs. This distrust of God revealed itself in their continual moans over lack of water, first at Marah, then at Rephidim (Exodus 15:24; 17:1-4) and in their sarcastic comments over God's ability to 'prepare a table in the wilderness' (verse 19; Exodus 16:2-3; see Psalm 23:5). Their reasoning is that God's power to give water miraculously and in abundance is no guarantee that he can provide food for the people (verse 20).

D. God's fury (verses 21–33)

Asaph uses God's reaction to the people's complaints recorded in Numbers 11:1-3 to express his response to their unbelief (verse 21). God in his grace continued to provide but he also indicated his hot displeasure at their attitude. Their lack of trust in God is emphasised again—'did not believe ... did not trust' (verse 22). In their extremity at the Red Sea the people had 'feared the Lord and believed the Lord' (Exodus 14:31) but they soon lost confidence in the one whom they had celebrated in song as 'my salvation' (Exodus 15:2). In spite of many more instances of God's gracious activity in feeding and caring for his people, 'they still sinned and did not believe his wonderful works' (verse 32).

Attention is drawn to two examples where God provided his people with food. The first is the vivid recollection of 'the bread ('grain')' from heaven' that rained down, the 'manna' as it was called (verse 24; Exodus 16:4, 35). Its heavenly origin is further expressed by the phrase 'angels' food' (literally 'bread of the valiant ones', verse 25; see Psalms 76:5, 'stout'; 103:20) and there was enough of it for everyone and it was satisfying ('food to the full'). Paul speaks of Israel eating 'spiritual food' for the manna was symbolic of Christ, as Jesus indicated when he spoke of himself as the true bread which came down from heaven (John 6:31-35; 1 Corinthians 10:3). As Israel grumbled ungratefully and despised God's gracious, miraculous provision so many of those to whom Jesus spoke grumbled, took offence and turned their backs on the one whom the Father had sent for their eternal well-being (John 6:41, 52, 61, 66).

The second example brings together two passages where God provided meat in the form of quails (Exodus 16:13; Numbers 11:31-34). He used winds from both south and east to 'rain' the birds on Israel's camp site as he had 'rained' the manna (verses 24, 26-28). The God who had shown extravagant grace in giving them water in abundance (verse 20) so overwhelmed them with food on the second occasion that it became a punishment for their greed (verses 29–31; see Numbers 11:33). Sinful cravings can lead to God's good gifts becoming a punishment (see James 1:13–17). It is a salutary reminder that sometimes God in his grace withholds desires that are not in our best interests.

The paragraph closes (verses 32–33) by summarising the forty-year wilderness period. Not only did the people continue to distrust despite continuing evidences of God's grace and power in his 'wondrous works' (see verses 4, 11; Numbers 14:11, 22–23), they 'still sinned' even in the face of God's wrath that was meant to discipline them and bring them to their senses. For this reason the whole generation that left Egypt died out, 'consumed' in the wilderness (see Numbers 14:33). Those years in the wilderness proved a miserable existence where life was brief, a mere 'breath' ('in futility', see verse 39; Ecclesiastes 7:15; 9:9) and uncertain, 'sudden terror' ('in fear', see Leviticus 26:16).

E. God's faithfulness despite Israel's unfaithfulness (verses 34–39)

This final paragraph seems to take in the judges' period when God's judgment on the people's sin led them to repent and call out to God for help (Judges 3:7–15) and this may also have happened during the wilderness wanderings. When God punished some of them ('slew them'), the rest expressed a temporary change of heart, they repented ('returned') and 'sought' help from God (verse 34). Only then did they call to mind that the 'Most High' (see verse 17) was their refuge ('rock'; see Deuteronomy 32:4, 15–18; Psalm 18:2) and their kinsman 'redeemer' who protects them (verse 35; see Psalm 19:14).

There follows a sad description of their hypocritical devotion, seeking to deceive God and deliberately lie to him. They were despising the special relationship that God had entered into with them ('his covenant') by their lack of commitment (see verse 10). The problem lay in the 'heart', at the very centre of their lives (see verse 8). It was not 'steadfast' (see Psalm 57:7). Using similar language from Isaiah, Jesus accused the religious leaders of his own day, of honouring God with their lips while their hearts were far from him (Isaiah 29:13; Mark 7:6).

The contrast between God and his people is most remarkable. While his people sinned 'in spite of' God's wrath (verses 31–32), God ('But he') showed 'compassion' despite their unfaithfulness and 'forgave' ('made

atonement for'; see Psalm 65:3) iniquity and on numerous occasions
he did not destroy the whole nation but turned his anger away and did
not arouse 'all his wrath' (verses 38–39). In this he displayed himself
(his 'name') as a God who is both 'merciful and gracious, long-suffering
... forgiving iniquity ...' and yet one who punishes the guilty (Exodus
34:5–7). This tension between God's anger and compassion is revealed
from Exodus to Deuteronomy (Exodus 32:9–14; Numbers 14:11–24;
Deuteronomy 4:31). The reason for God's patience in restraining his
anger is because he took account of their frailty ('flesh'; see Psalm 56:4)
and fleeting existence ('breath', a mere puff of 'wind'; verse 33 gives
another word with a similar idea; see Ecclesiastes 1:14). Psalms 90 and
103 in particular will develop further these themes of God's wrath and
compassion in relation to human weakness and the transient nature
of life. What an amazing God that he bears with wayward people like
ourselves and treats us with such compassion!

Second Review of Israel's history (verse 40–72)
Like an earnest preacher Asaph drives home his message by going
over the points he has already made but with the aim this time of
presenting the people with a future and a hope where the cycle of sin
and judgment is broken through the same God of all compassion.

Israel's forgetfulness (verses 40–42)
Unlike God who 'remembered' their weaknesses (verse 39), Israel
'did not remember' God's 'power' (literally 'his hand'; see Exodus
7:5; Deuteronomy 7:8) when he 'redeemed' them from the Egyptian
enemy (verse 42). The deliverance of his people from slavery was a
costly work. They were not bought with any human gifts. God acted
like a close relative and paid the price to set them free by exerting
his own outstretched 'hand'. It is a picture or type of our redemption
from slavery to sin and Satan by the precious blood of Christ (1 Peter
1:18–19).
It was because they were unmindful and forgot (see verse 11) that
they continually 'provoked' (or better, 'rebelled against') God and
repeatedly 'tempted' or 'tested' him (verses 40–41; see verse 56;
Numbers 14:22) by doubting his ability (see verse 19). They were like
the people who were continually asking Jesus for a sign when he had
presented them with many powerful acts (Mark 8:11–12; John 6:30).
All this brought the 'Holy One of Israel' grief and pain.[14] As in Isaiah's

prophecy (Isaiah 63:10), Asaph makes clear it is God's holiness that is affected by Israel's rebellion. Christians are likewise urged not to grieve the 'Holy Spirit of God' (Ephesians 4:30).

God's amazing activity (verses 43–55)

Mentioning the redemption from the enemy (verse 42), prompts a further recital of God's 'signs … wonders' in Egypt (verse 43; see verses 11–12; Deuteronomy 6:22). A more detailed description of those miraculous actions of God are given. Some examples of the 'plagues' that struck Egypt are mentioned but not in chronological order. First, the 'rivers into blood' (verse 44; Exodus 7:14–25), then 'swarms of flies' (verse 45; Exodus 8:20–32), 'frogs' (verse 45; Exodus 8:1–15), various types of 'locust' (verse 46; Exodus 10:1–20), 'hail' (verses 47–48; Exodus 9:13–35) and the death of the 'first-born' (verses 49–51; Exodus 11:1–10; 12:29–30). While God's wrath was always restrained toward Israel (see verse 38), the build-up of words expresses the full 'fierceness of his anger, wrath, indignation, and trouble' (verse 49) in the final plague when God sent 'angels of destruction' to destroy the descendants of Ham (see Genesis 10:6 where 'Mizraim' is the Hebrew for Egypt). It is a picture of the awesome end-time day of wrath (1 Thessalonians 1:10; 2 Thessalonians 1:7–9).

As in the previous review (verses 13–14, 'led'), God is likened to a shepherd leading his flock through the wilderness having 'overwhelmed their enemies' at the Red Sea, banishing Israel's fears (verses 52–53; see Exodus 14:13). There are also echoes of Moses' song in the concluding verses of the section, especially the sudden move from the exodus to the entry into Canaan (see Exodus 15:12–13). God guided and brought them to his 'holy border', a reference to the country that God had set apart for the holy nation and which he acquired by his powerful 'right hand'. It is further described as 'this mountain' referring to Canaan's hilly country (see Deuteronomy 3:25) but perhaps especially to Mount Zion (see verse 68), and its future in God's purposes as the place where he would dwell (verse 54; see Exodus 15:13, 17). God owned the land and he 'drove out' the previous occupants and allotted the territory (see Numbers 34:2; Joshua 13:6–7; 23:4) to 'the tribes of Israel'. The phrase 'by survey' refers to a measuring line for marking out areas of land (see Psalm 16:6; Amos 7:17).

Israel's sin (56–58)

The response of the people to God's gracious activity on their behalf
was the same after entrance into Canaan as in the wilderness. Like
their ancestors, they were unfaithful to their covenant commitments:
they 'turned aside' like an arrow shot from a bow that missed its target
(verse 57). They 'tested' (verse 56; see verses 18, 41) and 'rebelled against'
('provoked', see verses 8, 17, 40) the highest authority of all—'the Most
High God' (see verses 17, 35) and 'did not keep his testimonies' ('his
decrees'; see Deuteronomy 6:16–17). For the first time in the psalm
reference is made to the idolatry that arose after the death of Joshua
and the leaders that outlived him. God was provoked to anger by their
Canaanite pagan practices at the hill-shrines and, with the Second
Commandment concerning 'images' in mind, God is likened to a
husband whose passions are aroused when his wife proves unfaithful
(see Exodus 20: 4–6; Deuteronomy 5:8–9).

God's reaction (verses 59–64)

God's response to the people's rebellion was also the same after they
entered Canaan as it was in the wilderness—God 'heard' and 'was
furious' (see verse 21). He 'greatly abhorred' (or 'utterly rejected') his
people and the evidence of this was the destruction of the 'Shiloh'
tabernacle (verse 60; see Jeremiah 7:12–15; 26:6) and the capture of the
ark of the covenant by the Philistines (verse 61; see 1 Samuel 4).

The semi-permanent structure had been established there since the
days of Joshua (Joshua 18:1; 1 Samuel 1:3, 24; 3:3). In the centre of the
land, in Ephraimite territory, God had settled ('caused to dwell' rather
than 'had placed', verse 60), making his earthly home there among his
people (see Exodus 25:8). This was God's only earthly residence, implied
by the use of 'among men' (literally 'adam'—humanity). Eli's daughter-
in-law, the widow of one of his sons killed at that time, expressed
what is poetically portrayed here, by naming her child 'Ichabod' and
explaining, 'The glory has departed from Israel, for the ark of God
has been captured' (verses 61–64; 1 Samuel 4:19–22). To discipline
his people, God, in the fire of his wrath, allowed the symbol of his
stunning presence and importance to be taken into exile by the enemy
and the young men to be killed, a foretaste of what would happen
later when the Babylonians destroyed the Jerusalem temple. Ezekiel
saw in vision God's glory leaving the temple and moving toward the
east (Ezekiel 11:23). It is a sobering thought that God, in judgment, is

prepared to remove 'lampstands', i.e. churches (see Revelation 1:20; 2:5).

God's faithfulness despite Israel's unfaithfulness (verses 65–72)

The vivid imagery of the opening verses to this final section again expresses God's mercy and commitment to his covenant promises. There is a period of judgment but then comes the time for God to act on behalf of his people like someone awaking from sleep and like an excited warrior ('mighty man', verse 65) giving a joyful shout under the influence of wine. The enemy is driven back and put to perpetual dishonour (verse 66) which is what happened to the Philistines when, without human agency God humiliated them and their god (1 Samuel 5) and later when they were defeated under the leadership of Samuel, Saul and David.

The earlier reference to Ephraim (verses 9–11) and to the Ephraimite city of Shiloh and its sanctuary (verse 60) prepares for the transfer of influence and power from this dominant tribe of the north to Judah in the south with which the closing verses of the psalm are occupied. The ark never returned to Shiloh and Saul's dynasty associated with the northern tribes eventually collapsed (2 Samuel 2:9). The close link between Zion and David has already been emphasised in the introductory Psalm 2:6. God has firmly established this city of Zion and its sanctuary and he loves it (verses 68–69; see Psalm 87).

Though God had blessed Joseph and his two sons, particularly Ephraim, the younger (Genesis 48:14–22; 49:22–27) in whose territory God's sanctuary stood, in the end the descendants were by-passed. Two reasons are given: punishment on account of their sin (see verses 9–11) and God's sovereign choice (verses 67, 70). God in his purposes had in mind all along that from Judah, not Joseph, the true ruler of God's people would arise and that Mount Zion not Shiloh would be the place associated with God's special presence on earth. In a similar way, the first king of Israel was Saul of the tribe of Benjamin even though it was prophesied that the descendants of Judah would produce the royal line (Genesis 49:10). Saul's dynasty was rejected however, on account of his rebellious spirit and the kingdom handed over to David, the man after God's own heart (1 Chronicles 10:13–14; 1 Samuel 13:13–14; 15:22–23, 28). God's sovereignty and human responsibility are both acknowledged and we are not allowed to dismiss either in seeking to explain the mystery of God's ways.

The sovereignty of God's choice is highlighted by the description of David's humble origins and is a reminder of the truth that God 'does not see as man sees; for man looks at the outward appearance, but the LORD looks at the heart' (1 Samuel 16:7). From tending sheep God appointed David to 'shepherd' his people (2 Samuel 7:7–8), 'his inheritance' (verse 71; see Psalms 28:9; 74:2), shepherding and guiding (or 'led') them skilfully like the good shepherd himself (verse 72; see verses 14, 53; Isaiah 40:11). David's 'integrity' of heart is the pattern for his descendants to follow (1 Kings 9:4) for, despite grave wrongdoing, he remained loyal to God and did not worship false gods (1 Kings 11:4, 6; 2 Kings 22:2).

After the fall of Jerusalem in 587 BC, which is the context of a number of the surrounding psalms (see Psalms 74 and 79), this psalm, although composed during David's reign, will have been an encouragement to faithful Jews in exile. The psalm points forward to the fulfilment of God's purposes in the real shepherd of David's family line and to that Zion where God will be at home among his people for ever in the new creation. There is a future hope for the people of God in great David's greater Son, the 'Lion of the tribe of Judah', who, as the good shepherd, took the place of his people and became the 'Lamb slain' that he might shepherd them to fountains of life-giving water (Revelation 5:5–6; 7:17).

Psalm 79

For the Honour of God's Name

It would appear that this psalm was deliberately placed here immediately after the psalm that spoke of the rejection of Ephraim and the election of Judah, Zion and David. The hopes for the future with which that psalm ended were dramatically dashed by the events of 587 BC when Judah went into exile, God's sanctuary on the firmly established Mount Zion was destroyed and the Davidic monarchy was at an end with God's sheep scattered without a shepherd. Sadly, the people had taken to heart the encouragements of the psalm but had failed to heed the warnings (see Psalm 78:5-8). It was a feature of Israel's history as we read in 1 and 2 Kings and in the accusations and threats of prophets like Isaiah and Jeremiah. The picture of God's people like a flock of sheep provides another link with the surrounding psalms (verse 13; see Psalms 77:20; 78:70-72; 80:1).

This 'Psalm', one of a series associated with the 'Asaph' family of temple musicians and prophetic poets (Psalms 73-83), is closely related to Psalm 74 and describes the tragic situation that resulted from the fall of Jerusalem at the hands of Nebuchadnezzar's Babylonian army. There are indications in Jewish sources (1 Maccabees 7:16-17) that the psalm was used to express the people's distress during the desecration of the temple by Antiochus IV Epiphanes from 167-164 BC, and it has a permanent place in Jewish worship on the day they commemorate the destruction of Jerusalem. Christians have also employed this psalm especially during times of persecution. The early Christian leader, Jerome (c. 347–420), quoted it when Rome was invaded by the Visigoths in AD 410 and many French Protestant martyrs sang the psalm as they made their way to the scaffold.

Lament (verses 1–4)

With the briefest of introductions, ('O God'), the psalmist expresses the horrific situation that the enemy's actions have caused with a view to stirring God to action. Picking up the theme of God's 'inheritance' from the previous psalm (verse 1; Psalm 78:62, 71), he uses the word in this context, not of his people Israel, but to show how the 'nations', who are described later as those who do not acknowledge the true God (verse 6), have invaded his very own mount Zion (see Exodus 15:17). Not only that, these unclean pagans have 'defiled' the 'holy temple', God's earthly 'palace', by entering where only the priests and high priest were allowed (see Psalm 74:3–4). Ezekiel indicates that in fact the temple had been polluted by Israel before the enemy arrived so that the present situation was a punishment they deserved (Ezekiel 5:11; 23:38). The last line describing Jerusalem as in 'heaps' recalls the words of Micah 3:12 which are quoted by Jeremiah (Jeremiah 26:18) and more clearly acknowledges that this is a judgment from God.

The account of an eyewitness is evident in the description of how the people were affected and the shocking nature of the scene is made more poignant by emphasising that these were God's 'servants' (Psalms 34:22; 69:36), those committed to him ('your saints'; verse 2; see Psalm 50:5). It presses home the point that God is being dishonoured in the way they have been treated. Further pollution was evident in that their unburied corpses had become food for birds and beasts of prey (Deuteronomy 28:26) and instead of the blood of animals it was 'their blood' that was poured out like water around Jerusalem indicating the carnage that had taken place and the lack of survivors (verses 2–3).

In almost the exact words of Psalm 44:13 (see also Lamentations 5:1) the psalmist calls attention to the contempt in which they are held by neighbouring states (Daniel 9:16). Instead of Israel's enemies being put to 'a perpetual reproach' by God (Psalm 78:66), it is Israel who is being reviled and by implication God himself (see Psalm 74:10; see Isaiah 37:23–24).

The church of Jesus Christ, in times of persecution and weakness, ridiculed by the world, is encouraged to present the facts of the situation before God. It is not because God is not aware of what is going on but it brings his people to the end of themselves, to acknowledge their sins and to move them to seek God as never before in earnest prayer.

Prayer for deliverance (verses 5–12)

The cry 'How long, O LORD?' (verse 5; see Psalm 89:46) is the turning point from lament to supplication. Similar cries occur in Psalms 6:3; 13:1; 74:10 and 90:13. The calamity they are suffering, which is rightly seen as God's anger toward them, seems unending. Will God's passion, like a jealous husband (see Psalm 78:58: Deuteronomy 4:24) carry on burning like a fire till all are consumed? God had called for Israel's exclusive devotion and it is his people's unfaithfulness that has resulted in this wrath being revealed. In John's vision where the same cry is uttered by the martyrs (Revelation 6:10), there are a number of allusions to Psalm 79 including the reference to their 'blood' (verses 3, 10) and the 'beasts of the earth' (verse 2; see Revelation 6:8).

Action toward the enemy

But the cry of verse 5 looks for a time when that anger will subside toward them and instead fall on the enemy 'nations' and 'kingdoms'. The prayer, as Calvin observes, might be thought to be against the spirit of love but he shows that it is acceptable only when it is not motivated by the desire for personal revenge but rather for the good of God's people and with reference to God's just judgments. This prayer is according to God's word to Moses (Deuteronomy 30:7).

Two reasons are given why God should take action against the enemy. They are ones that Jeremiah used in his prayer (Jeremiah 10:25):

First, these nations have never acknowledged the true God nor worshipped him (verse 6). The petition seems to imply a similar concern to what Habakkuk had over God's using the pagan Babylonians to punish his own people. Surely it is upon the unrighteous nations who have no interest in God that his wrath should be poured out.

A second reason is the enemy's treatment of God's people—they have 'devoured Jacob' and Israel's 'dwelling-place' ('pasture ground' or a shepherd's abode, verse 7, see Jeremiah 33:12; but also used of God's habitation; see Exodus 15:13) has become desolate.

Forgiveness toward Israel

The psalmist acknowledges the wayward actions of earlier generations (see 2 Kings 24:3)[15] that resulted in this catastrophe but prays that God would no longer call them to mind. For God not to remember sins any more means they are forgiven (see Jeremiah 31:34). The urgent plea that God's 'mercies' or compassion would come quickly to meet them is made with the added motive to move God to action—'we have been brought very low' (verse 8).

A further argument in Asaph's prayer is the most powerful for it concerns God's nature ('your name's sake'), his honour ('the glory of your name') and because he is Israel's 'salvation' (verse 9; see Psalm 35:3). On this basis he appeals for help and deliverance and, freely acknowledging their own 'sins' or shortcomings, pleads for God to cover them ('provide atonement'; see Psalms 65:3; 78:38). God must act on Israel's behalf and change their situation to uphold the greatness of his name and to demonstrate the truth of his existence. The nations must be stopped from making their sarcastic comments. Christians acutely feel the derisive words of the world—'Where is their God?' (verse 10; see Psalm 42:3, 10; Joel 2:17)—when there is no evidence of him doing anything to alter unbearable situations. Is God really there? In addition, taking up what has been said earlier (see verses 2–3, 6) these nations who have been used by God to punish God's 'servants' (see verse 2) for their sins must themselves be punished for the atrocities they have committed (Isaiah 10:5–12).

Just retribution

The appeal includes the desire for this divine retribution to be witnessed by Israel, not for them to gloat but for them to see that God has acted justly and that their enemy can no longer threaten them (see Isaiah 66:24). Again, in order to move God to pity them, the people are described collectively like a 'prisoner' on death row, whose 'sighing' or 'groaning' (verse 11; see Psalm 102:20) ascends to God, similar to the groaning of Israel under Egyptian bondage that was heard by God (Exodus 2:24) who, at the Red Sea showed the greatness of his 'arm' ('power'; see Exodus 15:16). The petition closes by calling on God to take full vengeance ('sevenfold'; see Genesis 4:24; Leviticus 26:18, 21, 24) on those neighbouring states whose humiliating taunts (see verse 4) reflect badly on God. God is identified with his people (Isaiah 63:9) in the same way that Christ is identified with his church (see Acts 9:4).

Again, it is not personal vindictiveness that drives the prayer but a concern for God's honour.

Promise to give praise (verse 13)

The prayer concludes with the prospect of God's people giving thanks 'for ever' and recounting God's praises from one generation to the next (see Psalm 78:4). God had chosen them for this purpose (Isaiah 43:21). Everyone will see that they are a people shepherded by their God (see Psalms 100:3; 74:1; 80:1) even though at present all seems hopeless and the shepherd's pasture area is laid waste (see verse 7). It expresses great faith in the God who is able to change the distressing situation depicted in the earlier verses to one where the people anticipate declaring God's praises. Christians can testify with Peter that 'you were like sheep going astray but have now returned to the Shepherd and Overseer of your souls' (1 Peter 2:25).

This psalm is often thought to be out of tune with the spirit of Jesus. Yet it was our Lord who warned the religious leaders of his day that they belonged to the serpent's brood who had persecuted God's people throughout history and whose deaths will be avenged when God sentences them to hell (see Matthew 23:31-36). There are echoes of this psalm in John's vision of the third bowl where an angel praises God for judging righteously those who have murdered saints and prophets, with the 'Amen' coming from the martyrs, 'Lord God Almighty, true and righteous are your judgments' (see Revelation 16:5-7). The 'blood of Abel' and of all the martyrs rightly calls out for justice, but the 'blood of Jesus' speaks better things in that it provides atonement for the sins of all who call out to God for forgiveness (verse 9).

Psalm 80

God's Vine

How concerned are we for the unity of the people of God? Zeal for doctrinal orthodoxy and purity of worship, crucially important as they are, can sometimes blind us to the deep desire of God to see his people united in the bonds of love and peace as a showcase to the world. This is expressed particularly in Jesus' prayer for the church in John 17 and also by Paul in his letters to the churches. This concern is anticipated in the Old Testament. The message of Chronicles, for instance, is dominated by this strong sense of the fundamental unity of Israel, despite the schism that took place after Solomon's death. God himself did not abandon the northern tribes after the kingdom was divided but sent them great prophets like Elijah and Elisha, Jonah, Amos and Hosea and there were many there who had not bowed the knee to Baal (1 Kings 18:13; 19:18).

This psalm is an eye-opener in its concern for the descendants of Joseph who dominated the northern kingdom. It was composed by the Asaph family of Levites associated with the sanctuary in Jerusalem. 'Asaph' and his descendants were musicians with prophetic gifts and, with the rest of the tribe including the priests, were guardians and instructors of God's word through Moses (Deuteronomy 31:9, 24–26; 33:9–10; see Psalms 50 and 73–79). We are not sure when it was written but it may have been soon after the fall of Samaria, the capital of the northern kingdom of Israel, at the hands of the Assyrians in 722 BC (see 2 Kings 17), as the heading to the ancient Greek translation, the Septuagint, suggests—'concerning the Assyrian'. In contrast to the complacency of the affluent northerners who showed no grief for the affliction of Joseph even in the face of impending disaster (Amos 6:6), this psalmist, associated with the sanctuary in Jerusalem, expresses deep concern and urges God to come to the help of his afflicted people. Its present position is deliberate, taking its place alongside psalms that have spoken of the horrors of enemy action against Judah by the Babylonians (Psalms 74, 79). The psalm's opening call (verse 1) also follows naturally after the pastoral theme with which the previous psalm closed (see Psalm 79:13) and like Psalm 78 it makes reference to Ephraim.

To the familiar titles ('Chief Musician' and 'A Psalm') which clearly indicate that the poem was meant to be sung (see Psalm 4), there is added 'to "The Lilies"' (see Psalms 45, 69), a possible tune title, and 'A Testimony of Asaph'. The term 'Testimony' (see Psalm 60), suggests a close link with God's covenant with Israel for it is found many times in association with the ark, the Ten Commandments and the tabernacle (Exodus 16:34; 25:22; 38:21; Numbers 1:50) all indicating the unity of the people of God in the symbols of God's presence and his special relationship with Israel.

The refrain (verses 3, 7, 19) helps to divide up the psalm into appropriate sections.

Appealing to the Shepherd (verses 1–3)

The psalmist urgently seeks God's attention ('Give ear'; see Psalm 5:1) that he would reveal his stunning presence ('shine forth'; Deuteronomy 33:2; Psalm 50:2), activate his 'strength' from what appears to be his present inaction and indifference ('stir up'; see Psalms 7:6; 35:23) and come for the people's salvation. God is addressed with a unique expression as 'shepherd of Israel' (verse 1), although the picture of God as shepherd is a familiar one (see Psalms 23:1; 28:9) and a common feature of the Asaph psalms is the image of his people as sheep ('flock' verse 1; see Psalms 74:1; 77:20; 78:52, 71–72). It is a royal title that speaks of God's caring rule over his people and Jesus applies it to himself as 'the good shepherd' who cares and gives his life for the sheep (John 10:11–14).

He is further described as 'You who dwell *between* the cherubim' (verse 1; literally, 'a sitter of the cherubim'; see Numbers 7:89; 1 Samuel 4:4; 2 Samuel 6:2; Isaiah 37:16) which indicates his unique sovereignty. The original avoids actually saying that God is 'on' or 'between' the two cherubim that were either side of the ark on the mercy seat (Exodus 37:6–9). Though he had promised to be especially present on earth in the sanctuary above the ark, the phrase prevents us from thinking that the invisible God actually sat there. Other texts reveal that it was merely his footstool (Psalms 99:1, 5; 132:7). The earthly sanctuary was a picture of God's heavenly home (Exodus 25:9, 40) but even the heaven of heavens cannot contain God as Solomon confessed in his moving prayer at the dedication of the temple (1 Kings 8:27).

A most significant feature of this psalm is the way the psalmist identifies himself ('us', verses 2–3) with the northern tribes even though in a previous Asaph psalm these tribes headed by Ephraim have been by-passed on account of their sin in favour of Judah and the sanctuary in Jerusalem (see Psalm 78:9–11, 67–72).

Calling God, Israel's 'shepherd' (verse 1), calls to mind Jacob's dying words to 'Joseph' (Genesis 49:24) as well as his earlier reference when he was about to bless Joseph's sons, 'Ephraim and Manasseh', in which he spoke of God as the one who had 'fed' or better, 'shepherded', him all his life (Genesis 48:15). Interestingly, in addition to the two dominant tribes of the north linked with Joseph, 'Benjamin' is also mentioned (verse 2). These are all the descendants from Jacob's wife Rachel (Genesis 30:22–24; 35:16–18) and these tribes appear together on the west side in the arrangement of the tribes when encamped and on the march through the wilderness (Numbers 2:18–24). In this psalm these three represent all the northern tribes. Benjamin's land bordered north and south and Jerusalem actually lay in Benjamite territory but there were many from this tribe associated with the north in its rebellion against the rule of David's line. Saul's family and people like Shimei and Sheba, all Benjamites, showed their hostility toward David (2 Samuel 2:8–10; 16:5–8; 20:1–2; 1 Kings 12:16).

Using language reminiscent of the Aaronic blessing (see Numbers 6:24–26), the prayer urges God to show them favour, to show a smiling rather than a frowning face (see Psalms 4:6; 31:16; 67:1) and 'restore' them (literally 'cause us to return', verse 3). Experiencing the blessing of his presence would be the means of their salvation and restoration. This prayer contains several levels of meaning. It could mean a return from exile (see 1 Kings 8:34) or less specifically a restoration to a former happy state (see Psalm 53:6). But in the light of verse 18 a more spiritual dimension cannot be ruled out, so that the prayer includes a concern to be brought back to God (see Lamentations 5:21). This appeal is repeated in verses 7 and 19 but each time it is made with increasing force through the additional divine titles—'O God' ... 'O God of hosts' ... 'O LORD God of hosts'.

Protesting at God's anger (verses 4-7)

The psalm now views the people's present afflictions as the direct result of God's action, even though God uses agents like Assyria. Unusually in these psalms (see Psalms 42–83), appeal is made to God's covenant name the 'LORD' (Yahweh/Jehovah) and, as in Psalm 59:5, 'God of hosts'[16] is added to remind God of his powerful activity at the time of the exodus (see Psalm 24:10). Instead of God listening to the cries of his people, he is 'angry' (literally 'you have smoked'; see Psalm 74:1) against their prayer. The now familiar cry, 'How long?' (literally 'until when'; see Psalm 74:10), catches the concern of the people that this situation has gone on long enough.

Like the prayer of Psalm 42:3 a copious flow of 'tears' has replaced food and drink (verse 5) and as in the previous psalm, 'neighbours' (Psalm 79:4) as well as 'enemies' are involved in Israel's sad plight. They have become a 'strife', in the sense that people are engaged in legal wrangling over Israel's former territories (see Jeremiah 15:10), and they have also become the butt of jokes (verse 6). 'When God is displeased with his people we must expect to see them in tears and their enemies in triumph' (Matthew Henry).

The words of verse 3 are repeated in verse 7 but with the additional title 'hosts' as in verse 4, thus giving the plea more force.

Praying for the vine (verses 8-19)

The final section is in two parts with verse 14 occupying a pivotal point in the prayer.

The vine planted and ruined (verses 8-13)

Vines and vineyards were a recognised feature of Canaan even before Israel entered the land (Numbers 13:20, 24; Deuteronomy 6:11) so it is not surprising that the vine came to symbolise Israel with Jewish coins from the inter-testamental period featuring the vine emblem. Both vine and vineyard are often used in the Bible to picture Israel

(see Isaiah 5; Hosea 10:1). Its introduction in a psalm concerning the
Joseph tribes, may be due to Jacob's depiction of Joseph as 'a fruitful
vine' (Genesis 49:22). But the psalm, although primarily concerned
for the northern tribes, shows the unity of Israel. Under the image
of a vine, the nation's history from the time of the exodus is briefly
reviewed. Like a dedicated vinedresser, God had 'planted' Israel, the
vine, in Canaan after preparing the land by driving out its former
occupants (verse 8; see Psalms 44:2; 78:55). He had cared for it so that it
was firmly established and it filled the whole land, which was so during
the David-Solomon era, when it reached the Mediterranean 'Sea' and
the Euphrates 'River' (verses 9–11; see 2 Samuel 8:3; 1 Kings 4:21), in
fulfilment of God's word through Moses (Deuteronomy 11:24).

The history is presented to God as an important argument in the
prayer. If God does not listen to the cry of his people and take action to
restore their fortunes God would be rejecting his own hard work. Thus
the prayer continues against the background of their present sorry
position where wild unclean animals, a picture of the foreign nations
and neighbouring states (see verse 6), have invaded and ravaged the
land. The question 'Why?' (verse 12) strengthens the argument for it
is God who has allowed it to happen. Isaiah's allegory of the vine also
stresses God's action (Isaiah 5:5). The picture is of a protective hedge or
wall around the vineyard that has been broken down. Why would God
go to all that trouble to nurture the plant only to break down the walls
to allow all and sundry to enter and destroy the vine?

The psalm is not claiming, unlike Psalm 44, that the people see no
reason for the disaster. Like the previous psalm they are aware of their
own unfaithfulness resulting in God's anger toward them (verses 4, 14,
18) and the need to be brought back to God (see the constant refrain,
verses 3, 7, 19) but they do not want this state of affairs to go on and on
(see verse 4 and Psalm 79:5).

The vine restored (verses 14–19)

We might have expected the refrain after verse 13 and in fact verse 14 in
the original does begin like verse 7, 'O God of hosts return' but instead
of calling for God to cause them to return, the cry is for God to return
to them. This is intentional and draws special attention to the verse
which, for Alec Motyer, is of 'supreme importance' theologically. 'We
cannot be restored to God ... until first he *return*, reconciling himself to
us'. The psalmist pleads earnestly that God would not remain remote

and inactive concerning their plight but that he would 'visit' his 'vine', not to punish (Psalm 59:5) but to bless (Psalm 65:9). In this the psalm follows the example of Moses who twice asked the question 'Why?' after Israel's apostasy, before praying that God would 'turn' (Exodus 32:11–12).

The psalmist presses home the point made earlier that the Israel that finds itself in its present ravaged state 'burned with fire' and 'cut down' (verse 16) is the 'vineyard' (or more precisely the 'stock') that God's powerful 'right hand' had planted and the 'son' ('the branch'; see Genesis 49:22) that God 'made strong' for himself when he brought him out of Egypt (verse 15: Exodus 4:22–23). They 'perish' or 'are destroyed' because God's 'face' ('countenance'), instead of shining to bless, is set to 'rebuke' (verse 16).[17]

The importance of understanding that the term translated 'branch' is literally 'son' (verse 15) becomes clear when it reappears in verse 17 along with other words found in verse 15—'right hand' and 'made strong for yourself'. Here is a prayer of faith that calls on God to act in grace, and that looks to a 'son of man', a mere human (Psalm 8:4; Ezekiel 2:1, 3; etc.) yet heavenly (Daniel 7:13), an ideal Israel that represents God's people, and a royal figure like the one described in Psalm 2:7. The psalmist's desire is that God's 'hand be upon' this person not in judgment to destroy (see 1 Samuel 18:17; 26:9) but with favour, enabling him to succeed in the way he favoured Ezra and Nehemiah (Ezra 7:6; 8:31; Nehemiah 2:8).

The phrase 'man of your right hand' again takes us back to the opening of the psalm (verses 1–2), to Jacob's youngest son and brother to Joseph, Benjamin ('son of the right hand'; Genesis 35:18). The psalmist, on behalf of these rebellious northerners, represented by Rachel's descendants (Ephraim, Benjamin and Manasseh), looks to a future Benjamin, to the man at God's right hand (see Psalm 110:1) through whom God will bless the whole nation as God's vine. The Jewish Aramaic paraphrase of this psalm has no problem in translating 'son of man' as 'King Messiah'. Though the future Messiah is from Judah, it is in Joseph we are given a picture of Messiah's rule bringing life to a needy world, so it is not surprising to find Benjamin presented as a Messianic type.

There is an implied admission of guilt in verse 18 for the verb 'turn back' has been used in Psalm 78:57 of Israel's apostasy and lack of commitment that resulted in divine punishment. The belief of the psalmist is that through God's right hand man, life can be given to God's people ('revive us') so that God alone will be the object of their worship and trust—'we will call upon your name' (see Genesis 4:26; Psalms 18:3; 99:6). In the light of all this, for the third and final time, and invoking God in the fullest form—'O Lord God of hosts'—the refrain sums up the concerns of the whole psalm.

Jesus often used the vine imagery in his teaching but more significantly he pointed to himself as the true vine (John 15:1). In other words, he was indicating that he was true ideal Israel and all the living branches of the vine are the people of God united to Jesus. In Jesus we find the fulfilment of various strands of biblical prophecy and imagery. He is not only real Israel, God's firstborn son, but the son of man of Daniel 7 who represents God's people and the royal son who stands at God's right hand and whom he has made strong for himself. God has shone upon us in the gift of his unique Son. Of our Saviour alone can it be said that God's hand was upon him both in judgment as he stood in the place of rebels bearing the curse they deserved, and in blessing as he finished the work he came to accomplish. Through him we have life in all its fulness and can call upon his name as we come through him to the Father in prayer (see John 10:10; John 16:23–24; 1 Corinthians 1:2).

Psalm 81

A Call for God's People to Listen

This psalm, like the Letter to the Hebrews, encourages us to meet together for worship (Hebrews 10:25). Such worship includes not only singing with heartfelt praises and calling out to him in prayers of faith but listening to his Word with an obedient spirit. The last book of the Bible urges exclusive worship of the Triune God (Father, Son and Spirit) and gives examples of what that means: bowing before him in humble adoration, exalting him in our praises, making fervent prayers to him and listening to what the Spirit says through the word of the Son and Father (Revelation 1:17; 3:20-22; 4:8-11; 5:11-14; 6:10; 19:10; 22:9).

The psalm gives no precise indication of when it was written but we can probably assume that the 'Asaph' mentioned in the heading is the original prophetic musician appointed by David (see Psalms 50; 80). In addition to the now familiar title, 'To the Chief Musician' (see Psalm 4) there is added 'On an instrument of Gath' (literally 'on' or 'according to the Gittith'; see Psalm 8) which may well refer to the tune as much as to the musical instrument. There is a Jewish tradition that connects the term to Obed-Edom the 'Gittite' (a person from Gath) who was linked with Asaph at the time when the ark was removed from Obed-Edom's family home to Jerusalem (2 Samuel 6:11; 1 Chronicles 13:13-14; 16:4-6). If the word is associated with Gath (meaning 'winepress'), then it may also be calling attention to music associated with the festival of Tabernacles that celebrated the harvesting of the grapes (see verses 3, 10, 16; Leviticus 23:39).

There are close links with Psalms 50 and 95 in that the psalm is addressed throughout not to God but to God's people. It begins by calling them to worship because that is what God has ordained but it continues by urging the people to obey, reminding them of God's redeeming grace, warning them of the consequences of disobedience and encouraging them with words of blessing. It is placed appropriately at this point in Book 3, for it gives an explanation as to why the people have experienced the sufferings described in the previous psalms and serves to hearten God's people with a word of hope if only they would listen and respond accordingly. This message is of importance to the people of God today as the warning and encouraging passages of the New Testament indicate.

A call to a festival of rejoicing (verses 1–5)

The psalm opens with a rousing call to give a resounding joyful shout (Psalms 47:1; 66:1) to the God who is the 'strength' or 'refuge' of his people and 'the God of Jacob' (verse 1; see Psalm 46:7, 11). They are to produce music ('song') using the 'tambourine' ('timbrel', usually played by women when they danced; see Exodus 15:20; Judges 11:34; Psalm 150:4), the 'lyre' ('harp') and 'harp' ('lute'). For more comment on musical instruments and their use in worship see Psalm 150.[18]

Silver trumpet blasts announced the appointed festival times and the commencement of each new moon (month; Numbers 10:10) but, in addition, blowing the ram's horn (which is the 'trumpet' mentioned in verse 3), signalled the beginning of the holy seventh month which became for the Jews after the Babylonian exile their civil new year (Rosh Hashana), distinct from the religious new year that began with Passover (Exodus 12:2; Leviticus 23:24; Numbers 29:1). The 'full moon' would be the middle of the month when the third and final pilgrim festival, ('solemn feast', 1 Kings 8:2; John 7:2, 8–11, 37) took place, on the fifteenth day of the seventh month. It was known as 'Tabernacles' or 'Ingathering' (Exodus 23:16; Leviticus 23:34–43; Deuteronomy 16:16)[19] and we find that Jewish tradition links this psalm with the New Year and the Feast of Tabernacles.

The call to celebrate this particular festival is backed up by the reminder that God has laid this down for God's people to keep. It is a 'statute', an ordinance ('law'), a 'testimony' that 'the God of Jacob' (verse 4; see verse 1) has ordained for Israel. 'Joseph' (verse 5) is mentioned alongside Jacob (see Psalms 77:15; 78:67, 71), and, as in the previous psalm, it encourages the northerners, whose links with Judah were tenuous even in David's time (2 Samuel 20:1-2; 1 Kings 12:16, 20), to appreciate the unity of God's people and to see that the message is as much for them as for those in the south. Also, Joseph's name is used for all Israel on account of his exalted position in Egypt and as the saviour of his family (Genesis 49:26; 50:19-21; Exodus 1:8). It was at Sinai after their deliverance from Egypt that everything God had commanded was recorded in a document known as the Book of the Covenant (Exodus 24:7), which included the observance of the three great pilgrim festivals (Exodus 23:14-17). The first of those festivals, Passover and Unleavened Bread (Exodus 12:14, 24-25; 13:3-10), was actually instituted when God 'went throughout the land of Egypt' (verse 5) putting to death all the first-born (Exodus 11:4-5) but it is the final festival of Tabernacles that is uppermost in mind, which also reminded the people of the exodus period.

Two questions arise. Why is this particular festival so important to Asaph that he felt it necessary to draw special attention to it in this psalm and why should the final compilers of the Book of Psalms place it at this point? It is interesting that the first festival celebrated by Solomon after the building of the temple was Tabernacles (1 Kings 8:2) and it was the first festival to be kept by the returning exiles (Ezra 3:4). When Ezra arrived in Jerusalem it was at the end of the harvest season and he read the law to the assembled people and we are told how they kept the festival with great enthusiasm (Nehemiah 8:13-18). The occasion made it similar to the special sabbatical year when it was stipulated that the law was to be read to all the people during the festival of Tabernacles (Deuteronomy 31:10-13). This festival also features in Zechariah's prophecy as symbolic of the grand finale when the remnant of all the nations will be found worshipping the King in Jerusalem (Zechariah 14:16).

The Passover and Pentecost festivals have their fulfilment in Christ's death and the gift of the Spirit but the festival of Tabernacles or Ingathering awaits fulfilment when the elect from every nation have been gathered in at Christ's return. John sees the consummation of what this festival foreshadowed in his vision of the elect standing with palm branches in their hands (Revelation 7:9-17; 21:3-4). As John warned and encouraged the persecuted church to remain strong and rejoice in hope of the coming joy so it would seem those descendants of Asaph associated with Ezra placed this psalm after the previous laments to present a similar message to God's suffering people. It was a message that Asaph himself had originally given perhaps at the time of the Tabernacles festival both to encourage the whole nation to rejoice but at the same time warning them to be loyal in their worship of the true God so that they would continue to know harvest blessing.

That message is introduced in a rather cryptic way. On first reading, the words, 'I heard a language I did not understand' (verse 5), could be taken as Israel's description of life in Egypt, living among people speaking a foreign language and expressed by Asaph as if he had been there himself (hence the addition of '*while*' in many English versions). It fits the context better, however, to think of the words as an introduction to the message that follows (see Psalm 95:7). Asaph again speaks on behalf of the nation when he states that it is a message they had not acknowledged but which now they appreciate.

A message for God's people (verses 6–16)

The message is in two parts: first, it urges the people to listen, remembering God's gracious activity (verses 6–10); the second half also calls the people to listen but this time remembering God's judgment for disobedience (verses 11–16). Both parts end with the promise of abundance.

Listen and remember (verses 6–10)

God's activity is emphasised as the redemptive history is recounted ('I removed ... I delivered ... I answered ... I proved'). It covers their deliverance from Egyptian bondage to the Red Sea and into the wilderness (verses 6–7). The people are addressed as if they were present at the time of the exodus. There is solidarity with the original generation that came out of Egypt. God released them from the 'burden' of their slavery (Exodus 6:7) and they were free from the 'basket'-carrying servitude that characterised their oppression (verse 6). It is interesting that the term 'burden' is the word used to describe the 'forced labour' that Solomon imposed on 'the house of Joseph' and which Jeroboam, the future king of the rebellious northerners, was given the task of overseeing (1 Kings 11:28). When Israel saw the Egyptians pursuing them they were very afraid and 'cried out to the

Lord' (Exodus 14:10) but God answered them with action 'in the secret place of thunder' when the cloudy pillar of his presence protected them and was later witnessed at Sinai (verse 7; Exodus 14:19-20, 24; 19:16; Psalm 77:18). The 'waters of Meribah' (verse 7) probably refers to the first occasion when God 'tested' ('proved') Israel to see whether they would trust him but it ended with Israel testing God by putting him on trial (see Exodus 17:1-7; Deuteronomy 8:2; 33:8; see Psalm 95:8).

Remembering such amazing activity calls for a break or change before continuing and this is marked by the 'Selah' at the end of verse 7. Every Lord's Day provides Christians with the opportunity of meeting together to remember a greater redemption accomplished by our Lord Jesus Christ and to look forward with anticipation to the final harvest home when all his people will be raised and glorified in the new creation.

The words of verses 8 to 10 recall the language of Exodus and Deuteronomy. God summons his people Israel to 'hear' (or 'listen') that he might 'admonish' or 'testify against' them (verse 8; Deuteronomy 4:1; 5:1). There is also a close resemblance between these verses and the first Asaph psalm (see Psalm 50:7). There then follows a paraphrase of the opening lines to the Ten Commandments (Exodus 20:1-5; Deuteronomy 5:6-9). In view of the redemption from Egypt, their covenant God, 'the LORD' (Yahweh/Jehovah), demands total devotion— no strange foreign gods are to be worshipped (see Deuteronomy 32:12, 16). That same God, in view of the greater redemption from slavery to sin and Satan, demands that we look to his beloved Son and 'hear him', turning from all our idols to worship God alone (Mark 9:7; 1 John 5:21; Revelation 22:9).

As God had preserved them alive through Joseph, so the joy of the Tabernacles' festival reminded the people that God had amply provided for their physical needs throughout their wilderness wanderings and it encouraged them, in their harvest home celebrations, to look forward with hope and expectation to what God had in store in the future (see Deuteronomy 8:3-10; Psalm 107:9). 'Open your mouth wide and I will fill it' (verse 10) pictures the people like hungry fledglings with open beaks waiting for the parent bird to drop in the food they need (Psalm 103:5). Calvin comments that 'the reason why God's blessings drop upon us in a sparing and slender manner is, because our mouth is too narrow; and the reason why others are empty and famished is, because they keep their mouth completely shut.'

Listen and beware (verses 11–16)

As in the previous paragraph God calls for an obedient hearing and promises complete satisfaction. But this second part of the message begins, using the language of verse 8, to indicate that God's people ('my people ... Israel') did not 'hear' ('heed') and obey God's voice. There was a deliberate unwillingness to submit to God ('Israel would have none of me', verse 11) so God 'sent them' ('gave them over') in the obstinacy of their hearts 'to follow their own devices' (see Jeremiah 7:24; 13:10 where Jeremiah uses this language to condemn his people). Paul uses similar language when he speaks of God in his wrath giving people up to their own vile passions and debased minds (Romans 1:24-28). In the case of Israel instead of enjoying the plenty that Canaan offered, they were forced to remain in the wilderness for a further forty years.

There is a certain sadness in the way the final appeal is made—'Oh, that my people would listen to me ...' (verses 13–16). It is similar to Jesus' grief over Jerusalem's refusal to accept his overtures of love: 'How often I wanted to gather your children together, as a hen gathers her chicks under her wings, but you were not willing!' (Matthew 23:37-38). God's longing to care for his people who stubbornly refuse to obey his commandments ('walk in my ways', verse 13) is a theme in the prophets (see Isaiah 1:3, 19-20; Hosea 11:8). If only the people would listen then 'their enemies' (verses 14-15) would be subdued and they would be fully satisfied with the best of everything (verse 16; see verse 10). Their enemies are associated with the 'haters of the Lord' who are described as cringing before him ('pretend submission to him'; see Psalms 18:44; 66:3) and whose 'fate' (literally 'time'; see Psalm 31:15; Ezekiel 22:3; 30:3) would be forever (verse 15). As in Psalm 1, obedience is the key to knowing the choicest of God's gifts and they are reminded of this in the final verse of the covenant blessings for obedience—(Deuteronomy 28:1-14). The examples of God's liberality—'finest of wheat' and 'honey from the rock'—are taken from Moses' song (Deuteronomy 32:13-14).

In this way the message that recounts Israel's past failure to enjoy God's best is a challenge to those now hearing the psalm to end the story of unfaithfulness and disobedience and make the right choices. That same call comes to Christians. If we are to know Christ's fulness of joy we are urged to keep his commandments (John 15:9-14). Those who hear what the Spirit says to the churches are promised the right to eat 'from the tree of life' and to taste 'some of the hidden manna' (Revelation 2:7, 17). On the other hand, the future is bleak for those who reject the gospel. Having referred to Israel's unfaithfulness in the wilderness, the writer to the Hebrews urges believers, 'Let us therefore be diligent to enter that rest, lest anyone *should* fall after the same example of disobedience' (Hebrews 4:11).

Psalm 82

Judging the Powers That Be

This psalm is similar to the Asaph psalm in Book 2 where there is a grand gathering together to hear from God the judge (Psalm 50:1-5). It strongly affirms the truth of Psalm 2 that God is in ultimate charge and all authority in heaven and earth has been given to his Anointed King.

Although many commentators assume that God is the speaker in verses 2 to 7, there is a lot to be said for Calvin's view that the prophetic poet, Asaph, is the speaker throughout the whole psalm. Other psalms that speak of God's righteous judgment include Psalms 58 and 75. The ambiguity in the term 'gods' (verses 1 and 6) may be deliberate so that the meaning oscillates between earthly rulers and divine supernatural beings. Human rulers have their heavenly counterparts and are described by Paul as 'principalities and powers' (see Psalm 29:1).

Proclamation (verse 1)
Isaiah presents us with a picture of the Lord standing to pronounce judgment but in that situation it is clear that God is addressing the rulers of his people (Isaiah 3:13-15). Here the situation appears different. The picture is of God standing in the 'congregation of the mighty' ('divine assembly'; literally, 'the assembly of god'), judging among the 'gods'.[20] It is similar to the one described in the book of Job,

where the heavenly beings ('sons of the gods') both bad and good are subject to God (Job 1:6; 2:1). Micaiah ben Imlah, in his confrontation with Ahab and Jehoshaphat, as they sat on thrones arrayed in their royal splendour, pictured a heavenly assembly with the sovereign God on his throne determining events (1 Kings 22:10, 19–22). This heavenly assembly is mentioned again in the last psalm of Book 3 where they are called 'sons of gods' (or 'sons of the mighty', Psalm 89:6), a phrase that is used to describe heavenly beings in Psalm 29:1.

These 'gods' may well be associated with the angelic figures that represent the earthly rulers as in Daniel's vision of the 'prince of Persia' and the 'prince of Greece' (Daniel 10:13, 20–21).[21] The God of Israel who is the true and living God cannot be compared with such 'gods' (Exodus 15:11; Psalms 96:8; 135:5). Behind the events that have been mentioned in previous psalms concerning the pagan nations that have been used by God to punish his people Israel, there is an unseen heavenly world with which to reckon. Daniel was given a glimpse into this mysterious realm and it is that same spiritual world that is the focus in this psalm. Christians are caught up in this spiritual conflict. Paul speaks of receiving spiritual blessings 'in the heavenly places in Christ' (Ephesians 1:3) but later in his letter he states, as Sinclair Ferguson puts it, 'those heavenly places are the sphere in which the principalities and powers of darkness have to be engaged. Christian armour is the prerequisite for surviving the conflict' (see Ephesians 6:12–13).[22]

Pronouncement (verses 2–7)

Like David and so many of the prophets who denounced unjust rulers (see Psalm 58:1–2), Asaph speaks in God's name to the dark army of wickedness that lies behind all earthly rule. The 'How long?' (verse 2) that we have heard addressed to God many times in the psalms is here a protest and an implicit rebuke directed to those who are so influencing human rulers that they are perverting the cause of justice on earth by favouring the wicked. The 'Selah' at the close of verse 2, while it does not signal the end of a section, suggests a brief pause before presenting a positive statement on how justice should be exercised.

In Israel particularly, it was the duty of those in authority over the people, under the Sinai covenant, to support and defend the weak and vulnerable, such as the widow, the orphan, resident alien and the poor (verses 3–4; see Deuteronomy 10:17–19; 27:19). God's anointed king would do just that in his universal reign (Psalm 72:1-4, 12-14). The concern in this psalm is also universal in nature, and in the context of the psalms of Book 3 it is especially the oppression of God's people by foreign rulers, inspired as they are by these unseen forces, that is particularly in mind.

When the 'wicked' prosper at the expense of 'the poor and needy' (verse 4), who in the psalms are the righteous people of God (see Psalms 37:14; 74:21), they put in jeopardy the very moral fabric of society—'all the foundations of the earth are unstable' (verse 5; see Psalms 11:3; 96:10). The fallen mind of the wicked has lost the power to discern and think clearly—'They do not know nor ... understand' (Psalm 14:4; Isaiah 1:3; 44:18). Having abandoned the paths of uprightness, they walk about in the 'darkness' of ignorance and wickedness (see Proverbs 2:13; Isaiah 59:9-10).

Asaph then pronounces the fate of these 'gods'. He is ready to admit that they have been given great dignity and authority—'You are gods ... children (literally 'sons') of the Most High' (verse 6). But they are not worthy of the name, and certainly not like God's anointed Son (see Psalms 2:7; 45:6-7; 72:1-4, 17). Jesus used this verse in his dispute with the Jews when they accused him of blasphemy, arguing from the lesser to the greater (John 10:34). If these heavenly beings are called gods to whom this word was spoken how much more appropriate is its use for God's unique Son in whom all the fulness of God dwells. He has every right to call himself the Son of God. He did not need to grasp at being God for he was God in the fullest sense (John 1:1; Philippians 2:6; Colossians 2:9).

These 'gods', though having divine functions will all die like any 'human being' ('men'); they will 'fall like one of the princes' (verse 7; Daniel 10:13, 20-21). There may be an allusion to Adam (as the word for 'men' is 'adam'), who was made in the image of God and called God's son (Genesis 1:26-28; Luke 3:38). He had God-like authority to rule over the earth but on account of his disobedience the death sentence was pronounced on him (see Genesis 2:17; 3:17-19).

It is interesting that the Bible can depict earthly rulers in godlike, even angelic terms. The ruler of Babylon aspired, like Satan and the end-time Antichrist, to be as the Most High but is brought down by death to the lowest depths of the Pit (Isaiah 14:12-15; Daniel 11:36-37, 45; 2 Thessalonians 2:4, 7-9; Revelation 20:10). The king of Tyre and

Pharaoh of Egypt are likewise depicted as arrogantly seeking the status of God and are brought down to the grave (Ezekiel 28:11–19; 31:1–18). There is no dualism in the Bible with good and evil competing for supremacy. God is the supreme ruler. He has delegated authority in the heavenly realm as in the earthly. In both spheres God is still in control and brings angelic and human rulers to account. Every age produces its demigods and it is comforting to know that though God in his wise and inscrutable purposes allows them a certain amount of authority that can result in great suffering for God's people, their rule is limited and their punishment guaranteed.

Petition (verse 8)

The closing prayer brings us back to the situation in the opening verse. Asaph appeals for God the supreme ruler to 'arise' and 'judge' the whole earth (see Psalm 94:1–3). Against the background of the previous psalms where the enemy nations have done such damage to God's people, the psalm looks for God to act decisively to put the world to rights. Though Israel is his special inheritance (Psalm 28:9), the whole world ultimately belongs to him. He is the judge of all the earth, there is no one like him in all the earth and all the earth shall be filled with the glory of the Lord (see Genesis 18:25; Exodus 9:14; 19:5; Numbers 14:21; Psalm 24:1). It is because God reigns supreme that the nations will belong to him. Psalm 2 states that God has promised to give to his anointed one the nations for an inheritance and the ends of the earth for a possession (Psalm 2:8). The prince of this world was judged at the cross, the place where principalities and powers were disarmed, defeated and made subject to Christ (John 12:31–33; Colossians 2:15; 1 Peter 3:22). Paul also informed the Athenians concerning Jesus the Anointed One, that God 'has appointed a day on which he will judge the world in righteousness by the man whom he has ordained. He has given assurance of this to all, by raising him from the dead' (Acts 17:31). Kidner helpfully remarks, 'The psalm, having traversed some of the ground which Revelation will explore, ends very much as that book ends with its "Come, Lord Jesus!"'

Psalm 83

United Opposition Cursed

The 20th century produced many magazine articles and popular
books on prophetic topics concerning the hostile relations that
existed between the newly formed state of Israel in 1948 and the
surrounding Arab states. This psalm was seen as a prophetic preview
of the conflict in that region and there are some Christians today
who see verse 4 being fulfilled by those countries that are dedicated
to annihilating Israel as a nation. The situation in the Middle East
today certainly highlights the kind of experiences Israel faced in Old
Testament times, although the modern secular state of Israel must not
be confused with God's people of old.

Whatever our views on prophetic interpretation, our psalm is part
of Holy Scripture to be of help and encouragement to God's people
in all ages, when they face fierce opposition from the world. Some
commentators suggest that the background to this psalm was the
alliance against the kingdom of Judah during Jehoshaphat's reign
(2 Chronicles 20:1-30). However, the nations mentioned here are a
much larger group and perhaps refer not to a particular occasion but
represent, as Kidner suggests, 'the perennial aggression of the world
against God and His people'. It fits well with the context and themes
of the previous psalms in this third Book when Israel was smarting
after the awful effects of the Babylonian invasion and when Edom, a

pawn of the superpower, took advantage of Israel's predicament (see Psalm 137:7). It especially complements the previous psalm, for whereas Psalm 82 pulled back the curtain to view the unseen realm that affects earthly rulers, this psalm focuses attention on the world rulers in their opposition to God and his people. Both psalms are reminiscent of Psalm 2.

This is the last in the series of 'Asaph' psalms (see Psalm 73) and the heading contains the same combination of 'Song' and 'Psalm' that is found in Psalm 48 where further comment can be found. There are two main parts, with the 'Selah' in verse 8 indicating the close of the first section. The first half contains an initial call for action with compelling reasons (verses 1–8) while the second is a forceful prayer concerning the persecuting powers (verses 9–18).

Calling for God's attention (verses 1–8)

Plea (verse 1)
With no introduction such as is found in Psalm 28:1, the psalm begins immediately with an intense threefold appeal for God not to be silent and inactive (see Psalms 35:22; 39:12). The danger is great so the call is urgent.

Lament (verses 2–8)
Reasons are brought before God as to why he should take action. Asaph uses an important argument. These enemies of Israel are God's enemies—'your enemies'... 'those who hate you' (verse 2) and Israel is 'your people ... your sheltered ones' (verses 3). This last phrase suggests God's people are precious and need to be kept safe (see Psalms 27:5; 31:20) and is used by Ezekiel to describe the temple that God was allowing the enemy to pollute (Ezekiel 7:22). Saul of Tarsus found that in persecuting Christians he was persecuting Christ. It is most helpful for God's people to appreciate that the enemies of all things Christian are Christ's enemies as it encourages prayer, and reduces stress (see Philippians 4:6–7).

The enemies are like the roaring, raging waves ('tumult'; see Psalm 46:3, 6) confident in their rebellious hatred of God. They have devised cunning plans against God's people and colluded with others to see them realised (see Psalm 2:1–3). For a 'name' not to be remembered any more means that what the name signified has ceased to exist (see

Exodus 17:14). We do not need to take examples from recent history to show the lengths to which tyrants have gone to eradicate the name of Israel, the most obvious case in biblical times was Haman's crafty plans to exterminate the Jews (Esther 3). But bearing in mind the sinister forces of darkness mentioned in the previous psalm, we must not forget there is a war that has been operating since Eden to destroy God's 'seed' but the promise of Genesis 3:15 is that it will not succeed. There is a descendant, Jesus the Messiah, who has defeated the snake and his brood and shortly the God of peace will crush Satan under our feet (Romans 16:20).

Further details are given about the conspiracy to indicate the seriousness of the situation. Again it is emphasised that these plots are directed against God ('against you' verse 5; see verse 2). Ten enemy states that surround Israel have formed a league of nations ('form a confederacy' or more literally, 'made a covenant'). The list starts with the nations on the eastern side of Canaan and moves to the south and then west to the Mediterranean coastal region.

The people of Edom ('the tents of Edom' being a Hebrew idiom for the Edomite nation) and the Ishmaelites head the list, the one, descendants of Jacob's brother Esau (Genesis 36), the other, descendants of Abraham's son Ishmael, Isaac's older brother (Genesis 16:15–16; 25:12–18). Moab along with Ammon were descendants of Lot (verses 6–8; Genesis 19:36–38). The Hagarites, like the Ishmaelites, were nomads and descendants of Abraham through Hagar (1 Chronicles 5:10). There is uncertainty about the identity of Gebal. It was probably not the famous city known to the Greeks as Byblos (Ezekiel 27:9) but an area south of the Dead Sea near the Edomite city of Petra. Amalek was another nomadic tribe descended from Esau that lived south of Canaan and the first of Israel's foes when they left Egypt (Genesis 36:12, 16; Exodus 17:8–13). As here, Ammon and Amalek joined forces with Moab to defeat Israel in the period of the judges (Judges 3:13). On the western border Philistia lay to the south along what is the Gaza strip today, while Tyre was in the far north. In addition to these longstanding enemies of Israel the superpower Assyria is named, who used local vassal states like Moab and Ammon ('the children of Lot' verse 8) to keep rebel kingdoms in check. Assyria may be symbolic of world power in general for the name was used to signify Persian rule long after the empire had fallen (see Ezra 6:22). This may be the clue to viewing all ten nations as representative of the concerted opposition to

God's people, highlighted in the destruction of Jerusalem in 587 BC but seen throughout history and that will reach a climax before the final day of judgment (2 Thessalonians 2:1–12).

Most of the peoples mentioned were distant relatives of Israel and the reference to 'the children of Lot' (verse 8) draws attention to this. How sad it is that Christians down the centuries have often suffered more from those claiming to be followers of God and his Christ than from people of other beliefs! Reformers like John Calvin took heart from this psalm when they saw how the Pope had 'inflamed the whole world' against them and so can we when the world around us conspires together to obliterate those who go under the name 'Christian'.

Praying for action (verses 9–18)
From lament the psalm moves to petitioning God to defeat this league of enemy nations. It is in the form of an imprecation. In seeking deliverance, Asaph calls down curses on these enemies of God and his people.

Suggestions from history (verses 9–12)
Two notable occasions from the judges' period are used to remind God of his past activity in delivering Israel from vicious foes. The first relates to Gideon's victory over the Midianites (verse 9) and their leaders, Oreb, Zeeb, Zebah and Zalmunna (verse 11; see Judges 6–8). In the other incident, during the time of Barak and Deborah, the Canaanites led by Sisera and Jabin were roundly defeated at the river Kishon near Endor both of which are in the vicinity of Mount Tabor (verses 9–10; Judges 4–5). The psalm does not mention the names of the human deliverers in order to make clear that it was God who really saved Israel from their enemies.

Verse 12 again reminds God that the enemy's aim in taking possession of Canaan, is really an attack on God (see verse 2) for it is 'God's pastures' (see Psalms 23:2; 65:12) which he has given Israel to possess. It is a strong argument because throughout Scripture God takes special care of what belongs to him. Paul reminds the Corinthians that they are God's temple and 'If anyone defiles the temple of God, God will destroy him' (1 Corinthians 3:16–17).

Suggestions from nature (verses 13–15)
Asaph now uses imagery from the natural world in urging God to

act against the foe. The prayer becomes more intense and personal ('O my God', verse 13) as he calls for the anti-God league to become like a whirlwind of dust and like the 'chaff' that the wind drives away (see Psalm 1:4). We have all seen pictures of how bush fires spread with dramatic and frightening speed and it is that kind of scene that is suggested by the fire that runs through the forests that cover the mountain slopes (verse 14). It is one of utter devastation. The final picture is that of a terrifying storm of hurricane proportions and from which there is no escape (verse 15). In Isaiah 17:12–14 similar metaphors are found but there it speaks directly of what God will do in judgment on all who make war on God's people. The psalmist is only giving voice to what God has threatened to do to all his enemies.

Aim of the action (verses 16–18)

Up to this point we may have had the impression that Asaph was a typical zealous patriot calling down curses on the enemies of Israel that he might gloat over their downfall. But the psalm reveals neither a spirit of personal revenge nor a nationalistic hatred of the enemy. There is an overall positive purpose in calling for these curses. It is for the honour of God (see 2 Chronicles 20:6); it is that people will come to acknowledge that Israel's God, revealed under his covenant name 'the LORD' (Yahweh/Jehovah) is 'the Most High over all the earth' (verse 18; Ezekiel 6:7, 10; etc.). God is often called 'the Most High' in passages that have reference to other peoples and nations (see Genesis 14:18–20, 22; Deuteronomy 32:8; Psalm 7:17). Usually in these psalms (Psalms 42–83) the personal name for God ('the LORD'; Yahweh/Jehovah) is used sparingly but it appears twice in these closing verses, indicating that Israel's covenant-keeping God is not a local deity but God over all. It is commonly assumed in our relativistic age that the Christian God is just one among many gods that humans have invented. The God of Israel, however, is the God and Father of our Lord Jesus Christ and he is the living and true God (Jeremiah 10: 6–7, 10; 1 Thessalonians 1:9-10).

While the expression 'Fill their faces with shame' (verse 16) means that the proud enemy nations will be utterly humiliated as a result of God's action, to 'seek your name' suggests that it is with the aim of bringing them to worship 'the LORD' (verse 16). As Motyer comments, 'Sometimes people must be brought to nothing (13–15) *so that* they may be brought to God (16)'.

Verse 17 seems to contradict the aim of the previous verse. But if enemies do not willingly submit to God and seek him in worship, then there is nothing but confusion, continual dismay, shame and, as the opening psalms indicate (Psalms 1:6; 2:12), to 'perish'. Warnings of the future judgment are given in this life that we might come to our senses and flee from the wrath to come into the arms of Jesus who bore that wrath that all who submit to him with self-despairing trust might not perish but have everlasting life. But we can be sure there is a day coming when all will bow and acknowledge that Jesus is Lord to the glory of God the Father (Philippians 2:11).

Psalm 84

Delighting in God's Presence

In our busy day-to-day lives how much do we know of the psalmist's desires and appreciation of God? The Westminster Shorter Catechism begins by reminding us that the chief purpose of our lives is to glorify God and to enjoy him for ever. If we are seeking to honour God what do we know of the delightful privilege of enjoying him?

For those of the old covenant period, delighting in God was associated with the place that God had appointed to meet with his people. From David's time this came to be in Jerusalem in the sanctuary where the ark, the symbol of God's presence, was placed. Solomon eventually built the temple and there the infinite, transcendent God condescended to make his earthly home. Wanting to spend time with God in his temple was not the same as a Christian wanting to be in a church building all day. Everything about the old covenant sanctuary spoke about access to God and the blessing of God's presence. Under the new covenant, that presence can be known not only when Christians come together to worship but individually as we commune with the Father in the name of his Son and through the fellowship of the Spirit who indwells the believer. Not only is the corporate body of Christians meeting together seen as God's temple but each individual believer's body is a sanctuary where the triune God lives by the Holy Spirit and where rich personal fellowship with God can be enjoyed (John 14:23; Revelation 3:20) in the most difficult of circumstances.

The psalm heads up another series belonging to 'the sons of Korah' (see Psalm 42 for details) and like the one that began the first group (Psalms 42–49) it expresses love for God's sanctuary. But whereas Psalms 42–43 indicate that the psalmist was unable to attend the place of worship, this psalm suggests a pilgrim eagerly looking forward to being present for one of the pilgrim festivals. In addition to the familiar heading 'To the Chief Musician' (see Psalm 4) there is added 'On an instrument of Gath' (literally 'on' or 'according to the Gittith') which is included in the title to Psalms 8 and 81 and may suggest that the third great pilgrim festival of Tabernacles is in mind (see the introduction to those psalms for further information). Praise to God is implied as the psalmist expresses his desire for God's house, but overall it expresses trust in God with special concern for God's 'anointed' (verse 9). The 'Selah' at the close of verses 4 and 8 divides the psalm into its main sections.

Longing for God (verses 1–4)

The psalm begins not with an exclamation of how beautiful the sight of God's 'tabernacle' or 'dwelling place' is (see Psalms 43:3; 74:7), as our English versions suggest by the word 'lovely' (verse 1), but with an expression of great love for it—'How dear it is' or 'How beloved' (see Psalm 60:5). God is now addressed again by his covenant name, 'Lord' (Yahweh/Jehovah), a feature notable for its absence in so many of the psalms from 42 to 83, although the closing verses of Psalm 83 have prepared for this return to what was common in Book One. 'Lord of hosts' (verses 1 and 3; see Psalm 24:10) speaks of God as the all-powerful 'King' and may be used in these verses to emphasise that the 'Lord', the 'living God' (verse 2; see Psalm 42:2; Jeremiah 10:10), who has ordained to tabernacle among them in the Jerusalem sanctuary, is the one who has made the starry hosts and whom the myriad of angels worship (see Nehemiah 9:6). How amazing to be able to speak in such personal terms of this great ruler of the universe as 'my King and my God' (verse 3; see Psalms 5:2; 68:24; 44:4; 74:12; 83:13).

It is not surprising then to find the psalmist expressing not only love for this divine earthly palace with its open 'courts' (verse 2; Psalm 65:4) but a debilitating yearning ('longs ... faints') for it. But it is not for the temple as such but for the God of the temple that his whole being cries out. This is why the place is dear to him. God is there!

The psalmist likens himself to a bird that has found a home for itself in the temple buildings, a place of safety for rearing her young. God's 'altars' (verse 3) may be yet another way of referring to the whole temple but more probably the word is used to represent a place of refuge (see 1 Kings 1:50–51) and is a reminder that the altars of sacrifice and incense were the means whereby 'communion between God and man was possible' (Alexander). Motyer comments that 'the *altar* is the key to our security' and so we are encouraged to see here a picture of the place 'where sinners are reconciled to the Holy God and he to them'. It is a most privileged and fortunate position to be in ('Blessed' as in Psalm 1:1), to live in that secure and safe environment and regularly to praise God there.

Sparrows are, as John Stott, the preacher and keen bird-watcher once observed, 'the most ubiquitous birds in the world, constructing their nests in every available nook and cranny'. The 'swallow' is a scholarly guess, but Stott suggests the 'swift' that still visits the area in great numbers on migration and many nest now in the precincts of the mosque of Omar.

Strengthened by God (verses 5–8)

Not only are the regular worshippers at the temple, who live in or near Jerusalem, 'Blessed' but those who live far from God's sanctuary are also in a highly privileged position. These people who in thought are already on the pilgrim road to the temple ('whose heart is set on pilgrimage'; literally, 'the highways are in their hearts'; verse 5), do not need to be in the temple to know the protection and safety of God's 'strength' (see Exodus 15:2, 13). For the true worshippers, nothing can stop their thoughts from turning to reality as they finally make the journey in order to appear 'before God in Zion' (verse 7; see Exodus 23:17).

The pilgrim way is not an easy journey as the reference to the 'Valley of Baca' suggests (verse 6). We know of no such place in Canaan and 'Baca' is a word that means some kind of plant or tree and traditionally was rendered 'Mulberry or Balsam' (see 2 Samuel 5:23–24). It may be a play on the word for, in the original, the name is similar in sound to the word for 'weeping' (as indicated in the ancient versions like the Greek translation, the Septuagint). Despite the arid ground through which they must travel it is transformed into a spring by their attitude—'they make it a spring' (verse 6). But that positive attitude is due to God's strength; in fact they go 'from strength to strength' (verses 5 and 7). If the pilgrims were coming up to Jerusalem for the festival of Tabernacles in the seventh month (September-October time), they would pass through some very parched ground. This could easily be transformed, however, by the early rains that sometimes came before the festival started. The rain would leave literally 'blessings' (*berakot*), which in the original is another play on words, for it is similar to the word for 'pools' of water (*berekot;* verse 6).

Having arrived safely at the temple, the section closes with a solemn appeal for God to hear and answer the psalmist's prayer (verse 8). God is addressed as 'LORD God of hosts' (see Psalm 80:19) and as 'God of Jacob' (see Psalm 81:4), the first emphasising that Israel's covenant God is the all-powerful ruler of the universe and the second that he is their very own personal God.

Satisfied with God (verses 9–12)

The appeal for God to attend to the psalmist's prayer in the previous verse prepares for this particular petition for the king who is described as 'our shield' and 'your anointed' (verse 9). God is usually referred to as a 'shield' (see verse 11; Genesis 15:1; 2 Samuel 22:3; Psalm 3:3) but it can refer to human rulers (Psalm 47:9). The king, like the high priest (Leviticus 4:3) was 'anointed' with oil to symbolise that he was appointed, set apart and endowed by God for service among the people. The brief petition calls on God to look favourably ('look upon the face', verse 9) on the Davidic king that he might lead the people effectively, maintain the stability of the kingdom and give protection especially to the sanctuary in Zion and to those who worship there. God, the all-powerful 'King' (see verse 3) and protector ('shield' verse 11) of his people, rules through his special viceroy. It is with this background that we are to understand Jesus as the Messiah (the Anointed one; see Psalm 2). David and his royal descendants were types of God's real Anointed One and it is through him that God has overcome his enemies to give his people true security and the enjoyment of knowing his presence and help. It is not without significance that prayer for the king is made in the context of a psalm that has just spoken of God's presence in Zion (see Psalm 2:6).

The psalmist presents reasons (notice the 'For' or 'Because' at the beginning of verse 10) to back up his brief prayer for the king. It is important that God continues to help the Lord's anointed so that the country might be in a stable condition for pilgrims to continue to attend the central sanctuary. As a pilgrim in the temple courts, those few days spent worshipping at festival time is well worth the effort of the journey; it is better than thousands of days elsewhere (see Psalm 27:4–5).

I remember my minister encouraging me with verse 10 when as a young boy I gathered up the hymn books in the pews at the end of the evening service. The word 'door-keeper' may be too specific a translation for the original 'standing at the entrance'. Instead of thinking only of temple Levites guarding the entrance to the precincts or to the sanctuary itself, the verse may also be referring to pilgrims who had arrived at the doorway. Even to stand at the entrance to God's house was preferable to dwelling 'in the tents of wickedness' (verse 10). This catches the love that the pilgrim has for God's earthly dwelling-place (see verse 1) and serves as a reminder of the ungodly wicked that were introduced in Psalm 1.

Verse 11 explains why the pilgrim finds God's house such a satisfying experience. Even though it was a fleeting visit and a distant look in, this was not just better than nothing it was better than anything else, because God, their covenant 'LORD' (Yahweh/Jehovah), who had ordained to be present there, was their 'sun and shield'. They were in the presence of the ultimate king, their light and life ('sun'; see Psalms 27:1; 56:13) and their protector from all evil ('shield'; see Psalm 3:3). In John's vision of the New Jerusalem there was no need of a temple because the Lord God Almighty and the Lamb were its temple and there was no need of the sun because the glory of God illuminated it and the Lamb was its light (Revelation 21:22–23). The vision picks up words from the prophet Isaiah concerning the future Zion (Isaiah 60:19–20) and Malachi's 'sun of righteousness' who will arise 'with healing in his wings' (Malachi 4:2).

Their covenant God, the 'LORD', does more. He gives 'grace and glory' (or 'honour') and liberally supplies what is 'good' to those who 'walk uprightly'. The 'good' may, in the psalm's original context, be a reference to good harvests with which the three pilgrim festivals are associated, especially Tabernacles. On the other hand, as the first psalm in Book 3 has shown, God himself is Israel's 'good' and drawing near to God is the ultimate 'good' (Psalm 73:1, 28). 'In completeness' would be a better translation than 'uprightly'. This is what Abraham was challenged to be by God (Genesis 17:1). The term is used of sacrificial animals that were free from blemish. Noah and Job were not sinless but they were described as 'blameless' or 'complete' in that there was no noticeable blot on their characters.

Not everyone who enjoyed attending the temple worship at festival time is promised blessing. It is those whose lifestyle and attitude is pleasing to God, whether on pilgrimage or not, that are blessed with God's 'good'. We are dependent on God at all times and it is by his grace and favour that he honours us, enables us to live lives that are complete before him and blesses us richly. Jeremiah states that it is on account of our sins that God withholds good from his people (Jeremiah 5:25). By God's grace we are blessed with all spiritual blessings in the heavenly places in Christ (Ephesians 1:3).

Don Carson[23] considers Eric Liddell of *Chariots of Fire* fame as he ponders what the text means when it promises that God will withhold 'no good thing' from those whose walk is blameless. After his Olympic success Liddell became a missionary in China and was captured by the Japanese and died of a brain tumour aged forty-three, leaving a wife and three young daughters. Liddell's favourite hymn, Carson suggests, provides the best response:

Be still, my soul! The Lord is on thy side;
Bear patiently the cross of grief or pain;
Leave to thy God to order and provide;
In every change, He faithful will remain.
Be still, my soul! Thy best, thy heav'nly Friend
Through thorny ways leads to a joyful end.

The psalm ends with another 'blessed' or 'privileged' state (verse 12; see verses 4, 5) and it sums up the contentment expressed in this final section. It calls to mind the opening words of Psalm 1 and the closing words of Psalm 2. How fortunate is the person who 'trusts' the 'LORD of hosts' (see verses 1, 3, 8).

We do not need to go on pilgrimage in order to meet with God (John 4:21–24). Jesus promises that wherever two or three are met together in his name there he is among them (Matthew 18:20). The universal church of Christ is seen locally as the temple of God (2 Corinthians 6:16). It should be a joy for Christians to meet together for public worship where praise and prayer, the reading of the Scriptures, the hearing of God's Word and love for one another express the presence of God by his Spirit (1 Corinthians 14:25). On the other hand, Christians are pilgrims in this world (1 Peter 2:11) and we look to the ultimate beatific joy of the New Jerusalem where the dwelling of God is with his people and they shall see his face (Revelation 21:1–22:4).

Psalm 85

Praying for Revival

How concerned are we as Christians for the Church of God and for God to revive his work in times when it would seem the Church is under God's judgment? Here is a psalm that prays for deliverance from present troubles on the basis of what God has done in the past (verses 1-7) and looks forward with joy to a favourable answer (verses 8-13). It fits well with so many of the psalms in Book 3 that call out for relief and restoration against the background of God's anger and enemy action (see Psalms 74, 78-80, 83). The situation in which the people find themselves may relate to the period after the return from exile in Babylon when the initial enthusiasm of the Jews had waned and harvests had failed. Haggai prophesied in such circumstances (Haggai 1:6-11; see also Zechariah 1:12-17) and interestingly he referred to God giving 'glory' and 'peace' (Haggai 2:7, 9) such as we find in this psalm (verses 9-10).

This poem, another in a series belonging to the 'Korah' collection (see Psalm 84) to be used by the 'Chief Musician' (see Psalm 4), makes much use of a verb variously translated as 'brought back', 'turned', 'restore', 'again' and 'turn back' (verses 1, 3, 4, 6, 8).[24] It begins by referring to the land as God's ('your land'; verse 1) and closes by speaking of it as 'our land' (verse 12). There are close parallels with Psalms 44 and 80.

Past blessings (verses 1-3)

In the people's present distress, the psalmist on their behalf gains encouragement by looking back to God's gracious dealings with them in the past. It is a prayer addressed to their covenant God ('LORD'). The word translated 'favourable' has the idea of God's delight in the land that belongs to him (see Psalm 44:3) like a father delighting in his son (Proverbs 3:12). With the thought of God's wrath and the people's sin in the following lines (verses 2-3) the word 'favourable' also suggests God's gracious acceptance of the land and its people. Because of the people's rebellion against God, Jeremiah prophesied that God would punish them and not 'favourably accept' them even though they offered sacrifice (Jeremiah 14:10, 12). There can be no favourable acceptance by God without true repentance. An example of such an attitude is the earnest prayer of Daniel on behalf of his people (Daniel 9:1-19) and that prayer was answered, as was the prophecy of Jeremiah that had prompted Daniel's prayer, when God 'brought back the captivity of Jacob.'[25]

This acceptance and return from exile was the result not only of a change in the people—their repentant spirit, but as Motyer helpfully notes, 'a change in God'—the removal of his 'fury' ('wrath') and the heat of his 'anger' (see Psalm 38:1, 3) through the provision of an atonement that brought forgiveness (the bearing away of sin; see Leviticus 16:21-22) and the covering of their 'sin' (verses 2-3). Similar expressions have appeared in David's penitential psalms (see comments on Psalm 32:1, 5) and the passage also recalls Isaiah's prophecy of comfort (Isaiah 40:1-2). The 'Selah' suggests a momentary pause to take in the wonder of God's gracious activity in the middle of a passage where the LORD is the subject of every statement in verses 1 to 3. This whole scene that speaks of God having 'turned' from 'the fierceness' of his anger is a reminder of a pattern begun at Sinai when the people rebelled and Moses pleaded that God would turn from his burning wrath (Exodus 32:12).

The old Prayer Book of the Anglican Church appointed this psalm to be used on Christmas Day. It is a reminder of the grace of God toward our world in sending his Son to be the atoning sacrifice to appease God's wrath, that repentant sinners who trust the Saviour might know forgiveness and be brought back to God from the captivity to sin and Satan (1 John 4:4:9-10; 1 Peter 2:24-25).

Present distress (verses 4–7)

Fired by the knowledge of God's past mercies and acknowledging that God is Israel's great deliverer ('God of our salvation'), the psalmist pleads that what God has done for his people before, he will do again. Israel had sinned grievously once again, and God had responded as the covenant warnings indicated by expressing his anger toward them. Hence the cry to God—'Restore us' ('turn us') and that he would cause his 'anger' to cease. This particular word for anger suggests an indignation that is mixed with grief (see Psalm 31:9). There seems no end to God's anger. Unlike what is said in Psalm 30:5 about God's anger being for a 'moment', in this case it is being prolonged. So the question is similar to the 'how long' cries of previous psalms (Psalms 79:5; 80:4).

Out of this anguish comes an appeal on behalf of his people for God to 'revive us again' (literally 'will you turn, will you bring us to life'). Those needing to be revived are ones that are in a sorry state (see Psalm 80:18). They are as good as dead. We speak of people being revived after all their strength has gone or when at death's door artificial respiration revives them. God is the one who kills and makes alive (Deuteronomy 32:39) and Hosea, in calling Israel to return to the Lord, speaks in terms that were to be prophetic of Jesus as the true Israel: 'After two days he will revive us; on the third day he will raise us up, that we may live in his sight' (Hosea 6:2; Mark 9:31; Luke 24:7). The plea is for God to revisit them and raise them from their death-like state that they may be given a fresh reason for rejoicing in God. For God's people to be in a lifeless situation would be like a corpse unable to thank God or praise him (see Psalms 6:5; 30:9). Revival invariably leads to rejoicing. The revival that broke out among God's people with the special coming of the Spirit at Pentecost led to further experiences of the Spirit's presence enabling the apostles to witness 'with great power' and 'great grace was upon them all' (Acts 4:33). Then we read that 'great joy' was present in the Samaritan city as a result of Philip's visit (Acts 8:8).

The appeal is buttressed by this straightforward call (in place of the rhetorical negative question of the previous verse 6) that God would cause them to see and experience his 'steadfast love' ('mercy', verse 7; see Psalm 5:7), which is synonymous with granting them deliverance ('salvation') from their present distress (see verse 4). These verses are not far removed from Habakkuk's prayer that God would revive his work and in wrath would show compassion (Habakkuk 3:2).

The Church of Jesus Christ and individual Christians must have this same humble attitude. There is no mention in the psalm of threats from enemy action. All the emphasis is on the people's relationship to God, that his righteous anger might cease toward them and that he would favour them with a deliverance that would issue in joyful praise. We need to think less of the menacing forces arrayed against the Church and as Lloyd-Jones once said, 'be more concerned about the health and purity of the Church: most of all about the holiness of God and the sin of man.'[26]

Prospects bright (verses 8–13)

This second half of the psalm begins in a way that is reminiscent of Habakkuk's stance as he stopped to listen to what God would say (Habakkuk 2:1). If we desire revival it is important that we take to heart what God says in his word. The psalmist is assured of God's revealed promises concerning a state of well-being ('peace', verse 8) that results from knowing his deliverance. This is not the word of a false prophet who proclaims peace when there is no peace (Jeremiah 6:13–14) for it is a promise made to those who are described as God's 'saints', those committed to the Lord (see Psalm 30:4). In addition, there is an implied warning. The promise is made on condition that they do not 'turn' (verse 8) to the kind of folly that leads people to think they can live independently of God.

The following verses express more fully what this state of well-being will mean but again there is a proviso. God's 'salvation' (verse 9; see also verses 4 and 7) is near to those who revere him, to those in other words who turn from idols to worship God alone ('fear him'). Isaiah speaks in similar terms of God's salvation coming 'near' to his people (Isaiah 51:5; 56:1). That salvation in all its fulness is described in these closing verses but it begins with the removal of God's wrath from over us and the forgiveness of our sins (see verses 2–5).

The ultimate purpose of God in granting revival is that 'glory may dwell in our land' (verse 9). It should therefore be the Church's ultimate reason in praying for revival. The glory of God that settled on Mount Sinai (Exodus 24:16), the display and presence of God's stunning nature and importance (Exodus 33:18–34:7), is viewed as residing in the promised land. It is the glory that Ezekiel saw moving away east from the temple (Ezekiel 11:23; Psalm 78:59–64) that is to return not just to the temple area (Psalm 26:8; Ezekiel 43:2–5) but to the land. For the returned exiles, the land displayed no such glory and compared to Solomon's temple the structure they were building was a poor substitute. Haggai promises, however, that God will fill the temple with glory so that the 'glory of this latter temple shall be greater than the former' and as in our psalm it is associated with 'peace' (Haggai 2:7, 9). Isaiah also speaks of the 'glory of the LORD' being revealed and of his glory rising like the sun's light over his people and of the Gentile nations coming to that light (Isaiah 40:5; 60:1–2). God's glory results in his people's glory or honour (Psalm 84:11) as Isaiah suggests in his prophecy and what he sees starting with his people, spreads to encompass the whole world (Isaiah 62:2). It is interesting that Habakkuk also looks to a time when 'the earth will be filled with the knowledge of the glory of the LORD, as the waters cover the sea' (Habakkuk 2:14).

As a result of that initial revival associated with the Spirit's special coming at Pentecost the 'whole world was turned upside down' (Acts 17:6) and following the Great Awakening of the 18th century the gospel spread dramatically during the 19th century to reach every continent and many islands of the Atlantic, Indian and Pacific oceans. The ultimate fulfilment will be in the new creation when the earth will be literally filled with the glory of God and all opposition destroyed (Revelation 21:22–22:5).

The psalmist waxes lyrical as he presents in the final verses a word picture of this end-time state of well-being, previewed in those revivals that have for a time changed societies for the better. Only in the grand consummation of the new creation will there be that everlasting state of tranquillity and perfection where heaven and earth are one (Revelation 21:1–8). The festival of Tabernacles may be in the mind of the prophetic poet in his portrayal of the revival blessing (see Psalm 81:1–5). As in the joyful celebrations after a good harvest so this psalm looks to the fulfilment of the old covenant festival when all God's elect have been gathered in and God's grand and glorious future is an ever present reality.

God's unfailing love and faithfulness ('Mercy and truth', verse 10; see Exodus 34:6–7; Psalm 25:10), together with his 'righteousness and peace' (as the author of 'right order and well-being) are all working together to produce this eternal state of joy. Heaven and earth are one under the picture of faithfulness springing up from the earth and righteousness looking down from heaven (see 2 Peter 3:13). There is no withholding of the 'good' spoken of in the previous psalm (Psalm 84:11).

It is freely given so that the land produces as was promised under the old covenant blessings (Leviticus 26:4-6). Those physical blessings are literally fulfilled in the new creation for all who belong to the new covenant (Revelation 7:14-17; 21:4). Everything will be put right in the end ('righteousness') when the LORD comes to judge so that those walking in the pathway he has made will be secure. Plumer comments that 'Christ's example of righteousness and his glorious justifying righteousness *set*, or *put* us in the way of salvation.'[27]

Make your own this prayer of George Horne at the close of his comments on this psalm: 'Draw us, blessed Jesus, and we will run after thee, in the path of life; let thy mercy pardon us, thy truth enlighten us, thy righteousness direct us, to follow thee, O Lamb of God, whithersoever thou goest, through poverty, affliction, persecution, and death itself; that our portion may be for ever in thy kingdom of peace and love.'[28]

Psalm 86

The Servant of the Lord

There is something mysterious about prayer. Most people would confess that they have prayed at least some time during their lives and all over the world prayer of one kind or another is being offered by devotees of the various world religions. True prayer is fellowship with the living God through the means he has ordained—through his Son, Jesus Christ (John 14:6; 16:23-24; 1 Timothy 2:1-6). For James Montgomery the hymn-writer, 'Prayer is the Christian's vital breath'. Jesus gave his disciples a pattern prayer that provides us with a helpful framework for organising our prayers or even one to make our own and especially suitable as a communal prayer when the church gathers for worship.

Here is a psalm that directly addresses God from beginning to end. It is the second with the title 'A Prayer of David' (see Psalm 17) and it is an encouragement to us to be biblical in our praying. It is full of phrases and expressions that appear in other psalms (see also Psalm 71) and it especially draws on the language of the book of Exodus (see verses 5, 8, 15). Not that David looked up texts and strung different verses together to form this prayer. His mind was full of Scriptural phraseology and this fresh prayer flowed as a result of hiding God's word in his heart. Like a number of Bible prayers (see Nehemiah 9:5-15; Acts 4:24-28), the psalmist spends time telling of God's character and actions which then becomes an encouragement to faith as requests are made.

We can only speculate why a Davidic prayer is found at this point, the only one in Book 3, breaking into a series belonging to the 'sons of Korah'. Book 2 ended with the note that 'The prayers of David … are ended' (Psalm 72:20). Most of the psalms in Book 3 reflect the period from the destruction of Jerusalem in 587 BC through to the return from the Babylonian exile, so we can only conclude that the prophetic compilers saw this prayer of David as appropriate for such times. It also prepares us for the final psalm of Book 3 that is concerned with God's covenant with David.

Seven times the LORD (Yahweh/Jehovah) is referred to as the sovereign 'Lord' or 'Master' (verses 3, 4, 5, 8, 9, 12, 15) and, with that master-servant relationship in mind, David refers to himself humbly as God's 'servant' or as 'the son of your maidservant' (verses 2, 4, 16). A number of scholars have noted the way the psalm is structured, its use of key terms and phrases and how attention is drawn to the central point that highlights God's revealed character ('name') and David's desire to revere it (verses 10–11).

The Servant's appeal (verses 1–7)

The appeal envelops the whole section (see verse 1 and verses 6 and 7). Using familiar language in cries for help ('Bow down your ear … and hear me' but better translated 'Incline your ear and answer me', verse 1; see 2 Kings 19:16; Psalm 71:2; Daniel 9:18), David calls out to God under his covenant name 'LORD' (Yahweh/Jehovah). To reinforce his prayer a series of reasons are given introduced by the word 'for' (verses 1–5, 7).

Reason one: 'for I am poor and needy'. This does not mean David is in financial difficulties. It is descriptive of the humble, righteous person who is aware of personal weakness and need especially in the face of enemy action (see Psalm 35:10).

Reason two: 'for I am holy' (verse 2; see Psalm 85:8). He prays that his life might be kept safe for he is someone devoted to the God who is committed to him in love. The term 'holy' is from the same word family as the term for God's 'mercy' or 'faithful love' in verse 5. There is a loving commitment within the bonds of God's covenant (see Psalm 30:4). The phrases 'my God' and 'your servant' emphasise the very essence of the covenant which is often expressed as 'I will be your God and you shall be my people' (Leviticus 26:12; Jeremiah

30:22). David refers to himself humbly as God's 'servant'. Although this usage of 'servant' is similar to the respectful way in which a person would address a superior such as a ruler (2 Samuel 9:8), in this context it suggests an exclusive allegiance in the covenant relationship that puts God under an obligation to save him. God's honour would be at stake if he did not come to the aid of his servant who trusts him and is committed to him. God also spoke of David as he had done of Moses as 'my servant' (see the titles to Psalms 18 and 36; also 2 Samuel 7:5 and Psalm 78:70).

Reason three: 'for I cry to you all day long' (verse 3). It is an urgent concern. After referring to himself as 'servant' David appropriately calls on God to be 'merciful' or 'gracious' (see Psalm 4:1) using the term 'Lord' or 'my sovereign Lord' (not the same word as God's covenant name 'LORD', as in verse 1, which is translated in capital letters in the English versions) which calls attention to the master-servant relationship again.

Reason four: 'for to you ... I lift up my soul' or 'my whole being' (verse 4; see Psalm 25:1). It is to God alone he is making his appeal and not to any other god. He is totally committed to his Lord. The master-servant relationship becomes even more obvious as 'servant' and 'Lord' come together in the same verse. Added to his desire for God to be gracious and keep him in safety is the appeal for God to gladden his whole being ('rejoice the soul').

Reason five ('For you Lord, are good ...' verse 5) is based not on what David is and does but on what God is and does (verse 5). Only God is absolutely good as Jesus pointed out to the rich young ruler (Mark 10:17-18), and Book 3 has emphasised God's goodness (see Psalms 73:1, 28; 84:11; 85:12). God is 'good' and something of what that means to his people is spelled out in words that echo the proclamation of God's goodness and glory to Moses—'abundant in mercy' or 'abounding in faithful love' (Exodus 33:18-19; 34:6-7) to all who call. The sovereign Lord is 'ready to forgive'. The word used is not the one that speaks of God 'forgiving' sin in the sense of 'taking' it or 'carrying' it away (see Psalms 32:5; 85:2). It is used more sparingly and reserved for God alone. He alone is the one who can 'pardon' our sins (see Psalms 25:11; 103:3) and interestingly it is used by Moses as he pleads with God following the golden calf incident (Exodus 34: 9 'pardon our iniquity and our sin').

Reason six: 'for you will answer me' (verse 7). He makes his appeal for God to 'attend' to the voice of his entreaties (verse 6; see Psalm 5:1–2) and he can also 'call' on him (verse 5) in his trouble in the sure knowledge that God does answer prayer. 'Give ear' (verse 6) and 'answer me' (verse 7) take up the phrases 'your ear' and 'answer me' ('hear me') from verse 1. Unlike those who cried out from morning till evening, "'O Baal, hear us!" But there was no voice; no one answered' (1 Kings 18:26), the living God is the one who hears and answers prayer (1 Kings 18:37–38; Psalm 65:2).

The Servant's Master (verses 8–13)
To further support his plea, David praises God by confessing his faith in the God to whom he is committed. His sovereign Lord and Master is unique. He is unlike any other god that people worship or any heavenly being with earthly influence (see Psalm 82:1) and he does unique works (verse 8; see Exodus 15:11; Deuteronomy 3:24). It is because God is 'great', does wonders and is alone worthy of the name God ('You alone are God', verse 10; see Psalm 18:31) that the day must come when the 'nations' whom God has made 'shall come and worship' before this sovereign Lord and honour him (verse 9; see Acts 17:31). David makes a similar confession in his response to the covenant that God made with him (2 Samuel 7:22–24; see Psalms 22:27–28; 47:8). Isaiah also stresses the fact that there is no other God beside Israel's God and adds, 'to me every knee shall bow' (Isaiah 45:21–23), words that are taken up by Paul and applied to Jesus who as a result of his death and resurrection has been 'given the name which is above every name, that at the name of Jesus every knee shall bow ...' (Philippians 2:9–10). John sees the realisation of David and Paul's confession in the song of Moses and the Lamb where we have the closest parallel to our psalm: 'Great and marvellous are your works, Lord God Almighty ...! Who shall not fear you, O Lord, and glorify your name? For you alone are holy. For all nations shall come and worship before you ...' (Revelation 15:3–4).

This declaration of God's sovereignty over the nations is followed by David's personal confession concerning his desire to obey and revere this God whom he reverts to addressing as 'Lord' (Yahweh/Jehovah, verse 11; see verse 1). His God and sovereign Master is the covenant God of Israel and David prays that in his present troubles he will be guided aright along the course that God in his providence is taking him and live upon the promises of his word (see Psalms 25:4–5; 27:11). He is conscious, as every Christian ought to be, of the dangers of denying his God and giving the enemy cause to gloat. Pagans tended to spread their allegiance among the various gods they felt needed to be placated, whereas David desires a heart that is undivided in its loyalty and service to God ('unite my heart to fear your name' verse 11; see Jeremiah 32:39 in relation to the new covenant). Charles Wesley expresses this desire in his hymn, *Jesus, my strength, my hope*, where in the third verse he writes 'I want a true regard, a single, steady aim, Unmoved by threatening or reward, To Thee and Thy great name'. With his whole being (see Deuteronomy 6:5) he vows to 'praise' his divine Master in the sense of giving thanks for blessings received and honouring his name for ever. David gives a reason for this confession. It concerns God's character, his unfailing love ('mercy') that is 'great' toward him, seen especially in God's past action (or possibly with a view to a future action over his present trouble) in rescuing him from death ('from the depths of Sheol', verse 13; see Deuteronomy 32:22; Psalms 6:5; 18:5). In David's case the reference might be to the time of Absalom's rebellion but which becomes appropriate for the people of God during the period of the exile and in all periods of deep trouble.

The Servant's appeal (verses 14–17)

A brief indication of David's distressing situation is now given in words that are almost identical with Psalm 54:3, the main difference being that these 'violent' people are a well-organised 'assembly' ('mob', verse 14). What David might have expected from foreign enemies he is experiencing from those within Israel, from those like Ahithophel who were in league with David's son Absalom (see 2 Samuel 17:1–4). Christians through the ages have similarly been persecuted, often by organised gangs of arrogant and oppressive people with no regard for the living God. Daniel found fellow governors and satraps plotting to discredit him for his faith (see Daniel 6). In David's case he appeals to the character of God as revealed to Moses (verse 15; see Exodus 34:6).

From this firm basis David calls on God to 'turn' or 'face' toward him and be 'gracious' ('have mercy', verse 16; see verse 3 and Psalm 25:16; Numbers 6:25). The one whose strength is in the Lord is a happy and privileged person (Psalm 84:5) and David asks for that 'strength' (Psalm 22:19) to 'save' him in his difficult situation. He speaks of himself as God's 'servant' (verse 16) to draw attention once more to the master-servant relationship (see verses 2–5). It is for this reason he refers to God again as the sovereign 'Lord' in verse 15 and not under his covenant name 'LORD' as the quotation from Exodus 34:6 would have dictated. The phrase 'son of your maidservant' (verse 16; see Psalm 116:16; Exodus 23:12) underlines this relationship for it refers to a servant born in the house of the master. As a permanent member of the master's household the servant can be assured of his master's protection (Exodus 21:4).

David looks for 'a sign', not in this case like the 'signs and wonders' that brought judgment on Egypt, but a sign of some 'good' (verse 17; see Psalms 84:11; 85:12) that will shame those who hate him. He backs up his prayer with another reason ('for' or 'because you ... have helped me and comforted me'; see Psalms 54:4; 71:21), addressing God by his covenant name 'LORD' (see verses 1, 6, 11). This is the 'good' that he looks for that will signal God's support of him.

As David was God's royal servant (see Psalm 89:3, 20) as well as God's son (Psalm 89:26-27) so is our Lord Jesus (Acts 4:30). Isaiah views Israel collectively as the LORD's servant and the strength and help that David calls on God to give him so that the enemy might be disgraced is promised to God's people (Isaiah 41:9-12). But the prophet also sees one from Israel who is the ideal Israel and representative of his people who is called the Servant of the LORD and who knows God as his strength (Isaiah 42:1-4; 49:3-6). David in this prayer thus becomes a type of the Messiah as the Suffering Servant 'who, in the days of his flesh, when he had offered up prayers and supplications ... to him who was able to save him from death, and was heard because of his godly fear, though he was a Son, yet he learned obedience by the things which he suffered' (Hebrews 5:7).

Psalm 87

In Praise of the Eternal City

There are some beautiful cities in our world and if we have visited one then we are not slow in expressing our excitement at the sights and sounds that caught our attention. When Scotland's Protestant reformer, John Knox, visited Geneva, he was greatly impressed by the results of Calvin's influence on the city's church and its people. Writing to a friend he enthused that it was 'the most perfect school of Christ that ever was on the earth since the days of the apostles. In other places I confess Christ to be truly preached; but manners and religion so sincerely reformed I have not yet seen in any other place'.

This psalm in praise of Zion takes its place alongside other psalms that relate to Zion, including Psalms 46 and 48, and especially those in Book 3, like Psalms 76; 78:67-72; 84. However, Psalm 87 goes beyond anything previously sung, especially in its explicitly positive attitude to the pagan nations. The reference to the nations in Psalm 86:9 might account for our psalm being placed next to it. In the context of so many psalms dealing with the destruction of Jerusalem and its aftermath (see Psalms 74, 79, 80, 83, 85, 89), it stands out as a beacon of light and hope and can be compared to other passages in the prophets such as Isaiah 2:2-4; 35; 60-62 and Micah 4:1-5.

The Zion spoken of in this psalm has nothing to do with modern day

Zionism. Jerusalem today is nothing to write home about in terms of peace and joy. It only mirrors the bitterness and hatred that are present everywhere and the clash of races, cultures and religions that is found the world over. The city celebrated in this 'Song' (see Psalm 83) which belongs to the psalms 'of the sons of Korah' (see Psalms 84–85) has some associations with the city founded by David and the tabernacle and later the temple that was erected on Mount Zion (see Psalm 2:6). Ezekiel gives a stylised picture of this city that arises out of the one destroyed by the Babylonians (Ezekiel 40:2). The old city becomes symbolic of the heavenly holy Jerusalem which is the mother of us all (Galatians 4:26; Hebrews 12:22; Revelation 21:10). While the earthly city, as the prophets and Jesus taught, would be destroyed there is a new Zion depicted with a new temple and inhabited by citizens of a different order. Zion, in other words, personifies all God's worshipping people who belong to Jesus the Lamb of God (Revelation 7:4–17; 14:1–5).

After an introduction that speaks of God's love for Zion (verses 1–2), verse 3 announces an oracle from God that is given in verse 4. The following two verses restate and develop the message of verse 4 and the psalm ends by expressing the joy of the citizens (verse 7).

The city's founder (verses 1–3)

God founded it (verse 1)
The psalm begins abruptly with the truth that the LORD (Yahweh/ Jehovah) is the city's founder. In a prophecy that Isaiah proclaimed against the Philistines in the year that king Ahaz died it is stated again that the LORD 'founded Zion' (Isaiah 14:32; see 28:16). Unlike the cities of this world that are established by human beings this city owes its origins to God. Cain established a city and named it after his son (Genesis 4:17) and people built Babel in order to make a name for themselves (Genesis 11:4). These city-states had their day and influence but they have long ceased to exist. The same has been true of the great capital cities of past empires like Nineveh and Babylon. They lie ruined for the most part under sand and their treasures spread around the world museums.

This city of Zion is permanent and secure not only because God has founded it but because of its situation. It is founded 'in the holy mountains' (verse 1). Many times the psalms speak of Zion's 'holy hill' (see Psalms 2:6; 3:4; 15:1; 48:1). With the range of hills where Zion was located in mind, perhaps the plural is used to convey the greatness of the city. The mountains associated with Jerusalem become symbolic of this immense heavenly Zion (see Psalms 48:2-6; 125:2; 133:3; Isaiah 2:2). Israel's ancestors were interested in this city, not the earthly Jerusalem. Abraham had left a great civilization to live in tents in Canaan because he was waiting for that 'city which has foundations, whose builder and maker is God' (Hebrews 11:9-10). These patriarchs confessed they were resident aliens and pilgrims in this present world order. They believed God concerning the promised redeemer and that God had prepared a city for them (Hebrews 11:11-16).

This is one of the great themes of the Bible. Though the evil one has usurped power with the result that the whole world of rebellious human beings is under his dominion, God is preparing for himself a city-state where he is honoured and loved. Jesus Christ, God's Son, has established this city through his atoning death. He came into this world in the grip of the evil one, and dealt the decisive blow to Satan's power by paying the price of sin and experiencing the divine wrath that sinners deserve. Through belonging to Jesus the Messiah we belong to that heavenly city, which is why Paul could write to the Philippian believers that their citizenship is in heaven from where we eagerly await the Saviour (Philippians 3:20-21).

God is there (verse 1)

The mountain city is 'holy'. It is God who has set it apart for himself. The holy God has ordained to live there (Psalm 76:1-2). 'God is in the midst of her, she shall not be moved' (Psalm 46:5). It is the 'city of the great King. God is in her palaces' (Psalm 48:2-3). As God chose to live among Israel of old in the sanctuary on Mount Zion, with the ark symbolising God's presence, so he has ordained to dwell among his new covenant people (1 Corinthians 3:16-17). But this is a preview of what God has in store in the new creation. Ezekiel ends his vision of the end-time city by telling us that 'the name of the city from that day shall be: The LORD is there' (Ezekiel 48:35). The holy garden city that descends from God out of heaven and has the glory of God, is where God will be as much at home as he is in heaven (Revelation 21:2-3, 10-11, 22).

God loves it (verse 2)

The verse speaks of God's choice of Zion. It is not that God did not love 'all the dwellings of Jacob'. He did. The Spirit of God moved Balaam to bless instead of curse Israel with such words as, 'How lovely are your tents, O Jacob! Your dwellings, O Israel!' (Numbers 24:5). God loved all the places where Israel settled in the land, but he loved Zion's gates even more. It was at the city gates where people thronged, where business was conducted and where disputes were settled. The book of Nehemiah emphasises the importance of the walls and gates of 'the holy city' of Jerusalem filled with people consecrated to God yet falling short of the ideal (Nehemiah 10:28–29; 11:1, 18; 12:27–43; 13:1–31). Nevertheless, it pointed forward to the picture that this psalm paints. The 'gates' (see Psalm 24:7) figure much in Ezekiel and John's visions of the new Jerusalem (Ezekiel 40:6–37; Revelation 21:12–21). Zion's 'gates' stand for the city itself and its people meeting together as a worshipping company (Psalm 122:2).

This can be applied to the situation today. God loves each individual believer and each home where God is honoured but he loves even more all his people seen together as one great company of worshipping people. That is expressed locally as Christians meet as a church. We are not to neglect assembling together as believers (Hebrews 10:25). It is expressive of our unity in Christ and we should look on our gatherings as expressions and foretastes of the glories of the heavenly city. Under the new covenant 'you have come to Mount Zion and to the city of the living God, the heavenly Jerusalem ...' (Hebrews 12:12–24).

God owns it (verse 3)
It is described as the 'city of God' (see Psalm 48:1). Isaiah calls the people of God, 'The City of the LORD, Zion of the Holy One of Israel' (Isaiah 60:14).

In this verse it is the city itself that is addressed and we are told that God has some 'glorious' or 'weighty' things to say about it. It has a great reputation in general but some very significant facts are brought to our attention in the following verses. The 'Selah' suggests a pause before the message is proclaimed.

The citizens of the city (verses 4–7)
In verse 4 we have direct speech from God concerning its citizens and this is followed by comment that underlines what God says (verses 5–6). The psalm ends with a testimony by its citizens.

An international city (verse 4)

The citizens of Zion are not from one ethnic group. 'Rahab' is not a reference to the prostitute who hid the spies and who was saved from the destruction of Jericho. The name is spelt differently in the original. In ancient mythology 'Rahab' was a sea monster associated with the hostile primeval forces (see Psalm 89:10; Job 9:13 translated 'proud'; 26:12 translated 'storm'; Isaiah 51:9). It is used here as a nickname for Egypt (Isaiah 30:7) to draw attention to the threat that that nation had been to Israel over the centuries. 'Babylon' was the superpower that had recently destroyed Jerusalem and its temple and sent its people into exile. These two great enemies of Israel are represented in this city.

Israel had enemies closer to home. The Philistines ('Philistia'), along the western strip of what is Gaza today, were a continual menace from the time of the Judges through to David's reign and threatened Israel's existence. Also mentioned is 'Tyre' to the north-west from where Jezebel came with her pagan gods. These two people groups are among those listed in Psalm 83:7 who conspired against Israel yet they too are represented in the city. In addition to these nations that surrounded Israel, 'Ethiopia' ('Cush') covering the area now known as Sudan, is named as a representative of distant nations who belong to this city.

There have been hints already in the psalms concerning some of these nations and their associations with Messiah's rule (see Psalms 45:12; 68:31; 72:10). The prophets who often pronounce judgment on the foreign nations also look forward to the day when Israel's former enemies and distant foreigners will be one with God's people (see Isaiah 2:2–3; 19:18–25; Micah 4:1–8; Zechariah 2:11–12; 8:22–23; Malachi 1:11). John has that glorious picture of an innumerable company from 'all nations, tribes, peoples, and tongues, standing before the throne and before the Lamb ... saying "Salvation belongs to our God who sits on the throne and to the Lamb!"' (Revelation 7:9–10).

Its citizens know the Lord (verse 4)

There is some uncertainty over the translation 'to those who know me'. Is the divine oracle speaking to God's people about the nations mentioned (see Psalm 36:10) or does 'those who know me' refer to the nations themselves, so that 'to' means 'belonging to the number of those know me?' It seems better in context to understand the phrase in this latter sense. The citizens of the world, represented by these nations, are ones who 'know' the Lord. They not only acknowledge him by worshipping him alone but they have a personal relationship with God. This is what Jeremiah prophesied concerning those in the new covenant. Not all under the old Sinai covenant knew the Lord. But the prophet declares: 'they all shall know me, from the least of them to the greatest of them' (Jeremiah 31:33–34). It is through Jesus the Messiah and his atoning death that the new covenant is established (1 Corinthians 11:25) and it is by belonging to him we enjoy this relationship with God.

Its citizens are born there (verses 4–6)

This is the point that is stressed from the oracle of verse 4—'This one was born there'. When the Jews returned to Jerusalem from exile in Babylon it was a great concern to those in authority that each person could prove his Jewish descent and especially to ascertain who were of the priestly line. No foreigners were allowed in case they encouraged idolatry but difficulties arose when family records were missing as a result of the exile (Ezra 2:59–63; Nehemiah 7:5; 13:1–3). Concerning the heavenly city there are no such problems or worries.

The citizens of this city are not resident aliens, not foreigners with work permits. The nations are viewed as individuals, ideal persons and this is a more graphic way of presenting the truth that the representatives of all the nations have full citizenship rights. Each and every one of the nations is a natural born resident. It will be acknowledged by all that 'This one and that one were born in her' (verse 5). Everyone has a birth certificate marked 'Zion'! There are no mistakes and there is no fraudulent paperwork. They are all genuine citizens because Israel's covenant God, the 'LORD', is the registrar who does not misplace the records either! He records the names as he 'registers' the nations, 'This one was born there' (verse 6). In speaking of Christians coming to Mount Zion, the heavenly city, the writer to the Hebrews mentions that they come to the church or assembly 'of the firstborn who are registered in heaven ...' (Hebrews 12:23). The idea of a register of citizens calls to mind the record of those among the 'living' in Zion (Isaiah 4:3) and 'the book of life' (Psalm 69:28; Philippians 4:3; Revelation 3:5). Jesus encouraged his disciples not to rejoice so much in the fact that demons were subject to them but that their names were written in heaven (Luke 10:20).

Clearly a miraculous transformation is needed for people of various nationalities to find themselves citizens of this city. When Jesus spoke to Nicodemus about the need for a spiritual heavenly birth in order to enter the kingdom, such passages as this would probably have been in his mind (John 3:3-10). What is more, Paul saw the inclusion of the Gentiles with the Jews among Christ's people as the fulfilment of Old Testament prophecies and psalms like this. This was God's plan from the beginning. God blessed Abraham and his family so that all nations might be blessed (Genesis 12:1-3; Psalm 47:9). Gentiles, who are aliens have been brought near by the blood of Christ. They are no longer strangers and foreigners but 'fellow citizens with the saints and members of the household of God ... a holy temple in the Lord ... a habitation of God in the Spirit' (Ephesians 2:13-22).

Picking up the words of verse 1 it is again emphasised that God will 'establish' the city (see Psalm 48:8). Appropriately in the context of the nations, God is referred to as the 'Most High' (verse 5; see Psalms 7:17; 83:18).[29] The 'Selah' after verse 6 indicates a break before the final point is made.

Its citizens are fully satisfied (verse 7)

The psalm closes enigmatically with singers and instrumentalists uniting to express the feelings of all the citizens of Zion—'All my springs are in you'. The quotation suggests that they find their joy and fulfilment in this wonderful city. Although God is the founder and the one who makes the city what it is, the 'you' probably refers to the city. The song of the worshipping nations is that they find their satisfaction in this garden city. This is a place full of life and vitality. Psalm 46:4 speaks of 'a river whose streams shall make glad the city of God' and Ezekiel's future city has water issuing from the temple bringing life and fertility to the area (Ezekiel 47). The last book of the Bible takes up that picture of the garden city with the river of the water of life proceeding from God's throne (Revelation 22:1-2).

> See! the streams of living waters,
> springing from eternal love,
> well supply thy sons and daughters
> and all fear of want remove.[30]

Psalm 88

The Dark Night of the Soul

The poem, 'The Dark Night of the Soul', by the 16th century Spanish Roman Catholic mystic, St John of the Cross, relates the soul's difficult journey as it seeks to detach itself from the world and reach the light of union with God. That kind of mysticism is not biblical and owes more to ancient Greek philosophy, and this psalm gives no encouragement to such beliefs.

Though arguably the saddest in the collection, the psalm begins on a positive note addressing God by his covenant name 'LORD' and as the author of his salvation. God has revealed himself to the psalmist and a personal relationship already exists between them. But the psalm expresses the unrelieved darkness that he is presently experiencing. The realism of the situation described, where God is silent and no answers are forthcoming, is in itself an encouragement to believers. In some Christian groups a false piety has given people the impression that believers should never find themselves in such a predicament and no spiritual songs are sung to suggest an experience of this nature. It is reassuring to realise that God's word contains prayers that depict the kind of dark experiences through which Christians are sometimes led and confronts them in an open and honest way.

Martin Luther, the great Protestant Reformer, had many such dark periods in his life in which he spoke of 'the hiddenness of God'.

Christian hymn-writers, following the lead of our psalmist, have written similarly. In the second verse of Edward Mote's, *My hope is built on nothing less*, we sing: *When darkness veils His lovely face, I rest on His unchanging grace; In every high and stormy gale, My anchor holds within the veil.* The psalm encourages us to 'cling tenaciously to God in the dark' (Arthur G. Clarke) as Job did in his sufferings. Motyer likens the psalmist to Isaiah's description of the person who fears the Lord and obeys the Servant yet 'walks in darkness and has no light'. Isaiah urges such to 'trust in the name of the Lord and rely upon his God' (Isaiah 50:10).

Like Psalm 87, this is a 'Song' as well as a 'Psalm' belonging to the Korahites but in addition, like the heading to Psalm 80, it is for the 'Chief Musician' with perhaps a suggestion concerning the tune or instrument—'upon Mahalath' (see the heading to Psalm 53). The expression 'Leannoth', which is unique to this psalm, may be a part of the tune's name or a separate item about the psalm's content and associated with a verb meaning 'to humble' or 'to afflict' (see verse 7 'afflicted').[31]

The psalm is also one of the thirteen 'Contemplation' or teaching psalms (see Psalm 32) and the only one attributed to 'Heman the Ezrahite'. Heman was a famous Kohathite singer belonging to the Levites (1 Chronicles 6:33-38), involved in the prophetic music of the sanctuary along with Asaph and Ethan during David's kingship (1 Chronicles 15:17, 19; 25:1-7; see the heading to Psalm 89).

Three times Heman calls out to God (verses 1-2, 9b, 13) and in each case it is followed by a lament that speaks only of darkness and death with no relief whatever (verses 3-9a, 10-12, 14-18). This sad song introduces the 'Selah' not at two obvious places in the text but perhaps to suggest a pause at points where it was thought the subject matter was particularly harrowing, at the close of verses 7 and 10.

Like so many in Book 3, this psalm was placed here to express the feelings of God's people some time after the Babylonians had destroyed Jerusalem and its temple and carried off the bulk of the population into exile. Lamentations gives expression in poetry to this same darkness felt by the people of God at such a catastrophe.

Urgent appeal in affliction (verses 1–9a)

The psalm opens like many laments by the psalmist telling God that he has 'called out' to him continually, urging him to hear and receive his

prayer (verses 1-2; see Psalms 77:1-2; 86:1-3). Psalm 22:2 comes closest
to the cry of Heman. Kidner draws attention to Jesus' words, 'which
reveal God's sensitivity to these ceaseless cries, for all his apparent
indifference', in his comment after the parable of the unjust judge, 'And
shall God not avenge his own elect who cry out day and night to him,
though he bears long with them?' (Luke 18:7). For the psalmist hope lies
in the God of redemption and covenant promises ('LORD') whom he
can call 'my salvation' (verse 1; see Psalm 85:4).

Heman's plight is presented with a view to moving God to show
compassion and act to deliver him. Instead of being 'sated' or 'satisfied'
with the goodness of God's house (Psalm 65:4), his whole being is
'full of troubles' ('sated with evils', verse 3) so that he is like one who
is at death's door. While he uses the language of death and the 'grave'
('Sheol' verse 3), this does not mean that Heman was very ill and about
to die. The imagery of dying and the state of the dead is a graphic way
of expressing how the psalmist feels and the pressures he is under. It is
a death-like situation that he is enduring.

If a tomb was not available in a rock, dead bodies were buried in a
'pit' and this became symbolic of where a person under God's judgment
went after death (verse 4; see Psalm 28:1). He has become like a 'man
of vigour' (as the word for 'man' implies) who no longer has 'strength'
(verse 4). In verse 5 the psalmist likens himself to a dead soldier slain
on the battlefield, freed from the one he served (see Job 3:19), no longer
remembered (see Jeremiah 11:19) and without God's protection and
care ('cut off from your hand'; see Ezra 7:9).

The 'pit' features again in verse 6 and this time he considers that it
is God in his wrath who has brought him to what feels like the lowest
parts of the pit, pitch dark in the very depths of Sheol (see Psalms 63:9;
86:13; Ezekiel 26:20). Like a person drowned by a tidal wave (Psalm
69:2), so God in his wrath has 'afflicted' him (verse 7), picking up the
word Leannoth ('affliction') in the heading. He also believes it is God
who has distanced him from his intimate friends which is often seen
as aggravating the situation (Psalms 31:11; 38:11; 69:8). Like Job and
the Suffering Servant he is abhorred and despised by them (Job 19:13;
30:9-10; Isaiah 53:3). He feels shut in and unable to find a way out of
his predicament. His eye wastes away with grief (see Psalms 6:7; 31:9)
on account of his 'affliction' (see verse 7).

Urgent appeal with no answers (verses 9b–12)

Again Heman reminds God of how he has continually called out to him and 'spread out' (not 'stretched out' as in Psalm 44:20) his empty hands to Yahweh ('LORD' verse 9b) in his desperate need. He then wrestles with God in prayer by means of a series of rhetorical questions concerning death. Do they imply a negative or positive reply? In one sense the questions imply the answer 'no'. The psalmist speaks of what God does in this present life. It is here in this world that God shows his 'wonders' as he did at the time of the exodus (verses 10 and 12; see Psalm 77:11). God's 'loving-kindness' ('steadfast love'), his 'faithfulness' (verse 11) and his 'righteousness' as he acts to put things right (verse 12), are the divine characteristics that are so precious to Israel (Exodus 34:6) and they are experienced this side of the grave. Death ends all that gracious divine saving activity in the same way as a person whose body lies dead in a tomb cannot praise God (see Psalms 6:5; 30:9).

Death, the last enemy (1 Corinthians 15:26), is described using a variety of vivid images:

a. In the second half of verse 10 the word for 'dead'[32] is a poetic equivalent for the more regular word for the dead that appears in the first half of verse 10 (see Proverbs 2:18; Isaiah 26:14, 19).

b. The parallel expression to the usual word for 'grave' in verse 11 is 'destruction' (see Job 26:6; Proverbs 15:11), a term that surfaces in John's vision as the name of the angel of the bottomless pit—'Abaddon' (Revelation 9:11). The word expresses the point that the body perishes or is destroyed in the grave.

c. The grave or tomb is a place that is 'dark' (verse 12; see verse 6), the very opposite of walking 'in the light of the living' (Psalm 56:13).

d. It is also described as 'the land of forgetfulness' (verse 12; see verse 5). Not only are the dead soon forgotten (Psalms 6:5; 31:12) they also know nothing (Ecclesiastes 9:5, 10).

But these rhetorical questions can also imply an affirmative answer. The psalmist is in a death-like situation but he is not actually in the grave. He is alive and praying to Israel's God whose name is the 'LORD' (Yahweh/Jehovah, verse 9), who shows 'steadfast love', 'faithfulness' and 'righteousness' toward his people (verses 11–12). He can still do 'wonders' in the psalmist's present circumstances. Indirectly, then, Heman is appealing to God to rescue him and bring him up out of this 'grave' situation. He knows that God is able to do what seems impossible to humans.

There were examples in Old Testament times of God actually raising dead people to life again as happened during the ministries of Elijah and Elisha but these were rare occasions (1 Kings 17:17-24; 2 Kings 4:18-37). But David and the prophets anticipated that God would one day raise dead bodies to life (Psalm 16:10; Isaiah 26:19; Daniel 12:2).

Urgent appeal under divine wrath (verses 13–18)

Yet again Heman refers to his persistent pleadings to the 'LORD' (Yahweh/Jehovah, verse 13; see verses 1, 9b) using a different word for 'cried out' than the one in verse 1. Here it suggests 'crying out for help' (see Psalms 5:2; 18:41). The arrival of the morning light is often associated with renewed hope as well as marking the beginning of a new opportunity to resume prayer (Psalms 5:3; 30:5; 59:16). As he continues to wrestle with God his 'why' questions (verse 14) become challenges for God to take action. At present the psalmist knows only rejection ('cast off my soul', verse 14; see Psalms 43:2; 74:1; 77:7) and divine punishment ('hide your face from me'; see Psalm 13:1). The questioning implies that God can change the situation if he wishes. There is no confession of sin or any recognition that his grievous situation is due to any particular sin as we find in other psalms where God's wrath is felt. Heman seems to be in the same kind of situation as Job. He just cannot understand the reasons for his predicament. It is only those who have tasted God's goodness and love who can speak in these terms when they no longer experience the felt presence of God and despair that he is so distant.

As the psalmist's lament draws to a close, he brings together word pictures and themes he has used earlier. His whole life is viewed as an existence near to death. Through the years he has borne God's 'terrors' (Psalm 55:4-5) and is at a loss to do anything about them ('distraught', verse 15). He explains his situation as resulting from God's 'fierce wrath' (literally 'your burnings') that has 'gone over' him like the waves of the sea (Psalm 42:7). God's 'terrors' or 'dreadful assaults' have destroyed him (verse 16). Again the image of the sea is used in verse 17 (see verse 7) as he depicts God's terrors surrounding and closing in on him like an incoming tide trapping a person on a sand dune. God has removed 'loved one and friend' far from him (verse 18; see verse 8) and as for his 'acquaintances' only 'darkness' remains. The thought may be similar to Job's dark despair (Job 17:13-16) before God broke into his situation. The psalm ends abruptly but appropriately with the word 'darkness'.

The psalm is reminiscent, as we have seen, of Job's anguish but also of his persistence in prayer as he looked to God to bring light into his dark situation. Like Job, Heman did not curse God, he did not turn his back on God. The sufferings made him more determined to look to God and to call out to him in the darkness.

Heman reminds us that life in this present world order does not always have a happy ending. As the Preacher keeps on emphasising (Ecclesiastes 1:2), life for the believer as for the unbeliever, is fleeting and full of frustrating experiences. Believers can suffer severely all their lives with mental, physical and spiritual problems. Fine Christians are struck down with severe illnesses and become completely helpless through the effects of strokes and dementia. The 'groan' of creation is the groan of the believer too as we await the new creation and the redemption of the body (Romans 8:18–25).

We can appreciate why the Anglican *Book of Common Prayer* assigned this psalm to be read on Good Friday, for it gives some expression to what the Saviour must have experienced as he hung in pain and anguish on the cross. An eternity of suffering was crammed into those three dark hours as our Lord endured the full force of God's wrath. While Jesus could speak prophetically both of his death and resurrection on the third day and could endure the cross on account of the joy set before him, that did not mitigate in any way the intense pain and spiritual suffering he bore silently on that lonely tree accursed by God and humans. It is one thing to speak objectively about the sufferings of death and hell it is another actually to experience them. The Son of God in his humanity felt the full force of the darkness and horror of God-forsakenness.

In our darkest hour we can find comfort and hope in the God of our salvation.

We sing the praise of Him who died,
Of Him who died upon the cross;
The sinner's hope let men deride,
For this we count the world but loss.

The cross he bore is life and health,
Though shame and death to Him;
His people's hope, His people's wealth,
Their everlasting theme. (Thomas Kelly)

Psalm 89

Concern over God's King

We can expect agnostics and atheists to scoff at the gospel and its promises. But believers too can have deep concerns over God's big promises especially concerning Jesus' coming in power and glory to wind up this old world and to bring in the glory of the new order. All appearances seem against it and opposition to it is often reinforced with scientific arguments that seem to run counter to what God says in his Word. We can identify with this psalm and God's faithful people of old as they wrestled with the revealed truths concerning God and his Anointed (see Psalm 2), given the unpromising situations in which they found themselves. The background to the psalm is the covenant, or special agreement that God made with David, the details of which are recorded in 2 Samuel 7. It was made when David had the good idea of building a permanent 'house' for the ark. Instead, God speaks of building for David a permanent 'house' in the sense of a 'dynasty', while his son would be the one ordained to build a 'house' for God.

How do we deal with disappointment? Does God really promise something and then go back on his word? That is the concern of this psalm and it is an appropriate ending to Book 3 where the aftermath of the Babylonian exile has raised many issues concerning God's rule and the future of his people. Book 2 ended with a royal psalm that was full of hope for the king of David's line whereas this royal psalm, with the Davidic monarch gone, turns that hope into an urgent prayer of intercession. The psalm also has close links with Psalm 88 and picks up on those important characteristics of God such as his steadfast love, faithfulness and wondrous works (Psalm 88:10-12). Like the previous psalm it is a 'Contemplation' but this time belonging to 'Ethan' who is of the same 'Ezrahite' family of musicians as Heman and Asaph (1 Chronicles 6:44; 15:19). Along with Heman, he may also be identified as one of those famed for their wisdom (1 Kings 4:31). He is probably to be identified with Jeduthun (2 Chronicles 5:12; see the heading to Psalms 62 and 77). Maybe, like some of the psalms attributed to Asaph, it was composed by a member of Ethan's family who lived after the events of 587 BC.

The psalm bears some resemblance to Asaph's 'Contemplation' in Psalm 74 but whereas Asaph begins with lament and then recalls God's character and actions, this psalm works the other way round. First, Ethan celebrates the God who has made promises to David (verses 1–37) and then faces God with the grim reality that those promises seem to have been abandoned (verses 38–51). In this it resembles Psalm 44. These are not the words of a bitter cynic but a concerned believer who ends with an earnest prayer based on the knowledge of God's steadfast love. This is the way to work through our fears and disappointments.

The 'Selah' occurs four times at significant points in the psalm: at the end of the introduction in verse 4; after the development of the opening introduction that celebrates God's kingship and his promises to David in verse 37; after presenting the current situation in verse 45; and finally in the middle of the pleas for action in verse 48. The psalm closes in verse 52 with a doxology indicating the end of Book 3. While Psalm 72 ends Book 2 encouraging us to look forward to the universal reign of God's king, this psalm ends Book 3 by indicating how God has abandoned the king. But this does not mean that God has ceased to reign or that his purposes and promises have failed and the final two Books will make that clear. The concern of the psalmist is similar to the dashed hopes of the disciples when they saw Jesus, whom they confessed to be the Messiah, crucified and his dead body laid out in a tomb (Luke 24:21).

Introduction (verses 1–4)

The psalm commences with a firm commitment: 'I will sing'. Rather than the familiar phraseology of singing to the LORD (see Psalms 13:6; 96:1), he draws attention to the LORD's 'mercies' or 'acts of steadfast love'. This word associated with God's covenant with Israel and David together with God's 'faithfulness' to which he also wants to testify, is mentioned again in verse 2. God's steadfast love and faithfulness are two key terms in this psalm, each occurs seven times in the psalm. Also significant is the repetition of 'for ever' and the supporting phrases 'to all generations' and 'heavens' which indicate the permanent and unchangeable nature of God's loving commitment and faithfulness.

Verses 3 and 4 then introduce God's covenant with his 'chosen ... servant David' (see Psalms 78:70; 86:2), using terms from the first two verses to emphasise the binding nature of the special agreement, grounded as it is in God's character. God has promised to 'establish' (verses 2, 4) David's descendants 'for ever' (verses 1–2, 4) and 'built up ... build up' (verses 2, 4) his throne 'to all generations' (verses 1, 4). The details of the covenant are given in Nathan's prophecy to David (2 Samuel 7:7–17).

The following verses 5–37 develop what these opening lines have introduced.

God's character and kingship (verses 5–18)

The content of this paragraph comments on the first two verses of the introduction. Before viewing David's kingship we are taken to a higher level to remember who this God is who has made these promises to David no matter how improbable the present crisis has rendered them. His rule is celebrated.

God's cosmic rule unquestioned (verses 5–8)

The LORD's 'wonders' (see Psalm 88:10) and his 'faithfulness' (see verses 1–2) are praised in the heavenly congregation of 'holy ones' ('saints', verse 5; see also verse 7). In the original it is not the same term that is translated as 'saints' in other places (see Psalms 30:4; 79:2; 85:8) but the one describing supernatural beings such as angels (see Job 5:1; 15:15; Daniel 8:13). Like the worshipping company of God's people on earth (Psalm 22:22, 25), this congregation of heavenly beings gives honour and thanks to God (see Revelation 4:8–11).

The angelic beings are further described as 'sons of the mighty' ('sons

of gods', verse 6; see Psalm 29:1), 'the assembly (or better 'council')
of the saints' (verse 7; see verse 5; Jeremiah 23:18, 22) and the angelic
'hosts' in God's title 'LORD God of hosts' (verse 8; see Psalm 80:4).
There is no one in heaven like the 'LORD' and all who 'are around'
('surround') him greatly revere him ('feared', 'in reverence', verse 7).
'Who is mighty like you?' (verse 8) recalls the song of Moses (Exodus
15:11; Psalm 86:8). God is addressed in the original by a shorter form
of his personal name 'LORD' ('Yah', verse 8; see Psalm 68:4; Isaiah
12:2). Further reference is made to God's 'faithfulness' which, like the
heavenly beings, also 'surrounds' him (verse 7) as indeed it does the
whole paragraph (verse 8; see verse 5).

God's cosmic rule incomparable (verses 9–14)

God's power over creation is described using some of the language of
the ancient myths of Babylon and Canaan. The sea was always seen
by Israel as something to be feared and rightly so, for even today, as
we have witnessed recently in tidal surges and tsunamis, modern
sophisticated countries like the United States and Japan have looked on
helplessly in the face of such power. How awestruck the disciples were
when Jesus rebuked the wind and commanded the sea to be still so
that the result was 'a great calm' (Mark 4:39–41). The sea is personified
as 'Rahab' the monster of the water, similar to Leviathan (verse 10; see
Psalm 74:13–14; Isaiah 51:9), that God crushed and left slain as if on a
battlefield. This imagery moves naturally into thinking of God's victory
over Egypt at the Red Sea (see Psalm 87:4) where God scattered his
enemies by his own powerful action.

The previous paragraph ended by referring to one of God's great
characteristics and this one closes with a reminder of those divine
moral qualities that undergird his sovereign rule. God has absolute

There follows a glorious statement concerning God's ownership
of the whole universe and everything in it for he has created it all.
Impressive mountain peaks like 'Tabor' that rises from the north-east
corner of the Jezreel plain and distant 'Hermon' that is over five times
higher, join in acknowledging the greatness of God alone (verses 11–12).
The psalm refers again to God's 'mighty arm' (verse 13; see verse 10)
to re-emphasise by the addition of his 'right hand' lifted high, how
great, powerful and victorious he is. It was with a 'mighty hand and
by an outstretched arm' that God redeemed his people from Egyptian
bondage (Deuteronomy 5:15).

power but it is not corrupt or tyrannical. This is conveyed with the picture of his throne resting securely on the twin foundations of 'righteousness and justice' (verse 14; see Psalm 33:5). He is righteous and he does not act unfairly. God is also pictured as being assisted by aides. 'Mercy and truth' ('steadfast love and truthfulness', verse 14) are before God's presence ('before your face') to receive their orders from him.[33] What a blessing to know we are not ruled by impersonal fatalistic forces or by unpredictable malevolent immoral spirits.

God's cosmic rule appreciated (verses 15–18)

The people of God who have had occasion to join in celebratory worship with 'shouts of joy' ('joyful sound', verse 15; see Psalm 27:6 'sacrifices of joyful shouts') are highly privileged ('Blessed', 'How fortunate'; see Psalm 1:1). In what way are they fortunate?

First, they walk along with the LORD in the light of his personal presence ('light of your countenance', verse 15; see Psalms 4:6; 44:3; Numbers 6:24–27), which means that in their daily living they are in the privileged position of knowing Yahweh's favour. Christians are favoured people as they walk in God's light and have fellowship with him (1 John 1:5–7).

Second, they rejoice continually in God's character ('name'; see Psalm 20:1), riding high on account of that 'righteousness' that characterises God's rule (verse 16; see verse 14). We rejoice as believers in the righteousness of God displayed in the gospel.

Third, they can rejoice in this way because it is God who is the 'splendour' of their strength ('glory of their strength', verse 17; see Psalm 71:8). At this point the psalmist includes himself among God's people as he speaks of 'our horn' (verse 17b; see also 'our shield' and 'our king' in verse 18). It is according to God's good pleasure that they are able to triumph over their enemies. The 'horn' symbolises strength and when the animal's horn is held high it is ready to charge (see Psalm 75:4). Christians can say 'Surely in the LORD I have righteousness and strength' (Isaiah 45:24).

Finally, and as an introduction to what follows, the people are blessed because their king who is their protector ('our shield'; see Psalms 3:3; 47:9; 84:9) belongs to Yahweh ('LORD'), 'the Holy One of Israel' (verse 18; see Psalm 71:22). Christians know him as Jesus, the Lord's Anointed, and we sing, 'We rest on Thee, our Shield and our Defender ... and in Thy Name we go' (Edith Gilling Cherry).

God's covenant with David explained (verses 19-37)

This section develops the words of verses 3-4, the promise God made to David through Nathan the prophet (2 Samuel 7:4-17; 1 Chronicles 17:3-15). This covenant builds on the covenant promises to Abraham and Israel (see Genesis 12:1-3; 15:1-21; 17:1-21; Exodus 24:4-8; Leviticus 26:40-46).

God spoke 'in a vision' to the prophet Nathan (2 Samuel 7:17; 1 Chronicles 17:15) and he passed the message on to David who is referred to as God's 'committed one' ('holy one', verse 19) if we accept the reading of some Hebrew manuscripts. But the traditional Hebrew text reads 'faithful ones' (often translated 'saints', Psalm 85:8) and this may be reminding us that God spoke to two of his faithful prophets about David, first to Samuel and then to Nathan.

Promises of the covenant (verses 19-27)

The prophecy summarises God's messages to both prophets and begins by emphasising that it was God who chose David as he had chosen Israel in the first place (Deuteronomy 7:6-7) and favoured this 'warrior' or 'mighty one' with help. That 'help' (verse 19) is explained in verses 21 to 23. God promised to support and strengthen him. No enemy will get the better of him, in fact, all his 'wicked' foes ('son of wickedness' in verse 22 is someone characterised by wickedness; see Ephesians 2:2) will be decisively defeated (see 2 Samuel 7:9-10). People like Saul's family or Absalom were pawns of the devil and Jesus, whom David typifies, overcame the evil one throughout his life so that he could say as he approached his sacrificial death, 'the ruler of this world is coming, and he has nothing in me' (John 14:30).

God 'found' his 'servant' (verse 20; see verse 3); he had 'sought for himself a man after his own heart' (1 Samuel 13:14) and though Samuel 'anointed' him with sacred oil it was seen as God's act (1 Samuel 16:12-13; 2 Samuel 12:7). All the emphasis is on what God has done to indicate that David belongs to God and exercises authority on behalf of God. There are echoes of Psalm 2 here.

The Lord's 'faithfulness' and his 'steadfast love' ('mercy') will be David's close aides and all that God's 'name' represents will be to his advantage (verse 24) just as God's people celebrate in verses 16-17.

The 'sea' and 'rivers' (verse 25) probably speak of the waters that surround Israel's furthest borders like the Mediterranean and Red Sea, the river or brook of Egypt and the Euphrates. God promised that all that land would belong to Abraham's descendants (Genesis 15:18; Exodus 23:31) and it was during the David-Solomon era that the promise was realised (1Kings 4:21). It came to symbolise the worldwide dominion of the Lord's Anointed (see Psalms 2:8–9 and 72:8; Romans 4:13; Revelation 11:15). God is said to 'set' David's 'hand' and 'right hand' over the whole area (verse 25; see verse 13) so that in David we have a picture of the Lord's universal rule especially as verse 25 is seen in the context of verses 13–14.

Israel as a nation could speak of God as 'my Father' (Jeremiah 3:19) and be called God's 'first-born' (verse 27; Exodus 4:22). God was also the 'rock' of Israel's 'salvation' (Deuteronomy 32:15) and the nation was promised that if they obeyed God's covenant he would set them 'high above all nations of the earth' (Deuteronomy 28:1). What is said of Israel is here applied to Israel's king (verses 26–27; see 2 Samuel 7:14). Like a child in need calling out to its parent, so David can know God's fatherly protection. A first-born son enjoyed a privileged position, second only to the father. All the kings of the earth are under God's control but David is the most exalted—the word 'highest' when used of God is translated 'Most High' (see Psalm 83:18). David in these verses is a type of Christ who called on God as 'my God' and 'my Father' and committed himself to the rock of his salvation (Matthew 26:39, 42; John 20:17; Hebrews 5:7; 1 Peter 2:23). John begins his greetings to the churches with words reminiscent of verse 27, describing Jesus as 'the first-born from the dead, and the ruler over the kings of the earth' (Revelation 1:5).

Permanence of the covenant (verses 28–37)
This section develops what was said at the beginning of the psalm concerning the everlasting nature of God's promises to David (verses 1–4; see 2 Samuel 7: 13–16). The repetition of 'for ever' (verses 28–29) emphasises God's commitment to David and his descendants and makes the concerns of the final part of the psalm more poignant. God's 'steadfast love' ('mercy') is especially reserved for the king with whom this special relationship and agreement has been made ('covenant'; see Isaiah 55:3). The promise extends to David's descendants so that his dynasty will be as durable as the 'heavens' (verse 29; see Deuteronomy 11:21; Psalm 72:17). It is for this reason that David can refer to his 'throne' as the throne of the Lord's kingdom and Solomon is said to sit on 'the throne of the Lord' (1 Chronicles 28:5; 29:23; see Psalm 45:6).

It is also made clear that the Davidic monarch is to be true to the Lord. A warning is given in verses 30–32 (see 2 Samuel 17:14). If they failed to live by God's commandments (see Psalm 119 for the various terms for God's teaching) then they would be disciplined. The word 'break' (verse 31) is stronger in the original. It means 'to profane', to treat as common what God has set apart as special. The king was to have a copy of the law and to observe it all his life (Deuteronomy 17:18–20), being an example to his people of the man congratulated in Psalm 1. Reading consecutively through the psalms from the beginning, as Geoffrey Grogan remarks, helps us to 'see that the righteous conduct extolled in Psalm 1 should characterize the king of Psalm 2.'[34]

The 'rod' that God's king should be wielding (Psalm 2:9) God will use to punish the king for his rebellion ('transgression'). God also warns that he will inflict 'stripes' on account of the king's 'iniquity' or waywardness (verse 32). The 'stripe' or 'plague' is often used for a punishment from God (Genesis 12:17; Exodus 11:1) but also occurs many times to describe 'leprous' conditions (Leviticus 13:5–6, 17, etc.).[35] Interestingly, this is the term that Isaiah uses when referring to the punishment that the LORD's Servant suffered on account of his people's transgressions and iniquities—'by his stripes we are healed' (Isaiah 53:5).

Despite God's disciplining rod the promise to David will remain intact. God's 'steadfast love' and 'faithfulness' are again emphasised in the context of the special agreement he had made with David. The Davidic king might treat God's covenant statutes as something ordinary and easily dismissed, but God will not 'break', will not 'profane' his 'covenant' (verses 33–34). In order to make the point as clear as possible that God does not go back on his word (verse 34; see Isaiah 40:8), God goes on oath. The Letter to the Hebrews reminds us that people swear by someone greater than themselves. There is no one greater than God and for our benefit he condescends to show that his promises are true and irrevocable by swearing on his own eternal, infinite being (Hebrews 6:13–18). Here he swears by his 'holiness' (see Amos 6:8; Psalm 60:6), by that which makes God the one true God that he is. God cannot lie; it would be to go against his nature (1 Samuel 15:29; Titus 1:2). The way it is put in the original makes it into a curse. It suggests the unthinkable that if God does not keep his word he would himself be under God's curse. God's commitment to David is as strong as his commitment to Israel (verse 35; Numbers 23:19).

The concluding lines of God's promise again emphasise its permanent nature ('for ever', verses 36-37; see verses 28-29; 2 Samuel 7:16) with the sun and moon there as witnesses (see Psalm 72:5-7).

Crisis over the covenant (verses 38-52)

Having presented such a powerful statement concerning the Lord's irrevocable promises, the contrast with the reality depicted in the final verses could not be greater. The 'Selah' at the end of verse 37 is appropriately placed to mark the point where the psalm suddenly turns into lamentation. In this it is like Psalm 44 with a similar emphatic opening 'But you have cast off' addressed to God (verse 38; see Psalm 44:9). We are reminded of the disciples' dashed hopes as they made their weary way home from Jerusalem to Emmaus after witnessing their Messiah's death on the cross: 'But we were hoping that it was he who was going to redeem Israel' (Luke 24:21).

Lament (verses 38-45)

The deep concern is not that the Lord's anointed has been disciplined for that was built into the Davidic covenant (verses 30-32), but that God has so rejected his 'anointed' in his fury that he has 'renounced' his servant's covenant and 'profaned his crown' (verse 39). Like an unfaithful king who has treated God's law as nothing to be reverenced, so God has treated the 'crown', the symbol of the king's consecrated status (see verse 20) as nothing special but something to be thrown down to the earth (see verses 31, 34 and 44).

Verses 40 to 43 depict the destruction of the city's fortifications leaving the king and people vulnerable. The king represents his people and the city so that when something happens to them it is as if it is happening to the king. Instead of king and people rejoicing in their exalted position and knowing God's strength being in a position of power over the nations, it is the king's enemies that are exalted and strong and who are doing the rejoicing (see verses 16, 17, 24; Lamentations 2:17). Instead of being helped by God in battle the king has been hindered (verse 43). God has not been 'the rock' of his salvation in his time of need (verse 26).

What is said of the Davidic crown (verse 39) is said of his 'throne': it has been cast down to the earth (verse 44). This 'throne' that is to be like the heavens (see verse 29) for stability and endurance and is established for ever (verse 36) counts for nothing and his 'glory' or the 'pure radiant splendour' associated with the king as the Lord's representative has been brought to an end by God. Instead of honour there is only 'shame', his rule at an end while still a 'youth'. This was certainly the position of king Jehoiachin, who was deported to Babylon in 597 BC, when he was eighteen and after only three months on the throne (2 Kings 24:8-12). He languished in prison suffering the indignity of prison clothes and prison food for thirty-seven years until Nebuchadnezzar's successor showed him kindness (2 Kings 25:27-30). The 'Selah' (verse 45) marks the point where the lament turns to pleading with God that he would take action.

Prayer (verses 46–51)

His prayer is in two parts divided by the 'Selah' at the close of verse 48. In the first part (verses 46-48) the actual plea is, 'Remember how short my time is ...' (verse 47; see Psalm 39:4-5) and in the second part, 'Remember, Lord, the reproach of your servants ...' (verse 50; see Psalm 74:2). It is not that the psalmist believed that God forgets but it is a forceful way of urging God to take action on their behalf.

The cry of anguish, so often heard in laments, introduces the urgent plea. It goes up to Israel's covenant-keeping God: 'How long, Lord?' ('Until when, Yahweh?'; verse 46). In wording the cry is similar to Psalm 79:5. It is because of God's anger that he is hidden from them resulting in the desperate situation in which king and people find themselves. The psalmist speaks on behalf of all when he pleads the shortness of life and the inevitability of death. It is a subject taken up in the next psalm (Psalm 90), which introduces Book 4. Here the question is raised about the transitory nature of human life ('sons of men'). Surely God has not created human beings for a pointless existence ('futility', 'emptiness'; see Psalms 31:6; 41:6) where life on earth is so short and full of suffering? As strong as some people are ('man' as vigorous), they cannot escape death not even as a king.

In the second part of his prayer (verses 49-51), the psalmist, again representing his people, recalls those promises to David (verses 3, 35) and he introduces for the last time those terms employed throughout the psalm, namely, God's acts of steadfast love ('loving-kindnesses') and 'truth' (verse 49; see verse 1). He addresses God as 'Master' or sovereign 'Lord' and refers to God's people as 'your servants' (verses 49-50), which echoes the relationship depicted in Psalm 86:2-5, 15-16 between God and the king. King and people are still closely bound together and the psalmist speaks for all as he lays before God the scornful comments ('reproach') they are having to bear from many peoples who have seen what has happened to Israel and its king (verses 50–51; see verse 41). The implication behind the terms he uses is that because they are in this master-servant relationship the enemy action is reflecting badly on God. For God's servants to be dishonoured means God is being dishonoured. Also as God's servants it is expected that the master will protect them from their enemies.

Those suffering under grave persecution for the gospel's sake all their earthly lives can well appreciate something of the intensity of the psalmist's agony but the words of Jesus and his apostles do give encouragement to count it all joy when experiencing such trials. 'If you are reproached for the name of Christ, blessed are you, for the Spirit of glory and of God rests upon you' (1 Peter 4:14).

The psalm ends, like the previous one, with no resolution (verse 51; Psalm 88:18). But unlike Psalm 88 where the last word is 'darkness' here the psalm closes, as in the original, with 'your anointed'. In view of the promises to David, there is a future associated with the LORD's anointed. We are encouraged to watch this space.

Deportation to Babylon was the common lot for king and people. It was both the final curse of the Sinai covenant and God's rod for disciplining the king (verse 32). After announcing the destruction of the city and the exile as the final curse of the covenant on the people for their sins, the prophets often look forward to a new beginning with a Davidic king reigning over God's people (see Isaiah 9:7; 55:3–4; Jeremiah 23:5–6; Ezekiel 34:23–24; Hosea 3:4–5; Amos 9:11). The psalms of David in Book 5 also encourage us to look forward to the full realisation of God's promises to David (see especially Psalms 122:5; 132:1, 11, 17). Those promises are mentioned in the angel's announcement to Mary concerning the son she is to bear, 'the Lord God will give him the throne of his father David ... and of his kingdom there will be no end' (Luke 1:31–33).

What this psalm does is to teach us first of all that, like the old covenant made with Israel, failure on the part of humans does not come as a surprise to God for it is written into the agreement (Deuteronomy 31:14–29; 2 Samuel 7:14). But God does not abandon his promises, instead he works within the covenants he made with Israel and its king. God so arranged things that Jeremiah's new covenant and the blessing of salvation from sin's curse and the serpent's power might come to all nations through the Jews and that God's king might emerge from David's family line. At the same time the experiences of the people and their king under the wrath of God give a preview of what the true anointed one would undergo on behalf of all his people. He experienced the worst of all exiles as well as the cruel mocking scorn ('reproach') of the peoples as he hung upon the cross (see Psalm 69:9; Romans 15:3). As both the Lord's anointed and the suffering Servant of the Lord, God's disciplining rod which led to our peace was laid on him and with his stripes we are healed.

Doxology (verse 52)

It is the messianic hope that enables the prophetic editors to bring the Third Book to a conclusion on a positive note, even if it is a little short (see Psalms 41:13 and 72:18–19 for detailed comment).

Book Four

Despite many disappointments and the unhappy situation that had brought about the Babylonian exile and the loss of temple, city and king, God was still the sovereign Lord over all and concerned for his people's welfare. These are the themes celebrated in this particular part of the psalm collection. The people's sin has not only brought about the exile, it has brought to an apparent end the rule of David's line of kings. Like the prophet Isaiah, these psalms encourage and assure the people that God is still in charge of events. While people are like the grass that withers away, God and his word continue for ever (Isaiah 40:6-8). This, the smallest of the five books of the Psalter (Psalms 90-106), again reminds us of Psalm 2 that Israel's covenant LORD (Yahweh/Jehovah) is King and that he will act to favour Zion. These psalms also encourage the people to trust the Lord (Psalm 91), to thank him for his steadfast love (Psalm 92) and to look to him alone to fulfil his eternal purposes and the promises made to Abraham and David (Psalms 101, 103).

Psalm 90

God's Eternity and Human Frailty

This moving psalm is often read at funeral services and its contents are still sung at cenotaphs and solemn national occasions in the words of Isaac Watts' powerful hymn, 'O God, our help in ages past'. It deals with the brevity of human life against the backdrop of God's eternity.

Not many of the psalms in Book 4 have headings naming the author but this one does and it takes us back long before David's time. It simply reads, 'A Prayer of Moses the man of God'. The expression 'man of God' is applied to Moses in Deuteronomy 33:1 and by Caleb when speaking about the inheritance that Moses had sworn to give him in the land (Joshua 14:6). It is also applied to David (2 Chronicles 8:14; Nehemiah 12:24, 36) and especially to prophets like Elijah and Elisha (1 Kings 17:18, 24; 2 Kings 1:10; 4:7, 9, 21; etc.). The phrase emphasises the prophet's status in the eyes of the people, whereas 'servant' is the Lord's term for his prophets.

Although commentators have been reticent to accept at face value the Mosaic authorship of this psalm, there is every reason for doing so. As more modern scholars have noted, it has similarities to Moses' prayers and songs in Exodus and Deuteronomy as well as being a meditation on the early chapters of Genesis. What Ecclesiastes preaches,[36] this psalm prays. The fleeting nature of human life is not because that is how we were originally made but is the result of God's judgment on human sin. It is placed at this point in the Psalms to express the situation in which the people of God found themselves after the tragedy of the Babylonian invasion and deportations. Like Moses in the wilderness the Jewish exiles were without land, city, temple and king and they were living through a time when there was deep concern over the realisation of God's promises. It stands at the head of a series of psalms, some of which refer to Moses, where God is worshipped as the eternal king and saviour of his people. While the prayer emphasises the sense of sin it also encourages the people to trust God that he would make their own efforts successful.

The prayer follows on quite naturally from the previous psalm. It picks up themes from the lament section (Psalm 89:38-51) especially the references to God's wrath, the transitory nature of human life and the plaintive cry, 'How long?' (Psalm 89:46-48). The psalm begins by calling attention to God's eternity and stability in contrast to human frailty (verses 1-6), then considers God's wrath as a result of human sin (verses 7-12) and closes with pleas for wisdom and help in the light of God's grace (verses 13-17).

God's permanence and human frailty (verses 1-6)
The psalm begins, in the original text, not by addressing God by his covenant name 'Lord' (Yahweh/Jehovah) or even by the general word 'God', but by the term sovereign 'Lord' or 'Master' (verse 1; see Psalm 89:49-50) and it is balanced later in the prayer where God's people are referred to as 'servants' (verses 13, 16) and by a re-use of 'Lord' in the final verse. It is the relationship of master-servant that is in mind throughout even though the prayer does appeal to God by the name precious to his people from the time of the exodus (verse 13). The prayer begins with a strong affirmation. Israel's Lord and Master has been the 'home' or 'dwelling-place' in time past to people like Abraham, Isaac and Jacob and for his people he still is even when they are in the wilderness with no secure home. The same noun is used of God's heavenly home (Deuteronomy 26:15; see Psalm 26:8). Here, however, it is God himself who is the place of safety (see Psalm 71:3 where the same word is translated 'habitation'). A similar form of the word is used in the Blessing of Moses: 'The eternal God is your refuge ('dwelling-place') and underneath are the everlasting arms' (Deuteronomy 33:27). What a

blessing this truth has been to countless believers especially in times of deep sorrow and pain!

God is able to be such a permanent home because he has always existed. A vivid word picture presents God as giving birth to the mountains and earth's landmass. Even before creation God was there and at no point was there a moment when he was not there: 'from everlasting to everlasting, you are God' (verse 2).

By contrast, frail humans are reduced to a 'crushed' state ('destruction') by God in the same way as he 'crushed' or 'broke' Rahab the sea monster in pieces and as the king will crush the oppressor (Psalms 89:10; 72:4). The verb 'Return' (verse 3) usually signifies turning to God in repentance but that is not the context here and it may well be that Moses is thinking of God's curse on Adam where the same word is found—'till you return to the ground ... for dust you are and to dust you shall return' (Genesis 3:19). In this case 'crushed' may be a poetic way of speaking of 'dust' which is why the word appears in a number of modern English versions. The actual phrase 'return to the dust' will occur later in Psalm 104:29 (see also Job 10:9; 34:15). God's anger that gave rise to their being crushed to dust will be stressed in the next section. Here the emphasis is on the fleeting nature of human existence compared with God's eternity.

The point is restated showing that however long human life may appear to us it is in God's sight very insignificant. We get all excited when people reach a hundred and they receive a special card from the Queen. Proud empires that arise and flourish for a century or two quickly collapse and give way to new super-powers. People like Methuselah lived for nearly a thousand years but this does not impress God (see 2 Peter 3:8). To him it was like a day that has passed or a mere night 'watch' (verse 4; Exodus 14:24). The night was divided into three watches particularly for purposes of guard duty (Judges 7:19; Psalm 63:6). Even we humans are aware of how quickly time passes especially as we get older and look back on our lives. It seems so short to us.

Human life is fleeting and flimsy. We have seen in tsunamis how people are swept away in the flood ('flooded away', verse 5). Another picture of human life is that it is like 'sleep' perhaps in the sense of a dream. When we awake it has gone and is forgotten. Our lives can also be seen as 'grass' that can quickly grow and flourish in the early morning light and then by evening be cut down or wither (verse 6). As nature renews itself each day with fresh growth so we see in human life people and empires ever seeking to flourish yet ever fading and falling. *We blossom and flourish as leaves on the tree, And wither and perish—but nought changeth thee.*[37] The brevity of our lives is a common theme in the Bible (Psalm 37:2; Job 14:1-2; Isaiah 40:6-8; James 4:14).

God's wrath and human failure (7-12)

From looking at life in general ('man', 'children of men', and 'they' in verses 3 to 6), Moses becomes more personal in this section ('we' and 'our'). At the same time it indicates that the transient nature of human life is due to God's wrath on human sin. This is not, as some scholars suggest, a confession of sin by Israel under God's wrath for their own failure to live by God's law although the psalm could be used in that way. It is primarily a recognition by Moses of the truth presented in the early chapters of Genesis. Death is the penalty for human sin (see Genesis 2:17; 3:17; 5:5, 8, 11, etc.). Paul writes that 'through one man sin entered the world, and death through sin, and thus death spread to all men, because all sinned ... death reigned from Adam to Moses' (Romans 5:12). 'Whatever instrumental agencies may be employed to kill us, our real destroyer is the anger of our Maker' (Alexander).

Our mortality is the result of God's wrath and God's wrath is the result of our secret and open sins and so we are terrified and our lives decline and waste away like a murmur (verses 7-9). Nothing that we do is hidden from God. Secret faults are exposed to the light of his face (see Jeremiah 16:17; Hebrews 4:13).

Moses died when he was aged one hundred and twenty and Joshua when he was one hundred and ten. But these were exceptions. In general people were dying much earlier with some reaching the age of seventy and a few strong, healthy individuals managing to see their eightieth birthdays. We all know the adage that 'old age does not come on its own' and it expresses what is said here. There is nothing to boast about in our final years, for with age comes more 'labour and sorrow' and we swiftly pass from this earthly scene (verse 10). Henry Francis Lyte (1793-1847) catches the thought of the psalmist in his lines: *Swift to its close ebbs out life's little day; Earth's joys grow dim, its glories pass away.*[38]

The Preacher makes the same point in his great sermon on the transience of human life with 'labour' (or 'toil') being one of his favourite terms (see Ecclesiastes 1:3; 2:10-11, 19-21; etc.). Though there are always exceptions (see Psalm 73), this is the reality of life in this world for the vast majority as a result of that initial rebellion in Eden and it is compounded in those situations where God in his wrath gives people over to their sinful desires (Romans 1:18-32). It clearly resonated with God's people living after the fall of Jerusalem in 587 BC.

Who acknowledges and really takes any notice of the strength of God's raging anger at human sin in such a way as to give God the reverential respect that is due to him? (verse 11). People in general, and too often we Christians, can live our busy lives from day to day without appreciating the fundamental connection between our mortality, human rebellion against God and God's wrath. Moses therefore prays for himself and his people that they would understand this connection.

'So teach us' or 'cause us to know' (verse 12) picks up the 'who knows?' of verse 11. This is how to 'gain a heart of wisdom'. 'Counting our days' in the sense of realising just how short life really is, will encourage us to stop ignoring God and seek instead to live to honour him. The Preacher, as he stresses the transience of life and the need to fear God, also encourages us to use up the time we have in a profitable way and to enjoy the blessings that God gives during our fleeting lives (Ecclesiastes 9:7-10). In Jesus' parable of the rich farmer, God calls him a fool for thinking that all he had amassed belonged to him to enjoy forever with no thought of God (Luke 12:13-21).

God's grace invoked (13-17)

The prayer at the close of the previous section prepares us for this closing appeal addressed to the 'LORD' (Yahweh/Jehovah), the God of the covenant. Unlike Bernard Shaw in *Back to Methuselah* who saw the brevity of life as the supreme mockery of human effort, Moses is no cynic or prophet of despair.

There are several points in this plea:

First, in the light of the truth concerning God's displeasure at sin, the prayer urges God to 'Return' (verse 13) in the sense of turning from wrath to begin to act kindly toward them. With it comes the familiar desperate cry, 'How long?' (see Psalm 6:3) and a plea for God to 'relent' in the sense of 'show pity' ('have compassion') concerning his servants, in words reminiscent of Moses' song (Deuteronomy 32:36). Moses had also pleaded with God in a similar way after the golden calf incident (Exodus 32:12).

Second, the prayer asks that they might be fully satisfied with God's 'steadfast love' ('mercy'; see Psalms 63:5; 65:4) 'in the morning' ('early';

see Psalms 5:3; 46:5), and reminding us of the previous reference to the morning (verses 5–6). Instead of the typical human flourishing in the morning but withering by nightfall, Moses prays for God's unfailing love that will go on flourishing after the long night of trouble. Instead of 'all our days' passing away under God's wrath (verse 9), he prays that the people may be able to shout for joy and be glad during them (verse 14). This is something the Preacher also encouraged (see Ecclesiastes 3:12, 22; 5:19; 11:8–10). Verse 15 restates the plea asking that the time of affliction (see verse 10) would be compensated by a similar period of gladness. Interestingly, the poetic forms for 'days' and 'years' in the original are only found elsewhere in Moses' song (Deuteronomy 32:7) and thus give further witness to the truth of the heading.

Finally, the prayer urges God to give evidence of his steadfast love in a 'deed' ('work') that can be witnessed by God's people for generations to come and that their own 'work' would not be futile (verses 16–17). In place of seeing 'evil' experiences (verse 15) Moses prays that they and their children will see the 'majesty' or 'splendour' ('glory') of God and his work (verse 16; see Psalm 29:4).

In the closing lines of the prayer there is another reference to Israel's God as sovereign 'Lord' (not 'LORD'/Yahweh/Jehovah as in the AV and Revised AV), and thus the title for God envelops the whole psalm (verses 17; see verse 1). It comes appropriately after describing God's people as his 'servants' (verse 16) and the 'work' in which they are engaged. It draws attention to the master-servant relationship between the Lord and his people. The 'beauty' or 'desirableness' of the Lord that David wished to see (Psalm 27:4) is similar to what Moses prays here. He asks that it might be upon himself and his people. Without God all human achievement is a waste of time and of no lasting worth, whereas if his people have that proper reverence for God and commit their lives and all their hard work to him, not only will God's own 'action' live on to be enjoyed by future generations but their 'work' will too. Moses in his sermon to the people in the plains of Moab shortly before their entrance into Canaan often speaks of God's blessing on all the work of their hands as they obey him and the resulting joy they would experience (Deuteronomy 2:7; 14:29; 16:15; etc.). These blessings are all expressions of God's loving commitment toward his people that alone can fully satisfy the lives of God's people (see verse 14).

The salvation that God has accomplished in Christ far exceeds God's action in rescuing Israel from Egypt and leading them through to the promised land. God's amazing 'action' in redeeming lost sinners through Christ's death on the cross displays his matchless splendour like nothing else, and we pray that it will be known by our children and grandchildren and all generations to come. As we pray as Christians that God would 'establish the work of our hands' we are urged by Paul at the end of his great chapter on the resurrection hope to remain 'steadfast, immovable, always abounding in the work of the Lord, knowing that your labour is not in vain in the Lord' (1 Corinthians 15:58).

Psalm 91

Security in the Almighty

John Stott once pointed out that this psalm has the unusual distinction of being 'the only passage of Scripture which (at least in the sacred record) is quoted by the devil!'[39] The devil, of course, misapplied it when he urged Jesus to throw himself from the pinnacle of the temple and trust God's promise to send angels to protect him from harm (verses 11–12; see Matthew 4:6; Luke 4:10–11). It is a warning to us not to take verses out of context or to use Scripture in a bid to put God to the test. The psalm does not encourage us to act recklessly and imagine God will save us.

This is a psalm of assurance particularly when the going is tough. Its New Testament equivalent, as many commentators have pointed out, is Paul's triumphant words in Romans 8:31–39.

The psalm is closely connected in thought and language to Psalms 90 and 92 and like Psalm 90 there are some links to the song of Moses (Deuteronomy 32). Like most of the psalms in Book 4, it has no heading although there is a Jewish tradition that David was the author.[40] There are difficulties in understanding who is speaking to whom as the psalm proceeds, but it is useful to recognise that the switch from 'I' to 'you' to 'he' is a common feature of Hebrew poetry and does not in all cases mean a change of person.

There are good grounds for believing that the psalm is addressed primarily to the Davidic king as the Lord's Anointed, especially in his representative role as head of his people (see Psalms 2 and 72). Some of the language does remind us of David's psalms. The fact that the devil chose to tempt Jesus concerning his sonship using this psalm is a further indication that its contents were considered to refer to the messianic ruler (Matthew 4:5-7; Luke 4:9-12).

The psalm falls into two main sections with the first emphasising God's protection of those who belong to him (verses 1-13) and the second section consisting of God's confirmation of what has been said (verses 14-16).

Divine protection (verses 1-13)

It is in this first section that we are not sure who is speaking and to whom the words apply.

God our security (verses 1-2)

The first two verses are the key to the rest of the psalm for they emphasise who God is, and the close relationship that exists between God and his people. Everything about God encourages trust and those who take shelter in God will find protection.

In verse 1 the first two terms for God take us back to the days of Abraham where we first hear of 'Most High' on the lips of Melchizedek (Genesis 14:18-20; see Psalm 7:17) and the 'Almighty', the name that encouraged Abraham and his family to believe that nothing was impossible with God. This second name is used frequently in Job but only twice in the Psalms (Genesis 17:1; 35:11; see Psalm 68:14). Then, in verse 2, comes the name that became precious to Israel at the time of the exodus—'LORD' (Yahweh/Jehovah; Exodus 6:3). It spoke of God's special relationship with Israel and his commitment to them. For an individual to call this supreme being, 'My God', showed how personal that relationship was.

Verse 1 introduces the direct speech of the king in verse 2, who speaks on behalf of himself and his people. This God who can be personally addressed is a place of safety for his people. One who 'dwells' and 'lodges' ('abide') in the 'shelter' ('secret place') and 'shadow' of God knows him as a 'refuge' (see Psalm 62:8) and 'fortress' (Psalm 18:2). The 'secret place' is a place to hide from danger (Psalm 31:20) and 'shadow' suggests being kept safe like a chick under the wing of a bird (see Psalms 17:8; 36:7). Boaz speaks of Ruth the Moabitess committing herself to Israel's God 'under whose wings you have come for refuge' (Ruth 2:12). All these terms that speak of safety and security encourage confidence in God so it is no surprise to find the king declaring, 'in him I will trust' (verse 2).

Protection outlined (verses 3–8)

These verses present the various circumstances of life where that trust proves effective. The psalmist encourages the king ('you' singular), and by extension those whom the king represents, that God ('he') will rescue him from unexpected threats, whether they are human traps or fatal infectious diseases ('pestilence', verse 3). God acts, as suggested by the word 'shadow' in verse 1, like a mother bird protecting her young from dangerous predators and the king can 'take refuge' (verse 4) in the God whom he has already declared to be his 'refuge' (verse 2).

God's 'truth' in the sense of fidelity to his covenant promises (see Psalm 25:5), provides protection like a soldier's body 'shield' (verse 4; the same word is sometimes translated 'buckler' as in Psalm 35:2), while the word translated 'buckler' is only found here and may mean some other kind of large protective armour.

The following two verses give assurance that God will protect at all times, from the enemy arrows during the day and from scary night attacks, as well as deadly plagues and disasters that can strike at any hour (verses 5–6). Troops of a thousand or ten thousand may fall all around from plague or enemy action and yet the king and his people would be spared (verse 7). This was true of Israel when the plagues hit Egypt and God made a difference between his people and the Egyptians (Exodus 11:7). Major-General Sir Henry Havelock (1795–1857), a godly evangelical in the British army, had some remarkable escapes in battle that he attributed to God's protection.

There were occasions in Israel's history when they just stood still and watched as the wicked received the recompense ('reward', verse 8) they deserved. One notable occasion was at the Red Sea and another was under Joshua's leadership when Jericho fell (Exodus 14:13–14; Joshua 6:2). God will punish 'the wicked' (verse 8; see Psalm 1:4–6) and the righteous will 'see' justice done (see Psalm 54:7).

Trust in God's protection (verses 9–13)

In these verses the same theme of trust and God's protection is revisited. The psalmist includes himself with the king in making the

'LORD' (Yahweh) 'my refuge' (see verse 2). With strong emphasis on the 'you', in contrast to 'the wicked' of the previous verse, the psalm shows that as a result of making Israel's covenant-keeping and 'Most High' God his 'habitation' (verse 9; see Psalm 90:1), the king is assured that no 'harm' ('evil') or 'plague' will befall him or come near his 'tent' (verse 10, 'dwelling'). Spurgeon tells of an occasion during his early years in London when an outbreak of cholera occurred in his neighbourhood. He himself was preserved as he ministered among the sick and dying and was much encouraged in his spirit on reading verses 9 and 10 on a notice in the window of a shoemaker's shop.

The promise of verse 10 is effective 'because' ('for', verse 11) of God's 'angels' whose tasks include guarding God's faithful people (see Psalm 34:7) and carrying them so that they do not strike their foot against a stone that might cause serious injury or even death. The word for angel can be translated 'messenger' and is used for human and heavenly beings who are sent with a message (Genesis 19:1, 15; 32:1, 3; Deuteronomy 2:26). The heavenly army of angels is in the service and praise of God (Genesis 28:12; Hebrews 12:22; Revelation 5:11). God's angels that ministered to Jesus in his weakness (Matthew 4:11; Luke 22:43) also come to the aid of God's people (Acts 5:19-20; 12:7-11; Hebrews 1:14). Many in our day deny the reality of angels as they do the bodily resurrection of Jesus but this is nothing new, for the Jewish Sadducees two thousand years ago declared that 'there is no resurrection—and no angel or spirit' (Acts 23:8). Who knows what help Christians have received from these angelic beings, guarding them from perils seen and unseen! Elisha's servant was made aware of this angelic world that provided protection for him and his master (2 Kings 6:17; see Psalm 34:7).

To stress the point of God's keeping power, the two obvious dangers to people of the Middle East in those times were from the 'lion' and deadly snakes like the 'cobra' (verse 13), the one representing open violent attack, the other a more insidious and unsuspected danger. The creatures are used frequently to symbolise the wicked (see Psalm 58:3-6). God did, of course, urge our first parents as God's image bearers to have dominion over all these creatures and in the future new creation of Messiah's reign the young lion and cobra are mentioned as examples of the peace that will exist between humans and animals: 'they shall not hurt nor destroy in all my holy mountain' (Isaiah 11:1-9). Until that day comes God's people are assured that they are immortal until their work on earth is done. The words of Daniel's three friends give clear voice to this belief in their reply to Nebuchadnezzar's challenge to any god able to deliver a person from the fiery furnace for not worshipping him (Daniel 3:17–18).

In a book entitled *Shadow of the Almighty*, Elizabeth Elliott wrote of her husband Jim and of how he was killed along with four other fellow missionaries, all in their twenties, as they tried to bring God's message of salvation in Christ to an unreached tribe in Ecuador. Other missionaries have died young through disease and ill-health. Did that mean they did not trust God enough or that the claims made in this psalm are not true? Not at all! God has work for his people to do and when that work is finished he removes them to a better place where there is no more trouble. As it turned out, the men who killed those missionaries were later converted and turned to Christ. Jesus himself went through hell on the cross in his early thirties. A life cut short by human sin but also a fulfilled life, having accomplished all that God had purposed for him to do. God did not save him from death, thank the Lord, but he vindicated him on the resurrection morning and gave him the 'highest place that heaven affords' which is his by right.

Jesus alludes to this verse 13 (and possibly Deuteronomy 8:15) in his response to his disciples' excitement at the evidences of the authority they had been given in seeing demons subject to them in Jesus' name (Luke 10:17–20). The work of the seventy disciples is part of a series of events that will include king Messiah's defeat of Satan (that old serpent of Genesis 3) and his demons at the cross and their final destruction when he returns in glory (John 12:31–32; Colossians 2:15; Romans 16:20; Revelation 12:10–12; 20:1–3, 10). Whatever authority God gives his people over every form of evil in our world, our focus is to be on the secure standing we have with God by his grace. Jesus directed his disciples to a greater joy than any authority over evil spirits we may be given, namely, that our names are written in heaven. Believers are assured that they are secure in God and that nothing can destroy them. As Paul triumphantly declares, 'I am persuaded that neither death nor life, nor angels nor principalities nor powers, nor things present nor things to come, nor height nor depth, nor any other created thing, shall be able to separate us from the love of God which is in Christ Jesus our Lord' (Romans 8:38–39).

Divine confirmation (verses 14-16)

Here the message of the psalm is made more forcefully through this direct word from God about the king and this gives great encouragement to the people whom he represents. Such direct words from God are often found in the psalms (see Psalms 81:6-16; 87:4).

There are eight very emphatic promises that God makes concerning the king:

1. 'I will deliver him' (verses 14) suggests being rescued *from* the danger he was in.

2. 'I will set him on high' indicates the positive situation that results from the rescue. He has been brought *to* a safe place.

3. 'I will answer him' (verse 15) means that God will act to grant the king's requests (see Psalms 65:5; 86:7).

4. 'I *will be* with him in trouble' shows that God does not always prevent trouble from coming to God's king and people. However, as the 'I' with no verb following it suggests (note the italics which are used in the older versions to indicate additions to the original text where that is necessary in an English translation), the promise is that God is already present when distress comes to protect and deliver. This is our 'Immanuel' ('God with us'; Isaiah 7:14; 8:8, 10).

5. 'I will deliver him' is in the original a stronger verb than the one in verse 14 and suggests being drawn away or pulled out of a threatening situation.

6. I will 'honour him' or 'I will glorify him' takes the thought of verse 14 further for it suggests victory, vindication and respect.

7. 'With long life I will satisfy him' (verse 16) means the enjoyment of a full and purposeful life that is not cut short through divine punishment for disobedience. Long life was promised to Israel if they were true to the covenant and it was seen as a sign of God's favour (Exodus 20:12; Deuteronomy 30:20; Proverbs 3:2). Enoch did not live in this world as long as his father or children but he lived a fulfilled and complete life walking with God. Eternal life is begun in this life and continues even though we may die physically as Jesus explained to Martha (John 11:25-26).

8. I will 'show him my salvation' contains the idea of experiencing, entering into the enjoyment of that salvation (see Psalm 50:23).

The 'because' at the beginning and end of verse 14 makes it clear that all these promises are made to the one whom God declares 'has set his love upon me' and 'has known my name' (verse 14) and who 'shall call upon me' (verse 15; see Psalms 80:18; 86:5, 7). The phrases express the close relationship between the Lord and his anointed, and that he is a devoted worshipper who looks not to false gods but to the living God alone. To 'set love on' suggests a love that clings, a yearning love and is used by Moses of God's love for Israel (Deuteronomy 7:7; 10:15). The same word is used when Shechem's father spoke of how passionate his son's love was for Dinah, Jacob's daughter (Genesis 34:8; see Deuteronomy 21:11). To have 'known' God's name is more than to have acknowledged God. It means to be a friend of God, having a personal relationship with the Lord Almighty as he has revealed himself.

This psalm, like so many, speaks first and foremost of Jesus the Messiah. He is the king who was given these assurances of God's help and the promises of deliverance, vindication and glory. Previous psalms have presented similar assurances from God to his king (see Psalm 21). Christ our representative head has fully met the conditions and known the promises fulfilled through his own ministry in this world. But all who love God and belong to Jesus Christ can take to heart the words of this psalm and know the life and salvation that he has obtained.

Psalm 92

Communal Worship on God's Special Day

Isaac Watts (1674-1748) has a hymn based on this psalm that cleverly incorporates in the second verse what we are told in the heading. The verse begins 'Sweet is the day of sacred rest' and ends 'O may my heart in tune be found, Like David's harp of solemn sound!'[41] This is the only 'Psalm' with the heading 'A Song for the Sabbath day'. It is further evidence that the Sabbath, for the Jews of the Old Testament period, was not only a day of rest but a day when the people gathered for corporate worship. The Sabbath was a unique 'holy convocation' when, in addition to the daily offering of one lamb morning and night, two more lambs were offered and twice the amount of fine flour was used in the accompanying grain offering (Leviticus 23:3; Numbers 28:4-5, 9-10). Jesus, the Lord of the Sabbath, encouraged his disciples to meet together for worship on the Lord's Day, our Sunday, by appearing to his disciples as a group, morning and evening, and by sending the Holy Spirit at Pentecost as they met together on the first day of the week (John 20-21; Acts 2:1-4).[42] Interestingly, as so many calendars and diaries indicate, it is common nowadays to assume that Sunday is the seventh day rather than the first day of the week. Every day we are to worship and serve the Lord but we are urged to meet together to encourage one another and corporately to worship him in praise, thanksgiving, prayer and by the obedient response of our hearts to the preaching and teaching of God's word.

Every Lord's Day is a pointer to the final Day of the Lord when all God's people will not only be at rest from their present earthly labours but will be together worshipping God the Father and Jesus the Lamb in the eternal city. Ancient Jewish tradition considers this psalm to be 'a song for the time that is to come, for the day that shall be all Sabbath and rest in the life everlasting.'[43]

The everlasting LORD (Yahweh/Jehovah), the Most High, who is the 'habitation' of his people (Psalm 90:1) and of the king (Psalm 91:9) is in this psalm praised by king (verses 1-11) and people (verses 12-15) for his great works toward the righteous and the wicked. It brings to a fitting conclusion this introductory group of psalms with which Book 4 begins. The psalm is nicely balanced with a concern 'to declare' God's praises (see verses 2 and 15) surrounding the reasons for such celebration. A feature of Ancient Near Eastern poetry is detected in the psalm with what is called 'staircase' or 'climatic' parallelism where a first line, which is left as an incomplete sentence, is repeated and completed in the second line (see verse 9a: 'For behold, your enemies, O LORD'; 9b: 'For behold, your enemies shall perish').

Joyful praise (verses 1-3)

We are encouraged 'to give thanks' and 'sing praises' to the covenant-keeping 'LORD', who is the 'Most High' God (see Psalm 91:1, 9). It is 'good' not only in the sense that this is fitting (Psalm 54:6) but that it is a pleasant and enjoyable thing for God's people to do (see Psalm 147:1).

How are we to praise God? We are called to praise him by declaring what God has revealed about himself ('your name', verse 1; see Psalm 20:1). His loving commitment toward his people ('loving-kindness') and his 'faithfulness' are to figure prominently in our thoughts (verse 2; see Exodus 34:6). These two characteristics of God have been emphasised in Psalm 89. Our communal worship like our private devotions does not consist of mindless mutterings but intelligent speech that expresses who God is as well as what he has done.

This declaring is not only done in preaching but in 'song' (see the heading). We are encouraged to sing, to make music. The word for 'sing praises' is associated with the term 'psalm' which suggests singing that is accompanied by stringed instruments. Usually the instruments are mentioned in the heading but here they are included within the psalm. The 'ten-stringed instrument' may be the lute, to which is added the 'harp' (rather than 'lute') and 'lyre' (rather than 'harp'; verse 3; see Psalm 33:2 and Psalm 150). The phrase 'with harmonious sound' (verse 3), is a paraphrase of a term usually translated 'meditation' (see Psalms 9:16; 19:14). It is from the same word family as the verb 'to meditate' (see Psalm 1:2). In this context it suggests the musical sound of the lyre.

When are we to praise God? As the sacrifices were offered morning and evening at the sanctuary (Exodus 29:38–41) with offerings doubled on the Sabbath (Numbers 28:9–10) so God's people are to give praise every day and come together to offer praise on the Lord's Day, remembering that the whole day belongs to him, both morning and evening.

Reasons for praise (verses 4–11)
Attention has been drawn to those characteristics of God that are especially precious to God's people and it is the expression of his steadfast love and faithfulness that the psalm now highlights. God's 'action' ('work') has been mentioned in Psalm 90:16 and the phrase 'work of our hands' (Psalm 90:17) is now used of God's work ('the works of your hands' verse 4).

An example to follow (verses 4–5)
The psalmist is probably the king who was in overall charge of the sanctuary music (see 1 Chronicles 15:16; 25:2, 6). He encourages himself in praising God and by doing so leads the people in worship that is not only God honouring but enjoyable to all. As Isaac Watts pointed out in his hymn, *Come, we that love the Lord*, 'Religion never was designed to make our pleasures less'. Coming together to worship should bring gladness to our hearts and expressions of resounding joy ('triumph'; see Psalm 33:1) as we confess God's great work of redemption in Christ, foreshadowed for Israel through the redemption from Egypt.

God's works relating to redemption are 'great' (see Psalm 77:11–12). William Gadsby (1773–1844) praises God for his 'boundless works and ways' but speaks of redemption as his 'highest work'.[44] The greatness of God's works should lead us, as Matthew Henry observes, to consider the depths of his 'thoughts'. God's thoughts or plans that produce his great works are 'very deep' for they lie deep within the being of God. It is analogous to the comment of the psalmist about human thoughts

(Psalm 64:6). God's thoughts and plans are so different to what we would expect (Isaiah 40:13; 55:8–9) and led Paul to burst out in praise at the revelation of God's ways and purposes revealed in the Messiah: 'O the depth of the riches both of the wisdom and knowledge of God! How unsearchable are his judgments and his ways past finding out!' (Romans 11:33–36).

A position to avoid (verses 6–7)

It is clear from what is said in these verses that God's works must also include his providential dealings with the wicked. The 'senseless' person (see Psalms 49:10; 73:22) is not one who has a low I.Q. but someone who has no spiritual understanding. It is coupled with the word 'fool', one who is wise in his own eyes and lives without reference to God (see Psalm 14:1). The terms depict the unspiritual person who has no appreciation of God's wonderful works and ways. David speaks of them as having no regard for 'the works of the Lord, nor the operation of his hands' (Psalm 28:5). Paul describes this same person as the 'natural man' who 'does not receive the things of the Spirit of God, for they are foolishness to him; nor can he know them, because they are spiritually discerned' (1 Corinthians 2:14). Such people, now termed 'the wicked' and 'workers of iniquity' (verse 7; see Psalms 1:1; 10:4–6; 28:3) do not understand what is happening to them in life. They prosper like grass that flourishes and blossoms after the rains only to find that in the end it is destined to 'be destroyed for ever' (see Psalm 37:35–36).

Triumph over the enemies (verses 8–11)

Verse 8 is the central point of the psalm. It is a great affirmation of God's everlasting sovereignty and arises within the context of what happens to all God's enemies (see verses 6–7 and 9). Here is more reason to praise God. The word translated 'behold' and repeated, emphasises that it really is God's enemies who will 'perish' (verse 9) and all the supporting 'evil doers' will be dispersed like lion cubs when the old lion has perished (see Psalms 1:6; 2:12; Job 4:11). Alec Motyer makes the point that in calling the wicked of verse 7 God's enemies (verse 9) the 'adage that the Lord hates the sin but loves the sinner needs correction; those who set themselves against the Lord will find that he is personally set against them'.

The LORD who is 'on high' (verse 8) and who has made the king glad (verse 4) is the God who has also 'exalted' the king. He has been made strong and vigorous like a 'wild ox' whose 'horn' is held high ready to take on any attacker (verse 10; see Psalms 18:2; 75:4–5). The image of being 'anointed' (literally 'mixed') 'with fresh oil' like the grain offering (Leviticus 2:4; 7:12) conveys the idea of celebration and joy (see Psalms 23:5; 45:7; Isaiah 61:3). This glad celebration is because he has seen and heard that his enemies have been defeated. They are described as those who lie in wait to attack him (verse 11, 'my enemies'; literally 'my watchers'; see Psalms 27:11; 54:5) and who 'rise up against' him (Psalms 3:1; 86:14).

In the context of these verses it is clear that the king's enemies are the Lord's enemies and it is by God's help victory has been obtained. His eyes have not 'seen' in order to gloat but in relief and in satisfaction that justice has been done (see Psalm 91:8). This whole section recalls the close relationship between God and his king depicted in Psalm 2. Jesus the Messiah has been highly exalted and he is the one who has been appointed to judge and all his enemies will be brought low and punished.

God's blessing on king and people (verses 12–15)

In this final section attention is drawn first to the psalmist ('the righteous' one), to this kingly figure who in the previous section has triumphed over all his enemies. He is destined to be strong and majestic like the two kingly trees of the Near East, the palm and the cedar. The edible date palm can rise to a hundred feet, while the cedar of Lebanon was famous for its stately splendour. This righteous one does not 'flourish' like grass (see verse 7) but like trees that last and grow to great heights.

There is a shift now to the people who belong to the psalmist. They are one with him and they too 'flourish' like the smaller trees that were planted and grew in the temple courts. It is appropriate that having referred obliquely to the king there is also a reference to the temple as God's 'house' (see Psalm 52:8). Both God's leader and people thrive in the presence and under the protection of God (see Psalms 91:1; 27:4–5). They will 'bear fruit' even 'in old age' (verse 14; see Psalm 91:16) like the date palm and be 'fresh and flourishing' (literally 'fat and fresh') like trees bursting with sap and like 'fresh' olive oil (see verse 10). The word-picture is strongly reminiscent of the blessed man who is like a tree that brings forth fruit, whose leaf does not wither and who prospers in everything that he does (Psalm 1:3).

Verse 15 echoes words from Moses' song (Deuteronomy 32:4). Appropriately for a psalm assigned for use on the holy seventh day, God's covenant name 'LORD' (Yahweh/Jehovah) is used for the seventh and final time. The verb 'to declare' takes up the opening stimulus to proclaim the goodness of God's character (see verse 2). In the light of all that has been said within the psalm, leader and people can come together on God's special day to declare the greatness of his works. He is acclaimed as the psalmist's 'rock' (see Psalm 28:1). From his own experience the psalmist can testify that God is utterly dependable, one who is 'upright' (Psalm 25:8) and with no trace of 'injustice' or 'wickedness' ('unrighteousness'; see Psalms 58:2; 89:22). The wording 'no unrighteousness in him' reminds us of John's words that 'God is light and in him is no darkness at all' (1 John 1:5).

The 'song' is reminiscent of other poems like Psalms 37 and 73 in its focus on the contrast between the righteous and the wicked. But it also reminds us that we are more than conquerors in and through Christ the head of the Church who died and rose victorious and reigns on high with God the Father. As we gather together as Christians on the day specially set apart for communal worship, we are encouraged to honour God by proclaiming his worth in Scripture reading, prayer, song and preaching, and to delight ourselves in the Lord (Isaiah 58:13–14). Our Sabbath worship should be, as one writer puts it, 'the focus and culmination of a life that is daily and practically devoted to honouring God ... and to sharing in God's own creative delight.'[45]

Psalm 93

The LORD Reigns!

When the Old Testament people of God lost their independence and their king of David's family line after the Babylonian invasion of Jerusalem in 587 BC many were bewildered and disturbed. The psalms of Book 3 are used to express some of those heart-felt concerns for the future. It is no coincidence that this collection from Psalms 93 to 100 relating to God's rule is found here after the closing psalms of the previous Book (see Psalms 88 and 89).

These declarations of faith in God's universal kingship are not groundless chants to keep the faithful happy. They are based on good solid evidence. But the basic issue that Israel was slow to appreciate and which people today find hard to accept has to do with human sin and God's reaction to it. Israel and her earthly monarch repeated the folly of the original couple who were placed over the created order to rule on God's behalf. The Lord had been Israel's king from the time of the exodus (Exodus 15:18; Deuteronomy 33:5) but when, despite all his gracious warnings, they and their king abandoned him for other deities, God in his wrath gave them over to their enemies. This looked as if God's rule among his people was at an end. Far from it! It was serving his overall purposes for the salvation of humanity and the bringing in of that new creation where God will be appreciated as king the world over. A new day began to dawn when Jesus came preaching the good news concerning God's rule and calling people to repent and believe the gospel (Mark 1:14-15). Through Jesus the anointed king and his victory over sin and Satan, death and hell, the triune God Yahweh/Jehovah will be all in all (1 Corinthians 15:24-28).

Psalm 93 highlights his kingship over all the earth with the strong implication that it bears no comparison with the supposed claims of so-called gods like the Canaanite Baal, the Babylonian Marduk or any modern equivalent. The psalm deals with resistance to God's rule and shows that he had no difficulty in overcoming all opposition.

God's rule declared (verses 1-2)

'The LORD reigns' reminds us of the declaration that 'God reigns' in Psalm 47:8 where the theme is linked to the victory of Israel over the Canaanites. It is a proclamation like 'Absalom reigns in Hebron!' or 'Jehu is king!' (2 Samuel 15:10; 2 Kings 9:13). The Hebrew word order in our psalm does perhaps emphasise that it is Israel's God, the 'LORD' (Yahweh/Jehovah), known by the name precious to them from the time of the exodus, and no other god, who rules over all.

From earliest times kings have often been distinguished by their magnificent robes (1 Kings 22:10; Esther 6:8). They enhance the authority of the ruler. God's royal apparel is the 'majesty' of his being but the repetition of 'clothed' followed by 'girded himself' suggests in addition that he has equipped himself for battle. Equipped with 'strength' is the way David describes how he has been prepared for battle (2 Samuel 22:40; see 1 Samuel 17:38). Some impressive battle armour used by the kings of England is displayed in the Tower of London and this again, like the magnificent robes, is suggestive of a king's authority.

The evidence of the Lord's kingly authority is that the world is firmly 'established', as was Solomon's kingdom (1 Kings 2:12). Kingdoms might 'be moved' or 'totter' (see Psalms 46:6; 96:10) but not the inhabited 'world' of humans who live on the earth (see Psalm 24:1-2).

God is then directly addressed in verse 2 and it is made clear that this inhabited world of human beings is not to think, because it is firmly established, that it is in some way independent of God and has an eternal existence. As we humans discover more about our world, we are apt to think too highly of ourselves and imagine that we are the masters of our own destinies. Though this inhabited earth is firmly 'established' it is due to the one who is God 'from everlasting' (verse 2; see Psalm 90:2) and whose rule has been 'established' over all since the very beginning of creation. God's 'throne' is the symbol of his kingship as a whole. John has a picture of the creator God and of the heavenly creatures who 'give glory and honour and thanks to him who sits on the throne, who lives for ever and ever' (Revelation 4:8-11).

It is interesting that reference is made to the God who is everlasting and to his throne established 'from of old' (verse 2). Chronicles, written after the return from exile but with no Davidic king in sight, links David's throne to God's throne in a way that is not so noticeable in Kings. This ancient psalm may have been considered by the final compiler of the Book of Psalms an appropriate encouragement to a disappointed people with no earthly monarch to realise that all is not lost. God is still on the throne even though there is no Davidic monarch. The people are encouraged to remember that God has not abdicated or been removed and there are clear evidences from creation itself that this is so.

God's rule demonstrated (verses 3-4)

The psalmist, still addressing God by his covenant name, 'LORD', praises his authority over sea and water. What is said in these two verses reiterates and confirms the message of the first two verses. Despite occasional devastating floods and tsunamis, there is a general stability about the ordered world as God promised Noah in the aftermath of the great universal Flood (Genesis 8:1-22).

Like Psalm 92:9 we have in verse 3 another example of 'staircase parallelism', a feature of Ancient Near Eastern poetry where the second line repeats and completes the incomplete first line: a) 'The floods have lifted up, O Lord' b) 'The floods have lifted up their voices'. In addition, by repeating the lines about the 'floods' (literally 'rivers') lifting up 'their waves' (literally 'their din') we have a vivid picture of waves crashing relentlessly onto the beach at river estuaries. To people afraid of the sea it can be a threatening sight as the surges seem to want to overwhelm the land. The LORD, however, is not threatened by the pounding of the waves. He is 'on high' (see Psalm 92:8), more 'majestic' ('mightier'; the same word is translated 'excellent' in Psalm 8:1) than 'the noise of many waters' and the 'majestic' ('mighty') breakers of the sea (verse 4).

The Ancient Near Eastern myths indicate how the pagan gods had great difficulty controlling the original waters. This psalm, like

Psalm 29, indicates that the true God who revealed himself to Moses and his people, is the one who is in absolute control and he is a sure refuge to all who put their trust in him. In the Psalms, 'waters' can be used for any experience that tends to overwhelm God's people (see Psalms 18:16–19; 46:3) and it is comforting to know that the one who is 'mightier' or 'more magnificent' than the majestic sea breakers has promised that even 'when you pass through the waters, I will be with you; and through the rivers, they shall not overflow you' (Isaiah 43:2).

God's rule distinctive (verse 5)

This final verse is not a sudden change of subject. God's 'testimonies' are his solemn 'decrees' which include commands and promises. At the time of creation, God issued commands concerning the waters: 'Then God said, "Let the waters ... be gathered together ... and it was so"' (Genesis 1:6–10). Then after the Flood, in the covenant he made with Noah and his descendants, God issued a promise that he would never again destroy the world through the waters of a flood (Genesis 9:8–17). These 'testimonies' like the ones given to Moses and Israel in the covenant he made with them (see Psalms 25:10; 78:56), are very reliable, they 'are very sure'. They are 'the true sayings of God' (Revelation 19:9; 21:5; 22:6). As the feet of those who bring good tidings are 'beautiful' or 'befitting' (see Isaiah 52:7), so God's 'holiness' 'befits' ('adorns' or 'beautifies') his heavenly 'house', the palace in which is the 'throne' of the one proclaimed as king (verse 2). 'Holiness' is what makes God the God he is. It refers to the absolute difference that exists between God and everything else in the entire universe. That otherness of God includes ethical purity and truthfulness. His 'testimonies' are therefore expressive of his unique being.

The stability praised in this psalm enables scientists to function in their laboratories, astronomers to predict when the next total eclipse of the sun will take place, oceanographers to calculate the times of the tide and farmers to sow their seed in springtime and expect a harvest in the autumn. This same sovereign Lord of the universe is the God and Father of all who belong to Jesus, God's Son. We can be assured of his care and the decree concerning the eternal security of all his chosen ones.

When the south-west gale-force winds blew in from the sea, Martyn Lloyd-Jones' wife, Bethan, was often terrified, especially on the nights when her husband was away preaching. They lived in their South

Wales home only a short distance from the coastline and she feared the tide would engulf her house. One night, when an exceptionally severe gale was blowing, in her helpless despair she sank to her knees by her bedside and prayed that the Lord would hear her prayer and give her peace. He did! And she confessed that she never had any more fear of gales and tides.

Psalm 94

The Judge of All

If God really does rule over all, why do bad people seem to triumph? There are many examples where crime seems to pay and the wicked prosper. These are some of the thoughts that pass through our minds after reading Psalm 93. This psalm does not ignore or deny what we presently experience and the things we observe that go on in the world. At the same time the psalmist affirms God's sovereignty and that in the here and now, despite being unjustly treated, God's people can know his help and be assured that there is a day of reckoning when justice will be seen to be done. Unlike Psalm 93 and the psalms that follow, it does not actually speak of God as king, nevertheless, kingship in Israel involved judging (2 Samuel 15:2-6; Psalm 72:1-2) and it is that aspect of God's rule that is brought to our attention in this psalm.

There are no indications when the psalm was composed but it is placed at this point in Book 4 with the Babylonion exile (587 BC) and its aftermath in mind when Israel was oppressed by foreign nations. Jewish tradition relates how the Levites were singing the final verse when Solomon's temple was destroyed and then again when Herod's temple was razed to the ground by the Romans in AD 70. The psalm, while bearing some relationship to earlier laments, expresses strong trust in God right from the start. Paul quotes from the psalm (verse 11) in support of his statement that the wisdom of this world is foolishness with God (1 Corinthians 3:19–20).

Appeal for action (verses 1–2)

The psalm begins by appealing to the covenant 'LORD God' against the cruel oppressors of his people. We notice again a feature of ancient poetry, 'staircase parallelism', where the second line of the verse repeats the first line and completes the thought (see verse 3 and Psalms 92:9 and 93:3). It has the effect here of drawing special attention to the final words of the sentence—'shine forth!' (verse 1; see Psalm 80:1). It is the stunning, frightening presence of God's kingly majesty that the psalmist calls for, such as was displayed to Israel at Mount Sinai (Deuteronomy 33:2). We have a similar picture given to us of Jesus being 'revealed from heaven with his mighty angels in flaming fire taking vengeance' (2 Thessalonians 1:7–10). The idea of God 'shining' as he comes to judge has appeared earlier in Psalm 50:2. Moses had sung of God's coming to judge and to avenge the blood of his servants (Deuteronomy 32:36–43) and that is in the psalmist's mind here. Vengeance is something that rightly belongs to God (Deuteronomy 32:35). It is not for God's people to take the law into their own hands and repay evil for evil. We are to leave it to God or to God-appointed human authorities, to punish the guilty (Romans 12:19; 13:1–4). Where earthly judges fail, God is the supreme judge and all are accountable to the 'Judge of the earth' (verse 2). It reminds us of Abraham's prayer concerning Sodom, 'Shall not the Judge of all the earth do right?' (Genesis 18:25).

God's vengeance is not spiteful vindictiveness like those wanting to get their own back on someone who has hurt their pride (Ezekiel 25:15–17). Vengeance has to do with the establishment of justice, an important quality in what is expected of one who rules. God's vengeance is not arbitrary but true to God's righteous character. It brings deliverance and vindication for the oppressed and punishment for the oppressors (Isaiah 35:4). God is urged to 'Rise up' or more literally 'Lift yourself up' to assert his position as judge over those who have 'lifted themselves up' ('the proud' verse 2; Isaiah 2:12) against God and to 'reward' them according to what they deserve ('render punishment'; see Psalm 28:4).

Grounds for action (verses 3–7)

The cry 'how long?' (verse 3; see Psalms 6:3; 82:2) is an urgent appeal that 'the wicked' (see Psalm 1:1), who have triumphed long enough, would 'triumph' no longer. Again, we notice the 'stair-case parallelism' (see verse 1).

There follows a description of the wicked people. They are 'workers of iniquity' who 'utter' ('pour out' like a fountain) arrogant words (verse 4). What they say is left till the end of the section (verse 7). Their boast is that Israel's God, 'the LORD' ('Yah' in the original; see Psalm 68:4), 'the God of Jacob' (Psalm 20:1) is not concerned. They are like fools who believe that because no action has been taken against them thus far, they can do what they like with impunity (see Psalms 10:11; 14:1). It is a common belief among many to this day who would not call themselves atheists but who reckon that God has no real interest in what goes on in our world and takes no decisive action against evildoers.

These wicked people believe they can get away with crushing and afflicting God's covenant people ('your people … your heritage', verse 5; see Psalm 28:9). As I write Christians are being attacked and their houses and church buildings burnt in Pakistan and Nigeria by Muslim extremists. The most vulnerable in society, the ones the Law of Moses mentions as needing compassion (Exodus 22:21–22; Deuteronomy 10:18), the widow, the 'stranger' (the resident alien or migrant worker) and the fatherless, these are the ones who are at the sharp end of the injustice and violence (verse 6).

A word to fools (verses 8–11)

The words of this section addressed to the oppressors provide encouragement to God's people in their distress. They are described as 'senseless', they are behaving like animals among the people (see Psalms 49:10; 92:6 where the same word for 'fool' is also found). These arrogant thugs, either from within Israel or more probably foreign tyrants, who suggest that Israel's God does not bother to look or take notice of their wicked actions are warned to 'understand' or better 'consider, take note'. The psalmist takes up their own word in verse 7 and throws it back at them (verse 8). They need to learn the first principle of wisdom, which is the fear of the LORD (Proverbs 1:7).

The psalmist uses some logic to show the stupidity of the wicked in their own assessment of the situation. It is taken for granted that God is the creator who, like a gardener, has 'planted the ear' and like a potter has 'formed the eye'. They should have appreciated that the one responsible for sight and hearing can himself 'see' and 'hear' what they are doing. Furthermore, the God who disciplines or 'instructs' the nations, teaching human beings 'knowledge' (see Psalm 2:10) about himself and moral values (see Romans 1:19–20, 32), does 'rebuke' or 'correct'. Even before the final day of judgment dawns the wrath of God is already revealed against all human ungodliness and unrighteousness as God gives people over to their sinful desires (Romans 1:18, 24, 26, 28).

The Lord (Yahweh/Jehovah) is not only intimately aware of ('knows'; see Psalm 1:6) the activity of the oppressors of God's people but also of their evil thoughts (see Genesis 6:5). A final devastating point is made that unlike the thoughts and plans of God which are very deep (Psalm 92:5), the schemes of human beings ('man') are a mere breath with no substance in them (verse 11; see Psalm 39:5, 11; Ecclesiastes 1:2, 14). Paul uses this text to support his argument that the wisdom of this age is foolishness in God's sight, in order to convince the Corinthian believers that they too are fools if, as Gordon Fee comments, 'they do not take seriously this divine view of things' (1 Corinthians 3:20).[46]

An encouragement to the wise (verses 12–15)

From general divine discipline or instruction that is given to people and nations (verse 10) and by way of encouragement for the oppressed, the psalmist turns to the instruction that the 'Lord' ('Yah' in the original; see verse 7) gives to his people from his 'law' (verse 12; see Psalms 1:2; 19:7; 119:1). How 'blessed', 'how fortunate' (Psalm 1:1) is the person ('man' as in Psalm 88:4) who has this special revelation from God that is able to give that inner quietness of spirit even when the wicked are still attacking and before they receive their just retribution—'until the pit is dug' (see Psalms 35:7; 49:9; 55:23). Paul speaks of God's written word having been given for 'our learning, that we through the patience and comfort of the Scriptures might have hope' (Romans 15:4).

However hard the godly might find life in this world, the tyrants will not have the last word. The covenant-keeping God of Israel is the eternal king and universal judge who will put the world to rights. Even though God's people are 'crushed' and 'afflicted' (see verse 5) he will not be disloyal to his people by abandoning them (verse 14; see 1 Samuel 12:22). The same promises hold true for Christians (Hebrews 13:5–6). In the end justice ('judgment', verse 15) will be seen to be done as God's righteous standards are upheld ('righteousness') and all the 'upright in heart' (see Psalm 7:10) will be able to follow in its wake. Peter looks for this in the new creation in which the earth will be the home of righteousness (2 Peter 3:13).

Comfort that dispels anxiety (verses 16–19)

The section opens in verse 16 with rhetorical questions that are not expressions of despair but of confidence as the verses that follow indicate. It is Israel's covenant God, the LORD, who arises (see Psalm 3:7) to take action against the oppressors. The thought may be of someone to 'stand up' in court on behalf of the oppressed. He is the psalmist's 'help' (see Psalm 63:7) otherwise he would be lying silent in the grave (verse 17; see Psalms 6:5; 115:17). The LORD's constant love ('mercy') has kept him from falling when his foot stumbled (see Psalms 73:2; 91:12). Like Paul who could speak of conflicts outside and fears within (2 Corinthians 7:5), the psalmist has not only been afflicted with outward troubles but within he has known many anxious thoughts (see Psalm 139:23). He is able to confess, that despite everything, the Lord's comfort has brought him cheer ('delight my soul'; see Psalm 90:14).

Confident about the future (verses 20–23)

Again, the section opens with a rhetorical question (verse 20; see verse 16). Here it is made clear that the oppression is institutional. The seat of power is corrupt—it is literally 'a throne of destruction' because the life of the innocent and vulnerable are destroyed (verse 21; see verses 5–6).[47] Those who govern and make laws cause 'trouble' ('devise evil'), hence the need for righteous rule to be restored (see verse 15). There is no way in which the legal system of the oppressors is in partnership with God.

As the evil workers of verse 16 provide the background to the confident witness of verses 17 to 19, so verses 22 and 23 arise out of the trouble depicted in verses 20 and 21. The covenant God of Israel, the LORD, is the psalmist's 'defence' or 'high place' (see Psalm 59:1). He is the 'rock' (Psalm 28:1) where he can take 'refuge' (Psalm 14:6) from the enemies arrayed against him.

The final verse reaffirms the truth stressed at the beginning of the psalm with similar repetition to indicate the certainty of the divine action in destroying the enemies of God's people. Unlike the wicked who deal unjustly with the innocent, God's justice is fair and their punishment will fit their crimes. Sometimes God gives indications of this even in this life. A notable example was the way that scheming Haman was hanged on the gallows he had intended for the innocent Mordecai (Esther 7:10). There is a general principle God has built into the world that what people sow they will reap (see Galatians 6:7).

The psalmist is speaking for all God's oppressed people who find a safe haven in their God (see Psalm 18:2) and look with confidence to the divine punishment that their enemies justly deserve, as the 'our' in the final line of the psalm would suggest. Jesus encouraged his persecuted followers to pray persistently and not lose heart in the parable of the unjust judge. He concluded 'And shall God not avenge his own elect who cry out day and night to him, though he bears long with them? I tell you that he will avenge them speedily' (Luke 18:7–8; see also Revelation 6:9–11; 19:2–3).

Psalm 95

Worship and Warning

There has been renewed discussion and even division in recent decades over the form and content of what is appropriate when Christians gather together for worship. This psalm focuses our attention on the God we are called to adore (verses 1-7a) and that we are called to obey his word (verses 7b-11). Worship is, as Don Carson has put it, 'adoration and action'.[48] The progression from praise to hearing God's word is similar to Psalm 81.

The psalm is attributed to David by the writer to the Hebrews (see Hebrews 4:7),[49] but as with most of the psalms in this part of the collection there is no heading in the Hebrew text. It is placed in its present position for a number of good reasons. It fits with the immediate context of psalms relating to God's kingship by calling attention to God as king. The mention of the wilderness period also connects it to other psalms in Book 4 that refer back to Moses commencing with Psalm 90. More importantly, in view of the historical crisis arising out of the destruction of Jerusalem with the loss of temple and king, to which many of the psalms in Book 3 draw attention, this psalm, like others in Book 4, has an important place in encouraging the people of God in their wilderness-like situation. For the same reason the writer to the Hebrews uses this psalm to stress that Christians too are in a wilderness situation (Hebrews 3:7-4:13). We are pilgrims heading for that better country. Though we already belong to the heavenly city we are still in this old world. We are in a 'now' and a 'not yet' position as believers in Christ. Hebrews therefore urges Christians, through encouragements and warnings, to persevere to the end.

Call to adore with joy and awe (verses 1–7a)

From early centuries as Christians have gathered together on the Lord's Day this psalm has been used as a call to worship. The call to praise is in two parts: verses 1–5 ('O come ...!') and 6–7a ('O come ...').

Invitation to praise (verses 1–2)

The word 'come' (verse 1) means something like 'come on!' It is used in many different contexts to encourage a mutual speedy response as, for instance in Judah's call to sell their brother Joseph or the king of Judah's call to the king of Israel for them to face one another in battle (Genesis 37:27; 2 Chronicles 25:17). Here the psalmist calls his fellow worshippers ('let us') in Israel to join in giving a resounding cry of joy ('sing', verse 1), not necessarily in song (see Psalm 35:27), to their covenant-keeping 'LORD' (Yahweh/Jehovah). He is also described as 'the Rock of our salvation' (verse 1), a reminder that our ultimate safety resides in God and therefore he is the firm foundation of all our hopes (see Psalms 92:15; 94:22). The worshippers are also urged to 'raise a triumphant shout' ('shout joyfully'; see Psalm 47:1) like the applause of the people when the ark of the covenant came into the camp or when Saul was proclaimed king (1 Samuel 4:5; 10:24).

When the call to 'come' (verse 2) is renewed the verb means 'to meet'. It can be used in a hostile confrontational sense (see Psalms 17:13; 18:5, 18) but here it has the sense of meeting in a friendly way (see Isaiah 21:14; Psalms 21:3; 59:10). Through the appointed sacrifices the Old Testament people of God could come face to face with God ('his presence' or 'his face'). Now that Christ has offered the perfect, once for all sacrifice, the divine wrath that hung over us on account of our sins has been removed and we can through Jesus approach with boldness the 'face' of God (Ephesians 2:13, 18; Hebrews 10:11–12, 19–22). We are to do so with a thankful spirit and raise a 'triumphant shout' ('shout joyfully') with 'psalms', which suggests singing enthusiastically and jubilantly yet melodiously. Paul's exhortation to sing and make melody in our hearts to the Lord (Ephesians 5:19) does not mean he believed we should sing silently as opposed to singing with the voice. In this instance, the heart signifies the whole person and it is our duty as believers to honour God with our bodies by outwardly expressing in lip and voice the praise that wells up from our innermost beings.

Reasons for praise (verses 3–5)

Such communal worship is not to be mindless and uninformed like so much pagan worship. The word 'For' (verse 3) introduces the reasons why God is to be praised. Giving God the titles 'Lord' and 'Rock' (verse 1) already encourage the people to praise God for his covenant faithfulness and powerful deliverances. We are now informed that Israel's God is a 'great God' (see Psalm 86:10) and therefore greatly to be praised (see Psalms 48:1; 96:4). He is also 'the great King'. He is supreme over 'all gods' including false gods, angelic beings and other heavenly powers (see Psalms 29:1; 82:1; 89:6). The Assyrians boasted that their king was the great one (2 Kings 18:19, 28) and at the time when Sennacherib raided the land in Hezekiah's time, it did not look as if the Lord was greater than the Assyrian king. But appearances can deceive, as Sennacherib found out! When we confess God's greatness in our communal worship we are not whistling in the dark but expressing what God has revealed of himself both by word and action in our world. The Scriptures contain evidences of his greatness but they are themselves revelation of his uniqueness. But confessing God's greatness is still a confession of faith for we do not yet see all things in subjection to him.

Not only is God greater and higher than any potentate or supernatural being he is also the great creator and ruler of the world. The unexplored depths of the earth as well as the highest mountain summits belong to him for he made and fashioned all things including the sea and the dry land (Genesis 1:9-10; Psalms 24:1; 89:11). Among Israel's pagan neighbours, there was one god for the deep places, another for the heights and so on, but the true God made and owns the whole lot! As I write, marine researchers steering a remote-controlled submarine below the sea's surface between the Cayman Islands and Jamaica were excited to find newly discovered life forms around the world's deepest known hydrothermal vents where incredibly hot fluid gushes from volcanic chimneys. The pictures were amazing and a reminder of other hidden wonders yet to be explored but which God knows all about and of which he is in charge.

Invitation to praise (verse 6)

A different word for 'come' is used here and instead of an exclamation as in verse 1, this verb is an invitation to enter into God's presence. Complementing the call to exuberant worship is the summons to bow in humble submission before Yahweh ('LORD'). As we do so we are to remember that the God who made the sea (verse 5) is the one who has made us too—'our Maker' (verse 6).

The verbs to 'bow down' and 'kneel' are self explanatory but 'worship' means to 'prostrate oneself' (verse 6). They are all verbs to denote the respect and homage that are due to God. If our voices and faces are raised to sing joyful praises there is another aspect of worship where our backs and knees are bent to express submissive devotion. This side to worship is often missing among Christians, yet it is the example that meets us time and again as we view worship in heaven. The heavenly beings 'fall down' and worship God the Father and the Lamb (Revelation 5:8, 14; 19:4). When John was tempted on two occasions to fall down and worship the angel who was guiding him, he was told in no uncertain terms not to do so but to 'worship God' (Revelation 19:10; 22:8-9). Idolatrous worship before man-made images should in no way discourage believers from offering true homage before the invisible God.

Reason for praise (verse 7a)

It is right and proper that God's covenant people should humble themselves in worship before him, for he has chosen them to be his own special people (Exodus 19:5; Deuteronomy 7:6). The description of God as 'our God' is expressive of the special relationship between God and his people and is a reminder of the many occasions where God speaks of Israel as 'my people' and of himself as 'their God' (Exodus 5:1; 29:45; Jeremiah 31:33; 32:38). It picks up the earlier phrase 'our Maker' (verse 6) and indicates that God not only created them and everything else but that he 'made' his people for himself at the time of the exodus. The great God and King, the creator and ruler of the world, is the God who has formed a people for himself (Deuteronomy 32:18; Isaiah 43:1). Under the new covenant sealed by the atoning blood of Christ, God promises: 'I will be their God and they shall be my people' (Hebrews 8:6-13; Revelation 21:3). In Christ we are God's special people (1 Peter 2:9). We humble ourselves before God and wonder at God's grace: 'Why, O Lord, such love to me?'[50]

In addition, there is every reason for prostrating ourselves before God for he is the shepherd of his people. Kings were seen as shepherds of their people and sometimes their lands are described as 'pasture' (Jeremiah 25:36; Ezekiel 34:1–10). Israel is often depicted as a flock of sheep with God as the good shepherd who cares for his sheep (Psalms 23:1–4; 74:1; 79:13; 80:1; Ezekiel 34:11–31). The hand that rules over all (see verses 4–5) is the hand that also leads and guards 'the sheep of his hand'.

Christians have good reason to bow in worship as we remember that the Lord Jesus is 'the great shepherd of the sheep' (Hebrews 13:20) who gave his life for us and brings us into the one fold (John 10:11–16). Can you say with Peter, that 'you were like sheep going astray, but have now returned to the Shepherd and Overseer of your souls' (1 Peter 2:25)?

Call to listen with solemn warnings (verses 7b–11)

The psalm moves from head held high in triumphant praise to head bowed low in reverent homage to an ear alert to hear the voice of God. All three positions together form a biblical view of the kind of worship that is acceptable to God. Hearing God's word is often thought of as something separate from worship in many Christian assemblies whereas for the psalmist the loud praise and quiet prostration have been leading up to this culminating act—listening to God's word with a believing and submissive attitude that issues in a daily life of loving obedience to his will. This is Paul's call to those who have known God's salvation in Christ. We are to offer spiritual worship that involves the whole self, expressed through our bodies, in a life of obedience resulting in the kind of godly behaviour which he sets out before them (Romans 12:1–21). Communal worship in our Sunday gatherings must not be out of tune with the lives we lead the rest of the week.

The phrase, 'Today, if you will hear his voice' (verse 7b) is the introduction to a direct word from God, which the writer to the Hebrews attributes to the Holy Spirit (Hebrews 3:7). It is not a wistful longing as some have supposed with translations like 'if only' or 'O that you had listened'. This is a straightforward call to listen and not to be like the ungrateful and distrusting people who came out of Egypt. 'Today' is a very definite summons to seize the moment and respond positively to their God and Saviour. It is reminiscent of Moses' word to a new generation about to enter the land of promise (see Deuteronomy 15:15; 29:13). These 'today' references are days of God's grace, days of opportunity to receive with a believing heart God's saving message. Paul pleads with the Corinthian believers 'not to receive the grace of God in vain' and quotes Isaiah 49:8 in support and then concludes, 'Behold, now is the accepted time; behold, now is the day of salvation' (2 Corinthians 6:1-2).

Meribah ('rebellion') and Massah ('trial') recall what happened in the wilderness soon after Israel left Egypt on their way to Mount Sinai (Exodus 17:1-7). A similar event is described later (Numbers 20:2-13) but that is not in mind here. This first testing experience and the people's failure to trust God were symptomatic of their rebellious attitude (see Psalms 78:18, 41, 56; 81:7). The whole 'generation' that tramped through the wilderness over that forty-year period (verse 10), gave clear evidence of a hardness of heart, what Moses calls a 'stiff-neck' (verse 8; Deuteronomy 9:6, 13; 10:16). Despite the amazing 'work' the Lord had performed on their behalf in bringing them out of Egypt they still rebelled by testing him, like gold is tested, to see how true God was to his word (verse 9).

God was 'grieved' or 'disgusted' with that 'generation' for when they had the opportunity to enter Canaan they refused, wishing to believe the discouraging majority report concerning the land and dismissing the minority report of Joshua and Caleb (Numbers 14:1-10). They had gone 'astray in their hearts' like sheep and they did not take God seriously. There was a refusal to acknowledge ('know') the 'ways' in which God acted toward his people. They squandered their day of opportunity. God in his anger declared on oath that they would not enter the land of promise (verse 11; Numbers 14:21-23).

Canaan is described as God's 'rest' (verse 11), a familiar idea in Deuteronomy. It denotes the end of wandering and fighting, the safety, contentment and enjoyment of the inheritance that God had promised them and above all fellowship with God (Deuteronomy 3:20; 12:5-7, 9-10; 14:26; 23:14; 25:19; 27:7). In the book of Joshua we are shown how God did eventually bring a new generation of his people into Canaan under Joshua and how they found 'rest' there (Joshua 1:13, 15; 21:44; 22:4; 23:1).

The psalm ends abruptly but powerfully. If they listen to God's voice in his word, take heed to the warnings, and live obediently to the honour and praise of God, Israel would know that rest. That is what God promised in the covenant he made with the people at Sinai. But

instead of blessing they experienced, more often than not, the curses of
the covenant and eventually the final curse of removal from the land.
   Canaan was a pointer to a far more wonderful 'rest' for the people of
God of all nations. It is associated with that heavenly city, kingdom and
country (see Psalm 87; Hebrews 11:1–16; 12:22–24, 28; 13:14) The writer
to the Hebrews considers it to be God's good news (Hebrews 4:1–2). It
is both a present experience in Christ, entered into by faith (Hebrews
4:3; see Matthew 11:28–29), and a glorious future reality that we shall
enter when the new creation dawns at Christ's return (Hebrews
4:9–11; Revelation 14:13; 21:1–7). We are urged to enter while the day of
opportunity is there and warned not to be rebellious and unbelieving
and so forfeit that place of rest.

Psalm 96

Good News about the King

Here is a fine missionary psalm! It is one that Jews and Christians have long applied to the Messiah. Luther had no doubts that it concerned the kingdom of Christ and the spread of the gospel worldwide, a view that Calvin also shared.

Like the other psalms in this group (Psalms 93–99) it celebrates God's global supremacy as demonstrated in his acts of salvation, creation and judgment. It is placed here in Book 4 after the catastrophe of 587 BC and the end of David's dynasty to which many of the psalms in Book 3 refer. Seen in this context the psalm reassures God's people, living under foreign rule, that God has not abdicated. He is still in charge of everything.[51] Together with the preceding psalm, it forms a pair, with the first addressed to God's people and this psalm addressed to the whole world. But the song is truth for God's people to hear and sing. It has been given to encourage them to look beyond their immediate situation to what God has in store in fulfilment of his promise to Abraham and his descendants that all nations would be blessed through them.

There are echoes of this psalm in Isaiah's prophecies, particularly those in chapters 40 to 66, indicating that among the godly in Israel there existed a close fellowship that led to a common vocabulary that revealed itself in proclamation and praise. The Chronicler also includes a form of this psalm along with parts from Psalms 105 and 106 after his account of how the ark of the covenant was brought into the tabernacle at Jerusalem (1 Chronicles 16:1-7, 23-33). Like Psalm 94, our psalm uses a poetic form distinctive of very ancient poetry of the Near East (see verses 7 and 13).

It is a psalm of praise to the one true God, using throughout his covenant name, LORD (Yahweh/Jehovah), urging all to praise him who is the universal ruler and judge. He is worthy of worship on account of his superiority over the nations and their gods and in view of his coming to set everything right. Three times the psalm issues a call to praise and each time it is supported by reasons (verses 1-6, 7-10 and 11-13).

Proclaiming the King's glory (verses 1-6)

The call (verses 1-3)

The psalm begins with a threefold summons to 'sing' (verses 1-2a). It is addressed to 'all the earth' and the whole psalm does not lose this global vision.

To whom are they to sing? They are called to praise the God who revealed himself ('his name') to Israel by his covenant name, 'LORD' (Yahweh/Jehovah), the name precious to his people as a result of the redemption from Egypt (Exodus 3:13-15; 6:3-4; 34:5-7). Throughout the psalm only this name for God is used, its eleven occurrences emphasising that Israel's God is the true God and the whole world is called to bend the knee in adoration of him ('bless').

What are they to sing? It is described as a 'new song' (verse 1). This does not necessarily mean a brand new composition for some songs of the past can be sung afresh in the light of new information or experiences (see Psalm 33:3). For the inhabitants of the world it is a song they have never sung before so that for them it is new. In fact, the song relating to God's redemption will never grow old and is associated with the new creation (see Revelation 5:9; 14:3; 15:3-4).

What is the song's content? The song is about God's 'salvation' and the word 'proclaim' indicates that it is joyful news (verse 2; see Psalms 40:9; 68:11). It is the same good news that Isaiah proclaimed (Isaiah 40:9; 52:7). The deliverance from exile in Babylon, like the redemption from Egypt, was working in God's purposes toward the greater deliverance from sin and Satan through the Servant of the Lord and his atoning death (Isaiah 52:13–55:13). This psalm is indicating that God's past activity on behalf of Israel, when he displayed his stunning greatness ('his glory') and his amazing 'wonders' to the Egyptians (verse 3; see Psalms 9:1; 75:1), is a message to be declared to all nations and peoples. It points to the revelation of God's glorious character and action in Jesus the Messiah. Israel's God is the saviour of the world (John 1:29; 3:16; 4:42; Acts 4:12). Like the Lord's Supper (1 Corinthians 11:26), worshipping together in song includes the proclamation of God's saving work.

When is the song to be sung? It deserves to be sung all the time— 'from day to day' (verse 2), like the daily message proclaimed by the heavens (Psalm 19:2). This is not something to be left for special festival occasions. It is too good and important a subject to be kept just for holiday periods.

The reasons (verses 4–6)
These reasons (notice the word 'For' at the beginning of verses 4 and 5) for singing to the LORD and declaring his greatness also contain more content with which to praise and proclaim. We are reminded again that communal worship is not to be unthinking and unintelligible. Attention is drawn to the greatness of Israel's covenant God (see Psalms 48:1; 95:3) and therefore he cannot be praised too highly. He is worthy to be praised in a way that far excels all the compliments and adulation we may give to other people, things and experiences that have impressed us. He is to be praised 'greatly' and to be 'feared' or 'held in awe' above all the 'gods' of this world, above everything and everybody formidable and frightening (verse 4; see Psalm 86:8–10). What are these gods after all? They are worthless 'idols'! There is a play on words when the psalmist states that the 'gods' (*elohim*) of the people groups are 'nonentities' (*elilim*). It is favourite description of idols in Isaiah's prophecies (Isaiah 2:8, 20;19:1, 3; 41:24; 45:16; etc.). Moses warned the people not to turn to such 'nothings' (Leviticus 19:4) and Paul reminded the Corinthian believers that 'an idol is nothing in the world' and that there is 'no other God but one' (1 Corinthians 8:4).

In contrast to the pagan deities and to encourage praise, it is positively asserted that it is Israel's covenant-keeping God who is the real and living God who has shown his greatness and power in creation (see Revelation 14:6–7). He has made the heavens and in the heavenly sanctuary 'honour and majesty' (see Psalm 45:3) are like close aides, and they, along with 'strength' and 'splendour' ('beauty'), are associated with his royal excellence. The final two descriptions are applied to the ark of the covenant in Psalm 78:61. They are all displayed where God ordains to reveal himself. The earthly sanctuary where the ark was placed was a tiny yet significant earthly replica of God's heavenly home (Hebrews 8:5) and an anticipation of God seen in the flesh when Jesus, the Word lived on earth and the disciples saw his glory (John 1:14; 2:21).

Honouring the King's worth (verses 7–10)

The call (verses 7–9)

The threefold call 'Give ... give ... give' (verses 7–8) parallels the 'Sing ... sing ... sing' of verses 1 and 2. But for variety and emphasis, 'staircase parallelism' is used here where the second line repeats the first line ('Give to the Lord') but completes the thought ('glory and strength'; see Psalm 94:1, 3). The summons is addressed not to the heavenly beings as in Psalm 29:1 but to the 'kindreds' ('families'; Genesis 10:5, 18, etc.; 12:3) 'of the peoples' who worship nonentities (verse 7; see 'gods of the peoples' in verse 5). Although ultimately we cannot add to God's 'glory', to his stunning importance and 'strength', yet the call to 'give' does mean that what glory and strength God might give us we are to return to him in praise and proclamation (see Joshua 7:19). The opposite would be to boast of our own ego or that of others. God's 'name' (see Psalm 20:1) is worthy of all the praise we can offer him for as David confessed to God when the people had made their offerings for the building of the temple, 'all things come from you, and of your own we have given you' (1 Chronicles 29:14; see Psalm 29:1–2).

That the 'giving' involves more than acknowledging and praising is suggested by the following phrase 'bring an offering' which more precisely means to 'carry' a gift. The word for 'offering' (verse 8) suggests not only bringing a sacrificial offering to God but coming like subjects entering a king's palace 'courts' and showing their allegiance by carrying gifts or tribute to their sovereign. And the picture of subjects before an awesome ruler continues where they 'bow down' to the ground ('worship', verse 9; see Psalm 95:6) in the presence of the king who is arrayed in all his regal splendour. In this psalm we find it is before the majestic beauty of God's holiness (it is his majestic holiness not ours), that all earth's inhabitants are to prostrate themselves and tremble (see Psalms 2:11; 29:2).

The reasons (verse 10)

What is the motive for giving honour to the Lord? There is no 'for' introducing a reason but it is stated by implication in this verse. The facts that God reigns, that the inhabited world is firmly established and that he governs fairly are reason enough. It is the message we heard in Psalm 93:1. Israel along with all who come to know Israel's God needs to spread the news. Both Nebuchadnezzar the Babylonian king, and Darius the Persian king were humbled and brought to praise and proclaim Daniel's God as the one who reigns supreme (Daniel 4:34–37; 6:25–27).

It is the task of kings to rule and judge. The LORD, Israel's God, governs with 'uprightness' ('righteously') which means that he will be fair and impartial in his treatment of those who seek justice. That rule is already in evidence to those with an eye of faith but the day is coming when all will be brought to submit to the King of kings and Lord of lords.

An ancient marginal note by Christians crept into the text by mistake in some translations of the original so that the verse then read: 'Say among the nations, the Lord reigns from a cross.' It reminds us how the psalm was understood by the Early Church. Peter had already made clear to Cornelius and the other Gentiles with him that he had been appointed to preach and testify that Jesus was the one ordained by God to judge the living and the dead and that by believing in him they could be assured that their sins were forgiven (Acts 10:43). All judgment has been given to the Son and he shall reign and bring justice to the poor and needy (see Psalm 72:2, 4; Isaiah 11:4).

Rejoicing in the King's coming (verses 11–13)

The call (verses 11–12)

Next the whole world is called to 'rejoice' and 'be glad' and to make its contribution in praising God. Fields and trees join heaven, earth and sea in this poetic description of joyful shouts of praise to the LORD (Yahweh/Jehovah), Israel's God (verses 11–12). Isaiah uses similar language in expressing glad praises to God (Isaiah 44:23; 55:12).

The reason (verse 13)

The word 'For' introduces the reason for the joyful cosmic celebration. The LORD (Yahweh/Jehovah), Israel's God, 'is coming'. Again, 'staircase parallelism' is employed (see verse 7). It has the effect here of slowing the psalm down as it comes to this climatic point as well as acting as a poetic concluding refrain using word repetition ('he is coming'; see 'sing' and 'give' in verses 1 and 7). The build-up captures the excitement as we are finally told that this glorious majestic God is coming 'to judge the earth'. He is coming to set the world to rights. His rule will be true to his righteous character ('with righteousness') and will accord with his faithfulness ('his truth') not only in that he keeps his promises but in being absolutely impartial and truthful. It will mean punishing the wicked as well as vindicating the godly.

The New Testament makes clear that the LORD, Israel's God, to whom every knee must bow is identified with Jesus the Messiah who is also of David's family line. He is the real Davidic king who will administer justice and whose kingdom is an everlasting one. Paul applies to Jesus the words of Isaiah that the LORD (Yahweh/Jehovah) alone is saviour and that to him every knee must bow (Isaiah 45:22-23; Philippians 2:9-11). In a similar way, when the apostles first began preaching on the day of Pentecost, Peter, after quoting Joel's prophecy that whoever calls on the name of the LORD (Yahweh/Jehovah) will be saved, immediately drew the people's attention to Jesus. He also later made clear that there is salvation in no one else but in this name.

Psalm 97

Joy to all the Earth!

Josiah Conder (1789-1855) has a wonderful hymn that incorporates the sentiments of this, another psalm celebrating the LORD's kingship:

The Lord is King; lift up thy voice,
O earth, and all ye heavens rejoice!
From world to world the joy shall ring:
'The Lord Omnipotent is King!'

The Lord is King! Child of the dust,
The Judge of all the earth is just:
Holy and true are all His ways;
Let every creature speak His praise.

The truth that God reigns is good news for God's people, especially as they endure persecution. To a people dejected as a result of the destruction of Jerusalem and its temple and the loss of their king, such a reminder is an encouragement not to lose heart. The psalm does not ignore the reality of evil in the world and the power of wicked people, but the fact that God does rule and has acted and will act to destroy all opposition and to preserve and deliver his oppressed people is a great stimulus to faith and a message of hope to all who will listen. The whole book of Revelation had the same message to Christians suffering under Roman persecution and these passages of Scripture are also designed to raise the spirits of the suffering church today. 'The LORD reigns' is not a useless platitude to encourage the faithful to keep whistling in the dark when times are difficult but a reality grounded in what God has accomplished in Christ and which will be evident to all including the scoffers when the right moment comes for God finally to set everything right.

A word to all nations (verse 1)

This hymn of praise opens like Psalms 93 and 99 with the declaration that Israel's God 'reigns' but it also follows on from the previous psalm which adds the call for all to 'rejoice' and 'be glad' in God's kingship (Psalm 96:10-11). The 'multitude of isles' refers to the many far-flung 'coastal regions' of the Gentile world (see Genesis 10:5; Psalm 72:10; Isaiah 42:4, 10-12; etc.). That the 'LORD reigns' is a wonderful truth and it should thrill all our hearts. In reference to Christ we can also say that as a result of his atoning death, resurrection and ascension to God's right hand, the 'Lord has begun his reign' and shall reign till all his enemies are subdued.

God's appearance (verses 2-6)

The picture we are given of God is reminiscent of his appearance at Sinai in cloud, thick darkness, lightning and fire when even the mountains were affected (Exodus 19:16-18; Deuteronomy 5:22). Previous psalms have described God in this awesome way (see Psalms 18:8-9, 11, 15; 50:3; 77:16, 18) and his impressive presence is highlighted (notice the repetition of 'at the presence of') to indicate that Israel's God, the 'LORD' (Yahweh/Jehovah), is the sovereign ruler ('Lord') of the entire earth (verse 5).

This true and living God who is Lord of all is not like earthly dictators whose rule is often marred by corruption, exploitation and self-interest. The 'foundation of his throne', signifying the very structure on which the kingdom rests, is one that is characterised by 'righteousness and justice' (verse 2; see Psalm 33:5). God is the standard for determining what is right and his rule is based on right principles and on justice that entails right actions and fair decisions. He is concerned for right order and what is equitable and true.

For God's 'enemies', which incidentally are his people's oppressors, his righteousness and justice mean their destruction (verse 3). The peoples of the world will 'see' (verse 6) what is also proclaimed to them (Psalm 96:3), namely, a display of God's stunning greatness ('his glory'). An aspect of that 'glory' is God's 'righteousness' which the heavens themselves proclaim (verse 6; see Psalms 19:1; 50:6).

A word to idolaters (verse 7)

One of the great fundamental commandments that God revealed to Israel was that they should have no other gods nor make images nor worship before them (Exodus 20:3–5). Not only was Israel surrounded by pagan nations that worshipped false gods and made images to represent them, many within Israel became idolaters. It is one of the obvious evidences of a world in rebellion against God that it has suppressed the truth about the true God and 'worshipped and served the creature rather than the creator who is blessed for ever' (Romans 1:22–25). Prophets like Isaiah and Jeremiah were scathing in their treatment of idolatry (Isaiah 44:9–20; Jeremiah 10:1–16).

The world of idolaters and worshippers of false gods are to be shamed. They make great claims for what are 'nonentities' or 'nothings' ('idols'; see Psalm 96:5). And whatever can legitimately go under the name of 'gods' in the sense of supernatural beings such as angels and the principalities and powers that are associated with earthly rulers (see Psalm 82:1) are urged to worship God. The writer to the Hebrews may well have had this text in mind as he demonstrated Jesus' superiority to the angels (Hebrews 1:6).

God's supremacy (verses 8–9)

While shame and disappointment come to those who worship false gods, the people of God can rejoice and be glad on account of God's fair decisions ('judgments', verse 8; see verses 2–3) of which they have heard. Verse 8 is almost a word for word repeat of Psalm 48:11. Zion, the inhabitants of Jerusalem and its surrounding towns and villages ('daughters of Judah'; see Joshua 15:45 which reads literally 'Ekron and her daughters'), are ultimately the elect of God who belong to the Lamb, the Lord's Anointed (see Psalms 2:6; 87:2, 5; Revelation 14:1).

This is the God who is the 'LORD most high' over all the earth (see Psalm 83:18) and 'greatly exalted' (as in Psalm 47:9) 'above all gods' (verse 9). Again God's infinite superiority to all other power and influence is emphasised (see verse 7). God's activity among the Egyptians, the Canaanites, the Amalakites and the Philistines for instance, and the prophecies directed to many of them concerning their futures, indicate already his authority over the things they worship and the unseen rulers of this age that influence them. As Israel after 587 BC took comfort from this thought so too can we as we look at the powers that be and the influence they wield in our world.

A word to God's people (verses 10–12)

God's people are directly addressed in these final verses. God directed Israel to love him with all their beings (Deuteronomy 6:5) and here we have this lovely description of God's people as those 'who love the LORD' (see Psalm 5:11). The original is quite blunt: 'Lovers of Yahweh, hate evil!' (verse 10). Amos urged an apostate people to 'Hate evil, love good' (Amos 5:15) and David in Psalm 34:14 echoed the wisdom writers in his call to 'Depart from evil, and do good'. Perhaps in this context the evil in mind is the worship of false gods. The attraction to worship worthless idols is ever with us and twice the apostle who was himself exiled for his faith, is told in no uncertain terms not to fall down before an angel but to 'Worship God!' (Revelation 19:10; 22:9). With the demand comes the encouragement because those who are against evil are likely to find themselves in trouble from evildoers. God guards or 'preserves' the lives of his 'loyal ones' ('his saints'; see Psalms 4:3; 30:4) and rescues them from the power of the 'wicked' (verse 10; see Psalms 1:1; 28:3). Their covenant-keeping God (Yahweh/Jehovah) will never allow those who love him and are committed to him to be overcome by the evil one or by those associated with him. We still need to pray, 'Do not lead us into temptation, but deliver us from the evil one' (Matthew 6:13).

For these same people who are now described as in a right relationship with God and live straightforward lives ('righteous' and 'upright in heart'; see Psalms 1:5; 7:10) there is more encouragement. They can experience 'gladness'. This is because 'light is sown' (verse 11). Light when it is shone into the darkness dispels the gloom and makes people feel better and joyful. Thus the psalm ends as it began with a call to 'rejoice', only this time it is an invitation made to God's people, to those who have experienced the happiness that God's light has brought. They are also summoned to 'give thanks' to 'the remembrance of his holy name' or more simply to 'the memorial of his holiness' (verse 12; see Psalm 30:4).

Psalm 98

Rejoicing in the Rule of Righteousness

We need constant encouragements to sing praises to God just as Israel did, as we live under the shadow of powerful regimes opposed to the living God and all that he has revealed to be right and true. The people of God had experienced defeat and humiliation at the hands of the Babylonians and even when they returned to their own land by permission of the Persian authorities they still considered themselves in bondage. There was little to sing about. But this psalm, like some of the previous ones, urges us in the worst as well as the best of times to remember God's great plans and purposes and that we are on the victory side. There is a bright future when God puts all things right on the basis of the great saving work he has accomplished in Christ.

For the first time since Psalm 92 we have a heading even though it is very brief—'Psalm'. It is a reminder that it is a composition to be sung to musical accompaniment. There are many similarities between this and Psalm 96, especially in its opening and closing words. Like so many praise psalms there is the challenge to praise followed by motives for doing so. In Psalm 96 there were three calls to praise with accompanying reasons whereas here we have two calls with the word 'for' introducing the reasons, the second round being much fuller in its summons with a briefer time spent on the reasons (verses 1-3 and 4-9).

The LORD's universal kingship that Psalms 93-99 celebrate is marked by 'righteousness'. In this psalm we are told at the beginning that God has revealed his righteousness (verse 2) and it closes by telling us that his rule over the world will be 'with righteousness' (verse 9). It is not always possible for us to understand what is going on in world affairs and how everything will be resolved. These psalms, like Isaiah's prophecies (see especially chapters 40 to 55) encourage us to believe, in the most adverse circumstances, that the Lord is in charge in the rise and fall of world empires as well as in individual crisis situations and that right will prevail. Everything that happens on earth is working to a plan that is right. It will lead to the triumph of what is right and that 'right' will accord with God's righteous character and standards (see Psalm 94:15). 'Righteousness' is the very foundation of his rule and the heavens declare it (Psalm 97:2, 6). The truth of this is seen in the life, death and resurrection of Jesus. He revealed God's righteousness in his spotless life and ministry. His cross demonstrated God's righteousness in the condemnation of sin and Satan as Jesus experienced the judgment of God. The resurrection proclaimed God's righteousness in the vindication of his Son to the Father's side in glory. In the gospel the righteousness of God is revealed in all its wonder and power. All will see the kingdom of righteousness when the new creation dawns.

Praising God's salvation (verses 1-3)

It begins, like Psalm 96, with the call, 'sing to the LORD a new song!' (verse 1). It can be a song previously known but now in the light of a further appreciation or display of God's goodness the song comes to life in a fresh and meaningful way. On the other hand, as the heading suggests, the summons may be to sing a new composition, to sing a song of praise such as has never been heard before (see Psalms 33:3; 40:3; Isaiah 42:10). This psalm, though it has features and language similar to Psalm 96, is nevertheless unique.

It is in the reasons introduced by the word 'for' that we are shown what to sing about. God has done 'marvellous things' ('wonders'; see Psalms 9:1; 96:3). These wonders relate to the 'salvation' ('victory') that he has powerfully ('his right hand') and uniquely ('holy arm') achieved. He personally exerts himself for the benefit of his needy and broken people. The psalmist echoes phrases familiar from Isaiah's prophecy (see Isaiah 52:10; 59:16) and they help us to interpret aright our psalm.

In Isaiah, the 'salvation' accomplished and the 'righteousness' which it expresses and on which it is founded, is in the first place related to the deliverance from Babylonian captivity. But it points, like the deliverance from Egyptian bondage, to the deeper and more sinister spiritual problem of the people's slavery to sin and Satan that Isaiah unpacks from chapters 49 to 55. The powerful holy arm of the Lord that saves his people from their sins and brings them back to God is revealed in the work of the Suffering Servant who bears the sins of his people and receives the punishment that they deserve (Isaiah 53:1, 5). The Lord (Yahweh/Jehovah) is the one who, as the man of sorrows, undergoes this awesome task of atoning for sin so that his people ('the many') might be forgiven and be in a right legal standing before God (Isaiah 45:25; 53:11-12). What God has done for Israel is also shown to all 'the nations' (Isaiah 40:5; 52:15; 54-55) and Paul sees the fulfilment of Isaiah and by implication the words of verse 2 of our psalm as he preaches the gospel to the Gentile world (Romans 15:20-21).

The Lord's 'salvation', a term used in each of the first three verses, which his people have experienced is because he 'remembered'. This does not mean that God had a memory loss and then suddenly remembered. It emphasises that God had acted just as he had always said he would (see Genesis 8:1). When God makes promises he keeps his word by fulfilling those promises. He has acted in accordance with 'his loving commitment and truthfulness' ('his mercy and his faithfulness'; see Psalm 92:2) toward his covenant people ('the house of Israel'; verse 3). The redemption of God's people from exile was with a view to bringing people of all nations ('all the ends of the earth'; Isaiah 45:22) to see and enter into 'the salvation of our God' (Isaiah 52:10). God had made a great promise to Abraham that in blessing this chosen nation all nations would be blessed. Jesus indicated to the Samaritan woman that salvation is from the Jews but when the Samaritans believed they were able to confess that Jesus was the Messiah, 'the Saviour of the world' (John 4:22, 42). It also reminds us of Paul's language that the gospel is 'for the Jew first' and also for the Gentile nations (Romans 1:16).

Praising God's rule (verses 4-9)

The fact that this 'salvation' is for all nations is an encouragement for 'all the earth' (see Psalm 96:1, 9) to 'shout joyfully', to 'break out' and give a 'resounding cry' and 'make music' (see Psalms 47:1; 95:1–2). The first call did not address anyone in particular although the 'our God' (verse 3) implied the worshipping company of God's people. Now, in view of the universal salvation that Israel's covenant God has accomplished, the whole of creation is drawn in to praising him.

On the Sunday before the resurrection, as Jesus entered Jerusalem riding on a donkey to the loud acclaim of his followers, Matthew sees the event as the fulfilment of Zechariah's prophecy. That prophecy includes the word 'shout' (Zechariah 9:9) which is translated 'shout joyfully' in our psalm at verses 4 and 6. The word is often used for spontaneous shouts of joy and homage at the proclamation of a new king. When Saul was brought before the people by Samuel the people 'shouted' and they said 'Long live the king!' (1 Samuel 10:24).

The various musical instruments anticipate the joyful praise of the final Psalm 150. The 'harp' is better translated 'lyre' (see Psalm 33:2). This, along with the silver 'trumpets' (Numbers 10:2) and the ram's 'horn' (Psalms 47:5; 81:3), were used on special joyous occasions (Leviticus 25:9; 1 Chronicles 16:5–6). As such instruments were used at the proclamation of an earthly king (1 Kings 1:39; 2 Kings 11:14) it is understandable that they are drawn in here to celebrate the universal 'King' who is the 'LORD', (Yahweh/Jehovah). It was with the blast of the ram's horn that the people came to meet with God whose presence descended on Mount Sinai (see Exodus 19:13, 19).

The rest of the created world is called to join the joyful noise (verses 7–8; see Psalm 96:11–12). Here again the poetic imagery of rivers clapping their hands and hills shouting joyfully is reminiscent of Isaiah's language in a similar context (Isaiah 55:12).

At last the ultimate reason is given for this wholehearted and worldwide summons to praise. It is introduced again with the word 'For' (verse 9) and is almost a repeat of the final verse of Psalm 96:13 (see 1 Chronicles 16:33). The verb 'he is coming' found twice in that psalm introduces an important function of God's kingship, which is to judge the peoples of the world in a way that is true to his own righteous character and that is seen to be equitable and just (see Psalm 96:10). Israel's God, the LORD (Yahweh/Jehovah), is not only the cosmic ruler who has brought about a global salvation but the judge who will put the world to rights.

After the fall of all that Babylon represented, John heard the united voice of a great multitude in heaven, saying 'Alleluia! Salvation and glory and honour and power to our God! For true and righteous are his judgments, because he has judged the great prostitute who corrupted the earth with her fornication; and he has avenged on her the blood of his servants *shed* by her'. Then a little later a voice came from the throne, 'Praise our God, all you his servants and those who fear him, both small and great!' This is followed by a deafening roar from the great multitude, 'Alleluia! For the Lord God Omnipotent reigns!' (Revelation 19:1–6).

Psalm 99

Worshipping the Holy King

The previous psalm brought to a climax a truth about God that had been building up from Psalm 94—the revelation of God's righteousness (Psalm 98:2). This psalm emphasises the holiness of God by the threefold refrain that God 'is holy' (see verses 3, 5 and 9). Again, it is a truth concerning God's nature and character that has been frequently heard in these psalms in praise of God's kingship: 'holiness adorns your house' (Psalm 93:5); 'the beauty of holiness' (Psalm 96:9); 'his holy name' (Psalm 97:12); 'his holy arm' (Psalm 98:1). As we have seen in these psalms that extol God's rule, there is a close relationship with the message of Isaiah. The threefold reference to God as holy calls to mind the cry of the seraphim that Isaiah heard, 'Holy, holy, holy is the Lord of hosts; the whole earth is full of his glory' (Isaiah 6:3). That experience of the sovereign Lord, the universal King and Israel's covenant God (Yahweh/Jehovah) that Isaiah encountered in the year that king Uzziah died (Isaiah 6:3-5) so impressed him that throughout his book he refers to God twenty-six times as 'the Holy One' of his people which is more than all the other references in the Old Testament put together (see for instance, Isaiah 1:4; 5:19; 12:6; 30:15; 54:5; 55:5; 60:9, 14). The King whom Isaiah saw in all his glory is said by the apostle John to be Jesus (John 12:41). By implication, we have every reason to apply the words of our psalm to the Lord Jesus as Jehovah/Yahweh-Jesus.

Holiness is what makes God to be God. He is wholly different and set apart from everything and everybody else. His awesome otherness meant particularly that he was ethically pure and absolutely perfect and good. This made him so distinct from the kind of gods that were worshipped by the foreign nations and he called Israel to be holy like him by behaving in a morally upright way (see Leviticus 19:1-2). That same call comes to followers of the Lord Jesus (Matthew 5:48; 1 Peter 1:14-16).

Psalm 98 parallels Psalm 96 with its opening call to sing a new song, while this psalm parallels Psalm 97 in commencing with the proclamation that the 'Lord reigns' and is the last in a series that highlights God's kingship (see Psalms 93-99). They are placed here intentionally after the psalms of Book 3 that close with concern over the loss of the Davidic king and what that means not only concerning God's promises to David but in relation to God's rule and purposes. God's covenant name Lord (Yahweh/Jehovah) occurs seven times in this psalm, four times in the phrase 'Lord our God'. The number seven is used throughout the Bible to signify completeness. Perhaps the symbolism is employed to emphasise that Israel's God is still the covenant-keeping God despite all evidences to the contrary. It is also interesting that this concluding psalm concerning God's kingship mentions Moses and Samuel. The first psalm of Book 4 is attributed to Moses and this psalm has a number of links with Moses' song in Exodus 15 which also celebrates God's rule. Samuel opposed the wrong attitude of the people when they demanded an earthly monarch. He charged them with rejecting God as their king and drew attention to the oppressive nature of an earthly king's rule (1 Samuel 8:4-22). All this was important for the people in exile or those who had returned from the Babylonian captivity to take note of and appreciate as they looked to the future. It is likewise important for us as we seek to understand God's rule and the significance of King Jesus, the Son of God, who sits on his Father's throne (Revelation 3:21).

There are two refrains: we not only have the threefold statement that God is 'holy' (verses 3, 5 and 9) but a twofold call to 'exalt the Lord our God' (verses 5 and 9).

The awesome LORD (verses 1–3)

For the final time in the psalms the proclamation rings out, 'The LORD (Yahweh/Jehovah) reigns' (see Psalm 93:1). The God of Israel who is the universal king demonstrated his kingship to the Egyptians, to the chiefs of Edom, the valiant men of Moab and the inhabitants of Canaan so that the nations were in fear and dread (Exodus 15:14–15, 18; Deuteronomy 2:25). In the previous psalm the earth's inhabitants were urged to rejoice and the peoples of the world were judged with equity. Here, however, 'peoples tremble' and the 'earth' is 'shaken' ('moved') like a hanging basket. It relates to the end-time judgment to which those earlier historical episodes point.

Interestingly, the seat of God's kingly authority is Zion where, from the time of David, the earthly replica of the heavenly throne-room was the inner sanctuary where the ark was placed with 'the cherubim' on either side. The second Psalm speaks of the Lord reigning through his King on Mount Zion (Psalms 2:6; 97:8). Israel's God, the LORD, 'is great in Zion', the city of 'the great King' (verse 2; Psalms 48:1–2; 76:1–2). He is the only true world ruler who governs the world from this centre. It relates to all that has already been said about Zion as the true company of God's covenant people and accords with the prophecy often read on Remembrance Sunday or at Armistice Day services, concerning Zion as the centre of this universal kingdom (Isaiah 2:2–4).

Cherubs are associated with the original earthly sanctuary in Eden (see Genesis 3:24) and are depicted as winged creatures with human and animal faces (Ezekiel 41:18–19). The psalm, in the original Hebrew, is careful not to say that the invisible and infinite God dwells 'between' or 'on' them (see Psalm 80:1; 2 Samuel 6:2). Neither the ark nor the area above the ark was the symbol of God's throne. It was merely his 'footstool' (verse 5; 1 Chronicles 28:2; Isaiah 60:13) as indeed was the whole earth (Isaiah 66:1). But God's presence was certainly associated with the ark and the Jerusalem sanctuary.

Despite what opposition and oppression the people of God might be experiencing from foreign rulers, they are encouraged to believe that God is 'high above all the peoples' of the world (verse 2; see Psalm 47). All are directed to praise God's 'great and awesome name' (verse 3). God's nature and character, whatever God has revealed about himself, about the 'name' that he has, witnesses to his uniqueness. 'He is holy'. The holiness of God, unlike human beings who are given such titles, concerns his absolute moral integrity, his awesome purity that refuses to countenance sin, as well as his awe-inspiring majesty. The Philistines who experienced in their cities the overpowering presence of God in wrath, were brought to confess, 'Who is able to stand before this holy LORD God?' (1 Samuel 6:20). Isaiah, when he was confronted with a sight of the most holy God, cried out, 'Woe is me, for I am undone! because I am a man of unclean lips, and I dwell in the midst of a people of unclean lips; for my eyes have seen the King, the LORD of hosts' (Isaiah 6:5). We are brought low that we might be raised to sing his praises.

The lover of justice (verses 4–5)

As has been emphasised in previous psalms, Israel's God and King is completely unlike the rulers of this world as Samuel informed his people when they demanded a king like the other nations (1 Samuel 8:11-17). Though he has the 'strength' to crush all opposition, God does not abuse the power he has in the way we have seen, for instance, in the dictators of the 20th century. Power is needed to rule well but too often that power is corrupted by sinful self-seeking and aggrandisement. God's administration is governed by the rule of love (see Psalms 33:5; 37:28). The best of the David-Solomon era in Israel's history is held up as a type of God's perfect reign over his people 'Jacob' (see Psalm 44:4). His rule expresses his righteous character as he governs his people uprightly and justly.

As God is the high and lofty one (Isaiah 6:1; 57:15) and reigns high over all the peoples (verse 2), the call to God's people is to exalt (literally 'lift high') the LORD (Yahweh/Jehovah) God of Israel. How can mere human creatures exalt the one who is already exalted and infinitely higher than we are? We do so by acknowledging his greatness and declaring to others how great he is. Immediately following the summons to exalt God is the call to 'worship at his footstool'. To 'worship' means 'to bow down', 'to prostrate oneself' (see Psalms 29:2; 95:6). Matthew Henry comments: 'The more we abase ourselves, and the more prostrate we are before God, the more we exalt him.'

The 'footstool' is associated with the earthly temple and especially the ark of the covenant (see 1 Chronicles 28:2; Psalm 132:8). It not only symbolised God's presence among his people but it was associated with atonement and holiness. The high priest once a year, taking live coals in one hand from the incense altar went into the most holy place with the blood of the sin offerings and sprinkled it on and in front of the mercy seat that lay on top of the ark. This brought cleansing and holiness on account of the sinful impurity of the people (Leviticus 16:16, 19; Hebrews 9:3-9). Isaiah was cleansed from his sinful pollution through the symbolism of the live coal taken from the incense altar. As Job and Isaiah humbled themselves before God's presence and confessed their sin and unworthiness so we must have that same attitude of mind and heart and recognise that it is only through the finished work of Christ on the cross, to which those old covenant rituals pointed, that we can serve the living God (Hebrews 10:11-25).

The forgiving LORD (verses 6-9)

Our attention is drawn to the great leaders of Israel before the monarchy was established in Israel. These men, Moses, Aaron and Samuel, were great intercessors. They acted as mediators between God and the people. Although all three functioned as priests offering sacrifices (Leviticus 8:15-30; 9:1-22; 1 Samuel 9:13) it is their intercessory prayers that are particularly brought to our attention in the psalm. Moses and Samuel in particular were examples to the prophets who came after them of men who interceded with God on behalf of their people (see Jeremiah 15:1). They 'called upon' the God who had revealed his holy character under his covenant name LORD (Yahweh/Jehovah) and he 'answered them' (verse 6). There are many references to Moses' intercessions on behalf of his people from the time of the golden calf incident to the other occasions during the wilderness journey when the people rebelled against God and displayed ingratitude and unbelief (Exodus 32:11-30; Numbers 11:2; 14:13-19; 21:7; Deuteronomy 9:18-19). Moses actually prayed earnestly for his own brother and sister (Numbers 12:13; Deuteronomy 9:20). Aaron, the specially set apart priest, by his actions in making atonement for the people, saved his people from God's wrath (Numbers 16:44-48). Samuel also exercised an intercessory role on behalf of Israel (1 Samuel 7:8-9; 12:17-19, 23). These early leaders of Israel called out to God on Israel's behalf and the Lord answered them, speaking to them 'in the cloudy pillar' (verse 7). God talked to Moses and Aaron from the 'pillar of cloud' (Exodus 33:9; Numbers 12:5; Deuteronomy 31:15). We are not given any account of how God appeared to Samuel but this psalm suggests that his first encounters with God at the sanctuary at Shiloh may have been by means of the divine cloud (see 1 Samuel 3:10, 21).

These initial leaders in Israel also received and obeyed God's 'testimonies', his solemn declarations of how they should behave as his people. God's covenant law is also described as an 'ordinance' (or 'statute', verse 7; see Psalm 119:5). The God of Israel ('LORD our God'), 'answered' these faithful men who prayed on behalf of their people (verse 8), unlike the case of Saul, the first king of Israel, who received no answer when he looked to God for help (1 Samuel 28:5–6). The Lord finds the prayers of those who claim to follow him but have no time for God's word of instruction, detestable (Proverbs 28:9).

Although those early leaders like Moses and Samuel were not perfect and succumbed to sinful weaknesses they were not apostates like Saul. God answered their prayers and forgave them, even though the sinful deeds of both the intercessors and the people were not overlooked. The phrase 'God-who-forgives' (verse 8) expresses the wonderful truth that divine forgiveness means God is the one who 'bears away', 'carries the cost' of the people's rebellious deeds (see Psalms 32:5; 85:2; Leviticus 16:21–22; Isaiah 53:12). He does take vengeance on all wrongdoing. Moses and Aaron were disciplined for their sinful lapse and not allowed to lead the people into Canaan (Numbers 20:12). Sin is too serious for God to dismiss or ignore. The gospel shows how Jesus as God's sacrificial lamb, is the one who has 'taken away' the world's sin (John 1:29) and borne the cup of God's wrath and the curse that our sins deserve (Mark 14:36; Romans 3:25; Galatians 3:13; 1 John 2:2). If we had to pay the full cost of our rebellious actions we would all be damned for ever. Christ has paid the price at Calvary. Nevertheless, God does discipline his people for their sins (1 Corinthians 11:29–32; Hebrews 12:5–11). 'Forgiveness without discipline would make us spoilt children; discipline without forgiveness would break our hearts. Together they guarantee that while we can treat forgiveness as certain, we can never treat sin as negligible.' (Alec Motyer).

All this truth, filling out the meaning of God's holiness, presents us with further cause for praising Israel's covenant God and for submitting ourselves before him in humble adoration. The 'for' at the beginning of the closing line introduces us to the fundamental reason for our worship. For the fourth and final time God is given the title 'LORD our God' (see verses 5, 8 and 9a). It emphasises that it is the God who is in this special relationship with his people who is 'holy'. Significantly this fundamental attribute appears in reference to God for the third time. He is superlatively holy—'Holy, holy, holy is the Lord of hosts' (Isaiah 6:3; see Revelation 4:8).

In place of 'footstool' (verse 5) the refrain substitutes 'his holy hill' (verse 9), a reference to Zion's hill and its sanctuary (see Psalms 2:6; 3:4; 15:1; 43:3; 48:1). Our God is holy and is associated with a place that he has made holy. The earthly mountain becomes symbolic of heavenly realities about which the gospel speaks. Neither on Mount Gerizim with the Samaritans nor on the temple mount in Jerusalem with the Jews do we need to go to worship (John 4:20–24), but we come together to exalt our God and reverently bow our heads and hearts before him through Jesus remembering all that he has accomplished on the cross in order to bring us to God.

Psalm 100

The LORD, He is God

This psalm is best known in the metrical version originally composed by William Kethe, a friend of John Knox the Scottish reformer—'All people that on earth do dwell'. It is usually sung to a tune composed by Louis Bourgeois, one of John Calvin's musicians and known to posterity as the *Old Hundredth*. Queen Elizabeth I dismissed these metrical psalms as 'Geneva jigs' but the ordinary worshippers received them gladly for they were easier to remember and with more memorable melodies the whole congregation was enabled to sing heartily to the Lord. They had a profound influence on the Reformation in Scotland.

Psalm 100 provides a grand affirmation of the whole series celebrating God's kingship (Psalms 93–99). The psalm has a heading—'A Psalm of Thanksgiving'—the first of a short series in Book 4 where such headings are few and far between (see Psalms 90, 92, 98). It picks up the references to 'thanksgiving' and 'be thankful' in verse 4. Like the first part of Psalm 95 there is a two-fold call to worship (verses 1–2 and 4) and each time it is accompanied by reasons (verses 3 and 5).

Praise the LORD for he is God (verses 1–3)

Invitation to praise (verses 1–2)

Although some of our English versions use different words, the first verse is identical with the opening words of Psalm 98:4—'Give a resounding shout to the LORD, all the earth'. It is the kind of shout of joy and homage that is given to a king (see Psalm 47:1; Zechariah 9:9). As Calvin suggests, such an invitation to earth's inhabitants relates to the time when the people of God would be gathered out of different nations ('all the earth', verse 1; Psalms 96:1; 98:4; Exodus 9:14, 16; Numbers 14:21). The psalms like the prophets continually remind us that God's special relationship with Israel was with a view to blessing all nations as the promises made to Abraham indicate (Genesis 12:1-2).

This is strong encouragement to worship God; not that he needs us but because we were made to honour him and that is where we shall find our true satisfaction. As the Westminster Shorter Catechism puts it: 'Man's chief end is to glorify God and to enjoy him for ever'. 'Serve the LORD' (verse 2) implies that we are God's servants and a servant's whole object in life was to be in the service of his master. The verb to 'serve' has mainly been used in the psalms in relation to the messianic king (see Psalms 18:43; 22:30; 72:11) but its first appearance as here is in a summons to serve the LORD (Yahweh/Jehovah; Psalm 2:11).

Such service is not confined to what we do when we come together to worship. Those versions that translate 'serve' as 'worship' in this respect give a wrong impression. Though the context here suggests communal worship, as it does when God directed Moses to bring Israel out of Egypt to serve him at Sinai (Exodus 3:12), we must not limit this service to what we do as an assembly of God's people. This is an everyday commitment, where what happens in church is not out of step with how we live from day to day. Joshua urged this upon the people in his final sermon and the people responded, 'The LORD our God we will serve, and his voice we will obey' (Joshua 24:14-24). In the New Testament, Christians are exhorted in the light of God's mercies to 'present your bodies a living sacrifice, holy, acceptable to God, which is your reasonable (or 'spiritual') service' (Romans 12:1).

This service is not to be seen as a chore. We are to serve the Lord with 'gladness' (verse 2). While appreciating the reasons why some editors have altered the metrical version line from 'Him serve with mirth' to 'Him serve with fear' (see Psalm 2:11), they have completely lost the joyful, pleasurable nature of the service that this psalm encourages. Serving God is an enjoyable and fulfilling life.

For Israel under the old Sinai covenant, the call for them to 'Come before his presence with singing' (verse 2) meant coming to the central sanctuary where the ark, the symbol of his presence, was placed. With the new covenant now operating, Christians meet together in different places all round the world, as the Church of God seen locally, where God by his Spirit is present (1 Corinthians 3:16; Ephesians 2:22). It is as we are together with fellow believers that we are urged to teach and admonish one another as we sing with gratitude in our hearts to the Lord (Ephesians 5:19; Colossians 3:16).

Recognising who God is (verse 3)

The content and motives for praise are very important. 'Know' in the sense of knowledge cannot be discounted here. 'Knowledge is the mother of devotion and of all obedience: blind sacrifices will never please a seeing God' (Matthew Henry). The knowledge presented is of fundamental importance and for Israel the source of the knowledge was God's revelation of himself at the time of the exodus and the people's experience of his saving activity (Exodus 6:7; 29:46). That knowledge has been further increased in these end times with the revelation of the fulness of God in Jesus Christ and his saving activity through Christ's death and resurrection to which the exodus event pointed (Hebrews 1:1-4).

The first basic truth to inform his people's joyful praises is Yahweh/Jehovah's uniqueness as God—'the LORD, he *is* God' (verse 3). Although there are heavenly beings who can be called 'gods' (Psalms 82:1; 97:7-9) and in the religions of Israel's neighbours there was belief in many gods, only the God of Israel was the true and living God. To praise this one great absolute reality is to call the peoples of the world to reject all other gods as false and worthless and to worship him alone (Deuteronomy 6:13; Matthew 4:10; 1 Corinthians 8:6).

When Moses preached to a new generation of people about to enter Canaan, he reminded them of God's redeeming power in releasing the people from Egyptian bondage and added, 'To you it was shown, that you might know that the LORD himself is God' (or 'the LORD he *is* God'); there is none other besides him (Deuteronomy 4:35, 39). The same words were uttered by the people when God answered Elijah and sent fire to burn up his sacrifice—'The LORD, he *is* God! The LORD, he *is* God!' (1 Kings 18:39).

The second basic truth to give meaning and content to the people's praises, is that it is the Lord who is Israel's maker, not merely in the ultimate sense of the original creation but in forming them into a people for his glory (see Psalm 95:6; Deuteronomy 32:6; Isaiah 43:1, 21; 60:21). According to the Jews who preserved the Hebrew text we should read 'and we are his' rather than the not quite so appropriate 'and not we ourselves' (verse 3). This is the main point that because God has formed Israel, they belong to him in a special way. They are 'his people' whom he redeemed from Egypt. God is viewed as the shepherd whose flock they are—'the sheep of his pasture' (see Psalms 74:1; 95:7). The way God deals with Israel is a picture of what is true of the worldwide church of God (John 10:14-16; 1 Peter 2:25). We are not our own for we are bought with a price (1 Corinthians 6:20; 7:23). Our great God and Saviour Jesus Christ 'gave himself for us, that he might redeem us ... and purify for himself his own special people' (Titus 2:13-14; Deuteronomy 7:6).

But this knowledge is to be appreciated and acknowledged. When the psalm was written the world at large did not know about, let alone acknowledge, the 'LORD' (Yahweh/Jehovah), Israel's God. But the people were encouraged to look to the time when 'the earth will be filled with the knowledge of the glory of the Lord' (Habakkuk 2:14). As the gospel spread throughout the Roman empire Paul saw it as a fulfilment of psalms like this one (Romans 10:18; see Psalm 19:4). We look forward to the time when we shall see John's vision realised with people of every nation and language united in joyful acknowledgement of the LORD, revealed to us as Jesus who, along with the Father and Spirit, is the one true and living God.

Praise the LORD for he is good (verses 4-5)

There is now a second call to praise (verse 4). It is to be an important element in our praise of God to 'be thankful' (see Psalm 97:12). We are to show our appreciation of God and what he has done for us. When this thanksgiving is done in public worship it has the effect of testifying to others what great things we owe to God. Meeting together as Christians to sing praises to God involves teaching one another and Paul encourages the giving of thanks 'always for all things to God the Father in the name of our Lord Jesus Christ' (Ephesians 5:20; see

Colossians 3:17). One of the characteristics of the ungodly world under the wrath of God is its unthankful spirit (Romans 1:21). Let that not be true of any Christian! To 'bless his name' suggests bending the knee in adoration for all that God has revealed of his nature and character (see Psalm 96:2).

The gates and courts of the earthly Zion and sanctuary where Israel gathered to worship were pictures and shadowy outlines of the reality of God's heavenly city and palace (see Psalms 9:14; 24:7; 65:4; 84:2; 87:2; 96:8). Isaiah prophesies of the time when in the new creation 'all flesh shall come to worship before me' (Isaiah 66:23). It is through Jesus Christ that Gentiles as well as Jews can approach God's holy presence (Ephesians 2:13, 18). 'Therefore by him let us continually offer the sacrifice of praise to God, that is, the fruit of our lips, giving thanks to his name' (Hebrews 13:15).

The final verse is introduced with 'For' making the cause for praise explicit. There is every reason for praising God when we remember that the 'LORD *is* good' (see Psalms 25:8; 34:8; 86:5). Jesus made it clear that absolute goodness is found in God alone (Mark 10:18). That goodness is spelled out here in terms of the LORD's unending 'mercy' ('his enduring love'; see Psalm 26:3; Isaiah 54:8, 10) and 'truth' ('his faithfulness' or 'dependability'; see Psalms 89:1; 92:2). Jeremiah pictures all nations hearing of the good things that the Lord has done for his people in cleansing and pardoning them. The city is once more full of joy and gladness and the song of the worshippers echoes the closing words of this psalm: 'Praise the Lord of hosts, for the Lord is good, for his mercy endures for ever' (Jeremiah 33:11). Peter encourages the scattered church of Jesus Christ throughout our world in a similar way: 'But you are a chosen generation, a royal priesthood, a holy nation, his own special people, that you may proclaim the praises of him who called you out of darkness into his marvellous light ...' (1 Peter 2:9-10).

Psalm 101

Ruling with Integrity

It often happens after elections have taken place that the incoming leader who is to form a new government will make a glowing statement promising to operate in a much more open and transparent way than the previous administration. The sceptics smile and mutter that they have heard it all before and wait for the bright ideas and good intentions to fall by the wayside as revelations of moral failure and lack of integrity begin to emerge.

This psalm of David's is the king's resolve to rule with integrity and to make sure that the seat of government is kept free of corruption and intrigue, to reward plain honest work and to put an end to all who are bent on doing harm in the land. Most commentators over the centuries understand the psalm to be David's statement of intent that he drew up on becoming the recognised ruler of all Israel. It became a practice among a number of puritan families of the 17th century for expositions of this psalm to be used by ministers called to give a sermon when a couple set up a new home or when a family moved to a new house.

Good intentions are fine but the reality is that all of us fail to live up to the standards we set ourselves. The life of David is a prime example. As the Bible faithfully records, he came to grief in his own personal life and was unable to prevent intrigue and scandal developing within the royal family and court let alone silence all trouble-makers in the land.

Why then do we have this psalm and why is it placed in Book 4 and not perhaps in Books 1 or 2 where the majority of David's psalms are found?

The psalm clearly demonstrates what the ideal king of God's people should be like and how he should govern. By placing it here, after psalms that have drawn attention to the tragedy of loss of city, king and land as a result of the Babylonian invasion, the compilers of the psalm collection draw attention to the reason why they presently do not have a king of David's family line ruling in Jerusalem. The Davidic kings have failed to live up to the ideal and they have been disciplined, as God's covenant with David indicated. All attention in Book 4 has been on God's rule under his covenant name LORD (Yahweh/Jehovah) and, as we have seen, they have pointed to a fulfilment in Jesus Christ. Did this mean that there was no place any more for a Davidic king? Would there be need for the promises to David to be reinterpreted if Yahweh/Jehovah has become king instead? By including this psalm of David at this point the compilers encouraged the faithful in Israel not to lose heart and faith in God's word but to see a much bigger picture where the fulfilment of God's promises in the Messiah of David's line would also mean the reign of Yahweh. The ideal king, to which Psalms 2, 18, 45 and 72 also look, is only to be found in God's Son, 'Jesus Christ our Lord, who was born of the seed of David according to the flesh', who is also revealed as Yahweh/Jehovah (Romans 1:3–4; Philippians 2:5–11).

The king's commitment to personal integrity (verses 1–4)

In this song with musical accompaniment addressed to Yahweh (see Psalm 57:9 for 'sing' and 'sing praises'), David declares first, his intention to celebrate two essential qualities for governing God's people—'mercy' ('steadfast love') and 'justice' ('judgment'—decisions that are fair and God-honouring). They are characteristics of God's rule and what God expects from his people (see Psalms 5:7; 33:5; Hosea 12:6; Micah 6:8). Jesus condemned the scribes and Pharisees for neglecting these more important matters of the law (Matthew 23:23).

Second, the king is committed to behaving wisely and succeeding in a lifestyle that is marked by integrity ('perfect' in the sense of no obvious defect, verse 2; see 'blameless' Psalm 64:4). To 'behave wisely' includes the idea of acting wisely and prospering (see Psalm 2:10; Isaiah 52:13) and this is what marked out David even before he became king when he was in the service of Saul (1 Samuel 18:5, 14, 30). We are also told that he had no intention of acting the hypocrite but desired to be true to himself and his own household (verse 2). Many leaders in national life try to convince themselves and others that their private morality has little or no bearing on their public office. That was not how David saw it.

Surprisingly, in the middle of verse 2 David cries out 'when will you come to me?' He is clearly aware of the need of divine aid to keep such a commitment. But it might also be a plea like the 'how long?' cries of earlier psalms, looking for God to come to him to assure him of his presence in his lonely and difficult position as head of state.

From this positive aim of living in a way that is transparent and without obvious defect, David mentions dangers to avoid.

He undertakes not to desire anything that is 'wicked' (verse 3; literally 'Belial', 'worthless'; see Deuteronomy 13:13; Psalm 41:8; 2 Corinthians 6:15). Sadly, David later allowed his eyes to wander and to lead him into grievous sin (see 2 Samuel 11:2; Psalm 51).

In aiming at the highest standards, he hates the action of those who deviate from God's commandments and vows that such wayward action will not grip hold of him.

Finally, he will make sure that a 'perverse' or 'twisted' heart, the very opposite of the 'perfect' heart of verse 2, will keep far away from him and he will not 'acknowledge' ('know'), he will have nothing to do with 'evil' (verse 4).

The king's commitment to public integrity (verses 5–8)

A righteous king seeks to root out all corruption and intrigue from the royal household ('house', verse 7; see verse 2). Negatively, this will involve him putting an end to anyone who 'slanders his neighbour' in secret (verse 5; see James 4:11). Neither will he tolerate a person who has a 'haughty look' ('lofty of eyes') or a 'proud heart' ('wide of heart'). David had to contend with this kind of treatment under Saul's regime (see the heading to Psalm 18; also Psalm 52). What David seeks to eradicate tallies with those matters of which God disapproves (see Psalm 15:3).

On the other hand, David aims to recognise ('my eyes *shall be* on', verse 6) those who are 'faithful' and who, like the king, are committed to a lifestyle that is characterised by integrity ('perfect', see verse 2).

These are the people he wants working for him as part of the royal administration ('dwell with me ... serve me').

In order that everyone in the king's service gets the picture straight, David reverts to making more negative statements. People who will not be welcome to live in the king's household or to stand before him as government ministers are those who practise 'deceit' and tell 'lies' (verse 7). Among the thing the Lord hates are 'a proud look' and 'a lying tongue' (Proverbs 6:16–17). David was a man after God's own heart. He was also a type of the Christ who will banish from his heavenly city 'whoever loves and practises a lie' (Revelation 22:15). This closing vision that John gives us catches the point of the king's final vow in the eradication of all that is immoral or profane. Not only will the king 'destroy' all the 'wicked' in 'the land', he will 'cut off' from 'the city of the LORD' all the 'evil-doers' (verse 8; see Psalm 75:10). The word 'Early' translates 'to the mornings' which possibly means 'morning by morning'. It was one of the main duties of the king to administer justice and early mornings were seen as the best time to hear lawsuits at the city gate (Jeremiah 21:12). Tragically, and from within David's own household, Absalom organised a successful coup against his father by rising early, listening to cases and gradually duping the people into rebelling against God's anointed ruler (2 Samuel 15:2)

David's good intentions for himself and his kingdom were spoiled by his own sin and weakness. As Motyer comments, 'there is here an ideal which exposes David and his successors as inadequate and cries out for the perfect David-to-be'. The reference to 'the city of the LORD' (Yahweh/Jehovah; verse 8) also directs us to the heavenly city of the living God (see Psalm 87; Hebrews 11:10, 16; 12:22).

Psalm 102

The Eternal, Unchangeable King

Here is a prayer that sets the psalmist's own sufferings in the context of wider concerns for the kingdom of God. It is an encouragement to distressed and hard-pressed Christians living in a hostile environment who are concerned at God's slowness in taking action. Bearing in mind the fleeting nature of human life, it directs believers to view their sufferings against the backdrop of the eternal and unchangeable God's great purposes for his people. At the same time the compilers of the collection wish us to see this psalm as a concern for God's people as a whole, viewed under the symbolism of the city of Zion.

The unusual heading and opening verses have suggested to many that the psalm is a personal lament and it has been traditionally placed among the seven penitential psalms (see Psalm 6). In Jewish circles it is considered an appropriate psalm for a fast day and as a prayer for rain. There is however no explicit confession of sin or expression of penitence, although there is an implied recognition that the psalmist's plight is due to the wrath of God (verse 10). Declarations of confidence are found and the psalm concludes on an optimistic note grounded in the truth of God's eternity.

Some have suggested that David composed it during the crisis over Absalom's rebellion and its aftermath while others think it is the work of a royal descendant of David during the exile period. What is clear is that the contents are well suited to its present position in Book 4. Like Psalm 94, which also contains a lament and cry for help, it reminds us of the psalm that heads up this particular collection (compare Psalm 90 with Psalm 102:4, 10–11, 23–28). The psalms that have been placed in Book 4 whether authored by Moses, David and his musicians or unknown prophetic poets of the exile, all are employed to respond to the crisis depicted in the psalms of Book 3, many of which were composed to convey the shock of the Babylonian invasion that resulted in the loss of land, temple and king.

The previous psalm ended with a reference to 'the city of the LORD' and concern for Zion is one of the features of this psalm (see verses 13–16, 21). It also follows on well after so many of the psalms in Book 4 that proclaim the Lord's kingship as we are reminded again of the eternal creator God over-against all that is temporal and temporary.

The psalm has a unique heading. There is no reference to who wrote it or to any musical directions for its use. Instead, and in view of the deliberately ambiguous way it is written, it describes the feelings of the one who composed it—it is the 'prayer' (see Psalm 17) of one 'afflicted' (see Psalms 9:12; 94:5)—and yet at the same time it is for any poor sufferer who is 'overwhelmed' (see Psalm 61:2) who 'pours out his complaint (see Psalms 55:2; 62:8) before the LORD'. We are encouraged to make this psalm our own as we pray not only when we are in personal need but in our concern for the suffering church of God worldwide as well as its apparent weakness and failure especially in the western world.

Initial cry for help (verses 1–2)
Familiar terms are used in this extended appeal to the Lord to listen to his petition. Many of the prayers of David employ similar language—'Hear my prayer' (Psalm 4:1); 'Do not hide your face in the day of my trouble ... answer me speedily' (Psalms 59:16; 69:17); 'incline your ear' (Psalm 17:6). There is an earnestness and urgency about the plea. What do we know of such groaning in prayer?

Frail humanity (verses 3–11)
The emphasis on 'day' (verse 2) prepares for the references to 'days' (verses 3, 11) that act like brackets around this section of the psalm. They highlight the fleeting nature of our lives and when 'days' appears

later in the psalm it contrasts with the 'years' of God's eternity (verses 23–24).

Familiar pictures are used to describe the brevity of life and to indicate how the psalmist feels inwardly ('heart') and outwardly ('bones') in his anguish (verses 3–4; see Psalm 6:2). His life is like 'smoke' (Psalm 37:20; Isaiah 51:6) and 'grass' (Isaiah 40:6–8). The references to days 'consumed' and to a heart 'withered' like grass (see also verse 11) take us back to the opening psalm of Book 4 (Psalm 90:5–6). As is often the case when we are troubled he has no appetite. All he can do is groan and this has all led to him becoming nothing but skin and bone (verse 5; see Psalm 22:17). The description he gives of himself is like the anguish and despair depicted in Lamentations as a result of the fall of Jerusalem in 587 BC (see Lamentations 1:13; 3:4, 16). He likens his loneliness, isolation and sleeplessness to that of solitary birds of the night that inhabit desolate places (verse 6–7).

To add to the desperate situation enemies are taunting him and are using his unhappy condition in their curse formulas—'May I end up like that if I do not keep this oath'. Instead of a catch-word for blessing (see Genesis 12:2) he has become the very opposite. The poetry is superb for describing his condition. Similar to previous situations where the psalmist imagines himself feeding on his tears so here he uses the metaphor of eating 'ashes' and mixing his drink 'with weeping' (verse 9). Ashes were used when someone was in deep mourning like Job who sat among the ashes. Job also spoke of repenting in dust and ashes (Job 2:8; 42:6; see Isaiah 61:3).

The psalmist now describes his sufferings as due to God's 'indignation' (verse 10; see Psalm 38:3) and 'wrath' (Psalm 38:1). The words used for God's displeasure are extremely forceful and different from those found in Psalm 90:7. Again, the imagery is remarkable as he depicts God like a raging whirlwind that lifts him up and tosses him away, in much the same way as chaff is blown away in the wind (Psalm 1:4; Isaiah 41:15–16). As he began so in closing the lament the psalmist refers to the fleeting nature of his life as 'grass' that withers (verse 11; see verse 4) and to his 'days' (verse 3) which are now likened to a 'shadow' that lengthens as the sun goes down (see Psalm 109:23; Jeremiah 6:4).

Greatness of God (verses 12–17)

The contrast between God's eternity and human mortality is marked by a very emphatic 'But you' (verse 12; see Psalm 22:3, 9, 19) over against the 'and I' of verse 11. God is not merely said to 'endure for ever'. More precisely the original reads that the Lord will 'sit' forever (see Psalms 9:7; 29:10). He sits enthroned forever, reminding us again of the truth set out so powerfully in Psalms 95 to 99. God's fame ('remembrance of your name') will endure to all generations (see Lamentations 5:19).

The psalmist now anticipates that the God who rules from his eternal throne will 'arise' to take action. He will show compassion ('mercy' verse 13) on 'Zion'. God is in overall charge of events and at the set moment in his schedule he will intervene. This is very reassuring in all crisis experiences to know that he has his 'set time' (see Psalm 75:2; Habakkuk 2:3) for acting to further his plans and purposes. It was the right moment in his plan, 'when the fulness of time had come', that God sent his son into the world to redeem his people (Galatians 4:4). In the context of the fall of Jerusalem and the exile in Babylon, the psalm is similar to Isaiah's prophecy concerning the return from exile in which he speaks of comforting good news for Zion (Isaiah 30:18-19; 40:1-11; 51:1). Like Daniel, who when he had read Jeremiah's prophecy concerning the number of years set by God for Jerusalem to remain desolate, made his moving earnest prayer for God to have mercy and take action (Daniel 9:2; see Jeremiah 29:10), so the psalmist is similarly appealing to God that he would be gracious toward the city. It encourages God's people in every age to humble themselves before him and in a time of declension when the church of God is in a poor and perilous state, to cry out that he would favour his people with a little reviving before the ultimate day of the Lord comes.

God's servants, the worshipping company of his people, do delight in God's city and the prayer encourages God, who has been favourable to his land previously, to again favour the dust and stones of what is left of Zion (verse 14). When Sanballat heard that Nehemiah and the Jews were rebuilding the Jerusalem walls, he was furious and ridiculed their efforts: 'What are these feeble Jews doing? ... Will they revive the stones from the heaps of rubbish?' (Nehemiah 4:2). The psalmist prays in faith that this will happen because he knows that God is more interested in the future of Zion than his people are. In his mind is the honour of God. If Zion is restored then the nations will revere the Lord and the kings of the earth will recognise the stunning greatness of God (verse 15; see Psalm 105:15). The same sentiments are prophesied by Isaiah (Isaiah 59:19).

The prophetic psalmist is confident that Zion will be rebuilt (verse 16; see Psalms 51:18; 69:35) and that God will be seen in his majestic splendour. Again, the words recall Isaiah's vision of the glory of God arising and the Gentile nations coming to God's light (Isaiah 60:1-3). What happened with the return from exile was but a foretaste of even greater things as the prophets Haggai and Zechariah made clear. Thus God will turn to hear the prayer of the 'destitute', those stripped naked, and will not despise their pleas. The prayer of 'the afflicted' (see the heading) does not go unnoticed or unanswered by God but it is noticeable that they are completely helpless. As we come naked to Christ for forgiveness and salvation, so that same humility is necessary as we seek God to revive his work in our churches.

A message recorded for posterity (verses 18-22)
This part of the psalm underlines and expands much of what has been said in the previous paragraph. It looks again with expectation and assurance. Verse 12 spoke of future generations remembering God's name and one way of ensuring that 'the generation to come' will 'praise the LORD' ('Yah'; verse 18), is to have a written record of the promises that are to be fulfilled (see Habakkuk 2:2-3). There is not only a future for an afflicted believer but also for the church of Jesus Christ despised and ridiculed by the secularists of the day.

Like Isaiah and Hosea, the psalmist looks to a new era of blessing, like a new creation, when those not a people will be the people of God and those who had not obtained mercy will receive mercy (see Isaiah 43:15; Hosea 1:10-2:1; 2:23; 1 Peter 2:10). The 're-creation' of Israel from those exiled in Babylon was a preparation and picture of what God would bring about for people of all nations in Christ. Paul declared that 'we are his workmanship, created in Christ Jesus for good works' (Ephesians 2:10).

Those promises to be written down include:

Firstly, God has looked down from heaven, from the heights of his holy place ('his sanctuary', verse 19; see Lamentations 3:50) in the same way that he looked on his people in Egypt in their distress (Exodus 2:25). Solomon appealed to God that he would 'hear in heaven your dwelling-place' and forgive and 'maintain their cause' (1 Kings 8:49). Even closer is the wording that Moses taught the people to pray: 'Look down from your holy habitation, from heaven, and bless your people Israel ...' (Deuteronomy 26:15).

Secondly, God heard the 'groaning of the prisoner' and acted to free those who felt as if they were on death row—'appointed to death' (verse 20; see Psalm 79:11). It is true that the Jews in exile did not suffer the same kind of bondage experienced by Israel in Egypt (see Jeremiah 29) and some were reluctant to leave Babylon when they had the opportunity. But those who came back and saw a new temple built and a return to some kind of life back in Jerusalem, did not consider themselves free. They were still under the rule of foreigners and this is expressed in Ezra's prayer where he speaks of being 'slaves' (Ezra 9:9). The Levites too, in leading the people in prayer, speak of their great distress at being 'servants' in the land God gave to their fathers (Nehemiah 9:36–37).

Thirdly, it will result in recounting the great works of the Lord and praising his name in Zion. When Zion is restored all peoples and kingdoms of the world will be gathered there to pay homage ('serve'; see Psalm 100:2) to the LORD (Yahweh/Jehovah; verses 21–22). Isaiah presents a similar picture of Zion and the Gentile nations (Isaiah 2:1–4; 60–62; see also Zechariah 14:16).

The not-yet of the present (verses 23–28)
The psalmist's present position and, by implication, that of Zion is not forgotten. These verses present a summary of all that has been said. It returns briefly to the lament with which the psalm began (verses 23–24a; see verses 1–11) but then it looks again to God's eternity (verses 24b–27; see verse 12) and is able to end on a confident note (verse 28; see verses 13–22).

What the psalmist had experienced is how the people of Jerusalem felt after the fall of their city and the end of the monarchy. He felt strong as he lived his life, just as the city had seemed impregnable, but then he had been humbled. It is God who had done this. He had brought him to a premature end. In the same way the city's life had been brought low in the prime of life. 'He shortened my days' (verse 23) is similar to how the king's removal into exile is described (Psalm 89:45). Despite what is happening to him he makes an earnest plea ('O my God', verse 24) that he might not be 'taken up' in mid-life. The verb translated 'take away' is used for removal out of this life to be with God (see 1 Kings 2:1). This thought reminds him again of God's eternity.

The contrast between the 'my days' of the psalmist and the 'your years' of God is powerful (verse 24; see verse 2), expressing once more human frailty and God's eternity. God goes on and on 'throughout all generations' (see verse 12). He also goes back in time to 'of old', for he is the creator of the universe (verse 25; see Psalms 8:3; 33:6). The poetry is again superb as God's eternity and unchangeable nature are expressed. Heaven and earth, which to humans represent all that is stable and lasting (see Psalms 78:69; 104:5; 119:90), will grow old and perish. Like clothes that are worn out and need changing so the present universe will be changed. Isaiah similarly looks to the present order coming to an end and the creation of a new heavens and a new earth (Isaiah 34:4; 51:6; 65:17; 66:22). But God remains the one great Reality (literally, 'But you are he') and his 'years' have no ending (verse 27). The writer to the Hebrews, using the words of Haggai the prophet, speaks of heaven and earth being shaken by God so that the kingdom of God which cannot be shaken may remain (Hebrews 12:25–29).

The earthly life of the psalmist has an end and Amos spoke of an end for the people of Israel with the arrival of the final covenant curse and their removal from the land (Amos 8:2). For those living after the Babylonian invasion, it was a devastating experience as they saw the end to their once beautiful city and temple and the end of David's dynasty. Yet, as Jeremiah encouraged the exiles, the Lord had good plans for his people's well-being 'to give you a future and a hope' (Jeremiah 29:11). The psalmist likewise looks beyond his present predicament; and so for the people of the exile, the psalm encourages God's people to appreciate that they will not die out but will 'continue' (literally 'dwell') and be securely established in God's presence. The psalm ends with this glorious hope for God's 'servants' and their descendants in the new creation where they will serve him and see his face (verse 28; see verse 22; Psalms 22:30–31; 69:35–36). In that new Jerusalem there will be no more curse: no death, no sorrow, no crying, no pain, 'for the former things have passed away' (Revelation 21:4; 22:3–4). What the psalmist suffered and the exile that the Jews experienced became symbolic of what would happen to the Messiah when he endured God-forsakenness before being raised to glory to see the fruit of his sufferings in Jew and Gentile united in serving the Lord.

Amazingly, the ancient Greek version of the Psalms, translated by Jews living in Alexandria well before the Christian era interpreted the Hebrew text to mean that God was addressing the psalmist in these final verses 24b–28 so that the whole psalm is applied to the Messiah, with the lament anticipating his sufferings (verses 1–11) and

the following verses pointing to his exaltation and worldwide rule
(verses 12–22, 28). It means that there were Jews around during our
Lord's earthly ministry who understood the Messiah to be one with
God in creating and ruling over all. The writer to the Hebrews after
quoting from Psalm 45:6–7 appeals to this psalm, using the Greek
version of verses 25 to 27, in support of the deity of God's Son, Jesus
Christ (Hebrews 1:10–12; see also Hebrews 13:8).

Psalm 103

Praising the Compassionate King

Matthew Henry, the famous commentator, heads his comments on this psalm by saying that it 'calls more for devotion than exposition'. Every line encourages us to worship God with a humble, grateful spirit for the LORD's kindness and love toward us. One of the greatest hymns in the English language, by Henry Francis Lyte is based on this psalm, *Praise, my soul, the King of heaven.*

The psalm is attributed to 'David' and it heads up a group of praise psalms that brings Book 4 to a grand conclusion. It fits very comfortably next to Psalm 102 with its references to God's universal kingship and eternity and the frailty of human existence where life is compared to grass that flourishes but is quickly gone (Psalm 102:3-4, 11, 12, 25-27 and Psalm 103:15-17, 19). Like other psalms in Book 4 it provides a response to the tragedy of exile to which attention is drawn in so many of the psalms of Book 3. Psalm 102 has also highlighted the present position of those living at a time when the people of God were mourning the loss of their city, temple and king. But it also contains words of hope based on the unchangeable nature of Israel's covenant-keeping God and it may well be that Psalm 103 is a response to that glorious future for all nations obtained through the saving work of the LORD and his Anointed (see Psalm 102:12-22, 27-28). Like the book of Isaiah, it also speaks of God's forgiving grace. David's appreciation

of God's pardon gives a repentant Israel the hope of experiencing the
same divine forgiveness and the hope that God will not continue his
anger toward them for ever.

The psalm mentions Moses and the time of the exodus from Egypt
(verse 7) and this again is a feature of Book 4 with its first psalm being
a prayer of Moses (Psalm 90). It was the period when Israel received
revelation concerning God's covenant name 'Yahweh/Jehovah' (LORD;
Exodus 33:12-34:7). The great characteristics of God impressed upon
Moses and the people at that time included his 'steadfast love' ('mercy/
loving-kindness') and 'compassion' ('tender mercies/merciful/pity') and
these are the terms that keep appearing in this psalm (verses 4, 8, 11, 13,
17). Interestingly, as we saw in the previous psalm, there are a number
of similarities to Isaiah's prophecy in which God's faithful love and
compassion are celebrated (see especially Isaiah 40:4-6; 54:7-8, 10; 55:3,
7, 9; 63:7).

Encouraging personal worship (verses 1-5)

The psalm opens with David exhorting himself (see Psalm 42:5) to
worship Israel's covenant-keeping God ('LORD') with the whole of his
being. He does not use the word 'praise' but 'bless' which suggests
paying homage (see Psalm 34:1). When God blesses it is in order to give
us what we need but when we bless God we are giving expression to
our appreciation of his goodness toward us. The God who is so kind
and gracious toward his people is still 'holy' (verse 1). His name refers to
all that God has revealed about himself and this can be summed up by
the term 'holy' (see Psalms 5:12; 99).

Worshipping Yahweh/Jehovah is not a mindless activity but one
in which we are urged to call to mind 'all his benefits' (verse 2).
The British government hands out many benefits to those in need.
Sometimes they are referred to as entitlements but that is certainly
not the idea in the psalm. We, like Israel of old, do not deserve any of
God's 'payouts', as the psalm will indicate (see verses 8-10). Time and
again Moses warned Israel not to 'forget' (Deuteronomy 4:9, 23; 6:12;
8:11; 32:18) and too often whether from the government or elsewhere
we can take benefits for granted, count them as a right and show no
gratitude. Each of us is urged not to ignore but to deliberately recall
'all' his gracious provisions. The word 'all' occurs many times in this
psalm (verses 1-3, 6, 19, 21-22). As one commentator has put it, this
psalm 'affirms that God, who rules over all and does all good things

for all persons in need, is to be praised in all places by all creatures and things with all of their being' (J. Clinton McCann).

The little chorus runs, 'Count your blessings, name them one by one' and that is what David does in the following verses. God's gracious benefits include:

1. The forgiveness of 'all' his 'iniquities' or wayward acts (verse 3; see Psalm 32:1). A special word for forgiveness is used which in previous psalms has been translated 'pardon' or 'forgive' (Psalms 25:11; 86:5). It is used in Moses' prayer (Exodus 34:9) and by Isaiah (Isaiah 55:7).

2. The healing of 'all' his 'diseases'. Healing often followed pardon in cases where disease or other suffering was the direct result of sin. Moses pleaded for healing when Miriam sinned and was punished with leprosy (Numbers 12:13). Psalm 107:20 refers to Israel's sin, suffering and healing. God had promised that if they obeyed him then none of the diseases of Egypt would come to them and added, 'For I am the LORD who heals you' (Exodus 15:26). Kidner reminds us that while forgiveness is given immediately for those with a repentant spirit, healing is sometimes denied as in the case of David's own family situation after the Bathsheba incident (2 Samuel 12:13-23). We thank God for what healing he does give in this life but these are foretastes of the complete healing that will come for God's people with the redemption of our bodies on the great resurrection day (Romans 8:23; 1 Corinthians 15:51-53). Jesus' healing ministry was also a foretaste of the future glory and the result of his atoning death as Matthew indicates by identifying him with the suffering Servant (Matthew 8:16-17).

3. Redeeming his life from 'destruction' (literally 'pit' verse 4; see Psalm 16:10). While David could be referring to being delivered from a premature death, he probably has in mind that redemption from what our sins ultimately deserve: the hell prepared for the devil and his angels (see Psalm 49:7-9, 14-15). The return from exile, symbolic of the release from sin's bondage, was like a second exodus (Isaiah 51:10-11; 52:9). God acts like a next-of-kin to deliver his people, and, as the word implies, a cost is involved. The death of the Passover lamb was associated with the redemption from Egypt and likewise our redemption is at the cost of the precious blood of Christ.

4. Crowning him 'with loving-kindness' ('steadfast love') and 'tender mercies' ('compassion'). The God who 'surrounds' the righteous with favour (Psalm 5:12), who 'crowns' the king (Psalm 21:3) and is said to

'crown' the year with his goodness (Psalm 65:11), 'encircles' him with loving commitment and a heart of compassion (see Psalm 51:1).

5. Satisfying him with 'good' (see Psalms 34:12; 84:11; 85:12) so that youthful energy is renewed (verse 5). The translation 'your mouth' (literally 'your ornament') is a guess and it is better to understand the term 'ornament' as a colourful way of speaking of his soul (see Psalm 16:9 where 'glory' is used in a similar way). David is thinking, like Isaiah's promise later (Isaiah 40:31), of being made strong like an eagle as it soars effortlessly in the sky.

God's caring character (verses 6–18)

David now moves from the singular ('my soul' verses 1-2) to the plural ('us', 'our', 'we' verses 10, 12-14) to speak more generally of God's grace to his covenant people. God has acted on behalf of all his 'oppressed' people. His 'righteousness' is his commitment to act in accord with his righteous nature and his 'judgments' or 'justice' is the carrying out of that commitment. All this was especially seen in the days of Moses when God's ways and acts were made known in the way God delivered them out of Egyptian slavery and by humiliating Pharaoh ('I will execute judgment' Exodus 12:12) and led them through to Canaan ('all the righteous acts of the LORD', 1 Samuel 12:7). In addition, as God revealed to Moses at the time of the golden calf incident, the LORD (Yahweh/Jehovah) is also 'merciful and gracious', patient ('slow to anger') and showing steadfast love in abundance ('abounding in mercy', verse 8; see Exodus 34:6; James 5:11).

More is said about God's anger. As the righteous judge, God is consistently indignant toward the wicked (Psalm 7:11) and he will by no means clear the guilty (Exodus 34:7). But he is 'slow' in expressing that anger. God gave ample warning before the great Flood. Then again, the extermination of the Canaanites came after centuries of divine patience as God indicated to Abraham when he informed him that the sin of the Amorites was not yet full (Genesis 15:16). The apparent slowness of the end-time judgment is because of God's patience, 'not willing that any should perish but that all should come to repentance' (2 Peter 3:9). God was also patient with his own people despite numerous provocations soon after they left Egypt. David's statement that God 'will not always strive' ('contend', verse 9) is similar to what God says later through Isaiah, 'I will not contend for ever, nor will I always be angry' (Isaiah 57:16). How can the true God who is holy and righteous allow sinners to go on living? Surely they must be brought to justice. How can God not continue to be angry with his sinful people? It is not part of his nature to be angry. God's anger is momentary (Psalm 30:5). He *becomes* angry on account of sin because he is holy. On the other hand, God *is* love and he has devised a righteous way to justify sinners and appease his wrath (see Romans 3:21–26). Yes, God still disciplines his people but he does not deal with us in the way our failings and rebellious acts deserve (see Hebrews 12:5–11). The word for 'punished' (or 'rewarded') is associated with the word 'benefits' (verse 10; see verse 2). This is our God.

The reason for his forbearance is again emphasised as the psalm dwells upon divine forgiveness. It is all due to the unlimited extent of God's 'mercy', his 'steadfast love' toward those who 'fear him' (verse 11; see Psalm 57:10; Isaiah 55:6–9). To the ungodly wicked (see Psalm 1:4) who remain stubborn and unrepentant, there is no forgiveness. But for those like David who revere God, who humble themselves and confess their sins there are no restraints to God's loving commitment toward his people. Paul prays that we might be able to comprehend with all the saints 'what is the width and length and depth and height—to know the love of Christ which passes knowledge' (Ephesians 3:18–19). God's forgiveness removes our rebellious acts against his revealed will ('transgressions') as far away from us as it is possible for us to think (verse 12).

Micah expresses in similar language God's forgiving grace toward his people: 'Who is a God like you, pardoning iniquity and passing over the transgression of the remnant of his heritage? He does not retain his anger for ever, because he delights in mercy. He will again have compassion on us, and will subdue our iniquities. You will cast all our sins into the depths of the sea' (Micah 7:18–19).

From infinite measurements (heaven above earth and east from west), David now likens Israel's covenant-keeping God to a father who shows compassion toward his children in the way that a woman yearns with compassion toward her baby (1 Kings 3:26). Again, this fatherly concern is toward those who 'fear him' (verse 13; see verse 11). God is very aware of our physical frailty because he originally formed us from the dust (Genesis 2:7; 3:19). It is human weakness rather than moral corruption that arouses God's pity here. In a similar way Isaiah in his prayer to God confesses 'You are our Father; we are the clay, and you our potter; and all we are the work of your hand' (Isaiah 64:8).

The mention of human frailty leads David to contrast this with the everlasting nature of God's loving commitment toward those who belong to him. We are like grass and the flower of the field that flourishes with the early rains of winter, but come the hot winds of summer and there remains no evidence of greenery or colourful petals (see Isaiah 40:6-8). Cyprus and the Near East are similar in this respect as I found on a recent visit to the island. Everywhere looked so barren and brown but then I was shown the difference that the winter rains make to the landscape. It is a powerful picture of the fleeting nature of human life and one that Book 4 has emphasised already (see Psalms 90:5-6; 102:3-4, 11). God's 'loving commitment' ('mercy') and 'righteousness' (see verse 6) toward his people, on the other hand, are like God himself, 'from everlasting to everlasting' (verse 17; see Psalm 90:2). The expression 'children's children' (literally 'sons of sons') picks up the reference in the previous psalm to the 'children' of God's people (literally, 'sons of your servants', Psalm 102:28). Mary's hymn of praise, in response to God's amazing grace toward her, echoes these words: 'his mercy is on those who fear him from generation to generation' (Luke 1:50). Again, this commitment is made to those who 'fear him'. What this means is spelt out in verse 18. It concerns those who are loyal to the covenant and its requirements ('commandments' or more accurately 'precepts'; see Psalm 111:7). God's covenant people are called to live obediently within the covenant bond. That is as true under the new covenant as under the old Sinai agreement. To those whom God has called into the fellowship of his Son, the constant call is to live in obedience to the Lord's commandments (see John 14:15; Philippians 2:12; I Peter 1:13-25).

Encouraging universal worship (verses 19-22)

As David brings this wonderful psalm to a close he reminds us that Israel's covenant-keeping LORD is the universal sovereign. He rules over the whole universe from his heavenly throne (see Revelation 4:2). Again, this would have been particularly appropriate for God's people in exile under the rule of foreigners with their own city and God's earthly palace a heap of rubble. It recalls the many psalms of Book 4 that proclaim Yahweh's kingship (see Psalms 93-99). The truth about God's sovereignty prepares for this renewed call to 'Bless the LORD' (see verses 1-2) which includes not only the psalmist but the angelic armies of heaven and the whole created order—'all his works' (verses 20–22; see Psalm 96:11–12). God's angels have been mentioned in Psalm 91:11. They are seen as strong warrior-like beings who do the LORD's bidding (see Psalms 24:10; 29:1). Angels are God's messengers who are always ready to carry out his wishes (see Matthew 4:11; 2 Thessalonians 1:7; 1 Peter 3:22). By emphasising the angelic obedience to God—'do his word', 'heeding (listening to) the voice of his word' and 'do his pleasure'—they are presented as an example to God's people of willing submission in the service of God. In this way they encourage us to worship God aright as Lyte's hymn suggests in his line 'Angels, help us to adore him'.

The psalm ends as it began but now, in view of all that has been mentioned, there is even more reason and support for doing so! In the light of who God is and especially his steadfast love and compassion toward his weak and wayward people, David encourages himself and each generation of those who love the Lord and seek to do his will, to express their heart-felt devotion to him.

Psalm 104

Praising the King's Providential Care

H ere is a hymn that meditates on God's greatness and goodness in ruling the world he has created. Robert Grant's (1779–1838) fine hymn, a one-time favourite in school assemblies but sadly, fallen out of favour with secular authorities and the church at large, is based on this psalm:

> O worship the King, All glorious above;
> O gratefully sing His power and his love;
> Our shield and defender, the Ancient of Days,
> Pavilioned in splendour And girded with praise.

The psalm is linked to the previous one by the only other occurrence of the call to 'Bless the LORD, O my soul' with which they both begin and end. Whereas Psalm 103 tells of the LORD's unfailing love toward his people in salvation, this psalm considers his greatness in managing the world he has made. It takes up and develops the subject of God's creative 'works' briefly mentioned in the closing verse of the previous psalm, praising God's many 'works' (Psalm 104:24; see also verses 13 and 31). The psalm reminded Israel after the crisis spoken of in Book 3 concerning the loss of king, city and temple that God is the universal king who has created all things for his glory.

These two Psalms 103 and 104 together reminded the people that his saving work on their behalf was part of something massive that took into account the whole created order. The same point is made by Isaiah when he looks into the future and comforts the exiles in Babylon with good news, reminding them that the God of salvation is the God of creation (Isaiah 40) and showing, in the remainder of his great prophecy, how redemption from sin through the suffering Servant leads to the recreation of all things. Similarly, Paul indicated that the gospel that saves individuals from their sins and brings them back into fellowship with the creator God through Jesus, is about God's plan concerning the whole cosmos (see Romans 8:17-25; Ephesians 1:19-22; Colossians 1:20).

Psalm 104 can be seen as a meditation on Genesis 1-3 beginning with God's satisfaction with all he had made and his evaluation—'it was very good' (Genesis 1:31), but also taking into account human sin, its effects and eradication. A feature of this psalm is the way God can be addressed directly as 'you' and 'your' and then in the next breath spoken of indirectly as 'he' and 'his' (see for example verses 9-10, 19-20, 30-32). As Motyer comments, 'the Creator is both "he" and "you", a God observed in his works and also personally known'.

God's greatness and splendour (verses 1-4)

The psalmist stirs himself up to pay homage to Israel's covenant-keeping God, the King of creation—'Bless the Lord, O my soul!' (see Psalms 103:1; 42:5). Though God is so great and majestic, we are made to have a personal relationship with him—'O Lord my God' (verse 1). The greatness, 'honour' and 'majesty' of God's kingly splendour (see Psalms 93:1; 96:6) is seen in his creative activity. Producing light was the first of God's creative acts (Genesis 1:3-4) but here we are reminded that God is light and the source of all light in the expanding universe (verse 2; see Isaiah 40:22; Jeremiah 10:12; 1 Timothy 6:16; 1 John 1:5). While the Genesis account is presented in stately sober prose, the psalmist uses poetry to convey the truth of God's creation. We must therefore be careful not to take the colourful imagery in a literalistic way. The 'upper chamber' (verse 3; see verse 13) denotes the upper room of a house and God's heavenly dwelling is viewed as above the clouds or 'waters' of the firmament (see Genesis 1:7). He sits enthroned above many waters, as he did over the Flood (see Psalm 29:3, 10). The clouds that are moved across the sky by the wind are likened to God's chariots all expressive of a God who is not only transcendent over all but one who is continually active in his creation (see Psalm 18:10). We need to remind ourselves that God is not the pantheistic god of the New Agers who is to be identified with all that is created. Neither is God like the 18th and 19th century remote god of the deists, who believed that, having created and set in motion the universe, he left it to tick away like a clock.

God also makes his agents ('angels' or ministering spirits) like 'winds' ('spirits') and a 'flame of fire' (verse 4) carrying out swiftly and effectively all God's wishes on behalf of his people (Hebrews 1:14). The writer to the Hebrews quotes this verse as he did Psalm 102:25–27 to show how the Son is so much greater than the angels. Angels are in the service of God while the Son is one with God the Father (Hebrews 1:7–12).

The stability of the earth (verse 5–9)

These verses can be compared with similar poetic descriptions of creation in Job 38:3–30 and Proverbs 8:22–31. The earth is established on firm foundations (verse 5; see Psalm 93:1) but at first it was covered with water (Genesis 1:2). The verses depict poetically what is presented more prosaically in Genesis 1:9–10. There is nothing in the context to suggest that these particular verses are describing the account of the Flood, although that awesome event did mean a return to the conditions that existed before God separated the waters from the dry land and to an eventual recreation similar to Genesis 1 (see Genesis 7:17–20; 8:1–5, 13). The important point that is emphasised through the creation and Flood accounts is that God has set the boundaries of the ocean depths, and although tsunamis do occur and sea defences give way during tidal surges, the waters that cover so much of the earth will not 'return to cover the earth' (verse 9). Only on that one occasion did God allow the great deluge to happen as a punishment for human sin and as a preview of the final day of wrath when fire will be the instrument of judgment (2 Peter 3:5–7, 10–13).

Sustaining the earth (verses 10–18)

God's activity in caring for his creation is emphasised in this section where verses 16 to 18 provide a mirror image of verses 10 to 13 with verses 14 and 15 being the centre point. The waters, that seemed so threatening, are made to benefit the earth and its inhabitants. While rain 'waters' the mountains from the 'upper chambers' (verse 13; see verse 3), springs stream down from the 'hills' to provide drink for the animals (verses 10–11, 18) and to give nourishment to the trees (verses 12, 16) so that the birds can find a home in the branches and give voice to their satisfaction (verses 12, 17). Were it not for the rain, earth's land surface would become dry and parched but through God's activity ('your works'; see Psalm 103:22), it drinks in the water and is 'satisfied' (verse 13). The description of the hills and valleys flowing with water, providing food for animals and humans, echoes the view of Canaan given by Moses in contrast to the entirely different situation that existed in Egypt (Deuteronomy 11:10–12, 14–15).

God made the original unformed and uninhabitable earth (Genesis 1:2) into a habitable place so that humans and animals could thrive (Genesis 1:29–30) and that is the point to which our attention is drawn in verses 14 and 15. Long before 21st century humans became interested in ecology the psalmist was celebrating 'God's marvellous adaptation of the earth's resources to the needs of living creatures, and vice versa' (John Stott). Crops enabled people to produce 'bread' ('food'), 'wine' and olive 'oil', three of the most essential products for Israel but the phrase 'for the service of man' (verse 14) indicates that the psalm is not only thinking of Israelites but humanity in general. Despite the initial rebellion and the curse that God put on the ground (Genesis 3:17–19) God has continued to give these earthly benefits to all humanity. Paul informed the pagan people of Lystra that God had not left himself without witness 'in that he did good, gave us rain from heaven and fruitful seasons, filling our hearts with food and gladness' (Acts 14:17). Sadly, we abuse God's good provisions by excessive eating and drinking so, as Calvin points out, Paul had good reason for giving that prohibition, 'put on the Lord Jesus Christ, and make no provision for the flesh' (Romans 13:14). Self, as Lloyd-Jones stated, 'is the cause of all our troubles—drunkenness ... envying, strife—all these are but manifestations of self'.[52]

Regulating times and seasons (verses 19–23)

The Lord's providential care oversees the rhythm of night and day and holiday 'seasons' (see Genesis 1:4–5, 14–19). It is the moon that governs the timing of Israel's great festivals (Leviticus 23:4; 2 Chronicles 2:4; Ezra 3:5). The variation in Passover-Easter from year to year is based on when the full moon occurs during March-April. By God's decree, it is the sun that regulates day and night and God promised after the Flood that while the earth remained 'day and night shall not cease' (Genesis 8:22). The night is seen as providing safety for wild animals, represented by the 'young lions' (verse 21), to prowl under the cover of darkness. That is when they seek their prey. When dawn breaks they gather together to lie down in their dens. On the other hand, the sunrise is the time for humans to wake up and work until the sun goes down.

Scholars often draw attention to some similarities between this section of the psalm and the hymn of Pharaoh Akhenaton who died around 1336 BC. But interestingly, as if to counter the pagan Egyptian's devotion to the sun god, the psalm considers the moon before the sun and also emphasises God's role in controlling darkness as well as ensuring the sun's obedience as to when to set and rise each day.

Celebrating the wisdom of God (verses 24–30)

As the psalmist surveys the wonders of creation and God's continuing provisions for all his creatures, he cannot but burst out in praise: 'O LORD, how manifold are your works! in wisdom you have made them all' (verse 24; see Psalm 8:1). The variety and richness that we see in creation—scientists are still finding and are amazed by new life forms and species—witness to God's wisdom, to his skill and purposeful planning. This is a subject that is especially expounded in Proverbs (see Proverbs 3:19; 8:22–31). Wisdom, as the New Testament indicates, is especially associated with Jesus Christ, in whom are hid 'all the treasures of wisdom and knowledge' and by him and for him all things were created and it is through him that everything is sustained (Colossians 1:16–17; 2:3).

The earth is full of God's creations or 'possessions' even in the sea! Instead of the sinister 'deep' (verse 6), the 'great and wide sea' is a place teeming with life 'both small and great' (verse 25). The reference to 'Leviathan' might seem surprising but this creature, which in Ancient Near-Eastern mythology was a seven-headed dragon (see Psalm 74:14), is seen as one of God's large animals that he has made to romp around in the sea. Animals use the same sea as humans, the one for play, the other for trade as they sail from place to place in their 'ships' (verse 26).

What theologians describe as 'common grace' is presented to us here. God is good to all and sends rain and sunshine on all alike, whether righteous or unrighteous (Matthew 5:45). It is a demonstration of the richness of God's goodness, forbearance and long-suffering toward a rebellious people and such goodness is meant to lead us to repentance (Romans 2:4). All, people and animals, are dependent on God for their food and breath. These are the two basic ingredients for life on earth.

First, the psalm deals with food, a subject already considered in previous verses. The phrase 'in due season' continues the emphasis on times and seasons (see verses 19 to 23). Particularly in mind is God's promise that, 'While the earth remains, seedtime and harvest, and cold and heat, and winter and summer, and day and night shall not cease' (Genesis 8:22). Harvest is the time when God's hand is 'filled with good'. God gives the food that all seek but his creatures are also actively involved in gathering it in (verses 27-28; see Psalm 145:15-16).

From food, the psalm moves to 'breath' (verse 29). Lack of food can lead to loss of breath, but again, the emphasis is on God's active involvement in the giving and taking away of the breath of life. The verse alludes to the curse of death as a result of that initial great rebellion (Genesis 3:19) but there are also echoes of what God said at the time of the great Flood, especially the references to God's Spirit and the destruction of 'all flesh in which is the breath of life' (see Genesis 6:3, 17). When God turns away his face ('You hide your face') it means he is displeased and will discipline or punish people (see Deuteronomy 31:17; Psalm 13:1). David used similar wording when God 'troubled' him (Psalm 30:7). The word 'troubled' is a very strong term. It means to be dismayed or terrified (see Psalm 6:2-3). This is not the world before the Fall but life as it is at present. God, who graciously gives in his kindness to all, does also remove those benefits and then people and animals are greatly agitated. It is God who 'gathers up their breath', that vital element of life (see Genesis 2:7; 6:17; 7:22) and so 'they die and return to their dust'. Death is the result of Adam's sin. The same word 'die' or 'expire' is used in the account of the Flood (Genesis 7:21-22) while 'return to their dust' reminds us of Moses' prayer (Psalm 90:3; see Psalm 103:14) and God's words to Adam (Genesis 3:19). In a similar way the Preacher forcefully impresses on us the fragility of human and animal life and that in death 'the dust will return to the earth as it was, and the spirit will return to God who gave it' (Ecclesiastes 12:7; see Job 34:14-15).

Life continues on earth only because God wills it. The Lord who pronounced the death sentence in Eden also spoke of life and victory through the woman's 'seed' and Eve was given her name by Adam, 'because she was the mother of all living' (Genesis 3:15, 20). God is the one who creates life by his 'breath' or 'Spirit' (verse 30). The same Hebrew word can mean 'breath', 'wind' or 'spirit'. By using 'spirit' with or without a capital letter, we distinguish between our human breath and the divine breath with which we are animated. By using a capital ('Spirit') we remind ourselves that God by his Spirit works to give both physical and spiritual life (Genesis 1:2; Psalm 139:7; Romans 8:9). Every new life is amazing and wonderful and is the result of God's creative power. In picking up our food from the supermarket or having it delivered, we can sometimes forget that God is living and active in our world and that we are dependent on him seeing that 'he gives to all life, breath, and all things' (Acts 17:25). So too, with all the scientific advances of recent decades, we can assume we are in ultimate charge of life and death issues, whereas we need to remember that God is the creator and sustainer of our lives, in whom 'we live and move and have our being' (Acts 17:28).

He is also the one who keeps on renewing 'the face of the earth' (verse 30) from year to year in the same kind of way that David prayed that God would renew a steadfast spirit within him (Psalm 51:10). The God who renewed the earth after the desolation caused by the Flood is the one who is behind every renewal, whether after devastating natural or man-made disasters or the burst of new life in Spring-time. If this is true of God concerning his providential care of all life this must have been an encouragement to the people of the exile that he would also bring about the renewal promised by God through Moses and the prophets (Deuteronomy 30:1-10; Ezekiel 37; Hosea 1:10-2:1; etc.). It remains true for Christians today as we pray for a renewing and reviving of God's work that will eventually involve the renewing of all things when Jesus returns in glory (Matthew 19:28; Romans 8:19-22).

Concluding song of praise (verses 31-35)

The psalmist expresses the desires of his heart in this final outburst of devotion to God.

In the first place, he wishes to see the revelation of the LORD's stunning greatness and importance ('glory') continuing forever and that God will be able to 'rejoice' in 'his works' (verse 31; see verses 13, 24). These are the 'works' that were encouraged to worship the LORD (Psalm 103:22). Usually it is people who rejoice but this may be a more dramatic way of expressing what is more prosaically put at the end of the creation account: 'God saw everything that he had made, and indeed it was very good' (Genesis 1:31; see Proverbs 8:31). But as in verse 29 God's judgments must not be forgotten either. It only takes a look from him and the earth trembles, one touch and the hills smoke, language that reminds us of God appearing on Mount Sinai (Exodus 19:16, 18), but here speaking of God's wrath and indignation (Deuteronomy 32:22; Psalm 144:5–6). Though he is good he is not safe. He is a God to be feared for he is a consuming fire (Deuteronomy 4:24; Hebrews 12:29). It anticipates the psalmist's further wish in verse 35.

Secondly, the psalmist determines to spend the rest of his life (bearing in mind what he has said about the breath that God gives him in verse 29) singing and making music to Yahweh/Jehovah his God ('the LORD ... my God', verse 33; see Psalm 146:2). This psalm is an example of what he wishes to sing. It is his 'meditation' (verse 34; see Psalm 19:14) and he hopes it will be as 'pleasing' ('sweet') as righteous offerings (Malachi 3:4).

Thirdly, he desires that 'sinners', those whom the psalms have many times referred to as the ungodly 'wicked' (see Psalm 1:4), will come to an end ('consumed from the earth') and 'be no more' (verse 35). This world is not the perfect world that was originally created and even the world that was renewed after the Flood was still inhabited by sinners. The psalmist looks to the grand and final day of renewal and restoration in that new creation, the home of righteousness (2 Peter 3:13), when 'the cowardly, unbelieving, abominable, murderers, sexually immoral, sorcerers, idolaters, and all liars shall have their part in the lake which burns with fire and brimstone, which is the second death' (Revelation 21:8). These are people like Belshazzar, punished because he did not honour the God 'who holds your breath in his hand and owns all your ways' (Daniel 5:23; see verse 29).

The hymn concludes as it began with the psalmist taking himself in hand and urging himself to worship the LORD (see verse 1). Unlike Psalm 103 there is a further word to the whole worshipping congregation of God's covenant people to 'Praise the Lord' (literally 'Praise ye Yah', using the shorter form of Yahweh; see Psalm 68:18). We all know the Hebrew phrase as 'Hallelujah!' (see Psalms 105:45; 106:1, 48) and it is one that will be often heard in Book 5.

Psalm 105

Praising the LORD's Saving Activity

Count von Zinzendorf, the leader of the 18th century Moravian movement, has a hymn which includes the lines,

> O Lord, enlarge our scanty thought,
> To know the wonders thou hast wrought;
> Unloose our stammering tongues to tell
> Thy love immense, unsearchable.

Thinking about God's wonderful works on behalf of his people should excite us to praise him in song and speech. This is what our psalmist is seeking to do here. The first six verses encourage the people to praise God while the remainder of the poem explains why they should do so. It takes in the whole sweep of God's dealings with his people from the time of Abraham to the conquest of Canaan. What God did for Israel was in preparation for his even greater work in sending his Son to be the Saviour of the world.

The previous psalm exhorted a despondent people after the Babylonian exile to consider God's care of his people and to praise God especially for keeping his covenant with creation after the Flood. This psalm also urges the same people to praise God but this time by remembering God's covenant with Abraham and how the promises he made were wonderfully fulfilled in bringing the people out of Egypt and into the promised land. The first fifteen verses of this psalm are also found in the account of how David brought the ark of the covenant into Jerusalem (1 Chronicles 16:8–22; see Psalm 96).

Call to praise (verses 1–6)

The psalm opens urging the people to give thanks to Yahweh/Jehovah or acknowledge him for what he has done in the past and that has benefited each succeeding generation right up to the present. They are urged to 'call upon his name' (verse 1), which suggests in this context, not using God's name as the basis of prayer (see Psalm 116:4) but proclaiming it by making known his deeds among the people groups of the world. God's 'deeds' are those that are recounted in the rest of the psalm and they provide testimony to his reputation ('his name'), especially his power and sovereignty (see Isaiah 12:4).

They are further urged to sing, make music and 'meditate' ('talk', verse 2; see Psalm 1:2) concerning all God's 'wonderful acts' particularly in redeeming his people from slavery in Egypt (see Psalm 9:1). God's people are to 'boast' ('glory'; see Psalm 34:3) in all for which the 'holy name' Yahweh/Jehovah ('LORD') stands (verse 3). Those who 'seek' God's favourable look (see Psalm 27:8) in communal worship and prayer are exhorted to 'rejoice' and go on seeking him, drawing on his 'strength' and seeking his presence continually (verse 4). The terms used for seeking God are employed by the compiler of Chronicles to encourage God's people, now back in their own land after the exile, to look to the Lord for help rather than rely on the feeble aid that humans can give (1 Chronicles 5:20; 28:9; 2 Chronicles 15:2; 20:4). How Christ's church needs to be reminded of this constantly so that they do not fall into the trap of rushing into the frantic efforts that are sometimes made to further God's cause! Why is vital, urgent prayer so low down the list of priorities for many church ministers and members?

The people are urged again to call to mind what God did in Egypt at the time of the exodus ('marvellous works', verse 5; same as 'wondrous works', verse 2; Exodus 3:20). God's 'wonders' refer particularly to the 'plagues' that struck the Egyptians (Exodus 7:3; Psalm 78:43) while the 'judgments of his mouth' are about the Lord's great decisions concerning Pharaoh and his people (Exodus 6:6; 7:4; 12:12).

In this call to praise, the psalmist leaves till last the people he is addressing. This is in order to emphasise who they are and to prepare them for the primary reason why they are to give thanks and sing to the LORD (see verses 7–11). There was a long-running television series on BBC 1 entitled 'Who do you think you are?' where celebrities were shown how far back their ancestors could be traced, either from royal or humble origins. Here God's people are reminded that they are the 'seed' or 'offspring' of Abraham, and 'sons' or 'descendants' of Jacob (verse 6). They are Israel, God's 'chosen' people, and God is as committed to them as he was to Abraham 'his servant' (see verse 42; Genesis 26:24; Psalms 18 and 90). It is both a privileged and responsible position but it also means that they come under God's special care and protection. Jesus encourages his followers to appreciate that they are his servants and those who serve him will be honoured by God (John 12:26; 13:16; 15:15, 20). Paul also reminds Christians that if we belong to Christ, 'then you are Abraham's seed, and heirs according to the promise'. We belong 'to the household of faith' and can be called 'the Israel of God' (Galatians 3:29; 6:10, 16).

Reasons for praise (verses 7–45)
As in other praise psalms like Psalm 92, after the exhortation to give thanks and sing comes the reasons or motives for doing so, which at the same time provide more content to the praise psalm. In this case it is a historical overview of God's gracious and powerful activity on behalf of his people that is celebrated. What an encouragement to a forlorn people during or after the exile to read and sing these words!

1. The LORD's promises (verses 7–11)
Yahweh/Jehovah, Israel's God ('our God') is no local god, for his 'judicial decisions' ('judgments'; see verse 5) cover 'all the earth' (verse 7) which is why the 'peoples' of the world need to know him (verse 1). His rule is effective throughout the earth. Too often today we hear people speaking of the Christian God as if he were just one among many deities worshipped, whereas the God and Father of our Lord Jesus Christ is the only true and living God.

When it states that God 'remembered his covenant' (verse 8) it means that he has acted on what he has promised and has been doing so ever since he first entered into that special relationship and agreement with Abraham and he intends to keep on doing so 'for ever'. The 'thousand generations' (see Deuteronomy 7:9) also implies that he will continue keeping his word into the future. All God's words of promise are as authoritative and effective as his commands.

The covenant that God made with Abraham and which he renewed with the chosen line through Isaac and Jacob, concerned in essence the promise of many descendants and the gift of land (see Genesis 15:18; 17:2, 8; 26:3-4; 28:13-14). This covenant God originally 'made' (literally 'cut'; see Psalm 50:5) in a special sacrificial ritual in which God, under the symbols of smoke and fire, put himself under a solemn self-curse were he to fail to keep his promise (Genesis 15:9-12, 17-18; Jeremiah 34:18-20). It does not lapse with time but is a firm commitment for all time. It is like God's law, it is a 'statute' that is laid down in writing. The term 'Israel' draws in not only Jacob himself but his descendants. God has measured out ('the allotment'; see Psalm 78:55; Deuteronomy 32:9) the land of Canaan as their 'inheritance'. That land was a picture and symbol of the future inheritance that God has in store for all his people in the new creation (Matthew 5:5; Romans 4:13-18; Hebrews 6:12; 11:13-16; Revelation 21:1-7).

2. The Lord's protection (verses 12-15)

There was a time when the original family members were 'few in number' (verse 12). They had difficulty producing children and even Jacob's family could be numbered instead of being a people too many to count as God's promise had indicated (Genesis 22:17; 34:30; 46:27). Apart from a cemetery, Abraham and his family did not possess any land in Canaan but moved about like resident aliens (Genesis 23:4; 35:27; Hebrews 11:8-10, 13) among the Canaanites, the Philistines and the Egyptians.

To a people feeling the effects of God's curse during the exile, when they were scattered 'among the peoples' and left 'few in number among the nations' as God indicated to Moses (Deuteronomy 4:27; see Isaiah 1:9), such words would renew confidence and hope in God's promises. For Christians living under persecution or feeling the pressure of being a small minority we are encouraged to look with John at that great multitude which no one could number (Revelation 7:9).

God protected Abraham from kings like the Pharaoh of Egypt and Abimelech, king of Gerar (verse 14; see Genesis 12:17; 20:1-3). He also enabled him to obtain a notable victory over the kings of the east (Genesis 14). Abraham is spoken of as a prophet (Genesis 20:6-7) but the term probably applies more generally, like the word 'anointed' (verse 15; see Psalm 2:2), to all the original ancestors in that they were all specially chosen by God to carry out his purposes (see Isaiah 45:1 where it is used of the Persian king Cyrus). God prevented Abimelech from touching Sarah and we are also informed that the king of the Philistines later instructed his people not to touch Isaac or his wife (Genesis 26:11, 29).

3. The Lord's providence (verses 16–25)

These verses summarise the events surrounding Joseph's time in Egypt. It begins by showing God's providential care during a severe famine. Yahweh/Jehovah is seen as sovereign in that he summoned the famine and broke their life support ('provision of bread', literally 'staff of bread', verse 16) even in the land of Canaan. God did it then to indicate, as Matthew Henry suggests, 'that they might plainly see God designed them a better country than that was'. The same phrase 'supply/provision of bread' is used in connection with God's judgment on Jerusalem (Leviticus 26:26; Isaiah 3:1; Ezekiel 4:16; 5:16) so that this reference would again encourage God's people in exile to look for God to change their situation for the better and to see the period as a time of testing and refining his people (see verse 19; Jeremiah 9:7).

He planned for Joseph to be in that prominent position in Egypt after suffering great deprivations to provide wise government in times of hardship (verses 17–22; Genesis 37, 39–45). 'He sent a man before them' (verse 17) calls to mind those two remarkable statements that Joseph made to his brothers: 'God sent me before you to preserve a posterity for you in the earth ... So now it was not you who sent me here, but God' and then later, 'But as for you, you meant evil against me; but God meant it for good' (Genesis 45:7–8; 50:20). The people of God can be assured in every difficult circumstance of life that all things do work for good to those who love God (Romans 8:28).

From the time Joseph received those initial dreams of greatness that God gave him and which he shared with his family (Genesis 37) until he became the grand vizier of Egypt (Genesis 41:37–46) proved a period of severe testing but he came through all the stronger for it (verse 19). His 'wisdom' (verse 22) among the wise men of Egypt is comparable to Daniel's position among the Babylonian wise men (Daniel 2:48).

Joseph's father and family arrived in Egypt, called 'the land of Ham' (verse 23; Psalm 78:51; see Genesis 10:6 'Mizraim' being the Hebrew for Egypt), and 'sojourned' there. God's people increased in number, or more literally 'made his people very fruitful' (verse 24) so that eventually it provoked the hatred of the Egyptians and prompted them to form crafty policies to reduce the immigration figures (verse 25; Exodus 1:9–10).

4. The Lord's plagues (verses 26–36)

As it states in the exodus narrative (Exodus 3:10; 4:27–31), the LORD sent 'Moses his servant' (see Exodus 14:31) and his brother Aaron 'whom he had chosen' (verse 26; see Psalm 77:20). The plagues are specially mentioned using the familiar words 'signs' and 'wonders' (verse 27; see Exodus 7:3; Deuteronomy 6:22; 7:19; 26:8; 34:11; etc.). These miracles, like the miraculous signs of Jesus, reinforced God's message to Egypt (see John 12:37). As in all the previous episodes it is Yahweh/Jehovah who is actively involved not only in choosing his servants but in bringing about the various disasters, and the emphasis is on God's word and speech (verses 28, 31, 34; see verses 8, 19). Not all ten plagues are mentioned and the order is different to the Exodus account (see Exodus 7–12). Missing are the cattle disease and the boils. Enough are given to emphasise God's sovereignty over the Egyptians as well as over creation itself.

As expected the final plague that struck 'all' the first-born in Egypt (see Psalm 78:51) is placed last but the first disaster to be highlighted is the uncanny 'felt' darkness of the ninth plague that covered the land (verse 28; see Exodus 10:21–22). After this plague Moses spoke no more to Pharaoh (Exodus 10:28–29) and although the king's heart was hardened the death of the first-born that followed forced the Egyptians into submitting to God's words and letting Israel go free (verse 28). Darkness in many of the prophetic writings is used as a symbol of judgment, especially of Yahweh/Jehovah's day of disaster. Joel writes of 'the day of the LORD' as a 'day of darkness and gloominess, a day of clouds and thick darkness' (Joel 2:1–2; see also Amos 5:18, 20; Zephaniah 1:15). The Babylonian exile is seen as a pointer to the final day of judgment (Isaiah 13:9–11). God is said to live in thick darkness and that darkness of God's awesome, mysterious presence is what Abraham and later Moses experienced (Genesis 15:12; Exodus 20:21). A similar darkness enveloped the land when our Saviour bore God's wrath during those three hours as he hung upon the cross (Mark 15:33) so that none of his people might endure that outer darkness where there is weeping and gnashing of teeth.

5. The Lord's provision (verses 37–41)

In the end the Egyptians were glad to see the back of Israel and gave them items of gold and silver to send them on their way (verses 37–38; see Exodus 3:21–22; 11:2–3; 12:33, 35–36; 15:16). But it was Yahweh/Jehovah who had done it. He had brought them out loaded with precious metals and what is more, they had all made it, not one was too 'feeble' to escape (verse 37; Exodus 12:41, 51).

God also provided for his people's safety and guidance with the pillar of cloud and fire (verse 39; Exodus 13:21–22; Numbers 9:15–23; Psalm 78:14). The people of God today are similarly provided for and protected by God's presence (Isaiah 4:5–6).

> Round each habitation hovering,
> See! the cloud and fire appear,
> For a glory and a covering,
> Showing that the Lord is near.[53]

Psalm 91:1 presents a similar picture of security and we can be assured that as Christians journey to that celestial home that neither principalities nor powers can separate us from the love of God in Christ Jesus our Lord (Romans 8:38–39).

God also satisfied their hunger and thirst during the wilderness wanderings (verses 40–41; Psalm 78:16, 20, 25–27; see Exodus 16:4, 13; 17:1–7; Numbers 11:31). It is noticeable that no mention is made in this psalm to the people's grumbling and lack of faith. That is left for other psalms (Psalms 78; 106). This psalm is set here to encourage a new generation after the exile to look to the Lord for help and guidance that they might prosper once more. It all prepares for that end-time situation that Isaiah prophesies when the desert will blossom and the dry land will become springs of water to satisfy his chosen people (Isaiah 35:1; 41:18; 43:19–20).

6. Obedience (verses 42–45)

The psalm returns to the statement made in verses 8 and 9 concerning God's covenant with Abraham and his offspring. All that has been related thus far is proof that God has kept his 'holy promise' (literally 'holy word'; see verse 8). Yahweh/Jehovah brought out his 'chosen' people (verse 43; see verse 6) with joy and gladness to give them the 'lands of the Gentiles' as he had promised to Abraham (Genesis

15:13–16). They possessed the results of what the Canaanites had toiled to build up in terms of cities, houses and crops (verse 44; see Deuteronomy 6:10–11).

All this God did in order that his people might 'observe his statutes and keep his laws' (verse 45; see Deuteronomy 6:23–25). Up to this point there has been no mention of God's covenant at Sinai when God gave the law to his people. The way the psalm has been set out indicates that the keeping of God's laws is to be seen in the light of his gracious saving actions and provisions. There is to be nothing legalistic about their obedience. Keeping God's commandments is to be an expression of gratitude for all that God has done on their behalf. In the same way, Christians, as they view God's salvation that has come to them through Jesus Christ, are called to a life of obedience to God's will (Ephesians 4:17–32; Philippians 2:12–16; 1 Peter 1:13–21).

The 'Hallelujah' ('Praise the LORD', verse 45) is a fitting end to this praise psalm that has focused so much on the fulfilment of God's promises to Abraham. Those promises find that ultimate fulfilment in Christ and Christians should not be slow in praising the God from whom all blessings flow.

Psalm 106

Praising the LORD's Loving Commitment

As a number of commentators have observed, Psalms 105 and 106 are 'twin psalms' but they are certainly not identical! Psalm 105 reviews Israel's history to celebrate God's faithfulness to the promises made to Abraham without any mention of Israel's faithlessness. This psalm reviews the same history again to celebrate God's faithful love toward his people but this time it is highlighted by a confession of Israel's faithlessness. Like Psalm 105 and Psalm 96, parts of this psalm (verses 1 and 47-48) are similar to the song of thanksgiving that the Chronicler attached to the event of the ark's arrival in Jerusalem (1 Chronicles 16:34-36). In drawing attention to Israel's repeated ingratitude and sinfulness, Psalm 106 bears some resemblance to Psalm 78 but whereas the latter is a teaching psalm, this one is in the form of a confession of praise to God.

Whenever the psalm was originally composed it provides a fitting end to Book 4 and especially suits the situation of people coming to terms with the Babylonian invasion and its aftermath. Their hope lies in God's covenant faithfulness and compassion. In its confession of sin it calls to mind other moving prayers of the period like that of Daniel's in exile (Daniel 9:4-19) and those of the leaders of the people after the exile (Nehemiah 9:5-38). Such prayers remind us of the need to pray like this. Are God's people today so very different to wayward Israel? Do we not as Christians need to humble ourselves before God and acknowledge our own rebellious ways and the sad condition of the church in our country? This psalm encourages us to remember God's promises in his Word, to appeal to God's loving commitment to his people, to look in faith for God to change situations, to seek God's honour and to cry that God would save his people and bless his inheritance.

Praise and prayer begin and end the psalm while the bulk of the work records the sinfulness of the people and the grace of God from the time of the exodus through to their removal from the land of Canaan.

Praise and prayer (verses 1-5)

The psalm begins where the last two psalms ended with 'Praise Yah' ('Praise the LORD'). It is the first to begin in this way but it is a feature of many of the psalms in the final Book (see Psalms 111-113, 135, 146-150).

The call to 'give thanks' to Israel's covenant God, Yahweh/Jehovah, is found at the beginning of the previous psalm. Here a reason is immediately given—it is because he is 'good' and his 'steadfast love' ('mercy') goes on 'for ever' (verse 1; see Psalm 100:5; Jeremiah 33:11). The psalm will indicate how true this is, despite Israel's continuing unfaithfulness. We shall hear the invitation again in the opening psalm to Book 5 (Psalm 107:1; see also Psalms 118, 136). Isaiah makes mention of the LORD's 'faithful love' and kindness to Israel in a similar context to our psalm (Isaiah 63:7). In the New Testament we are constantly reminded to give thanks to God for blessings received, especially as we partake of the bread and wine at the Lord's Supper for there our attention is particularly drawn to God's amazing goodness and loving commitment.

Are the questions of verse 2 rhetorical, implying that no one can adequately praise God or celebrate his mighty acts? Previous psalms have encouraged us to praise God but with the hymn-writer Joseph Addison (1672-1719), we would have to admit that 'eternity's too short to utter all God's praise'.[54] Nevertheless, those who 'keep justice' and the one who 'does righteousness at all times' (see Isaiah 56:1) are among the privileged, happy people ('Blessed'; see Psalm 1:1) who can at least attempt to praise even if it is with 'stammering lips'. The sad fact was, as the psalm will relate, commitment to God and his people in the matter of righting wrongs and right relationships and right living were the very things lacking throughout Israel's history (Amos 5:7; Isaiah 5:7).

The prayer of verses 4 and 5 comes as a surprise, especially as it is expressed as a personal plea to be involved in God's gracious activity when he acts to deliver his people. Maybe the psalmist is speaking for all God's people or is expressing what each person in the community is encouraged to pray. They need delivering from their present situation—that is clear from the prayer at the close of the psalm. 'Remember me' (verse 4) is how Samson and Hannah earnestly called out to God in their need (Judges 16:28; 1 Samuel 1:11) and in a similar way the penitent thief prayed to the suffering Saviour: 'Remember me when you come into your kingdom' (Luke 23:42). The psalmist looks for the time when God will 'favour' his people and visit them with salvation. Isaiah uses similar language in speaking of the 'favourable' or 'acceptable' year of the Lord, words that Jesus read in the Nazareth synagogue and stated that the Scripture was fulfilled with his coming (Isaiah 61:2; Luke 4:19–21).

The 'benefit' (literally 'good', verse 5) refers to the gracious gifts that come from the LORD who is 'good' (verse 1). God's people are described as 'your chosen ones' (see Psalm 105:6, 26, 43), 'your nation' (Exodus 19:6; Psalm 83:4) and 'your inheritance' (Psalm 28:9) and the psalmist is eager to witness God's kindness toward his people, to share in their gladness and to boast ('glory'; see Psalm 105:3) in their God. In Christ, Gentiles as well as Jews are God's chosen ones, a holy nation and his own treasured possession (Ephesians 1:4, 18; 1 Peter 2:9) and we can rejoice in God that this is true of us now as we also look forward to the full realisation of God's salvation in the glory to come.

Confession (verses 6–12)

The psalmist, speaking for his people, acknowledges that as a nation they have no right to expect God to be gracious and help them in their present distress. They have broken the terms of the covenant that God made with his people at Sinai. The confession follows the pattern set by Solomon in his great prayer at the dedication of the temple. He envisaged a time when the people would suffer the final covenant curse of exile from the land, and suggested how penitent Israel might pray: 'We have sinned and done wrong, we have committed wickedness'

(1 Kings 8:47). The model prayer is employed by Daniel who also uses the same three verbs to denote their rebellious activity (Daniel 9:5).

It is difficult for individualistically-minded westerners to appreciate the solidarity which the psalmist and others recognise exists between them and their ancestors. The psalmist and those using this psalm in the exile share in the responsibility and guilt of former generations— 'We have sinned with our fathers' (verse 6). Not only are they one with the people of the past in their rebellion, but they also repeat their sins. As the various stages in the history of Israel are reviewed the common theme of covenant faithlessness stands out. At the same time God's covenant faithfulness shines all the brighter as he acts either directly or through a representative member of the community to save the nation from complete annihilation.

Israel's faithlessness was characteristic of their history from the start. No sooner had the people left Egypt than they began to criticise Moses and make rebellious comments. They did not have the wisdom to appreciate that the God who had shown them many expressions of his loving commitment ('the multitude of your mercies', verse 7) and had struck Egypt with a series of remarkable 'wonders', could save them from Pharaoh's army when they were blocked in at the Red Sea.

Yet God saved them, but it was not for their sake or anything they had done to merit it but 'for his name's sake' (see Psalm 79:9; Daniel 9:19). Israel at the Red Sea showed no signs of repentance for their lack of trust in God. Ezekiel, writing at the time of his people's exile, makes the same point. God acted in the exodus event 'for my name's sake' that his reputation should not be tainted or his character treated with disrespect by the Gentile nations (Ezekiel 20:9, 14, 22). That is how the Jewish exiles are encouraged to make their appeal to God—for his own glory's sake (see Ezekiel 36:22). Also included, is the thought that God is acting according to his nature and character. He is patient, faithful and committed to his people. The aim of God's action was that his 'mighty power' might be acknowledged not only by the enemy but by Israel herself (Exodus 14:4, 18, 31). Ezekiel sees the restoration of his people to their land in a similar light (Ezekiel 20:38, 42, 44).

As God 'rebuked' the waters at creation (verse 9; see Psalm 104:7) so we have this vivid picture of God's power over the sea, enabling his people to pass through the waters dry-shod (see Isaiah 63:13). In a similar way Jesus demonstrated his power over the natural elements and evil spirits and so pointed to his redeeming work and victory over all Satanic power through his cross and resurrection (Mark 1:25; 4:39; 8:33; 9:25; 10:45). The God who saved and redeemed his people through the water, destroyed the enemy through the same means (verses 10-11). There are echoes of verse 10 in the prophecy of Zacharias, John the Baptist's father (Luke 1:71).

The people's belief in God's word which resulted in them singing his praise (verse 12; see Exodus 14:31–15:1) is not seen as something to celebrate as the next section will indicate. Spurgeon aptly remarks: 'Between Israel singing and Israel sinning there was scarce a step'.

Israel's forgetfulness and God's displeasure (verses 13-33)

Various incidents during the wilderness period are related not necessarily in chronological order to illustrate Israel's continuing faithlessness and God's reaction both in wrath and grace. After the Red Sea miracle, the people quickly forgot the mighty deeds of Yahweh/Jehovah that had brought them out of Egypt and in their impatience they complained instead of waiting for God's counsel (verse 13).

Craving

The first occurrences of such mistrust were at the waters of Marah (Exodus 15:22-25), Massah and Meribah (Exodus 17:1-7) but the main focus is probably their craving for meat (verses 14-15; Numbers 11:4, 34). It was one of ten occasions when they put God to the test in the wilderness (see Numbers 14:22; Exodus 17:2, 7; Psalm 78:18). In wrath God gave them what they wanted only for many of them to die as a result (Numbers 11:33-34). Our Lord, as the true Israel, was driven into the wilderness by the Spirit to experience similar trials but he triumphed over Satan's temptations to obtain food and to put God to the test (Matthew 4:1-7).

Mutiny

Questioning the God-ordained leadership out of a spirit of jealousy was another indication of Israel's rebellious nature that was detrimental to the covenant community (verses 16-18). The reference is to the uprising under the leadership of Korah, Dathan and Abiram (Numbers 16), although only the latter two are named here (see Deuteronomy 11:6). Their punishment was to be swallowed alive by the earth while the followers of Korah were destroyed by fire. When it speaks of 'Aaron the saint of the LORD' (verse 16) it does not mean that he was especially eminent in personal holiness but that he was God's specially set apart priest to enter the most holy place of the tabernacle. A demon-possessed man recognised Jesus as 'the Holy One of God' (Mark 1:24).

Idolatry

A third example of Israel's unfaithfulness takes us back to the golden calf incident at the foot of Mount Sinai (verses 19-23; Exodus 32; Deuteronomy 9:8-21). 'Horeb' is the name for Sinai used mainly in Deuteronomy. Israel was unique among the religions of the Ancient Near East in having no image of their deity. Yet, contrary to the Second Commandment, they made a moulded image and began worshipping it. It is common for people to want an image of the god they worship, to have something to see and approach, and the bull calf seems to have been a familiar image by which to represent deity. But as God indicated, he cannot be represented by anything he has created. At Sinai/Horeb the people heard the voice of God and saw only fire and the thick dark cloud of his presence (Deuteronomy 4:11-12, 15-18). To bow down before what the people claimed to be an image of Yahweh/ Jehovah was to worship something other than the true God. They had 'changed their glory' for an animal that 'eats grass'! (verse 20). The choice of words expresses the contemptible nature of the action. God was Israel's 'splendour' or 'glory' (see Psalm 3:3; 1 Samuel 4:21). As Jeremiah puts it 'my people have changed their Glory for what does not profit' (Jeremiah 2:11). How could the stunning, awesome God be represented by any created object? Paul has in mind this verse in his condemnation of sinful human beings (Romans 1:23).

Israel had again forgotten (see verse 13) the God who had delivered them and done such amazing deeds both in Egypt ('the land of Ham' verse 22; see Psalm 105:23) and at the Red Sea. God had revealed himself by word and awesome deeds. This is how he was to be known and worshipped. For breaking so flagrantly the first commandments God was justified in wiping out the whole nation (verse 23). Moses, God's 'chosen one', is depicted as the great mediator and intercessor whose pleadings averted the divine wrath (Exodus 32:11-13, 31-32; Deuteronomy 9:25-29). He 'stood ... in the breach' like a fearless warrior standing at a point where the city wall had been breached to hold back the enemy (see Ezekiel 22:30). In this Moses foreshadows our Lord Jesus, God's chosen one, who went further than Moses, and actually bore the wrath of God so that idolatrous rebels might not experience the punishment that their sins deserve.

Doubting God
A further example of the people's faithlessness was their refusal to enter the 'pleasant land' (verse 24; see Jeremiah 3:19; Zechariah 7:14) of Canaan after hearing the depressing majority report of the spies (verses 24-27; Numbers 13-14). They preferred to listen to human opinion than to believe God's word (Numbers 14:11; see Psalm 78:22). The psalm depicts the people grumbling in their tents and refusing to listen to 'the voice of the LORD' (verse 25; see Numbers 14:22). The mighty voice of God that speaks through natural phenomena (see Psalm 29) had spoken words of assurance and yet they had undervalued it and preferred other voices, a repeat of Adam and Eve's sin.

God's judgment is then mentioned in terms of Yahweh/Jehovah's oath in which he swore to make them fall ('overthrow them', verse 26; Numbers 14:29) in the wilderness. The phrase 'he lifted up his hand' to them is an ancient gesture in swearing an oath (see Genesis 14:22; Ezekiel 20:23; Revelation 10:5-6). What God had sworn to give to Israel he now swears they will not receive (Numbers 14:30). The generation that left Egypt would not enter the good land they had despised (Numbers 14:29-35). Interestingly, the psalmist looks beyond the wilderness period to the final curse of exile as pronounced by Moses in the law—their offspring scattered and put to death among the nations (see Leviticus 26:33, 38; Ezekiel 20:23). This would have been a particularly sore reminder to those using this psalm during the Babylonian exile.

Apostasy
The next example of unfaithfulness is taken from near the end of their forty-year stay in the wilderness, when they were on the very border of Canaan. Israel sank even further into spiritual and moral failure by joining 'Baal of Peor' (verses 28-31; Numbers 25). 'Peor' was a mountain in Moab east of the Dead Sea associated with the god worshipped by the Moabites. The book of Numbers speaks of the Israelites eating the 'sacrifices of their gods' (Numbers 25:2) but the psalmist states that they 'ate sacrifices made to the dead' (verse 28). There is some evidence that these fellowship meals to pagan gods were associated with funeral observances (see Deuteronomy 18:9-11; 26:14; Isaiah

57:1–8 for practices relating to the dead). The apostasy provoked God's anger and it resulted in the people being struck down by an epidemic (Numbers 25:8–9).

The Zeal of Phinehas

Again we read of one man standing to intervene to prevent God's wrath from wiping out the whole nation (verse 30; see verse 23). Phinehas was the grandson of Aaron (Numbers 25:7) and his swift action in making atonement for the people satisfied the demands of justice and God praised him and the promise made to him guaranteed a future priestly line who would make atonement for the people (Numbers 25:10-13). The psalmist summarises God's response to Phinehas's action in words that recall what is said of Abram: and it 'was accounted to him for righteousness' (verse 31; Genesis 15:6). In Abram's case it was his faith in the promised offspring that was counted to him for righteousness (see Romans 4:3; Galatians 3:6), whereas here it was zealous action. The verb 'to account' has the idea of reckoning, thinking or esteeming (see 2 Samuel 19:19; Psalm 32:2). Kidner's comment is apt: 'happily it is Abram's faith we are to follow, not Phinehas's zeal!' Nevertheless, we see in Phinehas a foreshadowing of Christ's zeal on our behalf. Jesus, as our mediator and saviour, had that righteous status before God and as our perfect high priest and suffering Servant is able to justify many for 'he bore the sin of many and made intercession for the transgressors' (Isaiah 53:11-12; Hebrews 7:24-27).[55]

It is possible that this incident is also meant to call to mind Aaron's action when he mediated between the dead and living, an item not included in the account of the rebellion against Moses and Aaron (see verses 16–18; Numbers 16:46–48).

Moses' failure

However, even the best of human mediators fail and the next section refers to the occasion when Moses sinned by striking the rock in anger (verses 32–33; see Numbers 20:1–13). It was at Kadesh that the sad incident took place where the people again showed their unbelief over the lack of water and their desire to be back in Egypt. Although it was rebellion against God, Moses took it personally so that his rash words and action deprived him of the privilege of leading the people into Canaan. He had failed to honour the Lord (see Numbers 20:12).[56]

We thank God for Jesus, the true Servant of the Lord, of whom Moses was an imperfect type. 'He was oppressed and he was afflicted, yet he opened not his mouth' (Isaiah 53:7). He 'committed no sin ... who, when he was reviled, did not revile in return; when he suffered, he did not threaten' (1 Peter 2:22–23).

Israel's failure and God's faithfulness (verses 34–46)
The psalmist now recounts what happened when Israel settled in Canaan. It provides a summary of the history recorded in the books of Judges, Samuel and Kings. The Canaanites were to be destroyed (verse 34) but this was no arbitrary, unjust action. Their sin had come to full measure and it demanded their extermination (Genesis 15:16; Deuteronomy 7:2). Israel functioned as the instrument in executing the death sentence in the same way as Assyria and Babylon were later used to punish God's people. This was a special judgment before the great end-time judgment in the same way that the Flood and the destruction of Sodom and Gomorrah were seen. But Israel failed in their duty and this in itself became part of God's judgment on his own people (Judges 2:1–3). As Paul indicates, God's wrath seen in this world involves giving people over to their folly and vile affections (Romans 1:24).

After the initial period under Joshua and the elders who outlived him, Israel quickly began intermarrying with the Canaanites and adopting the customs and features of their religion (see Judges 3:5–6). This was all contrary to their position as a 'holy nation', dedicated to God and set apart from all other people groups. The 'land' that God had given them was also a holy place where the LORD had chosen to live among his people but it was being 'polluted' by their sinful activity in shedding innocent blood (verse 38; see Numbers 35:33–34; Jeremiah 3:1–2). Israel's transgression of God's covenant was a small-scale picture of the world's apostasy from the living God so that the whole earth was defiled because its inhabitants had broken the everlasting covenant between God and humanity and were ripe for the end-time curse of desolation (Isaiah 24:5).

They worshipped before 'idols' ('graven images') and this became a further temptation ('a snare') in Israel's downward slide into apostasy for it led them to engage in child sacrifices, which meant the shedding of 'innocent blood' (verses 37–38). When people depart from the living God the sanctity of human life is soon endangered (Jeremiah 19:4–5). The worship of idols is not a harmless pastime, rather it is associated with all that is evil and devilish (see Deuteronomy 32:16-17; 1 Corinthians 10:19-22). Not only the land but the people themselves are 'defiled' by their own immoral deeds and spiritual prostitution.

All this led to God's wrath being displayed against his own people. How tragic for God to say that he 'abhorred' his special possession ('inheritance', verse 40)! The psalmist then presents a summary of the recurring cycle of sin, punishment, cries for help, deliverance, followed by renewed apostasy that is such a feature of the early chapters of Judges (verses 40-43). Instead of ruling over the nations, the surrounding nations were too often ruling Israel as a result of their waywardness.

Their situation resembled the time of their bondage in Egypt when they cried to God and he remembered the covenant that he had made with their ancestors (verses 44-45; Exodus 2:25). The difference now lay in the fact that they were experiencing the curses of the Sinai covenant on account of their sins. But still, it is because of that special relationship God had with Abraham, Isaac and Jacob, that he continues to show the greatness of his loving commitment toward them (verse 45; Leviticus 26:42, 45; Psalm 105:8-11; see Luke 1:72). The fact that Israel 'did not remember the multitude of your mercies' does not stop God remembering and relenting 'according to the multitude of his mercies' (verse 45; see verse 7; Numbers 14:19). God is not like fickle people who change their plans according to unforeseen circumstances but he is gracious and changes his approach toward us according to his unchangeable nature and purposes.

The unusual expression 'He also made them to be pitied' (literally 'and he gave them to compassions', verse 46) is an idiom found in Solomon's prayer and in the account of Daniel's relationship with the chief eunuch (1 Kings 8:50; Daniel 1:9). Early evidence of such clemency toward captives is not recorded, but later, besides Daniel, we read of mercy being shown to king Jehoiachin, a descendant of David, by the Babylonians and of the goodwill of the kings of Persia toward the returning exiles (2 Kings 25:27-30; Ezra 1:2-4; 7:27-28).

Prayer and praise (verses 47-48)

As the psalm began, so it ends but as a mirror image, with prayer first and praise following (see verses 1-5). The thought of God's steadfast love that enables their captors to show compassion encourages this passionate prayer that God would act to 'save' and 'gather' his people in from the nations so that they may engage in the kind of praise with which the psalm began—'to give thanks to your holy name, and to triumph (or 'boast', see verse 5) in your praise' (verse 47; see verse 1 and Psalm 105:3). A number of Jews returned in stages from exile (see Ezra 2; 7–8:14; Nehemiah 7:4–73) but this was only the beginning and a preview of something much greater. Prophets like Isaiah look to the time when as a result of the suffering Servant's work, a universal call will go out and as a result of the gospel being preached there will be a gathering of God's people, the elect from every nation, into the heavenly Zion so that on the day when the Lord Jesus returns all his people will be together to inherit the land God has prepared for them (Psalm 87; Isaiah 55:1–7; 60:1–4; 62:10–12; Mark 13:26–27; Acts 15:14–19).

The first part of verse 48 (see 1 Chronicles 16:36; Luke 1:68) repeats the words found at the end of Psalm 41 while the second part calls the people to add their 'Amen!' and to 'Praise the LORD' ('Hallelujah!' see Revelation 19:4). In the Chronicles account it is reported that the people said their 'Amen' and 'praised the Lord'. When Moses commanded the people to pronounce the covenant curses from Mount Ebal, after each curse the people were also called to add their 'Amen!' (Deuteronomy 27:16–26). The congregation are invited to affirm what has been said and to add a final shout of praise to Yahweh/Jehovah, the God of the covenant. In this way Book 4 comes to an appropriate conclusion (see Psalms 41:13; 72:18–19; 89:52).

Book Five

Like book four, the psalms brought together in this final book from various authors including David are a response to the destruction of Jerusalem and its temple by the Babylonians in 587 BC, which is brought to our attention in many of the psalms of Book 3. They encourage God's people to place their trust in the living God. In contrast to the previous book, many of the psalms of book five suggest that the exile is over and a new beginning is dawning (compare Psalm 106:47 with Psalm 107:1-3).

The opening thanksgiving psalm is an appropriate introduction, for praise and thanksgiving dominate this final book. Psalms 108-110 are attributed to David, encouraging the people with further truth concerning the Lord's anointed. Two groups of psalms are included that recall the exodus from Egypt, and the people's return from Babylonian exile is seen as a second exodus. The first group (Psalms 113-118) is known by the rabbis as the 'Egyptian Hallel' and was sung at the family Passover celebrations, while the second group ('Songs of Ascent', Psalms 120-134) was associated with pilgrims journeying to the temple in Jerusalem. Separating the two groups is the majestic Psalm 119 with its celebration of God's law. Psalms 111 and 112 have already prepared the way for this massive psalm with their emphasis on godly wisdom that delights in God's word (Psalms 111:10; 112:1). Two psalms, one of praise and the other of thanks (Psalms 135, 136), follow the 'Song of Ascents' group, while in Psalm 137 there is a reminder of how impossible it was to sing the songs of Zion in exile.

Book Five continues with a group of eight psalms of David (Psalms 138-145), the last one being a magnificent praise psalm, bringing the David collection to a close. The whole Psalter then comes to a grand conclusion with the final 'Hallelujah' psalms (Psalms 146-150).

In book one there were eight beatitudes and these were placed in such a way as to draw attention to an important message concerning the happy state of the Lord's anointed king and those associated with him. Book Two only has one beatitude (Psalm 65:4) and Books Three and Four have four and two respectively (Psalms 84:4, 5, 12; 89:15; 94:12; 106:3) but they continue to remind us that the happy state consists of being in a right relationship with God. In Book Five there are ten beatitudes and they are scattered throughout in no particular order (Psalms 112:1; 119:1-2; 127:5; 128:1; 137:8, 9; 144:15ab; 146:5) but again they reinforce the message of Book One that God is committed to the poor and needy who find refuge in God, who delight to do God's revealed will and are concerned, like God and his anointed, that justice will prevail for God's oppressed people.

This final book also encourages the people to look forward to the full realisation of God's promises to David, promises that are mentioned in the angel Gabriel's announcement to Mary (Luke 1:31-33).

Psalm 107

Encouragements to Trust and Thank the LORD

Paul urges Christians to exercise a prophetic ministry when they meet together in communal worship by teaching and exhorting one another as they sing 'psalms and hymns and spiritual songs' (Colossians 3:16). The songs have a dual purpose: they are meant to bring praise to God but at the same time they instruct, reprimand and prod the congregation into living lives that honour God.

This psalm provides four illustrations, using the same phraseology each time, of God's goodness toward those in need in order to encourage all God's people to give thanks to their covenant-keeping God. The psalm draws to a close (verses 33–42) with a meditation on God's providential care of his needy people and ends with a word to the wise (verse 43; see Hosea 14:9) so that they might appreciate the steadfast love of the LORD. God's loving commitment toward his people is celebrated in this psalm and it answers the question raised in the closing psalm of Book Three: 'Lord, where are your former loving-kindnesses ('steadfast love')?' (Psalm 89:49). The psalm also has in mind the prayer that closes Book Four (Psalm 106:47) when it refers to God's redeemed people whom he has gathered out of the lands of the enemy (verse 2).

Unlike the three psalms that follow, there is no heading to this introductory psalm of Book Five and there is every likelihood that it was composed after the Jews had returned from the Babylonian exile. The return was a foreshadowing of what God would accomplish through the anointed one (the Messiah) of David's family line. Our psalmist encourages faith in the God of the impossible, or rather the God who when he makes promises to his people is committed to seeing them realised.

Call to give thanks (verses 1–3)

This psalm begins like Psalm 106:1 (apart from the opening 'Praise Yah'), and introduces its major themes: Israel's covenant God, Yahweh/Jehovah ('LORD') is 'good' and the enduring nature of his 'steadfast love' ('mercy', verse 1; see Jeremiah 33:11). The 'redeemed of the LORD' are encouraged to express their thanks (verse 2). They are people who have been rescued by their 'next-of-kin' from enemy hands and 'gathered' out of many lands and from all quarters (verse 3).[57] God had redeemed his people from Egyptian slavery and Isaiah sees that as symbolic of a greater redemption of which the return from Babylonian exile was an important preparation and picture. It symbolises the 'ransomed' or 'redeemed of the LORD' who have been delivered through the work of Zion's King who is revealed as the suffering Servant (Isaiah 35:10; 51:11; 62:12). As a result of what 'the arm of the Lord' has done in his Servant, people of all nations are 'gathered' together at Mount Zion (Isaiah 49:12; 60:4).

Deliverances from danger (verses 4–32)

The four examples of people being rescued are not taken from the four points of the compass as verse 3 might have led us to believe, although it is significant that the first example suggests the barrenness of the east (verses 4–9) and the last refers to the Mediterranean sea which lies to the west of Canaan (verses 23–32).[58] The same people are being considered in all four cases and the pictures of redemption do not necessarily relate in detail to incidents recorded in Israel's history.

Wanderers satisfied (verses 4–9)

First, the redeemed were like people wandering about in the desert. The same verb 'wander' is used by Isaiah to speak of people straying like lost sheep (Isaiah 53:6). They are faint with hunger and thirst, with 'no city to dwell in' (verses 4-5). It reminds us of Abraham and his family who lived in tents, as well as of all the unnamed of whom the world was not worthy, who wandered in deserts and mountains, awaiting the fulfilment of God's promises and longing for the city which has foundations (Hebrews 11:9-10, 37-39). Particularly in mind perhaps is Israel's journey through the wilderness after leaving Egypt which previews the Babylonian exile situation. Like Chronicles, this psalm encourages the people to pray and to call out in their distress to the God who is able to deliver and lead his people 'by the right way' to the city of Zion (verse 7). A similar picture is drawn by Isaiah to describe the spiritual state of the people whom God will redeem through the work of his Servant (Isaiah 40:3; 43:19-21; 48:17; 49:11-12). For Isaiah, the Persian ruler Cyrus, in his activity on behalf of the returning exiles from Babylon, foreshadowed the future Anointed one (Isaiah 45:1-2, 13).

Isaiah prophesies that 'the ransomed of the Lord shall return, and come to Zion with singing' (Isaiah 51:11). Our psalm calls for the redeemed to 'give thanks to the Lord', a refrain repeated after each example (verses 8, 15, 21, 31). The use of the term 'goodness' hides the fact that this is the same word translated 'mercy' and 'loving-kindness' (see verses 1, 43) referring to his steadfast love or loving commitment as he acts in answer to his people's cry. The 'children of men' (literally 'the sons of man') suggests frail ordinary humans are the recipients of God's grace. Jesus said, 'All that the Father gives me will come to me, and the one who comes to me I will by no means cast out' (John 6:37).

His 'wonderful works' refer especially to those amazing acts associated with the exodus from Egypt (Exodus 3:20; 15:11; see Psalms 105:2, 5; 106:7) and it is interesting that such wonders surround the new exodus associated with Jesus and his apostles (Acts 2:22, 43; 4:30; Romans 15:19; 2 Corinthians 12:12). God's deliverance is described in a way appropriate to the nature of the problem. Those hungry and thirsty in the desert are more than satisfied for they are filled with 'good' (verse 9; see Psalm 104:28; Jeremiah 31:25). Mary's psalm of praise speaks of filling the hungry with good things (Luke 1:53).

Derek Kidner reminds us that Jesus used such pictures of people lost, hungry, thirsty and faint in speaking of himself as 'the Way, the Bread and Water of life and the Giver of rest' (John 14:6; 6:35; 7:37; Matthew 11:28).

Prisoners released (verses 10–16)

The picture changes and those to be delivered are likened to prisoners experiencing the misery of lying in chains in a dark dungeon, remote from help (verses 10, 12; for 'shadow of death' see Psalm 23:4). It depicts very vividly the state of humanity in sin and recalls the words of Isaiah as he describes people who have rebelled against God's words and counsel (Isaiah 5:24; 8:19–9:2). Israel's rebellion at the Red Sea and in the wilderness (see Psalm 106:7, 33, 43) is a picture of people in general in their attitude to the 'Most High' (verse 11; see Psalm 7:17). But the people cried to God in their need and 'he saved them out of their distresses' (verse 13). God comes to the help of those who cannot help themselves. That is the gospel. They are rescued from their plight (verse 14; see verse 10; Jeremiah 30:8) and urged in the words of the refrain to 'give thanks to the Lord' (verse 15; see 8). The reason to confess God's steadfast love is again appropriate to the circumstances described: people who have been behind 'bars of iron' (verse 16; see verse 10 and Isaiah 45:2).

Zacharias uses the words of this psalm in his prophetic hymn as he speaks of God's Messiah coming 'to give light to those who sit in darkness and the shadow of death' (Luke 1:79). Luke then shows how Jesus sees himself as the fulfilment of passages like Isaiah 61:1–2. He had come to preach 'deliverance to the captives' and 'to set at liberty those who are oppressed' (Luke 4:18, 21).

The sick restored (verses 17–22)

The next picture is of people delivered from illnesses that are due to their sin. Not all sickness by any means is directly associated with sin as the case of Job makes clear (see also John 9:1–3), but Paul indicates that sin can lead to sickness and premature death (1 Corinthians 11:29–30). People who rebel against God are described as 'fools' (verse 17; see Psalm 14:1; Romans 1:22) and their sickness is self-inflicted. Sin's wages are death (Romans 6:23). They are pictured as loathing food and at death's door (verse 18). But they cried to the Lord and 'he saved them out of their distresses' (verse 19; see verse 13). The agent in their 'healing' is God's 'word' by which they were delivered from the pit of destruction (verse 20; see Lamentations 4:20). People who rejected 'the words of God' (verse 11) are brought to wholeness through 'his word'. Isaiah speaks of backsliders being healed (Isaiah 57:18) and of God's word accomplishing his purposes (Isaiah 55:11). The prophet also reveals that it is through the atoning death of the LORD's Servant that healing comes: 'by his stripes we are healed' (Isaiah 53:5). Hezekiah the king found himself near the gates of death but the word of the Lord came to Isaiah that spoke of Hezekiah's recovery from the sickness (Isaiah 38:4–10). Jesus healed people with a word and thereby demonstrated his saving power over the deep-seated sickness of sin— 'Your sins are forgiven' (Mark 2:5–12).

After the refrain of verse 21 (see verses 8, 15) thank offerings are to accompany the thanksgiving as tokens of gratitude and to bear testimony 'with rejoicing' ('with a resounding cry') to God's saving activity (verse 22; see Psalms 40:6; 50:14). Thank offerings were one type of peace offering (see Leviticus 7:11–18).

Seafarers saved (verses 23–32)

The scene changes and the redeemed are likened to mariners who have come through stormy seas and mountainous waves. Again, Isaiah has similar pictures. He calls on those 'who go down to the sea' to sing praises to God (Isaiah 42:10) and speaks comfort to those afflicted, who are 'tossed with tempest' (Isaiah 54:11). The sea spoke of danger and the threat of a watery grave and the psalm spends some time describing the effects of being on board ship in a severe windstorm. Reading it can make you feel seasick! God's 'wonders' include what we see happening in nature (verse 24; see Psalm 104:24–26). The God who made the sea sent the storm and this was what Jonah acknowledged and experienced so that the sailors on board ship with him 'were at their wits' end' (verse 25, 27; Jonah 1:4–5, 11). There was no way anyone could save the situation.

The cry goes up again to God and he brings them deliverance (verse 28; see verses 6, 13, 19). He stills the storm and calms the waves bringing gladness to people (verses 29–30; Psalm 65:7; Jonah 1:12, 15). As in the first picture the redeemed are brought safely home 'to their desired haven' (verse 30; see verse 7). As the LORD guided Israel to the rest of the promised land and as he would guide the Jews safely back after the Babylonian exile so he brings his storm-tossed afflicted ones to peace and rest as a result of God's saving work through his Servant (see Isaiah 53:5; 54:9–15). Jesus was drawing their attention to these same Old Testament passages when he stilled the storm on the Sea of Galilee (Mark 4:35–41).

Following the refrain (verse 31; see verse 21), the people are further urged to testify to God's steadfast love publicly (verse 32; see verse 22). They are encouraged to extol and praise God in the worshipping congregation and where the elders are sat together (see Psalm 22:22). The 'elders' were the tribal leaders and heads of families and represented Israel as a whole (Jeremiah 26:17; 29:1; Ezekiel 8:1; Ezra 6:7-8, 14). They often assembled at the city gate to administer justice (Proverbs 31:23; Lamentations 5:14). Public worship is encouraged throughout Scripture and the elders along with the other angelic beings set the example in the final book of the Bible (Revelation 7:11-12).

Recalling God's providential actions (verses 33-43)

This final section does not follow the pattern of the previous verses, although the emphasis on God's action toward his people continues and it picks up some of the words and ideas from the previous section. The language of Isaiah also echoes through the verses. It is in two main parts and both take us from trouble arising out of human sin to God's gracious action to bring about blessing (verses 33-38, 39-41). The psalm closes by encouraging the upright and wise to appreciate and rejoice in the LORD's steadfast love (verses 42-43).

First contrast (verses 33-38)

The God who turns fertile land into infertile on account of the wickedness of the people who live there (verses 33-34; see Isaiah 50:2), is the one who can reverse that situation so that the people are blessed (verses 35-38; see Isaiah 35:7; 41:18). It is possible that the psalmist has in mind the punishment meted out to Sodom and Gomorrah where 'barrenness' is literally 'saltiness' (verse 34). Those cities of the plain that Lot envied became barren, a salt marsh and unfruitful and that is the description of Canaan as a result of the final covenant curse (Genesis 13:10; 19:24-28; Deuteronomy 29:23). But what seems impossible to humans, God can change for the better so that the wilderness is changed into pools of water and 'a city for habitation' (verse 36; see verses 4 and 7) is established, filled with people who benefit from fruitful harvests (verse 37). This is a great encouragement to those suffering the Babylonian exile and who look with Isaiah for God to do a new thing when the Servant's work is completed and he pours out his Spirit on Israel's descendants and brings them to the heavenly city (Isaiah 43:19-21; 44:3-5; 49:19-21; 54:1; see Ezekiel

36:24–36). Those future blessings both spiritual and physical associated with the new covenant are described in terms similar to the blessings promised under the Sinai covenant (Deuteronomy 30:16).

Second contrast (verses 39–41)

The second part again contrasts the situation God's people were in at the time of the Babylonian invasion and their position after the restoration. They were brought low and their numbers were diminished through 'oppression, affliction (literally 'evil') and sorrow' (verse 39) that could either be a reference to the situation before the exile under weak and false shepherds of the people or to the foreign rulers. The God who punishes the leaders who have persecuted the humble needy people (verse 40; see Job 12:21, 24; Psalm 40:17) now sets the humble poor on high and protects them from affliction (verse 41). The passage again reminds us of Mary's hymn in which she praises the God who 'has put down the mighty from their thrones, and exalted the lowly' (Luke 1:52; see verse 9).

Conclusion (verses 42–43)

'This righteous providence of God', writes John Stott, 'both pleases the upright and silences the wicked' (verse 42). If we would be wise we need to observe the way in which God delivers the humble poor on the basis of his loving commitment toward his people. Even though they have failed him the Lord is always true to his word and continues to act in grace. 'Who is wise?' says Hosea, 'Let him understand these things. Who is prudent? Let him know them. For the ways of the Lord are right; the righteous walk in them, but transgressors stumble in them' (Hosea 14:9).

Our Lord Jesus recapitulated the experiences of Israel right through to a far more extreme and mysterious exile than that which the nation underwent. He experienced deprivations of various kinds and was afflicted and treated despicably especially by those in leadership positions. In his case there was no sin in him but the sins of his people were imputed to him and he suffered the consequences. He could identify with the psalmist and give thanks for the way God his Father brought him through all his troubles, from the very lowest position of death on a cross to being highly exalted and given the name which is above every name. This same Jesus demonstrated God's steadfast love. He is the God-Man who was able to feed the hungry, liberate those bound by Satan, bring healing and forgiveness to the sick and still the raging storm. This Jesus is our kinsman redeemer who has rescued his people from sin, Satan, death and hell and is now our risen Lord who will return in glory to put everything right once and for all.

Psalm 108

On the Victory Side with God

This is an interesting psalm because it looks as if parts of two previous psalms have been put together to form this 'Song'. The heading tells us that this is a 'Psalm of David', the first in a short series of three (Psalms 108-110). David must have had good reason to combine, with slight variation, the words of Psalm 57:7-11 with those of Psalm 60:5-12 to form this new psalm. Perhaps the Edomites presented a renewed threat. Whatever the initial reason it must be seen as a fresh psalm and not treated as merely a combination of the two previous psalms. We only need to go back to those psalms for more details concerning the various words and phrases used.

But why has the compiler of the whole collection of Psalms decided to use it here in Book 5 when parts of it have been heard before? It appears in this spot following on from Psalm 107 as a further means of comfort and support to God's people living in the aftermath of the Babylonian exile and their return to Canaan. There is something particularly moving, as Alexander Maclaren, in his exposition of this psalm observes, in summoning harp and lyre, 'which had hung silent on the willows of Babylon so long (see Psalm 137:1-3), to wake their ancient minstrelsy once more', as well as in the 'exultant confidence that the God who had led David to victory still leads His people'. The return from exile was a cause for celebration but the actual conditions after the return were far from ideal as we know from Ezra and Nehemiah and the prophecies of Haggai, Zechariah and Malachi. Psalm 108 continues the theme of praise in response to God's steadfast love which is so much a part of Psalm 107. It responds in particular to the question raised in Psalm 89:49 concerning God's promises to David. The psalm may also have been chosen because of its reference to Edom. The Edomites had rejoiced over the destruction of Jerusalem and had helped themselves to the booty (see Psalm 137:7; Obadiah verses 10–14).

In using this psalm of David in this new context, we see how God's word itself encourages us to apply the psalms to the different experiences we face and to the varying situations that affect the church. We await the grand consummation when all things will be renewed and glorified. Until then, as this psalm encourages us, we are to praise God among the nations and celebrate his steadfast love and pray for help to overcome the forces of darkness.

The psalm begins with praise and ends with a plea. It can be divided into two main parts (verses 1–6 and 7–13) and each ends with a prayer for God to help and bring deliverance (verses 5–6, 11–13).

Determination to praise (verses 1–4)

In the opening line the psalmist addresses God as he states his intention to sing and make music. His 'heart' and 'glory' (verse 1) refer to the whole of his being. He is ready and firmly set ('steadfast', verse 1) on praising 'the LORD' (verse 3). It is God's covenant name, Yahweh/Jehovah, that is used here not 'Lord' as in Psalm 57:9. He wishes to wake the dawn with his music as he gives thanks 'among the peoples ... among the nations' (verse 3). The psalm encourages the new generation after the exile not to remain dejected but to use their musical instruments in confessing God in this situation where they are under the gaze and rule of foreign powers. Yes, they do not have a king of David's line ruling over them but God has not forgotten his promises. He has had mercy upon them and brought them back to their land and they can therefore look in hope for God to keep his word to David. Therefore they can continue to sing with David of God's enduring love ('mercy') and faithfulness ('truth', verse 4) that are boundless and even reach down to them. And we can too! We are urged to make known the praises of the one who has done such great things for us. What is more the Church of Jesus Christ is singing praises to God in almost every people group the world over.

Prayer for deliverance (verses 5–6)

The refrain of Psalm 57:5 and 11 is used in this psalm to introduce the prayer that God would come to deliver his 'beloved'—the Hebrew word is used as a name for Solomon 'Jedidiah' (2 Samuel 12:25). Jeremiah speaks of Israel as God's beloved wife (Jeremiah 11:15). God's people, the ones he loves, need saving by God's powerful right hand (see Psalm 20:6). Just as a father or a husband would come to the aid of a beloved son or wife so the plea is for God to act to deliver the people he loves. What they need saving from is not mentioned at this point but is revealed later in the psalm. The psalmist looks for God to answer (not 'hear') him. By taking action on behalf of his people, this would be a demonstration of God's authority over all and a display of his stunning greatness. In the context of Israel's return from exile these words of David are used to urge God to act to carry further the work he has begun. In our situations we also use these words to call on our God who is indeed high over all to continue what he has begun and see the final fulfilment of all his promises in the new creation when all opposition will have been for ever removed.

Recalling God's authoritative word (verses 7–9)

Again, for the Jewish exiles this affirmation of God's lordship over the land of promise would have been a remarkably reassuring word. It also encourages Christians today to know that what God promised and did for Israel in bringing them back from exile to the land they thought was lost to them, is symbolic of the inheritance that God has in store for all his people. The land of Canaan is a picture of the future new earth that Christ's redeeming work on the cross has secured for all who love his appearing in glory.

People when they swear oaths usually do so by someone or something greater than themselves, the idea being that if they default on their promises it will result in their hurt and loss (see Hebrews 6:16; 1 Samuel 3:17; 2 Kings 6:31). When God goes on oath, he can only swear 'by himself' for there is no one greater (Hebrews 6:13; Genesis 22:16; Amos 4:2; 6:8; 8:7). God's 'holiness' is what makes God the unique being that he is. God swears by his own nature and character. In Psalm 89:35 mention is made of God's covenant with David in these terms:

'Once I have sworn by my holiness; I will not lie to David'. Hearing these words concerning the promised land would assure the people living without a Davidic king, that the promises made to David will not fail either. We praise God that all his promises find their fulfilment in Jesus the Anointed one (2 Corinthians 1:20).

God's promises concerning land went right back to Abraham and he confirmed them to Moses and the people before they entered. When Israel entered the land, in obedience to what had previously been arranged under Moses, it was allocated to the various tribes (Joshua 13–22). But it was made clear to the people that the land belonged to God and they were the tenants (Leviticus 25:23). The repeated emphasis in verses 7–9 on 'my' and 'mine' indicates who the rightful owner is. Again, these promises find their ultimate fulfilment through Jesus the Messiah.

As God is pictured parcelling out the land, and the whole land is covered by means of the places mentioned (see Psalm 60:6-8 for details), he does so with a note of triumph—'I will rejoice' or 'I will exult' (verse 7). To further emphasise the pleasure God has in allocating the land, instead of Philistia shouting out (see Psalm 60:8), it is God who shouts out in triumph (verse 9). God has made promises that concerned his people, the land and the enemy nations that surrounded them. He is the sovereign overlord and has these enemy states like Moab, Edom and Philistia under his control.

Prayer for deliverance (verses 10–13)

The reason for recalling God's oath now becomes clear. Edom had clearly gained an impressive victory over David's army and God had allowed this to happen by abandoning them to the enemy. Who is then going to lead David to Edom to take its stronghold capital city high up in the rocks? (verse 10). Has God spurned them? Is he no longer intending to go out with their armies? Again, these are the kind of questions that must have been in the minds of the Jews in exile and on their return to the land. Edom continued to be a problem to the community back in the land, as is suggested in Malachi 1:2-4. When the church of Jesus Christ finds herself surrounded by foes and threatened by persecution, are Christians to believe that God has abandoned his people and let them down?

This is the reason for the earlier prayer for deliverance and now the plea is again made with some urgency. They need help because of the trouble they are in and human promises of deliverance have no substance to them (Isaiah 30:7; Lamentations 4:17). But in view of what has been said about God's sovereignty over the enemy nations the psalm closes on a positive note. Through God they will be victorious and he will see to it that all their foes are humbled (verse 13). There is a part that God's people must play in defeating their enemies but they cannot do it alone.

We are called to work out our salvation but it is God who works within the believer to will and to do of his good pleasure (Philippians 2:12-13). Only through Christ who strengthens us can we do anything worthwhile to his glory. In all the troubles and distresses of this life we are more than conquerors through him who loved us and nothing can separate us from the love of God in Christ. Because Christ has conquered the evil one through his atoning death all his people are eternally secure. We are also assured that the God of peace will crush Satan under our feet shortly (Romans 16:20). The enemies of God represented under the symbol of Edom or Babylon can never thwart God's purposes. They will all be defeated and God's people will rule with Christ in the eternal kingdom (see Psalm 60:12).

Psalm 109

Human Hostility

This is the last and most terrible of the imprecatory psalms associated with David (see Psalms 35; 58; 69). An imprecatory psalm is one that calls down curses on people. Those who wish to show how un-Christian the Old Testament is refer to such a psalm as this. Verses 6–19 have been called a 'song of hate' and we can understand the reaction when you read 'Let his prayer become sin ... Let his children be fatherless and his wife a widow' (verses 7–9) and 'as he loved cursing, so let it come to him' (verse 17). It seems to go against all that we learn from Jesus who taught his followers: 'love your enemies, bless those who curse you, do good to those who hate you, and pray for those who spitefully use you and persecute you' (Matthew 5:44). How do we respond to these curses and can we use such prayers in private and public worship?

The psalm has sometimes been misused. John Calvin reports how a lady in France hired some Franciscan friars to curse her only son using the words of this psalm. There is no warrant in the Bible for employing such psalms in this way. Others follow an opposite path and believe the psalm's imprecation is 'recorded for our learning, not for our imitation' (see Kidner, vol. 2, p. 389). Spurgeon urged caution by suggesting these curses are not for ordinary people but for those in authority.

Understanding the Psalm

Some scholars seek to evade the difficulties by suggesting that verses 6 to 19 should be put in inverted commas and viewed as a quotation of what David's enemies were saying against him. The switch from the plural to the singular is used to support this idea. However, there is nothing in the text to indicate that these are the words of David's accusers. What is more, it does not avoid the difficulties because in verse 20 David associates himself with the sentiments of the previous verses, and the kind of curses found in this psalm are no different to those found in other imprecatory psalms.

There are similarities between this series of curses in verses 6–19 and the words of Jeremiah 18:19–23. Jeremiah is God's servant delivering God's message and in rejecting the servant they are rejecting God. In that context, the prophet calls on God to bring down the curses of the Sinai covenant, which is in effect the judgment that he was commissioned by God to preach. We must therefore be careful to see the biblical curses in the contexts in which they were given. They are not the impulsive sentiments of Christ's disciples when they called for heavenly fire to consume the Samaritan village that had refused to receive the Saviour (Luke 9:51–56). Their spirit was entirely wrong.

David's curses must also be viewed against the covenant background. Some of the expressions used are found in the curses associated with the Sinai covenant (see Exodus 22:22–24; Deuteronomy 27:15–26; 28:15–46). We must not forget the covenant that God made with Abraham and his descendants. While the Sinai covenant has had its day on account of the new covenant established through Christ and his cross (Hebrews 8:13), the covenant with Abraham continues through into the New Testament where the final blessing incorporates the Gentile nations—'in you all the families of the earth shall be blessed' (Genesis 12:3; Gal 3:6–29). That covenant also contained a curse on those who would treat God's people with contempt—'I will curse him who curses you' (Genesis 12:3). So in this psalm David is appealing to God to do as he has promised and the way in which the psalmist does it is typical of curse formulas of the time. Interestingly, David mentions the enemy loving to curse and not delighting in blessing (verse 17) and we find the enemy's curse is contrasted with God's blessing (verse 28).

The Abrahamic covenant is the only context in which Christians can use curses against their enemies. This accounts for Paul calling down God's curse on Alexander the coppersmith. For the harm that this man did to Paul, the apostle writes, 'May the Lord repay him according to his works' and warns Timothy to beware of him (2 Timothy 4:14-15). An example through symbolic action of a curse on people who disdain God's servants is one that Jesus gave to his disciples: they were to shake the dust off their feet when they left the city (Matthew 10:11-15). Christ also uttered curses on the Scribes and the Pharisees (Matthew 23) and twice the apostle Paul writes, 'let him be accursed', once in relation to those preaching a false gospel and once on those who do not love Jesus (Galatians 1:8-9; 1 Corinthians 16:22). The problem therefore is not between Old and New Testaments, or the words of Jesus against other passages of Scripture. The spirit of love is not confined to the New Testament and cursing and judgment not restricted to the Old.[59]

A Messianic Psalm

Returning to this psalm, the New Testament considers it to be very relevant to our Lord's situation and sees the curse of verse 8 fulfilled in Judas Iscariot who betrayed Jesus (see Acts 1:16-20). David's experience becomes symbolic of all that Jesus went through and worse and this psalm becomes his plea to God against those hypocrites within the covenant community who rejected him. Jesus identified himself with God's suffering people from Abel to Stephen and all the saints of God down the centuries who are persecuted for his sake. But of course, Christ's own death was not that of a martyr. His blood speaks better things than the blood of Abel for he died to liberate us from sin's bondage and bring us to God. It must be remembered that there are two appearings of Jesus, one to atone for the sins of his people, the other for their final salvation and judgment. This salvation will involve the complete eradication of all evil and the punishment of all the enemies of God and his people. First time round God sent his Son not to judge the world but to save it (John 3:17; 8:15; 12:47). For this reason Jesus stopped his reading of Isaiah 61:1-3 before the reference to the day of God's vengeance (Luke 4:17-21) and prayed for those who crucified him (Luke 21:34). When he returns in glory, it will be 'in flaming fire taking vengeance on all those who do not know God' or 'obey the gospel of our Lord Jesus Christ' (2 Thessalonians 1:8). In the book of Revelation, John encourages the persecuted church with a vision of the last judgment. We first view the martyrs crying out to God for vengeance and then see them finally rejoicing in the overthrow of all the political and religious forces of wickedness that have been arrayed against God and his people.

This psalm does not endorse taking personal revenge or hiring some holy person to call down curses on our behalf. 'We need the imprecatory psalms to remind us how serious it is to reject Christ and how awful the nature of God's judgment will be. When Christ comes again as judge the psalms of cursing will be accomplished.'[60] In our private devotions the psalm can be used to fill out our Lord's pattern prayer: 'thy kingdom come ... deliver us from evil' or when great evils have been carried out by wicked people which have affected us personally, our families, our churches or our communities. The psalm can be recited or sung by the church undergoing severe persecution or when enemies of the gospel have produced great havoc in church fellowships.

The Psalm in Context

The 'David' who wrote this 'Psalm' and who committed it to the 'Chief Musician' (see Psalm 4) to be used by the people of God in their worship, whose sins were not overlooked in the biblical records, is one who was noted for his kindness toward enemies like king Saul. Despite the many trials endured, he did not seek personal revenge but committed his case to God and left it with him to right wrongs and punish his persecutors. That must be our position as it was of our Lord himself.

The psalm's position in Book 5 is appropriate to the circumstances following the exile and the Jews' return to the promised land. God's people look for deliverance and vindication 'according to God's faithful love' which is good (verses 21, 26; see Psalms 107 and 108). They are assured that God will act on their behalf and can unite in praising him. The curses can apply to the enemies outside the covenant community like Edom (see Psalm 108), as well as those opponents from within. Not only David but Israel too in her sufferings foreshadows the sufferings of the Messiah while the treachery of Edom and of those within the Jewish community of the time become types of Judas' betrayal.

There are four main sections to the psalm. First there is the lament, describing the situation (verses 1-5) followed by the curses against the enemy (verses 6-20). The psalm continues with a plea that contains more indications of the troubles being faced (verses 21-29) and the psalm closes with a determination to praise God when deliverance comes (verses 30-31).

Seeking divine aid (verses 1-5)

The psalm begins in the original by addressing God—'O God of my praise' (verse 1), which is similar to Jeremiah's, 'you are my praise' (Jeremiah 17:14). There is actually no more praise until we get to the last two verses, yet this phrase is a reminder that the whole psalm is set in this context of David's God who is worthy of his praises. The enemy is active but God is silent (see Psalm 28:1).

He tells God his trouble. The wicked are speaking lies about him. There is hatred in their words and all for no just reason ('without a cause', verses 2-3; see Psalms 35:19; 69:4). David's complaint is similar to many of his laments in the first two Books (see Psalms 10:7; 52:4) and reminds us of Jesus' words to his disciples (John 15:25).

David has shown deep friendship ('love') to those who are now accusing him. Acts of goodwill and kindness have been repaid with evil and hatred (verse 5; see Psalms 35:12; 38:20). In all this his emphasis is on prayer and not on taking vengeance. Literally it reads 'but I—prayer' (see Psalm 120:7 'I—peace'). How true this was of our Lord and Stephen, the first Christian martyr who followed his master's example (Acts 7:54-60).

Praying for the punishment of foes (verses 6-20)

David appeals to God, the divine judge of all, that the enemy would receive strict justice, in other words, that the punishment would fit the crime. The principle is summed up in verse 17: 'As he loved cursing, so let it come to him; as he did not delight in blessing, so let it be far from him'. As the mouth of the wicked one had spoken against the psalmist so may a wicked one be set over him (compare verse 2 with verse 6). He asks that an 'accuser' (verse 6, from which we get the name 'Satan') might stand at the right hand of the accused so that when he is judged he will be found guilty and his own plea will fail leading to his condemnation (verse 7). Some of the terms found here are used of the devil, the arch-accuser of God's people (Job 1:6; 2:1; 1 Chronicles 21:1; Zechariah 3:1).

The enemy deserves to die because he slew 'the broken in heart' (verse 16). David calls for the enemy's premature death and for someone else to take over his official position (verse 8). Peter applied this verse to Judas Iscariot to show the necessity of replacing him, after first quoting Psalm 69:25 to explain his death (Acts 1:20). It was Jesus who said of Judas that it would have been better if he had never been born (Mark 14:21) and referred to him as one destined for hell ('son of perdition', John 17:12).

We know nothing of Judas' family situation but when an accused father and husband received the death sentence the family would be left destitute. Conventional imagery is used to show the plight of such people, with creditors and strangers seizing his assets. Again, the principle applies, as the accused showed no loving commitment to others but persecuted the humble poor believer (verse 16), so no such love is to be extended to him and his family (verse 12). The verses express the truth that the sins of the fathers are visited on the children (Exodus 20:5). John Donne's famous adage 'No man is an island' is barely understood by modern western individualistically-minded people. Grandparents as well as parents and children are all bound up together with us for better or for worse (verses 13–14; see Proverbs 20:7). These prayers, as Motyer observes, 'give expression to scriptural inevitabilities: this is what life is like under the rule of an awesome and holy God.' The curses only follow the punishments that the sins deserve in God's law. For example, false accusers will receive what they purposed would happen to the accused (Deuteronomy 19:15–21).

The imprecations come to a climax with this awful picture of the enemy who has delighted in cursing others being so overtaken with curses that it takes possession of the person within and without. Sin often contains its own punishment in people's lives.

The final verse brings this part of the psalm to a conclusion. We could take it as a continuation of the curses as in the translation, '*Let this be ...*' but it may also be translated as a prophetic statement: 'This is the Lord's reward to my accusers ...' (verse 20). 'This' refers to all the denunciations that have been mentioned and they apply to all who 'speak evil' of the Lord's anointed king (see Psalm 2).

Seeking divine aid (verses 21–29)

In this prayer, David brings his hurts and concerns to God. He does not take the law into his own hands and avenge the enemy. As a true believer, he understands that vengeance belongs to the Lord and he will repay at the proper time (Deuteronomy 32:35). The Christian, too, must take everything to the Lord in prayer and not seek personal revenge when persecutors accuse us falsely and say all kinds of evil against us (Romans 12:19). God will vindicate his people and punish their enemies on the day of judgment.

The sovereign 'Lord', Israel's covenant 'GOD' (Yahweh/Jehovah),[61] is the one to whom all God's oppressed people can look for redress. Appeal is made for deliverance on the grounds of God's 'faithful love' ('mercy') which is good (verse 21; see Psalms 107:1, 43; 108:4).

David then identifies himself with the 'poor and needy' (see Psalms 35:10; 40:17) whose 'heart is wounded' or 'pierced' (verse 22; see verse 16). The Servant was 'wounded' ('pierced') on account of our sins (Isaiah 53:5). The king likens himself to the ending of the day, when the shadows lengthen as the sun sets (see Psalm 102:11) and is gone like a locust that is shaken away by a strong wind (verse 23; see Exodus 10:19). In other words, David confesses his frail, vulnerable state. The imagery changes in verse 24 as again he laments his weak condition and the way he is being treated. People think of him as a lost cause (see Psalms 22:7-8; 69:10-12). Again, we think of how people mocked and shook their heads when they saw Jesus on the cross (Mark 15:29-32).

After this lament David again appeals for help to Yahweh/Jehovah his God to save him on the basis of his 'faithful love' ('mercy', verse 26; see verse 21). He wants people, especially his enemies, to see that his deliverance is due solely to God's power (verse 27). While his enemies may curse, he looks for God to bless him. God's blessing can overcome all human curses and those whose object was to shame David will themselves be shamed (verse 29; Psalm 71:13). We are reminded of God's words to Abraham, 'I will curse him who curses you' (Genesis 12:3).

Promising to give thanks (verses 30–31)

As often in laments, the psalm ends on a note of praise. David vows to give great thanks to God and to praise him openly among the throng of people. He considers himself among the 'poor' (verse 31; see verse 22). It refers to God's humble, obedient people who are often oppressed by the wicked. David is assured that not any accuser (verse 6; and not Satan as in Zechariah 3:1), but God himself will stand at his 'right hand' and deliver him from those who would 'condemn him'.

Like previous psalms of David, his experiences point us to those of our Lord Jesus. People who should have welcomed him turned against him and with hatred and lies plotted to kill him. He did not retaliate but committed his cause to God his Father and looked for vindication from him (Hebrews 5:7; 1 Peter 2:23). In all this, David foreshadows the Christ whom Isaiah prophesies in his portrayal of the suffering Servant. The Servant confidently cries, 'Surely the Lord GOD will help me; who is he who will condemn me?' (Isaiah 50:9). The Lord Jesus who was justified or vindicated in the Spirit by his resurrection (1 Timothy 3:16) is the one through whom all who rely on Christ for salvation are justified and will be vindicated on the day of resurrection and judgment (Romans 4:25; 8:33-34; 1 Thessalonians 4:13-18; Revelation 12:7-11).

Psalm 110

The Anointed King and Priest

The Old Testament passage most often quoted in the New Testament is this psalm. It is the third in a short series attributed to David (see Psalms 108-109). Jesus confirmed David's authorship when he drew the Pharisees' attention to its opening words by saying, 'How then does David in the Spirit call him Lord?' (Matthew 22:43-44).

As in Psalm 36, David is given a prophetic word. Rather than David's experience it is a direct word from God that is being disclosed to us. These divine oracles through David the prophet (see 2 Samuel 23:2) are introduced in verse 1 ('The LORD said ...') and verse 4 ('The Lord has sworn ...') with the other verses expanding on God's words (verses 2-3 and 5-7). To help in our understanding of this psalm, the introductory Psalm 2 becomes crucially important.

We might wonder why it is placed at this point in the psalm collection. Along with the earlier psalms of Book 5 (Psalms 107-109) this Davidic psalm is used by the final prophetic editor to encourage God's people at a time when instead of having a king of David's family line, they were being ruled by foreigners. They may have been given liberty to return to their homeland and to rebuild Jerusalem and the temple but they were still not free of Persian rule. The psalm is the sequel to Psalm 89 which laments the loss of the Davidic monarch.

Like Chronicles psalms such as this one encourage the faithful in Israel to look in hope to the fulfilment of God's special covenant with David (see 2 Samuel 7). The psalm promotes the expectation of a future Anointed One (Messiah) who will bring to realisation all God's promises relating to his rule over the nations.

It is the New Testament that helps us to interpret the psalm correctly. Not only does Jesus quote from it (Matthew 22:41-45; Mark 12:35-37; Luke 20:41-44) but it is used by Peter in his first sermon on the Day of Pentecost (Acts 2:34-35) and by the writer to the Hebrews (Hebrews 1:13; 5:6; 7:17, 21; 10:12-13).

Divine announcement (verse 1)

The psalm opens in a way typical of many of the prophetic oracles particularly Amos, Jeremiah and Ezekiel: 'The LORD said' (more literally, 'Utterance of Yahweh'; see Genesis 22:16; Isaiah 41:14; Jeremiah 1:8; etc.). This is the only place it occurs in the psalm collection. The covenant God ('LORD') makes this declaration to someone described as 'my Lord', which is a respectful way of speaking concerning a superior person. God directs this sovereign Lord to sit at his right hand, which means that he is being given a place of honour and authority alongside God (see Psalm 45:9; 1 Kings 2:19). Is David reporting what a prophet has said concerning him? That is how some take the words and suggest this is an oracle given to David at his coronation. It is true that the kings of David's family line were given a position of great influence. Chronicles refers to the Davidic king sitting 'on the throne of the kingdom of the LORD over Israel' and 'on the throne of the LORD as king' (1 Chronicles 28:5; 29:23; 2 Chronicles 9:8). Solomon is sitting on God's throne ruling under God over the kingdom of Israel. While it is important to remember verses like this that point to both David and Solomon in their kingly office over God's people as foreshadowing the future Messiah, that is not how Jesus saw this particular psalm (Mark 12:36).

It is David writing as a prophet who declares God's word about this superior person whom David calls 'my Lord'. The LORD, Yahweh/Jehovah, is speaking to the special Anointed King mentioned in Psalm 2:2, 6. Jesus saw it as a reference to himself as the Messiah (Mark 12:35-37) and Peter refers to it as a prophecy of Jesus' resurrection and exaltation to the Father's right hand (Acts 2:34-35; see Hebrews 1:3, 13). Interestingly, the call to David's Lord to sit at Yahweh's 'right hand' takes up words found in the closing verse of the previous psalm (Psalm 109:31) where it is Yahweh/Jehovah who is said to stand at the right hand of a humble poor believer like David (see also Psalm 110:5).

God's first announcement includes a promise that all the king's enemies will be under his feet. The picture of them being made a 'footstool' is similar to the symbolic action of Joshua's men when they were invited by him to put their feet on the necks of the Amorite kings as an encouragement to Israel that God would do this to all their enemies (Joshua 10:24). Psalm 72: 9 speaks in similar language of the king's foes licking the dust (see also Psalm 2:9). As a result of Christ's victorious death on the cross, by which he 'offered the one sacrifice for sins for ever' and so defeated Satan (see Genesis 3:15; Revelation 12:7–10), he has 'sat down at the right hand of God, from that time waiting till his enemies are made his footstool' (Hebrews 10:11–14). Christ is seated in that place of honour far above all principalities and powers and reigns there until all his enemies are under his feet (1 Corinthians 15:25; Ephesians 1:20–22; Philippians 2:9–11; 1 Peter 3:22). We either submit willingly, acknowledging him as Lord and Saviour or forcibly when he returns in glory.

Announcement explained (verses 2–3)

Although God is referred to in the third person—'The LORD shall send ...' (verse 2) it is quite normal in prophetic messages for direct and indirect speech to be used. The Messiah's powerful 'rod' or 'sceptre' (see Psalm 2:9) stands for his rule and authority as king. It is from 'Zion', where God dwells and the king reigns (Psalms 2:6; 20:2; 132:13), that God will extend Messiah's rule. The King's call to 'dominate' ('rule') the surrounding enemies has within it the promise that he will be victorious. It is prefigured in Solomon's dominion over all from the Euphrates to the Mediterranean (1 Kings 4:24; see Psalm 72:8).

A further encouraging promise is made in verse 3. Messiah's people will offer themselves freely ('volunteers'), like the freewill gifts that Israel gave for the construction of the tabernacle (Exodus 36:3–7). They will do this 'in the day of your power', which is the time when the King exercises the powerful rule mentioned in the previous verse. The language becomes highly figurative and it is difficult to know precisely how we should understand it. The first phrase, 'beauties of holiness' (see Psalms 29:2; 96:9) could refer to the Lord's people, those who are with the King in his victorious rule, arrayed in 'holy splendour'. The rest of the verse is similarly applied to Messiah's people who are like the refreshing dew that appears with the morning light ('the womb of the morning'). On the other hand, it is perhaps better to see the second half of the verse from 'in the beauties of holiness' as referring to the King. It is God's King who is clothed in 'majestic holiness' and who appears at the break of day ('the womb of the morning') like the early dew with all the liveliness and freshness of youth.[62] Similar metaphors are used by David in describing the ruler of God's people (2 Samuel 23:3-4). The life-giving, reviving properties of dew, like rain, were proverbial. Without it all vegetation would die during the hot, dry summers of Canaan (Genesis 27:28, 39; 2 Samuel 1:21; 1 Kings 17:1; Proverbs 19:12; Isaiah 26:19; Hosea 14:5).

Jesus the Messiah perfectly answers to this description. He is the all-conquering hero who comes with his people to rule with the rod of iron but he is also 'the Bright and Morning Star' who is full of life and energy (Revelation 19:11-16; 22:16).

Divine announcement (verse 4)

God's second announcement is made on oath—'The LORD has sworn ...'. This makes the announcement even more solemn and unalterable (see Psalm 89:35). It is again Israel's covenant God ('LORD') who makes the pronouncement and there is no possibility of going back on this word—'he will not relent'. God does not change his mind as humans do. He does not go against his eternal plans and purpose (Numbers 23:19). The announcement is made to the person spoken of in the previous verses, to David's 'Lord', the 'King of kings and Lord of lords' (Revelation 19:16). What is remarkable is that this King is declared to be a 'priest for ever'. He is commissioned once and for all to this office.

Normally in Israel and unlike the great rulers of Mesopotamia and Egypt, kings did not function as priests in making atonement for the sins of the people through animal and grain sacrifices, although they were allowed to pray on behalf of the people and to bless them. In the covenant God made with Israel at Mount Sinai, the office of priest in Israel was limited to one particular family of Levites, to Aaron and his descendants. Here we learn of a different priestly institution—'according to the order of Melchizedek'.

Also in Israel, the priest was not a king. While they had leadership functions, especially those who acted both as priest and judge, like Eli and Samuel, they were never crowned as kings. The cry for a king came from the people when Samuel was their leader. But the priesthood 'according to the order of Melchizedek' combines the offices of king and priest.

We read of Melchizedek ('My king is righteousness') at the welcome party for Abram after his victory over the four eastern kings who had invaded Canaan (Genesis 14:17–20). Like many ancient Near-Eastern rulers Melchizedek combined the offices of king and priest. As priest of God Most High he blessed Abram and he in turn recognised his priesthood as a representative of the God whom Abram worshipped and presented him with a tithe of the spoils of war. Clearly this priest-king knew and worshipped the true God, although no further details are given. He was ruler of the city-state of Salem, another name for Jerusalem (see Psalm 76:2). Interestingly, there was a king of Jerusalem in the days of Joshua who had a similar name, 'Adoni-zedek' ('My lord is righteousness'; see Joshua 10:1) but unlike Melchizedek, he was no different to the other Canaanite kings and perished with them when God used Israel to cleanse the land of its immoral filth.

When David conquered Jerusalem he made it his capital and it was from there he ruled, heir to this kind of priestly-kingship that Abraham acknowledged. It provides the background to this oracle given to David but the oracle does not refer to David but to his greater son, King Jesus, as the writer to the Hebrews makes clear. He is not a descendant of Levi and Aaron, but of Judah and David. He is the king of David's family line and he is also a priest but not from the order laid down in the Sinai covenant. On the contrary, this priestly institution is like the one that pre-dates Moses, from the time of Abraham. Jesus is both priest and king and thus follows 'the order of Melchizedek'.

It is significant that Isaiah in the first part of his prophecy portrays the future Messiah as a king from David's family line, whereas in the second part the same kind of language concerning his rule is applied to the Servant (Isaiah 42:1–4; see Isaiah 9:7) who is depicted as a priest who atones for the sins of God's people and makes intercession for them (Isaiah 52:13–53:12). Zechariah, one of the prophets of Israel after the return from exile, picks up this idea of linking the offices of priest and king in his prophecy of the coming Messiah. An elaborate crown is placed on the head of Joshua the high priest as a type of the coming King, 'the Branch', who 'shall sit and rule on his throne; so he shall be a priest on his throne' (Zechariah 6:9–15). The same prophet gives more details concerning the coming King (Zechariah 9:9–10). This psalm of

David, placed as it is in the final Book of the psalm collection, would have added weight to Zechariah's prophecy and encouraged the people to look with expectation to the coming Messiah.

This is another reason why the Sinai covenant is obsolete. With Jesus we have a better priesthood: one who is both the all-conquering king and on-going priest; one who perfectly understands us, having experienced human life in this world with all its troubles and woes; one who was tempted in all points like we are, yet remained sinless; one who offered himself as the perfect sacrifice for sin to end all such blood sacrifices; and one who ever lives to intercede for us (Hebrews 1:1-14; 5:6, 10; 6:20-7:28).

Announcement explained (verses 5–7)

The covenant God, Yahweh/Jehovah, is now referred to as the sovereign 'Lord' (verse 5; compare with verse 1) and is seen to be at the 'right hand' of this royal priest to give him protection and support (Psalms 16:8; 109:31). It is difficult to know whether the 3rd person singular pronoun 'he' in verses 5 to 7 refers to God or the King and it may be best to think of them acting as one. In God's strength the King is able to 'execute kings'. It is the 'rod of iron' theme by which he is victorious over all his foes 'in the day of his wrath' (see verse 2; Psalm 2:9). The scene is similar to the one presented in verses 2 and 3, except that here it is the second coming of the Messiah, that day of the King's anger when he comes to judge. This is the day of vengeance to which God's persecuted people look (see Psalm 109) and on account of which they bear patiently the cruelty and fury of their foes. We think of the dreadful atrocities committed against Christians throughout the centuries and especially during the 20th century and right up to the present as for instance in North Korea.

There is a day of reckoning. If these enemies of God and his people are not brought into submission through the conquests of the gospel during the present day of grace and salvation (Psalm 2:10-12; Acts 15:13-18) then they will be overthrown when he returns in power on the day of judgment (see Psalm 2:9). Verse 7, like the second half of verse 3 presents King Jesus refreshed and triumphant (see Psalms 3:3; 27:6). The scene is of total victory over all his foes and this is what we find in the final book of the Bible (Revelation 19:11-21; 20:7-15; 21:8; 22:15).

If we are uncomfortable with the picture of our Lord destroying his enemies, as it seems out of character with those passages that depict him as gentle and meek, John Calvin has this helpful answer: 'as a shepherd is gentle towards his flock, but fierce and formidable towards wolves and thieves; in like manner, Christ is kind and gentle towards those who commit themselves to his care, while they who wilfully and obstinately reject his yoke, shall feel with what awful and terrible power he is armed.' We are urged to repent and respond in faith to his gracious invitation to come to him.

Psalm 111

The Lord's Works and Will

I f Psalms 105 and 106 could be described as 'non-identical twins', Psalms 111 and 112 are more like an identical pair. But even identical twins have characters of their own and that is true of these two psalms. They are both alphabetic acrostic psalms which means we have an ABC structure (see Psalms 9–10, 25, 34, 37) where each of the twenty-two letters of the Hebrew alphabet are used in turn to commence a verse or parts of a verse.

These two psalms show great skill and remind us of the amazing variety of form and presentation that we find in God's Word. Both use all the letters of the Hebrew alphabet in record time by beginning each half of a verse with a new letter. In the final two verses of both psalms, each verse is divided into three parts and each part begins in turn with the remaining six letters. Together, these two psalms prepare us for Psalm 119 which is the mother of all alphabetic acrostics.

Psalm 111 follows Psalms 108:3 and 109:30 in giving thanks, as all are urged to do in Psalm 107:1, 8, 15, 21, 31. It is especially appropriate after the oracles concerning the Lord's Anointed Priest-King in the previous psalm. The psalm is placed here in Book 5 to encourage those who have returned from exile to see God's saving action as part of God's big storyline that began with the exodus from Egypt and will culminate in the saving and judging work of the coming Messiah.

Invitation to praise (verse 1)

Psalm 111 opens with the heading 'Praise the LORD!' ('Hallelujah'; see Psalm 104:35), the first in a series of three that begins in this way (Psalms 111–113). It stands outside the alphabetic structure and calls upon all to use the psalm in the praise of Israel's covenant God.

The psalmist is committed ('I will praise') to confessing or giving thanks to Yahweh/Jehovah ('LORD') with the whole of his being (see Psalm 86:11–12). But while it is personal he wishes to do it publicly where the 'upright' (Psalm 25:8) meet as a friendly 'company' ('assembly'; see Psalm 89:7), which he further describes as a 'congregation' (Psalm 1:5). Openly confessing thanks to those of similar mind and heart in church fellowship meetings is a great encouragement to faith especially in trying and difficult times.

Reasons for praise (verses 2–9)

Over the main entrance to the new Cavendish Laboratory that houses the University of Cambridge's prestigious physics department built in 1973, is the English text of verse 2 in the Coverdale translation: 'The works of the Lord are great; sought out of all them that have pleasure therein'. The same text in Latin is carved on the doors of the first Cavendish Laboratory of 1874. While the verse can certainly be applied to God's works of creation the context suggests that it is God's redemptive works that are in mind. The main theme of this thanksgiving hymn is the great works that God did for his people during the exodus period.

God's works (verses 2–7)

These works encourage investigation and people find delight in them (verse 2).

These works display the 'honourable and glorious' being of God (see Psalm 104:1) and they reveal his concern for what is right, 'righteousness' being one of God's enduring characteristics (verse 3).

These 'wonderful works', often a reference to God's victory over the Egyptians, are ones where God made a name for himself and by which he would be long remembered (Exodus 3:20; see Psalm 107:8, 15, 21, 31). They also indicated that God was 'gracious and full of compassion' (verse 4; see Exodus 34:6).

Included in God's works is the provision of 'food'[63] for his people who are said to revere him (Exodus 14:31). During the wilderness period he provided them with manna and quails (Exodus 16; Numbers 11). Through the exodus and wilderness God was continually mindful of 'his covenant' promises which he had made with Abraham and with the people at Sinai (verse 5; see Exodus 2:24; 6:5; 34:10, 27).

God's powerful works are seen not only during the exodus period (see Exodus 9:16; 15:6; 32:11) but in the way Israel was given Canaan as an inheritance (verse 6; Exodus 34:10-11). Israel's occupation of Canaan was a preview or picture of what God gives Messiah—'the nations for your inheritance' (Psalm 2:8).

God's works also show his 'verity and justice' or his 'reliability and judicial decisions' with regard to his people. Therefore what he requires them to do in his 'precepts' or 'detailed requirements' can be trusted (verse 7; see Psalm 19:7-9). This verse prepares us for the transition from God's works to his will for the people's lives.

God's will (verses 8–9)

God's commandments are not capricious but are firmly established. While our translation '*are* done' is possible, it is better to think not of the LORD's ordinances being done by God in 'truth and uprightness' (verse 8) but performed or obeyed faithfully and with integrity by his people. This alphabetical psalm is preparing us for a much fuller statement on this subject in Psalm 119.

The works of God in redeeming his people are introduced again but in this context they provide the background for how his people should live. It is in view of God's saving grace they are called to live a life pleasing to him (Exodus 20:1-2). In the same way Christians, who have known God's saving grace, are to live obedient lives (Romans 12:1-2). The covenant in this context refers to the commands of the covenant that God required his people to keep (verse 9; Exodus 20-24; Psalm 105:8).

The psalm reminds us that God has revealed himself ('his name'; see Psalm 20:1) both as 'holy and awesome'. God is, in other words, terrifyingly pure and unique (see Psalm 99:3). When the beaver in Lewis's *The Lion, the Witch and the Wardrobe* speaks about Aslan the lion, the children ask, 'Is he safe?' The beaver replies, 'Of course not, but he's good'.

Right response (verse 10)

The statement concerning the fearsome God in the previous verse prepares for this concluding word about fearing God. What is to be our response to this covenant God who is 'glorious in holiness, fearful in praises, doing wonders' (Exodus 15:11)? We are introduced to a fundamental principle that is stressed in the wisdom books of the Bible: 'The fear of the LORD is the beginning of wisdom' (Job 28:28; Proverbs 1:7; 9:10; see Psalms 19:9; 25:12; 34:11). Wisdom in the Bible is inseparable from knowledge and understanding (Job 28:12; Proverbs 1:2–7; 15:33) and there is a spiritual and ethical dimension to it. It includes a relationship with God and living a life that is pleasing to him. That is why fearing God is essential and foundational. Fear of God is more than giving him respect. It is being aware and knowing something of the reality of his awe-inspiring nature and character as he has revealed himself in Scripture. Such fear produces humility of spirit and concern lest we bring dishonour to his name.

Christians are called to 'cleanse ourselves from all filthiness of the flesh and spirit, perfecting holiness in the fear of God' and to 'work out your own salvation with fear and trembling' (2 Corinthians 7:1; Philippians 2:12). For Charles Bridges, the fear of the Lord is 'that affectionate reverence, by which the child of God bends himself humbly and carefully to his Father's law'.[64] All who do God's precepts (see verse 7) show they have a 'good understanding' (see Proverbs 3:4; 13:15).

The psalm ends as it began. The last letter of the Hebrew alphabet begins the word for 'praise' and matches the 'Hallelujah' ('Praise the LORD') at the head of verse 1. The LORD is worthy to be praised and in fact such praise will be enduring (literally 'standing') 'for ever'.

Psalm 112

The LORD's Wise Person

You could almost call Psalms 111 and 112 conjoined (Siamese) twins for where the one ends the other begins in praising and fearing the LORD. It is another alphabetic psalm and it follows the exact pattern of the previous one and even uses some identical terms and expressions. But it has a character of its own for whereas Psalm 111 praises God, this one celebrates the character and destiny of the one who fears God and seeks to follow his ways. It resembles Psalm 1 for after the initial heading, it begins and ends with exactly the same words, 'Blessed' and 'perish' and speaks of the 'righteous' and the 'wicked'. Its place in Book 5 encourages the returned exiles to live in a God-honouring way.

Introducing the wise person (verse 1)
Like Psalm 111 it opens with the heading 'Praise the LORD!' ('Hallelujah'; see Psalm 104:35), the second in a series of three that begins in this way (Psalms 111-113). Again, it stands outside the alphabetic structure and encourages all to use this psalm in praise of God. While the psalm focuses on the godly person we are not to praise the person but the God who has enabled this godly one to be conformed to the likeness of God.

The alphabetical poem commences by drawing attention to the

'blessed' person, the one who is to be congratulated (see Psalm 1:1). It is the one who 'fears the Lord' (Psalm 111:10) who is in this most happy and privileged position. Such godly fear, foundational to all true wisdom, finds its expression in delighting in God's commandments (see Psalm 1:2). A single individual is portrayed throughout, which suggests that the psalm is depicting the ideal person who represents all God's people. It bears some similarities to the godly life depicted in the alphabetic acrostic of Proverbs 31:10-31. The God-fearing wise man of this psalm and the God-fearing woman of Proverbs 31 both present the ideal successful life. As we saw in Psalm 1 it is Jesus who fulfils this role as prophesied by Isaiah. Messiah has the Spirit of wisdom, knowledge and of the fear of the LORD resting upon him (Isaiah 11:2).

Describing the wise person (verses 2–9)

The blessed life is expressed in Old Testament terms. First, the person is blessed with offspring who are like 'mighty' ones. They are described as if they were ancient heroes like Nimrod—'a mighty one on the earth' (Genesis 10:8). Family members who are 'upright' (see Psalm 111:1) will also enjoy God's blessing through this person's fear of God (verse 2).

'Wealth and riches' give another indication of blessing (see Proverbs 3:9-10; 22:4). The godly Job, before his testing experience, was blessed in this way (Job 1:1-3). Amazingly, what is said of God in the previous psalm, under the same letter of the alphabet—'and his righteousness endures for ever'—is applied to this person who fears God (verse 3)! His character reflects that of the LORD.

The godly person is also one who, like the LORD himself, is 'gracious and full of compassion, and righteous' (verse 4; see Psalm 111:4). Disciples of Christ are called to be perfect as their heavenly Father is perfect and to be merciful as the Father is merciful (Matthew 5:48; Luke 6:36). The first part of verse 4 should probably be understood to mean that this same person rises in the darkness to be a light to upright people. This person brings real relief to the upright in distressing times (Psalm 97:11).

The godly person is the one who is in a good position to be gracious in lending to others. When lending to others it is not with the aim of getting richer oneself as often happens. This individual is seeking to help the poor not to acquire easy money and does not take advantage of those less fortunate—'he will order his affairs with justice' (verse 5).

Being in this happy, fortunate position, there is no possibility of there being any alteration in this 'righteous' person's state—'he will never be shaken' and will be long remembered (verse 6; see Psalm 111:4).

The problems and tragedies of life do not terrify and undermine his stability because he is firmly 'trusting in the LORD' (verse 7). In Psalm 111:8 God's precepts stand fast, while here we are told that this godly person's heart 'stands fast' ('established') so that he continues to be without fear until he sees his foes put down (verse 8; Psalm 54:7). The hymn-writer expresses it as: 'Fear him, you saints, and you will then have nothing else to fear'.

The psalm emphasises the generosity of the godly person toward the poor. It went beyond lending without interest to giving to people who were in no position to repay (verse 9a). The verse is quoted by Paul as he encourages the Corinthian church to be cheerful givers (2 Corinthians 9:7–9). Again, his concern for what is right, like God's concern, is a characteristic that will stand for ever (see verse 3; Psalm 111:3).

Like an animal that raises its horn to indicate strength, God will give victory to this righteous person so that he will be honoured (verse 9b).

Proclaiming the happiness and privileged position of the godly is something that Jesus does in the Beatitudes at the beginning of the Sermon on the Mount. These are the people who are blessed: ones who are poor in spirit, who mourn, who are meek, who yearn for righteousness, who are merciful, pure in heart, peacemakers and persecuted for righteousness' sake. They are promised God's kingdom, that they will receive comfort, inherit the earth, be satisfied, obtain mercy, see God, be called sons of God and receive a heavenly reward (Matthew 5:3–12).

Concluding contrast (verse 10)

The psalm concludes with a brief reference to the wicked person. Such a one will see the triumph of the godly and it will provoke him to anger but, unable to change anything, he will melt away. His evil desires on the righteous will perish along with him (Proverbs 10:28). This is in contrast to the promise given to the needy: 'The expectation of the poor shall not perish for ever' (Psalm 9:18). To gnash the teeth pictures a person who is full of rage but powerless to do anything. It is a scene that Jesus often brings to our attention (Matthew 8:12; 13:42, 50; 22:13; 24:51; 25:30). Like the ending of Psalm 1 it presents a complete contrast to the way the psalm opens. 'O the happiness of the person who fears the Lord' whereas 'the desire of the wicked shall perish'. The call to praise the LORD (verse 1) means that besides praising God for the man who is blessed, there is a place for praising God that the wicked person's evil desires come to nothing (see Revelation 19:1–6).

Psalm 113

The Exalted LORD Exalts the Downcast

This is the third and final psalm in the series that begins with 'Praise the LORD' (see Psalms 111-112) and like the previous two it is concerned to exalt Israel's covenant God and to express concern for the needy, themes that unite these psalms to Psalm 107, which is the opening psalm to Book 5. They are placed at this point in the psalm collection to encourage a people dejected and in low spirits after the exile, to strengthen themselves in the Lord and to look expectantly for the fulfilment of all God's covenant promises. It has the same purpose for the Church today and individual believers, especially in distressing times when all things seem against us.

The psalm is the first of the so-called 'Hallel Psalms' (Praise Psalms) that run from Psalm 113 through to Psalm 118. They are also called by the Jews the 'Egyptian Hallel' (see the reference to Egypt in Psalm 114:1). According to Jewish tradition the singing of these six psalms was part of the ritual of the Passover meal. This may have been the practice when Jesus celebrated the festival on the night he was betrayed with Psalms 113-114 sung before the meal and Psalms 115-118 after it (see Mark 14:26). The application of these psalms to the exodus from Egypt encouraged the Early Church to use Psalms 113-114 and 118 on Easter

Day, for Jesus saw his death and resurrection in terms of an exodus as well as a redeeming work (Luke 9:31 'his decease/exodus'; Mark 10:45). The psalm begins and ends with 'Hallelujah' ('Praise the LORD'). Between these two general calls in the hymn God's people are urged to worship (verses 1–3) and reasons are given for doing so (verses 4–9). Those reasons include the kind of being God is (verses 4–6) and his actions on behalf of the downtrodden and disappointed (verses 7–9).

Call to praise the LORD (verses 1–3)

It is the 'servants of the LORD' who are urged to praise. In the singular, 'servant' is often used to describe leaders and prophets of the people like Moses, Joshua and David. Isaiah, in the second part of his prophecy (Isaiah 40–55), employs the term to speak of Israel as a whole (Isaiah 41:8; 42:19; 44:1–2, 21) and then of ideal Israel, the representative of God's people of all nations, who becomes the atoning sacrifice for sin (Isaiah 42:1; 49:3, 5–6; 52:13; 53:11). In the latter part of Isaiah's prophecy (Isaiah 56–66) it is the plural term that predominates and it refers to all God's people (Isaiah 56:6; 61:6; 65:9, 13–15). It is in this latter sense that 'servants' is used here (see Psalms 34:22; 69:36). Among the returned exiles, it was common practice to refer to themselves as God's servants (Ezra 5:11; Nehemiah 1:6, 10; etc.). It was both a privileged and responsible position. God's people are referred to in the last book of the Bible in this way. Those who are in the presence of God and the Lamb are 'his servants' who 'serve him' (Revelation 22:3; see Isaiah 61:6).

The divine name 'LORD' (Yahweh/Jehovah) appears in each of the first five verses, three times in the first verse, and in the seventh occurrence the familiar question, first heard at the Red Sea, is asked: 'Who is like the LORD (Yahweh/Jehovah)?' (verse 5). He is the incomparable God. In addition, 'name' occurs in each of the first three verses and is closely associated with 'Yahweh' ('LORD'), the great 'I am', the ever-present covenant-keeping God (Exodus 3:13–15). Its use here emphasises that God's 'praise' is in response to all that is revealed of God's character (verse 1; see Exodus 34:5–7).

All that God has revealed of himself under his special divine name is to issue in paying him homage ('blessed', verse 2; see Psalm 103:1) for he is worthy to be worshipped time without end ('from this time forth and for evermore'; verse 2) and universally ('from the rising of the sun to its going down', verse 3; see Psalm 50:1; Malachi 1:11).

The exalted LORD (verses 4-6)

The grounds for such praise are outlined. First, the hymn draws our attention to God's sovereignty. He is superior to all that is created, being 'high above' the Gentile nations (verse 4; see Psalms 46:10; 99:2; Isaiah 40:17) and 'his glory' or stunning importance, 'above the heavens' (see Psalm 57:5).

To ask the rhetorical question: 'Who is like the LORD our God?' (verse 5; see Psalm 71:19; Isaiah 40:18, 25) is to expect only one answer, 'No one!' He cannot be compared to anyone or anything. But Yahweh's uniqueness demonstrated so amazingly at the Red Sea (Exodus 15:11; see Deuteronomy 3:24) and in forgiving sin (Micah 7:18) is also displayed in his concern for the weak and the vulnerable (Psalm 35:10) as this psalm goes on to show.

Before mentioning that reason for praising God, the psalm presses home the point that the 'LORD' (Yahweh/Jehovah) is highly exalted. He sits enthroned 'on high' (verse 5). So transcendent is he that he 'humbles himself' to see the created order (verse 6; see 1 Kings 8:27).

Exalting the lowly (verses 7-9)

A second ground for praise is that this high and lofty God condescends to the most insignificant person on earth. The Lord's greatness is seen in his concern for those who cannot help themselves. The godly person of the previous psalm expresses the care that God has toward the poor and needy (see Psalm 112:9). Verses 7 and 8a borrow the language of Hannah's prayer of thanksgiving at giving birth to Samuel (1 Samuel 2:8). She who was barren and despised became the happy mother of a son. Every poor child of God can look up to the Lord for help in times of great need (Psalm 41:1). Normally God uses people, especially Christian brothers and sisters, to bring relief and the New Testament reminds Christians of their responsibilities in this area (Galatians 2:10; 6:10; James 2:15).

We have all seen pictures of those in abject poverty rummaging among the mountains of rubbish outside some of the world's vast cities. It is a powerful image of people in dire need. Both Hannah's prayer and the psalmist's hymn demonstrate what God does on a massive scale in Jesus Christ. The transcendent God stooped down to us in the Person of the Son, Jesus Christ, and humbled himself even to death on a cross (Philippians 2:5-8). He raises poor, needy sinners, who cannot save themselves, to sit in the heavenly places in Christ Jesus

(Ephesians 2:6). God's kingdom belongs to such who are of a humble contrite heart and Jesus encouraged his disciples with these words, 'Do not fear, little flock, for it is your Father's good pleasure to give you the kingdom' (Luke 12:32).

Interestingly, the Jewish Aramaic paraphrases of the Psalms interpret these final verses as God's restoration of Israel after its low state in exile. The psalm encouraged the people of God after the return from exile to look with Isaiah to the time after the Suffering Servant's work when barren Israel would see many children spreading out to all the nations (Isaiah 54:1-10; Luke 1:46-55). It points us to the results of Christ's atoning sacrifice on the cross, and to how the peoples of the earth are drawn to him in fulfilment of the promise to Abraham (Genesis 12:3; John 12:31-33; Galatians 3:13-14).

All this calls for a final 'Hallelujah' ('Praise the Lord', verse 9).

Psalm 114

The Presence of the Sovereign Lord

What does the Bible mean by the presence of God? Surely God is present everywhere at all times. There is not one single place where he is not present every moment of the day and night. While this is true, it is a truth that we accept on trust. This is what God has revealed in the Bible about himself and we take it by faith. However, God does, on occasions, make his presence objectively felt in our world. He has done this throughout the history of the Christian Church when the gospel has been preached in the power of the Holy Spirit. God's presence has brought people to their knees in repentance and then to jump for joy at the forgiveness of their sins. Whole communities have sometimes been affected by the presence of the living God. There is a day coming when the most stubborn cynic and ardent atheist will tremble at the presence of God when he comes to judge the world. Isaiah speaks of people entering into the rocks and hiding in the dust 'from the terror of the LORD and the glory of his majesty. The lofty looks of man shall be humbled, the haughtiness of men shall be bowed down, and the LORD alone shall be exalted in that day' (Isaiah 2:10-11, 19, 21; see Revelation 6:15-17).

When God brought Israel out of Egypt in fulfilment of his promises to Abraham it was to form them into a people who would display God to the world. He would live and walk among them and be their God and they would be his people. When the tabernacle was erected in the middle of the camp the glory of God's presence came upon it. The same thing happened when Solomon's temple was built. This psalm celebrates the presence of the Lord among his chosen people during the period from the exodus out of Egypt to the conquest of Canaan.

This is the second of the so-called 'Egyptian Hallel' psalms (see Psalm 113 for details). It is a very carefully crafted piece of Hebrew poetry with the Red Sea, Jordan and mountains and hills (verses 3–4, 5–6) being framed by references to God's presence (verses 1–2, 7–8). God's majesty and condescension that were highlighted in the previous psalm are applied in this psalm to God's activity in bringing his poor despised people out of Egypt (verses 1–2). It displays his sovereignty over creation (verses 3–6) as well as his concern to supply the needy (verse 8).

What Chronicles seeks to do through its history of Israel and what Haggai and Zechariah do through their prophecies, this psalm, like the previous ones in Book 5, encourage the people who returned from Babylon to be assured that God will not abandon what he has started and will keep all the promises he has made to Abraham, Moses and David. These psalms are also a comfort and encouragement to all God's oppressed people in every age. There is a divine principle that applies not only to the individual Christian but to God's work in general that 'he who has begun a good work in you will complete it until the day of Jesus Christ' (Philippians 1:6).

The psalm is a very unusual type of praise hymn. There is no call for praise but in a very dramatic and concise way it begins with reasons for praise and does not name God until near the end. After all the references to God's personal name in the previous psalm this one does not use the name Yahweh/Jehovah ('Lord') once.

Israel's beginnings (verses 1–2)

The phrase 'went (came) out of Egypt' is a standard way of speaking of the exodus event (see Deuteronomy 4:45–46; Joshua 2:10). 'The house of Jacob' parallels 'Israel' (verse 1) and indicates that the family who went into Egypt when Joseph was Pharaoh's vizier (Genesis 46:27) is the one that God formed into a nation set apart for him from the twelve tribes that came from the original twelve sons of Jacob (Exodus 19:3–6).

To the Israelites who spoke Hebrew, the language of the Egyptians was unintelligible and this only added to their sense of alienation.

When Joseph's brothers were speaking among themselves they were unaware at the time that Joseph could understand for he spoke to them through an interpreter (Genesis 42:23; see Isaiah 33:19). This reference to Israel's oppressors having a strange language would have resonated with God's people in exile under the Babylonians (see Isaiah 36:11, 13) as well as after their return, for the Jews were still under foreign rule (see Deuteronomy 28:49; Isaiah 28:11; Jeremiah 5:15).

From the exodus event of verse 1 the psalm moves to Canaan. The terse language of verse 2 is packed with ideas and we are probably meant to interpret it in a number of complementary ways. 'Judah' and 'Israel' are used in connection with the settlement of God's people in the land of promise and, by appearing in parallel statements, they could signify the whole land with Judah having the honour of being the place associated with Jerusalem and the temple. After Solomon, when the kingdom split into two, Judah came to denote the southern area that remained loyal to the royal line of David while Israel referred to the northern kingdom. Chronicles, written after the return from exile, applies the term Israel to the whole of God's people and that is probably the dominant thought here with Judah used as a parallel term.

Most unusual is the way we are left to assume that the pronouns in 'his sanctuary' (literally 'his holiness') and 'his dominion' refer to God. The psalm has made no mention of God up to this point and it is possible that the pronouns could be referring to 'the house of Jacob' (verse 1) and meaning that 'holiness' as well as 'dominion' refer to the whole holy land and realm as belonging to this family. Interestingly, the prophet Zechariah of the post exilic period, is the only biblical writer to refer to the 'holy land' (literally 'the land of the holiness'; see Zechariah 2:12; Exodus 15:17).

On the other hand, the words 'sanctuary' and 'dominion' could be speaking not of the land but of the nation and of God's presence among them. The words call to mind God's statement where he promises his covenant-keeping people that they will be 'a kingdom of priests and a holy nation' (Exodus 19:6) and Jeremiah speaks of Israel as 'holiness to the LORD' (Jeremiah 2:3). Leaving God's name to the closing lines makes its appearance all the more striking (see Psalm 24:7-10).

The exodus-conquest events (verses 3-6)

Using highly colourful poetry, the psalm provides more detail concerning the events referred to in verses 1 and 2. We are reminded first of the Red Sea incident (Exodus 14:10–31) and then of the crossing of the Jordan (Joshua 3). These two demonstrations of God's power over the waters (verse 3; see Psalm 29:3–4) are mentioned in Joshua's words to the people (Joshua 4:23). Motyer observes that the 'two "crossings" mark respectively coming out of Egypt and coming into Canaan'. Luther's comment is apt: 'We use this Psalm to give thanks unto Christ, who delivered us from the kingdom of darkness, and translated us into the kingdom of light, even into his own kingdom, the kingdom of God's dear Son, and led us forth into eternal life'.

Great trees are said to skip like calves in fright when the Lord thunders (Psalm 29:6) and that might be the thought behind the picture of mountains and hills skipping like lambs and rams (verse 4). It is a scene of terror rather than of joy. Mount Sinai became an awesome place with earthquake and electric storm expressing the presence of God in giving the Law. But the reference may also include the conquest of Canaan with the flocks on the mountains and hills jumping with fright during the military campaigns in the hill country (see Habakkuk 3:6).

The rhetorical questions emphasise what the psalmist wishes to make clear that God's activity in bringing his people out of slavery and into their promised inheritance was something momentous. These rivers and mountains are witnesses to the wonders of God's redemptive work and the establishment of his rule on earth in the Israelite nation. Nothing can stand in the way of the almighty, sovereign Saviour God. This becomes an exciting indication of what God is to accomplish as a result of the exodus from Babylonian exile which will culminate in Christ's redemptive work on the cross. The grand finale will be the redemption of the whole creation from bondage to decay and the end of the curse in the new heaven and new earth (Isaiah 55:12–13).

Israel's blessings (verses 7–8)

The reaction of the Red Sea, the river Jordan and the mountains should characterise the whole earth (see Psalms 96:9; 97:4–5). At the presence of the sovereign 'Lord' and Master who is Israel's God (verse 7, where 'the God of Jacob' picks up the reference to Jacob in verse 1), the whole inhabited earth is called to tremble. This is similar to John's vision of God's great white throne 'from whose face the earth and the heaven fled away' (Revelation 20:11). At the same time, this awe-inspiring

God is the one who reaches down to the thirsty and miraculously provides water in abundance from rock and flint-stone (verse 8). It poetically alludes to God's provision for Israel's needs in the wilderness (see Exodus 17:1-7; Numbers 20:2-13; Deuteronomy 8:15). Water is not only made to flee and turn back but to flow in abundance. After emphasising the majesty of God, the psalm ends like the previous one by showing God's loving care for his people. We can be assured that the God who redeems us from bondage to sin and Satan will sustain us to our journey's end.

Pools and springs of water in the desert are an indication of God's supernatural power to change things for the better. Isaiah uses similar picturesque language to indicate God's limitless ability (Isaiah 41:17-20; 43:20; 44:3). The return from exile was viewed as part of a much larger package that would be earth shattering and of great comfort to God's persecuted people (Hebrews 12:5-29). In this way again the psalm provided hope for God's people suffering the aftermath of exile. These passages prepare us for the words of Jesus who invited needy people burdened by sin to come to him for rest and who called out, 'If anyone thirsts, let him come to me and drink' (Matthew 11:28-30; John 7:37-38; see Revelation 22:17).

Psalm 115

Trust God not Idols

Here is a psalm that encourages the people to praise and trust God against a background of pressure from foreign influence and idolatry. Whenever it was originally written its place in this fifth book of the psalm collection is appropriate to the situation in which the Jews found themselves after the return from Babylonian exile. In a hostile environment where people taunt Christians concerning their trust in an unseen living God the psalm continues to instruct and counsel believers to trust him and to live to his honour and praise.

It is the third of the Jewish 'Hallel' or Praise psalms and the first of the four sung at the close of the Passover meal (see Psalm 113). The alternation between the first person plurals (see verses 1, 3, 12 and 18) and the second person (verses 14-15) together with the repetition of words and phrases has suggested to a number of scholars that the psalm was recited or sung antiphonally but there is no certainty about this.

Prayer concerning God's honour (verses 1-2)

Although God's people were not in a crisis situation they were nevertheless far from flourishing. The psalm acknowledges that it is God who has brought them through a notable deliverance. They take no credit to themselves for it—'Not unto us ... not unto us' (verse 1). It is due entirely to God's 'mercy' ('unfailing love') and 'truth' ('fidelity'). Daniel utters similar words in his great intercessory prayer (Daniel 9:18-19; see Ezekiel 36:22-23). William Wilberforce in 1807 expressed his political successes in winning his Yorkshire seat and in the passing of the Bill for the Abolition of the Slave Trade in these very words.

But the present position of God's people was far from ideal and the cry of verse 1 suggests that the people desired above all to see Israel's covenant-keeping God, the 'LORD', (Yahweh/Jehovah) honoured in the wider world rather than themselves. This would certainly be an appropriate psalm for the Jewish community recently returned from exile. Glad as they were to be back in their own land, they were still under foreign rule and considered themselves slaves to their Persian masters (Ezra 9:9). Such a situation reflected badly on God's good name and stunning greatness. God is worthy of 'glory', of honour (see Psalms 29:1-3, 9; 79:9).

All boasting in self-achievement must be excluded when the Church of Jesus Christ experiences seasons of revival and in times of pressure from the world we need to be more concerned about God's honour than our own standing in society.

The cynical question of the Gentile nations—'Where now is their God?' (verse 2; Psalm 79:10; Joel 2:17; see Psalm 42:3, 10; Micah 7:10) is one that should concern all who put their trust in the living and true God. If God's people are under any kind of pressure whether from alien forces or internal troubles it encourages these derisory comments. In the context of the following verses the taunt of the pagan foreigners might well have resulted from God's people having no image of God before whom they worshipped. Every other nation around them had gods that could be seen. It would seem absurd to the pagan nations to be worshipping a divine being who was not represented by some physical form.

God's sovereignty and human folly (verses 3-8)

The answer to the sneers and jokes is a confident confession of faith. It recalls the words of Psalm 2 where the nations and kings club together against the Lord and his Anointed while the sovereign God sits in the heavens and has the last laugh. God rules over all (Psalms 11:4; 103:19) and 'he does whatever he pleases' (verse 3; see Psalm 135:6; Ecclesiastes 8:3). The invisible God is not confined to a place on earth and he is no prisoner to circumstances. For the Jewish community recently returned from exile it would have been an enormous encouragement to hear these words spoken and to join in singing them. Whatever God's sovereign will ordains he sees it accomplished. The restoration of the Jews to their land was a clear indication of this, being prophesied by Moses and the true prophets who followed him (Leviticus 26:40-42; Deuteronomy 30:1-5; Jeremiah 29:10; Ezekiel 36:24). It also gave them further encouragement to believe that God's promises concerning the Anointed ruler would not fail either (2 Samuel 7:12-16; Psalms 2:6-9; 110:1-2).

The psalm then contrasts the living and true God ('our God' verse 3) with pagan gods ('their idols' verse 4; see Psalm 135:15-18). Of course, scholarship will tell you that we must make a distinction between an image and what it represents. The point is however, there is no reality behind the image other than the demonic (1 Corinthians 8:4-6; 10:19-20; 1 Thessalonians 1:9). The whole passage is similar to the prophetic denunciation of idols (Isaiah 40:18-20; 44:9-20; 47:5-7; Jeremiah 10:3-16) and is particularly reminiscent of the words of Moses (Deuteronomy 4:28). They might be visible, costly and impressive but they are dead and the work of humans. If the idol does not speak, see, hear, smell, feel, move or 'mutter' thoughts ('meditate'; see Psalms 1:2; 2:1), the question of verse 2 might very well be asked of the pagan nations: 'Where is your god?' If the godly become conformed to God's character (see Psalms 111 and 112), the makers of these images and those who rely on them become like their idols—shamed, blind, foolish and destined to perish (verse 8; see Psalm 97:7; Isaiah 45:16-17; Romans 1:21-23).

It is often forgotten that this sustained belief in one God with its denial of idolatry is among the great revelations of the Old Testament and set Israel and later the Jews apart from all other cultures. When as tourists we visit famous temples and shrines are we as provoked to grief and indignation as Paul was as he viewed the idols that filled the city of Athens? In this emotional response he was following God (Acts 17:16; see Psalm 106:28-29).

Call to trust the LORD (verses 9-11)

Following the contrast made between God and idols there is a very practical application. Idols are impotent whereas God is the almighty sovereign, so why fear these gods and those who trust them? Instead of trusting idols (verse 8) there is a three-fold call to 'trust in the 'LORD' (Yahweh/Jehovah). The first two groups mentioned, 'Israel' and 'house of Aaron' (verses 9–10) refer to the worshipping community and the priests. It is tempting to think of those 'who fear the Lord' (verse 11; see Psalms 34:7; 112:1) as representing foreigners who attach themselves to the God of Israel (see 1 Kings 8:41; Isaiah 56:6), people who by New Testament times would be known as 'God-fearers' (Acts 10:22, 35; 13:16, 26). On the other hand, it is used of the godly in Israel (Psalms 22:23; 111:5) so that the term may be gathering up all God's people under this one expression, like the 'small and great' in verse 13. Relying on idols is folly but trusting the living God of Israel is to rely on one who really can come to the aid of his people and defend them from their enemies—'He is their help and their shield' (see Psalm 33:20). Whether antiphonal singing or not, the repetition certainly emphasises the point.

Words of blessing (verses 12–15)

The same three groups representing the whole worshipping community of Israel (see verses 9–11) are mentioned again. In saying that the Lord had remembered them ('been mindful' verse 12) they may well be recalling the fundamental ground of their confidence, that God continues to remember the covenant he made with Abraham and his descendants through Isaac and Jacob (see Psalms 74:2; 106:45; Exodus 2:24).

For the people newly returned from exile, it would mean that God had responded to their plight and as in the first exodus he had acted to redeem them from their captivity in Babylon. For Christians today we also can say God has been mindful of us and in his Son Jesus Christ has redeemed us from the ultimate captivity to sin and Satan. This being so, God's people are assured that the Lord 'will bless' all those who fear the Lord (see Psalm 67:1), whether they are in leadership positions or ordinary members, whether they are insignificant or important people (verses 12–13; see Jeremiah 31:34). Mentioning 'small and great' may also suggest that these blessings are not earned but are the result of relying on God.

From the beginning blessing is associated with having many descendants (Genesis 1:28; 9:1) and this was promised to Abraham and Israel and prayed for by Moses (Genesis 12:2; 15:5; Deuteronomy 1:10–11). As a result of the Servant's atoning work Isaiah sees a great expansion in numbers (Isaiah 54:1–3; see Zechariah 10:8). Again, this would have been an encouragement to the returning exiles whose numbers were far smaller than those who entered Canaan under Joshua. Israel's covenant-keeping God is the one 'who made heaven and earth' (verse 15) and therefore he is in a position to give this blessing. It finds its ultimate realisation in Christ. All who belong to him are Abraham's offspring and they comprise a great multitude which no one can number of all nations and peoples (see Galatians 3:26–29; Revelation 7:9).

Determination to worship (verses 16–18)

Picking up the reference to heaven and earth in the previous verse, the psalm first reminds us of God's sovereignty. The 'heaven' is the Lord's heaven (see verse 3) and though the earth is his too, he has given it to human beings (literally 'to the sons of Adam'; verse 16). This is where he intends people to live and to have dominion (Genesis 1:28–30; Psalm 8:6–8). The new Jerusalem, made up of that innumerable company of God's people comes down out of heaven to the new earth (Revelation 21:1–2). God's gift to human beings is the earth. This is the eternal inheritance of all his people: 'Blessed are the meek for they shall inherit the earth' (Matthew 5:5). It is God's intention that those created in his image whom he has placed on the earth should praise and worship him. The future new earth will bring to a grand climax God's purposes in creating heaven and earth where human beings will fulfil their destiny to the honour of almighty God.

Though the dead are not beyond God's sphere of rule, they are in no position to praise and worship God for they have no bodies with which to speak and sing and bow the knee (verse 17; see Psalms 6:5; 30:9). The bodies of God's people lie silent in the earth (Psalm 94:17). Of course, our souls while absent from the body are present with the Lord. Christians are safe in Jesus Christ but their bodies wait for the day of resurrection. Here on this earth we are called to 'bless the Lord' or to worship with bowed knee, and this is where God's people will go on doing so to all eternity in the new creation (verse 18).

As with Psalm 113 this psalm closes appropriately with 'Hallelujah' ('Praise the Lord!' see Psalm 104:35).

Psalm 116

A Personal Testimony

I once heard a minister in one of the islands off the west coast of Scotland give a personal statement of God's dealings with him at a Sunday evening after-church meeting. Very effectively and movingly he used the opening words of this psalm to begin each part of his testimony.

The psalmist has experienced deliverance from a deadly peril and in expressing his relief he desires to show his gratitude in the presence of God's people at the Jerusalem sanctuary. We are not informed of the original circumstances out of which the psalm arose but its language recalls earlier psalms of David (see Psalms 18, 27, 31, 56). There is the possibility that the psalmist is speaking for Israel, the nation. Certainly, it is appropriately placed in this final part of the psalm collection to express the relief of the Jewish exiles newly returned to their own land. The Babylonian exile had been not only a bondage but a death-like situation and this psalm articulates their grateful thanks for God's gracious activity on their behalf. As Christians we too can use this thanksgiving psalm. With the commentator, George Horne (1730-1792), we can consider it 'as an evangelical hymn, in the mouth of a penitent, expressing his gratitude for salvation from sin and death.'

The psalm became part of the Hallel collection (Psalms 113-118) which was sung at the major Jewish festivals particularly the Passover (see the introduction to Psalm 113) and it has often been used in church circles in the celebration of the Lord's Supper.

Expression of thankfulness (verses 1–2)
The opening line actually reads, 'I love because the LORD has heard my voice ...' (verse 1) but of course the psalmist is confessing his love for the covenant God of Israel. This is the only place where such a testimony is made in the Old Testament although God calls Israel to love the LORD with all their beings and David urges God's people to do so (Deuteronomy 6:5; Psalm 31:23). On account of our rebellious natures, there would be no love for God were it not for God's prior love for us. There is always a 'because' in our confession of love for God. John writes, 'We love him because he first loved us' (1 John 4:19).

In his deep distress the psalmist has prayed to God to show him favour and he has listened to his pleas for grace ('supplications') and acted. Verse 2 is a restatement of verse 1 but here God is likened to someone leaning forward to catch every word (Psalm 31:2) and the psalmist resolves to 'call' out to him in thanksgiving 'as long as I live' (see verses 13, 17; Psalm 104:33).

Experience of trouble (verses 3–4)
The actual situation from which the psalmist has been rescued is not expressed but his 'trouble and sorrow' were deadly serious. 'The pains of death' (literally 'the cords of death') have encompassed him. It is as if he had been lassoed by death and it seemed impossible for him to escape the grave. But he called 'on the name of the LORD' (see Psalms 18:3, 6; 99:6; Genesis 4:26). His desperate earnest cry is recorded: 'O Lord, I implore you, deliver my soul' (verse 4). Peter, quoting the words of Joel that whoever calls on the name of the Lord will be saved, preached Jesus to the people (Acts 2:21–40). Jesus, who came of David's family line, is the one who put himself in the place of sinners and suffered unspeakable trouble and sorrow.

Resting in God's provision (verses 5–7)
The psalmist has called on 'the name of the LORD' for deliverance and now we understand the grounds of his confidence as he relates those characteristics associated with God's name: 'gracious', 'righteous' and 'merciful' (verse 5; see Psalms 86:15; 111:3–4; Exodus 34:6). While this

psalm starts out as a personal testimony, it encourages all God's people to see Israel's God ('LORD') as 'our God'.

The 'simple' (verse 6) are often the inexperienced and gullible (Proverbs1:4; 9:16; see Psalm 19:7) but here it probably means the weak and powerless, people like the psalmist who have been brought down to death's door and cannot help themselves. Again he refers to his deliverance, summing up what he has said in verses 3 and 4. The God of compassion has delivered him and has set things right. This God who is true to what he has revealed of himself, is the same God who brought his people back from their low state in exile and who has brought us back to God from our low state in bondage to sin and Satan (see Psalms 79:8; 107:39). He is indeed 'our God'!

The psalmist, who had been agitated and alarmed at the danger he was in, can now tell himself to return to a state of 'rest' (verse 7). When someone has been rescued from a crisis situation it often takes time to feel settled again. As in Psalm 42:5 it is not a sign of senility or mental weakness to talk to oneself (see also Psalm 103:1-2). Sometimes we need to take ourselves in hand and urge ourselves to action. The 'rest' or repose of the inner person is like the rest promised to Israel in the promised land (see Deuteronomy 12:9) and would have not gone unnoticed by those recently returned from exile. Christians are reminded of the words of Jesus who promised rest to those who are weary and heavily burdened by sin (Matthew 11:28).

All that the psalmist has experienced of God's grace can be summed up as the Lord having 'dealt bountifully' with him (verse 7; see verse 12; Psalms 13:6; 103:2).

Faith overcomes (verses 8-11)

In this confession of faith, which is a part of the psalmist's thanksgiving, God is now addressed directly. The words of verses 8 and 9 resemble those of Psalm 56:13. Not only could the Jewish exiles use this language to express their grateful thanks to God but Christians too can take these words upon their lips as they contemplate the salvation that God has accomplished through his Son, Jesus Christ. We are brought from death to life in Christ and he will keep us from stumbling. While we wait for the day when there will be no more tears we are thankful that even now we can rejoice through tears of sorrow (2 Corinthians 6:10; Ephesians 2:1; Jude 24; Revelation 7:17). Walking about in the presence of the Lord 'in the land of the living' (verse 9; see

Psalm 27:13), which is a poetic way for being alive, contrasts with 'the land of darkness' and the place of 'silence' (Job 10:21; Psalm 115:17).

Not only does the psalmist testify of his love ('I love', verse 1) but also of his faith ('I believed', verse 10). In verses 10 and 11 he returns to speak of the desperate state he was in before the Lord rescued him. He spoke of his own utter weakness ('I am greatly afflicted', verse 10) and in his consternation or alarm (rather than 'haste') he came to see that all human assistance was unreliable ('liars' in the sense of 'false', 'not to be trusted', verse 11; see Psalm 60:11). Paul uses the words of the psalmist to express his own faith in God when passing through near death experiences (2 Corinthians 4:13). He quotes, using the ancient Greek translation, the Septuagint (LXX), to show that despite the troubles he faces he relies on God and goes on proclaiming the good news. For both the psalmist and Paul it is faith in God that leads to speaking ('I believed, therefore I spoke', verse 10), whether in personal testimony or in preaching the gospel.

Gratitude for God's provisions (verses 12–14)

In the light of all the God-given, undeserved 'benefits'[65] (verse 12; see Psalm 103:2), what is his response to be? In what way can he repay such goodness?

There is no way humans can repay God. We expect the psalmist to say that he will give something in return but instead he states: 'I will take' and 'I will call' (verse 13). Most commentators suggest that 'the cup of salvation' refers to the drink offering where a prescribed amount of wine was poured out often in association with the other sacrifices. Unlike the other main offerings, very few details are given concerning this libation ritual in the Old Testament and a cup is never associated with it (see Exodus 29:40–41; Numbers 15:5–10; 28:7–8). In contrast to the cup of God's wrath (Psalm 75:8; Isaiah 51:17; Revelation 14:10), we have here the cup of God's full salvation. David can also say, 'You are my cup' (Psalm 16:5). There is no thought in this verse of the psalmist pouring out wine as a drink offering, rather it is a picture of him gratefully accepting the fulness of God's salvation and calling out to God in praise and thanksgiving. Christians, rescued from the pit of destruction, likewise take hold of this cup of salvation by faith and drink from it continuously for their spiritual well-being. Each time Christians partake of 'the cup of blessing' at the Lord's table (1 Corinthians 10:16; 11:25–26) they are symbolically indicating their appreciation of Christ's saving work and the continuing benefit they derive from it.

The reference to the cup of salvation encouraged the later Jewish use of this psalm at Passover time when four cups were shared during the course of the meal (see Psalm 113).

At the same time the promises ('vows', verse 14) that the psalmist has made he is determined to fulfil in the presence of all the worshipping company of God's people. This meant, in the old covenant context, offering peace offerings of the vow type (see Leviticus 7:16-18; 22:21). Vows are voluntary but once made they are to be kept. They express gratitude to God and testify to his grace and goodness. If we have committed ourselves to the Lord, make sure we do not go back on our word but rather encourage and exhort one another by meeting with God's people in public witness and devoted service to the glory of God and the blessing of others (Hebrews 10:23-25). The word 'now' does not mean 'immediately' or 'at once' but is used to emphasise his desire to vow and is more often found in earnest prayers or requests and often translated as 'I pray' (Genesis 18:3; Psalm 119:76).

Experience of trouble (verses 15-16)

As the psalmist reflects on the salvation he has received he sees it as an indication of God's concern for him. He therefore states the general principle that the death of God's loyal subjects ('saints', verse 15; see Psalm 30:4) is too 'costly' (a better rendering than 'precious') for him to treat lightly. For this reason the Lord has rescued him from the borders of death (verses 3, 8). In the same way God's Anointed ruler values the lives of all those under his care (Psalm 72:14; see Matthew 10:29-31). This accounts for the return of God's people from exile, for the failure of Haman to exterminate the Jews (Esther 9:23-28) and it still holds good for the Church of Jesus Christ under severe persecution. Death is the result of God's curse on human sin and is seen as unnatural and here we have a glimpse into God's own heart especially when he views the death of his faithful people. In order to bring about a righteous settlement, what a costly price he was willing to pay to overcome this last enemy through the death and resurrection of the Son, Jesus Christ.

The psalmist is one of God's saints or committed people and he indicates this by referring to himself as the LORD's 'servant' and emphasises it by adding 'the son of your maidservant' which makes him a home-born servant (verse 16; see Psalm 86:16; Exodus 23:12).

Though it speaks of a humble position it does give him security for he comes under his Master's protection. His 'bonds have been loosed' for the Master has released him from death's ropes and the restrictions of the grave (verse 3; see Psalm 107:10, 14) to bring him into the freedom of God's service (see Romans 6:22). George Matheson (1842–1906) puts it well in his hymn, 'Make me a captive, Lord, And then I shall be free'.

Expression of thankfulness (verses 17–19)

These final verses make more explicit what has already been stated in verses 13 and 14. For instance, the psalm closes by stressing that the payment of vows in the presence of God's people (verse 18; see verse 14) is offered 'in the courts of the LORD's house' in Jerusalem (verse 19). In addition, we are told that, in calling on the name of the LORD (see verse 4), the sacrifice of thanksgiving will be offered (verse 17). The psalmist shows his gratitude for God's salvation not by pouring out a drink offering but by means of a thank offering (see verse 13).

Both 'vow' and 'thanksgiving' sacrifices were special types of peace offerings and allowed the worshipper to receive back part of the sacrifice to share roast lamb, goat or beef with relatives and friends in the presence of the Lord at the sanctuary (Leviticus 3:1–17; 7:11–38).[66] Besides being of special interest to the newly returned exiles from Babylon, who had been for so long without their city and temple, this extra information reminds us that personal devotion which is a feature of this psalm ('I love ... I believed') is 'not in competition with the public, formal and localized expressions of godliness' (Kidner). Now that the once-for-all sacrifice of Christ has been offered the old covenant blood sacrifices have ceased. Nevertheless, we are urged to offer continually the sacrifice of praise and to give thanks to his name (Hebrews 13:15; see Ephesians 5:19–20).

Like the previous psalm it ends with Hallelujah ('Praise the Lord!'; see Psalm 104:35).

Psalm 117

Short Psalm, Large Topic

Matthew Henry comments that 'This psalm is short and sweet' and urges that it should be sung often not because it is short but because of the sweetness of it 'especially to us sinners of the Gentiles'.

While this is the shortest of all the psalms its message was not missed by the Apostle Paul who used it to celebrate God's saving work through Jesus the Messiah in gathering the Gentiles into God's family and to show that this was no afterthought in God's purposes (Romans 15:11).

This is the fifth of the so-called 'Egyptian Hallel' psalms (see Psalm 113) and, though brief, it has all the essential ingredients of a praise psalm with a call to praise God followed by reasons for doing so. Like the post-exilic prophets, Haggai and Zechariah, it encouraged the newly returned Jewish exiles to think big. They may be a tiny community in a world of superpowers and aggressive foes but the Lord's loving commitment and faithfulness toward them are overwhelmingly mighty and enduring and they are part of a massive project that is destined to encompass the whole world (see Daniel 2:44–45; 7:13–14, 18, 27). As Christians we are sometimes apt to forget the big picture as we grapple with difficulties in our local churches and communities.

The summons

'Oh, praise the LORD!' (verse 1). This same call that opens the psalm
appears again at the close. The fuller form of the divine name 'Yahweh'
('LORD') is used at the beginning, while the shorter form 'Yah' is found
at the end of the psalm ('hallelu-jah'; see Psalms 68:4; 104:35). In its
closing form it follows the pattern set by the previous two psalms. The
rarer word 'laud' or 'applaud' is coupled with this invitation to praise
(see Psalms 63:3; 145:4; 147:12a).

The summoned

We usually find the people of God encouraged to praise the LORD
(see Psalm 106:1, 48) but here it is the Gentile nations and people
groups of the world who are urged to 'praise' and 'laud' him (verse 1).
It is in tune with earlier psalms that have called on the whole earth to
sing and shout to the Lord, to rejoice and make a joyful noise to him
(Psalms 29:1-2; 96:1; 97:1; 100:1). Because the LORD (Yahweh/Jehovah)
is the unique, one and only true and living God, who has created and
continues to sustain the whole universe over which he is sovereign
(see Psalm 113:4-5), it follows that all 'Gentiles' and 'peoples' with their
various languages and tribal groupings should revere and praise him
and an earlier psalm has already indicated that they will do so (see
Psalm 86:9). This call to the Gentile nations is particularly appropriate
in the context of this group of psalms (Psalms 113-118) for it answers
the mocking remarks of the Gentiles quoted in Psalm 115:2 'Where now
is their God?'

That the nations are urged to praise the LORD as the one true God is
the fulfilment of God's purposes, first promised in Genesis (3:15; 12:1-3)
and expressed many times through the prophets (Isaiah 19:18-24;
Micah 4:1-3; Zechariah 2:11). How are the nations and peoples of the
world to hear and praise the LORD? The Church's great commission
as a result of Christ's death and resurrection is to preach the gospel in
every corner of the world as a witness to all the nations and to make
disciples of all the nations (Matthew 24:14; 28:18-20). 'For there is
no distinction between Jew and Greek for the same Lord over all is
rich to all who call upon him' and preachers are needed so that the
world might hear God's word concerning a Saviour and put their
trust in him (Romans 10:12-17). The Gentiles, those who were afar off
and opposed to God and his Anointed ruler (Psalm 2:1) are brought
near by the blood of Christ and made fellow-heirs of the same body

(Ephesians 3: 6). Nothing will hinder the fulfilment of God's great plan and we have John's vision of the elect from 'all nations, tribes, peoples, and tongues' standing before God's throne praising God and saying, 'Salvation belongs to our God who sits on the throne, and to the Lamb!' (Revelation 7:9–10).

We praise God that the promises made to Abraham have been realised in the salvation of sinners the world over.

> Ye Gentile sinners, ne'er forget
> The wormwood and the gall;
> Go spread your trophies at His feet,
> And crown Him Lord of all.[67]

The reason for the summons

Typical of the praise psalms, reasons are presented which at the same time provide content to the praise and, as often, they are introduced with the word 'For' (verse 2). The reasons for praising God are because of the Lord's loving commitment ('merciful kindness'; see Psalm 5:7) and his enduring reliability ('truth'; see Psalm 25:5). These two well-known characteristics of God find their first appearance together on the lips of Abraham's servant as he expresses thanksgiving to God for answered prayer (Genesis 24:27). The Lord is lovingly committed to his people and can be depended on to keep his word. These two words appear together a second time when God reveals himself to Moses after the golden calf incident (Exodus 34:6). David also brings the terms together as he considers the way the Lord has kept his promises despite his people's unfaithfulness (Psalm 25:10; see Psalms 36:5; 40:10; 86:15; 100:5).

This psalm acknowledges that the Lord's steadfast love is not only boundless (see Psalms 57:10; 108:4), it is formidable in its strength ('great' in the sense of warrior-like and mighty; see 'prevail' Exodus 17:11; 1 Chronicles 5:2; Psalm 65:3). The might of God's unfailing love that was first revealed to Pharaoh, an important representative of Gentile power at the time, in rescuing Israel from Egyptian slavery, has been repeated in a new exodus from the Babylonian exile. This same God has revealed the power of his steadfast love in the redemption of his people through Christ's death on the cross in full view of the principalities and powers. Through his atoning work at Calvary, Jesus the Messiah has overcome sin, Satan, death and hell. To have this strong, loving commitment 'over us' or 'upon us' (rather than 'toward us') means that God's people are wonderfully protected and secure. In addition, the Lᴏʀᴅ's 'truth' or 'reliability', which endures forever, is a reminder that when God makes promises he keeps his word. God's loving commitment that overshadows his people is 'the fountain of all our comforts' and his enduring faithfulness to his promises 'the foundation of all our hopes' (Matthew Henry).

Surprisingly, the reason why the Gentile nations and people groups are urged to praise God, is because God's loving kindness and faithfulness have been revealed in connection with his people ('us'). That 'us' means, in the first place, Israel. God made some amazing promises to Abraham and his descendants and it was due to those promises that God brought Jacob's offspring out of Egypt, formed them into a nation and entered into a covenant relationship with them at Mount Sinai. Despite Israel's unfaithfulness God remained true to his word and it was because of God's loving commitment to his people and to the promises he had made to Abraham that there was a return from exile to prepare for the climax of his promises in the coming of his Son, Jesus the Messiah. It was Jesus who said concerning his atoning death on the cross, his resurrection and ascension to God's right hand that in being lifted up he would draw people of all nationalities to him (John 12:20–33; see John 10:15–16). This was God's purpose all along that through Abraham all families of the earth might be blessed (Genesis 12:3).

Paul not only quotes verse 1 (Romans 15:11), he also has in mind what the whole psalm is saying. He refers to God's 'faithfulness' or 'truth' (Romans 15:8) in keeping promises made to Abraham, Isaac and Jacob that the Gentiles might glorify God for his 'mercy', which is how God's 'steadfast love' can sometimes be translated (Romans 15:9). This is the missionary aim of the apostle to the Gentiles and his letter to the Romans shows how the nations come to acknowledge the one true God through Jesus the Messiah.

Gentiles saved by God's grace can join Jewish believers in the Lord Jesus in praising and exalting this covenant-keeping Lᴏʀᴅ whose faithful love is over us and whose promises endure to all eternity. The final 'Hallelujah' ('Praise the Lᴏʀᴅ') is thus a call to Jew and Gentile, one body in Christ, to join in praise of 'the Father of our Lord Jesus Christ, from whom the whole family in heaven and earth is named' (Ephesians 3:14–15).

Psalm 118

Rejoicing in the Dawn of a New Era

Luther states, 'This is my psalm, my chosen psalm. I love them all; I love all Holy Scripture, which is my consolation and my life. But this psalm is nearest my heart ... It is my friend; dearer to me than all the honours and power of the earth.'

Like all the psalms since Psalm 110, it has no title but it is clearly a thanksgiving psalm where the psalmist speaks for himself and his people in giving testimony to God's help in a crisis situation. As in Isaiah's prophecy where Israel can refer both to the nation and to an individual who is viewed as ideal Israel and their representative, so in this psalm the psalmist expresses the nation's experience and foreshadows the one who became the ideal Israel and representative of all his people.

Though we have no idea when it was written, the psalm's contents, which call to mind the exodus theme, are appropriate for inclusion in this final book of the psalm collection. The psalms in Book 5 were placed there to give hope to those who had come through the Babylonian exile and had newly returned to the land of promise. It is no coincidence that our psalm begins and ends with the words that open Book 5 (Psalm 107:1) suggesting that this group of psalms (Psalms 107–118) was meant to provide encouragement to those facing continuing opposition. Together they indicate God's sovereignty over

309

the nations, his power to deliver and to overcome enemy activity and
to give God's people cause to praise and give thanks as they look to the
future with confidence in their covenant-keeping God and his ability to
act on behalf of his people.

The psalm was used later by the Jews at the Festival of Tabernacles
and, as the last of the 'Egyptian Hallel' (Praise) psalms, during the
Passover celebrations (see Psalm 113). It continues to be of comfort and
help to Christians and the Church as a whole. The New Testament's
use of this psalm indicates that we are to understand it as pointing us
to the Lord Jesus Christ, the one rejected by those who should have
known better but who was finally vindicated by God (Mark 11:9; 12:10–
11; Luke 13:35; Acts 4:11; Ephesians 2:20; 1 Peter 2:4–7).

As in Psalm 115, there are sections in the singular (verses 5–7, 10–12,
17–21, 28) and one in the plural (23–27), and together with the repetitive
phrases and the festive note (verse 27), they may indicate that the
psalm was originally to be sung or recited antiphonally as pilgrims
made their way to the sanctuary. Certainly we find parts of it sung by
the pilgrims on the way to Jerusalem when Jesus entered the city on a
donkey, as their words indicate (verse 25; Matthew 21:9).

Call to give thanks (verses 1–4)

The psalm is framed by this summons to give thanks (verses 1, 29) and
includes two well-known reasons—'for he is good!' and 'Because his
mercy endures for ever' (see Psalms 106:1; 107:1; 1 Chronicles 16:34;
Jeremiah 33:11). The second of these reasons acts as a refrain that is
repeated in the following three verses (see Psalm 136:1–26). As the
army went out to battle, King Jehoshaphat appointed the musicians
to sing the shortened version (2 Chronicles 20:21) while the full form
was heard when the builders laid the foundation of the temple after its
destruction by the Babylonians (Ezra 3:11). Giving thanks to the LORD
involves testifying to God's goodness and his enduring commitment
to his people. Three groups of people, 'Israel', the priests of Aaron's
family line and 'those who fear the LORD', are urged to join in, which is
probably a way of making sure no one is missed out (see Psalm 115:12–
13).

The testimony (verses 5–18)

The psalmist gives a brief summary of his experience and lessons are
drawn from it (verses 5–9). This is followed by a longer account (verses

10-14) leading to joyful expressions of gratitude for God's amazing deliverance (verses 15-18). The psalmist speaks for his people and we are reminded of the hostility surrounding the Lord and his Anointed and the help that comes to those belonging to the city of God (see Psalms 2; 46).

Review and reflection (verses 5-9)

First, he was in 'distress', 'hemmed in' like the tight situation described in Psalm 116:3 but he 'called' to the LORD and the LORD 'answered' by bringing him into a 'broad place' (verse 5; see Psalm 18:6, 19). When the people in Egypt cried out to God, he heard and responded to their call (Exodus 2:23-25). God's willingness to answer the cries of his people is one of the important truths that Chronicles wishes to impart after the return from exile (1 Chronicles 4:10; 5:20; 2 Chronicles 30:18-20) and a psalm like this would have also helped to strengthen the people's faith (Psalm 99:6).

Second, he confesses that 'The LORD is on my side' (literally, 'is for me', verse 6). Paul could similarly say, 'If God is for us who can be against us?' (Romans 8:31). If this is so, there is no need to fear human beings. This was David's assurance (see Psalm 56:9-11) and Hebrews quotes the Greek translation of these words to encourage persecuted Christians to find their contentment in the God who is able to uphold and provide for them (Hebrews 13:6). With the LORD on his side helping him the psalmist can look triumphantly on those who hate him (verse 7; Psalms 54:4, 7; 68:1; 112:8).

The considered response to this brief testimony (verses 8-9) is a memorable saying that all God's people can take to heart. Human help can fail and the best earthly leaders are unreliable (see Psalm 116:10-11) but we can have every confidence in the LORD. For the Jews under Persian rule, very aware that they owed their return from exile to Cyrus and that they were still dependent on help and protection from the Persian authorities, these words would have reminded them to look to the Lord not human agencies however powerful. The writer to the Hebrews in quoting verse 6 may have had the whole passage in mind, for he directs the believers away from cherished earthly leaders past and present to the unchangeable Christ who is the same yesterday, today and for ever (Hebrews 13:8). 'Blessed are all those who put their trust in him' (Psalm 2:12).

These main points of his testimony are so encouraging that they whet the appetite for a fuller account.

Detailed report (verses 10-14)

This more specific testimony stresses the psalmist's conviction as stated in verses 6 and 7. Hostile Gentile nations had always surrounded Israel and it was an ever-increasing threat as each successive verse with its repetitive lines suggests (verses 10-12). Over the centuries the Egyptians, the Philistines, the Edomites and the Syrians had been their chief foes, culminating in the advance of the superpower, Assyria. It was 'in the name of the LORD' that Israel had seen these nations cut off or destroyed, as witnessed in David's victory over Goliath and the deliverance of Israel during Hezekiah's reign (1 Samuel 17:45; 2 Kings 19:15-19, 32-34). Even under Persian rule the Jews were still surrounded by local enemies like the Samaritans but Nehemiah was given protection and completed the walls of Jerusalem with the Lord's help (Nehemiah 6:16). The vivid imagery of bees swarming around indicates their fearsome danger but the enemies are destroyed as easily as extinguishing a fire of thorns.

It is probably the exodus event that the psalmist has chiefly in mind when Israel was 'pushed' hard (verse 13) by the Egyptians with the people trapped between Pharaoh's army and the sea. They were wonderfully helped by the Lord and were able to sing praises to the God of their salvation. The opening words of Moses' victory song are quoted exactly—'The LORD is my strength and song, and he has become my salvation' (verse 14; see Exodus 15:2; Isaiah 12:2). The 'LORD' (Yahweh/Jehovah) not only saves but is himself that salvation, so that to know him is to know salvation.

As David and then Hezekiah are presented as types of the Christ, so the exodus becomes a type or pattern of God's activity, first in bringing the people back from exile in Babylon and then on to Christ's redeeming work on the cross. Vicious foes encircled our Lord as he was put to death by crucifixion but the Lord helped him and vindicated him. Through his death and resurrection he has disarmed principalities and powers and triumphed over them (Colossians 2:15). The Lord's people can expect persecution in this present world order but help comes through looking to the Lord (Acts 4:27). Prophets and apostles indicate that there will be a final great effort by the powers of darkness to overcome the Church of God that will end with the coming of

Christ in glory to judge the world and bring in the new creation. Our Lord saw the future destruction of Jerusalem in AD 70 as a preview of that coming time (Zechariah 14:2; 2 Thessalonians 2:1-12; Revelation 20:7-10).

Expressions of gratitude (verses 15–18)

The 'righteous' (verse 15; see Psalm 1:5) are those who are in a right legal position before God, 'whose life matches their profession'. In their homes they are heard voicing their joyful shouts at the deliverance. The threefold reference to God's 'right hand' recalls again the deliverance song at the Red Sea (verses 15-16; Exodus 15:6). God's people praise the LORD's own power that acts forcefully ('valiantly'; see Psalm 60:12) and signals victory ('the right hand of the Lord is exalted').

Against all the odds, the psalmist is able to declare that he did not die but survived to live another day in order to proclaim the LORD's (literally 'Yah's') activity (verse 17). This same 'LORD' had disciplined him severely but he had not been given over to death. It was a near death situation at the Red Sea and Paul can speak of the Israelites passing through the sea as symbolic of baptism (1 Corinthians 10:1-2). That disciplining experience taught them much of God's power and of their need to trust him. David had numerous death-like situations from which the Lord delivered him and Hezekiah's kingdom of Judah was saved a couple of times from a fate similar to what happened to the northern kingdom of Israel.

This psalm, whenever it was written, would have encouraged the Jews to see their captivity as a near-death situation in which they were severely disciplined and, in their case, it was directly due to their sins. Yet God did not give the nation over to death. Ezekiel the prophet in his vision of the valley of dry bones proclaims a future for the exiles in terms of the nation's resurrection. All this prepares us for the truth concerning the ideal Israel that finds its realisation in Jesus the Messiah, the Suffering Servant of Isaiah. On behalf and instead of his people he was disciplined and cut off even though he was sinless, yet he lived and was highly exalted (see Isaiah 52:13-53:12).

Communal praise (verses 19-29)

This second half of the psalm is itself framed by the theme of thanksgiving (verses 19, 28) and begins with a request to enter the sanctuary area for this purpose. The covenant community as a whole join in celebrating the deliverance and pray that God would continue his saving activity, with the psalmist adding another brief word of testimony and thanksgiving before the final exhortation to give thanks.

Approaching the sanctuary (verses 19–21)

The gates may refer to the gates of Zion (see Psalm 87:2) or to the main temple entrance where gatekeepers stood (see 2 Kings 25:18; Nehemiah 13:5). These 'gates of righteousness' are gates that belong to the 'LORD' (Yahweh/Jehovah) and through which only 'the righteous' may pass. The two verses together help explain each other. Whether the psalmist is thinking literally or figuratively the main idea is that he wishes to come where the people gather for worship (see Psalms 24:7; 100:4) to give thanks ('praise') and testify in the way the psalm has already being doing (verses 5–18).

The reason for this thanksgiving is that prayer has been answered (see verse 5) for he has personal dealings with this God who has chosen to be his salvation (see verse 14).

Acknowledging God's amazing activity (verses 22–24)

It is suggested that verse 22 was a proverbial saying that was used to indicate a reversal of fortunes. What was cast aside as worthless has been given a place of honour. The 'chief corner-stone' could either be a large foundation stone holding together at a corner of the building two walls of stone at right angles to each other or a keystone at the top of a building holding an arch together (see Ephesians 2:20).

In the experience of the psalmist the proverb could describe his deliverance from death to life. For the Jews recently returned to their homeland, it would have spoken of their former state in exile to their new beginning however insignificant they as well as their enemies might have thought it to be, with its inferior temple and city. Haggai and Zechariah certainly encouraged the people not to despise the day of small things but to think big. The glory of the later temple would far outstrip the former (Haggai 2:9; Zechariah 4:10).

While such parallels can be drawn from the history of Israel and the life of David concerning the psalmist's experience, the verse must also be seen against the background of the messianic prophecies relating to the 'stone' and to the Lord's unique Servant (Isaiah 8:14; 28:16; 42:1–4; 49:3–6; Zechariah 3:9; 4:7). The 'builders' of Isaiah's day, in the form of king Ahaz and the leaders of the people who rejected God's word concerning the Messiah, prefigure the rejection of Jesus by the Jewish leaders. This is how Jesus understood the psalm (Matthew 21:42) and Peter followed his Lord in applying it to the Jewish authorities and to all who refuse the gospel (Acts 4:10-12; 1 Peter 2:4-8).

Though discarded by those who should have known better, this precious stone has been raised to the highest place of honour. He who was despised and rejected by humans and treated as rubbish has been exalted far above all principalities and powers and given the name which is above every name (Isaiah 52:13; Ephesians 1:21; Philippians 2:9-11). This is indeed 'the Lord's doing' (verse 23) and it is one of God's amazing wonders (see Exodus 15:11), far greater even than all his signs and wonders in Egypt (Isaiah 53:10; Acts 2:23-24).

The 'day' (verse 24) relates to the new dawn resulting from God's wonderful activity in honouring the one rejected. God has brought about this amazing deliverance and change of fortune making possible this festive day when psalmist and people can join together at the sanctuary to 'rejoice and be glad' in the LORD. It is understandable why Christians should meet together to celebrate the wonders of God's grace in Jesus Christ on the day that Christ, the true Israel of God, rose from the dead. It was the risen Lord Jesus himself who encouraged ongoing use of the day for communal worship by making a point of meeting his disciples on this first day of the week (see John 20:1, 19, 26).

Appeal and Congratulations (verses 25–27)

In view of God's wonderful action, prayer is offered for continuing deliverance and success and a blessing is given to the psalmist who comes to the sanctuary with the authority of the Lord ('in the name of the Lord', verse 26), a blessing that is also addressed to others associated with him—'we have blessed you' (plural). The 'house of the LORD' that they have all come to is the temple from where the blessing is given and it ties up with verses 19-20 concerning entrance into the city and the temple courts. The earnest plea, 'Save now', or 'Save I pray' (verse 25), is the meaning of the 'Hosanna' that the crowd shouted when Jesus rode into Jerusalem (Mark 11:9-10). As Jesus was to do a little later in his confrontation with the chief priests and Pharisees, the people applied the words of this psalm to Jesus as the Messiah and used it to declare a blessing on him (see Matthew 21:9, 42). The 'coming one' became a title that the Jews used of the Messiah (see Matthew 11:3; Luke 7:19-20).

The psalmist speaking for himself and his people confesses belief that the 'LORD', the covenant God of Israel, is the all-powerful, sovereign God (*El*, verse 27). This affirmation recalls the words of the Israelites after hearing Joshua's sermon: 'We also will serve the LORD, for he is our God' (Joshua 24:18). It was this living and true God who had given them 'light'. He had turned their night into day (see verse 24) as he was to do for the Jews in Persia when Queen Esther's brave action saved her people from mass destruction, so that the 'Jews had light and gladness, joy and honour' (Esther 8:16). This saving, victorious 'light' (Psalm 27:1) certainly indicated God's presence and the shining of his face, as the priestly blessing conveyed (Numbers 6:25).

The final call to 'Bind the sacrifice with cords to the horns of the altar' (verse 27) is probably to be understood as urging the people to keep the festal sacrifice tied with cords until it was brought up to the horns of the altar. Although we have no clear evidence, some animals may well have been tied to the altar until they were slaughtered, just as we find people holding onto the horns of the altar, in their case hoping to be saved from such a fate (Exodus 21:14; 1 Kings 2:28). However, once the animal had been prepared and placed on the bronze altar for sacrifice there was no need, as in the case of Abraham's action with Isaac, for it to be tied down with ropes and there is no mention of such a procedure in the sacrificial laws.

The term for 'sacrifice' usually means 'pilgrim festival' but here it stands for the sacrifice made on such an occasion (see Exodus 23:18 where it reads literally, 'the fat of my festival'). In view of this association, we can understand more readily why the psalm came to be associated with the great Jewish festivals when the people were directed to come to the central place of worship to celebrate Passover, Pentecost or Tabernacles. As this was the last of the six psalms the Jews sang during the Passover meal (see Psalm 113), it is highly likely this is the one mentioned in the Gospels that Jesus and his disciples sang on the night he instituted the Lord's Supper, before rising to go to the Mount of Olives (Mark 14:26).

Final thanksgiving (verses 28–29)
The psalm closes by giving thanks and confessing that the sovereign, all-powerful God (*El*) of verse 27 is the psalmist's God ('my God'). The second reference to God is the more common form (*Elohim*) but again the personal relationship is strong—'my God'.

It is the desire of the psalmist to see this God exalted. We need to be constantly doing this in our own minds and encouraging others to do so. Particularly when we come together to worship we should be helping one another to see that the God who is high and lifted up, is lifted high in our thoughts. While verse 28 is a fitting end to the second part of the psalm (see verse 19) the final verse rounds off the whole by repeating the words of verse 1.

Psalm 119

The LORD's A to Z for Living

For Augustine (AD 354-430), the Latin theologian of North Africa, this psalm did not 'need an expositor but only a reader and a listener'. Nevertheless, over the centuries many, including Augustine have undertaken to comment on and expound the contents of this 'Great Psalm' for the benefit of God's people. The psalm seeks to drive home the importance of God's word for living a life that is pleasing to him as we journey through this world to the celestial city.

The current comments on this psalm are being written in the year that we remember the 200th anniversary of the birth of David Livingstone (1813-1873) the famous Scottish missionary and explorer of Africa. As a boy of nine he received the prize of a New Testament from his Sunday School teacher for repeating by heart the whole 176 verses.

The psalm's artistic structure

This is the most elaborate of the alphabetical acrostics in the psalm collection (see Psalms 9-10, 25, 34, 37, 111-112, 145), where each of the twenty-two letters of the Hebrew alphabet is used in turn to begin a verse. It would be like going through the English alphabet from A to Z with the first verse beginning with a word that started with the letter A and so on through the alphabet and ending with a verse whose first word commenced with Z. As we know if we have ever played the game of thinking of animals or birds beginning with different letters of the alphabet, it is easier with some letters than with others. There are plenty of words beginning with A but few when it comes to X. The same is true with some of the Hebrew letters and we can therefore appreciate the skill of the psalmist.

There are 22 sections to the psalm each with eight verses. Each verse in the first section begins with the first letter of the Hebrew alphabet (*Aleph*), each verse of the second section begins with the second letter (*Beth*) and so it continues through the entire alphabet, making it the longest psalm in the whole collection with its 176 verses (22 letters x 8 verses for each letter).

God's Word like nature is varied and colourful and not drab. But this psalm's artistic structure is not merely for art's sake. The form assists the memory, impresses the truth upon the reader and aids reflection.

The psalm's theme

Being an alphabetical psalm, it does not seem to have any clearly marked development of ideas. One attempt to find some overall movement of thought has been to see how lament and petition which are strongly present in the first half (see for instance verses 17–24), give way to more praise and assurance in the second (see verses 169–176). A low point in the psalm is detected in verses 81–88 after which we find a marked upturn in verses 89–96. There is a clear introduction in the opening verses that highlights the blessed state of those who keep God's word (verses 1–3) and the psalm closes on a note of praise with a final plea to God his master and shepherd.

In most of the sections various topics are raised but the one big message concerns God's specially revealed truth. The psalm rings the changes using eight different terms for God's Word: *torah* (law, instruction), *'edoth* (testimonies, declarations), *piqqudim* (precepts, requirements), *huqqim* (statutes, decrees) *mitswoth* (commandments), *mishpat* (judgments, rulings), *dabar* (word) and *imrah* (promise, saying, statement). This may be the reason why eight verses are used for each letter of the alphabet although, apart from section eight (*Heth*; verses 57–64), not all eight terms are used in each section. Under the first letter (*Aleph*), for instance, verse 3 contains none of the terms and two verses use the same word 'statutes' (verses 5, 8), thus leaving 'judgments', 'word' and 'promise' out altogether. Besides verse 3, only three other verses omit the terms for God's word (verses 84, 90, 122).

God's 'way' (*derek*) is also a synonym for God's revealed will for our lives
and occurs in two verses where the other terms are not used (verses 3,
37), as well as in parallel with 'precepts' (verse 15; see Psalm 18:21).

In this psalm we are not only shown the multi-faceted nature
of God's word and its vital significance for our lives but what our
response ought to be to God himself. There is no dichotomy between
trusting God and trusting his word. The psalm encourages us to
delight in God's revelation, to treasure what he has to say and to live
our daily lives in the light of it. In this it resembles Psalm 19, where
six of the terms found here for God's word are used, and where we are
given good reason to keep it. But it is Psalm 1 that has provided the
groundwork for understanding this 'giant among the psalms' (Kidner).
There we are informed of the two basic groups in the world, the godly
and the wicked (also translated 'ungodly'). The godly are the righteous
who 'delight' in 'the law of the LORD' and, as in this psalm, we are urged
not to be involved in the 'way of sinners' (Psalm 1:1-2) but to follow
God's ways.

The psalm's messianic character

We need to see the connection that is made in the psalms between the
law and the king. Psalm 1 has already encouraged us in this direction
by its close link with Psalm 2 and the messianic ruler mentioned
there. The Israelite king was to have a copy of the law with which he
was to familiarise himself throughout his entire reign (Deuteronomy
17:14-20). Prior to kingship being allowed in Israel, Moses commanded
Joshua to meditate on God's law (Joshua 1:7-8) thus making him a type
of the future ruler. It is interesting that with the new king crowned
after the awful episode with queen Athaliah, the priest gave king
Joash the 'testimony', which is one of the words for God's law in this
psalm (2 Kings 11:12; see also 1 Kings 2:2-3; 9:4-7). Obedience to God's
law was to be wholehearted (see 2 Kings 23:3), a point that is strongly
emphasised in our psalm. One commentator argues that it might have
been the prayer of the deposed king Jehoiachin as he looked for the
restoration of the Davidic monarchy. This was the young king who
was taken into exile by the Babylonians. Later, at the end of 2 Kings,
we read of an upturn in the king's fortunes when he was released
from prison and given a place of honour by the Babylonian king and
this did act as a reassuring pointer to the future of David's family line.
Certainly, this psalm was a prayer that Jesus, the Servant of the Lord,

could make his own as he followed the path that God had set before him, identifying himself with sinners and suffering on their behalf.

The psalm's place in the collection

There is no title to this prayer psalm but it is placed after a group of psalms, none of which has a title indicating authorship or any clue concerning usage (Psalms 111–118), but it comes before a large collection of pilgrim psalms each of which is headed 'A Song of Ascents' (Psalms 120-134). The previous psalms have emphasised the Lord's saving goodness and it is in the light of God's gracious love that we have Psalm 119 that encourages God's people to love his commandments and do them. This is no legalistic religion that is being presented to us. Psalms 113 to 118, in particular, which were used by the Jews at the Passover festival, function like the introduction to the Ten Commandments, where God's redeeming grace is celebrated before the law for his covenant people is given (Exodus 20:2). The arrangement of the psalms is deliberate and encouraged the people of God living after the return from Babyonian exile as well as the people of God today, living in the period when all the types and pointers have been fulfilled in Jesus and his atoning death, to rest in a finished redemptive work, to love and keep his commandments, and to recognise that God's covenant community is a pilgrim people singing in expectation of the future glory in the heavenly city and temple when they will see the King in all his glory.

While the psalm does not refer to the exodus, promised land, Jerusalem, the temple and its worship or to important figures like Abraham, Jacob, Moses or David, it does address Israel's God by the name that became precious to his people at the time of the exodus. He is the 'LORD' (Yahweh/Jehovah), the living and true God who kept promises made to Abraham and who showed his sovereign power in rescuing Israel from the Pharaoh and forming them into a nation set apart for himself with laws the envy of the ancient world. This special, personal name is found twenty-three times in the psalm and we must therefore keep in mind that the psalmist is writing against the background of God's redemptive grace and loving commitment toward his people. In one place only is the more general word used and even there it is personalised as 'my God' (verse 115).

As in English and other languages, the letters of the Hebrew alphabet have names and these are often mentioned in Bible versions alongside the Hebrew characters as headings to the section. Such headings are not in the original text but indicate which letters are being used to begin each verse of every new section. Often the key word in a section is due to it beginning with the Hebrew letter for that particular section. For example 'and' in the *waw* section (verses 41–48), 'remember' in the *zayin* section (verses 49–56), 'good' in the *teth* section (verses 65–72) and 'come to an end' in the *kaph* section (verses 81–88).

1. The happy situation (The *Aleph* section; verses 1–8)

The first three verses form the introduction both to the section and the whole psalm. It opens with two beatitudes ('Blessed', verses 1–2) in a way that reminds us of how the whole collection began (see Psalms 1:1; 2:12). Unlike what we often find in today's western world, the privileged people, the people to be envied are people of integrity, whose 'way of life' is irreproachable ('undefiled') as they follow the 'way' that God has revealed.

God's 'law' is his spoken and written instruction and his 'testimonies' are those declarations associated with God's covenant with Israel (Exodus 31:18; Deuteronomy 4:45; Psalm 25:10) and are part of God's revealed will. Other terms used to describe God's teaching in this section include his 'precepts' (verse 4) which is a term only found in the Psalms (see Psalm 103:18 where it is often translated 'commandments', and Psalm 111:7), his 'statutes' (verses 5, 8 and used of God's 'decree' in Psalm 2:7), his 'commandments' (verse 6) and his 'righteous judgments', meaning his 'judicial decisions' or 'rulings' that are expressive of his righteous character (verse 7).

There is a whole person involvement in doing God's will, where an inner attitude ('the whole heart', verse 2) is expressed in outward actions ('keep', verses 2, 4, 5, 8). While 'walking' is associated with living the godly life, 'keeping' speaks more directly of observing God's commandments. There is no idea of legalistic duty but of an enthusiastic endeavour to obey God. Deuteronomy encouraged a love for God from the heart that would issue in joyful obedience, but it also recognised the need for a circumcised heart to produce this kind of devotion (Deuteronomy 5:29; 6:4–6; 10:16; 30:6). This is the new birth of which Jesus spoke and is essential if we are to have this love for God that would keep his commandments sincerely (John 3:3–8; 1 Peter 1:22–23). Those who have this spiritual birth, receive Jesus as Saviour and

Lord and out of love for him keep his commandments (John 1:12-13; 14:15).

From verse 4, the psalmist moves from general statements (verses 1-3) to addressing God directly and personally. It is God himself who has commanded these 'orders' or 'precepts' to be carefully kept (see Deuteronomy 24:8) and the psalmist appeals to God for help in obeying what he has decreed ('statutes'). He wishes to be firmly committed ('directed' or 'established') to keeping them. This is a reminder that without divine help Christians quickly lose heart and begin dragging their feet. For this reason the apostles are constantly urging believers to press on in the faith and to live lives pleasing to God. As the psalmist looks at all God's commands he is concerned that if he does not keep them it will lead to shame. That shame can mean a guilty conscience as well as being disgraced in the eyes of others. Being abandoned by God, for instance, would be an obvious case (see verse 8).

It is the psalmist's desire to 'give thanks' ('praise', verse 7) with 'uprightness of heart'. David wished to give thanks with a 'whole' heart (Psalms 9:1; 138:1) and similar to the general statement of verse 2, is a concern that there would be no conflict between inner attitude and outward expression of thanks as he learns of God's righteous rulings. His prayer of verse 5 becomes a commitment in verse 8—'I will keep your statutes'. The final cry suggests there are times when God does abandon his people either to test their faith, to discipline them or for other more mysterious spiritual reasons known only to God as happened in Job's case. When such times come, and it would seem that the psalmist was in such a situation, his plea is that he would not be 'utterly' abandoned. Jesus always did his Father's will and yet he was abandoned on the cross, with all its attendant disgrace (see Psalm 22:1; Mark 15:34).

2. The purifying word (The *Beth* section; verses 9-16)

The reference to the young person is reminiscent of Proverbs' interest in instructing the young, like parents teaching their children (Proverbs 1:4, 8; 2:1; 3:1; 4:1; etc.; see Psalm 34:11-14). Purity of life is to be a concern of every believer of whatever age and temptation does not stop when we reach a certain time of life. Nevertheless, the earlier we appreciate the need to keep our path pure and to use the means God has given to help us, the better it will be for us. Paul's young colleague, Timothy, was urged to be an example to believers 'in purity' by keeping himself pure (1 Timothy 4:12; 5:22) and to flee from youthful desires (2 Timothy 2:21-22). Only when we have been cleansed by the Spirit's regenerating work can we begin to live a life of purity (Titus 3:5). God's 'word' (verse 9), which includes commands and promises, is an important cleaning instrument, counteracting all the filth that proceeds from the agents of this world's ruler. Paul speaks of the church of Jesus Christ made pure by a spiritual cleansing that is accomplished through the purifying word of the gospel (Ephesians 5:26). Jesus made a similar statement when he spoke of his followers being cleansed and sanctified through the word he had spoken (John 15:3; 17:7).

Recognising how easy it is to stray from God's way, he seeks God with his whole being (verse 10) after the manner of verse 2. He also asks that God would be like the wise teacher of Proverbs and 'teach' him the 'statutes' of the law. Interestingly, this prayer comes in the context of worshipping God—'Blessed are you, O LORD' (verse 12; see 1 Chronicles 29:10; Psalm 28:6). It reminds us that learning from God's word and applying it to ourselves is an important part of worship. But the psalmist also appreciates that he has the responsibility of making use of this word that God has given for spiritual growth and purity of life.

In his prayer the psalmist tells of his own activity:

1. He has 'hidden', he has 'treasured up' God's 'word' in his innermost being (verse 11). While this more poetic term for 'word' usually denotes a 'saying' or 'promise', in this context it stands for God's commanding word. Learning God's word 'by heart' is good but it needs to be stored up 'in the heart'. Only by being a part of our lives will it truly shape our thinking, our attitudes and the way we live that we might not 'sin' against God. In this way we can be kept clean and resist temptation.

2. He has 'declared' with his 'lips' all the decisions that have come from God's 'mouth' (verse 13). Storing up God's word within him was for the purpose of recounting it to others by lip as well as by life.

3. He has 'rejoiced' in what God's 'testimonies' or 'declarations' have said about godly living as if he had all the riches in the world. There is no suggestion of God's laws being burdensome. The psalmist will later state that he prefers God's instruction to gold and riches (verses 72, 127).

He tells of desires:

1. He will 'meditate' ('muse'; see Psalm 77:6, 12) and 'contemplate' ('look', verse 15; see verse 6) God's 'ways', which is another way of

speaking of God's 'precepts' (see verse 4). Mulling over God's word and regarding what it is saying as important shows how diligent the psalmist was in seeking to live a clean life before the holy God.

2. As he has rejoiced so he will continue to 'delight' in God's 'statutes'. The danger of forgetting God's gracious acts and his covenant is mentioned several times by Moses as he urges obedience to God's law (Deuteronomy 4:9, 23, 31) and the psalmist is aware of this and makes his declaration not to forget.

3. The comforting word (The *Gimel* section; verses 17–24)

The hints of trouble in verses 6 and 8 are made plain in these verses. To live a life pleasing to God as he directs in his word, will lead to persecution by the ungodly, wicked world that opposes God and hates his people. God's name is not mentioned in this section but he is addressed in a prayer that is similar to a lament.

The Lord's 'servant' (verses 17, 23; see Psalm 18), who is seeking to be loyal to God and his instruction, is under threat and feels like a 'stranger' ('resident alien', verse 19) in his own country. He has become like a sojourner who has taken up residence in another country but with no rights of ownership (see Psalm 39:12). It was this kind of insecurity that the Jews felt back in their own land after the exile, with enemies in the ascendancy causing difficulties to people like Nehemiah. The enemies of the Jews are typical of the ones spoken of here as the 'proud' or 'arrogant', leaders ('princes') of communities like Sanballat and Tobiah who scoff and plot together against the psalmist (verses 21–23; see Nehemiah 2:10; 4:1, 7–8; 6:1–2). They 'stray' (or 'wander', see verse 10) from God's commandments and are rebuked and 'cursed' by God for breaking his law (see verse 118).

Christians are also resident aliens in this present world order (Hebrews 11:13; 1 Peter 2:11). Though we can enjoy good relationships with non-Christian friends, work colleagues and family members, it should be our testimony that we find true friendship and fellowship among God's people.

The psalmist responds to this persecution by making his requests known to God:

1. He, the servant, seeks the bounty of his Master's goodness (Psalms 13:5; 103:2; 116:7) to sustain his life so that he may continue to obey God's word (verse 17).

2. He prays that God would 'open' or better 'uncover' his eyes to

'look at' (see verses 6, 15) the wonders of God's law (see verse 129). This is the prayer that faithful Scripture Union readers use before their daily reading from the Bible. God's instruction is a miracle of divine grace. To have in our hands God's infallible word is itself a wonder but that word is also filled with truth concerning the wonders of God's works (see verse 27). But without divine help we fail to appreciate how amazing it is to have God's law to direct our lives or to understand what God is saying there. Spiritual things, said Paul, must be spiritually discerned (1 Corinthians 2:11-12). As Christians we constantly need God's Spirit to take away all that clouds and dims our understanding of God's word.

3. He may be a stranger in his own land but he prays that God will not 'hide' his commandments from him (verse 19) and he expresses the intensity of his longing ('breaks with longing') for God's rulings. He feels shattered (verse 20).

4. He prays for relief from persecution ('Remove' or 'Roll away', verse 22) for it is on account of his loyalty to God's word that he is suffering. He backs up these requests by reminding God that he has kept his declarations and 'muses' on his statutes which he finds a 'delight' for they have become his 'counsellors' or 'advisers'. God's word not only instructs, it reproves and corrects and equips us for every good work (2 Timothy 3:16).

The psalmist's experience pictures what the real Servant of the Lord endured during his earthly life. He came into the world he had made, was like a stranger even among his own people while he kept God's law in the ultimate sense (John 1:10-11; 17:4; Hebrews 4:15). He was despised and scorned and the rulers of this world plotted against him. On behalf of others, Jesus also endured the curse of the law that Jewish and Gentile persecutors who put their trust in Christ and his atoning work might be saved from the coming wrath (Galatians 3:10-14).

4. The way of truth (The *Daleth* section; verses 25–32)

Five verses in this section begin with the noun 'way' (*derek*; verses 26, 27, 29, 30, 32) and as in its earlier appearances is used either in the singular or plural for God's demands (verse 27; see verses 3, 15) or for a way of living or life-style (verses 26, 29, 30, 32; verses 1, 5, 9, 14).

The psalmist continues to feel the effects of enemy action. Suffering has brought him to a death-like situation. His life 'clings to the dust' (verse 25; see Psalm 22:29) and he 'melts' in tears of grief ('heaviness' verse 28; see Proverbs 10:1). Is he to experience 'shame' (verse 31) for choosing 'the way of truth' (verse 30) over-against those who are on 'the way of lying' ('falsehood' verse 29)? The two ways of Psalm 1 are again presented to us.

The psalmist is so low that he is as good as dead. Physically, mentally and spiritually he needs reviving and he knows that only God can do this and so he appeals to him—'revive me' (verse 25). The basis of his plea is God's 'word' which contains many gracious and precious promises. Even though God knows all our ways (Psalm 139:3), the psalmist has 'declared' to God his 'ways'. There is nothing in the context to favour the idea that the psalmist is recounting to God his own sinful way of life. Rather, what he has proclaimed to God is his present low situation on account of his commitment to God, a feature of lament psalms, and he has been answered. Nevertheless, he is aware of his human frailty and the danger of forgetting God's law as well as his need to know more so he prays that God would continue to 'teach' him his statutes.

He also asks for 'understanding' concerning the 'way' of God's requirements ('precepts', verse 27) so that he can further muse ('meditate'; see verse 23) on the wonders of God's acts of deliverance. It is in the context of God's saving activity that all the divine instructions for God's people are given (see Exodus 20:1-2; Romans 12:1). The psalmist also needs to be strengthened ('set up', 'established') as a result of his great grief (verse 28). Again, it is in accordance with God's word he asks for this. In verse 22 he had requested release from the persecution he was facing and it may be that here he pleads that the false accusations referred to in verse 23 will be removed from him (verse 29). It is also possible, at the same time, that he is aware of the temptation that this 'way of lying' poses for him as well and for this reason asks for it to be removed.

But he is also conscious of his own responsibility in keeping to 'the way of truth' (or 'faithfulness') that he has 'chosen' (verse 30). That is why he prays that God would favour him with his teaching ('grant me your law graciously', verse 29) and speaks of setting before him God's rulings and clinging (see verse 25) to his declarations (verses 30-31). There is no tension in the psalmist's mind between grace and law. Instead of running to evil (Proverbs 1:16) he speaks of running 'in the way' of God's commandments (verse 32). To 'walk' is

the usual way of referring to living in accordance with God's will (see
verses 1, 4; Galatians 6:16; Ephesians 2:10; 1 Thessalonians 4:1; etc.).
To 'run' suggests an enthusiasm for obeying God's commandments
(see Proverbs 4:11-12) which is the result of his mind and inner being
('heart') having been enlarged by God. His understanding has been
broadened (see 1 Kings 4:29).

5. Humble requests (The *He* section; verses 33-40)

In this whole section the psalmist recognises his spiritual need so that
every verse is a plea to the 'Lord', the God of the covenant: 'Teach me
... Give me ... Make me walk ... Incline my heart ...' and so on. Each of
these requests for God's help is in order that the psalmist might keep
God's teaching and rulings. He wishes to be totally committed ('to the
end', verse 33) in observing God's word with his whole being (verse 34).
The needs he expresses in these requests can be summarised as a plea
for life: 'Revive me' (verses 37, 40), one with which the previous section
opened (verse 25). The psalmist is eager to do God's will and loves his
commandments. He is spiritually alive otherwise he could not please
God or 'delight' in his law (verse 35; see Romans 8:8; 7:22). But he is
aware that godly people can lose heart, grow weary in well-doing and
begin dragging their feet instead of running (see verse 32). Christians
are all prone to wander from the God they love. Persecution is also
a factor and this is what brought the psalmist low (verses 17, 22-23,
25). His plea again is that God would deliver him from the taunts and
censorious comments of his enemies by turning away the dreaded
'reproach' he has been enduring (verse 39; see verse 22). God's judicial
decisions with regard to the enemy are good and fitting.

There is, however, another issue about which a godly person is
concerned. The psalmist is aware of the temptation to be attracted
to 'worthless things' ('emptiness', verse 37). This is the particular
matter that led him to ask to be revived. The word translated
'worthless' is applied to worthless conduct, speech, actions and false
prophecy (see Psalms 41:6; 60:11; Ezekiel 12:24). It is used especially
when speaking of idols (Psalms 24:4; 31:6). In this sense it closely
parallels the previous line where the psalmist prays that he will not
be inclined to 'covetousness' ('gain'; verse 36). Among the items Paul
lists which Christians are to put to death, is 'covetousness, which is
idolatry' (Colossians 3:5). Consumerism thrives on the human sin of

covetousness. An obsession with possessing and gaining what this world has to offer takes over people's lives.

We need God's help to have our eyes drawn away from seeing what is valueless and to have that life that inclines our whole beings (mind, affections, will) toward God's declarations (verse 36). The psalmist is committed to God as one who reveres him ('fearing you') as a 'servant' and looks to the Master for support and the fulfilment of his words of promise (verse 38). 'There he is' ('Behold') longing for God's precepts. He in no way wished to have a divided or half-hearted devotion toward God and his word, so he renews his plea to be revived (verse 40) on the strength of his trust in a God who is righteous and will act according to character (see Psalm 5:8).

6. Desire and commitment (The *Waw* section; verses 41-48)

There are very few words beginning with this Hebrew consonant but there is one familiar word and he employs it to begin each verse. It is the conjunction often translated 'and' but it can mean 'also', 'so', 'then', and 'but' depending on the context. Joining all the verses together by means of this letter 'and' produces a sequence of thought within the section. It also joins the whole to what has gone before as if to say 'and this also I desire'.

The previous section was full of requests and this section opens with an earnest desire that the LORD's 'unfailing love' ('mercies') would come to him. His foes are still there accusing him falsely ('reproaches' or 'taunts', verse 42, see verse 39) and he appeals to Israel's God who has entered into a special relationship with his people. God is committed to them in love and the psalmist can look to him for help and deliverance according to his 'word' of promise (verse 41). When the people of Israel were suffering in Egypt, they cried to God and he acted according to promises made to Abraham (Exodus 2:24). The 'answer' that he looks for to combat his foes will be God's action vindicating him (verse 41). Jesus is the prime example for he received the false accusations at his trial and the taunts of his enemies as he hung on the cross. But he trusted God and his word and waited for him to vindicate him on the resurrection morning. The great accuser of God's people is Satan and he is the father of lies and all opposition to God's people emanates from this source.

As for the psalmist, he places his hope in God's 'ordinances', his judicial decisions, and therefore prays that his desire to testify to God's faithful word will never be taken away from him (verse 43). This in turn is a motive for continuing to remain loyal to God's law and never giving up ('continually for ever and ever', verse 44).

Instead of experiencing the restraints that the enemy puts upon him, God's deliverance will mean freedom. He will be able to 'walk about' in a 'wide place' ('at liberty', verse 45; see Psalms 18:19; 118:5). Trusting God and living to please him is not drudgery and bondage but true liberty.

Furthermore, he is determined to speak of God's declarations before 'kings'. Ezra and Nehemiah, as well as Daniel, were not ashamed to testify before the great emperors of their day, just as Paul was not ashamed to preach the gospel in Rome where Nero had his palace. The psalmist testifies to his love for God's commandments. Love for God means that we shall love his word of promise and command. Jesus said that if we love him we will keep his commandments (John 14:15). The psalmist also vows to delight in them (verse 47; see verse 35) as he worships God and muses on his statutes (verse 48; see verses 15, 23, 27). Worship is expressed by hands raised toward heaven (Psalm 63:4) and is often a sign of prayer (Psalm 28:2; 1 Timothy 2:8). The outward action is to be symbolic of an inner attitude of worship and dependence on God (Lamentations 3:41).

7. The word of promise and comfort (The *Zayin* section; verses 49–56)

'Remember' is the key word in this section (verses 49, 52, 55) as the original begins with the letter *zayin*. From prayers and desires the psalmist moves to statements of his commitment to God. Twice he uses God's covenant name 'LORD' (Yahweh/Jehovah, verses 52, 55), which draws attention to the special relationship between God and his people. He begins, however, by drawing attention to his position as God's 'servant' (verse 49; see verses 17, 23, 38) and calls on God as his master and sovereign to be mindful of the 'word' that he has been given and which is the ground of his 'hope'. That 'word' is associated with covenant promises (see Psalm 105:8, 42). When God remembers it means that he acts in accordance with those promises (see Exodus 2:24). God promised to be true to his people and it is this that gives the psalmist 'comfort' in his 'affliction' (verse 50). It is a word that has brought him 'life' (see verses 17, 25, 40).

The psalmist's foes are still causing him trouble as the word 'affliction' suggests and they are described as the 'proud' (verse 51). They are people like the one named in Proverbs as 'the scoffer', who acts with arrogant pride (Proverbs 21:24). The psalmist also includes among them the 'wicked' (verse 53; see Psalm 1:4) who have abandoned God's law and are mocking him greatly. Despite all this he has not been tempted to follow them in turning aside from God's law (verse 51). Far from it! He speaks of the righteous 'indignation' that has gripped him not because of what the wicked are doing to the psalmist but because of the enemy's disregard for God's instruction. The word for 'indignation' is a rare one that refers to the scorching east wind that is used to describe God's awesome end time judgment (verse 53; see Psalm 11:6).

In contrast to his enemies, the psalmist finds God's statutes a subject for 'songs' even though he feels like a stranger in his own country on account of the persecution (verse 54; see verse 19). It is unlikely that the phrase 'house of my pilgrimage' (or 'sojourning') refers to the temple or to his own bodily tent (see 2 Corinthians 5:1–5).

Having asked God to remember his words of promise and command and act accordingly (verse 41), the psalmist states how he has remembered God's decisions from 'of old' which have resulted in him finding comfort there (verse 52). In addition, he remembers the 'LORD' (Yahweh/Jehovah) and all that his 'name' stands for (see Exodus 3:13–14; 34:5–7) at night as well as in the daytime and has kept his law (verse 55). The LORD is not a yesterday god but the living God who is there for his people at all times and in all situations. This is the comfort that he enjoys because he has been loyal to God's precepts (verse 56).

8. The Lord's unfailing love (The *Heth* section; verses 57–64)

This is the only section where the eight verses use in turn all eight terms for God's revealed truth. The section opens and closes with the psalmist addressing the covenant God of Israel, 'O LORD' (Yahweh/Jehovah, verses 57, 64) and confessing that God is his 'portion' and that the land or 'earth' is 'full' of God's 'faithful love' ('mercy'; see Psalm 33:5). In Israel, the tribe of Levi was set apart from the rest of the tribes with no land allotted them. Instead they had the Lord as their allotted 'portion' (Numbers 18:20; Deuteronomy 10:9). Not only that, God chose Israel from among all the nations to be the Lord's 'portion' or special allocation (Deuteronomy 32:9).

Individual members of the covenant community like the psalmist could also speak of knowing God in this special personal way (see Psalms 16:5; 73:26). God's loving commitment was especially seen toward his covenant people in Canaan but like the Lord's glory the whole earth is full of it (Psalms 33:5; 104:10–30; Isaiah 6:3). Canaan, like David's old city, is a preview and pointer to the new creation when the earth will be full of God's glory and loving commitment (Hebrews 11:10, 13–16; Revelation 21:3–4). Like the psalmist, Paul could speak of God in very personal terms as 'my God' (Romans 1:8; 1 Corinthians 1:4) and encourages the Philippian believers with the promise that 'My God shall supply all your need according to his riches in glory by Christ Jesus' (Philippians 4:19). What an allocation to have this God for one's own!

In this special relationship the psalmist is committed to obeying God's 'words' (verse 57; see verses 55–56) and looks to the Lord to teach him more of his statutes (verse 64). For this he needs God's favour which he has sought wholeheartedly and prays that God would 'be gracious' ('merciful') and appeals to God's 'statement of promise' ('word'; verse 58).

The psalmist has considered his own 'ways' (verse 59; see verse 26), which is always a wise thing to do, knowing how prone those who love God are to go astray (verse 67). The feet that originally began to walk in the ways of the Lord need to be re-directed constantly in the way God has directed in his 'declarations' ('testimonies'), like a car veering off a straight road if the steering wheel is not adjusted slightly from time to time. We have a built-in tendency to veer off course (Galatians 5:17). Nevertheless, the psalmist is eager to get back on the track revealed in God's 'commandments' (verse 60) and in times of opposition from the enemy he has not 'forgotten' God's 'law' (verse 61). He uses the picture of a hunter capturing animals with 'cords' or 'ropes' to describe his oppression by the 'wicked' (see Psalm 140:5). This is the opposition from the 'brood of vipers' felt by all God's people, who belong to the 'seed of the woman', from the time of Abel to the present (Genesis 3:15; 4:25; Matthew 3:7; 12:34; 23:33).

The psalmist is eager to get up at midnight to give thanks on account of God's righteous 'judicial decisions' ('judgments', verse 62; see verses 7, 55), in contrast to Pharaoh and the Egyptians who rose in the middle of the night to lament the results of God's judicial decision in the death of their first-born (Exodus 12:29–30). Those who love and revere the

Lord by keeping his 'precepts' identify with others of the same mind. They are relatives in the faith, brothers and sisters in the Lord who encourage and help each other (Malachi 3:16-18; Ephesians 5:19-21; Hebrews 10:24-25; 12:12-13). The section closes with a confession to the LORD, 'The earth ... is full of your mercy' (or 'steadfast love'; see Psalm 33:5) and a prayer 'Teach me your statutes' (see verses 12, 26). Everywhere the psalmist looked there were indications of God's loving commitment toward the whole world and not just to Israel. Sadly, few were committed to God in return. The psalmist is concerned about his own faithfulness to God and therefore seeks the aid of the divine wisdom teacher.

9. The Lord's goodness in affliction (The *Teth* section; verses 65-72)

The adjective translated variously as 'good', 'well' and 'better' (verses 65, 68, 71, 72), the noun for 'goodness' (see verse 66) and the verb 'do good' (verse 68) dominate this section. It is from a position of being 'afflicted' or 'humbled' (verse 67) that the psalmist celebrates God's goodness. He acknowledges that he had strayed unintentionally but he is back on track, keeping God's word. Whether the thick-skinned 'proud' (verses 69-70; see verse 51) who have 'smeared' (rather than 'forged') like plaster the character of the psalmist by their lies (see Job 13:4; 14:17) were responsible for the psalmist's affliction is not clear but it has all been for the spiritual good of the psalmist.

Though he comes as a 'servant' to a master (see verse 17), he addresses God by his special personal name ('O LORD'), and confesses that God has done for him what is good just as his word promised (verse 68). As a result he prays that God would teach him 'goodness' (see Psalm 25:7) in the matter of discernment ('judgment') and 'knowledge' (verse 66). This goodness will include what is morally right and will result in a pleasing outcome. Believing God's commandments is an important ingredient to the fulfilment of this request.

God is good and all that he does is good and learning God's laws is to learn goodness for God's law is good (verse 68; see Psalm 73:1; Romans 7:12). God's goodness is seen in his providential dealings with the psalmist. Affliction is used by God to discipline his people for their good. It brings us back to God, to be taught from his word and wholeheartedly to keep his precepts (verses 67, 69, 71). The 'law' or instruction that comes from the 'mouth' of God is therefore far more precious than all that this world holds valuable (verse 72; see Psalm 19:10).

10. Made to bear witness (The *Yodh* section; verses 73–80)

The affliction of the previous section reappears here (verse 75) together with the 'proud' who have treated the psalmist wrongfully with their false allegations (verse 78). He also refers again to those companions who revere God (verses 74, 79; see verse 63). In the first half of this section the psalmist addresses the 'LORD' and witnesses to two important truths concerning God and himself.

First, he confesses that God has 'made' him like a vessel in the potter's hand and 'established' or 'prepared' ('fashioned', verse 73) him as if he were setting up a dynasty (Psalm 9:7). The same two verbs are used by Moses in his song concerning Israel: 'Has he not made you and established you?' (Deuteronomy 32:6). From this confession comes the plea that he would be given understanding so that he could learn God's commandments. Being made in God's image involves not only the skill to rule (see Genesis 1:28) but to have a personal relationship with God and the ability to 'understand' things. However much we think we know of God's word there is always more to learn.

Second, he makes a strong affirmation: 'I know ...' (verse 75). He acknowledges that God's judicial decisions are right (see verse 7) and recognises that it was 'in faithfulness' to his covenant stipulations that God had 'afflicted' him by allowing his foes to humiliate him. This is the reason those who fear God can be glad when they see the psalmist and like him they will be able to place their hope in God's word. Cruel people who are responsible for their actions are used by God to discipline his people and to fulfil even deeper and more awesome divine purposes as in the case of Job. The Suffering Servant was oppressed and afflicted yet it fulfilled the divine plan (Isaiah 53:7, 10). Though cruel hands put Jesus on the cross it was according to God's 'carefully planned intention' (Acts 2:23).

The remaining verses are all earnest prayers of a 'servant' who looks to the heavenly master for the protection and support he has promised in his word. He pleads that God's unfailing love would be his comfort (verse 76) and that God's compassion ('tender mercies') would come to him so that his whole life might be renewed (see verses 37, 40), seeing that God's law is his delight (verse 77). In addition, he prays that the proud will be shamed while he sets himself to muse on God's precepts (verse 78; see verse 48). He closes first with a prayer for his fellow companions who revere God and who 'know' God's declarations. It would appear that these friends have believed some of the lies of the psalmist's proud foes so the psalmist prays that they will not remain aloof from him but 'turn' to him and find encouragement through the way he has been able to persevere in his afflictions (verse 79). Finally, he prays for himself that he will be blameless (have no obvious blemish) in the light of God's statutes so that he might suffer no shame (verse 80).

11. Trusting God's word in severe persecution (The *Kaph* section; verses 81–88)

The psalmist does not use God's covenant name in this section but it is an earnest appeal to God similar to David's laments and reminds us of Jesus' strong cries in the Garden of Gethsemane (Mark 14:32–42). It is clear that the suffering he has been enduring from proud enemies is so intense that it has brought him to death's door. This is the lowest point in the whole psalm.

The key term in this section is variously translated as 'faints' (verse 81), 'fail' (verse 82) and 'make an end of' (verse 87). In the opening two verses the verb has the idea of 'coming to an end'. As the Korahite author 'faints' for the LORD's courts (Psalm 84:2) so our psalmist 'faints' or has 'come to an end' of himself with longing for God's deliverance. He has no strength left in him but he is not in total despair for in his darkest hour he still has the light of God's 'word' and in that he hopes and waits (verse 81). The following verse underlines the point, but this time it is particularly his 'eyes' that have 'come to an end'. They 'fail' through looking for God to fulfil his 'word', his 'statement of promise'. As yet he has not received the comfort that God holds out to his people (verse 82; see Isaiah 12:1–2; 49:13; Jeremiah 31:13).

His plight is desperate. One reason for this is the mounting opposition from his foes who do not live according to God's law. It is not so much the particular activity that is against God's law but the 'proud' themselves who do not live by it (verses 85). It would be better to translate: 'The proud ... who do not act according to your law'. They are pursuing him with 'falsehood'; ('wrongfully', verse 86); they are like hunters digging 'pits' to trap an animal (verse 85) and have all but finished him on earth ('made an end of me', verse 87).

What really hurts, however, is the fact that God is silent and has not intervened on behalf of his servant even though he has not forgotten or abandoned God's laws which he confesses are truthful in contrast to the deceitfulness of his foes (verses 83, 86, 87). The psalmist likens himself to a 'wineskin in smoke' (verse 83; see 'clouds' in Psalm 148:8) and although the precise nature of the illustration remains unclear to us it suggests that he is in a distressing and dangerous position. Perhaps these leather bottles were hung up near a fire where thick smoke would rise and damage them.[68] He wonders when these days of suffering will come to an end. When will God vindicate him by acting in justice to punish his persecutors (verse 84)? All he can do is cry 'Help!' (verse 86) like a person trapped in a house full of smoke.

Even so, the psalmist is not in despair. He continues to believe in God's 'steadfast love' ('loving kindness') and on the basis of it pleads as before for God to restore his life ('Revive me', see verses 25, 37, 40) so that he can continue to live a life of obedience to God's revealed will ('the testimony of your mouth', verse 88; see verse 72).

The psalmist prefigures Jesus the Messiah 'who, in the days of his flesh ... offered up prayers and supplications with vehement cries and tears to him who was able to save him from death, and was heard because of his godly fear' (Hebrews 5:7). The great enemy was judged and our Saviour was vindicated by his bodily resurrection and ascension. Paul suffered great persecution for Christ's sake and on one occasion despaired even of life, yet the God who raised Jesus delivered him, and Paul knew that he would deliver both him and all believers in the ultimate sense from every enemy action (2 Corinthians 1:8-11; see also 4:7-15).

12. The Lord's eternal word (The *Lamedh* section; verses 89–96)

At this point the second half of this great spiritual poem begins. Mention is still made of his 'affliction' (verse 92; see verses 67, 75) and his 'wicked' foes who are out to 'destroy' him (verse 95; see verses 61, 87) but the tone is much more upbeat and positive. His prayer for life has been granted. He would have perished in his affliction but he has been given 'life' through God's word (verses 92–93).

It opens full of confidence in the divine 'word' as the psalmist addresses God by his personal covenantal name, 'Lord' (Yahweh/Jehovah). 'For ever' like the other terms and expressions in the following verses such as 'settled' ('stands firm', verse 89), 'all generations' (literally 'to generation and generation', verse 90), 'abides' ('stands', verse 90) and 'continue to this day' ('stand today', verse 91) emphasises time ongoing into the future. God, his word and his reliability are constants in a world of changing situations (see Psalm 89:1-2). All scientists, atheists included, believe in the scientific laws that have been discovered and on the basis of these basic principles they continue their investigations, make their predictions and send people into space. They take it for granted that those laws can be understood and expressed in human language. These so-called natural laws are, in fact, the laws of God and that is what the psalmist emphasises in these opening verses. The stability of God's word and the created order stand firm to this day for they are God's 'servants' (verse 91). It is important to remember that the scientific laws, the whole universe and all that is in it are the result of God's creative activity and they serve and obey the creator.

For the psalmist, God's specially revealed teaching is his 'delight' (verse 92; see verse 77). If this had not been true he confesses that he would have perished in his trouble. He had not forgotten nor will he ever abandon God's word (verse 93). There he had found comfort and hope, knowing that God's word is trustworthy and that he has everything under control. This is his delight: it is uplifting, reassuring and revives his spirits. He also places himself willingly in a servant position, 'I am yours' (verse 94), and looks to God his heavenly master to 'save' him. In adding, 'for I have sought your precepts', the psalmist is not suggesting that he has earned God's deliverance but expressing his commitment to God and his word. In spite of the enemy he is determined to give even more attention to understanding God's 'testimonies' (verse 95).

The section ends with a contrast between God's commanding word which is 'very wide' ('exceedingly broad', verse 96) and the end of all earthly perfection. God's promise to Noah about the regularity and continuity of times and seasons had an end in sight: 'while the earth remains' (Genesis 8:22). As the Lord brought an end to all flesh in the Flood (Genesis 6:13), the psalmist has seen that the present laws that govern the created order will come to an end, yet God's command remains sure and firmly fixed (verse 89). Jesus said, 'Heaven and earth will pass away, but my words will by no means pass away' (Mark 13:31). It is through his work on the cross that we can look forward beyond the 'end' of all things to a new creation in which righteousness dwells (Colossians 1:15–20; 2 Peter 3:10–13).

13. Wisdom from God's word (The *Mem* section; verses 97–104)

There are no prayers in this section, only declarations. Despite the many words beginning with the letter 'm', the psalmist confines himself to the exclamation 'How!' (verses 97, 103) and to one preposition translated 'from' and 'through' (verses 101, 102, 104) and that is also used to form comparisons ('than', 'more than'; see verses 98, 99, 100).

The psalmist continues on the positive note begun in the previous section and opens by blurting out his love for God's law (verse 97). He has already mentioned to God that he loves his commandments and delights in them (verses 47–48), but he expresses himself here in an even more enthusiastic way. Another exclamation toward the end of the section indicates how sweet God's sayings are to his taste (verse 103). David expressed his delight in God's word using similar language (Psalm 19:10; see also Ezekiel 3:3).

That love is not merely spoken it is expressed in action. He has made God's law his 'meditation' continually by reflecting on what it says and talking about it (verses 97, 99). Love for God's word is an indication of love for God himself. Israel was called to love the Lord with all their beings and God's words were to be at the very centre of their beings. It was to be part of their personal lives as well as their home and family life (Deuteronomy 6:4–9). Jesus said to his disciples that if they loved him they would keep his commandments (John 14:15). The psalmist has also kept God's precepts, has held back his feet from entering every evil path (verses 100–101) and has hated every path of falsehood (verse 104).

The important point that he wishes to stress in this section is that God is his teacher by means of his word. In verse 102 he stresses that it is God himself ('you yourself') who has taught him (see Psalm 25:8–9). The God-breathed Scriptures are given to teach us and make us wise about salvation through faith in Jesus the Messiah but we need God's Spirit to enlighten our minds and give us understanding (2 Timothy 3:15–17; John 16:13; 1 Corinthians 2:6–16). George Horne remarks that the heavenly Teacher is unlike all others in this one great respect that 'with the lesson, he bestoweth on the scholar both a disposition to learn and an ability to perform'.

The result of this teaching is that the psalmist is 'wiser than' his wicked 'enemies' despite their ingenious plotting and scheming (verse 98; see verse 95). They are the arrogant fools who have suppressed the truth about God revealed in creation and rejected God's specially revealed will in his word (verses 21, 53, 85; see Psalm 14:1–4; Romans 1:21–23; 3:9–19). The psalmist has God's commandments ever with him for they have become part of his life (see verse 11).

In addition, he goes further and mentions that he has 'more understanding than all my teachers' (verse 99). There were various sources for gaining understanding about life. In the first place, it was the task of parents to train their children (Deuteronomy 4:4–9, 20–25; Proverbs 1:8; 31:1). Much common-sense wisdom used to be gained this way. Other tutors would be involved later depending on their children's future employment. Daniel and his three friends were taught the language and literature of the Chaldeans (Daniel 1:4). But without that heavenly wisdom that comes from God to appreciate and understand God's truth such tutors are sadly lacking in understanding what is really important. There is an anointing, as John indicates, that means we have no need of teachers (1 John 2:27).

One further group he mentions: 'the ancients' (verse 100). These could be the older men or elders of the community who were revered for their experience, settled disputes at the city gate, witnessed legal transactions and offered advice when asked (Joshua 20:4; Ruth 4:2–11; 1 Kings 20:8). There is much knowledge and wisdom in the world, much of it helpful and important but true wisdom does not necessarily depend on life-long experience. If their insights are based purely on human wisdom developed over the years they are again lacking that vital element. True wisdom is revering God and keeping away from all that is dishonourable in God's sight. It is an understanding that results from meditating on God's word and that leads to obedience (see verse 56).

In comparing himself to these various groups of people he is not boasting in his own abilities nor is he undervaluing the importance of the knowledge of experience, common-sense wisdom and other avenues of knowledge. What he is doing is bearing witness to his Teacher and the textbook he is using and applying to his life.

14. The light of the LORD's word (The *Nun* section; verses 105-112)

Affliction still troubles the psalmist (verse 107) and there is a wicked enemy to face (verses 109-110) and this is true for all God's people throughout their earthly pilgrimage (Acts 14:22). We have a saying, 'I took my life in my hands', and it is based on such biblical statements as this (see Judges 12:3; 1 Samuel 19:5). The psalmist is carrying his very life ('person', 'soul') on the palm of his hand, meaning he is risking his life. To follow God's teaching provokes the enemies of God to persecute the righteous yet the psalmist continues to live by it and does not forget it (verse 109). The danger from traps set by the wicked is real enough but that makes no difference as the psalmist is determined not to stray from God's precepts (verse 110).

In the light of these ongoing trials, the psalmist presents new pleas. After a section with no direct reference to the LORD, the psalmist calls out twice to the covenant God of Israel, 'O LORD' (verses 107-108). His life has been greatly weakened and so he appeals to the God of the covenant for 'life' (see verse 77), which covers ongoing spiritual as well as physical life, because that is what God directs in his word (verse 107; Leviticus 18:5; Deuteronomy 6:24).

The second plea takes an unusual turn and indicates that the positive note began at verse 89 is still present. Like offering to the Lord animal and food sacrifices for him to accept (Leviticus 1:4; 7:18), the psalmist asks God to accept 'the freewill offerings' of his mouth (verse 108). The voluntary offerings included blood sacrifices of the peace offering type, which were not actually required in the law but presented as grateful acts of devotion to God (Leviticus 7:16) as well as gifts offered for the construction of the tabernacle and temple (Exodus 35:29; 2 Chronicles 31:14; Ezra 1:4). Here the psalmist brings to God spontaneous offerings of a verbal nature ('of my mouth'). At the end of Psalm 19, David offers 'the words of my mouth' as well as 'the meditation of my heart' as an offering for God to accept (Psalm 19:14). Such offerings from a humble spirit will include praise and thanksgiving as well as the prayer that the psalmist offers here (Psalms 50:14; 51:15-17; Hosea 14:2; Hebrews 13:15). Coupled with his humble desire freely to offer praise and prayer that God will accept is his plea for the Lord to teach him his judicial rulings ('judgments', verse 108). Knowing God's decisions revealed in his word will result in further spontaneous acts of praise and prayer.

Surrounding his lament and prayers are important statements

concerning his attitude to God's word. On a dark night treading an unfamiliar footpath in the countryside without a light it can be quite dangerous and we can miss the right way. Following on the wisdom theme of the previous section, the psalmist speaks of life as a 'path' (verse 105; see Proverbs 1–9). If we are to walk safely it is important to have God's revealed 'word' as our 'lamp' that acts as a 'light' for every step we take on the journey through life. In view of this, the psalmist has gone on oath to keep God's righteous rulings ('judgments', verse 106; see verses 7, 62).

In the final verses which form a frame round this section the psalmist returns to tell us more about how he views God's word. He has taken God's 'testimonies' as his 'heritage for ever' (verse 111). Not only is the Lord himself his allotted portion (verse 57), but he sees the Lord's declarations as his inherited possession like Canaan was to be Israel's inheritance (Exodus 23:30). At a time when Canaan is no longer theirs but part of the Persian empire 'beyond the River' (Ezra 4:10–11, 17, 20), the godly psalmist sees God's word as a possession that no human authority can take from him. These testimonies of God are something about which he can really rejoice. This enthusiasm for God's law is not sentimental emotionalism but an emotion that is coupled with a commitment to perform God's statutes 'for ever'. Having asked God to 'incline' his heart (verse 36), the psalmist now sees his own responsibility for inclining his mind, affections and will to do God's will 'to the end' (verse 112; see verse 33).

15. For and against God (The *Samekh* section; verses 113–120)

At the centre of this section the psalmist prays for safety (verses 116–117) while either side are statements of love, loyalty and awe addressed to the one whom he calls for the first and only time in this psalm, 'my God' (verse 115).

In contrast to his own single-minded aim to perform God's laws (see verse 112), he hates the 'double-minded' (verse 113), those who, metaphorically speaking, sit on the fence and cannot make up their minds whether to be committed to God's law or not. Elijah spoke to people like this who were faltering between two opinions when he challenged his people on Mount Carmel to decide one way or the other, Baal or Yahweh/Jehovah (1 Kings 18:21). Jesus said you cannot serve and be loyal to two masters at the same time (Matthew 6:24). The verbs 'love' and 'hate' in the Old Testament can often mean 'for' and 'against' and that is the idea here (see Psalm 97:10). Loving God's laws means more than having an emotional attachment to them, it includes a commitment to obey them. Likewise, hating the double-minded involves repudiating the attitude. This section gives further examples of what the psalmist is for and against.

He shows his opposition to wrongdoing by addressing the 'evil-doers' directly and indicates that he is thoroughly against their way of life (verse 115; see Psalm 1). At the end-time judgment Jesus will use these words to supporters who turn out to be workers of lawlessness (Matthew 7:23). The psalmist shows which side he is on by making statements concerning God's rejection of those who stray from his statutes on account of their deceit and falsehood (verse 118) and of God's action in putting away 'all the wicked of the earth' which he describes as 'dross' (verse 119). Dross is the impurity that comes to the surface when metal is refined in the fire (see 1 Corinthians 3:11–15). It is possible that the 'wicked of the earth' could mean in this context the rebels within the land of Israel (see Psalm 28:3).

On the other hand, the psalmist indicates his love for God and his law: by waiting expectantly for his word that speaks of comfort and blessing (verse 114); by his determination to keep God's commandments (verse 115); and by thinking of the fate of the wicked which encourages him in his loving commitment to God's testimonies (verse 119). While God puts away the wicked the psalmist has found God to be his 'hiding place' (verse 114; see Psalms 32:7; 61:4) and 'shield' (see Psalms 3:3; 28:7; etc.). The final verse reminds us that though God is good and kind and can be trusted and loved, he is not one that humans can tame. 'He's not safe but he is good'.[69] God is holy and a consuming fire (Isaiah 6:1–5; Hebrews 12:29). This view of God and of his awesome judgments that causes the flesh to bristle is a far cry from the casual, complacent approach that we can so often exhibit as Christians in our communal worship and personal lives.

It is in the context of his loving loyalty to God and commitment to his will despite continuing opposition that the psalmist prays to be upheld, sustained in his resolve to do God's will so that he might continue to live and find deliverance just as God's word indicated. Otherwise, if God does not meet these requests the psalmist would be made to look stupid, that his hope had been misplaced and this would bring, by implication, dishonour to God for it is on the basis of God's word that his requests are made (verses 116–117). As it is put in other psalms, for God not to act would cause the enemy to say, 'Where is your God?' (Psalms 42:3, 10; 79:10; 115:2). These are bold arguments that Christians can also bring to God.

16. Doing and timing (The *Ayin* section; verses 121–128)

Words beginning with the letter for this section include the verb translated variously as 'do', 'deal' and 'act', the nouns 'surety', 'eyes' and 'servant' and the 'therefore' that occurs twice in the final two verses. Three times 'servant' appears, which is another term commencing with this letter, and on the third occasion it stands as the opening word right at the centre of the section: 'I am your servant' (verse 125).

The section is unique in that it begins with two verses that do not include any direct or indirect reference to God's specially revealed word (verses 121–122; see also verse 84). It is what the psalmist has done that is emphasised (verse 121). Though the word for 'justice' is the same as God's judicial rulings at the close of the previous section (verse 120) it does not refer to God's righteous judgments but to the psalmist's obedience to God's law in his concern for the poor and vulnerable in society. Oppression of the poor is evidence of the perversion of 'justice and righteousness' (Ecclesiastes 5:8). These two qualities God loves and are the foundation of his kingly rule (Psalms 33:5; 89:14) and so the psalmist has good reason to appeal to God not to be left to the mercy of the 'proud' who would oppress him (verse 122; see verse 85). The oppressors are gaining the upper hand. It seems to be a losing battle and it is as if the psalmist is now being sued for unpaid debts and looks to God to take responsibility for paying them. The servant-master relationship that he has with the Lord means he can expect to come under the divine master's protection and help. Hezekiah uses the same word for 'surety' (translated 'undertake' or 'pledge' in some versions), as he cries out in his helplessness to the Lord who is oppressing him in judgment (Isaiah 38:14).

The psalmist's lament continues in verse 123 with words reminiscent of verses 81–82 and then he prays, again from the position of a servant, that God would act according to his 'steadfast love' ('mercy', verse 124; see Psalm 109:21) and teach him more about God's statutes. If he is to know and do God's 'testimonies' then he must be given 'understanding' (verse 125). The servant-master relationship is not to be isolated from God's covenant relationship with his people. It is an aspect of that relationship which emphasises the psalmist's willing submission and devotion to God and at the same time the protection and help that he can expect from God, his lord and master.

It is clear that despite the psalmist's efforts the situation in which he finds himself is beyond his efforts to transform. The first part of verse 126 can be taken as a direct address to God: 'It is time for working, Lord' or as a statement, 'It is time for the Lord to work'. Whichever translation is taken the point is that there is great need for Israel's covenant Lord to do something and the rest of the verse is certainly a prayer to God. Although the psalmist is seeking to demonstrate the characteristics of God in society (verse 121), the oppressors are undermining that good work, attacking him personally and 'they have regarded your law as void'. These arrogant oppressors have gained the ascendency, violated the covenant stipulations so that the covenant itself is as good as dead (see Isaiah 24:5; Jeremiah 11:10).

Desperate days call for desperate cries that God would change the situation for the better. We must give God no rest till he establishes and makes his people a praise in the earth (Isaiah 62:7). Every revival of true religion is a foretaste of the final transformation of all things when the earth will be full of the glory of God. Before that grand finale, we are warned that the professing church will pass through seasons of great declension and apostasy (1 Timothy 4:1; 2 Timothy 3:1–9). In such periods God's people call out for God to do something by sending a season of refreshing (Acts 3:19). God's time, however, is the right time and while we pray persistently we also wait patiently (Luke 11:5–13; 18:1–8).

But the last verses both begin with 'Therefore'. The psalmist is not inactive while he looks for God to act. He continues to 'love' God's commandments in the sense of being committed to keeping them in his daily life for they are more precious than the best quality gold (verse 127). Although it may not be politically correct and against the trends of the day, the psalmist continues to regard God's precepts as 'straight' ('right') and is opposed to every 'path of falsehood' (verse 128).

17. Wonders and blessing (The *Pe* section; verses 129–136)

Human oppression is still evident (verse 134) and the psalmist has such a deep concern about those who do not keep God's law that 'channels of water' run down from his eyes (verse 136). It is an expression of his sincere love for God and his word and this is obvious from the way he begins the section.

As he has indicated earlier, God's declarations are 'wonderful' (see verses 18, 27). They are all part of God's amazing miraculous activity like the wonders that God displayed before Pharaoh (Exodus 3:20). God's word delivered through people with their own distinctive styles of expression is itself a wonder and it is a 'wonder' that God has actually given us this revelation of his will for our lives. In addition, God's word tells us of the wonders he has done. The wonders performed at the exodus point to the greatest wonder of all, Jesus Christ God's Son our Saviour, who is a called the 'Wonderful Counsellor' (literally 'a wonder of a counsellor', Isaiah 9:6). God was in Christ reconciling a lost world to himself (2 Corinthians 5:19).

No wonder the psalmist desires to keep these wonderful words of life! But God's words are not a wonder to everyone. There are proud oppressors who reject God's law but the psalmist is particularly interested in the 'simple' (verse 130; see Psalm 19:7). This is a wisdom term often found in Proverbs for the naive and gullible. They are not like the 'fool' whose mind is closed to the truth and lives contrary to God's law. The 'simple' are the uncommitted, easily seduced but they are open-minded enough to be shaped aright and improved (Proverbs 1:4, 22; 7:7; 9:1–6).

For understanding to be given to people like the 'simple', they need the light of God's words (see verse 105). In fact, for all to appreciate the wonders of God's law eyes need to be opened (verse 18). The 'entrance' refers to God's activity illuminating the mind to appreciate his words as the truth is proclaimed by word and gospel sacraments. Jesus 'opened the Scriptures' to his disciples, showing from the Old Testament the necessity of his death and resurrection and 'opened their understanding that they might comprehend the Scriptures' (Luke 24:24–27, 32, 44–47).

God's commandments are not only for the simple. The psalmist confesses his own longing for them like the craving and panting of an animal in need of food and water (see Psalms 42:1–2; 63:1). Job relates how people waited silently and eagerly for his counsel like a mouth open wide for the spring rain (Job 29:23). It leads the psalmist into prayer for God's blessing. First, he prays in language reminiscent of the priestly blessing of Numbers 6:24–26 that the Lord would 'look upon me and be merciful to me' (verse 132) which more literally reads,

'Turn to me and be gracious to me'. Interestingly, he adds that he is not asking for some random favour but something that is according to a practice revealed in God's word for which people who love God's name can apply.

His next request shows his concern to live in a way that pleases God. He has mentioned his own responsibility in turning his feet to walk according to God's directions and in restraining them from going in an evil way (verses 59, 101), but he realises his need of God's help to 'direct' or 'establish' his 'steps' (verse 133). God does this as suggested in verse 105 by the light of his word. In addition, he wishes to be controlled by God rather than be ruled by any sin. This may have been in Paul's mind when he wrote about sin not having dominion over us (Romans 6:14). Because of our position in Christ, Christians are no longer under the rule of sin and death and therefore are enabled by God's grace not to allow any sin to master us. The psalmist also appeals to God to 'redeem' him in the sense of liberate him from human oppression (verse 134; see Psalms 26:11; 78:42). Just as God redeemed Israel from Egyptian slavery to serve the Lord, so he prays that he might be free to observe God's precepts (see Exodus 3:12; 6:6; 8:1, 20; 9:1, 13; etc.). God has redeemed his people so that they might be zealous for good works (Titus 2:14).

His final plea returns to his first petition (see verse 132) as he asks for the blessing of God's smile upon him (verse 135; see Numbers 6:25; Psalm 31:16). The blessing sought is not material prosperity but a concern for God's laws. He can never have enough teaching about God's statutes. As a child, Jesus was ever eager to learn more from the teachers of God's law in the temple (Luke 2:46). That is why, like the psalmist (verse 136), Jesus expressed such deep sorrow over those who should have known better but who were rebelling against God's law by rejecting him (Luke 19:41-44). Paul likewise speaks of his sorrow and continuing grief over Israel's rejection of Christ as well as over those who professed to be Christians but turned out to be enemies of the cross of Christ (Romans 9:1-5; Philippians 3:18-19).

18. The righteous God and his righteous word (The *Tsadhe* section; verses 137-144)

The key term is 'righteousness' prompted by the initial letter for this section. It occurs four times as a noun, twice to introduce a verse (verses 142, 144) and twice elsewhere (a second occurrence in verse 142 and translated 'righteous' in verse 138). The adjective 'righteous' is also used to open the section (verse 137). It is the LORD who is 'righteous', the opening verse declares, and the closing verse announces that 'righteousness' characterises God's testimonies (see also verse 138). God has perfectly expressed himself in his written word. God's righteousness is a righteousness 'for ever' (verse 142) and the righteousness of his testimonies are also 'for ever' (verse 144).

'Righteousness' is one of God's great attributes and it is the foundation of his universal rule (Psalm 97:2). He is the standard for what is right and he always acts in a way that is true to his righteous character. God's righteous standard was shown to Israel in the covenant law and is most wonderfully displayed in the gospel (Romans 1:16-17; 3:21-26). The rules and regulations, the instruction and decisions contained in God's written word through Moses are uppermost in mind here. Because God is righteous, his 'rulings' ('judgments') are 'upright' ('straight', verse 137), which is what the psalmist considered them to be (verse 128). As there is only one God, his is the universal standard even though people try to claim that his right is wrong and their wrong is right. He restates the point in the next verse. God's 'testimonies' or 'declarations' that he has commanded are also 'righteous' and 'fully trustworthy' ('very faithful', verse 138; see verse 86). God is not an arbitrary, inconsistent God and his 'law is truth' ('reliable', verse 142). The psalmist speaks of God's word as 'very pure'. It has been tested like metal is refined and has not been debased by foreign and inferior elements (see Psalms 12:6; 18:30).

In praising the righteousness of the LORD and his word, the psalmist expresses his own loyalty and love (verse 140; see verse 127). The precious, changeless nature of God's word far outweighs the taunts of his enemies who deliberately put God and his words out of their minds (verse 139). God's 'servant' may be 'small' or 'insignificant' and 'despised' in the eyes of his foes (see Judges 6:15; Psalm 68:27; Micah 5:2), but he does not forget God's precepts (verses 140-141). He continues to delight in his commandments despite the 'trouble and anguish' that have overtaken him (verse 143). In fact, the psalmist refers to an all-consuming zeal, a passion for God's honour on seeing the way people are behaving toward God's words (see Psalm 69:9). His final prayer is that God would enable him to understand and so practise God's declarations in order to energise him for continuing life-long service (verse 144).

We are reminded of the despised and rejected Lord Jesus Christ, the Lord's Servant (Isaiah 53:3), whose zeal for God consumed him (John 2:17). He delighted in God's commandments when trouble and anguish were all around him (Psalm 40:8; John 8:29). In his high-priestly prayer he spoke of the truth of God's word (John 17:17). This same Jesus endured the cross, despising the shame (Hebrews 12:2) and encourages his followers to run along the same track.

19. Near and far (The *Qoph* section; verses 145–152)

The psalmist begins the first two verses with calls to the LORD ('I cry out', verses 145–146). He follows this by two verses commencing with the verb 'to precede' or 'go before': he has 'preceded' the dawn ('rise before', verse 147) as well as the night watches ('awake through', verse 148). The final verse also begins with a term from the same word family ('of old', verse 152). Toward the end he employs another pair that is translated as 'drawn near' and 'near' (verses 150–151). This leaves the word 'voice' to begin the verse that acts as a turning point in the section (verse 149) with its call for life in accordance with God's steadfast love ('loving-kindness') and judicial ruling ('judgment'). The urgency and intensity of the psalmist's pleas are indicated by his threefold calling out to God (verses 145–147) and by his addressing him three times using his covenant name, 'LORD' (Yahweh/Jehovah; verses 145, 149, 151).

Alec Motyer suggests that the two halves of this section correspond to James 4:8 where we read, 'Draw near to God' (see verses 145–148) 'and he will draw near to you' (see verses 149–152).

Prayer means coming near to God (see Psalm 73:28). The psalmist does so sincerely with his whole being and also with a desire to obey God's statutes and testimonies (verses 145–146). 'Without serious moral commitment, intercession is merely self-seeking' (Motyer). He is in great distress because of people who pursue 'malicious mischief' ('wickedness', verse 150). Long hours are spent in prayer (see previous verses 55, 62, 97). He is up before the dawn[70] crying for help and his eyes are open before the last of the night 'watches' (see Psalm 63:6). In his need for deliverance and life (verses 146–147, 149) he is helped by musing ('meditate') on God's word (verse 148). Over long periods of intercession it is important that God's word informs our minds and encourages us as we persevere in prayer. The psalmist's hope is in God's word (verse 147) and his prayer rests on the Lord's loving commitment and just decision (verse 149).

True prayer will result in God coming near and this was the psalmist's experience—'You are near, O LORD' (verse 151; see Psalms 34:18; 69:18). Kidner notes that the threat from the enemy is not glossed over—'They draw near' (verse 150)—but by using similar wording for the Lord's presence, the threat 'is put in perspective by a bigger fact.' These foes who are near the psalmist are 'far' from God's law and as such they are 'far' from salvation as the next section indicates (verse 155). The wicked schemes of the enemy cannot succeed in the end for though they may claim to be in the covenant community their behaviour indicates they are not committed to obeying him. On the other hand, the psalmist who has been meditating on God's word finds the commandments trustworthy guides to a life pleasing to the Lord. God's testimonies have been the psalmist's study for some time and he acknowledges that they stand for ever (verse 152; see verse 144).

This intimate, personal relationship that God has with people committed to him in loving obedience, is something that can be felt and it brings relief and assurance. God's Servant was assured of vindication through the Lord's nearness to him (Isaiah 50:8) and in Jesus' experience as he prayed intensely in the Garden of Gethsemane, he knew God's presence and angelic help (Luke 22:39-46) and God did vindicate him by his resurrection. Jesus' parable concerning the widow and the judge was for the purpose of encouraging persistent prayer. The Lord's people should always pray and not lose heart. Jesus ends by saying, 'And shall not God vindicate his own elect who cry out day and night to him though he bears long with them?' (Luke 18:1-8).

20. See and revive (The *Resh* section; verses 153-160)

Two verbs dominate this section, each occurring three times: 'see' (verse 158 and translated 'consider' in verses 153, 159), which is used in each case to begin the verse, and 'revive' (or 'give life'; verses 154, 156, 159) which is always found in the second half of a verse.

The psalmist begins by asking God to look at ('see', 'consider') his 'affliction' and he closes by requesting him to see ('consider') his 'love' (verse 159). God saw his people's 'affliction' in Egypt and acted to 'deliver' them (Exodus 3:7-8). The persecuted church in Jerusalem raised their voices to heaven and urged the Lord to 'look on their threats' (Acts 4:29). These afflictions and threats are all part of a long-standing war that has been raging ever since our first parents believed the evil one rather than God. The psalmist's sufferings have been mentioned many times, particularly in verses 81–88 and in this lament he refers to his 'many' persecutors and enemies (verse 157). Such 'wicked' people are not interested in God's statutes (verse 155) and as he sees ('I see') these 'treacherous' persons he is 'disgusted' by them because they do not observe God's word (verse 158; see Psalm 139:21). They claim to belong to the covenant community but their attitude and actions clearly indicate they are apostates. God's promises of 'salvation' are far from them in that they can only expect God to punish them for their disobedience (verse 155).

At the same time the psalmist reminds God that he is committed to the covenant stipulations. He loves God's precepts and does not forget or turn away from his 'law' and 'testimonies' (verses 153, 157, 159). It is from this position as a loyal member that he prays that God would plead his cause and act as a kinsman redeemer. It is as if the psalmist is on trial and the enemy considers him guilty. He therefore calls on God to intervene for him and rescue him from the plight in which he finds himself (see Psalm 43:1; 69:18).

It is in this context of deliverance that the theme of 'life' is introduced. The verb 'to give life' has occurred frequently in the psalm (verses 25, 37, 40, 50, 88, 93, 107) and can be used for to 'keep alive' or to 'make alive' in the sense of 'restore life' either physically or spiritually. Life, like salvation, in this context, should be thought of in the widest of senses. The psalmist claims this gift of life on the basis of God's promised word (verse 154) and the greatness of his compassion ('tender mercies', verse 156). He wished to be delivered from the false accusations and restored to the community but a spiritual reviving cannot be ignored. He prays according to God's steadfast love that he will be revived (verse 159) and this has a much more restorative, spiritual aspect to it (see verses 37, 93).

The final verse is a strong declaration concerning God's word. He confesses his faith in the truthfulness or reliability of the sum total of God's word (see Psalm 139:17) and that God's righteous rulings stand for ever. This means as Jesus emphasised that 'till heaven and earth pass away, one jot or one tittle will by no means pass from the law till all is fulfilled' (Matthew 5:18). The Lord Jesus is faithful and true and so also are the words that proceed from the throne of God and the Lamb

(Revelation 3:14; 19:11; 21:5; 22:6). This faithful Lord has promised to establish and guard us from the evil one (2 Thessalonians 3:3).

21. Praise, peace, joy and commitment (The *Sin/Shin* section; verses 161–168)

The penultimate letter of the Hebrew alphabet can be pronounced in two ways and the difference proved to be a matter of life and death for the Ephraimites who, when asked to say 'Shibboleth' could only say 'Sibboleth' (Judges 12:5–6). Some words beginning with this letter are pronounced 's' (verses 161–162, 166) while others are pronounced 'sh' (verses 163–165, 167–168). One of the psalmist's favourite words, 'keep', is reserved for the final two verses ('My soul keeps', 'I keep').

After the threefold use of 'LORD' in the previous section the divine name is entirely absent in these verses (see also sections 3, 11, 13, 15, 17), which is not surprising as there are no direct petitions either. His persecutors are mentioned first but only briefly as most of the section is taken up with expressions of joy and commitment. The 'Princes' have been mentioned earlier (see verse 23) and it is not clear why these leaders wish to make life hard for the psalmist. What is clear is that they have no just reason for harassing him (verse 161; see Psalm 35:7). Significantly, he is not in awe of them whatever their claims and standing in the community. The holy 'awe' he has for God's 'word' is because of the awe he feels when contemplating God himself (see verse 120). It is most liberating to be freed from that servile fear of humans and instead to have that profound reverence for the awesome God that is deeply concerned not to offend him. *Fear Him, ye saints, and you will then Have nothing else to fear.*[71] At the same time *The terrors of law and of God*, as Augustus Toplady confessed, *With me can have nothing to do; My Saviour's obedience and blood Hide all my transgressions from view*[72] and perfect love casts out fear (1 John 4:18). This is not paralysing dread but an awe and reverence that co-exist freely with love.

It is this freedom from the fear of people that enables the psalmist to rejoice over every statement or saying of God, the kind of joy someone has who has just found much plunder ('great treasure' or 'spoil', verse 162; see 1 Samuel 30:16). Isaiah speaks of the joy at the announcement of the Messiah: it is like people who 'rejoice when they divide the spoil' (Isaiah 9:3). He has expressed his 'love' of God's law numerous times (verse 163; see verses 97, 113, 119, etc.) as well as his opposition to ('hate') and his abhorrence of all that is false ('lying'; see verses 104, 128). Such loving commitment to God's law leads to 'praise' all day long (verse 164; see Psalm 55:17) or with 'seven' symbolising completion it may mean that he praises God fully. This praise is because of God's righteous rulings which speak of his promises and give directions for our lives.

One of the great benefits of a loving commitment to God and his law is 'great peace' (verse 165). Only here in the psalm does the word 'peace' occur. It speaks of a state of wholeness and well-being. In this context, it clearly relates particularly to an inner condition. Although outward circumstances are far from peaceful, people like the psalmist can know an inner peace that is God-given and Christ purchased (John 14:27). When persecuted for no good reason it means their conscience is clear before God and they can live with themselves. This 'great' peace arises out of their loving commitment to God's teaching and despite all the hazards of life they continue in God's way and do not fall away ('stumble'). Lying behind this peaceful condition is a relationship with God where people like the psalmist are in a right legal position with God through faith in God's promised Messiah (see Genesis 15:6; Romans 5:1). Such believers can rejoice with hope for the 'salvation' that is nearer to them now than when they first believed (verse 166; see Genesis 49:18; Romans 5:2; 13:11). Those who are in this relationship with God 'keep' his commandments. They are not burdensome (1 John 5:3). God's people, Christ's disciples, love them 'exceedingly' and the whole person ('My soul') is involved as they 'perform' them (verses 167–168).

Jesus is himself the perfect example of loving God's word and delighting to do his will and it is on account of his righteous life and atoning death that sinners who look to him alone for salvation can stand upright in God's presence and live out their lives before God's scrutiny—'all my ways are before you' (verse 168; see Hebrews 4:13).

22. Closing prayer (The *Taw* section; verses 169–176)

While the previous section offered no petitions, this final one is full of prayer from beginning to end and twice he appeals to God by the name that became so precious to Israel from the time of the exodus— 'LORD' (verses 169, 174; see Exodus 3:14-15, 6:3; 34:5-7). The two verses beginning 'My lips' and 'My tongue' can also be read as prayers: 'Let my lips' and 'Let my tongue' (verses 171–172). Only verse 174 contains no plea but even there he certainly expresses his longing to God. In many ways the section summarises the whole poem with the psalmist's call for understanding, deliverance and help and his acknowledgement of God's law and concern for life. The verses in this section go in pairs: prayers for a hearing (verses 169-170); ability to praise (verses 171-172); asking and longing for help (verses 173-174); and prayers for life and to be shepherded (verses 175-176).

Unlike the section that brings the first half of the psalm to a close (verses 81-88), a strong positive note is present, especially with the references to praising God and delighting in his word. There is no mention of the psalmist's enemies but surprisingly, the psalm ends not with notes of praise, as he does earlier, but with the honest recognition that he is prone to wander like a lost sheep and continually needs the heavenly Shepherd to seek him out. The psalmist can be upbeat but he is no triumphalist.

The section begins with an urgent ringing 'cry' that is offered to God like a sacrifice ('draw near before', verse 169; see 1 Samuel 14:36). He prays that his 'supplication' or 'plea for grace' will be acceptable to God (verse 170). In this humble way the psalmist makes his request known to God for 'understanding' (see verses 27, 34, 73, etc.) and deliverance (see verse 153) according to God's word of promise.

The following two petitions amount to implicit promises, which is why our translation has 'My lips shall utter praise ... My tongue shall speak of your word' (verses 171-172). The word translated 'utter' or 'pour out' pictures the 'praise' gushing out like water (see Psalms 19:2; 145:7). Such eager and free flowing praise is in the confident expectation that God will 'teach' him his statutes (see verses 12, 26, 33, 64, 68, 124, 135). As 'tongue' parallels 'lips' so 'speak of your word' parallels 'utter praise'. The word translated 'speak' usually means 'answer' and is used here as an enthusiastic response to God's word of promise and command, especially in view of the fact that 'all' God's commandments are in accord with his righteous character (see verse 7).

The psalmist prays for the supporting 'help' of God's powerful 'hand' and expresses his longing for 'salvation' (verses 173-174). In both cases he supports his desires by appealing to his wholehearted commitment to God's teaching and commands. He has 'chosen' to follow and obey God's precepts as Moses directed Israel (Deuteronomy 30:15-20) and his 'delight' is in his law (see verses 77, 81). God's deliverance will mean the preservation of his life and this will enable the psalmist's whole being to praise God. Therefore he prays for life and asks that God's rulings, which include directions on how to live as well as promises to those who obey, would help and guide him on his journey through this world.

In this closing and longer than usual sentence and with the concerns of the previous verse in mind, the psalmist humbly confesses that he has strayed 'like a lost sheep'. In what sense is he a lost, dying sheep? From all that the psalmist has written in this long poem it is clear that he is a true member of the covenant community. He has neither abandoned God's way revealed in his law nor, as he states in his final words, forgotten God's commandments (see verses 16, 83, 93, 109, 141, 153). His foes are the ones who have not only strayed from God's law, they have gone far from it and abandoned it altogether (verses 21, 139, 150). In addition, he speaks of himself as the Lord's 'servant' (see verses 16–17, 23, 38, 125, etc.). He has committed himself to the Lord for willing service.

The psalmist is therefore not suggesting that he is an apostate but he is acknowledging his sinful failures and inconsistencies, something of which every true Christian is conscious. 'If we say that we have no sin, we deceive ourselves, and the truth is not in us' (1 John 1:8). That is why we constantly need reviving and why we look for the consummation of God's work of salvation in Christ.

Although he does not address God as Shepherd that is the implication when the psalmist speaks of himself like a lost sheep. God is the 'shepherd of Israel' who led his people through the wilderness by the hand of Moses and Aaron (Psalms 77:20; 80:1). His appeal for God to 'seek' him also suggests the shepherd image. Usually it is the psalmist who seeks the Lord and his precepts (verses 2, 10, 45, 94). Here the seeking suggests someone searching with a view to finding (Nehemiah 7:64; 12:27; Psalm 37:36). The good shepherd seeks what is lost and brings them back (Ezekiel 34:16) as in Jesus' parable (Luke 15:4). In fact, Jesus speaks of himself as the good shepherd who came to seek and save the lost and to give his life a ransom for many (Mark 10:45; Luke 19:10). He came to gather in the lost sheep of the house of Israel and the other sheep from among the Gentiles so that there might be one flock and one shepherd (Matthew 10:6; 15:24; John 10:16). The Bible's last book pictures the Lamb shepherding the whole company of God's people from all nations and leading them to springs of living water (Revelation 7:17).

'A Song of Ascents'

The following fifteen psalms (Psalms 120–134) all have this same heading which occurs nowhere else. Four of the psalms making up this little collection were written by David (Psalms 122, 124, 131, 133), one by Solomon (Psalm 127) and the rest by unknown authors. They were probably brought together and each given this title 'A Song of Ascents' after the Babylonian exile as a group of short (except for Psalm 132), easy to memorize psalms that pilgrims could sing as they made their way to the temple in Jerusalem. The numerous references in these psalms to 'Zion' and 'Jerusalem' support this view. We know that groups of people on pilgrimage to Jerusalem for the three great annual festivals of Passover, Pentecost and Tabernacles, did sing en route (see Psalm 42;4; Isaiah 30:29). The word translated 'ascents' is also used for 'steps' or 'stairs' (Nehemiah 3:15; 12:37; Ezekiel 40:6) and belongs to the same word family as the verb 'to go up' which is sometimes employed to describe worshippers going up to the central sanctuary at festival time (1 Samuel 1:3; Psalm 122:4).

A notable feature of these psalms is the use made of stair-like repetition where the same word is repeated as if leading the reader along step by step. It is especially appropriate for the songs of ascent. We see its use particularly clearly in Psalm 121 with the words 'help', 'slumber' and 'keep'.

The contents of this special group of psalms often include references to everyday life as well as to national concerns and both would be appropriate on the lips of ordinary pilgrims coming together for these special festive occasions. A progression can be detected from the difficulties and trials faced by the pilgrims (Psalms 120-131) to the blessing and joy of being together in Zion at the sanctuary (Psalms 132-134).

Such psalms placed here in this fifth book of the whole psalm collection would have been a real encouragement to the returned Jewish exiles from Babylon in view of their ongoing problems and depressing circumstances. For Christians today they remind us of our privileged situation in Christ. The Zion we, as pilgrims, are marching toward, is the Zion to which we already belong by God's grace. When Christians gather as a church for communal worship it should be a small-scale view of this spiritual city to which we belong. Such gatherings should be the highlight of our week, where hearts as well as feet 'go up' to the place of meeting, a little taste of heaven on earth and a preview of the great day of the Lord.

Psalm 120

In the World But Not of It

Whatever the origins of Psalm 120, it is placed here in Book 5 at the head of these pilgrim psalms by the inspired editor to express the continuing concerns of God's people after their return from exile. As Christians passing through this world dominated by Satan's influence, similar troubles face us and the psalm encourages us to press on toward the heavenly city looking to Jesus, our triumphant leader and saviour, who has journeyed ahead of us. The psalmist is portrayed as an alien (verse 5) who recalls a past answer to prayer (verse 1). This serves as the basis for a further petition (verse 2) on account of a new crisis that has developed (verses 3–4) and the psalm closes with a lament describing the psalmist's plight (verses 5–7), which adds urgency to his appeal for the Lord's help. It is in the final section that we find the first example of what scholars term staircase repetition, a characteristic of these pilgrim psalms. The verb 'dwell' in verse 5 is repeated in verse 6 and 'peace' in verse 6 is taken up in verse 7.

Past deliverance acknowledged (verse 1)
In his 'distress' (see Psalm 118:5) the psalmist had called out to the covenant-keeping God ('LORD') and had been heard (see Psalm 3:4). When God is said to have heard the pleas of his people it means he has acted to deliver them. The restrictive, distressing situation the psalmist

had been in is very appropriate in describing the people's situation as captives in Babylon. God had heard the prayers of people like Daniel (Daniel 6:10-11; 9:1-19) and they had returned to their homeland.

Earnest appeal (verse 2)

Recalling the past action of God in answer to prayer encourages this new plea. David was frequently troubled by those who propagated false rumours and engaged in deceit (see Psalm 31:18) and the previous psalm also refers to the same problem (Psalm 119:69, 78). The Samaritans used such tactics to hinder the Jews from rebuilding the temple and to oppose Nehemiah's work in rebuilding the city walls (Ezra 4; Nehemiah 6:1-9). False accusations were brought against Jesus which led to his being sentenced to death and the Christian can expect similar treatment from those who hate God and his Messiah (Matthew 5:11). The God who delivered Jesus from death on the resurrection morning and who has delivered believers in Jesus from the worst of exiles through his Son our Saviour, can be looked to for help when the enemy accuses his people falsely (see 1 Peter 3:16).

Enemy addressed (verses 3-4)

The psalmist now turns to address the liars and using poetic imagery expresses his certainty that the enemy will receive divine justice. Though the wounds from false tongues are hurtful and damaging, those who utter such lies will be destroyed in a much more terrifying and painful way. The rhetorical question in verse 3 asks what punishment from God is appropriate for such malicious lies. In the original, the way the question is formed is derived from the curse formula, 'The Lord do so to you and more also' (see 1 Samuel 3:17). The answer in verse 4 uses illustrations that suggest the punishment fits the crime (see Psalm 28:3-4). As the enemy's false words have been like deadly arrows (Psalm 64:3-4) and like a burning fire (Proverbs 16:27) so God's judgment will be like a warrior's sharp arrows and like the burning charcoal of a broom tree that retains its heat for some considerable time (see Psalm 7:11-13). The two images could be combined to suggest that the arrows were like fiery darts (Psalm 11:6). People may snigger at hell-fire preaching but the reality of God's just punishment of sinners is far worse than any metaphor can convey.

It will be noticed that the psalmist does not take the law into his own hands and retaliate like for like but leaves God to vindicate him and to punish the enemy. This is how Jesus taught his disciples to deal with persecutors and he himself led by example.

Situation described (verses 5–7)

The lament begins with an impassioned cry of grief and he describes his situation as if he is a resident alien in foreign parts with no citizenship rights. 'Meshech' (verse 5) lies north of Canaan near the Black Sea in modern-day Turkey (1 Chronicles 1:5; Ezekiel 38:2) while 'Kedar' is a nomadic Arab tribe in the desert area to the east and south of Canaan (Genesis 25:13; Isaiah 21:13–17). Not only does he feel like a foreigner but he considers himself to be like someone who has settled among hostile foreigners (verse 6). The psalmist is all for 'peace' and although he desires and proposes peaceful relationships, the people he is among only want war. They are hostile toward him and insist on giving him a hard time (verse 7). This closing remark also indicates that the psalmist had done nothing to warrant such a reaction. It reminds us again of the hostility and hatred that was directed against Jesus by the Jewish authorities. He came and settled among his own people yet they despised and rejected him for no sound reason. Yet Jesus remained meek in the face of unprovoked attacks. His disciples also live as resident aliens in a world that opposes God and his people. They live in the world but they do not belong to the world (John 17:14–18). Nevertheless, they are to follow this way of peace (Romans 12:18; 2 Corinthians 13:11; 1 Peter 2:11–12; 3:8–17; Hebrews 12:14) and commit themselves to the God who has promised to vindicate them at the right moment. 'Shall God not avenge (vindicate) his own elect who cry out day and night to him though he bears long with them?' (Luke 18:7–8).

Psalm 121

Kept by the LORD

From a situation of distress in the previous psalm, this second of the pilgrim songs (see Psalm 120) expresses trust in the covenant-keeping LORD, the creator of heaven and earth, who is the protector of his people. The psalm, one of the most well-known, has been of special encouragement to God's people down the centuries and often used as a prayer before departing on a journey or leaving loved ones behind.[73]

The promises found here make the song similar to Psalm 91 but they are presented as a confession of faith for the benefit of God's people. We do not know when the psalm was originally written or by whom but the inspired editor has included it here to be a stimulus to God's people in the period following the return from exile, to give them hope and confidence as they face the hardships of life. The reference to distant mountains, the concern with safety and the need for protection from the sun's heat and the dangers of the night makes it particularly appropriate as a song to be sung by the faithful on their way to one of the annual festivals in Jerusalem. There is a change from the first person singular in verses 1 and 2 to the second person singular from verse 2 onward. Either the psalmist moves from speaking about himself to speaking to himself or he begins by speaking for himself and his people and then shifts to addressing his people as if they were a single

individual. This is quite a common practice where God regards Israel as
his son or servant and addresses them in the singular.

Jesus was ideal Israel and he knew the reality of this psalm in his own
experience from birth to the death of the cross. The promises of this
psalm apply to his followers too. Christians can be assured that united
to Christ they are safe and secure despite all that the devil might throw
at them.

A notable feature of the psalm's form is the stair-like repetition
where the same word is repeated as if leading the reader along step by
step. 'My help' is repeated in verses 1 and 2, 'slumber' appears twice in
verses 3 and 4 and then 'he who keeps' and 'keeper' occurs three times
in verses 3 to 5 and the same verb is used again three times in verses 7
and 8 but translated 'preserve'.

Declaration of trust (verses 1-2)

Is the psalmist looking longingly toward mount Zion and the hills that
surround her? Or is he looking anxiously at the mountains ahead that
spell danger and difficulty? The wider context of these pilgrim psalms
(Psalms 120-134) would suggest a positive looking forward to Zion's
hill (see Psalm 125). But the question that immediately follows (verse 1)
takes his thoughts of help beyond the earthly city and its temple. His
help comes from the covenant God of Israel ('LORD') who is the creator
of the whole universe (verse 2; see Psalms 115:15; 124:8; Isaiah 37:16).
The mountains themselves are impressive and everything associated
with mount Zion is wonderful but God is greater for it is he who made
all things. The apostles in the face of stiff opposition from the Jewish
authorities raised their voices together in prayer and addressed God as
the one 'who made heaven and earth' (Acts 4:24).

Divine protection (verses 3-6)

The picture of a foot slipping (see Psalms 17:5; 38:16; 66:9) on a rough
path is appropriate when thinking of pilgrims journeying to Jerusalem
(verse 3). Motyer writes: 'The Lord who redeemed (Exodus 6:6) his son
Israel (Exodus 4:22) will not now lose him on his way home!' God has
committed himself to his people so that he will keep us from falling
and bring us safely to our heavenly destination (Jude 24). Whatever
difficulties we do encounter, whether through our own fault or not,
God uses them for our good.

Though the psalms sometimes speak as if God is asleep and needs to be awakened, this is only a way of urging him not to be inactive any longer but to answer the pleas of the psalmist. In actual fact, the one 'who keeps Israel' does not slumber or sleep (verses 3–4). He is not like a guard who drops off to sleep while on duty. To have such a one to keep watch means we can sleep in our beds and feel secure (see Psalm 4:8). Israel's God, 'the LORD', is the best of guardians for he gives full protection day and night (verses 5–6). The 'shade' reminds us of being under the shadow of the Almighty (Psalm 91:1) while standing at the 'right hand' means that God is ready at his side to defend and shelter him (verse 5; see Psalm 109:31).

In the sub-tropical Middle East, the sun can be fierce and dangerous for travellers walking through the hills. A full moon was also frightening to the ancients but it could also indicate a hard frost (see Jeremiah 36:30). Both sun and moon are used here poetically to emphasise that the Lord's protection is constant and covers every threat and eventuality, day or night. Insurance companies encourage us to take out comprehensive policies for our peace of mind. God's people can have every confidence that they are fully protected.

Divine preservation (verses 7–8)

The word for 'keep' (verses 3–5) reappears and is translated 'preserve' in these closing verses. It is a word that recalls the exodus and the priestly blessing which begins, 'The Lord bless you and keep you' and ends 'and give you peace' (Numbers 6:24–26). Joshua was able to confess at the end of his life that the Lord who had brought them out of Egypt 'preserved us in all the way that we went' (Joshua 24:17; see Numbers 14:9). One of the blessings for obedience under the Sinai covenant was that Israel would be blessed 'when you come in' and blessed 'when you go out' (Deuteronomy 28:6). Such assurance of the LORD's overall protection of his people in their 'going out' and 'coming in' (verse 8) could be applied not only to their daily work (see Psalm 104:23; Deuteronomy 31:2) but when they went out to wage war against their enemies (Joshua 14:11), when they went out into exile and returned as well as in their going on pilgrimage to the annual festivals and returning home. This divine care and protection is 'from this time forth, and even for evermore' (verse 8; see Psalms 113:2; 115:18). Through all the busyness of our lives as believers, we are assured of God's keeping power (see 1 Peter 1:5) preserving us from all harm ('all evil', verse 7) until we reach the end of our earthly pilgrimage.

Psalm 122

The Beautiful City of God

Though not original to Watts' hymn *Come, we that love the Lord,* Dr Robert Lowry's chorus catches something of the abiding truth of this psalm: 'We're marching to Zion ... the beautiful city of God.' As Christians we belong to that heavenly city and are marching toward it. Do we love God's city which is made up of brothers and sisters in the Lord? Do we prize this city more highly than all the architectural splendours of the world?

Of all the pilgrim psalms (Psalms 120–134) this is most clearly a song of pilgrimage (see Psalm 120 for the heading 'A Song of Ascents'). Within this group of psalms it is the first of four attributed to David. Although the name Zion is not used, it has close associations with the Zion songs (Psalms 46; 48; 65; 84; 87). Interestingly, the psalm begins and closes with 'the house of the LORD' (verses 1, 9), while at the centre is the reference to 'the house of David' (verse 5). Jerusalem is known as the 'city of God' only in the Psalms (Psalms 46:4; 87:3) and the 'city of David' many times in the historical books but not in the Psalms (2 Samuel 5:7, 9; 6:12; Nehemiah 12:37; also Isaiah 22:9). This encourages us to think of these references to Jerusalem and Zion in the psalms as pointing to a heavenly reality that is comprised of all God's people (see Isaiah 35:10; 51:11; Hebrews 11:10, 16; 12:22–24).

The three references to 'house' recall David's desire, in view of the house he had built for himself and family, to construct a house that would serve as God's earthly palace. In God's special promises to David there is a play on the word 'house'. God did not allow David to build him a house (that is, a temple), but instead God would build David a house in the sense of a lasting dynasty (2 Samuel 7:1–17). David draws these themes together in this psalm and it reminds us of Psalm 2 where God rules through his Anointed king. David's greater son and Lord is associated with the dwelling of God among his people in the city of God (Psalm 110:1).

From the point of view of a pilgrim using these songs, the psalm completes a trilogy that begins with distress caused by enemies (Psalm 120) followed by the difficulties of the journey (Psalm 121) and ends with rejoicing at being in the city where God has made his home (Psalm 122). Again, we find step-like parallelism where words are repeated and taken further in the following lines ('Jerusalem', 'tribes' and 'thrones' in verses 3–5), which is a feature of these pilgrim songs (see Psalms 120:5–7; 121:1–4, 7–8).

Glad anticipation (verses 1–2)

David speaks for God's people as they enter the gates of Jerusalem and look excitedly at the prospect of coming near to God's sanctuary (verses 1–2). It was a rare privilege for those living further than a Sabbath day's journey, to visit the capital city where the ark, the symbol of God's presence, was housed in the tabernacle that David had erected, before Solomon's temple was built. It was required in the Mosaic Law that adult males should appear at the central sanctuary three times a year for the festivals of Passover, Pentecost and Tabernacles (Exodus 23:14–17; Deuteronomy 16:16–17). When the central sanctuary was at Shiloh, Samuel's father and family attended only once a year (1 Samuel 1:3, 7, 21). For whole families to make the journey to Jerusalem was quite a treat but expensive and for safety reasons they generally travelled in groups, just as Joseph and Mary with Jesus joined the Nazareth contingent of pilgrims for the annual Passover festival (see Luke 2:41–44).

Isaiah uses David's phraseology to describe Gentile nations joining Jewish people in coming to the LORD's mountain, to the place where Israel's God makes his home (Isaiah 2:3). This prophecy began to be fulfilled at Pentecost when Peter preached and three thousand were added to the Church (Acts 2:9–11). It gives support for understanding

Psalm 122 in the light of Christ's coming with the people of God of all nationalities seeking God's presence as they meet together.

How pleased and blessed was I To hear the people cry, 'Come let us seek our God today!' are the opening words of Isaac Watts' paraphrase of this psalm and they express the joy that Christians are to have at meeting together on the Lord's Day. While our individual lives should be expressing daily our worship of God we are urged to gather for communal worship and it should gladden our hearts that we can come together as God's people to sing, pray and hear God's word read and preached. As we make the effort of coming near to God in this way may we know God coming near to us by his Spirit and speaking to us all through the preached word and by the mutual love and concern we have for one another.

Praising the city (verses 3-5)

The reasons for the people's joy are spelled out in more detail in these verses. First, the city itself is wonderful (verse 3), then it expresses the unity of God's people (verse 4) and thirdly, it is governed well under God's appointed ruler (verse 5).

The first example in this psalm of 'step' parallelism is found here where the word 'Jerusalem' ends the previous verse and is repeated at the beginning of verse 3 which goes on to give more information about the city. It emphasises the joy at seeing the city so compact and well-suited for receiving its visitors from all the tribes of Israel. We are reminded of an earlier psalm that urges the people to 'Walk about Zion, and go all around her. Count her towers; Mark well her bulwarks; consider her palaces' (Psalm 48:12).

Using step parallelism again, the tribes that go up to the city are not described, as so often in the Bible, as 'the tribes of Israel' (Psalm 78:55) but uniquely as 'the tribes of the LORD' (literally 'tribes of Yah', verse 4). This gathering of the tribes was an expression of their united devotion to the covenant God of Israel. The phrase 'to the Testimony of Israel' (literally 'a testimony to Israel') in the New King James version makes 'Testimony' a name for God but this is very unlikely. It refers rather to God's decree instructing male Israelites to visit the central sanctuary every year at the annual festivals (Exodus 23:14-17; see Psalm 81:4-5). The loyalty of Israel's clans to God's commandment was seen in these festal gatherings at the central sanctuary in Jerusalem where they gave thanks for all that the name 'LORD' (Yahweh/Jehovah) stood for. All the pilgrimage festivals were connected with harvest and all celebrated aspects of the exodus and the journey to Canaan, so that thanksgiving to God was a special feature of these occasions.

Jerusalem is also the home of God's appointed ruler. For a third time in this psalm the step-like pattern is used to emphasise that the 'thrones' (verse 5), the centre of civic life where just decisions ('judgment') were to be made, belong to David and his family line (see 1 Samuel 7:12-16). Like the judges that ruled over the tribes before the monarchy was established in Israel, the king's advice was sought in resolving disputes that could not be settled locally (1 Samuel 15:2-6; 1 Kings 3:28). In addition, he had the task of organising the affairs of the whole country and deciding foreign policy. We are told that 'David administered judgment and justice to all his people' (2 Samuel 8:15). In this David acted as God's viceroy (see Psalm 9:4, 8) and foreshadowed Messiah's reign (Isaiah 9:7; 11:3-5).

The enthusiasm for this city is not out of place, for an earlier psalm has indicated that the Lord who loves all the dwellings of Jacob, loves even more the gates of the city where his pilgrim people enter and where everything is put to rights (Psalm 87:2).

Praying for the city (verses 6–9)

While right decisions make for peace, wrong decisions often lead to dissension and disunity as happened after the death of Solomon (1 Kings 12:16). Those seeing and enjoying the blessing of good government and contented people will take seriously the exhortation to pray that it would long continue. Under the just rule of the Prince of Peace, justice and peace go hand in hand (Isaiah 9:7).

There is an obvious play on the name of the city in which the shortened form 'Salem' (see Psalm 76:2; Hebrews 7:1-2) is similar in sound to the name for peace (*shalom*). In fact, the 'sh' sound in Hebrew occurs in the first four words ('pray', 'peace', 'Jerusalem' and 'prosper', verse 6) making it a fine example of alliteration. It is also interesting that as the name 'Jerusalem' has been mentioned three times in the psalm, so the word 'peace' occurs three times in these final verses. As Grogan suggests, it would seem that the psalmist is praying that the city 'will live up to its name'.[74]

The exhortation to 'Pray' or, more exactly, to 'ask for' peace is followed by an example of the kind of prayer that is to be offered and the English versions rightly place the latter part of verse 6 and the whole of verse 7 in inverted commas. It is in the form of a two-part blessing. First, the prayer seeks a blessing on those who love the city—'May they prosper' (verse 6). The verb 'prosper' in the first instance means to 'be secure', 'quiet' and 'at ease' (Job 3:26; 12:6) but then it can indicate the success that such security brings—'to thrive' or 'flourish' (Jeremiah 12:1). Second, there is a blessing on the city itself—'peace be within your walls, prosperity (or 'security') within your palaces'. Both 'walls' (often translated 'bulwarks' or 'ramparts') and 'palaces' ('citadels') are also found together in the description of Zion (Psalm 48:3, 13).

In addition to this twofold blessing for Jerusalem's well-being there is a final brief benediction on behalf of all the family of God who live there: 'Peace be within you' (verse 8). David's brothers and companions are his faithful fellow Israelites who are found worshipping together within the city walls. It is because the LORD (Yahweh/Jehovah), their covenant-keeping God, has made his home there that David seeks by prayer the 'good' of the city (verse 9; see Psalm 125:4). The psalm began with the glad prospect of going to 'the house of the LORD' (verse 1) and it closes with this commitment to pray for the city because that is where 'the house of the LORD' is (verse 9). The presence of the Lord among his people is what makes this city so wonderful.

To the exiles newly returned from Babylon, with the city walls and temple demolished as well as later when a temple was built that looked so inferior to that of Solomon's magnificent structure, a psalm like this would have encouraged the people to look with the eye of faith beyond what the physical eye could see to that city described by the prophets. Isaiah records the song of God's people, 'We have a strong city; God will appoint salvation for walls and bulwarks. Open the gates, that the righteous nation which keeps the truth may enter in. You will keep him in perfect peace, whose mind is stayed on you ...' (Isaiah 26:1-2). It is Isaiah who also prophesies of the prosperity of the LORD's city (Isaiah 60). John in his vision of the new Jerusalem sees the city gates inscribed with the names of the twelve tribes of Israel and the city walls named after the twelve apostles to emphasise the unity of God's people whether under the old or new covenant (Revelation 21:12-14; see Psalm 122:4).

While the disciples and others admired the beauty and splendour of Herod's temple that made Jerusalem so attractive, Jesus saw the city and wept over it saying, 'If you had known, even you, especially in this your day, the things that make for your peace! But now they are

hidden from your eyes.' And he went on to prophesy its destruction
(Luke 19:41–44; 21:5–24). Jesus also taught that through his death and
resurrection he would raise up a temple that would last. The Church
that he died to redeem consists of his people who are being built up
into a living temple in the Lord (Ephesians 2:19–22). All who trust
Jesus Christ are also citizens of the heavenly Jerusalem and this new
Jerusalem will be revealed in the new creation (Revelation 21:1–2).
After the Holy Spirit was given to the Church on the day of Pentecost,
the gospel went out from Jerusalem to Rome as Acts makes clear and
in fulfilment of Jesus' words. For Paul, the old Jerusalem represented
all that was anti-Gospel, whereas Jew and Gentile in Christ belong to
the Jerusalem which is above. We pray for the peace and prosperity
of this city until all whose names are in the book of life are brought
in and the Lamb and his people are for ever together in the home of
righteousness, where there are no tears and no curse.

Psalm 123

The Need for Divine Grace

Each of the previous pilgrim psalms (see Psalm 120 on 'Song of Ascents') has been characterised by a word that has special significance for that psalm: in Psalm 120 it was the 'tongue'; in Psalm 121 it was 'keep'; in Psalm 122 it was 'Jerusalem'. Here in this prayer psalm it is God's 'mercy' or better his 'grace' that is the dominant theme. The cry for divine favour arises out of deep distress caused by those who hold the godly in contempt. Psalm 120 depicted a similar oppressive situation but instead of being affected by the enemy's lying tongue, the people of God are subject to ridicule and scorn.

Whenever it was originally written, the editor of the collection found this psalm of particular relevance to the Jews after their return from the Babylonian exile, especially to pilgrims on their way to the sanctuary for the annual festivals like Passover, Pentecost and Tabernacles. As we find from Nehemiah the Jews endured various forms of persecution (Nehemiah 2:19; 4:4). The Christian, too, who seeks to be faithful to Jesus Christ, can expect to receive similar treatment and be made to feel small and stupid. How ridiculous to be spending your day in church on Sunday when you could be out enjoying yourself or catching up on jobs around the house!

Seeking the LORD's attention (verses 1-2)

The opening is like Psalm 121:1 but emphasises even more strongly that it is to God the psalmist is looking for help—'Unto you' (verse 1a), and 'so our eyes *look* to the LORD our God' (verse 2b). David mentions how his eyes '*are* ever towards the LORD' (Psalm 25:15). Speaking on behalf of his people ('I' in verse 1 becomes 'our' and 'us' in verse 2), the psalmist looks expectantly for God to come to their assistance. It is interesting that we have priests after the exile named Elioenai or Elihoenai ('Unto the LORD are my eyes'; see Ezra 8:4; 10:22, 27; Nehemiah 12:41).

We can look with confidence and hope to the sovereign God who is high over all. He has ordained to make heaven his home—'who dwells in the heavens' (verse 1; see Psalms 11:4; 103:19). Jesus encouraged his disciples to pray to God as 'Our Father in heaven' (Matthew 6:9). From there he laughs at the stupidity of humans who club together to fight against him and his Anointed (Psalm 2:4). It is because he is the transcendent God that he can act on behalf of his people.

As servants and maids look to their masters and mistresses for protection and the provision of their needs so the attitude of God's people in their distress is one of reverent trust as they seek God's favour ('mercy'). We come before God with no rights of our own. Just as it was by God's grace that he entered into a covenant relationship with a people he had rescued from slavery to serve the Lord, so Christians have been redeemed by God and called to be in the service of the King of kings. We look to the Lord as Israel was encouraged to do, conscious that we owe all to him. This LORD (Yahweh/Jehovah) is our covenant God too (see Psalm 113:5). In prayer we come into the presence of the sovereign Lord who has committed himself to us and in our trouble we petition him until we receive the grace we need. The God of all grace is 'able to make all grace abound toward' us (2 Corinthians 9:8).

Prayer for favour (verses 3-4)

We are now introduced to the petition and the reason for the impassioned cry. The plea for God's 'grace' is repeated, underlining the urgency of the request—'Have mercy on us, O LORD, have mercy on us!' (or better 'Be gracious, O LORD, be gracious'; verse 3; see Psalms 4:1; 6:2; 25:16). Though they do not deserve it, they plead God's favour, for grace is God's unmerited favour. Why are God's people in need of his grace? The rest of verse 3 begins to give the answer with more detail given in verse 4 and use is made of 'step' parallelism, a feature of these psalms, where 'exceedingly filled' is repeated in the following line with added information (see Psalm 120).

The verb translated 'filled' can be used for someone who has eaten well and is satisfied. Here it stands for having a surfeit of shame. Sometimes we speak of having our fill of trouble. That is the thought here. God's people have endured great shame and ridicule (see Psalms 44:13; 79:4). It was the kind of situation that Nehemiah described when Sanballat and his cronies laughed at them, first for wanting to build the city walls and then when they saw the walls they were building (Nehemiah 2:19; 4:1-3).

The people responsible for inflicting this scorn and derision on God's people are described as the wealthy, who feel secure ('who are at ease'; see Isaiah 32:9; Amos 6:1; Zechariah 1:15). They are the haughty, exalted ones ('the proud') who look down on God's people. It is no coincidence, then, that the psalmist's cry at the beginning is to the God who dwells in the heavens who really is high and lifted up.

There are people like Richard Dawkins who take it upon themselves to treat Christians with contempt and ridicule the Bible and Christian values. They proudly advertise that there is probably no God and encourage people to relax and enjoy themselves. While this does not at present result in too much harassment it could well lead in time to a general hostility and persecution of Christians. Pilgrims on the way to the celestial city must remember they are resident aliens in this present world order and can expect such treatment. Christians have a great sympathetic high priest and we are encouraged to 'come boldly to the throne of grace, that we may obtain mercy and find grace to help in time of need' (Hebrews 4:16). 'But may the God of all grace, who called us to his eternal glory by Christ Jesus, after you have suffered a while, perfect, establish, strengthen, and settle you' (1 Peter 5:10).

Psalm 124

The Great Escape

H ere is a thanksgiving psalm that David penned after he and his people escaped from a most dangerous situation. 2 Samuel 5:17–25 gives us a clue to the kind of occasions when David looked to God for help and wisdom as the Philistines sought to put an end to his rule in the same way they had destroyed Saul's kingdom. The escape is due entirely to Israel's covenant God. The previous psalm had offered an urgent prayer for God to be gracious and come to the aid of those facing ridicule and shame, while this psalm offers thanks and humbly acknowledges that help and deliverance has come from the Lord 'who made heaven and earth' (verse 8; see Psalm 121:2).

The editor of the whole collection considered this psalm 'Of David' to be particularly appropriate at this point in Book 5 to express the people's appreciation of God's action in delivering them from the Babylonian captivity. It would also have reminded the people on pilgrimage to the Jerusalem sanctuary (see Psalm 120 for 'Song of Ascents') of the great escape from Egyptian bondage and the deliverance at the Red Sea. Christians likewise can use this psalm to express thanksgiving to God for the greatest escape of all—deliverance from the bondage of sin and Satan through Christ's redeeming work on the cross. We sing with the saints in heaven, 'Salvation *belongs* to our God who sits on the throne, and to the Lamb' (Revelation 7:10).

The thanksgiving psalm is in the form of a testimony for it does not address God directly but speaks appreciatively of the help and deliverance they have received from the LORD, their covenant God. As Paul urges Christians, the people of God are encouraged to speak to one another in such songs, for it builds up confidence in God and shows to unbelievers that the LORD is the living and true God who hears and answers prayer.

What might have been (verses 1–5)

These five verses form one long sentence with two 'If' clauses (verses 1–2) and three 'Then' clauses (verses 3–5). More literally the psalm opens: 'If it were not Yahweh who was for us'. Before going any further, the psalmist urges Israel to take part in making the confession (see Psalms 107:2; 118:2–4; 129:1) and a little more detail is given of the grave situation—'when men rose up against us' (verse 2). The more literal translation highlights the opposites 'for us' ('on our side'; verses 1–2) and 'against us' (verses 2–3). If God is not for us then God's people have no way of escape from the enemy. Those who rise up against them are much too powerful.

Two graphic images are used to convey the hopelessness of the situation without God's help. The godly would be like prey in an animal's mouth (verse 3). This is what the enemy thought had happened when Jerusalem was attacked by the Babylonians (Lamentations 2:16). The language also reminds us of Korah and his companions when God in his anger brought about their swift destruction as the earth opened its mouth and swallowed them alive (Numbers 16:30–33). The Jews experienced the fury of the enemy in Nehemiah's day (Nehemiah 4:1, 7).

In verses 4 and 5 the image changes and their situation without God's help would have been as dangerous as being in a dry river bed, suddenly overwhelmed with a deluge of water. Some of the dry wadi beds of Judea are very steep-sided. If there is a thunderstorm in the mountains a raging torrent can quickly rush down giving anyone in the wadi little chance of escaping.

In Christ, believers can take comfort in knowing that nothing can separate us from the love of God and that the devil and all his evil associates cannot finally overcome God's people. If God be 'for us', writes Paul, who can be 'against us?' (Romans 8:31).

Worshipping the LORD (verses 6-8)

David at this point offers praise for God's gracious intervention on behalf of his people. The Lord (Yahweh/Jehovah) is to be 'blessed' (verse 6) which includes paying him homage and expressing appreciation for all that he has done to save them from the enemy's clutches (see Psalms 41:13; 103:1-2). Two further illustrations indicate the extreme danger the people would be in but for the Lord's intervention. The enemy is likened to a wild animal but God has saved his people from its jaws (verse 6; see Psalm 7:2). God's people have had a narrow escape like a bird from a fowler's broken trap (verse 7; see Psalm 91:3).

The final verse presses home the fact that their freedom is due to their covenant God and this is an encouragement to all those reading and singing this psalm to know that this same God will come to the aid of his distressed people. The 'name of the Lord' is a way of summing up God's revealed character. Our help is in the living God who has made himself known as one who keeps his promises and is all-powerful to save his people from the most impossible of situations. He is, after all, 'the LORD who made heaven and earth' (verse 8; see Psalm 121:2).

This is the God who has sent his Son to free us from our sins and who is able to present us faultless before his presence with exceeding joy (Jude 24; Revelation 1:5). If you are to have God on your side you must know his Son, Jesus Christ, as your Saviour and Lord. It is to those who belong to God through Jesus that this sure promise of help is given. 'Therefore let those who suffer according to the will of God commit their souls to him in doing good, as to a faithful Creator' (1 Peter 4:19).

Psalm 125

The Security of God's People

Security dominates every aspect of our society from security codes for internet banking to security cameras in town centres. Besides national security all kinds of security systems are in place to prevent fraud, theft and other serious criminal activity. There are other situations where technology is of no help in giving people security. Our western relativistic world where the old absolutes are called into question can make people feel very insecure. You may also be concerned about the future well-being of the Church of Jesus Christ in your country. This psalm addresses such issues.

A pattern seems to be emerging in these Songs of Ascents (see Psalm 120). The editor has so arranged them that the second three Ascents songs (Psalms 123–125) follow the thought of the first three (Psalms 120–122). They begin with prayers of relief from distress (Psalms 120, 123), then there is a confident looking to the help that God gives (Psalms 121, 124), and finally we are assured of the peace and security that characterises God's city (Psalms 122, 125). This movement toward Jerusalem fits well with these psalms associated with pilgrimage to the annual festivals at the city's sanctuary. We do not know when this psalm was originally composed but it was an appropriate one to include at this point especially as the returned exiles from Babylon were being harassed and oppressed by foreigners opposed to their

Psalms 73-150

existence as well as by ungodly elements within their own community. Its concerns can be reapplied to the many situations the people of God continue to face as they live as pilgrims heading for the eternal city.

Declaration of confidence (verses 1–3)

This declaration is presented in both a positive and negative way. To adapt Motyer's helpful outline, we have:

1. A believing community that finds its security in the LORD (verses 1–2)

In their communal expression of trust in their covenant God they are likened to 'Mount Zion'. David had achieved a notable victory in taking this strong settlement from the Jebusites (2 Samuel 5:6-7). The city of David built on this mountain made it a secure place. But it is the Lord who makes this city what it is in God's purposes and it becomes symbolic of the eternal city of God which Abraham was looking forward to seeing (Hebrews 11:10, 16). This is the city that 'cannot be moved' when everything else is shaken to bits (verse 1; see Psalms 46:5; 48:8; Hebrews 12:26-28). To trust the God of Zion is to be eternally secure—'abides (literally 'sits') for ever'.

In addition, the people of God are assured of his protection (verse 2). The original city of Jerusalem was so surrounded by a ring of larger mountains that it was almost impossible to see it from a distance. It provided a measure of shelter and security from attack. This is used here as a picture of the Lord's protective presence (see Psalm 34:7; Zechariah 2:5). Zion stands for the people of God and they are the ones who are shielded by him in the present and on into the unending future. Outside the Psalms the phrase 'from this time forth and for ever' (verse 2) is used only by Isaiah and Micah (Psalms 113:2; 115:18; 121:8; 131:3; Isaiah 9:7; 59:21; Micah 4:7).

All who belong to God through Jesus are given eternal life. Jesus said, 'they shall never perish; neither shall anyone snatch them out of my hand. My Father, who has given them to me, is greater than all; and no one is able to snatch them out of my Father's hand. I and my Father are one' (John 10:28-29).

A sovereign Protector I have
Unseen yet for ever at hand,
Unchangeably faithful to save,

Almighty to rule and command.
He smiles, and my comforts abound;
His grace as the dew shall descend;
And walls of salvation surround
The soul He delights to defend. (Augustus Toplady)

2. A threatened community waiting on God to remove oppressive rule (verse 3)

Verse 3 describes the kind of situation the Jews experienced in their own land after returning from exile. As in the days of Joshua, it speaks of the land 'allotted' to the people (see Joshua 14:2; 18:10). God had given the land to his people ('the righteous') for their possession. They cast lots but the outcome was not by chance because 'its every decision is from the LORD' (Proverbs 16:33). Wicked foreign officials were in the ascendancy and this made life difficult for God's people. Because of the truth declared in the opening verses they are assured that they will not remain under these oppressors perpetually. The 'sceptre' (used also of the shepherd's 'rod' or 'club'; see Psalm 23:4) is a symbol of power and rule (Genesis 49:10; Psalms 2:9; 45:6) and 'sceptre of wickedness' refers to evil oppressors like the Assyrian and Babylonian kings. Isaiah speaks of their burdensome rule ('rod') being broken (Isaiah 9:4; 14:4-5; 30:31). In Nehemiah's time it was Sanballat and his associates who were oppressing the Jews (Nehemiah 2:10; 6:1-14).

Another reason why God's people are assured that their oppressors' power will not continue is for their own spiritual good. The ascendancy of evil rulers may lead the righteous to meddle with sinful activities—'reach out their hand to iniquity'. They may be tempted to follow the ungodly regime and engage in unbrotherly practices (see Nehemiah 5) or even to abandon their faith in God and worship pagan gods.

This assurance reminds us of Paul's words that though temptations come to God's people, 'God is faithful, who will not allow you to be tempted beyond what you are able, but with the temptation will also make the way of escape, that you may be able to bear it' (1 Corinthians 10:13). We are also warned by Jesus that 'because lawlessness will abound, the love of many will grow cold. But he who endures to the end shall be saved' (Matthew 24:12-13). The Bible encourages Christians to believe that all God's elect will persevere to the end and be saved for eternity. This does not mean that the believer can sit back and presume all will be well. If God has worked salvation within us then we are to work it out in our daily lives with God's help, for it is he who enables us to will and do according to his good will. God's word, prayer, living obediently as he has shown us in his word and engaging with others in Christian fellowship and worship are the particular means God uses to help us persevere in the faith.

Prayer for God's promised blessings (verses 4-5)

The promised assurances lead into prayer. God's people are those who 'trust in the LORD' (verse 1) and they are described as 'the righteous' (verse 3). That is their status by God's grace. The people who are truly the LORD's in the Old Testament period are in the same position as Christians under the new covenant. Our right legal standing before God is by grace alone and through faith alone in God's promised Messiah. From this position, we are called to live 'good', 'upright' lives and not be like hypocrites with a veneer of goodness but pursue an uprightness that is centred in our innermost beings—'upright in their hearts' (verse 4; Psalm 7:10; Proverbs 2:21).

The 'good' for which the psalmist prays relates to God's promises associated with the covenant he made with their ancestors (see for example Genesis 12:1-3; and compare 2 Samuel 7:28). God promises that 'he who puts his trust in me shall possess the land, and shall inherit my holy mountain' (Isaiah 57:13; see 60:21; 65:9). Those who are of a humble and contrite heart are assured by Jesus that they will inherit the earth (Matthew 5:5).

There are people in the community who are morally warped and twisted who 'turn aside to their crooked ways' (verse 5). They belong to 'the workers of iniquity' whom the Lord will lead away to the punishment they deserve (see Psalms 1:6; 28:3). Malachi accuses the corrupt priests of departing from the way and causing many to stumble at the law (Malachi 2:8-9). Our Lord warns that there will be those who have claimed to speak and act in Christ's name whom he will disown on the day of judgment with the words, 'I never knew you; depart from me, you who practise lawlessness!' (Matthew 7:23).

The desire for peace (Psalm 120:7) and the prayer for peace (Psalm 122:6-8) are now followed by the benediction: 'Peace be upon Israel!' (see Psalm 128:6; see Numbers 6:26). This peace relates not merely to a cessation of war and unrest but to a state of well-being and prosperity in the land. It contrasts with the fate of all those who turn aside to follow the crooked ways of the ungodly wicked. There is no peace for the wicked (Isaiah 48:22; 57:21) but for the true Israel of God, who are of a contrite and humble spirit, the LORD says, 'Peace, peace to him who is far off and to him who is near ... and I will heal him' (Isaiah 57:19). Paul writes that Christ himself is our peace who has made Jew and Gentile one by breaking down the dividing wall. When the gospel was proclaimed to the Ephesians, Christ 'came and preached peace to you who were afar off and to those who were near. For through him we both have access by one Spirit to the Father' (Ephesians 2:14-18). An eternal state of peace and security will exist when that holy city comes down to fill the new earth, where sorrow and pain will be no more and all the unbelievers and the immoral will have their part in the lake of fire, which is the second death (Revelation 21:1-8).

As the apostle Paul draws his letter to the Galatians to a close he writes: 'And as many as walk according to this rule, peace and mercy be upon them, and upon the Israel of God' (Galatians 6:16).

Psalm 126

Restoration of Zion's Fortunes

Psalm 85 has urged God to revive what he has done in the past and this psalm seems to reflect a similar situation. However, there is no mention of God's anger on account of the people's sin or of his forgiveness of their sins such as we find in Psalm 85. We have no idea how the psalm came to be originally written but there were many occasions in Israel's history when they experienced sudden reversals of fortune. The psalm does bear some similarities to the circumstances depicted by the prophet Joel. What we do know is that the editor of our psalm collection has placed it among the pilgrim psalms (see Psalm 120 for 'A Song of Ascents') to express the feelings of the returned exiles from Babylon.

After the initial excitement of the return brought about through the decree of Cyrus the Persian emperor in 537 BC the Jews were soon brought down to earth by the harsh realities of life during the period before Ezra arrived in Jerusalem (see Ezra 1-6; Haggai 1) and later on in Nehemiah's time.

The psalm looks back to a recent experience where they have been delivered by God and remembers the joy of the people and the impression made on the surrounding nations. Now trouble has come to them again and prayer is offered that he would again come and change the situation for the better. Like Psalms 120 and 123 it is a prayer psalm for relief from the trouble they are experiencing (see the introduction to Psalm 125).

As Christians we look back on God's great redeeming work in Christ but there is constant need to pray that God would complete what he has begun in us. Likewise, we pray for the reviving of God's work in our churches. God has intervened on behalf of his people in the past and for that we must be eternally grateful. But we need to evaluate that past in a biblical way, commit the present to the Lord so that we do not become dry and apathetic but look to the future that God has revealed in his Word.

Recollection of God's past activity (verses 1-3)

The opening line does not actually speak of the Lᴏʀᴅ bringing captives back to Zion, it speaks rather of the 'restoration of Zion' not the 'captivity of Zion'.[75] There has been a great restoring almost like someone being brought back to life again. Zion is used to describe the people of God (see Isaiah 49:14). When the Lord brought about this change in Israel's fortunes it was like waking up after a wonderful dream and finding the dream was a reality. This was certainly the experience of the newly returned exiles from Babylon. Prophets like Jeremiah and Isaiah had seen visions of this reality and had prophesied of this day (Isaiah 44:24-45:13; Jeremiah 29:8-11; 31:23-26) and now it had all come true. Moses had spoken of the people's conversion and of a return from captivity after the final curse of exile had taken its course (Deuteronomy 30:1-3).

Laughter and singing are expressions of joy. When they were in exile the people were sad and in no condition to sing (Psalm 137:1-6). Something of the gladness of the returned exiles is recorded when the foundations of the temple were laid (Ezra 3:11-13). Often the enemies of Israel sarcastically called out 'Where is their God?' (Psalms 79:10; 115:2) but here the surrounding nations were made aware of what great things God had done for his people (verse 2). We know that it resulted in the adversaries of the Jews, who had ulterior motives, wanting to join in the project to rebuild the temple (Ezra 4:1-4). This return with its consequent rejoicing is seen by Isaiah as a type of the greater return that would result from the work of God's Servant when 'all the ends of the earth shall see the salvation of our God' (Isaiah 52:8-10; see Ezekiel 36:36).

What is being said among the nations, God's people can echo and be glad about (verse 3). The step-like parallelism is a feature of these songs of Ascent (see Psalm 120). Similarly, Joel called on the people to 'be glad and rejoice, for the LORD has done marvellous things' (Joel 2:20-21). The demon-possessed man healed by Jesus did as he was commanded and went home and began proclaiming the 'great things' God had done for him and they were all amazed (Luke 8:39).

Prayer for further action (verses 4-6)

In the light of God's action in the past, the psalm makes this plea that God would act again on behalf of his people (verse 4). The phraseology is similar but not quite the same as in verse 1. Here the word 'captivity' is used although it does appear in contexts that suggest other kinds of deprivation. It describes, for instance, the restoration of Job's fortunes (Job 42:10; see Psalms 14:7; 53:6; 85:2). Looking back nostalgically at 'the good old days' can lead to inactivity and dejection but a right attitude to the past can give hope and encourage prayer for future blessing.

Whatever the original situation the psalm depicts, it expresses the concerns of the Jews newly returned to their own land from the Babylonian exile. They may be back where they belong but life is far from easy and they need God to change things for the better.

The 'streams' that could be so destructive (see Psalm 124:4) also speak of blessing when there has been a lack of rain (Psalm 126:4). After a long dry summer the winter rains fill the wadis or water courses transforming the parched ground in the 'South' (the Negev) with fresh green life overnight. The prayer is that God would dramatically alter the situations in which they find themselves (see Isaiah 35:1).

Continuing the agricultural illustration the psalm acknowledges that we are called to 'sow in tears' (verse 5). Sowing seed is hard work and there is a measure of uncertainty over the results. Nevertheless, if the Lord answers their prayers then there will be a harvest which they can 'reap in joy'. James uses this picture of a farmer waiting for the rains to encourage Christians to be patient and persevere to the end (James 5:7-8).

The concluding verse restates the previous verse but does so in a very emphatic way. We could translate more literally: 'He who certainly goes crying, carrying a basket of seed, will certainly come with a shout of joy carrying his sheaves'. The psalmist is confident that God will answer his prayer. It is to encourage the returned exiles to pray earnestly to God and look with confidence for answers to their prayers that the psalm is placed at this point in the whole collection.

This is a picture of what God is able to do in the spiritual realm when he raises people who are dead in sins to newness of life in Jesus Christ. It also expresses the cry of God's people that he would revive his work in times when the outlook seems bleak and uncertain. Jesus used the same illustration to depict the Gentile harvest of which the Samaritan believers were a small but significant sign (John 4:35-42).

God is able to change things dramatically and unexpectedly. Sowing the good seed of God's gospel is hard work and there is often little to show for it. We are assured, however, that our labour is not pointless in the Lord. There will be a harvest and we look forward with great anticipation to that day when all the elect will have been gathered in. What a time of rejoicing that will be! We pray for foretastes of that occasion as we see many responding to the good news such as we find in Acts 2 on the day of Pentecost when three thousand responded to Peter's preaching. There we see the sentiments of Psalm 126 and the prophecy of Joel 2:28-32 brought together.

Psalm 127

Without God there is No Future

The heading of this 'Song of Ascents' (see Psalm 120) adds that it is 'Of Solomon'. While four of these songs belong to David (Psalms 122, 124, 131, 133) this is the only one attributed to Solomon. There may be a more subtle reference to Solomon in the expression 'his beloved' (verse 2) for it reminds us of the special name given him by God, 'Jedidiah' ('Beloved of the LORD'; see 2 Samuel 12:25). Solomon was renowned for his wisdom and this song is a teaching psalm in the wisdom tradition of Proverbs like Psalms 37 and 49. It was left to Solomon to build a house for the Lord and to be the first in a long family line descending from David that would eventually end with the Messiah, the Anointed One. In this psalm we have the Old Testament equivalent of Jesus' words to his disciples when he said 'without me you can do nothing' (John 15:5).

The editor of the collection saw how appropriate the psalm was to the situation in which the returned exiles from Babylon found themselves as they settled down once more in their own land to rebuild the city and temple, to repopulate the area and to await the Messiah who would come from David's family line. Singing this psalm as they journeyed on pilgrimage to Jerusalem for the annual festivals encouraged the people to place their faith and hope in God. What is said about an earthly city, temple and family applies to the spiritual family, temple and city that arise out of these Old Testament types.

There are two clear parts to this song and one of the ways the two belong together is by means of a play on words. In the original Hebrew, the words for 'builds' and 'children' (literally 'sons') have similar sounds. Also there is a play on the word for 'house' (verse 1) which is not only used to describe a physical structure but applied figuratively for a family line or dynasty (see 2 Samuel 7:2, 11–13) and this is the sense in verses 3–5. The main message that binds the two parts together is the truth that nothing lasting can be accomplished without the LORD. Each part ends with an encouraging word (see verses 2d and 5).

The worthless efforts of humans and the grace of God (verses 1–2)

In Ecclesiastes, the Preacher's main point is to show how transient human life is, whether we are believers or not. It is pressed home in the New Testament by James using the same kind of language: 'For what is your life? it is even a vapour that appears for a little time and then vanishes away' (James 4:14; see Psalm 39). This psalm uses a different word for vanity which means 'emptiness' or 'nothingness'. It has been translated 'idly' and 'vain' in previous psalms (Psalms 12:2; 41:6; 60:11; 108:12) and is used in the Third Commandment for taking up the name of God for no good purpose ('in vain'; Exodus 20:7). The word describes idols and other worthless things (Psalms 31:6; 119:37).

It is therefore a strong term to use. Builders can spend a great deal of hard work ('labour') on erecting a fine house all to no avail if God is not in it. Whether building a place to live in, constructing a house or temple to serve as God's earthly home (2 Samuel 7:5) or raising a family (Deuteronomy 25:9; Ruth 4:11) it can all go sadly wrong without God's involvement. We can apply this to the building of God's spiritual house, which is the implication in Jesus' words in his allegory of the vine. Only in union with Jesus Christ can we bear much fruit whether in terms of personal spiritual progress or new Christians added to the Church (John 15:1–5, 16).

Similarly, Israel's covenant God, the LORD, must be as much engaged in the task of guarding the city as the watchmen who stay awake through the night watches. Again, while the city of Jerusalem might be particularly in mind it applies also to the people of Zion. As the prophet was called to be a watchman in Israel so preachers and pastors, as overseers, are responsible for guarding the flock of God.

The psalm is not denying the place of human responsibility or activity in general daily life or in connection with the local church. It is God who has ordained that human beings should work hard and there is no place for laziness (see Proverbs 6:6-11). He has also given responsibility to church officers as those who will one day give an account of their ministries on the day of judgment (1 Corinthians 3:13-14; James 3:1). But no human, however hard he or she works or however meticulous they may be in covering every eventuality, can be sure of how future events will unfold. Those who framed the Welsh Calvinistic Methodist Confession of Faith of 1823 made every effort to see that it would remain the denomination's confession for the rest of time. It was even stated in law that no one was to raise questions about changing it. This did not prevent those opposed to its contents from steering the denomination away from the fundamentals of the faith. We must realise that human beings with the best of intentions do not have ultimate control of what they plan and execute. When a dreadful calamity takes place in a city, there is often a public inquiry to see if blame can be attached to somebody or to an organization and to learn lessons so that such a situation could never happen again. But frail humanity cannot foresee every eventuality. In the end, we must confess that God alone can prevent a city from being attacked or devastated by flood or fire and he alone can keep a church true to Bible principles.

Similar to the Preacher's words, the song discourages an over anxious spirit that busies itself from morning until evening weighed down with every care imaginable, never even taking a break for lunch. It also encourages us to receive from God's hand the good gifts to aid us during our short and uncertain pilgrimage through this world (Ecclesiastes 2:20-24). The 'bread of sorrows' (or 'toils' verse 3) is a reminder of the curse put on humans after the initial rebellion in Eden (Genesis 3:17, 19). Without God our feverish activity is all wasted. But it is saying more. If we believe that God is involved in all our legitimate God-given activities, we can relax in a good sense and cast all our cares upon the Lord knowing that he cares for us. Although some of us tend to think otherwise, none of us is indispensable and we must never suppose that everything depends on us and act as if God did not exist. In fact, it is because of God's care for his people that he has given the blessing of 'sleep'. This is a gift from God to his 'beloved one' (see Psalm 60:5), to the one he loves, and it is not to be despised. We need to rest and sleep, it is God alone who neither slumbers nor sleeps.

Not too far removed from the thought of this psalm is Jesus' reply to Martha's complaint about her sister Mary. Martha was overwhelmed and troubled about many things and in the busyness of her life she was forgetting the most important person (Luke 10: 41-42).

The blessings of a large family (verses 3-5)

The opening word, 'Behold' not only draws our attention to this final example where yet another ordinary human activity is to be viewed in relation to God, it also suggests a measure of excitement. This could be conveyed by translating, 'Children really are a heritage from the LORD'. The word for 'children' is literally 'sons' (see verses 3-4). This does not mean in Israel that daughters were despised and treated as unwanted. Far from it! They were to be respected and cared for and joined with the rest of the family in joyful worship of God (Deuteronomy 12:12, 18). Of Ruth it was said that she was better to Naomi than seven sons (Ruth 4:15). But for the people of God in the Old Testament era the concern was to have sons who would continue the family name and the godly looked forward to the special royal descendant who would gain the victory over the snake and his evil descendants (Genesis 3:15). The final two verses of this song suggest why sons are so important.

Henry VIII went to extreme lengths to obtain a male heir to the throne of England and Wales and presents us with a notable example of someone who did not trust God in the way this psalm encourages. Solomon had many wives contrary to God's law, but we only read of one son and Matthew Henry adds, 'for those that desire children as a heritage from the Lord must receive them in the way that he is pleased to give them, by lawful marriage to one wife'. At a time when the very word 'marriage' is being redefined by the lawmakers of the world, this is a salutary remark.

The term 'heritage' (verse 3), usually translated 'inheritance', is often used when speaking of Canaan as God's gift to Israel (Psalm 105:11) but it sometimes denotes God's people as his possession (Psalm 106:40). Here we are taught that children are not the result of human achievement but gifts from God. The 'fruit of the womb' is another way of describing children (see Genesis 30:2) and 'reward', as in God's encouragement to Abram (Genesis 15:1), suggests that this is God's gift rather than something earned. While humans are encouraged by God to procreate (Genesis 1:28) it is God who 'opens' or 'closes' the womb (Genesis 20:18; 29:31).

Sons are seen particularly as a great support and defence to the family. If they are born during the early part of a marriage, which is the meaning of 'children (sons) of one's youth' (verse 4), the sons will normally have reached their prime when their parents get older. As 'arrows in the hand of a warrior' so these sons will be in a position to defend the family when the father becomes frail. The simile concerning 'arrows' is continued in verse 5 which opens with a beatitude: 'Happy is the man who has his quiver full of them'. This strong father is in a blessed and very fortunate position (see Psalm 1:1). The implication is that it is the Lord who has filled his quiver with these many sons.

The city 'gate' was the place where business was transacted and legal disputes settled (see 2 Samuel 15:2; Psalm 69:12). These sons in the prime of life will not act like wimps when false accusations are made against the family. Eliphaz, one of Job's comforters, gives a contrasting picture to the one presented here. A man cursed finds his sons crushed in the gate with no deliverer (Job 5:4).

What is said of the human family is to be true of God's family, the Church. At a period when the western world seems to be turning its back on Christianity, there is the danger for church leaders to look anxiously around for ways of gaining new converts. While we are urged to go and make disciples of all nations and burdened to pray for a reviving of God's work in our time, we must never get into the situation of thinking we must frantically try to do God's work for him as if he were not in full command of the situation. Worry on the one hand and self-confidence on the other are symptoms of unbelief. The gates of Zion will be filled with the sons and daughters of the Lord to the eternal praise of God and his Anointed one.

'Be anxious for nothing, but in everything by prayer and supplication, with thanksgiving, let your requests be made known to God; and the peace of God, which surpasses all understanding, will guard your hearts and minds through Christ Jesus' (Philippians 4:6–7).

Psalm 128

The Well-being of Family and Community

The order of service for the solemnisation of marriage that I found helpful in my ministry contained a statement setting out reasons why it was ordained. It ended with these words, 'It was ordained for the good of society, which can only be strong and healthy when family life is honoured and preserved'. The statement is given biblical support by this psalm which starts with the godly man, then moves to his family and ends with the well-being of the covenant community.

There is a close link with the previous psalm with its reference to the gift of children and the happy position of the father (Psalm 127:3–5). Like the previous psalm this 'Song of Ascents' (see Psalm 120) is a wisdom or teaching song but with a prayer at the end on behalf of Israel. Psalm 126 looked to God for blessing on the community, Psalm 127 taught that trust in God not restless activity leads to blessing and Psalm 128 makes clear that blessing comes from the Lord.

We are not told who wrote the psalm or when it was written but the compiler of the Psalms found it a fitting one to add to his collection of pilgrim songs. For the newly returned exiles from Babylon this psalm would have encouraged the Jews to live godly lives and to knuckle down to work, produce offspring and to have the interests of God's covenant community at heart. It assured those living under foreign rule and experiencing all kinds of depressing situations that, if they were truly devoted to God, they could not be in a better position. As pilgrims journeyed to Jerusalem for the annual festivals, singing such a song as this would have inspired confidence and trust in God.

That same godly attitude is to be the hallmark of believers in every age. Christians, whether married or not, are to encourage hard work and be concerned for the well-being of home and family life. This psalm should also encourage us to remember one another as members of the heavenly Jerusalem. By our membership and support of the work of the local church family in its life and witness to Jesus Christ we are involved in that city which will one day fill the whole earth.

A pattern observed in the earlier pilgrim songs (see Psalm 125) continues with Psalms 126 to 128 forming a third group of three songs and again the movement is toward Zion. As with the previous two groups, the opening psalm (Psalm 126) expresses some distress ('tears'), the second encourages trust in God (Psalm 127) and the final psalm speaks of security (Psalm 128).

The happy family home (verses 1–4)

Happiness declared (verse 1)
The Song begins in a similar way to Psalm 112:1 and also reminds us of Psalm 1. What makes for a happy home? The head of the household must be godly, showing the characteristics of a righteous, wise person—'one who fears the Lord' (see Psalm 34:7, 9) and this involves living according to God's revealed will ('who walks in his ways'; see Psalm 119:3). Those who live according to God's law and keep his commandments are among the happy, fortunate people (Psalm 119:1–2). Jesus our Righteousness and Saviour is the perfect example of one who revered, loved and obeyed God.

Happiness described (verses 2–4)
After the general statement, the psalm speaks to the individual husband and father (verses 2–3). What does it mean to be in this blessed, happy state?

First, the man can have confidence that he can enjoy the results of his work in contrast to the feverish anxious toil mentioned in the previous psalm (Psalm 127:2). More literally, the first part of verse 2 reads 'The labour of your hands you will surely eat'. Verse 2 ends as verse 1 begins by pronouncing the man to be highly privileged. Most English versions give rather tame translations such as 'You *shall be* happy' but the original is more dynamic and needs to read something like 'Oh how blessed you are!' This is followed by 'well with you' (literally 'good to you!') meaning the good things God has in store for his people (see Psalm 125:4).

Second, the man is promised that his wife will have many children. The first blessing was to the original couple when God said 'Be fruitful and multiply, and fill the earth', a blessing that was repeated after the Flood (Genesis 1:28; 9:1). As in Genesis 3:16-19, the man works the ground and the woman gives birth to children and that is still what generally happens throughout the world. It is more or less assumed today that if a healthy couple want children they will be able to have them. But even with all our modern medical advancements it still cannot be a certainty. In ancient times having children was not taken for granted and for Jews living in the Persian period this promise of a wife with many children meant a great deal. She is likened to a vine loaded with fruit. Of course, this is not the woman's only function in life and Proverbs shows that besides her responsibilities 'in the very heart' of her own house (verse 3) she can have duties in the wider world (Proverbs 31:10-31).

We are given a lovely picture of a household with mother and father and their offspring around the table at mealtime. As in Psalm 127, the word for 'children' is 'sons' (verse 3) but here it can rightly be translated more generally. They are likened to a vigorous olive tree with its many shoots (Psalm 52:8; Hosea 14:6). Both the vine and the olive were important trees for the ancient Israelites and Israel herself is likened to both the vine and olive tree (see Psalm 80:8; Isaiah 5:2; John 15:1; Jeremiah 11:16; Romans 11:17, 24).

As I write, marriage in many countries of the western world is being redefined, but it must be remembered that from the beginning of creation it involved the lifelong union of one man and one woman. It symbolises the mystical union between Christ the bridegroom and his wife the Church (Ephesians 5:22-33; see Psalm 45). In fact, not only marriage, but family life and work are all brought together by the apostle Paul as he instructs Christians in living the Spirit-filled life (Ephesians 5:15-6:9). The communion table expresses something of the

unity of God's family in Christ and we look forward to the day when all
the children of the heavenly King will be gathered together on Mount
Zion (Revelation 7:9–17; 14:1–5).

Whereas the same word translated 'blessed' and 'happy' in verses 1
and 2 is used for the blessed state of the one who fears the Lord, here
in verse 4 the more common term for blessing is found and it indicates
how that happy position has been achieved (see Psalm 67:1). 'Behold'
or 'take notice of' this, the psalmist says, for thus shall the God-fearing
man be blessed by God. This word to 'be blessed' is the opposite of to
be cursed. It describes the good things that God gives to his people.
Such good gifts would include having many descendants, plenty of
food on the table and freedom from enemy attack. Being blessed in this
way produces the happy or 'blessed' state of verses 1–3.

These temporal blessings were important to the life of Israel until
the coming of Messiah. Under the new covenant, such blessings
are not the chief concern, but to those who seek first the kingdom
of God and his righteousness, earthly blessings are often added.
But Jesus indicates that when parents, children and other family
members must be given up for Christ's and the gospel's sake we are
promised that we shall 'receive a hundredfold now in this time—
houses and brothers and sisters and mothers and children and lands,
with persecution—and in the age to come, eternal life' (Mark 10:29–30).
At the resurrection Christians are also promised that they will 'inherit
all things' (Revelation 21:7). What temporal blessings Christians receive
now are but shadows of the real eternal good things in a new creation
where there will be no more curse.

The closing benediction (verses 5–6)

The family is the basic unit of society and good homes are important
for the well-being of community life. It is the Lord who blesses
his people and blessing on individual families leads to blessing in
the community and when there is stability and prosperity in the
community this adds to the welfare of family life. For this ideal
picture of a happy family to become a reality prayer is needed. As
one commentator puts it, 'Blessedness is not viewed as an automatic
consequence of one's actions—it is a divine gift.'[76]

In these final verses the focus moves from the home to the city. It
was in Zion or Jerusalem that God had ordained to live among his
people (Psalms 46:5; 48:3). This was the place where God ruled the

nation through his appointed representative of David's family line (see Psalm 20:2, 9). Earthly Zion and its Davidic king were only types of the heavenly city and the Lord's true Anointed one as Psalm 2 indicates. The references to this city remind us of previous songs in this series (Psalms 122:1-2, 6-9; 125:1-2; 126:1).

To experience the Lord's blessing from Zion is to look with joy at the 'good' things that it offers (verse 5; see Psalm 65:4). In other words, people find their satisfaction in this prosperous city belonging to God (see Psalm 87:7) throughout the days of their life. Descendants are seen as prolonging the life of the family. To see one's grandchildren is to see one's life renewed with each new generation as well as to experience a long and fulfilled life.

Like Psalm 125:5, this song ends with the same prayer for 'peace' to be upon God's people, 'Israel' (verse 6). The prophet Zechariah writing in the period after the return from exile, encourages his people with a graphic picture of the peace and security of Jerusalem as a place where old people feel safe in the streets and which is full of children playing happily together (Zechariah 8:4-5). Alexander observes that the whole of chapter 8 of Zechariah is a prophetic commentary on this psalm. It becomes symbolic of the eternal city of God for which Abraham and others looked.

The people of God came on pilgrimage to Jerusalem for the annual festivals as an expression of their loyalty to the covenant-keeping God, 'the LORD'. There they would worship God and seek his blessing for their family (compare 1 Samuel 1). Blessing is mediated from Zion. Christians can come by faith to Mount Zion where Jesus, the mediator of the new covenant, is. It is there we are to draw near and find grace to help in time of need. At the same time we are not to forsake meeting with fellow believers and being blessed through the encouragement and support of one another (Hebrews 10:19-25; 12:22-24) for this is a foretaste of the joys to come. As believers we look forward with the psalmist to being part of that new Jerusalem that will descend from heaven to fill the new earth.

Psalm 129

Zion's Enemies

This 'Song of Ascents' (see Psalm 120) first testifies to the Lord's faithfulness in preserving his people throughout their long years of suffering (verses 1–4) and prays that all future attempts to destroy them will have no success (verses 5–8). There is no record of when the psalm was originally written but it is an appropriate song for the newly returned exiles from Babylon. They had come through many trials and afflictions and, as we learn from Nehemiah they still faced much opposition from those who hated all that Jerusalem stood for. The Church of Jesus Christ can use this psalm as we give thanks to God for keeping his people through wave after wave of persecution and face with confidence whatever God's enemies might throw at his Church in the future. The gates of Hades cannot prevail against the Church of Jesus Christ.

Psalm 129 begins the fourth triad of pilgrim psalms (see Psalms 125 and 128) and, in recalling the past as it faces the present and future, it is similar to Psalm 126, the one that begins the third triad (see Psalm 126). Distress and trouble feature strongly in the opening psalm to each triad (see Psalms 120, 123, 126).

Recollecting the Lord's faithfulness (verses 1–4)

The nation speaks as if it were one person—'Many a time they have afflicted me ...' (verse 1). This is confirmed by the invitation for 'Israel' to join in what is being said (verses 1–2; see Psalm 124:1–2). God indicated to Moses that Israel as a people was to be viewed as God's first-born son and Pharaoh was told to let God's son go free (Exodus 4:22–23). In addition, the worshipping company of God's people in the first part of the psalm is identified with the hated and oppressed city of Zion in the second half (see verse 5).

The nation had known affliction from its 'youth'. This is a reference to the beginnings of Israel as a people specially chosen by God. The prophets spoke of the time of the exodus and wilderness wanderings as the period of Israel's early years: 'As in the days of her youth, as in the day when she came up from the land of Egypt' and 'When Israel was a child I loved him, and out of Egypt I called my son' (Hosea 2:15; 11:1; see Jeremiah 2:2; Ezekiel 23:3). They began life as a nation pursued by the Egyptians at the Red Sea and attacked by the Amalekites in the wilderness (Exodus 14; 17:8–13). All down the centuries they were oppressed by one enemy after another: the Midianites, Moabites, Edomites and the Philistines, and later by the Assyrians and Babylonians. But these assailants had not been allowed to annihilate God's people and, in fact, they outlived all their aggressors.

The brutality of the oppressors is vividly portrayed by this picture of Israel on its back like a plot of ground being ploughed and formed into furrows ready for the farmer to sow his seed. A similar scene is prophesied by Micah: 'Zion shall be ploughed like a field' (Micah 3:12; see Isaiah 51:23). The enemies of God's people in every age have endeavoured to do their worst to 'wear out the saints of the Most High' (Daniel 7:25) but they have not succeeded. Why? Verse 4 gives us the answer. God has not been mentioned up to this point. But suddenly, and using his covenant name 'Lord' (Yahweh/Jehovah), God is seen to be the one responsible for keeping his people from extinction. Interestingly, it does not speak first of his actions on behalf of Israel but of his character—'The Lord is righteous'. God remains true to himself. He had revealed himself to Moses as the ever-present one who keeps his promises and who would redeem his people from their bondage (Exodus 6:2–8). He is the one who has 'cut in pieces the cords of the wicked' (verse 4). The Lord is the one has broken the power of all his people's enemies. He cut Israel free from the Egyptians and, for those first using this psalm as a pilgrim song, he had most recently cut them free from the Babylonians.

Jesus Christ, the ideal Israel and her representative, was himself oppressed from the beginning of his life on earth when Herod sought to have him destroyed. Matthew relates the incident of how Jesus was taken to Egypt until the death of Herod and quotes Hosea's prophecy 'Out of Egypt I called my son' (Matthew 2:15). Christ's sufferings led him to the cross but there he triumphed over the great enemy of God and of his people. He gave his back to those who smote him (Isaiah 50:6) that he might free us from our slavery to sin and Satan. Christians are taught that they too will suffer persecution and the history of the Christian Church right up to the present is a story of opposition and oppression for God's true people. But the Israel of God continues and will overcome through him who loved them and gave himself for them. Who are the over-comers arrayed in white robes? They are 'the ones who come out of the great tribulation and washed their robes and made them white in the blood of the Lamb' (Revelation 7:13–14). We thank God that the rulers of this age who have persecuted the people of God soon wither and fade away but the city of God remains.

Declaration of confidence (verses 5–8)

As in Psalm 126 recalling God's past deliverances encourages hope for the future. The verbs in these verses can be taken either as statements of confidence ('All those who hate Zion shall be put to shame ... They shall be as the grass ... Those who pass them by will not say') or, with most English versions, as a prayer for judgment ('Let all those who hate Zion be put to shame ...').

As a prayer it is not one of personal vindictiveness but arises out of a sincere concern for God's cause. It must be viewed in the light of Psalm 2 which teaches that all who do not submit to God and his Anointed will experience the divine wrath. God's people have a duty to pray that all who are engaged in a hate campaign against Zion will be thwarted in their attempts (verse 5).

The desire is that the enemies of God's people would become like grassy weeds that spring up on rooftops made of soil but soon wither under the heat of the sun (verse 6; see Isaiah 37:27). The simile is taken further in verses 7 and 8 so that the grassy roof is seen as a cornfield that produces nothing for reapers to pluck with their hands or gather into bundles under their arms. And instead of passers-by encouraging the reapers with a word of blessing, no such greeting would be given. It is a prayer that those who hate Zion and seek her destruction would be unsuccessful in their attempts.

The words of verse 8 remind us of the story of Ruth where Boaz calls out to the reapers of the barley harvest, 'The Lord be with you!' and they reply, 'The Lord bless you!' (Ruth 2:4). In contrast to the blessing on God's people at the close of the previous psalm (Psalm 128:5) no blessing is to be offered here. Those who are bent on persecuting the Church of Jesus Christ cannot be encouraged in what they are doing. The apostle John declares that those who teach false doctrine are not to be greeted with such blessings, 'for he who greets him shares in his evil deeds' (2 John 11).

Not to be blessed means to be under God's curse. God said to Abraham that he would bless those who blessed him and would curse those who cursed him (Genesis 12:3). Those who afflict God's people touch the apple of his eye (see Deuteronomy 32:10; Psalm 17:8; Zechariah 2:8). Jesus identified himself with those whom Saul of Tarsus was persecuting. The prayer of this psalm, however, does not forbid Christians to pray for the conversion of their persecutors and we are thankful to God that many since Paul's day who have mistreated and even murdered God's servants have been brought to repentance and trusted Christ to save them.

Psalm 130

The Forgiveness of God's People

For Luther this was one of the 'Pauline Psalms' (the others being Psalms 32, 51 and 143) and he composed a superb hymn based upon it: *From deep distress I cry to Thee, Lord, hear me, I implore Thee.* For the great Puritan theologian, John Owen, the words of this psalm, particularly verse 4, had a significant impact on his personal life as a Christian, so much so that in a massive exposition of the psalm most of it is taken up with the contents of verse 4.[77] The same verse of this psalm brought comfort to John Bunyan when he was convicted of sin. John Wesley, just prior to his famous Aldersgate Street experience, had attended evensong at St Paul's Cathedral and was much affected when the anthem sung was Psalm 130. In fact, this psalm has had an important place in the Church's worship from at least the time of Augustine, bishop of Hippo in North Africa (AD 354–430), when it became the sixth of the seven 'penitential psalms' (see Psalm 6 for the full list).

The eleventh 'Song of Ascents' (see Psalm 120) expresses both penitence (verses 1–4) and confidence (verses 5–8). Following a pattern within this pilgrim group of psalms, it stresses Israel's dependence on their covenant God (see Psalms 121, 124, 127) after a psalm that implied trouble from oppressors (Psalm 129; see also Psalms 120, 123, 126). Other features common to these pilgrim psalms, include the stair-like parallelism and the repetition of words (see 'voice' in verse 2 and 'watch for the morning' in verse 6).

It is a psalm that the final compiler to the whole collection considered applicable to the situation of a humbled people who had recently returned from exile in Babylon. They were ones who realised that the captivity was on account of Israel's grave sin in serving other gods. There are similarities in this psalm to the great prayers of Daniel 9, Ezra 9 and Nehemiah 1 and 9 and in fact, the noun translated 'forgiveness' or 'pardon' in verse 4 is only used elsewhere in the confession of sin by Daniel and the people of Nehemiah's time (Daniel 9:9 'To the Lord our God *belong* mercy and forgiveness'; Nehemiah 9:17 'ready to pardon'). The psalmist may be speaking on behalf of the nation (as David does in Psalm 122), in which his own personal penitent words express the feelings of the community and this would fit with the assurances addressed to Israel at the end of the psalm (verses 7–8). It is therefore a psalm that serves both the individual believer and the community of faith.

The cry (verses 1–2)

The psalmist's call from the 'depths' is like Jonah's prayer to the Lord from the belly of the fish (Jonah 2:1–2). Isaiah uses the term 'depths' to describe a real watery situation when God divided the Red Sea to make a way for his redeemed people to cross (Isaiah 51:10). In a lamentation over Tyre's fall, the word is used figuratively (Ezekiel 27:34). Its only other occurrence is in Psalm 69:2, 14 where again it is used metaphorically for an overwhelming distressing experience. Often the sea is used to suggest being overcome by death. While Jonah was literally in the sea, he can speak of calling out from the 'belly of Sheol' for it seemed to him that he was at death's door (Jonah 2:2). Thus the psalmist was in a death-like situation and as we see from the next section this was on account of sin. It was because of the people's 'death' in captivity due to their apostasy that Daniel prayed as he did. Paul describes our position before conversion as being dead in trespasses and sins (Ephesians 2:1, 5).

In addition to using God's personal covenant name 'Lord' (Yahweh/ Jehovah, verse 1), the psalmist couples it with 'Lord' (verse 2), a reminder that he is the sovereign God. The next couple of sections also use these two names for God (verses 3, 5–6) perhaps to emphasise not only the covenantal relationship but the psalmist's lowly but privileged position as a servant looking to his master. This is a heart-felt cry that God would take notice of his 'supplication', a term that in this context has the idea of pleading for God's 'favour'.

We are taught in these verses, as Matthew Henry suggests, that whatever condition we are in 'to continue calling upon God' and 'to assure ourselves of an answer of peace from him'.

The confession (verses 3–4)

The verb 'should mark' (verse 3) is, in the original, the word more commonly translated 'to keep' or 'to guard' and in this context suggests that if God were to 'keep' in his mind all our offences, instead of putting them out of mind (see Jeremiah 31:34; Micah 7:18–19), what hope would there be for us. There is a similar use of the verb 'to keep' with reference to God watching or not watching our sins in Job 10:14; 14:16–17. The word 'stand' is an appropriate one when thinking of a guilty person standing before the Judge of all the earth. Who can stand upright before the holy, righteous God? Who can maintain one's innocence or endure the sentence pronounced? The ungodly cannot stand in the judgment (Psalm 1:5). Who can stand before God's wrath when he appears for judgment? (Nahum 1:6; Malachi 3:2). There is a clear implication of what Solomon makes explicit that all are guilty of sin before God (1 Kings 8:46). The last of Luther's Pauline psalms emphasises the same point (Psalm 143:2; see also Psalm 14:3).

Since no one can stand, our only hope is in God's gracious act of forgiveness. This must not be seen as something automatic as Voltaire blasphemously stated: 'God forgives because it is his business'. The covenant God of Israel and their sovereign Lord does the impossible—he forgives his wayward people and disobedient servants. He does not keep watch on our sins. Sinners are able to stand and not cringe in his presence. Why? Because with the Lord there is 'forgiveness' (verse 4; it is a word only found here and in the prayers of Nehemiah 9:17 and Daniel 9:9). The people in the days of Ezra, who had heard God's Law read to them, confessed their sins and as they did so they reminded themselves of God's forgiveness after Israel had made the golden calf at the foot of Mount Sinai. They recalled God's words to Moses (Exodus 34:6) as they prayed, 'But you are God, ready to pardon, gracious and merciful, slow to anger, abundant in kindness, and did not forsake them' (Nehemiah 9:17).

The first benefit mentioned in Psalm 103:3 is that God is one 'who forgives all your iniquities'. This act of grace when rightly received by humble, repentant sinners does not trivialise forgiveness or lead to the kind of presumption suggested in Voltaire's words. It should have the opposite effect. God's pardoning grace is given so that we might have that relationship with God that is expressed in a godly reverence and awe, amazed at such mercy and love to wretched, wayward creatures. This attitude is the opposite to the thinking of those whom Paul has in mind when he writes, 'Shall we sin that grace may abound?'

The confidence (verses 5–6)
The psalmist, confident of God's amazing grace in forgiving sinners, now speaks of his desire for God. Some take the waiting (see Psalms 27:14; 40:1) for the LORD and his word as an indication that he is still looking for that assuring word of forgiveness while others see it as an expression of ongoing trust in God, looking for continued assurances from the Lord in times of stress and difficulty. In the context of the restoration of the Jews from Babylonian exile it could well mean the promised blessings that are to accompany the forgiveness of their sins and the return to their land such as we find in the prophecies of Isaiah. As watchmen guarding a city during the night wait in anticipation for the break of day (see Psalm 127:1) so the psalmist's whole being is committed to waiting expectantly for what God has promised in his word (see Psalm 119:49, 81, 114, 147; Isaiah 33:2; Micah 7:7).

The communication (verses 7–8)
God's people as a whole, here called 'Israel' (see Psalm 73:1; see Romans 9:6; Galatians 6:16), are likewise urged to trust and eagerly look to their covenant Lord in sure hope of his loving commitment ('mercy') and his 'abundant redemption'. 'Where sin abounded, grace abounded much more.' (Romans 5:20). Not only is God's faithful love 'with' him but so too is his 'redemption' (verse 7) as was his 'forgiveness' (verse 4).

While 'redemption' is often used with reference to slavery to the Egyptians or Babylonians (Psalm 111:9; Isaiah 50:2) in this context it speaks of deliverance from sin and its consequences. The verb 'redeem' or 'ransom' (verse 8) comes from the same word family as the term 'redemption' in verse 7 and conveys the idea of paying a price to set free someone who is in slavery (Exodus 13:13, 15; Psalm 49:7). Whatever it costs, he will 'ransom' (verse 8) his people from 'all their iniquities', from all their wayward acts, just as Hosea speaks of ransoming them from the power of the grave (Hosea 13:14).

These Old Testament passages look to our Lord Jesus, the Messiah, who paid the price for our redemption at Calvary's cross. Jesus came to 'save his people from their sins' (Matthew 1:21). He also taught that he had come to give his life a 'ransom for many' (Mark 10:45) and Paul speaks of the one mediator, the man Christ Jesus, 'who gave himself a ransom for all' (1 Timothy 2:5-6). Our great God and Saviour Jesus Christ 'gave himself for us that he might redeem us from every lawless deed and purify for himself his own special people, zealous for good works' (Titus 2:13-14). God's people, the Israel of God, are redeemed from bondage to sin and Satan by the blood of Jesus so that we too might 'fear' God (see verse 4) by living to please him and not giving way to sinful desires and the temptations of the devil. As in this psalm, Paul closely associates our redemption with the forgiveness of our sins—'In him we have redemption through his blood, the forgiveness of sins, according to the riches of his grace' (Ephesians 1:7).

Psalm 131

Calm and Content

Some modern commentators are of the opinion that this short psalm was written by a woman with a child in her arms (see verse 2). In the Bible we do have songs and prayers by women such as Miriam who led the ladies in singing after the deliverance at the Red Sea. Deborah accompanied by Barak sang after the defeat of Sisera and Hannah's prayer of thanksgiving is recorded after the birth of her son Samuel (Exodus 15:20-21; Judges 5; 1 Samuel 2:1-10). In place of scholarly speculation, however, we are informed in the title to this 'Song of Ascents' that it is 'Of David', which means it is accredited to him along with Psalms 122 and 124 within this group of pilgrim psalms (see also Psalm 133).

David's expression of humility and his desires for his people are used by the final editor to the psalm collection at a time when God's people were back in their own land. Many of them seem to have been very discontented with their situation and were remembering the 'good old days' of which their fathers had spoken. In this context the psalm, like Jeremiah's word to Baruch, aims to calm those with grandiose expectations: 'Do you seek great things for yourself? Do not seek them' (Jeremiah 45:5). We all need to hear the message of the psalm and calmly trust the living God who has everything under control. How agitated we can become through our sinful desires and ambitions for

403

ourselves and those we love! The church of Jesus Christ also needs to take to heart David's words and have that same confidence in God instead of feverishly seeking to attract support and influence like the worldly wise.

The step-like parallelism, a feature of these pilgrim psalms, can be seen in verse 2 with the repetition of the phrase 'like a weaned child'.

A confession to God (verses 1–2)

What David is not (verse 1)

At first glance we might consider David's words to be the height of pride and presumption: 'LORD, my heart is not haughty' (literally 'not high'). It sounds as if David is addressing God like the self-righteous Pharisee in Jesus' parable (Luke 18:9-14). Surely anyone who thinks he is humble needs to remember Jeremiah's words that 'The heart is deceitful above all things and desperately wicked; who can know it?' (Jeremiah 17:9). But Jeremiah goes on to state that it is the Lord who searches the heart and David comes before God like an open book. And as Peter confessed to Jesus, 'Lord, you know all things; you know that I love you' (John 21:17), so David's confession to God is sincere and true. The 'heart' here refers to the root of David's whole being and he declares that he has this humble and self-effacing spirit. Eyes that are 'lofty' suggest an arrogant attitude and the Lord is against such people (see Psalms 18:27; 101:5; Proverbs 6:16-19).

The temptation to pride is in us all and becomes especially acute if God places us in positions of responsibility. The heart of king Uzziah became lifted up with pride with the result that God disciplined him. Similarly, good king Hezekiah began to have too high an opinion of himself but he humbled himself of his pride so that God's wrath was averted (2 Chronicles 26:16; 32:25; see Proverbs 18:12). We are urged by Paul to have that lowly mind which esteems others better than ourselves (Philippians 2:3).

David's greater Son provides the perfect example. Though as God he was truly high and lifted up, he humbled himself and became obedient even to the point of being willing to die the death of the cross. As the man Christ Jesus, he was 'gentle and lowly in heart' (Matthew 11:29) and chose to look on those who were the lowest and least respected in society to bring them help and salvation.

God is seen as the one who does 'great matters/things' (Psalms 71:19;

106:21). The word translated 'profound' (or 'wonderful') is likewise used of God's activity especially his great wonders demonstrated in delivering the Israelites from Egyptian slavery (Psalms 71:17; 78:11). David has not gone about seeking to act as if he were God. That has always been a danger for those who gain positions of power, whether in a country or a church. The prince of Tyre had arrogant thoughts of greatness, to be godlike and to understand mysteries (see Ezekiel 28:2–6). David was not like that and neither should any of God's people be.

What David is (verse 2)
In place of the negatives of verse 1 we have this very positive statement. The word 'Surely' does not adequately convey the emphatic way in which the verse opens. It is in the form of an oath so that a word like 'Rather' or a strong 'But' would be better.

David's contented spirit is likened to a child that has recently been weaned from mother's milk and has learned to rest quietly in her embrace and not cry to be suckled ('with his mother' is better translated more literally as 'upon his mother'; Isaiah 28:9). Children were weaned in Israel from about the age of three. David's 'soul' is David the person, soothed and quiet as if he is nursing himself—'my soul within me' or more literally 'upon me'. Jesus once used a little child as a visual aid when teaching his disciples humility (Matthew 18:1–5). He himself was the perfect example of one who calmly and quietly committed himself to God his Father. In that attitude he was led as a lamb to the slaughter and prayed on the cross, 'Father, into your hands I commit my spirit' (Isaiah 53:7; Luke 23:46).

A challenge to the people (verse 3)
In the final verse David urges Israel to learn the lesson that he has learned and to look to God for the future with quiet confidence. David never forced God's hand but waited God's time for him to be acknowledged as king over his people. In placing the psalm at this point the editor sees the need again to encourage God's people after the Babylonian exile to rest in the Lord and wait patiently for him and not to run ahead of God (see Psalm 130:7). Our great example, Jesus Christ, waited God's time to be exalted and God's people today must have that same quiet confidence in God and his timing. That 'hope' or 'waiting' spoken of in the previous psalm, the Israel of God throughout

the ages are to possess—'from this time forth and for ever' (see Psalm 125:2).

Psalm 132

The LORD's City and His Anointed

L ike the author of Chronicles, the compiler of the psalm collection has placed this psalm in Book 5 to encourage the Jews living in the period after their return from exile in Babylon to look forward with anticipation to a grand and glorious future for God's people. Both Chronicles and this 'Song of Ascents' (see Psalm 120) highlight the importance of the LORD's anointed ruler from David's family line and of the city where God ordained to live among his people.

We are not given any details concerning the author of the psalm but it recalls how David brought the Ark into Jerusalem and God's special promises to David. Solomon certainly used verses 8 and 9 of the Psalm at the time of the dedication of the newly built temple (2 Chronicles 6:41). It is a well-constructed psalm that falls into two parts. One way of dividing the psalm is to see both parts beginning with prayer (verses 1, 10), followed by an oath (verses 2-5, 11-12) and ending with desires for the Lord's presence among his people, among both the temple ministers and God's faithful people (verses 6-9, 13-16). The psalm concludes with the promise of victory for the Lord's anointed ruler (verses 17-18). Perhaps a better way of viewing the psalm is to take the first ten verses as a prayer concerning David and the remaining verses as referring to God's promises to David, with each part beginning and ending with reference to David (verses 1–2 and 10, verses 11–12 and 17–18). This, the thirteenth and longest 'Song of Ascents', should be read in conjunction with Psalms 2, 72 and 89 for the theme of the LORD's Anointed, Psalms 24, 46, 48 and 87 for the Zion theme and Numbers 10:35–36, 2 Samuel 6 and Psalm 68 for the references to the ark of the covenant.

Prayer for the Davidic ruler (verses 1–10)

The actual prayer frames the section (verses 1–2, 10) with David's vow (verses 3–5) and the people's determination (verses 6–9) providing substance to the prayer.

The prayer (verse 1)

This prayer to 'remember David' (verse 1) is a call for God to act for the sake of David. It would seem that Solomon, David's son, who now occupied his father's throne, is making this request as he himself calls to mind the special promises God made to David. We often find the verb 'remember' in contexts associated with God's covenant promises. God remembered his covenant with Noah and all flesh (Genesis 9:15–16). When the Israelites groaned under their bondage in Egypt, God remembered the covenant he had made with their forefathers (Exodus 2:24). It must not be thought that God ever forgets anything, but it is a vivid way of either drawing attention to the fact that God never goes back on his word or urging God to take action according to his promises.

David's 'afflictions' are especially mentioned. They refer, as the Hebrew word suggests and as verses 2 to 5 indicate, to all the frustrating, humbling experiences he endured in bringing the ark of the covenant into Jerusalem and the 'much trouble' involved in preparing for a temple that he was not allowed to see built (2 Samuel 6–7; 1 Chronicles 22:14). Though the historical books of Samuel and Chronicles do not record the oath that David 'swore to the LORD' (verse 2) it certainly accords with the information that is given concerning his strong desire to build a house for God in his new capital city (2 Samuel 7:1–2; 1 Chronicles 22). In asking God to remember David, the psalmist has this oath especially in mind which is why verse 2 opens with 'How he swore ...' or 'In which he swore ...' It was in the form of a vow. David 'vowed' to the covenant God of Israel, 'LORD' (Yahweh/Jehovah), who is also described, literally, as 'the Mighty One of Jacob' (see Genesis 49:24;

Isaiah 1:24; 49:26; 60:16). God has absolute power and nothing can hinder his activity. He is both mighty to save and to destroy.

David's oath (verses 3–5)

The idiom used in the original is like Psalm 131:2. David is prepared to fall under God's curse if he fails to carry out what he has committed himself to do. He reveals his determination to bring the ark of the covenant, the symbol of God's presence among his people, to its 'dwelling-place' in Jerusalem so that the 'LORD', 'the Mighty One of Jacob' might have a suitable place to live on earth among his people (verse 5; see 1 Chronicles 13–16). He speaks of the 'chamber' or tent of his own house and the 'comfort' (literally 'couch') 'of my bed' (verse 3). Using proverbial language ('sleep to my eyes ... slumber to my eyelids', verse 4; see Proverbs 6:4), David indicates that he cannot rest until he has carried out what he promised. Bringing the ark to Jerusalem was a first step to building a permanent, magnificent or multi-roomed 'dwelling-place' or 'tabernacle' (verse 5; see verse 7; Psalms 74:7; 84:1).[78] He himself had a fine home and his desire was for God to have an appropriate place to settle (2 Samuel 7:2).

The phrase 'until I find a place for the Lord' (verse 5) may have been in Jesus' mind when he said, 'Foxes have holes and birds of the air have nests, but the Son of Man has nowhere to lay his head' (Matthew 8:20). It is a significant comment from the one who is described as God and who was made flesh and lived ('tabernacled') among us (John 1:14). Christians should be as concerned and determined as David in preparing their own hearts as a suitable place for God to live. Jesus made a promise to those who would love him and keep his commandments that the triune God, Father and Son by the Spirit, would come and 'make our home with him' (John 14:23).

The nation's concern (verses 6–9)

David along with his people are the 'we' and 'us' in this part of the psalm (verses 6–7). 'Ephrathah' is the area in which Bethlehem was situated and from where David came (Ruth 4:11; 1 Samuel 17:12; see Micah 5:2). Rachel, Jacob's beloved wife, was also buried in the vicinity (Genesis 35:19; 48:7). The 'it' (verse 6) refers to the dwelling-place of the ark.[79] In Ephrathah David and his people had heard of where the ark was housed and they searched and found its dwelling-place 'in the fields of the woods' (verse 6). The word for 'wood' is 'Jaar' and the reference could be a poetic way of referring to Kirjath Jaarim (City of Woods or Forest City), the place where the ark was brought when it was returned by the Philistines and housed in Abinadab's home 'on the hill'. Kirjath Jaarim was also known as 'Baale Judah' and it lay on the Judah-Benjamin border (Joshua 18:14-15; 1 Chronicles 13:6). There the ark remained for twenty years, neglected throughout Saul's reign (1 Samuel 7:1-2; 1 Chronicles 13:3) until David and the people came to collect it and bring it to Jerusalem (2 Samuel 6:2-4).

With the ark settled in Jerusalem on Mount Zion, the people come and worship at this central sanctuary. No reference is made of anyone going to Kirjath Jaarim to worship but here is a picture of worshippers encouraging one another to come together to God's 'tabernacle' or 'dwelling-place' (verse 7; see verse 5). They 'worship' (literally, 'bow down') toward the ark, the symbol of God's presence. God is enthroned in the heavens above the cherubim but the ark in the sanctuary is likened to his 'footstool' (see Psalm 99:5; 1 Chronicles 28:2).

The phrase 'Arise, O LORD' takes us back to the time when the ark led the people through the wilderness (verse 8; Numbers 10:35; see Psalm 68:1). The ark went before the people 'to search out a resting place for them' (Numbers 10:33). Now the call is for the ark to arise for its final resting place in Zion, the city of God. This ark was not only a pledge and token of God's presence but also of his power ('you and the ark of your strength'). But God refused to be manipulated by his people and on one notable occasion showed them that they could not treat the ark like a lucky charm or mascot (see 1 Samuel 4; Psalm 78:61).

Verses 8 and 9 are used by Solomon at the close of his prayer at the time of the dedication of the temple after the ark had been brought into the inner sanctuary and the divine glory cloud had filled God's house (2 Chronicles 5:2-14; 6:40-41). But whereas the psalm speaks of God's priests 'clothed with righteousness', Chronicles refers to them being 'clothed with salvation'. The terms are in some instances almost synonymous but 'righteousness' means to be in a right legal standing before God whereas 'salvation' has a broader meaning (see verse 16). To be 'clothed' with righteousness is to be seen, like the high priest, Joshua, not with the filthy garments of sinfulness but in rich, clean clothes that are acceptable to the righteous God (Zechariah 3:3-5). They are to engage in their priestly work as those who have been made righteous in this unique way. God's 'saints' (see Psalm 30:4) are those committed to God and his people. They are encouraged to give resounding shouts of joy. In the parallel passage the prayer is that they will rejoice in God's 'goodness' (2 Chronicles 6:41).

The prayer resumes (verse 10)

This brings to completion the first half of the psalm and returns to the opening plea to remember David. All that has followed has been in support of that initial plea. David is God's 'servant' (see the heading to Psalms 18 and 36) who is a man after God's own heart. He has an interest in serving God and has not been neglectful of the symbol of God's presence but has been concerned that the Lord might live among his people in a permanent home. David the king is the Lord's anointed one who has had oil poured on his head in a symbolic action to indicate his special status as ruler of God's people. Accompanying that action the Lord's Spirit also came upon him (see 1 Samuel 16:13; 1 Chronicles 11:3; Psalm 89:20).

This verse too has its parallel at the very close of Solomon's prayer (2 Chronicles 6:42). Each king of David's line was the Lord's anointed. The prayer is for blessing on David and his successors, that God would not reject them as he had done king Saul. In Psalm 84:9 the prayer is in a positive form: 'look upon the face of your anointed'. To 'turn away the face' is for the person making the request to be turned away. The phrase is only used elsewhere in the Old Testament when Adonijah makes the cheeky request to Bathsheba, Solomon's mother, to have Abishag as wife and when later Bathsheba brings the request to king Solomon. There it is translated 'do not deny me', 'do not refuse me' and 'I will not refuse you' (1 Kings 2:16, 17, 20). Many times requests are made for God to hear and answer prayer for 'David's sake' (1 Kings 11:12–13; 15:4; 2 Kings 8:19; etc.). Psalm 2 has referred to the LORD's 'Anointed' and the prophets look forward to a new David who will unite God's people and bring blessing to all nations (Ezekiel 34:23–24; 37:24; Hosea 3:5; Amos 9:11). It is to this 'Anointed' that the psalm ultimately looks.

The Lord's promises concerning the Davidic ruler (verses 11–18)

The second half of the psalm picks up the various items raised in the prayer. Balancing the oath that David swore to the Lord, we are informed that the Lord swore an oath to David. The psalmist is alluding to the promises made to David at the time when the king was eager to build a house for the Lord (2 Samuel 7:12–16). They were repeated to Solomon after his dedicatory prayer (1 Kings 9:1–5). God had given David this pledge ('truth', verse 11; see 2 Samuel 7:28) which is here described as a 'covenant' (verse 12; Psalm 89:3, 35–36, 49; see Isaiah 55:3). Unlike what happened later in the northern kingdom of Israel where dynasties came and went in rapid succession, God had promised David that 'he would set up' his descendants ('seed') after him (2 Samuel 7:12), the 'fruit' of his body (verse 11), and they would sit on David's throne. If his descendants remained loyal to what God expected of them as leaders over God's people, which included abiding by the commandments and 'testimonies' laid out in the Sinai covenant (Deuteronomy 17:14–20), then 'sons also shall sit upon your throne for evermore' (verse 12; see 2 Samuel 7:14–16).

The psalm then turns to God's election of 'Zion' as the place of God's earthly 'habitation' and 'resting place' which again balances the concerns of the prayer in the first part of the psalm (verses 13–14; see verses 5, 7–8). David's choice of Jerusalem as his capital, where the ark was eventually brought and where the temple was built, was in God's purpose all along and is expressed in Solomon's speech and prayer (1 Kings 8:44, 48; 2 Chronicles 6:5–6, 34, 38). The earthly city then becomes symbolic of the real, heavenly city where the Lord's Anointed, David's greater Son, reigns with his people (Hebrews 12:22; Revelation 14:1; 21–22).

Promises are made about the city and its people, which include the blessing of abundant supplies and food enough to satisfy the poor (see Psalm 87:7). Taking up the earlier words, God is committed to answering the psalmist's prayer in a fuller way than was requested. Zion's priests will be clothed with 'salvation' of which 'righteousness' is an essential ingredient (see 2 Chronicles 6:41), and her saints will 'shout aloud for joy' (see verse 9).

The promises that God makes in this second half of the psalm are framed, like the prayer, with references to David and the LORD's Anointed (verses 11–12, 17–18; see verses 1–2, 10). Thus the psalm closes with the promise that in Zion ('there', verse 17) God will make David's 'horn' to 'sprout' or 'spring up', a reference to the king's strength flourishing (see Psalm 75:4). Jeremiah uses the noun 'sprout' or 'growth', usually translated 'Branch', to refer to a future righteous ruler of David's family tree (Jeremiah 23:5). God also promises to 'prepare' or 'set in order' a 'lamp' for his anointed one. The lamp symbolises light and the psalmist may well have in his mind the several burners on the golden candlestick which were always kept alight in the tabernacle (Exodus 25:37; Leviticus 24:4). David is called the 'lamp of Israel' (2 Samuel 21:17) and when the prospect seems bleak for Judah and its kings of Davidic descent the historical narratives point back to the promises referred to in this psalm. During Jehoram's reign we read, 'Yet the Lord would not destroy the house of David, because of the covenant that he had made with David ... to give a lamp to him and to his sons for ever' (2 Chronicles 21:7; see 2 Kings 8:19). In the light of such promises the Jews after the return from Babylon would have been encouraged to look with hope to the re-establishment of David's rule as they worked to rebuild the temple and the walls of Jerusalem.

The final verse promises that with God's help the king will conquer his enemies. Instead of being clothed with deliverance they will be covered in 'shame' (see verses 9, 16; Psalm 35:26). On the other hand, the king's 'crown shall flourish'. The usual word for crown is not used but a term from the same word family as Nazirite (Numbers 6:1–21). It symbolised the king's consecration to the Lord (see Psalm 89:39). This was the term for the golden crown that was placed on top of the high priest's turban (Exodus 29:6; 39:30–31; Leviticus 8:9). The verb 'flourish' is one that is associated with grass flourishing and flowers blossoming (Psalms 90:6; 103:15) but is used here to describe the sparkling, shining nature of the royal headdress.

All this reminds us of Psalm 72 with its picture of peace, prosperity and prestige associated with the divine ruler. The editor encouraged his people to sing this psalm as a pilgrim song to keep God's promises to David alive in the people's minds and hearts. Hundreds of years later, Zacharias the priest, on hearing that Mary, a young relative of Elizabeth his wife, was to give birth to the Lord's Anointed, was filled with the Holy Spirit and praised God. In Jesus the Messiah, the Lord God of Israel had 'raised up a horn of salvation' in the house of his servant David and 'the dayspring from on high' had visited them 'to give light to those who sit in darkness and the shadow of death' (Luke 1:68–79).

Psalm 133

The Unity of the LORD's Family

A loving, united family is all too rare and even when there is peace between parents and children the wider family can often cause friction and a souring of relationships. The local church family, made up as it is of saints who still sin, often finds itself torn apart by personality clashes, self-interest and pride. God's holy nation, Israel, was made up of those whose tribal loyalties often came before national concerns. When David first became king the northern tribes continued to support one of Saul's descendants and later in David's reign not only did he face a rebellion by his own son Absalom, but some of the northern tribes tried to break away from his rule (2 Samuel 2:4, 8-11; 15-18; 20:1-22). After the death of Solomon the kingdom did divide permanently with the majority of tribes setting up their own state system and religion in opposition to Jerusalem and its king (1 Kings 12).

This little psalm, the fourteenth 'Song of Ascents' (see Psalm 120), is by David and he may have composed it after all Israel had met to acknowledge him as king (2 Samuel 5:1-5). The editor of the psalm collection has placed it among the pilgrim songs to encourage fresh hope in all that God had promised by the prophets concerning the future despite the catastrophe of exile in Babylon. It also provided encouragement to travellers on their way to the annual festivals in Jerusalem to keep their sights on the goal—God's presence with his people gathered together in Zion. The prophet Zechariah, as he encouraged the people to complete the building of the temple after the return from exile, provides a commentary on this psalm that points us forward to the coming of Christ and the unity between God's people from all nations (Zechariah 8).

The last three songs in this series, of which this is the second, all emphasise the importance of Zion and God's blessings associated with it. Its emphasis on unity is a theme picked up by the Chronicler in his history of the nation. Even more than in the other historical books, Chronicles stresses those times when 'all Israel' were brought together (1 Chronicles 9:1; 11:1, 4; 13:5; etc.; 2 Chronicles 11:13; 24:5; 29:24; 30:1, 5–6; 31:1; 35:3).

Paul could well have used this psalm to express his joy at seeing the union that Christ had brought about between Jew and Gentile through his atoning death. To the Galatians he wrote, 'For you are all sons of God through faith in Christ Jesus ... There is neither Jew nor Greek, there is neither slave nor free, there is neither male nor female; for you are all one in Christ Jesus' (Galatians 3:26–28). Writing to the Ephesian church made up of Gentiles as well as Jews, he taught that Christ himself 'is our peace, who has made both one, and has broken down the middle wall of division ... For through him we both have access by one Spirit to the Father' (Ephesians 2:14–18). For this reason Paul later urges the believers to 'keep the unity of the Spirit in the bond of peace' (Ephesians 4:3).

Commending unity (verse 1)

The first word 'Behold' conveys David's enthusiasm as he makes this statement, which could be translated, 'How good and how pleasant it really is for ...!' This proverb-like saying was, for David, no commonplace remark. For the people of God to show their unity as brothers within the covenant community, especially during festival time at the central sanctuary in Jerusalem, was a remarkable phenomenon. To see people from the various tribes living together and sitting together after worshipping together was for David something 'good' and 'pleasant' or 'delightful'. This last adjective is used by David to describe Saul and Jonathan in their lives (2 Samuel 1:23).

Comparing unity (verses 2–3a)

Two illustrations are used to show what this unity is like. Repetition with the step-like pattern that we have noted as a feature of many of these pilgrim psalms is present in these verses. The word 'good' in verse 1 appears again but is translated 'precious' (verse 2), 'beard' is repeated and in the original the same verb 'descending' is used three times and translated as 'running down' in verse 2 and 'descending' in verse 3a. All this is done for poetic effect and emphasis.

The oil of gladness and unity (verse 2)

'Good oil', meaning costly, perfumed oil, on the head can sometimes symbolise joy (Psalm 23:5; Ecclesiastes 9:7–8; Isaiah 61:3). If the oil reached the beard it meant that it had not been merely smeared on the head but poured.

The second reference to the 'beard' introduces 'Aaron', the high priest, so that we are to think of this 'good oil' as that special anointing oil that spoke of consecration to the Lord's service and of the Spirit's influence (see Exodus 29:7; Leviticus 8:12). Kings were likewise anointed with oil, hence the phrase in the Books of Samuel to 'the Lord's anointed' or 'messiah' (1 Samuel 16:6; 2 Samuel 19:21; see Psalm 2:2) which was then applied to Jesus the Messiah (or 'Christ' in Greek) in the New Testament.

The anointing oil that trickled down Aaron's beard onto 'the edge (literally 'mouth') of his garments', meant that it reached down to the opening at the neck of the high priest's official robe (see Exodus 28:32). This is David's first picture of God's covenant community of twelve tribes bound together by a common heritage that included redemption from slavery and a commitment to a life of service to the God of Abraham who had entered into a special relationship with them and had called them to gather round his central dwelling-place where the high priest ministered on behalf of all the people.

Believers today from every background and culture are bound together in the Lord who loved them and gave himself for them, redeemed by the precious blood of Christ and committed to serving him daily. The communion meal reminds Christians of their unity in the Lord as they partake of the one loaf and the cup of blessing (1 Corinthians 10:16–17).

The dew that promotes life (verse 3a)

This second illustration was important to the people of the Middle East during the hot summer period when there was no rain. To have no dew could be as bad as having no rain (1 Kings 17:1; Haggai 1:10). When Isaac blessed Jacob and later spoke to Esau he referred 'to the dew of heaven' (Genesis 27:28, 39). Dew ensures life and fertility (Hosea 14:5).

'Hermon' was the highest of Israel's mountain range and lay in the north-east (see Psalms 42:6; 89:12) and its peaks remained snow-capped even in the summer. The dew that descended on Hermon was said to be particularly heavy but that same dew also descended upon the smaller hills surrounding Zion that lay much further south. Both received the same life-giving moisture that refreshed and sustained the vegetation. All Israel, north and south, were united in being recipients of this all-important means to mature the fruit and other crops. The dew illustration is especially appropriate for the closing statement of the psalm.

Consequence of unity (verse 3b)

It is there in Zion, the place where all Israel gathered as a united people, that 'the LORD commanded the blessing' (see Psalm 24:5). God's 'blessing' is the opposite of his curse and the death-like situations associated with it. Blessing is spelled out as 'life for evermore'. There in Zion where God ordained to meet with his people is the source of this life in all its fulness. 'All my springs are in you' sing Zion's musicians (Psalm 87:7).

As Jesus prayed for himself and his people he stated that eternal life is to know the only true God and Jesus Christ who was sent by the Father. He also prayed that all true believers would be one and made perfect in one and so view his glory (John 17). Where we see it we are encouraged not to take it for granted but to guard and maintain it. It is scandalous the way those who claim to be Christians sometimes behave toward fellow believers within local churches and in the wider Christian community. Instead of encouraging one another in the great biblical truths of the gospel to live to please and serve the Lord, we look for opportunities to denounce and rubbish those who do not follow our own narrow culture-bound views that we claim are more biblical to the faith once delivered to the saints. No wonder we are experiencing so little blessing in terms of true spiritual vitality and conversions.

Psalm 134

Blessing the LORD and Being Blessed by Him

This is the fifteenth and final 'Song of Ascents' (see Psalm 120). There is nothing to indicate when it was originally composed but for the editor of the psalm collection the references to the sanctuary in Zion and the final benediction provided a fitting conclusion to this series of pilgrim songs that began with a distressed member of the community feeling like a foreigner among people who hated peace. The psalm is also closely related to the previous one. Both psalms are introduced with 'Behold', both are addressed not to the LORD but to other people and both end with the LORD's blessing. In fact, the final three psalms in this series of 'Ascent' songs all focus our attention on Zion, the city where God had ordained to live among his people and to bless them. There the people worshipped together peacefully and found security and blessing. It is an ideal picture of the city to which Abraham looked forward and to which the people of God have already come by faith as a result of Christ's finished work on the cross (Hebrews 11:10, 16; 12:22–24). These psalms point us to the reality that is depicted by John in his vision of the holy city, the new Jerusalem, that came down from heaven to fill the new earth (Revelation 21:1–4, 10–27).

Exhortation (verse 1–2)

The psalm opens like the previous song on an enthusiastic note ('Behold'; see Psalm 133:1), only this time it is a call to worship. We could translate the opening line: 'Come now, bless the Lord'. The word translated 'bless' did originally suggest kneeling in homage to a superior person (See Psalm 103:1) and that background is appropriate in reference to God's 'servants'. They are to worship with a submissive, reverent spirit before the covenant God of Israel. The exhortation to worship ('bless the Lord') is repeated at the end of verse 2, thus providing a frame round the first part of the psalm.

Who are these servants? They could be God's people in general and the term is used in this way particularly after the return from exile (see Psalm 113:1). However, the reference in this psalm to these servants standing in God's house at night and lifting up their hands would indicate especially the priests and possibly the other Levite clans who had the responsibility of guarding and caring for the tabernacle and whose later functions involved the musical side of temple worship. In the Mosaic Law the tribe of Levi was set apart by God to carry the ark of the covenant and 'to stand before the Lord to minister to him and to bless in his name' (Deuteronomy 10:8; 21:5). In the time of Nehemiah we are told that the Jews rejoiced 'over the priests and Levites who ministered' (literally 'who stood') in the temple (Nehemiah 12:44).

Though 'night' may not mean that worship went on all night long (see Psalm 92:2), Levites had duties that involved them in working day and night (1 Chronicles 9:27, 33). We also read that during festivals more activities went on at night (Isaiah 30:29). To 'lift up' the hands toward the 'sanctuary' ('holy place'), like bending the knee, was a symbolic gesture. It signified a humble spirit, appealing to God in an attitude of dependence (see Psalm 28:2). David speaks of lifting up his hands in worship (Psalm 63:4). A similar gesture involved spreading out the hands to God, which is how Moses pleaded with God to stop the plague of hail (Exodus 9:29). It was also with hands outspread that Solomon stood before the altar and offered his great prayer at the dedication of the newly built temple. Such physical expressions could often become mere outward forms and superstitious acts with no inner reality so that the people at the time of the destruction of Jerusalem were encouraged to lift up their hearts as well as their hands as they made confession of their sins (Lamentations 3:41; see Isaiah 1:15). Paul exhorts Timothy that 'the men pray everywhere, lifting up holy hands, without wrath and doubting' (1 Timothy 2:8).

Although this psalm may well be addressed especially to the priests and Levites it can be applied under the new covenant to all God's people, whether they are set apart to be ministers of the gospel or not. Isaiah, in the latter part of his long prophecy, can speak of a new situation after the coming of Christ. The old barriers between Jew and Gentile and priests and laity will be broken down so that a Gentile can become a priest and a Levite and all God's people from the nations of the world will be servants of the Lord (Isaiah 56:6–8; 65:13–16; 66:21).

Benediction (verse 3)

When Aaron was first set apart as high priest he 'lifted his hand toward the people' and 'blessed them' (Leviticus 9:22) and this would seem to be the background to this final verse. The words also remind us of the priestly blessing that begins, 'The LORD bless you and keep you' (Numbers 6:23–27). As in that passage the 'you' is singular. This could mean either that each individual Israelite is blessed or that the whole company of God's people viewed collectively as God's son is blessed. It is 'from Zion' that the blessing flows (see Psalms 128:5; 133:3) for that is where God has ordained to live among his people. The earthly city and sanctuary are symbolic of the heavenly reality.

The 'LORD', (Yahweh/Jehovah), the covenant-keeping God of Israel who has made his home in Zion, is the one 'who made heaven and earth' (see Psalms 115:15; 121:2; 124:8). How amazing that such a God against whom we have rebelled, should bless us! Concerning the difference between us blessing God and God blessing us, Motyer helpfully puts it like this: 'When he "blesses" us he reviews our needs and meets them; when we bless him we review his excellencies and worship him'.

Psalm 135

Praising the LORD, Supreme over All

This psalm is what Derek Kidner calls 'an anthology of praise' for every verse has wording identical to other parts of the Old Testament. Despite these many allusions and quotations it does not read as if someone has deliberately set about cutting and pasting a verse from here and there out of the biblical texts. The unknown author from the period after the return from exile has so imbibed God's word that we are presented with a fresh expression of praise to the living God which has a character all of its own. It is constructed in such a way as to highlight examples of God's sovereignty from Israel's early history (verses 8–14). By this means, God's people are encouraged to praise him for his goodness toward them (verses 1–4 and 19–21) and for the way he exercises his power in the world in contrast to the impotence of the nations' idols (verses 5–7 and 15–18). This theme would have been an encouragement to the Jews after their return from exile when they were still living under foreign rule to put their trust in the LORD God of Israel. It serves a similar purpose for God's people today who are often smarting under oppressive regimes that hate God and Jesus his Anointed one.

The editor of the psalm collection has purposely placed the psalm to follow the final 'Song of Ascents'. It provides content to the exhortation for the Lord's servants to worship (see Psalm 134:1 and Psalm 135:1-2) and along with the following psalm (Psalm 136), it acts as an appendix to the Songs of Ascents. It is also interesting to find that the psalm opens and closes with 'Hallelujah' ('Praise the Lord', verses 1, 21) and brings to mind Psalms 111 to 118. This has the effect of forming a frame around Psalms 119 to 134 and drawing our attention to the importance of God's words of instruction and of his presence in Zion.

Call to praise (verses 1–4)

The opening words are similar to Psalm 113:1 but they are used in such a way as to link up with the first two verses of Psalm 134. Rather than 'bless', as in the previous psalm, the term 'praise' is employed, which includes the idea of boasting in God and honouring him. The 'servants of the Lord' in this psalm probably include not only the priests and Levites (see Psalm 134:1) but, as the final section suggests, all God's people (see Psalm 113:1). Verse 2 however draws our attention particularly to those who minister in the temple precincts or 'courts' (see Psalms 96:8; 134:1), which is described as 'the house of the LORD' and 'the house of our God', this last phrase being a particular favourite with Ezra and Nehemiah (Ezra 8:17, 25, 30; Nehemiah 10:32–39).

Verse 3 is similar to Psalm 147:1 except that here, instead of the act of praising God being a 'pleasant' or 'lovely' duty, it is God himself who is delightful. We are encouraged, then, to praise God for he is 'good' (see Psalms 34:8; 118:1) and to 'make music' ('sing praises') to this 'LORD' whose character or reputation ('name', verse 1, 3) is 'delightful' ('pleasant').

As often in praise psalms reasons are presented why people are to praise God. The first ground for praise is the Lord's character (verse 3), whereas in verse 4 it is the Lord's choice of Israel. 'Jacob', the father of the nation, was given the new name of 'Israel' by God to remind him of the incident at Peniel and as a sign of God's blessing and covenant promises (Genesis 32:28; 35:9–15).

The God who originally chose scheming Jacob and his family of twelve sons formed their descendants into a nation to be his own valuable possession ('special treasure'; Exodus 19:5; Deuteronomy 14:2; 26:18). It is a word that describes a king's personal treasures of gold and silver (1 Chronicles 29:2; Ecclesiastes 2:8). Malachi employs the term to describe those who feared the Lord and meditated on his name (Malachi 3:17). In the New Testament, we find Paul and Peter using Greek equivalents to describe Christians as God's own treasured possession (Titus 2:14; 1 Peter 2:9). The word found in the older English versions was 'peculiar' and led to the formation of a Christian denomination known as 'The Peculiar People'! Of course the word did not mean strange or odd but 'special'.

Seven times the name 'Lord' is found in these verses (both Yahweh/Jehovah and the shortened form Yah/Jah, as in hallelu-jah, are used) to emphasise the association of God's personal covenant name with this nation he had loved and chosen to be set apart for his honour and praise (Exodus 3:14-15; 6:3-4; 19:5-6; Deuteronomy 7:6-8).

The Lord above all gods (verses 5-7)

The psalmist speaks for all God's people as he makes this confession of faith. He begins emphatically, 'Because I myself know'. Here is another reason for praising the 'Lord' and he includes his people with himself when he refers to God as 'our Lord' (verse 5). He acknowledges that the 'Lord' is not only good and delightful but also 'great', and as Jethro likewise confessed, this sovereign 'Lord' of Israel is 'above all gods' (see Exodus 18:11, 'I know that the Lord is greater than all the gods').

Verses 6 and 7 echo Psalm 115:3 and Jeremiah 10:13; 51:16. God is not limited in the way that humans and their gods are confined by time, space and ability. He reigns over all and rain clouds, electric storms and wind are all subject to his command. Similar wording is used in Jeremiah's attack on idolatry (Jeremiah 10:1-16). Throughout Israel's history all the nations that surrounded them and to which they were later in subjection worshipped and served the creature rather than the creator. In Israel alone as a result of God's revelation to them was there this belief in the one universal ruler to whom the people were commanded to commit themselves fully and exclusively in worship and service. In this they were to be a light to the world concerning the knowledge of the one true and living God. Christians have the same calling in the multi-religious societies in which they live.

The Lord's sovereignty illustrated (verses 8-14)

The power of God displayed in the world of nature was particularly seen in Israel's early history from the exodus to the conquest of Canaan. What happened at the Red Sea as well as at Sinai may be in the psalmist's mind in the previous verse (Exodus 15:8, 10; 19:16; see Psalm 18:7-15). This naturally leads him to give more specific examples of the Lord's powerful activity against what were considered immovable obstacles. Verse 8 refers to the tenth plague that destroyed all the first-born of Egypt, 'both of man and beast' (see Exodus 12:29). This was the final curse to fall on the Egyptians but it was one of many 'signs and wonders' to hit the very heart of the country (Deuteronomy 6:22; see Psalms 65:8; 71:7; 78:43). Addressing Egypt herself ('in the midst of you, O Egypt', verse 9) brings the history alive and adds to the vividness of the account.

God's rule is emphasised in the defeat of 'many nations' and the slaying of 'mighty kings', including 'Sihon king of the Amorites' and 'Og king of Bashan' on the east bank of the Jordan, and 'all the kingdoms of Canaan' to the west of the river. The account of Israel's victory over Sihon and Og recorded in Numbers 21:21–35 is especially seen as evidence of the Lord's greatness and it is referred to a number of times in Deuteronomy and Joshua as well as in other parts of the Old Testament (for example Deuteronomy 2:24–3:11; Joshua 2:10; 9:10; 1 Kings 4:19; Jeremiah 48:45; Nehemiah 9:22).

The lands belonging to these nations both east and west of the Jordan the Lord gave to Israel his people as their inheritance (see Psalms 105:11; 136:21–22). Canaan becomes a picture or prototype of the inheritance God has prepared for all those who love him. It is through Christ's victory on the cross over principalities and powers and the ruler of the darkness of this world that this inheritance is given to his people. Jesus said, 'Blessed are the meek, for they shall inherit the earth' (Matthew 5:5).

This central section of the psalm closes by celebrating the 'Lord's' (Yahweh/Jehovah) reputation ('name') and 'renown' or 'fame' (literally 'remembrance', verse 13). This fame results from his activity in redeeming and delivering his people from their enemies and bringing them into the land of promise. Similar words appear in Psalm 102:12. They also echo the words of God to Moses as he announced how he was to be known to the Israelites in Egypt (Exodus 3:15). He is the great 'I am', not a yesterday god who is unable to deal with the problems of today and tomorrow but the ever-present one to whom the people can look for the future. Our Lord Jesus Christ is the unchangeable one who is the same yesterday, today and for ever (Hebrews 13:8).

The final verse is a quotation from the Song of Moses in Deuteronomy 32:36. Because the Lord is over the nations as well as Israel, the psalmist is confident that, moved with 'compassion' for 'his people', who are also described as 'his servants', he will 'administer justice' ('judge') by vindicating them (see Psalm 72:2). But as the context of Moses' song reveals, Israel must come to that position of helplessness and not be looking in their need to other gods to help them. This promise that the Lord would pity them and right all the wrongs of his oppressed people would have been especially applicable to those suffering hardship and persecution after the return from exile. The same promises hold true for Christians in all their trials and suffering for the sake of Christ.

The useless gods of the nations (verses 15–18)

The mention of the false gods in the Song of Moses brings to the psalmist's mind the words of Psalm 115 to which he has already alluded in verse 6. Apart from minor differences, this whole section reproduces verses 4 to 6 and verse 8 (see Psalm 115 for more detailed comment). Whereas these beautifully made and costly idols and the gods they represent are completely impotent to respond to those who worship them and pray to them, the implication is that Israel's Lord is not like that for he is the living God who hears and answers prayer (see Jeremiah 10:1-16). Those who trust these senseless gods become senseless themselves.

Call to worship (verses 19–21)

Psalm 115 is still in the psalmist's mind but instead of assuring the covenant community of God's blessing on the religious leaders and all who fear the Lord (Psalm 115:12-13), our psalm concludes by urging Israel, its religious leaders and those 'who fear the Lord', to 'bless the Lord' (see Psalm 103:1). The phrase 'house of Israel' means those belonging to Israel, just as 'house of Aaron' and 'house of Levi' refer to Aaron's and Levi's households, in this case their descendants living at the time when the psalm was composed.

'Blessed be the LORD' (verse 21; see Exodus 18:10; Psalm 28:6) becomes in the New Testament 'Blessed be the God and Father of our Lord Jesus Christ' (2 Corinthians 1:3; Ephesians 1:3; 1 Peter 1:3). This homage was to go out from Zion for it was there that God ordained to live among his people (Psalm 132:13-14) and it was from there that God blessed his people (see Psalms 128:5; 133:3). It was in Jerusalem where the Christian Church first met that the Spirit of God descended and filled his people and from there the wonderful works of God were declared to people from every nation and the good news of the gospel proclaimed (Acts 2:1-11). From Jerusalem the gospel spreads to the ends of the earth so that every part of the world wherever God's people assemble becomes a spiritual Jerusalem where homage is paid to the God and Father of our Lord Jesus Christ (see John 4:20-24). We look forward to the consummation when Zion's city, the new Jerusalem made up of God's people from all nations, will be seen in the new creation.

As the psalm began so it concludes with a fitting response— Hallelujah! 'Praise the Lord!'

Psalm 136

Confessing the LORD's Enduring Love

If ever anyone needed biblical warrant for singing choruses this is it! There are some Christians who complain when spiritual songs are repeated three or four times. Here is a psalm that repeats the chorus twenty-six times! One Jewish tradition claims this psalm to be the 'Great Hallel' ('Great Praise') while another tradition sees it as the final psalm of the 'Great Praise' that began with Psalm 120.

The psalm belongs with the previous one to form a kind of appendix to the Songs of Ascents (Psalms 120–134). Both psalms begin and end with exhortations to worship God either in praise or thanksgiving. Reasons are also presented for doing so. This psalm expands on what is briefly mentioned in Psalm 135 and uses some of its expressions.

The distinctive feature of this psalm is the refrain that appears at the close of each verse. This is not the first time it has been heard. It is used at the beginning of Psalms 106 and 107 and at the beginning and end of Psalm 118. When Solomon had finished praying at the dedication of the temple all the people worshipped and praised God with the words of this refrain when the heavenly fire consumed the sacrifices and the glory of the Lord filled the sanctuary (2 Chronicles 7:1–3; see also 5:13). Jehoshaphat arranged for singers to praise God with this refrain as they went out to battle against the enemy (2 Chronicles 20:21). The same refrain was heard again by the priests and Levites when the temple foundations were laid after Israel's return from exile (Ezra 3:11). It cannot be said with certainty that the words were used as a choral or congregational response after a leader introduced the first half of each verse.

God's people are urged to give thanks to Israel's covenant-keeping God, the 'Lord' (Yahweh/Jehovah) and sovereign over all (verses 1-3, 26), who is the God of creation (verses 4-9), the deliverer of his people (verses 10-15), their guide and conqueror (verses 16-24), who also provides for all his creatures (verse 25). Every action of God toward his creation in general and his people in particular is evidence of his amazing love and commitment and this is acknowledged in each verse.

Call to acknowledge God (verses 1-3)

This opening call is identical to the introductory words of Psalms 106, 107 and 118. The previous psalm (Psalm 135:1, 3, 19-21) urged God's people to praise and worship the Lord while this one speaks of our duty to offer thanks. To 'give thanks' includes the idea of confession and acknowledgement of God and what he has done. The psalm encourages God's people to call to mind the being and activity of God and to express that in grateful adoration.

We are first reminded of who God is—he is 'good' (see Psalms 34:8; 100:5). Good is the opposite of all that is bad (Leviticus 27:10) and in the ultimate sense, as Jesus indicated, only God is good (2 Chronicles 30:18; Mark 10:18). The good God entered into a special relationship with his people that he might do them good (Deuteronomy 6:24; 8:16; 10:13). One Old Testament theologian writes: 'to speak of God as good is to affirm that the Lord is the source of all that makes life possible and worthwhile, the deliverer of those in trouble and distress, the one who, in making this whole universe, marked it forever as "very good".'[80]

Coupled with God's goodness is his 'mercy' or better his 'unfailing love'. The loving commitment shown within a marriage relationship is a picture of God's steadfast love toward his people. But while death ends the marriage vows, God's love within the covenant relationship has no end; it *'endures* for ever'.

The psalm also speaks of God's sovereignty for he is 'the God of gods' and 'the Lord of lords' (verses 2-3). This terminology reflects Moses' words to Israel: 'For the Lord your God is God of gods and Lord of lords, the great God ...' (Deuteronomy 10:17). Neither Moses nor the psalmist is implying that the true God heads up a pantheon of gods. The phraseology expresses the superlative and indicates that God is the one supreme Being and ruling Lord of all. A similar phrase 'holy of holies' means the 'most holy'. It also means that while there are supernatural beings that can be called gods (see Psalm 82; 1 Corinthians 8:5-6; 10:19-20), in reality there is only one true and living God (see Deuteronomy 4:35, 39). Whatever god or kingly figure people look up to or worship, the God of Israel is superior to them and he is in ultimate charge.

Creator (verses 4-9)

Following the call to give thanks to God in the first three verses, the repeated 'To him who ...' at the beginning of each verse from verse 4 to verse 25 makes it into a very long sentence. God is the one who 'alone' does 'great wonders' (verse 4; see Psalm 72:18). Often God's 'wonders' has reference to the plagues of Egypt and the deliverance of his people at the Red Sea (Exodus 3:20; 11:10; 15:11; Psalms 105:27; 106:7). But the term can also refer to God's wonders in creation (see Psalm 107:24). The psalmist may therefore have both creation and the exodus event in mind as a preliminary statement covering all that is to follow. God is unique in that he alone can create and overcome all opposition to rescue his people and bring them to the inheritance he has prepared for them. God's plans and purposes are never thwarted (see Isaiah 45:18-22; Daniel 6:26-27).

God's work of creation displays his 'wisdom' (verse 5). The words resemble an earlier psalm, 'O Lord, how manifold are your works! in wisdom you have made them all' (Psalm 104:24) and the statement in Proverbs: 'The Lord by wisdom founded the earth; by understanding he established the heavens' (Proverbs 3:19; see Jeremiah 10:12).

Some examples of his creative power are given beginning with the 'earth' (verse 6). Whereas the Genesis account presents the creation in stately prose, we have here a highly poetic description of the earth 'laid out' or 'spread out', as if beating out a thin sheet of metal, to cover over the waters (see Psalm 24:2; Isaiah 42:5).

God is the maker of the 'great lights' (verse 7). The psalm can be compared to the Genesis text at this point although the wording is different. The sun and moon are actually named here instead of being referred to as the greater and lesser lights and the stars are included with the moon in ruling the night (verses 8-9; see Genesis 1:16-18). Far from being gods to be worshipped as in pagan thought, these heavenly bodies are made by God and serve his purposes in determining the length of day and night.

The wisdom and power of God seen in creation bear witness to God's unfailing love.

Saviour (verses 10–15)

More space is now given to God's activity in rescuing Israel from Egypt and bringing them to Canaan. As in the previous psalm, it moves immediately from nature to the final plague that 'struck' Egypt by killing all their 'firstborn' (verse 10; see Psalm 135:8; Exodus 12:12-13, 27, 29). The phraseology of the next two verses (verses 11-12) is taken from Deuteronomy where many times we are informed of how God 'brought out' his people from Egypt 'with a strong hand and with an outstretched arm' (Deuteronomy 5:15; 9:29; 26:8). Israel's deliverance from bondage was an amazing demonstration of God's power and it was capped by God's action at the Red Sea bringing his people safely through the sea and gaining a notable victory over Pharaoh and his army (verses 13-15; see Exodus 14:21-31). The word translated 'overthrew' is literally 'shook off' (verse 15) and is taken from the Exodus account (Exodus 14:27). It suggests the effortless way the Lord shook off Pharaoh's army as if it were an insect on his arm (see Psalm 109:23).

Again, God's action in saving Israel from the Egyptians demonstrates his commitment to his people. It pictures the greater work of God in rescuing his people from slavery to sin and Satan. Jesus spoke of his atoning death as the occasion when the ruler of this world would be cast out and people of all nations drawn to himself (John 12:31-32). Pharaoh was one of the snake's offspring (Genesis 3:15) and his overthrow pointed to the fatal blow that Christ would minister to the devil, that old snake, through his cross and resurrection (John 16:11; Revelation 12:9-11).

Conqueror (verses 16–22)

The psalm moves on to depict God's guidance of his people through their wilderness wanderings (verse 16; see Psalm 78:52-53). Nothing is said of Sinai and the giving of the law or of the people's sinfulness. All the emphasis is on God's action in rescuing his people from an alien power and leading them safely home to the land promised to their forefathers. All this speaks of his unfailing love toward them. Paul encourages Christians with the promise that this same God who is Paul's God 'shall supply all your need according to his riches in glory by Christ Jesus' (Philippians 4:19).

God not only struck the Egyptians (verse 10) but he did the same to 'great' and 'famous kings' (verses 17-18). They are named as 'Sihon king of the Amorites' and 'Og king of Bashan' (verses 19-20; see Psalm 135:11). These two kings would not allow Israel to pass through their territory and each in turn came out to engage in battle and on both occasions Israel gained the victory over them (Numbers 21:21-35). Their names reappear many times throughout the Old Testament for they represented the first of a long line of Canaanite kings who were defeated by Israel (Deuteronomy 1:4; 3:1-13; Joshua 2:10; 9:10; 1 Kings 4:19; Nehemiah 9:22). The psalm makes it clear that it was God who really gave Israel the victory over them and it witnessed once more to his unfailing love.

Like the previous psalm, following the reference to Sihon and Og, mention is made of the land gifted by God to Israel for 'a heritage' or 'inheritance' as it is more commonly translated in Deuteronomy and Joshua (verses 21-22; see Deuteronomy 4:21; 15:4; etc.; Joshua 1:6; 11:23). Almost identical wording is found in the previous Psalm 135:12 including the repetition of the word 'heritage' except that in our psalm the refrain is added each time which has the effect of emphasising even more the importance of this gift from God. The phrase, 'their land' (verse 21), not only refers to the land belonging to Sihon and Og where the tribes of Reuben, Gad and half of Manasseh settled, but to the whole of Canaan (see Psalm 135:11-12). That land east of the Jordan represented the whole Canaanite country and became, in effect, a foretaste and guarantee of Israel's possession of the entire land that God had promised them.

Instead of referring to Israel as 'his people' (see Psalm 135:12), the nation is described as God's 'servant' (verse 22) in the singular. This is a title first employed by Isaiah to speak of the nation Israel as he introduced that unique person, the Servant of the Lord, the ideal Israel, who would be all that Israel never was and who would become an atoning sacrifice for his people's sins (Isaiah 41:8; 42:1, 19; 44:1-2; 49:3; 52:13). Jeremiah is the only other Old Testament writer to refer to Israel in this way (Jeremiah 30:10; 46:27-28).

Christians belong to the Israel of God and Israel's inheritance in Canaan is a picture of what Christ our conqueror and saviour has obtained for his people. We give thanks 'to the Father who has qualified us to be partakers of the inheritance of the saints in the light.' (Colossians 1:12). God's unfailing love does indeed have no end!

Carer (verses 23–25)

While these verses could be a summary of verses 10–22, it is more likely to be the experiences that Israel suffered during the judges' period or more probably it is referring to more recent events including the Babylonian exile and the conditions that prevailed after the Jews returned to their land. The psalmist includes himself in these final verses by the use of 'us' and 'our' (verses 23–24). God had brought them low by removing them from their land but he also remembered them as he promised Moses (Leviticus 26:42, 45) and 'rescued' (literally 'tore apart' or 'snatched away') them from those who caused them distress. The refrain becomes even more significant in the light of Jerusalem's destruction and the people's removal to Babylon. They have been torn or snatched away from a new bondage and returned to their land. Truly God's steadfast covenant love does last!

Christians think of their 'lowly state' in spiritual bondage and the way God has graciously 'delivered us from the power of darkness and translated us into the kingdom of the Son of his love, in whom we have redemption through his blood ...' (Colossians 1:13–14). In view of God's amazing kindness and grace, can we be weary and bored of repeating, 'for his steadfast love endures for ever'?

The final verse that brings to a close the long sentence (verse 25; see verse 4) returns to the universal theme begun in verses 4 to 9. God who created heaven and earth provides for the needs of 'all flesh', a reminder of God's promises to Noah and 'all flesh' after the Flood (Genesis 9:11, 15–17). Despite what people teach and say, we live in a world that God made and as we eat our 'daily bread' we give thanks to the one who fills 'our hearts with food and gladness' (Matthew 6:11; Acts 14:15–17). 'Every good gift and every perfect gift is from above, and comes down from the Father of lights' (James 1:17).

Call to acknowledge God (verse 26)

Following the many reasons for thanking God, the closing verse returns to the opening call. We are urged to give thanks to 'the God of heaven', a title often employed when speaking to pagans and especially prominent from the time of the exile (for example, Genesis 24:3, 7;

2 Chronicles 36:23; Ezra 5:12; Nehemiah 1:4; 2:4; Daniel 2:19; Jonah 1:9). It is also an appropriate one in this context. It reminds us again that the LORD, Israel's God, is the one God who has created heaven and earth and to whom all flesh look for sustenance.

The whole psalm helps us to appreciate what God's loving commitment means, its universal dimension and its enduring nature. It is because his steadfast love is for ever that 'God so loved the world that he gave his only begotten Son, that whoever believes in him should not perish but have everlasting life' (John 3:16).

Psalm 137

Zion remembered, Babylon destroyed

Like Charles Dickens' novel *A Tale of Two Cities* concerning London and Paris at the time of the French Revolution, this psalm is about two cities: Babylon and Jerusalem. It presents us with a theme that runs through the Bible and which ends with a description of Babylon's fall and Jerusalem's glory.

Though the psalm has no heading, its contents indicate that it was written during the Babylonian exile (587-539 BC)[81] or immediately after when the pain of that experience was still fresh in the mind of the psalmist. This communal lament indicates how traumatic and devastating the exile was for God's people. Yet God was with them in the exile and true to his promise he had brought them back. This psalm should be compared with David's imprecatory Psalm 109 and its place at this point in the psalm collection, after two hymns that have encouraged praise and thanksgiving, is quite deliberate and purposeful. God had continued to remember them and had acted to release them from their foes and the chorus running through Psalm 136 highlights God's commitment toward them. In this way Book 5 (Psalms 107–150) helped the community newly returned from exile to move forward in faith and to look with confidence to the fulfilling of all God's promises in the coming of God's Anointed King and Priest (see Psalms 2, 110).

Throughout the history of the Christian Church, Christians have

434

suffered greatly for their faith and the 21st century is proving to be no exception with Sudanese and Nigerian believers facing the cruellest atrocities imaginable. There is no thought of personal vengeance but the psalm encourages Christians to look to God to punish their persecutors. The psalm must be read in the light of the final book of the Bible which was written to encourage fellow believers pressured by false religion and state persecution.

The psalmist begins by recollecting the situation of the Jews in exile as they considered what the Babylonians had done to Jerusalem and its people (verses 1–4). A vow of loyalty to Jerusalem follows (verses 5–6) and the psalm concludes with a cry to God for justice against treacherous Edomites and ends confidently in the knowledge that God will fulfil his promises in punishing the brutal Babylonians (verses 7–9).

Recollection (verses 1–4)[82]

For the exiles living in the Babylonian plain between the Tigris and the Euphrates, there were many pleasing features about their situation and when opportunity came to return to Canaan some who had settled well made no effort to move back. This would have been especially true of those who had grown up in Babylon and had got on in life. Relaxing under shady trees along the banks of the Euphrates or some of the smaller streams and artificial irrigation canals was very appealing when compared with Jerusalem and its hilly terrain. The strength of the temptation to feel happy and content with their pleasant surroundings and to forget Jerusalem is suggested by the force of the oath in verses 5 and 6.

Those whose interests rose above personal advantage and earthly pleasures could only weep as they sat and 'remembered Zion' (verse 1). Like Moses, who chose 'to suffer affliction with the people of God than to enjoy the passing pleasures of sin' (Hebrews 11:24–26), the psalmist and those like him considered all that Zion meant. This was the place that God had chosen to live among his worshipping people. God's many precious promises made to king David were associated with this place (see Psalm 132).

The 'willows' (verse 2) or the Euphrates poplars that resemble willows were along the banks 'in the midst' of these waterways and not in far away forests. Hanging up their 'harps' (or 'lyres'; see Psalm 98:5) on the trees may have been a symbolic gesture indicating that they were in no mood to sing praises. The lyre is often associated with joyful praise (see Psalms 33:2; 92:1-4; 108:2).

To make matters worse their captors, also referred to as 'those who plundered us' (some think the rare word could mean 'our tormentors'), are asking them to sing one of the 'songs of Zion', songs which can also be termed 'the LORD's song' ('the song of Yahweh/Jehovah'). Their cruel demand seems to be for the purpose of entertainment which is how our text understands it by rendering the word often translated 'gladness' as 'mirth'. How could they sing songs like David's joyful Psalm 122! When Jerusalem fell to the Babylonians we read of those who clapped their hands in glee and poked fun at the songs of Zion that spoke of the city as 'The perfection of beauty, the joy of the whole earth' (Lamentations 2:15; see Psalm 48:1-3). Seen in this light, their request was sarcastic and for God's people to humour them would be like rubbing salt into open wounds as well as encouraging the enemy to continue in their blasphemous activity. Their musical instruments would remain hung up on the trees.

It is not that God's people could never sing praise to God on foreign soil. If the nations of the world are urged to praise the Lord then Israel can praise God wherever they are, as happened when they crossed the Red Sea and Pharaoh's army was destroyed (Exodus 15:1-21). Their present circumstances were different. The reason why the people were in a 'foreign land' (verse 4) was because of God's judgment on the nation for its apostasy. The removal from their own land was a divine punishment and they were in a death-like situation where 'the dead do not praise the Lord' (Psalm 115:17). Daniel in his intercessory prayer confesses the sin of the people and the justice of the great disaster and calls on God to turn away his furious anger from God's city. It was not a time for singing but for deep contrition and cries for mercy and forgiveness (Daniel 9:4-19).

Reaffirmation (verses 5-6)

But for the godly Jews, refusal to sing 'the LORD's song' did not mean they intended blocking out of their minds all thoughts of Jerusalem. These verses express a great love for the old city that was now in ruins. Painful though it was to think of the city's present state, the covenant community, humbled as a result of the exile, cannot forget where they belong and hold the city and all it stood for in the highest esteem. Though Babylon's city and waterways were impressive, it is Jerusalem that is raised up in the mind of the poet above anything else in which they might delight. As Motyer puts it, 'Babylon was his address, Jerusalem his home'. Love for Jerusalem was not divorced from love for God and his cause in the world. They belonged together because that is where God had ordained to meet with his people and where he had given king David great and precious promises.

This confession of the psalmist's loyalty to Zion (notice the singular 'I' and 'my'), a commitment that spoke for all the godly, is in the form of a self curse formula and is directed to Jerusalem as if it were a person—'If I forget you, O Jerusalem ... If I do not remember you' (verse 5). If ever the psalmist were to forget Jerusalem then it would be impossible for him to make music and sing. He is calling down a curse that his right hand would cease for ever to pluck a stringed instrument and that his tongue would be permanently stuck to his palate so that he would no longer be able to sing. God's people in Babylon looked to God's promises of a return, a new beginning like a new exodus that would lead to the coming of the Servant King of Isaiah's prophecies and a new day when Zion would be transformed.

What is said here is a reminder to Christians of our heavenly citizenship. We are sojourners and pilgrims in this world and we are to seek and set our minds on those things above where Christ is (Colossians 3:1-2; 1 Peter 2:11). 'For our citizenship is in heaven, from which we also eagerly wait for the Saviour, the Lord Jesus Christ' (Philippians 3:20).

Retribution (verses 7-9)
Many Christians wish the psalm had ended at verse 6. The final verses appear to be out of keeping with the spirit of Christ who taught his disciples to love their enemies and do good to those who hate them and to bless and not curse (Luke 6:27-29). But these verses, like the previous lines, are part of God's word and cannot be brushed aside as sub-Christian, pre-Christian or an expression of sinful attitudes that must not be followed.

Against Edom (verse 7)
The word 'remember' appears again (see verse 6) this time in a prayer to God. The psalmist calls on the covenant God of Israel ('LORD', that is, 'Yahweh/Jehovah') to 'Remember against the sons of Edom', in the sense of bringing a legal case to bear against the Edomites

for their attitude over the fall of Jerusalem. This use of 'remember' is taken up a couple of times by Nehemiah in his short prayers for God to punish treacherous enemies and those who would defile the priesthood (Nehemiah 6:14; 13:29). The 'day of Jerusalem' is the day of God's judgment on the city (Lamentations 1:12; 2:1). Obadiah the prophet speaks a number of times concerning this calamitous 'day' for Jerusalem as he describes how the Edomites rejoiced to see the city's destruction and prevented many of the city's inhabitants from escaping (verses 10–14). Our psalmist shows how they urged the Babylonians to completely destroy the city: 'Raze *it*, raze *it*, to its very foundation'.

Israel and Edom were the descendants of Isaac and Rebekah's twin sons, Jacob and Esau, yet the Edomites behaved treacherously and encouraged the Babylonians in their destruction of Jerusalem (Ezekiel 25:12; 35:5). They were intent on seeing the end of God's rule on earth. For the psalmist Edom is symbolic of all worldly opposition to God and his people. Obadiah viewed Edom in the same way and ended his prophecy against Edom with the promise of deliverance for Mount Zion, of God's people possessing their possessions, of Esau doomed and the triumph of God's rule—'the kingdom shall be the Lord's' (verses 17–21; see Psalm 22:28).

The curse on Edom is therefore to be viewed in the light of God's word through prophets like Obadiah and Ezekiel and as a pointer to God's judgment on all who take their stand against God, his Anointed and the people who belong to him (see Psalm 2).

Against Babylon (verses 8–9)

After the prayer to God for the Edomites to receive the punishment they deserve the psalm moves to the Babylonians, the idiom 'daughter of Babylon' (verse 8) standing for the city itself in all its attractiveness (see Psalm 45:12; Isaiah 47:1). There is no prayer for the city's destruction but a confident statement that she will be 'destroyed'. This is because prophets like Isaiah had long ago declared that the instrument that God would use to punish Judah would itself be punished (Isaiah 13; 47:1; Jeremiah 50).

In addition, the psalmist congratulates ('Happy', or 'Blessed' as in Psalm 1:1 and 2:12) the one who will do to Babylon what she did to Jerusalem. It is a retribution that is commensurate with the crime committed. Modern western sentimentality does not like the final words of this psalm but warfare is brutal and barbaric and takes no special account of women and children. In fact, an enemy might especially target children, for that would mean putting an end to a nation's future (see Psalm 109:13). Recent international treaties concerning rules of engagement did not apply in the ancient world although God made it known that he did punish nations for war crimes (see Amos 1).

Seizing infants and dashing them against the rock was a vivid if gruesome way of indicating the end of a nation's future. There are many instances in the Old Testament and other ancient writings of the Middle East of the use of this kind of phraseology (see 2 Kings 8:12; Hosea 10:14; Nahum 3:10; Jeremiah 13:14). Jeremiah speaks of the utter destruction of Babylon as breaking in pieces not only the nation but man and woman, old and young (Jeremiah 51:20-23). This kind of language should not be taken literally any more than we take the 'daughter of Babylon' literally. It expressed in the language of the day the total defeat of the enemy. The same verb 'to dash' is used in Psalm 2:9 of the Anointed One who will 'dash in pieces' the rebellious nations.

As in the case of Edom, prophets had written of Babylon's defeat and both the city and its king were seen as symbolic of the great opponent of God and of his people (Isaiah 14). The psalm's expression of satisfaction at the destruction of Babylon is no different to the rejoicing over Babylon's fall in the final book of the Bible. A voice from heaven describes the punishment in terms of strict justice: 'Render to her just as she rendered to you and repay her double according to her works ...' and it ends 'Rejoice over her, O heaven, and you holy apostles and prophets, for God has avenged you on her!' (Revelation 18:6-7, 20). As one writer has put it, 'Edom and Babylon were the ancient examples of "Antichrist", as were Judas and false teachers in the early church'.[83] All these judgment passages are meant as warnings to us to submit to the Son before the awesome day of the Lord comes (Psalm 2:10-12) and the following psalm mentions kings who have humbly submitted and offered praise to God (Psalm 138:4-6). The Lord's Anointed tasted the worst that humans could do in the physical torture he endured on the cross but he also experienced the full cup of the Lord's wrath so that all who repent and put their trust in the Saviour might not endure that terrible and indescribable second death. It is the holy and righteous Jesus, the one appointed to be the final judge, who can be congratulated for righting all wrongs and punishing the enemies of God and his people.

Psalm 138

Earthly Kings Join the LORD's Anointed in Thanksgiving

We begin another series of psalms by 'David' (Psalms 138-145) before the final Hallelujahs (Psalms 146-150). This psalm is placed here appropriately after Psalms 135-137 for it expresses the thanksgiving that was encouraged in Psalm 136. In addition, by referring to the kings of the earth who will also give thanks (verses 4-6) the psalm provides a contrast to the punishments meted out to the nations intransigently opposed to God and his people (Psalm 137:7-9). This psalm that arose out of David's own circumstances is used by the final editor to the whole psalm collection to encourage praise and prayer among the returned exiles from Babylon. They still experienced many difficulties as David did but the psalm inspired hope and reassured them that the best was yet to be. Christians too are taught in this psalm to be wholehearted in giving thanks to God for his steadfast love and to have confidence in God concerning the future.

Personal thanksgiving (verses 1-3)

The psalm encourages the people to take up their instruments (see Psalm 137:2) and 'make music' ('sing praises') as they 'praise' or better give thankful testimony to God (see Psalms 7:17; 136:1). David pledges to give thanks:

- sincerely—'with my whole heart' (see Psalms 9:1; 119:2) means with one's whole being.
- boldly—'before the gods', that is, before the other deities that the nations worship (see Psalms 135:5, 15–18; 136:2–3) or the angelic beings that represent these nations (see Psalm 82:1).[84]
- reverently—'I will worship' (literally 'I will bow down'; see Psalm 29:2).
- biblically—'towards your holy temple' (see Psalm 5:7) as God had directed. Under the old covenant the people were to direct their prayers and worship toward the Jerusalem temple (see 1 Kings 8:48; Daniel 6:10). Though the temple was not built in David's time, the tabernacle was sometimes called God's temple (as in the Hebrew of 1 Samuel 1:9). It was David who brought the ark of the covenant into the tabernacle at Jerusalem and it was before the Lord in the tabernacle that David sat and gave thanks to God after receiving great promises concerning his royal descendants (2 Samuel 7:18). However, it may be the heavenly temple that David has in mind here (see Psalm 18:6). Since the coming of Christ and his once-for-all atoning sacrifice at Calvary the Jerusalem sanctuary has had its day (see John 4:20–26). We worship and give thanks, whether personally or communally by coming directly by faith into the heavenly temple through our great high priest and mediator Jesus Christ (Hebrews 10:12, 19–22).

Reasons for giving thanks (verse 2)

'Your loving-kindness and your truth' ('loving commitment and faithfulness')—two of God's great characteristics revealed to Moses (Exodus 34:6; but see Genesis 24:27) that frequently appear together, although the first is often translated 'mercy' (see Psalms 25:10; 40:11; 57:3).

'you have magnified your word above all your name'—God has made his word so great that it even surpasses the fame or reputation ('name') he already has. Perhaps David had in mind the amazing promises that God had given him in 2 Samuel 7 concerning his descendants on the throne of Israel. The inspired editor saw how particularly encouraging such words would have been to the post-exilic community recently returned from exile, with no prospect of being free of foreign rule or of a king of their own of Davidic descent. In Jesus Christ, who according to the flesh, is a descendant of David, God's promises have been wonderfully fulfilled, although we still await the grand consummation when the King will be seen in all his beauty (Isaiah 33:17).

'you answered me' (verse 3)—David testifies that God has heard his pleas for help and has come to his assistance by making him brave and strong.[85] God revitalised him in his hour of need. We think of the early church praying after being told by the Jewish authorities not to speak or teach any more in the name of Jesus. They included the words of Psalm 2 in their prayers and we are told that they were all filled afresh with the Spirit and 'spoke the word of God with boldness' (Acts 4:23–31).

Universal thanksgiving (verses 4–6)

King David's thankful testimony leads the way for other kings to follow his example. His influence on foreign nations and their kings is noted by the biblical historian. Hiram king of Tyre loved David and worshipped the Lord (1 Kings 5:1, 7). Other psalms speak of the nations coming to recognise and praise Israel's God (Psalms 22:27–28; 47:9; 72:10–11; 117:1), but only here do we find the prospect of kings from other nations giving thanks (where 'shall praise' in verse 4 is again 'confessing thanks'; see verse 1). They will acknowledge the 'Lord' (here for the first time in the psalm God is actually named), Israel's covenant-keeping God. Four times his special personal name is used in this short paragraph.

David is assured that these kings will confess the Lord when they hear God's 'words' (verse 4) including God's word and promises spoken of in verse 2. In Psalm 119: 46 the poet declares: 'I will speak of your testimonies also before kings, and will not be ashamed'. Personal testimony is helpful and encouraging but it is the words that proceed from the 'mouth' of God that are inerrant, authoritative and stand for ever (Deuteronomy 8:3; Isaiah 1:20; 40:5, 8). He speaks prophetically of the time when the nations of the world represented by their rulers will hear the gospel and will themselves 'sing' of God's saving 'ways' (verse 5; see Psalm 103:7). The good word of God sounded out from Jerusalem to reach the ends of the earth (Isaiah 2:3; Luke 24:46–47). God's words and ways reveal the 'glory', the stunning importance of the Lord. The Lord is great (Psalm 135:5) for 'great' is his glory.

We see 'his glory in a blaze'[86] in the person and redeeming work of Jesus. When the Word, who was with God and who was God, was made flesh, the apostle John declared, 'we beheld his glory, the glory as of the only begotten of the Father, full of grace and truth' (John 1:14; Isaiah 40:5; 60:1).

The kings are brought to see that it is the Lord who 'is on high' (verse 6). He and not the kings is 'the lofty one who inhabits eternity and whose name his holy' (Isaiah 57:15). Yet, though he is so high, kings and all who submit and 'kiss the Son', find that the Lord 'regards' (literally 'sees'), looks with favour and kindness on the 'lowly' (see Psalms 2:10-12; 136:23). As for the 'proud', they are known by God 'from afar'. He is very aware of whom these haughty people are but they have no personal relationship with him. They are kept at a distance. This was the theme of Hannah's prayer, echoes of which are found in Mary's praise psalm (1 Samuel 2:1-10; Luke 1:46-55; see Psalm 113:4-9). God dwells with those who are of a humble contrite spirit and revives them. The penitent tax collector was accepted rather than the self-righteous Pharisee and Jesus added, 'for everyone who exalts himself will be abased, and he who humbles himself will be exalted' (Luke 18:9-14).

Statement of trust (verses 7–8)

Beside the distressing situations that afflict the rest of humanity there are additional troubles that God's people must face. In this world, said Jesus to his disciples, 'you will have tribulation; but be of good cheer, I have overcome the world' (John 16:33).

David was aware of such times of distress and comforted himself in the sure knowledge that God cares for his people. His opening words remind us of his earlier testimony that though he walks through the dark valley where death lurks he will have no fear of evil for God is with him and will refresh and vindicate him in the presence of his enemies (Psalm 23:4-5). While walking through trouble and feeling the heat from the wrath of his enemies he is assured that God will preserve his life ('revive me') and stretch out that strong divine right hand to deliver him (see Psalms 30:3; 60:5; 71:20). It is a lovely picture like a father stretching out a hand to grasp his child who is in danger.

The real Davidic king, the Lord Jesus Christ, walked on earth amid distress, carrying our sorrows and bearing our sins. God revived him by raising him from the dead and setting him at his own right hand in glory. There he ever lives as our high priest who feels for his people in all their troubles and who by his Spirit comes to their aid to revive and grant deliverance from the power of their enemies including Satan their leader.

The first part of the final verse is difficult as the English versions show. Literally it reads: 'The LORD will bring to an end for me'. The same verb has appeared in Psalm 57:2 in a similar context and the words may be taken in two different ways—it could either be that God will complete the good purpose that he has for David and his descendants that would end with the coming of the Anointed One or that he will indeed bring to an end the troubles that David has faced. Either way the steadfast love of Israel's covenant-keeping God, the 'LORD', lasts for ever, reminding us of the refrain of Psalm 136.

A final plea urges God not to 'forsake' (literally 'to drop', 'to let fall') the works of his hands. This could mean that David, while confident of God's ability to bring all his troubles to an end, does not have a presumptuous spirit but appeals to God not to abandon his acts of deliverance (see 'works of your hands' in Psalms 92:4; 111:2, 6–7; 118:17). On the other hand, if David has in mind the completion of all God's purposes concerning him, he again does not take this for granted but urges God not to 'let go' his covenant people who can also be described as 'the work of my hands' (see Isaiah 60:21; 64:8). In the end both possible meanings result in the complete salvation that Christ has purchased and promised (see Romans 8:30; 1 Corinthians 15:51–53; Philippians 1:6). Such certainty does not make prayer superfluous; it encourages it. As Matthew Henry explains: David 'turns his expectation into a petition.'

Psalm 139

The God who Knows and Sees Everything

The writer to the Hebrews sums up the contents of this well-known prayer psalm: 'And there is no creature hidden from his sight, but all things *are* naked and open to the eyes of him to whom we *must give* account' (Hebrews 4:13). There is another New Testament text that must be considered alongside to indicate the relational aspect of God's knowledge: 'The Lord knows those who are his' (2 Timothy 2:19; see Psalm 1:6).

In this 'Psalm of David' belonging to the musical director's collection ('To the Chief Musician' see Psalm 4) it is not so much the 'intensely personal' nature of the psalm that stands out as the greatness of David's God, the 'LORD'. He is the living and true God who is all-knowing and everywhere present. It can be both a frightening and a reassuring truth. The passing reference to God's knowledge in the previous psalm (Psalm 138:6) becomes the key theme of this psalm, with the verb 'to know' or the noun 'knowledge' found six times with God as the subject (verses 1-2, 4, 6, 23) and once of David's knowledge (verse 14).

David begins by adoring the God who knows everything about him (verses 1-6), then indicates that there is nowhere he could go to escape

446

from God (verses 7–12) and supports these convictions by showing how God has been intimately involved in the origins and development of David's life from before birth and will continue to be into the future (verses 13–18). In view of this David takes his stand on God's side against all who are opposed to God and ends by surrendering himself to God's all-searching eye and by desiring to be guided by God (verses 19–24).

For the people newly returned from the Babylonian exile, this psalm along with the others in Book 5 would have served as a great encouragement as well as a searching and humbling challenge to remain faithful to God in the context of a world in rebellion against the Lord and his Anointed. Christians too, surrounded as we are by a hostile world that hates the God and Father of our Lord Jesus Christ, can find comfort but not complacency in this precious psalm.

God's knowledge is wonderful (verses 1–6)

The psalm begins where it ends and summarises the whole psalm—'O Lord, you have searched me and known me' (verse 1; see verse 23). It is addressed to Israel's covenant-keeping God, special to God's people from the time of the exodus (Exodus 3:13–14; 6:3; 34:5–7). Jesus is given this name which is above every name (Philippians 2:9–11; Isaiah 45:22–25).

The verb 'to search' speaks of a thorough investigation and this deep scrutiny resulted in knowing all there is to know about the psalmist (see Psalm 44:21). David, of course, is not implying that God was ignorant of him until he undertook a long and detailed examination like a medical specialist. It is David's way of vividly expressing the truth that God is all-knowing and therefore knows the thoughts and intentions of his own heart (see Jeremiah 12:3). God's knowledge when used with reference to his people must not be thought of as a cold, scientific-like knowledge but one that involves personal intimacy (Genesis 18:17–19).

His 'sitting' and 'rising' cover all of David's activities. Everything that he is involved in throughout his life and all his intentions are known and understood by God even though he dwells 'afar off' in heaven (verse 2; Psalm 138:6). God is associated with heaven, transcendent, high, reigning over his creation, but that does not mean he has no interest in his creation. Jeremiah makes clear that God is one who is near at hand as well as one who is far away (Jeremiah 23:23). Verse 3 presses home the truth of verse 2 using picture language. David's 'path' and his 'lying down' (literally his 'lair') have been thoroughly inspected. The verb translated 'comprehend' is literally 'scatter' and is used of sifting or winnowing in order to separate the grain from the chaff. God is also 'acquainted' or 'familiar' with all David's 'ways', with all he does (see Psalm 119:26). God knows us more intimately than we know ourselves.

Further truth is given in verse 4 to underline what has already been said. The Lord knows everything that David says as well as what he does. Words express thoughts and if thoughts do not escape him neither do words. So knowledgeable is God of his every word and action, it is as if David has been hemmed in by God on all sides. The word translated 'hedged' is used of a city 'besieged' (2 Samuel 11:1) or of items that need to be 'bound' (Ezekiel 5:3). David is also aware of God's hand over him. To someone who hates God this is an awful thought but for David it is awesome. Such divine knowledge is too wonderful for him; it is knowledge that belongs to God alone. This is the God who knows each one of us just as thoroughly as he knew David and what a comfort that is if we know God as our heavenly Father through Jesus his Son, our Saviour.

God's presence is inescapable (verses 7–12)

The idea of God's presence, suggested in verse 5 comes to prominence in these verses. Even if David wished to escape God's scrutiny, there was no place where he could hide. The greatest comparisons possible are mentioned: the heights of 'heaven' and the depths of 'Sheol' ('hell'; verse 8; see Psalm 6:5). If he could travel at the speed of the dawn ('the wings of the morning') to beyond the western horizon ('the uttermost parts of the sea', that is, the Mediterranean) and settle there (verse 9), it would make no difference. God by his powerful 'right hand' (see Psalm 74:11) would still be there to guide and support him (verse 10). One more hypothetical suggestion is presented. David reasons that even if darkness should 'cover' him ('fall on me', verse 11),[87] it would be daylight as far as God was concerned. Darkness makes no difference to God for to him darkness and light are the same (verse 12).[88]

Adam and Eve tried to hide among the trees from God's presence and Jonah tried to flee from the presence of the Lord by hiding in the hull of a ship bound in the opposite direction to where God had directed him to go (Genesis 3:8; Jonah 1:3). Only a guilty conscience would wish to evade God (Amos 9:2). The parallel expressions indicate the close relationship between God's 'presence' (literally 'face') and God's 'Spirit' (verse 7; see Psalm 51:11). It is by the Holy Spirit that God the Father and God the Son make their home in the life of the believer (John 14:15–18, 23).

God's creative work is marvellous (verses 13–18)

The God who knows and surrounds him and from whom there is no possibility of hiding is the God who has been involved in David's origins. He continues to address God and speaks of his 'inner parts' being 'formed' by God (verse 13).[89] David's 'inner parts' (literally 'kidneys'), translated 'reins' in the older English versions, often refers to the emotions or conscience (see Psalms 7:9; 26:2). In referring to being 'covered' (or better 'weaved', 'knitted together') he is speaking of the earliest stages of development in his mother's womb. God was not only active to create at the beginning of time but also specially concerned with each individual so that nothing is the result of chance happenings.

At this point David gives thanks to God ('praise'; see Psalm 136:1) as he contemplates these awesome things. He is himself a wonder ('wonderfully made'); he is a walking miracle! God's works are 'marvellous' (verse 14) and David fully acknowledges this. Modern scientific advancements in our understanding of the human body and pre-natal scans continue to testify to the amazement that David expresses. God's involvement in the development of the foetus should also make anyone contemplating terminating a pregnancy without good reason think twice about it.

Some of the terms found here express God's activity in delivering Israel from Egypt. God's regenerating, saving work in the life of a Christian should also move us to amazement and to thank God for his miraculous activity.

David returns in verse 15 to contemplate the way God was active in his embryonic development (see verse 13). The growth of his bodily 'frame' (literally 'bone') in the womb was not hidden from God's view. Until the invention of medical scanning machines it was impossible to observe the process that takes place in the secrecy of the womb. The 'lowest parts of the earth' parallels 'secret' and is another expression for the womb where the embryo was 'skilfully wrought' (literally 'weave') like an intricate piece of embroidery. Again, David emphasises that

God saw every aspect of his embryonic state ('my substance, being yet
unformed', verse 16; see Job 10:11).[90]

Medical science is only now catching up with what David goes on to
indicate in the second half of verse 16, that a person's life after birth is
already mapped out before birth in the very earliest stages of the baby's
existence (Job 14:5). Everything is written in God's 'book' (see Psalm
69:28). The whole life of David is all there in essence in its embryonic
state. While a number of scientists and philosophers are inclined to
believe in determinism and to minimise human responsibility, the
Bible teaches that while God has foreordained everything that happens
it stresses equally that people make their own decisions and God holds
them responsible for their actions.

For a second time (see verse 14), David is moved to adore the
'precious' or 'splendid' nature of God's thoughts (verse 17; see Psalm
36:7). These are the vast 'thoughts' that God has concerning the whole
of David's life. God knows David's thoughts (verse 2) but David cannot
begin to comprehend God's thoughts. To count the sum total would be
like counting the grains of sand on the seashore. What is more, when
David is asleep and not meditating on God, he is not separated from
God so that he can say 'when I awake, I am still with you' (verse 18).

Zeal for God (verses 19–24)
The sudden change of tone and subject is not as surprising as it might
seem. Having spent time contemplating the God who is not limited as
we are and who knows him better than he knows himself and who has
recorded the details of his life before he was born, David turns first to
those who oppose this God and then asks God to test his own sincerity.

Concern for God's honour (verses 19–22)
In this psalm there is no thought of enemies threatening his own
life. David is interested in God's honour not personal vindictiveness.
It is scandalous that wicked, murderous people exist. They are an
affront to God and he wishes them gone and to have no associations
with them (verse 19). These 'enemies' of God speak deceptively and
blasphemously, treating the LORD's holy character and reputation
with disdain (verse 20). David is totally opposed to those who 'rise up'
against God. He loathes and hates completely (which is the sense of
'perfect' in this context) these enemies of God whom he regards as his
enemies too (verses 21–22; see Psalm 5:8–10).

The Early Church theologian, Augustine of North Africa, noted that it is as God's enemies they can be hated for their wickedness but loved as human beings. David's hatred is the hatred that the holy God has for all opposition to his rule. The word 'hate' refers here to a settled active opposition. As the Old Testament scholar, E. J. Young, states, 'it proceeded from no evil emotion' and he comments further, 'Had David not hated, he would have desired the success of evil and the downfall of God Himself'.[91] These verses should be read along with those two introductory psalms that speak of the wicked and the hostile enemies of God and his Anointed (Psalms 1–2).

Calvin makes the point that we are quick to defend ourselves when others wrong us but 'are abundantly timid and cowardly in defending the glory of God'. At the same time he urges Christians to seek the good of all and if possible they are to be 'reclaimed by kindness'.

Concern for his personal sincerity (verses 23–24)

David returns to the thought with which he started and responds submissively to the reality that he has earlier described. He humbly invites the God who has searched and known him to search and know his 'heart', to know what is deep within him. 'The heart is deceitful above all things, and desperately wicked; who can know it?' states the Lord and then goes on to say, 'I, the LORD, search the heart, I test the mind ...' (Jeremiah 17:9–10; compare 11:20). David desires God to 'try' or 'test' him to know his 'anxieties' or 'disturbing concerns' (verse 23; see Psalm 94:19). How sincere is his own fervour for God? Is there a 'wicked way' in him? The word for 'wicked' (verse 24) is not the usual one but means 'pain' or 'hurt'. It suggests a way that is hurtful, that pains either God or people or both.

As he reveals in this prayer, David was no hypocrite. What about us? Is our own outward zeal for God a smoke-screen that hides secret sin, selfish motives and personal grudges? These are grievous to God, and Christians are urged not to grieve the Holy Spirit of God (Ephesians 4:30). We are encouraged to submit to God's all-searching eye.

The psalm ends with David asking God to guide him in the 'way everlasting' (verse 24). This expression, unique in the Old Testament, can be taken to mean that David is praying to be led in the old way, the good way that people like Abraham and Moses have followed in the past. God spoke through Jeremiah exhorting the people to 'Stand in the ways and see, and ask for the old paths, where the good way is and walk in it' (Jeremiah 6:16). But it is probably better to interpret the phrase as referring to the way that goes on into the future. It is the opposite to the way of the wicked that leads to destruction (see Psalm 1:6). This, in fact, is also the ancient way. It is 'the path of life' that leads to God's presence where there is fulness of joy and pleasures for evermore (Psalm 16:11). 'In the way of righteousness there is life, and in its pathway there is no death' (Proverbs 12:28; see Matthew 7:13–14). This is the way of God's good news in Jesus Christ. Repenting of our waywardness and hypocrisy we come with self-despairing trust to our Saviour who alone can lead us in the way everlasting.

Psalm 140

The LORD's Anointed
Prays for Deliverance

This is the last 'Psalm of David' that includes in its title 'To the Chief Musician' (see Psalms 4, 138–139) and good use is made of the 'Selah' that appears for the first time in this final Book of the psalm collection (verses 3, 5, 8; see Psalm 3). As in the two previous psalms in this series by David trouble from his enemies who are also God's enemies (Psalms 138:7; 139:22) is never far away and it rises to the surface once more in this psalm. There were many occasions when violent and wicked people were determined to be rid of David. He was the LORD's anointed whom God loved and David in turn loved his Lord. In all his trials and sufferings he is depicted as a type of our Lord Jesus and also of all the persecuted who are united by faith to Christ. In every distressing experience and trouble of life Christians are encouraged by this psalm 'to carry everything to God in prayer'.

Again, as we have seen in all the psalms of Book 5, these songs and prayers provided the Jews who had returned home after the Babylonian exile with expressions of confidence in the Lord despite severe provocation from those who hated them. Psalms like this one also provided Paul with biblical support for his contention that all humanity stands condemned before God (see verse 3 and Romans 3:13).

Prayer for deliverance (verses 1–5)

The opening call is typical of David's prayers for help (see Psalm 6:4). He prays to be rescued and 'preserved' from these exceptionally 'violent' and 'evil' men (verse 1) who secretly plan evil things and continually stir up war. While the tongue can be sharpened like a sword (Psalm 64:3) it can also be like the venomous snake's forked tongue (see Psalm 58:4). A pause of some kind is suggested by the 'Selah' at the end of verse 3 before the second appeal to the 'Lord' begins in verses 4 and 5, after which there is another pause.

He prays similarly, as in verse 1, for God to 'keep' and 'preserve' him from the clutches of these exceptionally 'violent' people who are now equated with the 'wicked'. They want to see him 'thrown down' (see Psalm 118:13; the original suggests something stronger than 'stumble'). These evil people, described also as 'proud' or 'arrogant', have tried to trap David like a hunter with snares and nets.

The enemies of God's people will use all kinds of devices as they seek to destroy God's people. It was especially obvious in the lengths to which the opponents of Jesus went to trap him (Mark 12:13). Paul writes of death-like experiences from which the Lord delivered him and he could testify at the end of his life that he experienced deliverance from 'the mouth of the lion', which may be a veiled reference to Caesar, and that 'the Lord will deliver me from every evil work and preserve me for his heavenly kingdom' (2 Corinthians 1:10; 2 Timothy 4:17–18).

Profession of confidence (verses 6–8)

As he makes a further appeal to God to hear his prayer for grace ('supplications'; see Psalm 28:2), he does so in the confident knowledge that the 'Lord' (Yahweh/Jehovah; translated 'God' in verse 7), the covenant God of Israel, is his God (verse 6; see Psalms 16:2; 31:14). He has a personal relationship with the one whom he also reveres as the sovereign 'Lord' (verse 7) who is described in this unique way as his strong deliverer ('the strength of my salvation'). He gives an example of what he means. When he had all the necessary armour for battle (literally 'the day of weapons') it was God who 'covered' his unprotected head. David was able to strike Goliath at his most vulnerable point which was his forehead (1 Samuel 17:49). Paul uses the imagery of the soldier to describe the Christian's spiritual armour in the war against the devil and his evil forces (Ephesians 6:10–17).

The greatest weapon that God's servants have is prayer, as Paul knew when he asked the Thessalonians to pray for him and his fellow companions that the gospel might spread freely and that they 'may be delivered from unreasonable and wicked men; for not all have faith' (2 Thessalonians 3:1-2; see Ephesians 6:18-20). David likewise prays that the evil desires and plans of the wicked will not succeed (verse 8). 'The weapons of our warfare', declared Paul, 'are not carnal but mighty in God for pulling down strongholds, casting down arguments and every high thing that exalts itself against the knowledge of God, bringing every thought into captivity to the obedience of Christ and being ready to punish all disobedience when your obedience is fulfilled' (2 Corinthians 10:4-6).

Prayer for justice (verses 9–11)

In David's concern for justice to be done, he does not take personal vengeance but, as God through Moses had made clear (Deuteronomy 32:35), he leaves it for God to punish the wicked. David uses vivid imagery that picks up some of the language of verse 5 to make the point that the retribution to fall on the enemy will be just and appropriate. What the enemy planned for David they will experience (see Psalm 35:7-8). Paul was similarly harassed by those who wished to harm him. Alexander the coppersmith was one such person and Paul left it to the Lord to 'repay him according to his works' (2 Timothy 4:14).

Profession of faith (verses 12–13)

Like his 'I said' of verse 6, his 'I know' is a statement of confidence that God will hear and rescue him. What he has prayed for in verses 9–11 is expressed in legal terms as God's policy toward those who are poor and needy—he 'gives justice' ('maintain the cause') and 'right decisions' ('justice', verse 12; see Psalm 9:4). Like David the 'afflicted' (or 'poor') and 'poor' ('needy') are not necessarily materially impoverished but represent the devout, persecuted people of God who have that humble spirit enabling them to look to God for help (see Psalm 9:18; Matthew 5:3; Luke 6:20).

As the wicked are described at the beginning of the psalm in different ways (verses 1, 4), so now at the close the humble poor can also be termed the 'righteous' and 'upright' (see Psalms 1:5-6; 7:10; 32:11). They can stand upright in God's presence for God has accepted them.

Already the godly can give thanks and sit in God's presence because of Christ's victory on the cross over the dark powers of evil but there is a final day coming when they will be delivered out of all their troubles and will give thanks and confess his name and dwell in his presence for ever (see Psalms 23:6; 27:4).

Psalm 141

The LORD's Anointed Prays when Tempted and Threatened

This 'Psalm of David' reminds us of the prayer Jesus taught his disciples when he included the words 'Lead us not into temptation but deliver us from the evil one' (Matthew 6:13). It has a number of similarities to the previous psalm where the wicked lay traps for the godly and David prays that he will be rescued and that his enemies will fall into their own nets. However, in this psalm David is also aware of how easy it is to be influenced by the thinking and actions of the wicked and prays that he himself will be kept from behaving in a similar way.

As the leader of his people, the prayer psalm is also on behalf of the covenant community and, as with the previous psalms of Book 5, brought warning as well as encouragement to God's people newly returned from exile in Babylon. Christians too are shown the importance of being alert as well as prayerful. We are to seek God's help in guarding our own speech and in taking refuge in our God who has promised never to leave or abandon us.

Cry of help (verses 1–2)

In deep distress David calls on the covenant God of Israel to hurry

457

to his aid (verse 1). The expressions used are familiar from earlier psalms (see Psalms 4:1; 22:19; 38:22; 40:13). He sees his prayer as 'incense' smoke rising from the altar (Exodus 30:7-8; Leviticus 2:2) and the 'lifting up' of his hands, a gesture that accompanied heartfelt prayer (Psalms 28:2; 63:4; 1 Timothy 2:8), as an 'evening sacrifice'. Animals were sacrificed on a daily basis, morning and evening (Exodus 29:38-42), and maybe this prayer was first offered in the evening, just as David's prayer in Psalm 5:3 is associated with the morning (see also Psalm 88:13). We find Daniel's great intercessory prayer was offered at the time of the evening offering (Daniel 9:21; see also Ezra 9:5). In Psalm 55:17 David speaks of praying three times—evening, morning and midday—and this had been Daniel's custom in exile (Daniel 6:10). The apostle John, in his vision of the Lamb with the scroll, sees 'golden bowls full of incense, which are the prayers of the saints' (Revelation 5:8).

Prayer to remain loyal (verses 3–6)

The verbs 'to keep' ('guard') and 'to preserve' ('keep watch') are used in the previous psalm (Psalm 140:1, 4) as David pleads to be rescued from his wicked enemies and their evil talk. Here he is praying that he will be kept from falling into the ways of his foes (verse 3; see Psalm 140:3, 9). How easy it is to follow evil influences! Proverbs has much to say on watching what we say (Proverbs 13:3; 21:23; see also Psalms 34:13; 39:1; James 3:1-12) and the prophet Micah uses a similar phrase to guarding the door of one's lips but in a different context (Micah 7:5).

David is aware that it is from the heart that the mouth speaks and wicked works are hatched so he prays that God would help him deal with his innermost being. Jesus said that it is what 'comes out of a man, that defiles a man. For from within, out of the heart of men, proceed evil thoughts' and evil actions (Mark 7:15-23). David is aware that to sit down at table with those who 'work iniquity' is dangerous to his own moral and spiritual well-being. Partaking of their 'delicacies' suggests much more than ordinary interaction with ungodly people (see Daniel 1:5-16). It implies joining in their activities and becoming 'one of the boys' (see Psalm 1:1). Peer pressure to conform can be difficult to resist. Paul warns the Corinthian believers not to be unequally yoked together with unbelievers and to flee from idolatry and immoral practices (1 Corinthians 6:18; 10:14; 2 Corinthians 6:14-16).

He is willing to receive discipline from a righteous friend even if it hurts. Such a wake-up call would be a 'kindness' (an act of 'faithful love'). This is reminiscent of the wisdom words: 'Rebuke a wise man, and he will love you' and 'Faithful are the wounds of a friend' (Proverbs 9:8; 27:6) David welcomes rebuke as a blessing in the same way as a person welcomes festive oil (verse 5; Psalms 23:5; 104:15). The apostle Paul was forced to rebuke his fellow apostle Peter when he was in the wrong for confining his table fellowship to Jewish believers (Galatians 2:11–12). After that incident Peter was still able to call him 'our beloved brother Paul' (2 Peter 3:15). Christians, including church leaders, need to have the grace and humility to receive discipline and the wisdom and grace to give it when needed.

It is difficult to work out the meaning of verse 6 but it must be viewed in the context of David's prayer 'against the deeds of the wicked' (literally 'against their evil deeds', verse 5). Only when the wicked 'judges' who make bad decisions are themselves judged by being thrown by the sides of the rock (see Psalm 137:9), will they find out to their cost how 'sweet' David's words were. The wording, as in Psalm 137, may be metaphorical for being permanently removed from office but we know in Jesus' case there was an attempt to punish him for his words by literally throwing him down a cliff (Luke 4:29; see also 2 Chronicles 25:12).

Cry for help (verses 7–10)

Michael Wilcock[92] helpfully shows how the psalm is about the spoken word and he considers the contents under the headings of 'urgent words' (verses 1–3, 7–10), 'guarded words' (verse 4) and 'well-spoken words' (verses 5–6). The final verses return to the urgent appeal of David's opening words. He seeks protection from the snares of sinful people and prays for action against them.

David, speaking for all God's people by the introduction of 'our' in verse 7,[93] indicates in graphic picture language how they have been brought to death's door. They are like people whose bones are scattered, like clods broken up by the farmer's plough, which is similar to Ezekiel's imagery (Ezekiel 37).

In this death-like situation for David and his people, and understood perfectly by those who had been exiles in Babylon, he looks up to God and seeks refuge in his time of need (see Psalm 25:15). He prays for God's protection from the 'workers of iniquity' who are out to catch him like an animal or bird. The picture of 'snares', 'traps' and 'nets' is similar to the previous psalm (Psalm 140:5). He prays that he will escape safely (literally 'while I shall pass by') while his opponents all fall into their own nets (see Psalms 9:15–16; 57:6).

The enemies of God's people cannot win in the end. Though Satan and his disciples seek to harm them their time is short. Our Saviour, Jesus Christ, who himself experienced the kinds of temptations and troubles that David endured only to a deeper and greater extent, has already judged the prince of this world at the cross. While all God's enemies will eventually fall and perish, God's people will triumph with the Saviour to all eternity.

Psalm 142

The LORD's Anointed
Prays when Lonely

There are sad people in the world who are full of self-pity and complain that no one cares when in fact if they only stopped to think and look around there are family and friends who take an interest in them and do what they can for them although they are often not appreciated. David's expressions of loneliness are not of that self-centred nature. Like Psalms 140 and 141, this prayer is aware of those who have 'set a snare' (verse 3) for him but, unlike in the previous two, persecution by strong opponents have brought him to a position where he is imprisoned and no one cares.

The heading to this psalm is the only one in Book 5 to indicate where the 'Prayer' was composed—'in the cave' (see Psalm 57). Spurgeon adds this comment, 'Caves make good closets for prayer; their gloom and solitude are helpful to the exercise of devotion. Had David prayed as much in his palace as he did in his cave, he might never have fallen into the act which brought such misery upon his later days.'

It seems the occasion was the time before he became king when he was on his own, fleeing from Saul who was out to kill him. David does not wallow in self-pity but indicates where he finds relief. The heading describes this as 'A Contemplation of David' (see Psalm 32). It is part of

461

the psalm collection with the object of instructing us in prayer and this psalm did that for the Jews after their return from exile in Babylon, still persecuted and vulnerable, and feeling imprisoned by foreign powers. It also was there for Jesus as he meditated on its contents during his lonely experiences with enemies maligning him and seeking his destruction, and with family and friends who did not understand him. As Christians we can learn from this prayer in those situations when we are ostracised for our faith.

A feature of this psalm is the way it employs the phraseology of other psalms or more likely this psalm has been an inspiration in the formation of the other psalms. It encourages us to use the words of Scripture in our praying. As God speaks to us as we read his Word so we can use his Word back to him in prayer.

Announcement (verses 1-2)
David tells us how he will call out to the 'LORD', the God of the covenant (see Psalm 77:1). He was in a personal relationship with God so he knew where to go in time of need. To the LORD he makes his 'supplication' or his prayer for God's grace (Psalm 30:8). His 'complaint' (literally 'murmuring' often translated 'meditation') to God he says 'I pour out' (see Psalms 42:4; 62:8). As God's people have done in every age he will declare before God his 'trouble' (Psalms 77:2; 107:6, 13, 19, 28). Jesus did the same in his distress especially in the Garden of Gethsemane and the Church in its earliest days poured out its concerns in the face of persecution (Acts 4:24-31; 12:5, 12).

Prayer of assurance and distress (verses 3-4)
Speaking directly to God, David is assured that God knew his situation ('my path') when he was 'exhausted' or 'faint' ('overwhelmed', verse 3; Psalm 77:3). A similar phrase is used by Jonah in his prayer to God (Jonah 2:7). David's enemies have set a trap for him to fall into but he expects God to see that he has no one at his right hand to give him support (Psalm 109:31). He has no one who 'acknowledges' or recognises him as a friend (see Ruth 2:10). In addition, he has no 'place of escape' ('refuge'; see Psalm 59:17) and 'no one cares' about his life. The implication is that he is looking to the Lord to care for him and to be at his right hand and his refuge. David's desolate state prefigures the sufferings of Christ on behalf of his people.

Appeal to God to hear and act (verses 5–7)

From his vulnerable, lonely position, David cries out in his need to the covenant Lord, 'You are my refuge' (verse 5; Psalms 14:6; 46:1). It encourages Christians in every trial and difficult situation to call out with confidence to God in this way. God is David's 'portion in the land of the living', meaning that for David God was everything to him in this life as well as beyond the grave (see Psalms 16:5; 73:26; 119:57). Possessing the Lord was far more important than inheriting a piece of land in Canaan. God not land was David's security. Spurgeon remarks, 'There is no living in the land of the living like living upon the living God.'

In his low condition David calls out to God to listen to his cries as he prays to be delivered from his 'persecutors' ('pursuers'), like Saul and his men who keep on pursuing him (1 Samuel 24:14). In David's psalm of praise after he had been delivered from all his enemies including Saul, he used the same language, speaking of God having delivered him 'from my strong enemy, from those who hated me; for they were too strong for me' (2 Samuel 22:18; Psalm 18:17).

In his closing words, David pleads that God would bring him out of his prison-like situation in the cave where he is confined. He longs to be let out so that he might give thanks ('praise'; see Psalm 136:1) to God. Instead of having enemies 'surround' him, who are described in an earlier psalm like strong bulls of Bashan (Psalm 22:12), he will have the 'righteous' around him hearing his testimony of how God has dealt 'bountifully' with him (see Psalms 13:6; 116:7). To 'deal bountifully' is sometimes translated 'rewarded' or 'recompensed' and this word also occurs in David's hymn of praise at the end of 2 Samuel (2 Samuel 22:21; see Psalm 18:20).

The Christ, David's descendant, was rescued from even stronger persecutors and from a greater confinement than was ever experienced by David. He was brought out from death and exalted to God's right hand and now is surrounded by the spirits of the righteous who die in the Lord. All the strong forces of evil and darkness that seek to persecute God's people cannot overcome those who belong to Jesus Christ. Those brought out from that death in trespasses and sins (see Isaiah 42:7) and made alive in Christ will also be raised bodily to live and reign with Christ in the glory of the new creation.

Psalm 143

The Lord's Anointed Prays in a Crisis

This is the sixth in the series of psalms attributed to 'David' (see Psalms 138-145). The ancient Greek translation adds a note to the heading claiming that it was written when the king was being pursued by his son Absalom. There is no other evidence for this and the psalm is more likely to have arisen around the same time as the previous one, when David was being hunted by Saul. The psalm is closely linked to Psalm 142 with the same vocabulary re-appearing— 'supplication(s)' (verse 1; Psalm 142:1), 'spirit overwhelmed within me' (verse 4; Psalm 142:3), 'persecuted' or 'persecutors' (verse 3; Psalm 142:6), 'deliver' (verse 9; Psalm 142:5-6). Augustine of Hippo in North Africa (AD 354-430) had no doubt that in viewing David's life we see 'another David ... even our Lord Jesus Christ'.

While the Early Church considered this psalm to be the last of the seven penitential psalms (see Psalm 6), Luther regarded it as the fourth and final 'Pauline Psalm' (see Psalm 130). Both Luther and the Early Church Fathers were thinking particularly of verse 2 with its statement about universal guilt and Paul's use of the text in Romans and Galatians as he teaches justification by faith alone and not on the basis of human works.

This prayer psalm is in two parts with the last 'Selah' of the psalm collection and indicating in this context the end of the first part (verse

464

6). David, the LORD's 'servant' (verses 2, 12), after urging God to hear his cries, first of all describes his situation, recollects God's past works and confesses his longing for God before presenting, in the second half of the psalm, eleven fervent pleas. For the people living back in their homeland after the exile it presented them with encouragements to pray to God despite their failures. They are urged to do so with a penitent spirit looking to the Lord for forgiveness and help in all their difficult situations. It acts similarly for God's people today as we recognise our dependence on God's grace alone and seek him in all our trials to direct our path and deliver us from all our foes.

The lament (verses 1-6)

Before presenting the dire situation in which he finds himself, David first calls on his covenant LORD to listen to his prayer and supplications (or better, his pleas for God's grace; see Psalm 142:1). The opening expressions are often heard as introductions to prayer psalms (Psalms 5:1; 17:1) Though God is more ready to hear than we are to call on him, we cannot take him for granted but are to approach him humbly as Abraham did, recognising that we are 'dust and ashes' and are coming to the sovereign Lord of the universe (Genesis 18:27, 31). Casual, glib requests are just as offensive to him as sanctimonious prayers.

David's appeal (verse 2)

He appeals to God's character as he seeks God to act on his behalf. God's 'faithfulness' means he can be trusted and will therefore carry out the promises he has made. His 'righteousness' means that God will always act according to his own upright standard (see Psalm 36:5-6). He then introduces in verse 2 a request not heard before in these laments. Often in psalms of this nature where enemies are out to destroy him, David declares his innocence (see Psalms 17:3-4; 26:1-6). There were occasions when he was persecuted by enemies who maligned him for no good reason and like Job he insisted that he was innocent of the sins of which he was accused.

In this prayer, David is aware of his own sinful nature and the appeal arises out of what he has said in verse 1. He is pleading not on the basis of his own righteous deeds for he realises that they are but filthy rags in God's sight (Isaiah 64:6). He has no merit or works of his own by which he could expect God to accept and answer his requests. Daniel likewise appealed to God's righteousness not to his or his people's righteousness (Daniel 9:16, 18).

David, as God's 'servant' (see verse 12), pleads that he will not be dealt with in strict justice. He confesses that according to God's own righteous character, for he is the ultimate and perfect standard for what is right, 'no one living is righteous' (verse 2; see Psalms 14:2–3; 130:3). His law reveals that standard and we all fall short. By God's law we are guilty and condemned (Romans 3:19–20; 1 Corinthians 15:56; Galatians 2:16). Solomon in his prayer of dedication acknowledged the complementary truth that there is 'no one who does not sin' (1 Kings 8:46). If God acted toward us on the basis of justice no one would be accepted by him, all would be condemned.

We are not acquitted by God and pardoned of all our sins on the basis of our works or even on the basis of our works plus God's grace but solely through God's unmerited favour (Romans 3:23–24, 28; Titus 3:7). However, God has acted in faithfulness and righteousness through his gift of righteousness in Jesus Christ (Philippians 3:9).

David's concerns (verses 3–6)

The reason for David's opening call to God in verse 1 is because ('For') he is being pursued ('persecuted') by an enemy who has 'crushed' him to the ground and made him live in darkness as if he were in the realm of the dead (verse 3; see Lamentations 3:6). As in the previous psalm he describes how his 'spirit is overwhelmed' (or 'faints') within him (Psalm 142:3) and his inner being is 'distressed' or 'appalled' (see Psalm 40:15). The description of his circumstances may be a vivid way of referring to the darkness of the cave where he was forced to live (see the heading to Psalm 142).

As often in prayers of this nature, David recollects God's past actions (see Psalms 44:1–3; 77:5) which give hope that he will act again in the present crisis. The wording is similar to Asaph's psalm with the three verbs 'remember', 'meditate' (see Psalm 1:2) and 'muse' (or 'talk') all re-appearing (Psalm 77: 11–12). To 'spread out' or 'stretch out' the hands in prayer symbolises David's dependence on God (see Psalms 44:20; 88:9). He further confesses his longing for God, again in language reminiscent of other psalms (Psalm 63:1; see Psalm 42:1–2).

Though he deserves to be pursed to death if God acts according to strict justice David appeals to his covenant-keeping God to be merciful and to act on his behalf according to his faithful, righteous character (compare Psalm 7:4–5). The 'Selah' brings the first part of his prayer to a close (see Psalm 3:2).

The pleas (verses 7–12)

Arising out of his knowledge of the LORD's past mercies, these eleven petitions express the urgency of his need and his confidence that God will respond. They also indicate that his first concern was not deliverance from trouble but a longing for God which accords with his confession of verse 6.

1. 'Answer me speedily' (verse 7)—He urges God to be quick in answering his petition for his 'spirit fails' (A similar expression is found in Psalm 84:2).

2. 'Do not hide your face from me'—He seeks to know God's gracious presence or else he will be as good as dead. The 'pit' often stands for death under God's wrath (see Psalms 28:1; 88:4). Both these petitions in verse 8 have appeared earlier (see Psalms 69:17; 102:2).

3. 'Cause me to hear your loving-kindness' (verse 8)—While other psalms speak of proclaiming God's faithful love 'in the morning', David wants God to speak to him of it at that time. The morning came to signify the prospect of fresh hope and deliverance (Psalms 46:5; 59:16; 92:2). God's 'loving-kindness' ('loving commitment') is the assurance that God will not let his servant down but that he will come to his aid for his 'trust' is in God (see Psalm 9:10).

4. 'Cause me to know the way in which I should walk'—David now pleads for God's guidance. It is one of the important prayers of Psalm 119 that God's way might be known. Again, his plea comes from a desire for God—'I lift up my soul to you' (see Psalms 25:1; 86:4).

5. 'Deliver me' (verse 9)—It is from such desires for God that he calls out to his covenant God, 'LORD', to be rescued from his enemies (see Psalm 59:1). As in verse 8 another expression of confidence follows in which he confesses that he has taken cover in the LORD—'in you I take shelter' (literally 'to you I have covered').

6. 'Teach me' (verse 10)—is a familiar desire in Psalm 119 (Psalm 119:12) and Psalm 25:4–5 utters a similar prayer that David would do God's good pleasure ('will') which he reveals to his servants

(see Psalm 40:8). Again, he confesses his covenant relationship to
God—'you are my God' (see Psalms 31:14; 40:5).

7. 'Lead me'—The phrase, 'Your Spirit is good', is probably better
   read as part of the plea: 'Let your good Spirit lead me'. The prayer
   of the people in the days of Ezra and Nehemiah gives voice to
   a similar expression: 'You also gave your good Spirit to instruct
   them' (Nehemiah 9:20). The dangers of life are likened to uneven
   ground and David prays that God's good Spirit will lead him
   in a 'land of uprightness'. An almost identical phrase occurs
   elsewhere for the desert 'table-land' or 'plateau' (Deuteronomy
   4:43; see Jeremiah 48:21), so that David might be using it in a
   figurative sense for 'level ground' (see similar thoughts in Psalms
   26:12; 27:11).

8. 'Revive me' (verse 11)—This is another desire common to Psalm
   119 (Psalm 119:25). David prays that he will be given fresh life or
   restored to life from the death-like situation he finds himself
   in (see verses 3–4; Psalm 138:7). It is not for his own sake or for
   anything that David has merited that he prays but for the sake of
   his covenant God ('Lord'; see verses 1–2).

9. 'Bring my soul out of trouble'—shows again the close link with
   the previous psalm (Psalm 142:2). Referring to God's covenant
   name in the first half of verse 11, leads David to appeal to God's
   'righteousness' which he mentions at the beginning of the psalm
   (verse 1).

10. 'Cut off my enemies' (verse 12)—He prays on the basis of God's
    revealed character, his 'loving commitment' toward him ('in your
    mercy'), that his enemies will be destroyed (see Psalm 18:40).

11. 'Destroy all those who afflict my soul'—In the context of God's
    covenant promises, those who 'oppress' ('afflict') God's people
    are to be eradicated. For David to pray that his troubles may be
    removed will naturally involve the destruction of his enemies.
    Calling for an end to his persecutors is not a desire for personal
    revenge but for God's justice to be established. His final plea
    draws attention to his 'servant' position before God (see verse 2).
    While this does indicate a lowly status it also means he can count
    on his Master's protection (see Psalm 116:16).

As God's servants, Christians can hold God to his promises for
protection and deliverance from their enemies. Until God's time for us
to be removed from this earthly scene we can pray similar prayers with

confidence as we seek God for himself so that we might have this rich relationship with him.

George Horne, an 18th century clergyman, following Paul's example, used this psalm in a spiritual way. He saw it not only as a prayer for pardon that acknowledges the impossibility of being justified except by grace alone, but as a pointer to the gravity of our position in sin. To rescue us sinners, our Saviour was himself forsaken on the cross, his spirit overwhelmed and appalled and his body laid out in the darkness of the grave. We stretch out our hands to the one whose hands were stretched out in love for us upon the cross and experienced the removal of God's gracious presence. The penitent believer prays to be delivered from the evil one and to be directed in a way that is pleasing to God through the influences of the Holy Spirit and eventually brought out of all trouble to triumph finally with our Saviour in the glory of the new creation when all God's enemies will have been removed.

Psalm 144

The Song of the Servant-King

While all four of the previous psalms may well have been originally composed before David took the throne of Israel, when he was pursued from cave to cave by Saul, this one relates to a later period when, as king, he was in trouble from foreign attack. It has many links with David's song of thanksgiving for deliverance from all his enemies including Saul (Psalm 18) but this psalm also includes a prayer for deliverance.

Many Christians are concerned by the wars and bloodshed that figure so prominently in the Old Testament. Why does the Bible give so much space to it and why do psalms like this one seem to encourage fighting as we see from the very first verse? The early chapters of Genesis give us an important clue. When our first parents sinned as a result of the snake's temptation, God passed sentence on the devil-possessed snake and all those who would follow him. As he did so he made an announcement about a war that will rage in this world. God instigated this war when he said to the snake, 'I will put enmity between you and the woman and between your seed and her seed ...' (Genesis 3:15). The woman's seed or descendants include all God's people and the snake's seed includes not only evil spirits but humans who are in the power of the Evil One. One descendant of the woman's in particular will engage the snake himself in battle and 'though two had wounds, there conquered One—And Jesus was his name', as the hymn-writer so powerfully puts it.[94]

The setting apart of Israel was with a view to the coming of the Saviour of the world. Israel's battles against her pagan neighbours were symbolic of this deeper spiritual battle but at the same time expressed the demonic antagonism toward God and the people he had chosen to be a light to the nations. It all comes to a head in Jesus, who is the seed of the woman who bruises Satan's head. He who was God in the flesh was despised and rejected. Jew and Gentile, the religious and secular authorities, all clubbed together to put him to death. But by his cross and resurrection Christ triumphs. Jesus paid the penalty for his people's sins, he redeemed them to God by his blood and gained the victory over the snake and his hold over humanity in sin. The devil, though decisively defeated, still makes war with Christ's people. Unlike under the old covenant, new covenant warfare is not fleshly but entirely spiritual. We do battle not against flesh and blood but against spiritual wickedness in the heavenlies. We are called to fight the good fight of faith and win the nations for Christ not with earthly weapons but with the armour that God supplies.

For the people living back in their own land after the Babylonian exile, still under foreign rule with no king of David's line in Jerusalem, this psalm like all the ones in this final Book 5 encouraged them to look with confidence to the God who rules over all. The post-exilic community could identify with the 'foreigners' and their empty words (verses 7, 11; see Ezra 4; Nehemiah 4–6). But it kept alive the hope that God would bring to a grand climax the promises he had made to David (verses 9–10) and set up the future idyllic situation for Zion of which the prophets also spoke (verses 12–15; see Isaiah 2:1–4; Amos 9:11–15; etc.).

David begins his prayer by focusing on God, his defender and the giver of stability while humans, who are so full of themselves, are shown to be transient (verses 1–4). He prays for deliverance from present dangers and his confidence in ultimate success is seen in his song of praise (verses 5–10). A further plea is made on behalf of himself and his people as he looks with expectation to future peace and stability (verses 11–15).

Honouring the LORD (verses 1–2)

David prepares for prayer by worshipping God. 'Blessed' implies bending the knee in submission and respect. The opening lines recall verses from Psalm 18. The Lord is described as his 'Rock' (Psalm 18:46; see Deuteronomy 32:4) who grants success in battle by giving skill to the soldier's hands and fingers ('trains my hands for war ...' (verse 1; Psalm 18:34). The battle is the Lord's (1 Samuel 17:47; 2 Chronicles 20:15-17). In one sense his people do nothing to win the battle but at the same time he gives his servants the equipment and help to gain the victory (see Ephesians 6:10-20).

All David's descriptions of God in verse 2 are found in Psalm 18:2 apart from this unique title 'my loving-kindness' ('steadfast love'). God not only provides protection but he is committed to David by a loving bond (see Psalm 59:10, 17) so that God's people are brought in submission under his rule. At first the northern tribes of Israel looked to one of Saul's sons but eventually submitted to David who then reigned over 'all Israel' (2 Samuel 5:1-5; see Psalm 18:47). In this David becomes a type of the Messiah, where God's people of all nations come under the rule of King Jesus (see Psalms 18:43; 72:8).

Human insignificance (verses 3–4)

In view of God's greatness and his goodness toward him, David is staggered as he thinks of himself as a frail human being with a fleeting existence. He is about to pray to God for help yet he comes not from a position of arrogant over-confidence but as a humble suppliant. Similar sentiments are found in Psalm 89:47-48 but in that psalm they appear as part of the psalmist's appeal for God to show his steadfast love and keep his promises at a time when the Babylonians had put an end to the Davidic rule.

The opening words, 'LORD, what is man ...?', remind us of Psalm 8 which also expresses astonishment that God should pay attention to mere mortals. Why should God bother with David? His statement about humanity's transitory nature is not new. He makes a similar point in Psalm 39:4-6 and it is emphasised by the Preacher of Ecclesiastes, where the word 'vanity' is literally 'breath' as here (Ecclesiastes 6:12; 8:13). James 4:14 also states: 'What is your life? It is even a vapour (or 'breath') that appears for a little time and then vanishes away'. David does not take what he has said in the first two verses for granted. As John Kent (1766-1843) wrote, *Say, while lost in holy wonder, 'Why, O Lord, such love to me?' Hallelujah! Grace shall reign eternally.*[95]

Psalm 8:4 is applied to Jesus by the writer to the Hebrews (Hebrews 2:6) and we do well to reflect on the truth that our Lord humbled himself by taking frail flesh and died the death of the cross to gain the victory over the dark powers of evil that God's people might see Satan under their feet.

Praying for divine intervention (verses 5–8)

David now calls on God to act and he uses language reminiscent of God's presence at Mount Sinai when the mountain smoked and the lightning flashed (verses 5–6; Exodus 19:18–19). What he is able to thank God for doing in Psalm 18 he prays that he will do against his present enemy (verse 6; see Psalm 18:14). It is significant that his trust is not in his own weapons to scatter and defeat the foe but in his covenant-keeping God, the 'LORD' (verse 5). The picture language David uses changes in verse 7 as he calls on God to 'stretch out' his hand from heaven to 'rescue' ('snatch away') and 'deliver' him 'out of great waters' (see Psalm 18:16). It is only at the end of verse 7 that specific mention is made of the enemy whom he describes in verse 8 as a deceptive, strong, foreign foe. It may be that the reference to the 'right hand' of the enemy has in mind the raising of the right hand in swearing an oath (Deuteronomy 32:40). This alien enemy's activity belies the tokens of truthfulness. It reminds us of the great enemy of God's people whom Jesus described as a liar from the beginning and the father of lies (John 8:44).

Singing God's praises (verses 9–10)

Anticipating the victory that God will bring about, David promises to sing 'a new song' to God (verse 9; see Psalm 33:2–3). This could mean a new composition in view of an amazing deliverance (see Isaiah 42:10) but it could equally well be a graphic way of indicating an enthusiastic response as they celebrate with the music of a 'ten-stringed harp' God's triumph over the enemy. At the end of this present world order, such a song will be sung to celebrate the defeat of all evil and sin as a result of the Lamb's redeeming work (Revelation 5:9–10).

In speaking of God's 'salvation to kings' (verse 10), David makes a general statement that applies to the whole line of kings who would follow the Lord in the way that David did, before referring particularly to 'David, his servant', who prefigures the future Messiah (1 Kings 15:3, 5, 11; 2 Kings 14:3; etc.; Jeremiah 30:9; 33:15; Ezekiel 34:23–24; Hosea 3:5).

God 'delivers' (literally 'snatch away', 'set free'; and also found in verses 7 and 11) 'from the deadly (literally 'evil') sword' (see Psalm 22:20).

Our Saviour, of David's family line, gained the victory over the great enemy of God and his people at Calvary's cross. In the language of John, he was 'caught up to God and his throne' at his resurrection, escaping the devil who had the power of death (Revelation 12:4–5; see Hebrews 2:14).

Praying for the nation's prosperity (verses 11–15)

The words of verse 11 repeat verse 7 in order to continue the prayer begun at verse 5 that God would 'rescue' ('snatch away') and 'deliver' David from the clutches of the foreign enemies. It is with the long-term results of this rescue in mind that David is calling on God for present action. The deliverance of the Lord's Anointed will bring about a fulness of life that is reminiscent of the covenant blessings of Deuteronomy 28:1–14 (see Leviticus 26:1–13). They are the kind of blessings described by the prophets after the final curse of the covenant has taken place (Hosea 3:5; Amos 9:13–15; Micah 4:4). In the new society there will be peace and prosperity. The young men will be strong and healthy and the young women pictures of elegance and beauty (verse 12). There will be no shortage of food with plenty of sheep in the fields and oxen well laden with the fruits of the harvest (verse 13–14a). No enemy will breach the city walls ('breaking in'; verse 14; see Nehemiah 1:3; 2:13), no further exile ('going out'; see Ezekiel 12:4; Amos 4:3) and no more cries of complaint and distress in the streets. A similar situation concerning Zion is described in Psalm 132:13–18.

The psalm ends with two beatitudes—'O how fortunate', how 'happy are the people …' to whom it happens like this and 'whose God is the LORD' (verse 15; see Psalms 1:1; 33:12). The people of God are in this blessed and highly privileged state because the 'LORD', (Yahweh/ Jehovah), is their God (see Psalm 2:12). It is because of the covenant relationship they have with him that this blissful future is theirs. David has taken to heart the promised blessing that Moses gave Israel shortly before his death: 'Happy are you, O Israel! Who is like you, a people saved by the LORD' (Deuteronomy 33:29). As a result of the Servant-King's atoning work for the people's sins, Isaiah can speak of the security of God's steadfast love to David and ends with that idyllic picture of peace and joy with no more curse (Isaiah 55:1–13). This is the future of which the apostles write concerning the glorified state in that new earth where righteousness dwells (Romans 8:18–25; 2 Peter 3:13; Revelation 21–22).

Psalm 145

Praising the LORD's Universal Rule

Here is a magnificent praise psalm and the only one with the heading 'Praise of David'. It is the last in a series of psalms by David (Psalms 138–145), and a fitting conclusion in Book 5 to a collection that began in Book 1 with psalms by David before the final 'Hallelujahs' (Psalms 146–150). Josiah Conder (1789–1855), a Congregational lay preacher and poet, catches the main emphasis of this psalm when he writes:

> The Lord is King; lift up thy voice,
> O earth, and all ye heavens rejoice!
> From world to world the joy shall ring:
> 'The Lord Omnipotent is King!'

In this well-constructed poem each verse begins with a different letter of the Hebrew alphabet in sequence. It is the last of the acrostic psalms like Psalm 119 only instead of using eight verses for each consecutive character of the twenty-two letter Hebrew alphabet, just one verse is devoted to each letter as is the case with the other acrostic poems (see Psalms 9–10, 25, 34, 37, 111, 112). With a twenty-two letter Hebrew alphabet we might have expected the same number of verses but there are only twenty-one. This is because in

476

the middle (between verses 13 and 14), the equivalent letter to our 'N' is missing. Many modern English versions have followed the ancient Greek translation which supplies the missing verse and a Hebrew manuscript found among the Dead Sea Scrolls gives added weight to this position. However, it is equally possible that David omitted the N line deliberately and in fact, it is something that David generally did, as his other acrostic psalms also omit letters and sometimes add a letter that has already been used (see Psalms 9–10, 25, 34, 37).

This psalm is an A to Z of praise to God the King who rules over the entire universe. The term 'kingdom' occurs four times right at the centre of the hymn (verses 11–13) and interestingly, the letters of the alphabet that begin verses 11 to 13 (K, L, M) happen to form the word for 'king' when read in reverse order (MLK). The missing N line serves to draw attention to this word play which emphasises God's sovereignty in the most glowing of terms. The King's greatness and goodness is worthy of celebration to all eternity by all his subjects. Particularly in the latter half of the psalm the word translated 'all' or 'every' occurs many times (seventeen times altogether in the original) and this gives added emphasis to the universal nature of God's rule.

When the inspired editor to the psalm collection placed this psalm here, there was no king of David's line ruling over the people. They were still being governed by foreign rulers. It is therefore highly significant that we have this final psalm of David that so powerfully asserts God's overall sovereignty. God is on the throne and the people can be assured that the purposes of God will come to the grand conclusion through his Anointed ruler that was announced in Psalm 2. Christians join in this praise psalm in the light of all that God has done through his Anointed one, Jesus the Messiah, and look forward to the consummation when Jesus will be seen with all his people in the new creation so that the triune God may be all in all (1 Corinthians 15:28).

Commitment to praise (verses 1–2)

The psalm begins by announcing the theme developed in the rest of the poem—God's kingship. David the king desires to exalt God the King—'I will extol you' (see Psalm 30:1) and give him never-ending worship. He acknowledges the LORD, the covenant-keeping God, as 'my God' and ultimately the only 'King' there is (literally it reads 'the King'). To 'bless his name' is to express on bended knee all that God has revealed about himself (see Psalms 2:1; 103:1). David commits himself to reverent worship 'every day'. Worship and 'praise' is to be frequent as well as long lasting.

Reasons for praise (verses 3–9)

Praising God is not to be unintelligible gibberish but full of content that informs the mind and witnesses to God's being and character.

The first reason for such worship and praise is because of the LORD's greatness (verses 3–6). It is with the words of verse 3 that Augustine of Hippo opens his famous *Confessions*. God is the only one who can rightly be called 'great' without qualification (Psalms 48:1; 86:10) and as such he deserves very much to be praised (Psalm 96:4). The word 'great' is often used unthinkingly for anything we like from ice-cream to a football match. Here it is used deliberately to express God's incomprehensible, 'unsearchable greatness'. But we can only know what he chooses to reveal about himself.

David not only thinks of himself as praising God throughout his lifetime and beyond, but he sees generations after him continuing to 'laud' or 'commend' ('praise'; a different verb from verses 2 and 3) God's deeds and 'declare' his 'mighty acts' (verse 4; see Psalm 106:2). There is a build-up of words to express God's 'majesty' which is glorious and splendid (verse 5; see Psalm 45:3). David wants to muse or 'meditate' on God's person and his 'wondrous works' (see Psalm 77:12). God has shown such remarkable wonders throughout Israel's history but especially at the time of the exodus (Psalms 105:2, 5; 106:7; 107:8, 15, 21, 31). Others will talk of these mighty 'awesome acts' and David joins them in recounting these evidences of God's 'greatness' (verse 6).

A second reason for praising God is on account of his 'great goodness' which includes his 'righteousness' (verse 7). God's 'goodness' depicts how great God is. People will look at those mighty acts of God and 'will utter' or 'pour forth' the memory of God's goodness. In other words, they will call them to mind or commemorate them as indications of God's kindness and will give 'shouts of joy' ('sing'; see Psalm 33:1) because God has acted according to his righteous standards.

God is not only great but 'gracious and full of compassion' and these characteristics of God along with his patience ('slow to anger') and his great loving commitment ('great in mercy') also indicate his goodness, as God revealed to Moses (verse 8; Exodus 33:19; 34:6–7). It is not only to Israel that God has been good, there is a further reason for praising God and that is because his generosity and kindness extends to the whole world, to 'all' indiscriminately and his 'tender mercies' or 'compassions' (see Psalm 51:1) are over all that he has made (verse 9). These statements again show that he is indeed the supreme King over all.

Praising God's glorious rule (verses 10–13)

In the light of what has been said about God's goodness toward all that he has made in verse 9, 'all' these 'works' have been made in order to 'give thanks' ('praise'; see Psalm 136:1). The whole creation is to acknowledge Israel's God ('LORD'), and his 'saints' (see Psalm 30:4), those belonging to the covenant community who are committed to God and his people, will reverently bend the knee in worship ('bless').

This leads David to introduce the stunning importance of God's 'kingdom', the term appearing four times in these verses. David has already stated that God's kingdom 'rules over all' (Psalm 103:19) and now he shows how the whole creation is to speak of its 'glory' and 'power' (verse 11). The ending to Jesus' model prayer picks up these words: 'for yours is the kingdom and the power and the glory' (Matthew 6:13). Talking of God's universal rule is a witness to humanity of his 'mighty acts' (verse 12; see verse 4) and of the majestic glory of the kingdom. It is a reign that is for all eternity and so is a rule that will be known by all generations to come. Again, these powerful lines press home the truth that the LORD (Yahweh/Jehovah) is King. Nebuchadnezzar uttered the same words as he praised Daniel's God (Daniel 4:3, 34).

Praising God's righteous rule (verses 14–20)

More reasons for praising God's goodness are presented in these verses. Unlike the powerful rulers of the ancient world and much of the modern, the 'LORD' shows his kindness in his concern for the poor and needy. He 'upholds' or 'supports' all those who 'fall' and 'raises up' all who are 'bowed down' (verse 14). This encourages God's people to cast all their care upon the Lord 'for he cares for you' (1 Peter 5:7). The God who supports is also the God who sustains. All who look expectantly to God for sustenance he feeds at the proper time. God is not tight-fisted but his hand is 'open' so that every living thing is satisfied as a result of God's providential goodness (verses 15–16). David, no doubt, has in mind God's covenant with Noah and the whole creation that while the earth remains seedtime and harvest would not cease (Genesis 8:22; see similar language in Psalm 104:27–28).

God also shows himself to be 'righteous' and 'gracious' in 'all his ways' and 'all his works' (verse 17). He is concerned to do the right and that includes punishing those who oppress and persecute the righteous. God's ways are parallel to God's works (see also Psalm 103:7) and refer to God's plans and ways of acting. The word translated 'gracious' is from the same word family as the term for God's faithful love and usually refers to people who show their commitment to God in practical ways and is often translated 'holy', 'godly' or 'kind' (see Psalms 30:4; 86:2). This is the only place in the psalms where it is used of God and it expresses his 'kind commitment' (see also Jeremiah 3:12 where it is translated 'merciful').

David turns next to encourage God's people, those who are within the covenant community. If God is so kind to all how much more so toward his people! Though God is the King of the universe he is 'near' to those who 'call upon him in truth' (verse 18). God is present everywhere (Psalm 139) yet he presences himself in a special way among his people. James encourages us to draw near to God 'and he will draw near to you' (James 4:8). The phrase 'in truth' means sincerely and earnestly and is not dissimilar to Jesus' words to the Samaritan woman concerning worshipping God 'in spirit and in truth' (John 4:24; see Isaiah 10:20). Isaiah speaks of those who draw near in worship with their lips but their hearts are far from the Lord (Isaiah 29:13). Those who are truly committed to God alone, who call on God in truth, are those who revere and love him (verses 19–20). God, for his part, is graciously committed to them. David is assured that the LORD who satisfies the 'desire' or 'goodwill' of every living thing (verse 16) will fulfil the 'desire' or 'good pleasure' of his people by saving and protecting them (verses 19–20). Jesus said that if God feeds the birds and takes care of his creation he will certainly provide for his people who are of 'more value' than birds (Matthew 6:25–30). To 'save' his people does mean that all the 'wicked', who have oppressed and sought to destroy them, will themselves be destroyed. Paul was able to testify at the end of his life: 'I was delivered out of the mouth of the lion. And the Lord will deliver me from every evil work and preserve me for his heavenly kingdom' (2 Timothy 4:17–18).

Commitment to praise (verse 21)

David returns to where he began with the desire to speak the Lord's 'praise', using the same word that is found in the heading. Having emphasised the universal nature of God's rule it is also fitting to close by indicating that 'all flesh', meaning, in this context, every living creature (see Psalm 65:2), will 'bless' the unique, pure God of Israel ('his holy name'; see Psalm 33:21) who has specially revealed himself under the name 'Lord' (Yahweh/Jehovah).

It is the conviction of the whole Bible that despite what we see in this fallen world of people enslaved by sin and Satan and full of pain, deprivation and sorrow, God rules over all and he is working out his purposes despite human frailty and folly and the devilish power of Satan so that all will eventually acknowledge that the kingdom is the Lord's (Daniel 7:27; Obadiah 21; Revelation 12:10).

Psalm 146

The Happy Worshipper

The psalm collection is brought to a fitting close with a coda of praise. Each of the final five begin and end with a summons to all to 'Praise the Lord' (*hallelu yah;* see Psalms 113-118). Among the many who have been inspired to write hymns of praise based on this psalm, Isaac Watts' *I'll praise my Maker while I've breath* is perhaps the best known.

Along with praise this psalm instructs and recalls the two introductory psalms (Psalms 1-2) with which the whole collection begins. We are urged not to put our trust in human rulers, while, on the other hand, it speaks of the happy state of those who put their trust in the Lord and reminds us of God's care of the righteous as well as the ruin of the wicked.

The psalm also has close contacts with the previous one in theme and phraseology. It opens as Psalm 145 began and ended by praising the Lord while the psalmist lives (verses 1-2; Psalm 145:2, 21). Both psalms acknowledge that God's reign is for ever (verse 10; Psalm 145:13). Help is to be found in the Lord who gives food to the hungry (verses 5, 7; Psalm 145:15-16). The Lord raises those bowed down, cares for the needy and punishes the wicked (verses 8-9; Psalm 145:14, 18-20). There are echoes too of other parts from the psalm collection.

Introductory summons (verse 1a)

It is difficult to know whether the initial communal call 'Praise the LORD!' ('Praise Yah') is a title like 'Praise of David' in the previous psalm (see also Psalm 111) or an integral part of the psalm. Supporting the view that it was intended to be part of the whole, the psalm has a similar concluding call for all to praise the Lord thus forming a frame around the psalm. In addition, the reference to Zion in verse 10 may also suggest that the introductory summons like the closing call is addressed particularly to the united company of God's worshipping people and therefore part of the psalm. Whatever conclusion we come to, it is important to remember that the psalm titles belong with the rest of the text as part of Holy Scripture. They are not like the bold-type headings that Bible editors use to indicate each psalm's content.

Personal commitment to praise (verses 1b-2)

As Spurgeon notes, the psalmist practises what he preaches, for after calling all to praise, he immediately encourages himself to do the same—'Praise the LORD, O my soul!' The closing words of Psalm 104:35 reverses what we have here, for the psalmist first summons himself to worship before ending with a communal call to praise the Lord. We do need to stir up our whole beings to engage in this holy activity.

The psalmist also vows to 'Hallelujah' the God who has revealed himself so wonderfully under this special name of 'LORD' ('Yahweh/ Jehovah') and to make music to him throughout his life. His words recall Psalm 104:33—'while I live ... while I have my being'. The dead, as earlier psalms have indicated, are in no position to praise God, for their bodies lie silent in the grave (see Psalms 6:5; 30:9; 115:17). It is here on earth with our whole selves, body and spirit, that we are called to praise the Lord. Only when we are resurrected to that new life on earth will we again be able to praise God with our whole beings.

Warning against trusting humans (verses 3-4)

Many of the psalms urge us to trust the Lord, but like Psalm 118:8-9 this one directs us not to place our trust in 'leaders' ('princes') however great their influence and power. They cannot bring 'help' (literally 'salvation'). Though they may mean well in making their promises and plans for the future, the best of people are still 'human' ('son of man'; see Psalm 8:4) and as a result of God's judgment on humanity after the initial rebellion in Eden, they die and their plans perish with them (see

Psalms 76:12; 144:4). The Preacher impresses on us the same truth that when the spirit goes the body of dust returns to the ground (verse 4; Ecclesiastes 12:7; see Genesis 3:19; Psalm 104:29).

Nonconformity at the end of the 19th century put its trust in Lloyd George, the Welsh Liberal Prime Minister, others later idolised the Scottish Ramsay MacDonald, the first Labour Prime Minister. More recently, there are those who nostalgically look back to the English Conservative Margaret Thatcher, the first woman Prime Minister. Christians too are tempted to put their trust in big names in the evangelical world. Can religious leaders save us? Can their ideas and plans revive the work of God? Leaders come and go. Only the Lord remains 'unchangeably faithful to save' (see Isaiah 45:21-22; Acts 4:12).

Encouragements to trust the Lord (verses 5–9)

In contrast to frail humanity the psalm congratulates those who have Israel's God for their 'help' and 'expectantly wait' ('hope'; Psalm 119:116 and similar to Psalm 145:15) on him. The term 'Happy' declares the blessed condition of the person—'O how fortunate' (see Psalms 1:1; 2:12). To be in a personal relationship with 'the God of Jacob', Israel's covenant 'LORD', 'who made heaven and earth' (verse 6; see Psalms 115:15; 134:3), is to be in a most privileged position. The 'God of Jacob' who was so gracious and kind to him through all his distressing experiences is Zion's refuge and strength (Psalm 46:7, 11) and a great encouragement to a people newly returned from the Babylonian exile (see verse 10).

The psalm continues to emphasise who God is and to spell out his greatness and goodness, in much the same way as in the previous psalm. While the sea was feared as a dangerous place and often used symbolically to express the powerful forces arrayed against God, it is part of his creation and subject to him along with all of nature's teeming life. Unlike the god of the deists and the liberals who it was believed had created the world then left it to tick away on its own to fend for itself, the living and true God 'keeps truth' or better, keeps faith for ever. In his covenant with Noah and all his creatures God promises to care and provide for all (Genesis 8:22; 9:8-17).

The psalm continues in verses 7 to 9 to indicate why knowing this God means being in such a blessed position. God 'executes justice for the oppressed' by taking up their cause, by vindicating them against fierce, unscrupulous opponents (see Psalm 103:6). He also feeds the hungry and releases the prisoners (see Psalm 107:5, 9). There are good reasons why God allows his people to go hungry, to be put in prison and suffer sorrow and hardship. He disciplined his people, for instance, by using the Babylonians to take them captive, to reduce to rubble their city and temple and to remove their king. But he can also restore and bring deliverance. He can open blind eyes and lift up those who are bowed down (see Psalm 145:14). Isaiah spoke in similar terms of the creator God who sends his Servant to 'open blind eyes, to bring out prisoners from the prison' (Isaiah 42:7) and comforts Zion that the Lord their Maker will free the captives and provide food for them (Isaiah 51:13-14). Those Jews back in their land after exile in Babylon still considered themselves to be in bondage. Such words from the prophets and the psalms gave hope to the people.

Still more encouragements are given for being in this blessed state of trusting the living God for help and deliverance rather than humans. Israel's covenant-keeping God, the 'Lord' is one who 'loves the righteous', those who are in a right legal relationship with God (see Psalm 1:5-6). They love him (Psalm 145:20) and he loves them. That love extends to the vulnerable within the community, to people like the 'resident aliens' ('strangers'; see Psalm 39:12), 'the fatherless and widow' (verse 9). It was because of God's own compassion for the poor and dispossessed that he commanded his people to show them special concern (Deuteronomy 10:18-19; see Psalms 68:5-6; 82:3). The same God who 'watches over' and 'relieves' his oppressed people, 'turns upside down' the 'wicked' (Psalm 1:6). The verb 'turn upside down' is often translated 'to be bent, be crooked' and is used for those who are morally 'bent' in the sense of perverting justice and falsifying scales (Job 8:3; Amos 8:5). For those who are themselves 'bent' in their dealings with God's people God will make sure that their punishment fits their crimes. He will make their path crooked so that they do not succeed in their evil intentions (see Psalm 145:20).

What is said of the Lord in verse 8 is true of the Messiah. This same Lord (Yahweh/Jehovah) appeared in the flesh as the man Christ Jesus. When the disciples of John the Baptist who was languishing in prison, came to Jesus asking whether he was the Messiah, Jesus replied, 'Go and tell John the things you have seen and heard: that the blind see, the lame walk, the lepers are cleansed, the deaf hear, the dead are raised, the poor have the gospel preached to them' (Luke 7:22). Jesus drew their attention to these miracles because this is what the prophets had foretold would happen. Isaiah particularly speaks in these very terms of a future in which the glory of God would be seen and Zion would be full of joy (Isaiah 35:5–6). Jesus not only used his miracles to point to spiritual realities but to give foretastes of the future glory. As has been already noted, Isaiah also speaks of God's Suffering Servant as the one who would bring sight to the blind and freedom for the prisoners (Isaiah 42:7) and in the passage from Isaiah that Jesus read in the synagogue at Nazareth, he claimed that it was being fulfilled in his ministry (Isaiah 61:1–2; Luke 4:16–21). The LORD and his Anointed One are so closely associated that they are one God and yet they are two Persons (see Psalms 45 and 110). The truth of the triune God so clearly revealed in the New Testament, is not absent from the Old Testament revelation.

Concluding message and summons (verse 10)

While the rulers of this world quickly pass from the scene (see verse 4), Israel's God 'reigns for ever' (see Psalm 145:13; Exodus 15:18; Psalm 29:10). This is good news for 'Zion' (see Psalms 2:6; 87:1–7). Isaiah, similarly, pictures messengers announcing this same gospel to Zion: 'Your God reigns!' (Isaiah 52:7). The God of the psalmist ('my God', verse 2) is the God of everyone who is in the happy position described in verse 5 ('his God'). He is also the God of the whole company of God's people now and for all succeeding generations ('your God'). 'Hallelujah' is the only appropriate response, yet the Lord knows us better than we know ourselves and so we need this closing exhortation, 'Praise the LORD!'

Psalm 147

Praising the LORD is Pleasurable

This is a magnificent praise psalm in which calls to praise are supported by reasons for doing so. It is a fine example of synonymous parallelism which is one of the features of Hebrew poetry. In almost every verse the second line restates the thought of the first line often in a more dramatic way. There are some similarities of language with the previous psalm as well as other psalms and parts of the Old Testament.

The psalm focuses alternately on concerns for creation in general and his people in particular and there is good reason for thinking that it was composed after the return of the Jews from Babylonian exile. It provided the people with encouragements to praise God for what he was doing among them in re-building the temple and city walls, and in bringing healing and restoration to the people. The mention of creation may, as in the prophet Isaiah's messages of hope, point towards seeing the return as a new creative work that will lead to the renewal of all things in a new creation. It emphasises that there is no God like the LORD and that he is deserving of praise. The psalm encourages Christians to praise the creator God for his providential care and for what he is doing through Christ and his Spirit in building his Church.

There are three sections to the psalm, each beginning with a call to praise or sing (verses 1, 7 and 12) and each time good grounds are given for doing so. Worshipping God in word and song is meant to be done intelligently and with understanding.

Call to praise with reasons (verses 1–6)

The initial call to everyone to 'Praise the Lord!' ('hallelu-yah') is not merely the title but an integral part of the psalm providing the first of three exhortations to praise. With the final 'Praise the LORD' (verse 20) it also acts as a frame around the whole psalm.

The call is immediately followed by reasons—note the 'for' in each line of verse 1.[96] But they are not the usual reasons that we expect. Rather than immediately giving us content for praise the psalmist first shows that 'to sing praises' (or better 'to make music') to 'our God' is doing something that is 'good' and that it is 'pleasant' to make this 'beautiful' or 'fitting' expression of 'praise'.

These initial explanations make us wonder what is coming next. We are urged to engage in this good and pleasant occupation of praising God when we consider what the 'LORD' is doing for his people (verses 2–3, 6). He is the same sovereign 'Lord' who shows his greatness and the might of his power by numbering and naming all the stars and whose own understanding cannot in the same way be measured by anyone else (verses 4–5; the word for 'infinite' is translated 'number' in the previous verse). God's knowledge and control of the stars and infinite understanding reminds us of Isaiah's phraseology as he comforted his people (Isaiah 40:26, 28). It means that God is well able to undertake his new, re-creating work among his people.

As in Isaiah, the return of his people from exile is but the initial stage in God's plan for a worldwide gathering together of his elect when the heavenly Jerusalem will finally be built up (see Isaiah 11:12; 4:2–6; Psalms 51:18; 102:16). Jesus speaks of his coming on the clouds of heaven with power and great glory and of sending his angels to 'gather together his elect from the four winds, from one end of heaven to the other' (Matthew 24:31). The apostle John also records how the high priest's words concerning the death of one man for the people were prophetic in that Jesus would die for the nation and he adds, 'and not for that nation only, but also that he would gather together in one the children of God who were scattered abroad' (John 11:51–52).

Again echoing the words of Isaiah, the psalmist shows how this same God, Israel's 'LORD', will heal 'the broken-hearted' and bind up 'their wounds' (verse 3; see Isaiah 61:1; Luke 4:18). The psalm also affirms that God 'relieves' the humble ('lifts up the humble'; see Psalms 146: 9; 149:4) and punishes the 'wicked' by casting them down to the earth (verse 6; see Psalms 1:5-6; 145:20), meaning that they are utterly defeated and humiliated. Mary's song speaks of bringing down the mighty from their seats and exalting the lowly (Luke 1:52; see 1 Samuel 2:6-8). In Jesus Christ, we see one who, in obedience to God's will, humbled himself even to the death of the cross and who was raised up by God to the highest place of all. In Christ his people also will be vindicated while Satan will be crushed under their feet (Romans 16:20).

The 'wicked', as the psalms have indicated, not only include cruel opponents of the righteous but also proud hypocrites who offer sacrifice and are seen to prosper especially at the expense of the needy.

Call to sing with thanksgiving (verses 7-11)

The second exhortation to all is to 'sing'[97] to the LORD 'with thanksgiving' and to 'make music' (see verse 1) with the lyre ('harp'). The one who is engaged in this creative activity on behalf of his people is 'our God' (verse 7) and they are to express their gratitude for his goodness.

Surprisingly, nothing more is said about God's support and care of his people. Instead we have a hymn-like piece that shows how God brings the clouds across the sky to produce rain for the dry earth to make the grass grow on the bare mountains so that the cattle can graze and the young ravens' cries can be relieved (verses 8-9; see Job 38:34, 41; Psalm 104:14). God cares for both the domesticated and wild creatures and if he feeds even the ravens then says Jesus, 'Of how much more value are you than the birds?' We ought not to be worrying about our lives in that way but seeking rather the kingdom of God (Luke 12:22-34).

The psalm therefore encourages us to revere the Lord and to put our trust and hope in his unfailing love ('mercy'). It is people like this in whom the Lord 'takes pleasure' (verse 11) and not in what humans admire as powerful and strong. In the ancient world it was the war-horse and the swift running legs of a man that thrilled people and made them feel secure and invincible (verse 10; see Psalm 33:17-18; Isaiah 31:1-3) just as the modern world delights in the latest military hardware or fast cars.

Call to praise with reasons (verses 12–20)

The third and final exhortation urges the people belonging to the city that God is building ('Jerusalem'/'Zion'; see Psalms 48, 87, 122), to 'extol' ('praise' as in Psalm 145:4) and 'praise' their God, the LORD (Yahweh/ Jehovah). This section further develops what has already been said in the previous section (see verses 1, 10–11). He has made his people secure so that no enemy can enter within the city's walls for God has 'strengthened the bars' of the gates (verse 13). What Nehemiah was literally doing in building the walls and gates of the city (Nehemiah 3:1–7:3), God has done for the city he has prepared for his people (Hebrews 11:16). He has also blessed their children. There is peace for the borders are secure and there is plenty of the finest food to eat (verse 15; see Psalm 81:16). It is a picture of the world order in the new creation.

This is the God who is actively involved in managing the whole of creation. His word is like a messenger running swiftly to carry out the king's wishes. It is a poetic way of showing God's complete control of the seasons from winter's frost and snow to the wind that thaws and allows the frozen waters to flow (verses 15–18). The psalmist may well have had in mind the mountains of Lebanon and the Hermon range with the snow and ice melting to replenish the streams and rivers.

The same divine commanding 'word' (verse 15) that operates in controlling the elements and the seasons, revealed his will to Israel in the form of 'statutes' and 'judgments' (verse 19; see Psalms 78:5; 119:5, 7). Moses, in urging the people to keep the commandments that God gave them, pointed to their uniqueness as a people, set apart for God. Unlike the generally accepted view where a nation's greatness was assessed by its size, wealth and military might, Israel was to be seen as unique on account of its special personal relationship with God. In addition, Moses states, 'What great nation is there that has such statutes and righteous judgments as are in all this law which I set before you this day?' (Deuteronomy 4:7–8). This is the background to the psalmist's words, 'He has not dealt thus with any nation' (verse 20). God's people are privileged in having special revelation from God while other nations only have God's general revelation in creation (see Psalm 19). Israel was not meant to keep this knowledge to themselves but to be a light to the nations but they failed through disobedience and apostasy. This psalm draws attention to Israel's uniqueness in having this special revelation and relationship with God so that his people might be encouraged in their new situation after the exile to see God's amazing grace toward them and to prepare them for making God's will known to the nations. It is through the Lord's Suffering Servant who is the true Israel that light and salvation have come to the Gentile world (Isaiah 49:3, 5-6).

It is a wonderful privilege to possess the Bible in our own language. While the world gropes around in ignorance despite the witness to God's eternal power and Godhead in creation, we have revelation that makes us wise about salvation through faith in the Word made flesh. This special revelation fully equips us for every good work God wants us to do. The only fitting and proper response is 'Praise the Lord' (verse 20).

Psalm 148

Universal Praise to the LORD

Important messages that governments want everyone to hear are usually broadcast over the radio or on the television. More recently, items of interest or concern that people wish to distribute widely are sent over the internet and received on personal computers or mobile phones. The psalmist uses the widest possible network in summoning everyone to praise the Lord.

This is the third in a series of praise psalms with which the entire psalm collection comes to a dramatic climax (Psalms 146-150). Unlike the previous psalm which laid emphasis on the grounds for praise with only brief calls to praise the LORD, this psalm is quite the opposite for it is full of exhortations to praise (verses 1-4, 7-12) with only two concise reasons for doing so (verses 5-6, 13-14). Between the opening and closing Hallelujah ('Praise the LORD') the psalm first calls for praise from the heavenly regions (verses 1-6) and then urges the same from the earth (verses 7-14). Everything and everybody are urged to praise the Lord, reinforced by the word 'all' which appears nine times throughout the psalm. The motives for praise include God's creative and sustaining activity (verses 5-6), his stunning character and greatness (verse 13) and his saving purposes through the nation of Israel (verse 14).

While the whole of creation speaks of God's glory it also groans along with the people of God awaiting the day of cosmic transformation, resurrection and the end of the curse (Romans 8:19–23). Only then will the whole creation be perfectly united in the praise of Yahweh/ Jehovah, the triune God, free from suffering, catastrophe, tears and death.

Praise from the world above (verses 1–6)

The familiar summons for all to 'Praise the LORD' ('hallelu yah'; see Psalm 146:1) is followed immediately by the call for this praise to come 'from the heavens', from those 'in the heights' (verse 1).[98] Included in this heavenly sphere is the 'heaven of heavens' (verse 4), which is a Hebrew way of expressing the superlative like 'holy of holies'. It is similar to Paul's 'third heaven' which as Calvin shows is another way of saying 'what is highest and most complete' (2 Corinthians 12:2). This 'highest heavens' is the place which God has chosen to call home and where the angelic armies ('hosts') also live (verse 2). These supernatural beings carry out God's commands (see Psalms 82:1; 91:11; 103:20–21).

The heavenly sphere also refers to the sky where other armies are seen like the sun, moon and starry lights (verse 3; see Isaiah 40:26). As for the 'waters above the heavens' (verse 4), this is a poetic way of referring to the rain clouds (see Genesis 1:7; 7:11; 8:2). 'All' beings in the unseen spirit world as well as 'all' the things that are visible in the sky above are urged to praise God.

Why should they praise Israel's God, the 'LORD'? Praise is due from them because by his sovereign command they were created in the first place (verse 5). The psalmist is recalling Genesis 1 and similar words are found in Psalm 33:6 and 9. Furthermore, God also permanently orders and maintains what he has created. No one and nothing can alter his decrees. The entire world above us both spiritual and physical is to bear witness to Yahweh/Jehovah, the Creator.

This passage clearly indicates that there is no place for the worship of angels as some were tempted to do in New Testament times and later. The apostles Paul and John and the writer to the Hebrews warn us of the temptation (Colossians 2:18; Hebrews 1:4–14; Revelation 19:10; 22:8–9). The other real danger is to believe that our futures are determined by the stars. Both stars and angels are creations of the living God and they both witness to the creator and ruler of all.

It is immensely reassuring that until God decides to end this present order no stray asteroid, no activity in the sun, no chance happening from outer space, no human stupidity, can bring this ordered universe to an end (see Genesis 8:22). That is not to say that humans are not held responsible for environmental pollution or that they can do what they like with impunity.

Praise from the world below (verses 7-14)

Now the call is to 'Praise the LORD' ('hallelu yahweh') 'from the earth' (verse 7; compare verse 1). First, the 'sea creatures' and all that are in the 'depths' of the sea are mentioned (see Genesis 1:2, 21; Psalms 33:7; 74:13). The mysterious 'depths' and the monsters of the sea are also part of God's creation and powerfully witness to God's greatness and are not to be revered or worshipped as was common in the pagan world.

'Fire', caused by lightning, and 'hail', together with 'snow and clouds' and 'stormy wind' all fulfil God's commanding 'word' (verse 8; see Psalm 147:15-18). The word for 'clouds' is usually translated 'smoke' but here it is used for mist or steam that often appears when the sun rises and warms the ground or other wet surfaces. 'Mountains and all hills' brings us to the earth itself and the mention of 'fruitful trees' like the fig and olive, and the mighty 'cedars' all of which would catch the eye of a person in Israel, represent all vegetation (verse 9). Wild animals and cattle, creeping things and birds are all exhorted to contribute to God's praise (verse 10).

Lastly, as in Genesis 1, the psalmist moves from nature and animals to the world of people, the pinnacle of God's creative activity (Psalm 8:5-8). All humanity is to join in the praise from the great and powerful to ordinary men and women, to young and old (verses 11-12). The wording is reminiscent of Joel's prophecy concerning the outpouring of God's Spirit on all flesh, including sons and daughters, old men and young, menservants and maidservants (Joel 2:28-29). All alike 'from the earth', animate and inanimate, are to praise the Lord's 'name' just as all 'from the heavens' are to do (verse 13; see verse 5). Again, reasons are stated why praise should be given to the LORD.

The first reason is because he alone is God. In contrast to the tall cedars of Lebanon and to the high and mighty among earth's rulers, God is the only one who is truly 'exalted' (verse 13; Isaiah 12:4). His royal splendour or majesty ('glory') places him far above everything mentioned in the previous verses from the earth below to the highest heaven.

A second reason for praise is on account of 'his people', who are described as 'his saints' (see Psalm 30:4), 'the children of Israel' (literally 'sons of Israel') and 'a people near to him' (verse 14). This last expression is used of the priests who approach the Lord in the sanctuary (Leviticus 10:3). It suggests a more personal and special relationship and is related to the other idea of the Lord coming near to all who call upon him in truth (Psalm 145:18; James 4:8). Praise is due from all creation not only because of God's activity in creation (verses 5-6) but also because of his activity with regard to Israel. God's people are in a unique position. They are the means by which people the world over and of all ages and stations in life can praise God. 'Salvation' said Jesus, 'is of the Jews' (John 4:22). God, to whom the whole earth belongs, made them to be a kingdom of priests and a nation set apart for himself as his special treasure (Exodus 19:5-6). That ministry continues through all who are united to Christ, who are redeemed through the blood of the Lamb. They are described by Peter who echoes the words of Moses, 'But you are a chosen generation, a royal priesthood, a holy nation, his own special people, that you may proclaim the praises of him who called you out of darkness into his marvellous light' (1 Peter 2:9).

'He has raised up a horn for his people' is a better translation than 'he has exalted the horn of his people' (verse 14). The 'horn' often symbolises strength and in Daniel's visions horns denote kings (Psalm 75:4; Daniel 7:7-8; 8:3). Although it is generally assumed that the meaning is that God has given fresh strength to his people so that they might bring him the praise that is due to him, there is another more satisfying interpretation. The 'horn' is not identical with the 'saints', rather it stands for David and his line of kings (see Psalm 132:17) and is a reminder, especially to the post-exilic community that God had not forgotten the promises he had made to David.

As for the difficult phrase 'the praise of all his saints' (literally, 'a praise to all his saints') this suggests that the anointed king of David's family line is the praise of all his people.[99] God's people, 'the children of Israel' (literally 'the sons of Israel') are described as 'saints' (the 'committed'; see Psalms 30:4; 149:1) and a 'people near to him' (see Leviticus 10:3). The New Testament shows that the real, genuine king of David's line is Jesus of Jewish stock. Through his perfect life, atoning death and victorious resurrection to God's right hand he has redeemed the true Israel of God from all backgrounds and races to be to the praise of God. In Christ Jesus those who were once far off 'have been

made near'. Jew and Gentile have access by one Spirit to the Father by
the blood of Jesus (Ephesians 2:13, 17–18). All creation including angels
and nature will join in the praise, for reconciliation comes through the
Anointed one whom God has appointed to sum up the whole universe
(Ephesians 1:10; Colossians 1:20–22; Revelation 5:9–14). This calls for
the final Hallelujah ('Praise the Lord!').

Psalm 149

A Song for the LORD's People

Where the previous psalm ends with its reference to Israel (Psalm 148:14) this psalm from beginning to end is for God's people to sing. It falls into two main sections with the first half following the pattern of a praise psalm by urging praise (verses 1–3) and presenting the reasons for so doing (verse 4). The second half also begins with a fresh call to praise (verse 5) but then suddenly and uniquely for a praise psalm a military note is introduced (verses 6) which ends with retribution for the nations and royal honour for God's people (verses 7–9). The whole is again held together by 'Praise the LORD' (verses 1, 9), as in the three previous psalms.

We shall first look at the contents of the psalm and then consider what it meant for the people who first sang it and how we are to apply it.

Zion's worship (verses 1–4)

The initial call to 'Praise the LORD' (*hallelu yah*) is followed immediately by an exhortation to 'sing' God's 'praise' in a 'new song' to the 'LORD'. Calls to sing a 'new song' have been heard a number of times (see Psalms 33:3; 96:1; 98:1) and on two occasions David states he has a new song to sing (Psalms 40:3; 144:9). Fresh outpourings of praise are to be expected when we consider who the living God is and his activity

497

in salvation and judgment. Isaiah issues a similar exhortation to sing a new song but his summons is to the whole world. Here the call is narrower. The people urged to sing and praise are described as 'the congregation of saints' (verse 1). They are the worshipping assembly of God's faithful people (Psalm 1:5).

Various words and expressions are used to describe God's people in these verses. The term 'congregation' or 'assembly' is used for God's covenant community and the New Testament equivalent is translated 'church', not in the sense of a building but of a group of people who gather together to worship God.[100] They are called 'saints' in the sense of having a mutually loving and committed relationship with God and his people (see Psalm 30:4). As often in Chronicles, 'Israel' is employed for all God's people irrespective of tribal and political distinctions. These same people are also referred to as 'the children of Zion' (literally 'sons of Zion'). This unique phrase as far as Psalms is concerned is only found in a couple of other places (Lamentations 4:2; Joel 2:23). In the light of what the Babylonians had done in destroying Zion's city and its temple, the expression introduces a tender note that takes account of their feelings. These 'precious sons of Zion' (Lamentations 4:2) who have lamented over their city, can 'be glad' ('be joyful') and 'rejoice' in their God. This is the last reference to Zion, the temple-city where God made his home on earth from the time of David and Solomon. It was seen by the Old Testament prophets as a little model of God's ultimate purpose to make the whole earth a holy mountain and temple garden city (Daniel 2:34–35, 44–45; see also Isaiah 54:2–3; Revelation 21:2–3).

Speaking of God as their 'Maker' and 'King' (verse 2) recalls the words of Isaiah as he prophesies of the new beginning after the Babylonian exile—'I am the LORD, your Holy One, the Creator of Israel, your King' (Isaiah 43:15; see 44:6; 51:13; 54:5). The God who formed Israel into a nation at the time of the exodus is doing a new creation work with them that will lead eventually to the creation of new heavens and a new earth (Isaiah 65:17; 66:22).

God's people are urged to praise the living God who has revealed his character and actions especially under the 'name' of the LORD (Yahweh/Jehovah). They are encouraged to 'praise' and 'make music' ('sing praises') using 'dance' and 'the tambourine and lyre' ('timbrel and harp'; verse 3; see Exodus 15:20; Judges 11:34; 1 Samuel 18:6). These means of praise are found again in the final hymn (see Psalm 150:3–4). Singing, dancing and making music are signs of joy especially after a time of sadness and mourning. Jeremiah speaks in a similar way as he prophesies the future hope for God's people in the return from exile, the new beginning for Zion and the new covenant (Jeremiah 31:4, 13).

Why are God's people to worship him in song and dance to the accompaniment of musical instruments? The answer is not what we expect. Instead of mentioning aspects of God's character or itemising some of his mighty actions on behalf of Israel we are told that it is because the LORD 'takes pleasure' or 'delight' in his people (verse 4; see Psalm 147:11). The same word is used by God with reference to his special Servant who represents and symbolises ideal Israel and ends up suffering in their place. 'Behold! My Servant whom I uphold, my Elect One in whom my soul delights' (Isaiah 42:1). It is amazing that God should take delight in people who had sinned so woefully. But they had been humbled or afflicted (see Psalm 9:12 for 'humble') as a result of the punishment they had received from God at the hands of the Babylonians and now he had adorned ('beautify') them 'with salvation'. The same word is used by Ezra when praising God for the Persian king's help toward beautifying the house of the Lord (Ezra 7:27). The people of Zion will again see themselves like precious metal (see Lamentations 4:2). Isaiah's words also come to mind where he states that the LORD has 'glorified' ('beautified') his 'humble' or 'afflicted' people (Isaiah 54:11; 55:5; 60:9) in their deliverance. One writer comments that the cry of the humble poor 'resounds from one end of the Psalter to the other' and that here finally their liberation is affirmed.[101]

Zion's warfare (verses 5–9)

God's 'saints' (see verse 1) are issued with a fresh call to 'exult' ('be joyful') in the 'glory' that is coming to them (verse 5). Instead of languishing in grief 'on their beds' (see Psalm 6:6) they can give ringing shouts of joy ('sing aloud'; see Psalm 33:1). The 'high praises' of God are to be in their mouth but instead of musical instruments in their hands there is a 'two-edged sword' (verse 6). When Nehemiah's men were building the walls of Jerusalem, they worked with a trowel and carried a sword at their side (Nehemiah 4: 13–18). But they also recognised their dependence on the Lord by praying to him believing that he would fight for them (Nehemiah 4:9, 20). The Chronicler, also writing in the post-exilic period to encourage the people of God in his day, draws attention to an outstanding military victory during the time of

Jehoshaphat that highlights such themes as prayer, worship, reliance
on God and faithfulness to him (2 Chronicles 20).

The psalm, however, is not about enemies seeking to attack Israel,
but of Israel being used by God, as they were against the Canaanites, to
be the instrument in punishing the rebellious nations. As Babylon was
God's tool in disciplining his people so Israel is to be the instrument in
carrying out God's retributive justice. Vengeance belongs to God but he
often uses human agents, sometimes without them realising it, to carry
out his purposes. Unlike the earlier punishments, there is something
very final and all-encompassing about this judgment scene against
the 'nations' and 'peoples' (verse 7). The rulers of this world ('kings'
and 'nobles') are all finally and thoroughly defeated as the 'chains' and
'fetters of iron' signify (verse 8; see Psalm 2).

This is no nationalistic war of aggression but an action that accords
with God's righteous sentence already set out in writing. This 'written
judgment' (verse 9) may well refer to God's eternal decrees associated
with his book of destiny (see Psalms 69:28; 139:16; Revelation 20:12,
15). It is a decree revealed in the written Law of Moses as well as in
the prophetic writings (see Deuteronomy 32:41; Isaiah 61:2 'the day
of vengeance of our God'). The final day of vengeance also means
ultimate vindication and salvation for God's people (Isaiah 63:4).
Isaiah's prophecies again come close to the language of the psalm
(Isaiah 45:14; 49:23). To be involved in this final overthrow will be
'honour' for all those who love him and are loyal to him ('saints'). They
were deprived of such status when they were punished and sent into
exile but now they will share in God's sovereign rule, the word 'honour'
being often associated with royal 'splendour' or 'majesty' (see Psalms
29:4; 96:6). The concluding 'Praise the LORD' is a natural and obvious
concluding call and response that matches the opening words.

How is this psalm to be understood?

Many in our western world today find the contents of this psalm
offensive and there are some professing Christians who are
embarrassed by its language and disapprove of its use. How are we
to interpret these references to God's people executing vengeance
on the nations? Are we to envisage Jews in the future doing this to
their enemies? If we then read and sing the psalm in the light of
Christ's coming and the new covenant, and understand the 'saints',
the 'children of Zion' as all those belonging to Jesus Christ, how

can Christians sing of executing vengeance on the nations? Does not the New Testament emphasise with quotations from the Old Testament that vengeance belongs to the Lord (see Deuteronomy 32:35, 41; Romans 12:19; Hebrews 10:30)? How can Christians talk of executing punishment on the peoples of the world? Does not Paul indicate that it is Jesus, at his second coming, who will take vengeance (2 Thessalonians 1:7–10)?

Some points to bear in mind

1. This victory hymn must be read alongside Psalm 2.[102] In both, mention is made of the 'nations' and 'peoples' along with their 'kings' and others in positions of power. The big difference is that in Psalm 2 it is the LORD's Anointed who is appointed to deal with the world leaders whereas here the task is given to the LORD's people. At the same time, the emphasis is on the LORD's Anointed as King on Mount Zion in Psalm 2, but here there is no reference to the Messiah, only to the LORD (Yahweh/Jehovah) as king and his people as the sons of Zion. Interestingly, there is a similar move in Isaiah from viewing the ruler of David's line who will punish the wicked of the earth in the first part of his prophecy to emphasising the LORD as king and Zion's people as the servants of God. In Daniel's vision of the world empires and the Ancient of Days, there is the same shift. In the vision Daniel sees the heavenly Man ('Son of Man') receiving the kingdom with all nations serving him, whereas in the interpretation no mention is made of the heavenly Man, it is the 'saints of the Most High' who are given the kingdom (Daniel 7:13–14, 22–27).

The New Testament indicates that Jesus is the heavenly Man, the Davidic ruler, who stands on Mount Zion with God's elect people from all nations (Mark 14:61–62; Luke 1:32–33; Revelation 14:1). All those who are united to Christ by faith will rule with Jesus, judging humans and angels (1 Corinthians 6:2–3). When Jesus Christ returns in power to take vengeance on those who do not know God or obey the gospel, he comes 'with all his saints' (1 Thessalonians 3:13; 2 Thessalonians 1:8–10). God has appointed the day in which he will judge the world in righteousness by the man whom he has ordained. God's vindication of Jesus in raising him up from the dead is his guarantee that this will happen (Acts 17:31). Jesus is seen in John's vision of the rider on the white horse, who will rule with a rod of iron and tread the winepress of God's wrath when all rule opposed to God will be destroyed.

2. Jesus Christ is the federal head and representative of his people. Those who are his loyal and loving servants are all bound up in him. This important truth is emphasised in both the Old and New Testaments. Isaiah is the prophet who especially teaches this using the name 'Israel'. While in his earlier chapters he prophesies the coming of a king of David's family line who will set the world to rights, after prophesying the Babylonian invasion he brings comfort and hope by shining the spotlight on God's Servant. Israel as a people is God's servant in the same way as the nation is designated God's son. The nation, however, proves to be disobedient, spiritually blind and deaf (Isaiah 42:19–20). But from the nation, there is an ideal Israel, who will fulfil God's purposes (Isaiah 42:1–9). This is God's special Servant who is called 'Israel' and yet he is distinct from the disobedient nation for he has been appointed to bring Israel back to the Lord (Isaiah 49:3, 5). Through the Servant's work on behalf of Israel and for them, God's people of all nations become the Lord's many servants and are united to him (Isaiah 52:13–53:12; 65:8–16). The future rule of justice and peace promised to the Davidic king that Isaiah presents in the earlier prophecies is fulfilled through the Servant's obedience in becoming a curse and being punished in the place of his people. He is the light to lighten the Gentiles and the glory of his people Israel (Isaiah 9:6–7; 42:1–7; 49:5–6; Luke 2:32). The only 'honour' or 'royal splendour' accorded God's people is on account of Jesus, the Messiah and Servant of the Lord.

3. The words of this psalm must be taken as a prophecy relating to the great judgment day. There is no justification in the text for the Church of Jesus Christ to fight with physical weapons. Sadly the 'two-edged sword' has been interpreted literally. Jesus Christ made it clear that his rule was not like that of earthly rulers and Paul on several occasions emphasised that the weapons of our warfare are not fleshly (2 Corinthians 10:3–6). The military language used in the New Testament is to draw attention to the fact that Christians are at war but our enemies are spiritual in nature. Human beings are pawns in the hands of the evil one, so that we wrestle not against flesh and blood but against spiritual wickedness in the heavenly places and God has given us spiritual armour with which to defend ourselves and spiritual weapons with which to fight (Ephesians 6:10–20; 1 Thessalonians 5:8). The Christian's 'two-edged sword' is the Bible and God's gospel which church leaders are called to preach (2 Timothy 4:2; Hebrews 4:12). A

spiritual victory was won on Calvary's cross by Jesus the Messiah over Satan and his rule when his penal substitutionary sacrifice ended the devil's hold on the nations (John 12:31–33; 16:11; Colossians 2:13–15; Revelation 12:7–12). The final battle resulting in the complete elimination of the evil one and those associated with him, will likewise involve not physical arms but the sharp sword of Messiah's word (Revelation 19:15).

4. If the 'two-edged sword' is not to be taken literally, then those who use this and the final psalm in support of introducing 'dance' into the church's communal worship had better think again! And contrary to the suggestions of some scholars, there is no such custom in Israel of a sword-dance although in much later times there is evidence of Jews engaging in a fire dance during the Tabernacles festival. While whirling and dancing were practised both formally and informally in Israel there is no evidence of dancing as a recognised part of temple worship. Spontaneous expressions of joy in jumping and dancing are features of new life and spiritual awakening and these must be clearly differentiated from liturgical dances. Does this mean that musical instruments are also to be treated in a spiritual way and therefore have no place in public worship? This question will be discussed in the next psalm (see Psalm 150).

5. In the aftermath of the Babylonian invasion and the end of the monarchy, the emphasis in the final Books is on the LORD (Yahweh/Jehovah) as King. This prepares us for the appearance of Messiah as Yahweh/Jehovah in the flesh. The only Saviour, Yahweh/Jehovah, whose name is above every name and before whom everyone must bow down is associated with Jesus (Isaiah 45:21–25; Philippians 2:9–11). After reciting the passage from Joel that everyone who calls on the name of the LORD (Yahweh/Jehovah) will be saved, Peter preached Jesus to the people and urged them to be baptised in the name of Jesus Christ (Acts 2:16–22, 36–38).

Psalm 150

The Final Call to Praise

Here is the *Hallelujah Chorus* of the Old Testament! This closing psalm brings the whole collection to a grand and glorious conclusion as well as being the final praise psalm that completes Book 5 (Psalms 107-150; see Psalms 41:13; 72:18-19; 89:52; 106:48). It is especially appropriate after the psalm that speaks of the end-time judgment when all opposition to God's rule will be ended and the unrepentant punished. In the same way the New Testament Hallelujahs come when the enemies of God's people, symbolised under the name of 'Babylon the Great', have all been defeated and punished: 'Praise our God, all you his servants and those who fear him, both small and great ... alleluia! For the Lord God Omnipotent reigns' (Revelation 19:5-6).

The psalm from beginning to end is one long call to praise with the familiar opening and closing hallelujahs framing the whole. There is nothing more to be said apart from the briefest of reasons for praise in verse 2. The call to praise is itself an expression of praise and while the Psalms come to a close, 'praise shall never end ... Eternity will prolong, but never end the strain' (Henry Law).[103]

The who, where and why of praise (verses 1-2)

The opening verse is a reminder that praise is to be offered to the

'LORD' ('Praise the LORD'; the original is *hallelu yah*), the covenant-keeping God of Israel, who is also the one true, living and powerful 'God' ('Praise God' in the original is *hallelu-el*). As the whole psalm collection has made clear, he is the God of creation and redemption, the God who provides and cares for his creation and the God who will judge the world righteously, vindicate his oppressed people and be victorious over all his foes.

God is to be praised 'in his sanctuary' and 'in his mighty firmament'. His 'sanctuary' ('holiness') could refer to the temple in Jerusalem or to his heavenly home, the earthly being symbolic of the heavenly and an indication that the high and holy God ordains to be present among his people as they come near through atoning sacrifice (Psalms 11:4; 68:24). Perhaps both the heavenly and the earthly are intended (see Psalm 148:1, 7). God's 'mighty firmament' (see Genesis 1:6-7) could, in this context, also be referring to heaven (see Psalm 148:4). Across and above the vast expanse God is to be praised. The two phrases together may be indicating that heaven and earth are to unite in praising God.

Plenty of content and reasons for praise have been given in the other praise psalms. They are summarised in verse 2 as his person and work. First, attention is drawn to his works—'his mighty acts'. These will include his activity in creation and salvation, in preservation and judgment (see Psalms 20:6; 66:7; 106:2; 145:4, 11-12). Secondly, his person is described as 'his excellent greatness'. The psalmist cannot give adequate expression to the immensity of God. God is supremely and surpassingly great (literally 'the muchness of his greatness'). We praise God for who he is as well as for what he has done. The greatness of God was particularly expressed in Psalm 145.

The how of praise (verses 3-5)

God can be praised not only with words but with musical instruments. Different sounds are mentioned. The 'sound of the trumpet' is really the 'blast' from the ram's 'horn' (verse 3). This is the most frequently named instrument in the Old Testament. It was the instrument used to announce the beginning of the holy seventh month, which after the exile became the Jewish civil new year (see Psalm 81:3) as well as to announce the Jubilee year which commenced on the Day of Atonement (Leviticus 25:9). The loud blast of the horn also signalled important events like a coronation and was used in times of war as a call to arms or retreat or to proclaim victory (2 Samuel 15:10; Nehemiah

4:18-20; Jeremiah 6:1; 2 Samuel 18:16; 1 Samuel 13:3). When David brought the ark to Jerusalem with shouts of joy and dancing there were blasts from the ram's horn and during the solemn covenant renewal oath as part of king Asa's religious reforms the rams' horns as well as the silver trumpets were employed (2 Chronicles 15:14). Clearly, the blasts of the horn were not meant to play tunes or keep time but were reserved for special occasions and for the giving of signals. Nevertheless, even if they were not used for regular communal worship the horn-blasts when sounded were to be to the praise of God.[104]

The 'lute and harp' (verse 3) would be better translated 'harp and lyre'. These are melodious stringed instruments that are useful in accompanying singing. They are often mentioned together especially as musical background aids in songs of praise to the LORD (see 1 Samuel 10:5; Psalms 33:2; 57:8). The 'lyre' ('harp') is the most commonly mentioned stringed instrument in the Old Testament and widely used in the ancient Near East. Jubal is said to have been the first to invent it (Genesis 4:21). The chosen line and those who are godly are not necessarily the ones who are the most intelligent or inventive. Contrary to what some misguided Christians believe, the people of God through the ages have made use of the skills and musical abilities of ungodly people. It was the lyre that David used to comfort Saul (1 Samuel 16:23). The instrument was employed at social functions (Genesis 31:27; Isaiah 5:11-12) and along with other instruments was used by the roaming prophets (1 Samuel 10:5) and by the Levite musicians (2 Chronicles 5:12; Nehemiah 12:27). As for the 'harp' ('lute') this was very similar to the 'lyre'. Some harps had ten strings (Psalms 33:2; 144:9) while others may have had more or less (see Psalm 92:3).

The 'timbrel and dance' ('tambourine and dance', verse 4; see Psalm 149:3) often appear together (Exodus 15:20; Judges 11:34; 1 Samuel 18:6-7; Job 21:11-12). The 'timbrel' was a hand held drum and, as in the ancient Near East generally, it was an instrument used by women. It was played at banquets and other joyful social occasions (Isaiah 5:12; Jeremiah 31:4). There is no evidence it formed part of temple worship but it was used by the roaming prophets in their praises and at special religious functions outside the temple (1 Samuel 10:5; 2 Samuel 6:5; 1 Chronicles 13:8).

As for the 'stringed instruments and flutes' (verse 4) the first term only occurs here and is perhaps used as a general word for stringed instruments. The word 'flutes' (or 'pipe') only appears four times in the Old Testament. Jubal is said to be the first to play the instrument (Genesis 4:21) and Job refers to it a couple of times (Job 21:12; 30:31). Perhaps it was a kind of lute or like the previous term it might stand for wind instruments in general.

The 'loud cymbals' and the 'high sounding cymbals' are literally 'cymbals of hearing' and 'cymbals of shouting' the former suggesting a more mellow sound and the latter a loud clash. Paul may have had this one in mind when he spoke of the 'clanging cymbal' (1 Corinthians 13:1). The term used here for 'cymbal' is a percussion instrument that is only mentioned at the time David brought the ark to Jerusalem (2 Samuel 6:5). Another term from the same Hebrew word family is used in the parallel verse in 1 Chronicles 13:8 and this is the more common form found a number of times in Chronicles, Ezra and Nehemiah. It was employed on special occasions (1 Chronicles 15:19; 16:5, 42; 2 Chronicles 5:12–13; Ezra 3:10; Nehemiah 12:27) as well as in the regular worship of the temple (1 Chronicles 25:6; 2 Chronicles 29:25).

The extent of praise (verse 6)

It ends on a 'breath-taking and breath-claiming note'.[105] With Psalm 148:7–12 in mind with its call to animals as well as people to praise the Lord the phrase 'everything that has breath' need not be limited to humans. Everything that has 'the breath of life' (Genesis 7:22) is summoned to praise Israel's God, 'the LORD' (Yahweh/Jehovah). However, 'everything that has breath' (or more precisely 'all breath') is particularly associated with human beings (Deuteronomy 20:16; 1 Kings 15:29) who are differentiated from animals in their creation. Only of humans are we told that it was God who breathed into them the breath of life (Genesis 2:7). There is a special close relationship between God and those created in his image and likeness. The final 'Praise the Lord' (hallelu-yah) is again a fitting conclusion both to the closing psalm and the entire collection. Psalm 150 is the goal of Psalm 1 and as Erich Zenger comments, 'Human happiness ... is perfected in the praise of YHWH' [that is Yahweh/Jehovah].[106] Perhaps this is the reason why the rabbis gave the title 'Praises' to the whole psalm collection.

'Praise God more every day you live. Praise Him more in private. Praise Him more in public. Praise Him more in your own family. Praise

Him above all in your own heart. This is the way to be in tune for heaven.' (J. C. Ryle)[107]

Poetry and Music
in Christian worship

Humans can bring praise to God indirectly and directly by their words and actions (Matthew 5:16; Colossians 3:17). Praising God with words is the reason why the praise psalms give us content and grounds for praise. Such praise can be uttered in ordinary prose or in poetry. The Psalms give us examples of praise using poetic forms. Poetry is music in words and can express more movingly and memorably what we wish to convey.

The psalms also encourage us to sing the poetic words as well as read them and that introduces us to the subject of music in the worship of God. Poetry lends itself better than prose for singing purposes. The psalms can be chanted using the words as we find them in the various vernacular versions or they can be cleverly re-translated to form them into set rhythms, metres and rhymes and sung to popular tunes and ballads or specially composed melodies and often harmonised in the style of a Bach chorale. Such attempts have met with varying degrees of success. A well respected example in English is the Scottish Metrical Psalter of 1650. It keeps as faithfully as possible to the Hebrew text but its language and poetry are often stilted and contrived. The metrical version of Psalm 23 is one of the best and most widely known of them all and begins, *The Lord's my Shepherd, I'll not want.*

We can sing without instrumental accompaniment and we often find children and grown-ups singing to themselves, particularly when they are happy. Even weeping can involve music that can vary in pitch and sound depending on the cultural expressions of sorrow by grieving people. It was a characteristic of some Welsh preachers particularly in the 19th century to be so taken with their subject that their preaching turned into a kind of singing called the 'hwyl'. Besides making music with the voice, humans have invented musical instruments that produce different types of sound. We read of a descendant of Cain who was the first to use some of the earliest and simplest string and wind instruments, like the lyre and pipe, to make music (Genesis 4:21). The musical instruments mentioned in the Old Testament can be used on their own, like other human activities, to make music in praise of the Lord, which is the implication in Psalm 150. They can also be employed to accompany and aid human voices to sing in tune and keep in time, so that poetry set to music with instrumental accompaniment brings praise to God. Stringed instruments, which included lyres and harps, along with cymbals were the musical instruments employed in the regular temple worship to accompany the singing under the direction of the Asaph musicians (1 Chronicles 25:6; 2 Chronicles 29:25). Other special religious occasions of a joyful nature outside the sanctuary worship brought together a wider selection of musical instruments.

The people of God under the new covenant are encouraged to sing and mention is made of 'psalms and hymns and spiritual songs' (Colossians 3:16; see also Ephesians 5:19). It is difficult to distinguish between the terms for all three are used interchangeably in the headings to the ancient Greek translation of the Psalter.[108] To limit these references to the Old Testament psalm collection as some do, is to go beyond the evidence. If that was Paul's intention, the term 'Psalms' would have been sufficient to describe the whole collection and that is the way that Luke, Paul's close associate, referred to the collection when he described how the risen Lord Jesus drew the disciples attention to the book of Psalms along with the rest of Scripture as a witness to Christ's sufferings and the glory that would follow (Luke 24:44).

John Calvin, following many of the Christian leaders of the early Christian centuries, argues against the use of musical instruments to accompany the psalm singing in public worship. Unusually for Calvin, his arguments are not based on good biblical evidence. To suggest that musical instruments are no more useful in celebrating the praises of God 'than the burning of incense, the lighting up of lamps and the restoration of the other shadows of the law' is not a valid argument.[109] While the ceremonial law and all the tabernacle furnishings are symbolic of Christ and his priestly work, the same cannot be said of musical instruments. They are not used to symbolise anything but are like the suggested tunes, merely aids to singing the words. For this reason harps can find a place in the heavenly worship (Revelation 5:8; 14:2). Calvin's association of musical instruments with images is also suspect. While the Second Commandment bans the use of images it does not prohibit the use of musical accompaniment. We agree with Calvin that New Testament communal worship is to be kept simple and uncomplicated and nothing should take away from centring our thoughts on the living God, his gospel and his will for our lives. However, instrumental accompaniment that is unobtrusive can be helpful to congregational singing and is certainly no less biblical than a precentor standing in front of a congregation to introduce the tune and keep everyone in time.

Paul draws the attention of Christians to a fundamental requirement for the true worship and praise of God by his people. He speaks of singing songs and making music 'in your heart to the Lord' (Ephesians 5:19) and of singing with thankfulness 'in your hearts to the Lord' (Colossians 3:16). As Iain Murray has stated, 'Even the employment of the best manual of praise is no guarantee of true worship ... Our first need is for a thankful heart and for the spirit of praise.'[110]

Bibliography

I have profited from the following commentaries, some of them not by evangelicals. They are referred to in the commentary by their surname:

Alexander, Joseph A., *The Psalms Translated and Explained*, (reprinted from the 1864 Edinburgh edition), Grand Rapids: Zondervan.

Calvin, John, *Commentary on the Psalms of David* 2 Vols. Translated by James Anderson (The Ages Digital Library Commentary).

Goldingay, John, *Psalms* 3 vols., Baker Academic, vol. 1, 2006; vol. 2, 2007; vol. 3, 2008.

Henry, Matthew, *Bible Commentary* (Many editions and online).

Hossfeld, Frank-Lothar & Zenger, Erich, *Psalms 2: A Commentary on Psalms 51–100*; *Psalms 3: A Commentary on Psalms 101–150*, English translated by Linda M. Maloney, (Hermeneia series), Minneapolis: Fortress Press, 2005/2011.

Kidner, Derek, *Psalms* 2 vols. (Tyndale Old Testament Commentaries), Leicester: IVP, 1973/75.

McCann, J. Clinton, 'The Book of Psalms: Introduction, Commentary and Reflections' in *The New Interpreter's Bible* Vol. IV, Abingdon Press, 1996.

Motyer, J. Alec, 'The Psalms' in *New Bible Commentary* 21st Century Edition, (editors D. A. Carson, R. T. France, J. A. Motyer, G. J. Wenham), Leicester: IVP, 1994.

Spurgeon, Charles H. *Treasury of David* (Many editions and on line).

Wilson, Gerald H., *Psalms* Vol. 1 (The NIV Application Commentary). Zondervan, 2002.

Particularly interesting is Peter Gradenwitz, *The Music of Israel: From the Biblical Era to Modern Times*, 2nd edition (Portland, Oregon: Amadeus Press, 1996).

Endnotes

1. See Mesopotamian city laments in W. C. Bouzard, *We have heard with our ears, O God*, Scholars Press, 1997.

2. 'Slippery' is used elsewhere for 'flattery' and 'deception', while the translation 'destruction' means 'deceptions' but with slight alteration in Hebrew vowel pointing could be 'destruction' or 'ruin' as it must be in Psalm 74:3.

3. Augustus Toplady's hymn *Object of my first desire*.

4. See Genesis 41:44 and compare a similar phrase in Genesis 29:1 where the literal reading is 'Jacob lifted up his feet and went to the land of the sons of the east'.

5. The literal translation is 'They have set up their signs (as) signs'.

6. The Hebrew could also read: 'they (i.e. people) recount your wondrous works' as we find in other psalms (9:1; 26:7; 71:17).

7. The original is more vivid—'not from the place of going out (of the sun) or from the place of evening and not from the wilderness'.

8. The phraseology is Kidner's.

9. From Charles Wesley's hymn *O for a thousand tongues to sing*.

10. The word for 'song' is 'stringed instruments' (see Psalm 69:12).

11. Translations differ because the original can give a variety of senses. It could be literally rendered: 'This is my sickness/grief: the years of the right hand of the Most High' or 'This is my sickness/grief: the changing of the right hand of the Most High'. NIV on slender grounds translates 'appeal' instead of 'sickness' The older translations supplied 'remember' from the following verse but there is no 'But' in the original. On balance the first half looks back to the 'sickness' or 'wound' of his affliction whereas the second half of the verse prepares us for the positive attitude that follows.

12. The same word is used for both stupidity and confidence (Ecclesiastes 7:25; Proverbs 3:26).

13. Dale Ralph Davis, *Judges*, Christian Focus, 2000, p.107.

14. The word translated 'limited' only occurs here but in view of the parallel verb 'grieved' it would be better rendered 'pained' or 'vexed'.

15. The phrase 'iniquities of our forefathers' rather than 'former iniquities' (see Jeremiah 11:10).

16. Literally it reads 'Yahweh, God, Hosts' ('Lord, God, All-powerful') as in all the psalms where it appears (Psalms 59:5; 69:6; 80:4, 7, 14, 19; 84:8) apart from Psalm 89:8 where it reads 'Yahweh God of hosts' which is the usual form in the rest of the O.T.

17. It is out of keeping with the context to suggest that the verb 'they perish' should be interpreted as a call for their enemies to be destroyed and translated 'May they perish' as in ESV which also introduces without warrant a third person plural form 'They have burned ... they have cut it down'. A prayer for vengeance is clear in the previous psalm but not in this one.

18. See Calvin on Psalm 81 for his argument against the use of instruments.

19. For details concerning the festivals see Philip Eveson, *Beauty of Holiness*, chs. 26–27.

20. Another suggestion is that Israel, the people of God, is the 'mighty congregation' or 'great assembly' with the term 'god' used to express the superlative as in 'mighty cedars (literally 'cedars of god') in Psalm 80:10. But although Israel as the people of God could be addressed in Deuteronomy 14:1 as 'sons belonging to Yahweh your God' which is a possible parallel to 'sons of the Most High' (verse 6), they are never called 'gods'.

21. A popular view understands 'gods' as judges on the basis of Exodus 21:6; 22:9, 28 where the same term 'gods' is used. Although many scholars dismiss this view and understand the Exodus verses as referring to God himself and not human deputies, it may well be that the judicial authorities in Israel were seen as representing God.

22. Sinclair B. Ferguson *Daniel* in The Communicator's Commentary series, edited by Lloyd J. Ogilvie, Word Books, 1988, p. 216.

23. D. A. Carson *For the Love of God*, IVP, 1998, for May 29.

24. A different part of the verb is used in Psalm 80 verse 14 and a different form of it in verses 3, 7, 19.

25. An alternative translation 'restore the fortunes of Jacob' (see Psalm 14:7) is generally accepted today although the traditional rendering is what the rabbis believed to be correct.

26. D. Martyn Lloyd-Jones, *From Fear to Faith,* IVP, 1953, p. 65.

27. W. S. Plumer, *Psalms*, Banner of Truth, p. 803.

28. George Horne, *Commentary on the Psalms*, Old Paths Publications reprint 1997 from an 1835 edition.

29. Some think that the phrase 'most high' could refer to Zion, established and exalted above the hills (see Isaiah 2:2).

30. From John Newton's hymn, *Glorious things of thee are spoken.*

31. It could also be associated with a rarely used verb for singing.

32. The Hebrew word *rephaim* refers not to ghosts or dead spirits but to corpses in a grave. See Bruce K. Waltke, *The Book of Proverbs Chapters 1-15* (The New International Commentary on the Old Testament), Eerdmans, 2004, p. 232.

33. Literally it reads 'they shall be before your face' which suggests 'being in the presence of' rather than 'going in front' as forerunners.

34. G. Grogan, *Psalms* (The Two Horizons Old Testament Commentary), Eerdmans, 2008, p. 156.

35. See Philip Eveson *Beauty of Holiness*, pp. 172-3.

36. The word often translated 'vanity' in Ecclesiastes literally means 'breath' or 'vapour' and is better rendered in that book as 'transient' or 'temporary'.

37. From the hymn, *Immortal, invisible, God only wise* by Walter Chalmers Smith (1824-1908).

38. From the hymn, *Abide with me: fast falls the eventide.*

39. John R.W. Stott, *The Canticles and Selected Psalms,* Hodder and Stoughton, London, 1966, p. 119.

40. The Septuagint (LXX) has 'Praise of a Song by David' while in one of the Dead Sea Scroll documents found at Qumran a version of the psalm appears with the heading 'Of David' (11Q11).

41. From the hymn, *Sweet is the work, my God, my King.*

42. For further details see *The Book of Origins*, pp. 48-56 and *The Beauty of Holiness* pp. 304-310.

43. Rabbinic oral tradition as recorded in the Mishnah *Tamid* 7.

44. From Gadsby's hymn *O what matchless condescension.*

45. Norman Wirzba, *Living the Sabbath*, Brazos Press, 2006, p. 22.

46. Gordon Fee, 1 Corinthians, NICNT, p. 152.

47. The AV as well as the Revised AV has turned to the Greek translation (the LXX) for 'throne of iniquity'.

48. D. A. Carson, ed., *Worship: Adoration and Action*, Baker, 1993.

49. Hebrews follows the heading in the ancient Greek translation (the LXX).

50. From John Kent's hymn, *Sovereign grace o'er sin abounding*.

51. It is with this background in mind that the LXX has the heading 'When the house was built after the exile. Song of David'.

52. D. Martyn Lloyd-Jones, Romans 13, p. 322.

53. John Newton, *Glorious things of thee are spoken*.

54. From the hymn *When all Thy mercies, O my God*.

55. Tom Holland's view (see *Contours of Pauline Theology*, Christian Focus Mentor Imprint, 2004, p. 223) that 'counted as righteous' means 'brought into the covenant' is not proved by comparing Psalm 106:31 and Numbers 25:10–13. He fails to appreciate that Phinehas was already in a covenant relationship with God. The covenant of peace pertained to God's continuing grace to Israel in guaranteeing a perpetual priesthood.

56. There is uncertainty as to whether 'spirit' refers to God's Spirit or the spirit of Moses. The immediate context would suggest Moses' spirit but texts like Isaiah 63:10 and Psalm 78:40 might suggest God's Spirit.

57. The Hebrew text has 'from the sea' and there is no need to emend to read 'from the south'. As people were taken by ship to Egypt so they will return by sea (Deuteronomy 28:68).

58. The translation 'west' in verse 3 actually reads 'from the sea'.

59. I am indebted to John N. Day, *Crying for Justice*, Kregel, 2005 for his insights.

60. Richard P. Belcher, *The Messiah and the Psalms*, Mentor Imprint, Christian Focus, 2006, p. 83.

61. Notice GOD in capitals is employed instead of LORD in capitals for God's personal name to save confusion when the term 'Lord' is also used in the address.

62. 'Youth' is plural and in the only other place where it is used it means 'youthful' or 'youth' not 'young men' (Ecclesiastes 11:9–10).

63. The word is often used of a wild beast's prey but it is found elsewhere as a poetic equivalent for food (Proverbs 31:15; Malachi 3:10).

64. Charles Bridges, *An Exposition of Proverbs* (1846), The Sovereign Grace Book Club edition 1959, pp. 3–4.

65. The word only occurs here but it belongs to the same word family as the verb 'deal bountifully' in verse 7.

66. See Philip H. Eveson, *The Beauty of Holiness*, pp. 96–102.

67. From the hymn *All hail the power of Jesus' Name!* by Edward Perronet and John Rippon.

68. Apart from Psalm 148:8 the only other place where this word for smoke (or 'cloud') is found is Genesis 19:28 where it describes the destruction of the cities of the plain as 'the smoke of a furnace'.

69. The quotation is from C. S. Lewis' book *The Lion, the Witch and the Wardrobe*.

70. The 'dawning' is actually the 'twilight' in Hebrew, which could mean before the darkness of the night just as much as before the full light of the morning.

71. From the hymn by Tate and Brady *Through all the changing scenes of life*.

72. From Toplady's hymn, *A debtor to mercy alone*.

73. It is unique within this group of psalms in that there is a slight variation in the Hebrew title, not obvious in the English translations, which emphasises that the song is to be used for pilgrimage purposes. We could convey the sense with 'for the ascents' rather than 'of the ascents'.

74. *Psalms*, Geoffrey Grogan, Eerdmans, 2008, p. 201.

75. The phrase is literally 'return a returning of Zion'. Many emend 'returning' to the more common form found in verse 4 'captivity' but there is no need for this change.

76. Craig C. Broyles, *Psalms* (New International Biblical Commentary), Paternoster Press, 1999, p. 465.

77. See 'A Practical Exposition upon Psalm cxxx,' in *The Works of John Owen*, vol. 6, pp. 325–648. Octavius Winslow was a descendant of one of the Pilgrim Fathers and spoke in 1861 at the opening of Spurgeon's Tabernacle in London on this psalm (see *Soul-Depths Soul-Heights, An exposition of Psalm 130*, Octavius Winslow, Banner of Truth, 2006).

78. The word is in the plural, which may suggest either a place of many rooms or a large imposing structure.

79. The 'it' is feminine singular and so does not refer directly to the 'ark' which is masculine. It may be referring to the singular feminine noun 'dwelling-place' or to a combination of both which is often indicated by the feminine form.

80. Patrick D. Miller, 'Psalm 136:1–9, 23–26', *Interpretation* 48 (1995), p. 391.

81. Some from Judah were taken into exile as early as 606 BC, including Daniel and his three friends (Daniel 1:1–6). This would account for Jeremiah's prophecy of an exile of seventy years (Jeremiah 29:9–11; Daniel 9:2).

82. I am dependent on Arthur G. Clarke's *Analytical Studies in the Psalms* for these titles.

83. John N. Day, *Crying for Justice*, Kregel, 2005, p. 72.

84. The Greek translation (the Septuagint) translates the word as 'angels' (see Psalms 8:5; 29:1–2; 96:4).

85. The Hebrew is difficult but that seems to be the sense of the phrase which literally reads 'you will set me up in my soul with strength'.

86. See William Gadsby's hymn, *O what matchless condescension*.

87. The Hebrew verb used is 'to bruise' as in Genesis 3:15.

88. The second half of verse 11 could be read as continuing the thought of the first half: 'the light will be night around me.'

89. The same word 'formed' is found in Proverbs 8:22 ('possessed' in some versions) and is used as another term for 'create' and sometimes means to 'gain' or 'possess' (Genesis 4:1; see also Genesis 14:19, 22).

90. The one word in Hebrew is translated variously as 'unformed body' or 'my substance yet being unperfect'.

91. Edward J. Young, *Psalm 129 A Study in the Omniscience of God*, Banner of Truth, 1965, p. 105.

92. Michael Wilcock, *The Message of Psalms 73–150: Songs for the People of God*, Bible Speaks Today, IVP, 2001.

93. The NIV inserts 'They will say' and understands verse 7 to be the words of the judges in verse 6, but there are no good grounds for this.

94. From William Williams' hymn translated by Bobi Jones *In Eden—sad indeed that day*.

95. From Kent's hymn *Sovereign grace o'er sin abounding*.

96. A number of modern English versions like the NIV consider the initial call to praise to be a title 'outside the metrical arrangement' and translate the 'for' in each case as a mark of emphasis ('Surely it is good') or an exclamation—'How good ...! How pleasant ...!' But the grounds for doing this are weak.

97. It is an unusual word which may suggest responsive singing (see Exodus 15:21; 32:18; 1 Samuel 18:7).

98. The second 'Praise the LORD' is literally 'hallelu yahweh'.

99. Another view is that God's people show forth 'the praise' of God by being God's unique people.

100. The Old Testament Greek version, the Septuagint (LXX), translated the Hebrew word by *ekklesia* and this same Greek word is used in the New Testament for 'church'.

101. Jean-Luc Vesco quoted by Gordon J. Wenham *Psalms As Torah*, Baker Academic, 2012, p. 118.

102. Remember also that the ideal 'man' of Psalm 1 is associated with the king of Psalm 2.

103. Henry Law, *Daily Prayer and Praise*, Vol. 2 (Psalms 76–150), Banner of Truth edition, 2000, p. 292.

104. A different word for 'trumpet' is used for the longer silver wind instrument.

105. J. Clinton-McCann, 'The Book of Psalms' in *The New Interpreter's Bible* Vol. IV, Abingdon Press, 1996, p. 1278.

106. F. Hossfeld and E. Zenger, *Psalms 3*, p. 664.

107. Quoted on the inside cover of Iain H. Murray's book *Should the Psalter be the Only Hymnal of the Church?* Banner of Truth, 2001.

108. The original Hebrew does not use a precise term for hymn in the headings only *mizmor* (psalm) and *shir* (song). The nearest equivalent would be *tehillah* (praise; see Psalm 145) but the Septuagint uses the Greek equivalent for praise (*ainesis*) not the word for hymn. Our English terms are derived from the Greek words *psalmos*, *hymnos* and *ode*.

109. See Calvin on Psalm 81 for his argument against the use of instruments.

110. See *Should the Psalter be the Only Hymnal of the Church?* mentioned above, p. 30.